# Adelaide &
# South Australia

Susannah Farfor, George Dunford, Jill Kirby

# Contents

| | | | |
|---|---|---|---|
| Highlights | 4 | Barossa Valley | 159 |
| Getting Started | 9 | The Mid-North | 170 |
| Itineraries | 12 | Yorke Peninsula | 183 |
| The Authors | 15 | Flinders Ranges | 195 |
| Snapshot | 17 | Eyre Peninsula & West Coast | 216 |
| History | 18 | Outback | 234 |
| The Culture | 24 | Directory | 251 |
| Environment | 30 | Transport | 265 |
| South Australia Outdoors | 37 | Health | 276 |
| Food & Drink | 43 | Glossary | 281 |
| Wineries | 48 | Behind the Scenes | 283 |
| Adelaide | 59 | Index | 289 |
| Adelaide Hills | 86 | Legend | 296 |
| Fleurieu Peninsula | 98 | | |
| Kangaroo Island | 113 | | |
| Murray River | 127 | | |
| The Southeast | 142 | | |

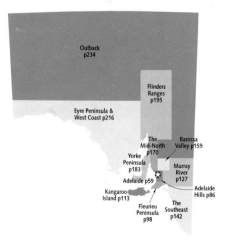

Outback p234

Flinders Ranges p195

Eyre Peninsula & West Coast p216

The Mid-North p170

Barossa Valley p159

Yorke Peninsula p183

Murray River p127

Adelaide p59

Adelaide Hills p86

Kangaroo Island p113

Fleurieu Peninsula p98

The Southeast p142

# Destination Adelaide & South Australia

Charming and often underestimated, leafy Adelaide is Australia's cultural capital. This big town with a big heart and a hefty dose of hedonism knows how to put on a show – such as the internationally renowned biennial Adelaide Festival of Arts, Womadelaide and the Adelaide Fringe. Start your gastronomic odyssey of this restaurant-soaked capital in the superb Central Market, but leave time to indulge in some of the best galleries and museums in the country.

Midsummer is perfect for sundowners at an Adelaide beach hotel. Even better, in the winter you can sip a red in front of an open fire in a converted stone stable cellar at one of the premium gourmet and wine regions, including the Barossa Valley, right on Adelaide's doorstep.

Meandering through the state and down to the sea is the mighty Murray River, once the inland highway of Australia. South Australia's rugged coastline is regularly visited by southern right whales and harbours sheltered bays and some of the country's finest surf beaches.

On magical Kangaroo Island, you can experience abundant and accessible wildlife in its own habitat – seals, sea lions, penguins, kangaroos, koalas, platypuses – and revive yourself with the wonderful feeling of being surrounded by nature no matter where you are on the island.

Obtain highs of another kind atop the Flinders Ranges, inhaling the breathtaking ancient landscape.

South Australia is by far the country's driest state, and as for space, 80% of its vast area is home to only 1% of its population. The hues of the remote and dry outback provide endless inspiration for artists' palettes.

South Australia's diverse attractions span its landscape from the charming city of **Adelaide** (p59), and the wine and gourmet regions of the **Adelaide Hills** (p86), **Barossa Valley** (p159) and **Clare Valley** (p174) to some of Australia's loneliest yet most compelling country in the **outback** (p234). Then there are the fine beaches on the **Fleurieu Peninsula** (p98), top surfing on **Eyre Peninsula** (p218) and **Yorke Peninsula** (p183), the wildlife wonderland of **Kangaroo Island** (p113) and the majestic **Flinders Ranges** (p195).

RICHARD I'ANSON

Quench your thirst for knowledge at the South Australian Museum (p63), Adelaide

Take in the rugged, wind- and salt-parched coastline of the Eyre Peninsula (p218)

MANFRED GOTTSCHALK

View Adelaide's skyline from the tranquil Torrens River (p61)

CHRIS MELI

PAUL SINCLAIR

Bushwalk through landscapes of awe-inspiring ancient beauty in the Flinders Ranges National Park (p210)

JON ARMSTRONG

Climb the sandhills at Coo-rong National Park (p146)

Explore well-preserved, historical Quorn (p206)

ANDREW MARSHALL & LEANNE WALKER

Relax among the vineyards of the
Barossa Valley (p159)

Ride this charming old rattler to
Glenelg (p82)

Wander the nature tracks in Mt Lofty Botanic Garden (p89), Adelaide Hills

Catch a game at the world's most beautiful cricket ground (p67), Adelaide

RICHARD I'ANSON

RICHARD I'ANSON

Visit the stark and arid but colourful hills of the Breakaways (p246), near Coober Pedy

Enjoy the rare sight of Lake Eyre in flood, Lake Eyre National Park (p247)

JASON EDWARDS

RICHARD I'AN

Take the double-decker horse-drawn tram to boulder-strewn Granite Island (p107)

GRANT DIXON

Lap up the seclusion of Flinders Chase National Park (p125)

Puzzle over why the Blue Lake is so blue, Mt Gambier (p150)

RICHARD I'AN

# Getting Started

Travellers to South Australia (SA) will be greeted by a well-oiled tourism machine, primed to cater for every traveller's budget and whim. It can be a good place to experience Australia in a relatively more compact form through arts- and festivals-hub Adelaide, white sandy beaches, fabulous gourmet regions, and plenty of opportunities to experience the natural landscape and its creatures.

## WHEN TO GO

Truth be told, any time is a good time to be *somewhere* in SA. South Australia has a Mediterranean climate of hot, dry summers and cool winters. Generally, spring and autumn give the greatest flexibility for a short visit because you can combine highlights of the whole state while avoiding extremes of weather. In summer (December to February) South Australians flock like migrating birds to the coast, where most days are warm enough for swimming and lazing around outdoors. In the north it's generally too hot to do anything much except slump under an air-conditioner with a cold drink. Generally, the further north you go, the hotter and drier the weather gets. Daily maximums of around 35°C are common in the outback from late spring through to early autumn (November to March).

See Climate (p254) in the Directory for more information.

In winter, when the south is often cold and wet, the outback beckons with its mild to warm days and clear skies. It's cool – often freezing – at nights. This kills off the bushflies, which in the warmer months can be an absolute nightmare.

Late winter (August) and early spring (September to November) usually bring out the magnificent wild flowers, which bloom all the way from the coastal heath up through the mallee and into the Flinders Ranges and outback.

An important consideration when travelling in SA is school holidays. The main holiday period is from mid-December to late January, with fortnight holidays also occurring early to mid-April, late June to mid-July, and late September to mid-October. South Australian families take to the road (and the air) en masse at these times. As a result, the roads are cluttered with caravans, accommodation can be booked out, prices rise and things become a little hectic, particularly during Christmas and Easter.

---

### DON'T LEAVE HOME WITHOUT...

- Your bathing suit – a must for coastal explorations
- A palate geared up for sampling SA's many gastronomic delights
- Double-checking the visa situation (p263)
- Sunscreen, sunglasses and a hat to deflect ultrafierce UV rays (p280)
- Extra-strength insect repellent to fend off merciless flies and mosquitoes (p255)
- Good maps if you are heading to the outback (p260)
- A satellite phone or HF/UHF radio if you're really going out bush
- Extra water – the heat will be more than you're used to

## COSTS & MONEY

Recently the Australian dollar has strengthened considerably against the US dollar and the British pound. Despite this, holidays in Oz can still be quite economical for international visitors, with reasonably priced accommodation, and excellent-value food and general everyday costs. This is especially true of Adelaide.

How much you should budget for depends on what kind of traveller you are and how you'll be occupying yourself. Seeing the sights, having a good time, staying in decent places and enjoying the often wonderful food will cost you $100 to $150 per person per day (based on twin share). But you can easily spend much more. At the low-cost end, if you camp or stay in hostels, cook your own meals, avoid big nights out in the pub and catch buses everywhere, you could probably manage on $45 per day; for a budget that realistically enables you to have a good time, set aside $60 per day. These low-cost figures don't include long-haul trips, which can punish the budget wallet. Travellers with a demanding brood in tow will find there are many ways to keep kids inexpensively satisfied, including beach and park visits, camping grounds and motels equipped with pools and games rooms, junior-sized restaurant meals and youth/family concessions for attractions. For more information on travelling with children see p253.

## TRAVEL LITERATURE

Before you head to SA, pick up some travel literature to help inspire your planning phase.

In *The Dog Fence,* James Woodford tracks life along the 5400km fence from Surfers Paradise in Queensland to the Bight near the Western Australian border, which cuts through the Great Victorian Desert, Coober Pedy, Moon Plain and the road to Oodnadatta.

Roff Martin Smith writes about his nine-month, 10,000km journey of discovery into Australia in *Cold Beer and Crocodiles: A Bicycle Journey into Australia,* which sees him working the pedals along the Nullarbor, Eyre coast and into the Barossa.

For comfortably predictable reading, pick up a copy of Bill Bryson's *Down Under* in which the humorist takes his usual well-rehearsed pot-shots at a large target. *Australia: True Stories of Life Down Under* is a collection of short travellers' tales by various well-known authors.

Any of Len Beadell's books give a humorous account of life and adventure in the bush. *Outback Highways* draws stories from each of his books.

In *All Things Bright and Beautiful* Susan Mitchell explores Adelaide's social structure and how the Snowtown murders, dubbed the 'body-in-the-barrel murders', could have occurred in this civilised and cultured city.

Geoffrey Blainey's award-winning *Triumph of the Nomads* chronicles the life of Australia's original inhabitants and convincingly demolishes the myth that the Aborigines were 'primitive' people trapped on a hostile continent.

*Flinders Ranges Dreaming* by Dorothy Tunbridge is a collection of 50 Dreamtime *stories* from the Adnyamathanha of the northern Flinders Ranges.

## INTERNET RESOURCES

**South Australian Tourism Commission** (www.southaustralia.com) The state's tourism site has vast amounts of information on accommodation and activities, and links to other useful sites.
**Department for Environment & Heritage** (DEH; www.environment.sa.gov.au/parks) Official site with details on SA parks and conservation areas.

3

# TOP FIVES
## MUST-SEE FILMS

One of the best places to do your essential trip preparation is on a comfy couch with a bowl of popcorn in one hand and the remote in the other. Head down to your local video store to pick up these classic SA flicks. See also p27.

- *The Tracker* (2002)
  Director: Rolf de Heer
- *The Adventure of Priscilla, Queen of the Desert* (1993)
  Director: Stephan Elliott
- *Gallipoli* (1980)
  Director: Peter Weir
- *Breaker Morant* (1980)
  Director: Bruce Beresford
- *Storm Boy* (1976)
  Director: Henri Safran

## FESTIVALS & EVENTS

If there's one thing South Australians know, it's how to put on a show and get out to celebrate. Adelaide boasts some of Australia's best arts and cultural events, including:

- Adelaide Festival of the Arts (p71)
  March in even-numbered years
- Adelaide Fringe (p71)
  March in even-numbered years
- Womadelaide (p71)
  March in odd-numbered years
- South Australian Country Music Festival & Awards (p131) June
- Barossa Vintage Festival (p163)
  April in odd-numbered years

**Adelaide Review** (www.adelaidereview.com.au) Adelaide's fortnightly cultural publication with listings on what's happening in and around town.

**Encyclopaedia of SA Culture** (saculture.com) An amusing take on life in SA.

**Commonwealth Bureau of Meteorology** (www.bom.gov.au/weather/sa) Up-to-the-minute information on SA weather and warnings.

**Lonely Planet** (www.lonelyplanet.com) Succinct summaries, links to other sites and the Thorn Tree bulletin board.

# Itineraries
## CLASSIC ROUTES

### CRUISING THE SOUTHERN COAST                    Two Weeks

Head along the Gulf St Vincent coast via the wine region of **McLaren Vale** (p101) to the wonderland of **Kangaroo Island** (p113). Next cruise along the Encounter Coast of the Fleurieu Peninsula, keeping an eye out for whales in season, and stop for a swim and beachside lunch at the Flying Fish Café in **Port Elliot** (p109). Then travel through Goolwa and out to the **Murray Mouth** (p110) to watch the dredges at work. Continue on to the pretty Scottish-heritage town of **Strathalbyn** (p94) and cross the Murray on the punt, veering south to the pelican-popular **Coorong** (p146). Explore the dunes, beach and saltpans, and gain a valuable insight into the Ngarrindjeri culture.

Continue via sheltered bays along the rugged coast – perhaps picking up a fresh lobster – and on to hamletlike **Robe** (p147). Marvel at the implausible Blue Lake and explore the terraced gardens of Umpherston sinkhole near **Mt Gambier** (p150), and sample the 'terra rosa' wines of **Coonawarra** (p153).

From here, visit the bird haven of **Bool Lagoon** (p156), and ancient marsupial fossils and bats in the heritage-listed caves of **Naracoorte** (p156) before heading back to Adelaide through the **Adelaide Hills** (p86).

Visit the gourmet and wine regions of McLaren Vale and Coonawarra, spot wildlife on Kangaroo Island and the Fleurieu Peninsula and enjoy the views from the Adelaide Hills. Covering the 1100km of this journey will take about two weeks.

## CENTRAL ODYSSEY (THE NORTH)          **Two to Three Weeks**

From Adelaide, point your vehicle north, passing through the epicurean playgrounds of the **Barossa** (p159) and **Clare Valleys** (p174). Travel through sheep and wheat country along the Barrier Hwy to historic **Burra** (p180), which lives on the memories of its copper-mining past. From here, head north then west to the old railway towns of **Quorn** (p206) and **Hawker** (p208), and the dramatic bluffs and gum-lined creeks of the **Flinders Ranges** (p195). Lace up your walking boots and pack your camera with plenty of film to snap magnificent **Wilpena Pound** (p211) and wildlife, and examine the sacred Aboriginal paintings etched into Arkaroo Rock. Continue north through **Parachilna Gorge** (p214) and **Leigh Creek** (p214) then take the scenic route to explore the **Gammon Ranges** (p214), if your vehicle will allow it, and learn timeless Adnyamathanha lore at the Aboriginal-run Iga Warta centre.

Head north from Leigh Creek to **Marree** (p247), once a hub for camel teams and the Great Northern Railway. Join the rugged **Oodnadatta Track** (p247), following the route of the old Overland Telegraph Line and the Great Northern Railway past **Lake Eyre** (p235) – especially if you're lucky enough to experience it at its bird-filled best – to **Oodnadatta** (p248). Next cut south to explore the lunar landscapes surrounding the opal town of **Coober Pedy** (p240).

From here, continue south along the bitumen to Adelaide, but before hitting the city allow time for a quick detour to do absolutely nothing in the relaxed fishing/holiday town of **Port Broughton** (p194) on the Yorke Peninsula.

**Sip wine in the Barossa and Clare Valleys, ponder the lives of past copper miners in Burra, walk in the Flinders Ranges and explore SA's vast outback. Before heading back to civilisation check out underground life at Coober Pedy and relax on the beach on the Eyre Peninsula. Expect to take two to three weeks for this 2500km itinerary.**

# TAILORED TRIPS

## WANDERING THE VINES

Prime your taste buds and get ready to stock your cellar. Start your odyssey in South Australia's gourmet and wine districts, peppered with charismatic towns and settlers' stone cottages, in the hills east of Adelaide. Take in views of the city, sample refreshing cool-climate wines, then get a culture shock in German-heritage **Hahndorf** (p91). Head north through farmland and gnarled gum trees to **Eden Valley** (p169), home of renowned Henschke wines

and the back door to the **Barossa Valley** (p159). Try the Barossa's powerful reds and then sober up with lunch at Maggie Beer's Farm Shop.

Continue through picturesque countryside to the **Clare Valley** (p174) via **Kapunda** (p178), veering into local artists studios. Hire a bike and pedal the Riesling Trail, resting up at a quaint B&B or the atmospheric Rising Sun Hotel.

Veer east towards the Riverland via lakeside **Barmera** (p135), sipping wines at ecofriendly winery-cum–bird reserve, Banrock Station.

Head south to the **Coonawarra region** (p153) and pretty **Penola** (p154) to sample golden Chardonnay and peppery Shiraz. Next, check out the world-first wines in **Langhorne Creek** (p112), antique-filled **Strathalbyn** (p94), and peruse the galleries in the gastronomes' stomping ground of **McLaren Vale** (p101) and **Willunga** (p102) on your way back to the 'big smoke' (well…).

## WILD WONDERLAND

Keep your eye out for dolphins as you cruise along the Gulf St Vincent coast to magical Kangaroo Island.

Get a hawk's-eye view of penguin life in **Penneshaw** (p121) and ponder life at the isolated lightstations that oversee the rugged coastline. Take the South Coast Rd, walking by water birds at **Murray Lagoon** (p124) and traversing the beach at **Seal Bay** (p124). Climb the sculpted inland sand dunes of **Little Sahara** (p124), surf off pristine beaches near **Vivonne Bay** (p124), climb

into the earth at the **Kelly Hill Caves** (p124), and spy tree-top fur-balls on a koala walk before entering the wildlife holy grail of **Flinders Chase National Park** (p125). New Zealand fur seals frolic under the impressive rock frame of **Admirals Arch** (p126), and the colourful lichen-covered **Remarkable Rocks** (p126) are truly…remarkable.

Slip into calmer water on the north coast and take the plunge into underwater gardens on an organised dive. At **American River** (p120), walk through the glossy black cockatoos' she-oak feeding grounds and along the foreshore to spy pelicans and water birds.

Anything you miss here can be spotted at **Cleland Wildlife Park** (p89) in the Adelaide Hills.

# The Authors

### SUSANNAH FARFOR
**Coordinating Author**

Susannah is a Melbourne-based writer and editor whose work covers adventure travel and food publications (including the Qantas and Virgin Blue in-flight magazines, *SportDiving,* the *Age Good Food Guide* and *Age Cheap Eats*). For this title she surfed the coasts, hiked the hills, explored caves and put an oenology course to good use by quaffing wines along with South Australia's (SA) array of gourmet produce. Fascinated by the more remote regions of Australia, she has travelled in every state and also wrote Lonely Planet's *Northern Territory* guidebook. Susannah researched and wrote the Adelaide, Adelaide Hills, Fleurieu Peninsula, Kangaroo Island, and introductory and end chapters for this title.

#### My South Australia

My favourite SA trip started near Coonawarra (p153); I then dropped down to Mt Gambier see the morning mist reveal the incredible Blue Lake (p152). I hiked in the Coorong (p146) and swam at beaches along the Encounter Coast (p105) before ferrying to Kangaroo Island for a walk with penguins (p121). Next stop: Adelaide (p59), via the gourmet region of McLaren Vale (p101). I perused Adelaide's galleries (p63) and museums (p63), absorbed the colourful market (p67), feasted in great restaurants (p75) and checked out the West End scene (p76). In the Adelaide Hills I mingled with wildlife at Cleland Wildlife Park (p89), then indulged at Henschke Winery (p56) and Maggie Beer's Farm Shop & Restaurant (p168) in the Barossa Valley.

### GEORGE DUNFORD

Long family road trips squabbling with his sisters were George Dunford's first experiences of SA. With advice from a host of SA expat informers, George headed out to Coober Pedy, the dry Nullarbor and, most inhospitable of all, Baxter Detention Centre. After a few flat tyres, speeding fines and a blown gasket George returned to freelance writing in Melbourne, but he misses the ubiquitous pub-meal parma. George wrote the Yorke Peninsula, Flinders Ranges, Eyre Peninsula & West Coast and Outback chapters for this title.

### JILL KIRBY

After leaving England to travel the world, Jill made Australia home in 1995, exploring the country both as a backpacker and as a journalist/TV producer. Bowled over by SA's lifestyle, she moved to Adelaide, producing local TV programmes and writing about SA for the electronic and print media. Her love of beaches, wine and wildlife keeps her exploring this glorious state. Jill wrote the South Australia chapter for the 2004 *Australia* guide. In this guide she wrote and researched the Wineries, Murray River, the Southeast, the Barossa Valley and Mid-North chapters.

## CONTRIBUTING AUTHORS

**Professor Tim Flannery** wrote the Environment chapter. Tim's a naturalist and explorer and the author of a number of award-winning books, including *The Future Eaters, Throwim Way Leg* (an account of his adventures as a biologist working in New Guinea) and the landmark ecological history of North America, *The Eternal Frontier*. His latest book, written about Australia, is *Country*. Tim lives in Adelaide, where he is director of the South Australian Museum and a professor at the University of Adelaide.

**Dr David Millar** wrote the Health chapter. David is a travel medicine specialist, diving doctor and lecturer in wilderness medicine who graduated in Hobart, Tasmania. He has worked as an expedition doctor with the Maritime Museum of Western Australia, accompanying a variety of expeditions around Australia. David is currently a medical director with Travel Doctor in Auckland.

# Snapshot

Hot conversation topics in South Australia (SA) revolve around environmental concerns, particularly water, as the state has so little of it. An oft-heard phrase here is that this is 'the driest state in the world's driest country…' Of particular focus is providing a panacea to the gasping Murray River, and to stem the rising salination catastrophe. In 2004, SA, Victoria and New South Wales agreed to introduce measures to reduce evaporation rates from farmers' irrigation channels and restore some of the Murray's flow. Currently, a team of dredges works 24 hours per day to keep the river's mouth open. The government is also starting to clean up dirty rivers, which at times transport untreated sewage into the sea.

Water and environmental factors also affect SA's vines, and passionate quaffers ruminate over whether it will be a good or great year for their favoured drop. When talk of water runs dry, conversation turns to football, cricket or any motor sport roaring through town. The rivalry between fans of Australian Football League (AFL) teams Port Power and the Crows provides plenty of banter.

Despite its bountiful pleasures, SA fights an ongoing battle to keep its grip on big business (and jobs) in the state, and the urge to 'keep up' with the country's larger cities is a powerful one. In 2004, a car manufacturing plant closed down its Adelaide operations despite government subsidies, and the head of News Corp, Rupert Murdoch, was given the keys to the city before walking out and leaving the door open.

The response to the uncertainty generated from terrorism and world events in recent years has been a leaning towards conservatism, with the 2004 federal election seeing the emergence of the SA-based Family First Party from its Assemblies of God roots. In contrast to basic Christian values, and human rights, has been the mandatory detention of asylum seekers, including children, in SA's remote Woomera and Baxter Detention Centres (see p220).

Despite Adelaide's outward conservatism, this progressive state has led social reform in Australia for more than a century, particularly during the '60s and '70s. Many changes regarding Aboriginal land rights, capital punishment, sexual discrimination and racial discrimination are rooted here, and it was the first state to give both women and Aborigines the vote. Flamboyant former premier Don Dunstan's name is never far away from Adelaide's artistic and cultural core. Having created both the successful South Australian Film Corporation and the State Opera of South Australia, his government's legacy can be seen in the ongoing strong arts focus.

**FAST FACTS**

Population: 1,527,000

Area: 984,400 sq km

GSP (Gross State Product) per head growth: 3.7%

Proportion of Australian GDP: 6.6%

Unemployment rate: 6.4%

Median age: 38.2, the oldest in Australia

Official unemployment: 5.8%

Koalas on Kangaroo Island: approximately 30,000

Percentage of Australian wine originating in SA: 46%

# History

## ABORIGINAL SETTLEMENT & SOCIETY

Mystery shrouds many aspects of Australian prehistory; however it is now believed that the ancestors of today's Aborigines came across the sea from Southeast Asia at least 46,000 years ago. Although much of Australia is now arid, those early migrants found a much wetter continent, with vast forests and lakes teeming with food resources. With these favourable conditions, the Aboriginal people populated most of the continent within a relatively short period.

Australian Aboriginal society has the longest continuous cultural history in the world. In South Australia (SA), the earliest known relics of the Aboriginal occupation are rock carvings near Olary which have been dated at 43,000 years, making them 16,000 years older than the Neanderthal carvings of Europe.

At the time of European settlement, SA is thought to have been populated by approximately 12,000 Aboriginal people living in 43 tribal groups throughout the region. Even the hostile Simpson Desert was occupied on a year-round basis, thanks to water obtained from scattered permanent wells. Knowledge and skills developed over thousands of years enabled Aboriginal people to utilise their environment to the fullest, while an intimate understanding of animal behaviour and plant ecology ensured that serious food shortages were rare.

Aborigines also traded goods across Australia, using routes that followed the paths of Dreamtime ancestors. One trade route ran from Lake Alexandrina through the Flinders Ranges and southwest Queensland to the Gulf of Carpentaria. Along with practical commodities and items of spiritual significance, songs and dances were also traded.

The History Trust of South Australia is a rich resource for enquiring minds (www.history.gov.sa.au).

## EUROPEAN EXPLORATION

In 1627 the Dutch ship *Gulden Zeepaard* recorded the first European sighting of the SA coast. The French ships *Recherche* and *L'Esperance* followed in 1792, and the first British explorer on the scene was Lieutenant James Grant, in 1800. While sailing along the southeast coast, Grant named several key features including Mt Gambier and Mt Schank.

Keen to beat the French in charting the huge unknown chunks of Australian coastline, the English sent Matthew Flinders in command of the *Investigator*. Reaching Fowlers Bay in January 1802, he sailed east, charting and naming Spencer and St Vincent Gulfs, and Kangaroo Island. His journey ended speculation of a north–south channel dividing Australia; much of the data he collected is still in use today.

On 8 April 1802, Flinders unexpectedly met the French ship *Le Géographe* anchored in what became known as Encounter Bay. The French, under Captain Nicholas Baudin, had sailed from the east, also surveying the coast, and the two captains exchanged information on their respective discoveries over dinner on Baudin's ship.

In 1829, Captain Charles Sturt headed inland from Sydney determined to find out where the westward flowing rivers of New South Wales (NSW)

TIMELINE **60,000–40,000 BC** | **AD 1627**

The exact date is debatable, but Aborigines arrive and settle in Australia during this period | Dutch captain Francois Thijssen, aboard *Gulden Zeepaard*, is the first European to sight the coast of SA

went. At the Murrumbidgee River he rowed downstream until meeting a large waterway he called the Murray. A month later he reached Lake Alexandrina and discovered where the Murray flowed into the sea.

His glowing reports on the region attracted the attention of the National Colonisation Society, a radical group of English colonial reformers who proposed that a colony should be based on planned immigration with land sales, rather than free grants of land. Such a colony would be self-supporting with no need for subsidy from the British Government.

In *The Dig Tree*, Sarah Murgatroyd weaves an engaging tale out of the desperately tragic journey of Burke and Wills' ill-fated expedition to be the first Europeans to cross Australia from south to north in 1860–61.

## COLONISATION

In 1834 the British Parliament passed the SA Colonisation Act, inspired by the ideas of the colonial reformers. This made SA the only Australian colony established entirely by free settlers, a distinction many South Australians are only too happy to highlight.

The first official settlement was established in 1836 at Kingscote on Kangaroo Island. However, colonial surveyor-general Colonel William Light selected Adelaide as the site for the capital. The first governor, Captain John Hindmarsh, landed at present-day Glenelg on 28 December 1836, and proclaimed the Province of South Australia that day.

Despite its optimistic beginning, the colony was on the verge of collapse two years later. Immigrants were unemployed and farming had barely started owing to the lack of surveyed land. A vigorous programme of land surveys was instigated and by 1841 about 1000 sq km had been made available for settlement, and Adelaide had grown from a collection of huts into something approximating a town. But progress came at a price: the construction of numerous public buildings and other works drained colonial coffers; supported migration ceased, employment was hard to come by and SA plunged into its first recession.

By 1843 things were looking up – wool was being exported and wheat farms were producing a surplus, creating a short supply of harvesting labour and prompting the recommencement of immigration and a rapid increase in population. Discoveries of rich copper lodes at Kapunda and Burra around this time boosted both confidence and the economy. The infant colony was finally on its feet, and just over a decade later it was one of the world's major producers of copper, with pastoral leases reaching the northern Flinders Ranges.

## EARLY IMMIGRANTS

The first immigrants to arrive in SA were mainly poor English, Scots and Irish with agricultural or trade experience. About 12,000 landed in the first four years of settlement; the colony's policy was to select young married couples to encourage natural population increase and foster interest in SA's future.

Another group of settlers were the 800 German farmers and artisans, mainly Lutherans fleeing religious persecution, who arrived between 1838 and 1841. One of their first villages was Hahndorf, in the Adelaide Hills. A second group of 5400 hard-working Germans had arrived by 1850, and many more followed during the next decade. They settled mainly in the Adelaide Hills and the Barossa Valley, where the soil and climate were

Mary Penfold, who emigrated in 1844 with her doctor husband, Christopher, became a skilled vigneron after cofounding the famed Penfold's winery.

| 1802 | 1836 |
| --- | --- |
| Captain Matthew Flinders, on *Investigator*, extensively charts the SA coastline | The first official settlement in SA is established at Kingscote on Kangaroo Island |

similar to the wine-growing areas of their homeland, and established vineyards and the beginnings of the SA wine industry.

Thousands of Cornish people came to SA following the discovery of copper in the 1840s. Skilled miners and builders, they developed a strong subculture in the areas they settled.

## SECOND-WAVE EXPLORERS

South Australia's first 30 years saw a number of important exploring achievements. Between 1839 and 1841 Edward John Eyre made the first traverse of the Flinders Ranges; his enthusiastic reports of potential agricultural land in the Mid-North area gave impetus to that region's settlement.

In 1839, Charles Bonney drove the first herd of cattle from Melbourne to Adelaide via Mt Gambier, establishing a safer alternative to the Murray River stock route from NSW and opening up the lower Southeast, which became one of the colony's finest agricultural areas.

Five years later, Charles Sturt set off with a whaleboat to look for the oft-speculated-upon inland sea, but after 18 months of hardship he abandoned it in a waterless red expanse of stones and sand hills. If nothing else, he had discovered the Simpson Desert, one of Australia's most inhospitable regions.

Perhaps SA's greatest explorer, John MacDouall Stuart made several epic forays into the interior between 1858 and 1862. His successful crossing of the continent from south to north opened up a route for a telegraph line between Adelaide and Darwin, and led to SA taking control of the Northern Territory (NT) in 1863.

## COPPER, WHEAT & WOOL

The mining of copper at Kapunda, Burra, Moonta and Kadina helped save SA from bankruptcy on several occasions. By the 1870s, SA had replaced Cornwall as the leading copper producer in the British Empire, making many people in SA wealthy. It also left a legacy of fine public buildings in mining towns and Adelaide, including the University of Adelaide, founded in 1874 with grants made from mine profits.

Adelaide became the first Australian capital city to be connected by telegraph with London in 1872, and to a waterborne sewerage system in 1881.

In 1865, SA had half of all land under wheat in Australia. However, overcropping had already begun to exhaust the soils in the Adelaide Hills and Fleurieu Peninsula. When more land was opened in the 1870s, there was a mass exodus from these regions. The wheat boom which followed resulted in the creation of many towns, particularly in the Mid-North and southern Flinders Ranges, along with new railway and port facilities. By 1880 the Willochra Plain in the central Flinders Ranges were under the plough, and enthusiastic trumpeting of 'a rich golden harvest' extended to the NT. Sanity returned with the onset of drought in the mid-1880s.

If wheat was SA's foundation, wool was its wealth. Sheep farmers opened up the country for settlement, particularly in more distant areas, yet as with wheat growers, the first pastoralists had little if any understanding of the natural environment. A tendency to overestimate carrying capacity led to gross overstocking and with no pasture kept in reserve ruin came to many in the 1865 drought.

| 1862 | 1894 |
|---|---|
| John MacDouall Stuart makes the first south–north crossing of the continent | South Australian women are the first in the British Empire permitted to vote, and the first in the world eligible to stand for Parliament |

Then as now, the wool industry was based on merinos, with SA breeders developing a strain better suited to semiarid conditions.

## SELF-GOVERNMENT TO FEDERATION

South Australia was initially governed by a body combining representatives from the colony's Board of Commissioners and the British Government. However, SA's financial problems in the early 1840s upset the British Government, which had to pay off the debts. It abolished the board in 1842 and made SA an ordinary Crown colony. In 1856 a new act created the SA Parliament, giving SA the most democratic constitution of any Australian colony.

Recession returned in the mid-1860s with copper again helping stave off bankruptcy. Increasing prosperity was reflected in the growth of the transport and communications system; by 1890 railways connected Adelaide to Oodnadatta in the north, Melbourne to the east, and Cockburn to the northeast. There were also 3200km of sealed roads and more than 100 steamboats engaged in trade on the Murray River by 1878.

Following John MacDouall Stuart's explorations, SA gained control of the NT (previously part of NSW) and in 1870 work commenced on an overland telegraph line to Darwin. Completed in just two years, this ambitious undertaking linked SA to the world telegraph network.

The drought of the early 1880s heralded a general recession lasting until 1900. Public debt mounted, and in desperation the government became the first in Australia to introduce income tax. When this proved inadequate, agricultural development schemes offered new farmers blocks of land and government loans, which resulted in significant irrigation projects along the Murray, and the draining of vast seasonal swamps in the Southeast.

A number of reforms were passed by the SA Parliament during this period, including the establishment of Australia's first Juvenile Court in 1890 and the granting of free education in 1891. In 1894, SA became the first Australian colony to recognise women's right to vote in parliamentary elections, and the first place in the world to allow women to stand for parliament.

Catherine Helen Spence was Australia's first professional female journalist and political candidate, and a key feminist influence in the state's social and political reform.

## EARLY 20TH CENTURY

South Australia experienced slow but steady growth following amalgamation of colonies into the Commonwealth of Australia in 1901. Manufacturing became increasingly important, particularly in the field of heavy engineering. The Port Pirie smelter was enlarged during WWI, and was soon producing 10% of the world's lead, as well as silver and zinc.

The war was a time of division in SA. Before 1914 the state had several German place-names, but in a fit of anti-German zeal these were either anglicised or replaced. Many were reinstated during 1936's centennial celebrations, when the German settlers' huge contribution to SA's development was officially recognised.

The early 1920s brought brief prosperity before a four-year drought led into the Great Depression. While all states suffered during this period, SA fared worst of all: in 1931 more than 70,000 people out of a population of 575,000 were dependent on welfare.

| 1901 | 1967 |
|---|---|
| The Commonwealth of Australia is created and SA becomes a state | Non-Aboriginal Australians vote to give Aborigines and Torres Strait Islanders citizen status |

**THE STOLEN GENERATION, LAND RIGHTS & SECRET WOMEN'S BUSINESS**

By the early 1900s, legislation to segregate and 'protect' Aboriginal people imposed restrictions on their rights to own property or seek employment. The Aboriginals Ordinance of 1918 authorised the state to remove children from Aboriginal mothers and place them in foster homes or institutional care if the father was suspected to be non-Aboriginal. This practice continued until the 1960s, resulting in bitterness that persists to this day, especially among those now known as the 'Stolen Generation'.

After WWII, 'assimilation' of Aboriginal people became the government's stated aim. To this end, Aboriginal rights were subjugated even further, with the government controlling where Aborigines could live and even whom they could marry.

South Australia was the first state to give Aboriginal people title to their land and a degree of control over their own affairs, thanks to three historic pieces of land rights legislation; the Aboriginal Lands Trust Act (1966), the Pitjantjatjara Land Rights Act (1981) and the Maralinga Tjarutja Land Rights Act (1984). Land held under Aboriginal freehold title cannot be sold, entry is restricted and no development can take place without the traditional owners' permission.

In 1967 non-Aboriginal Australians voted to give Aborigines and Torres Strait Islanders citizen status, including the right to vote. The years since have seen an ongoing coming to terms with the past. Where 'assimilation' was once the goal, now it is 'reconciliation'.

But cultural clashes still occur, exemplified in SA by the politically and culturally divisive Hindmarsh Bridge controversy. First proposed in 1988, the bridge's construction was blocked due to concerns by Ngarrindjeri women regarding the spiritual and cultural significance of the site. A series of court battles followed, pitting Aboriginal beliefs against development, culminating in 1995's Royal Commission which ruled that the claims and evidence of Aboriginal secret women's business were fabricated.

Further court appeals were launched, and in August 2001 the Federal Court's findings directly contradicted those of the Royal Commission, ruling against the developers on all counts and concluding that the evidence presented was not fabricated. Unfortunately this vindication came five months after the bridge had been officially opened, and the decade-long situation was a step backwards for reconciliation, made worse by the media's often flawed coverage.

Industrial development quickened during WWII; the first water pipeline was built from Morgan to Whyalla, ship building commenced at Whyalla, and the Leigh Creek coalfields were opened up for electricity production. In 1948 work began on the Woomera rocket range northwest of Port Augusta.

## LATE 20TH CENTURY TO PRESENT DAY

Momentum continued into the 1950s, encouraged by a booming market and protective tariffs on imported goods. Shifting from a rural economy to a predominantly industrial one, SA captured a relatively large share of the national growth in industry and overseas migration.

In 1965 the Labor Party came to power after 26 years of Liberal (conservative) rule. One of the new government's first reforms was an act prohibiting racial discrimination, the first in Australia. By this time the state's economy and population growth were stagnating, revealing the shortcomings of economic dependence on the manufacture of motor vehicles and household appliances. Overseas competition and deepening industrial recession saw the last ship built at Whyalla roll down the slipway in 1978.

| 1976 | 1983 |
|---|---|
| Huge deposits of uranium, copper, silver and gold are discovered at Roxby Downs | Ash Wednesday bushfires in SA and Victoria kill 76 people |

Although the 1970s were a difficult time for SA, controversial Labor premier Don Dunstan's government could claim several important achievements, including the creation of the South Australian Film Corporation (1972) and the State Opera of South Australia (1976). Major reforms included the Sexual Discrimination Act (1975), and improved legislation dealing with women's issues, capital punishment and Aboriginal land rights.

Hopes for economic recovery followed the 1976 discovery of huge deposits of uranium, copper, silver and gold at Roxby Downs, coupled with oil and gas finds in the Cooper Basin throughout the 1970s. While the mining industry prospered through the 1980s and 1990s, manufacturing-based industries fared poorly, and by 1989 the rural sector was also in crisis, due to drought, soaring interest rates and tumbling commodity prices.

South Australia's economy has remained somewhat sluggish, although the 2004 completion of the railway linking Adelaide with Darwin's cargo port is a positive sign, as it creates a direct link between SA and the markets of Asia and beyond. Tourism is also increasingly important, with travellers drawn by a range of festivals of international repute.

| 2001 | 2004 |
|---|---|
| The state is put on the questionable human rights map through Australia's policy of putting asylum seekers in detention in SA's outback | The completion of the Ghan rail line to Darwin creates a direct link between SA and the markets of Asia |

# The Culture

## REGIONAL IDENTITY

Despite the stereotype of tanned, outback-dwelling, muscle-bound, croc-wrestlers, most Australians are urban and urbane – more comfortable wrangling a bruschetta-and-macchiato brunch than wrestling an over-sized reptile.

As much as Australians are shaped by their isolation from the rest of the world, South Australians are removed an additional step – from the majority of the Australian population that lives along the eastern coastline. Another point of difference (slight or otherwise) is their ancestry from free settlers rather than convict colonies. The conservative Christian backbone of South Australia (SA) has given it a reputation for wowserism, though history shows a well-developed progressive streak whose reasoned debate has delivered many social reforms that now form social policies Australiawide.

Humour is often used as a social levelling tool in Australia. For those not familiar with its unique character, a first encounter with Australian humour can be a confusing experience, mixing self-deprecation, sarcasm and irony.

Social interaction, particularly 'down the pub', is often a mix of jokes, amusing anecdotes and personal teasing. Visitors can be shocked to hear best mates trading insults (taking the piss) until they realise it's meant in the nicest possible way. Swear words are often used as close terms of affection, and if you're being teased it can mean that you are liked and are being accepted in the group.

## LIFESTYLE

Around 83% of South Australians live in Adelaide, where they thrive on a high standard of living, sandy beaches, lush parklands, fantastic cafés and restaurants, and a laid-back atmosphere that makes it seem more like a large country town than a city. The beach holiday is still very much the annual summer pilgrimage for most families, who flock to the beach (many dragging caravans) in search of long, lazy, sun-kissed days on the sand and in the surf.

The majority of folks rate home ownership very highly. Inside the average South Australian middle-class suburban home, you'll probably find a married heterosexual couple, though it is becoming increasingly likely they will be de facto, or in their second marriage. Our 'dad and mum' couple will have an average of 1.4 children, probably called Joshua and

In *The Tyranny of Distance*, Geoffrey Blainey explores Australia's development – from Cook's voyages and the hardships faced by early settlers through to its challenges today – and discusses how Australia's geographic remoteness has shaped its history and identity.

Make sure you're always in on the joke with Lonely Planet's *Australian Phrasebook*, which has 250 pages of rhyming slang, Aussie expressions, Aboriginal languages, national songs and other cultural titbits.

### CROW-EATERS

Aussies love a nickname, and citizens of most states have one (whether they like it or not). In Queensland you'll knock back a beer in a bar full of Banana-benders (or Cane Toads), in New South Wales you'll sit among a crowd of Cockroaches at the footy (in fact the name Cockroaches comes from the Rugby League State of Origin), in Western Australia, you'll enter the world of Sandgropers (named for a relative of the grasshopper who loves to burrow in sandy soils), and in Tasmania you'll trek alongside a bunch of (rather unimaginatively named) Apple-eaters. But once you arrive in SA, you'll rub shoulders with Crow-eaters. Life was so hard in SA that the colonials were likely to run short of sheep and be forced to eat crows – hence the nickname Crow-eaters. There's not much eating on a crow.

Emily, Australia's names of the moment (and yes, Kylie is still popular). But the birth rate has been falling over the last few years.

## POPULATION

The most recent census (2001) counted some 18,970,000 people in Australia. South Australia has less than 8% of that population – an estimated 1,527,000 in 2003. Among Australian states and territories, SA has the highest concentration of its population living in the capital city. The largest towns outside Adelaide are Whyalla and Mt Gambier. Only around 1% of all South Australians live in the dry outback, which makes up around 80% of the state's land area. This amounts to a density of 0.02 persons per sq km. However, the spread is by no means even, as more than 50% of the outback region's population lives in its four main towns: Coober Pedy, Leigh Creek, Roxby Downs and Woomera.

Although less than in other states, 25% of the population in SA is foreign-born, with the majority coming from the UK (8.5%), Italy (1.7%) and Germany (0.9%), with other significant communities emigrating from Greece and Asia. Around 1.6% of the state's population identify as being of Aboriginal origin.

Despite the extraordinarily low population density, population policy is fiercely debated in Australia. Opponents of increased immigration argue the dry Australian landscape can't sustain more people (among other arguments); others say population growth is an economic imperative, particularly considering Australia's declining birth rates.

## SPORT

Sport is an obsession throughout Australia, and there's no sport that arouses more passion than Australian rules football (AFL or Aussie rules; http://afl.com.au). A fast, tactical and physical game featuring spectacular marking and bone-crushing tackles, Aussie rules is unique – only Gaelic football is anything like it. Although there are some enthusiastic punch-ups on the field, the crowds are noisy but law-abiding. The national competition originally developed from the Victorian league, it has featured successful teams from other states for several years including SA's Port Adelaide (http://portadelaidefc.com.au), 2004 premiership winners, and the Adelaide Crows (http://afc.com.au), which won the premiership in 1997 and 1998. You can catch a match from March to August (with the finals in September) at **AAMI Stadium** ( ☎ 08-8268 2088; Turner Dr, West Lakes).

> When the wind is blowing and the land is firm, land yachties head out to sail on dry lakes and across the desert.

Soccer is very much a poor cousin: it's widely played on an amateur basis and is slowly gaining in popularity, but the national league is only semiprofessional.

Grand slam tennis ace and SA-homeboy Lleyton Hewitt became the youngest year-end world number one ever in 2001 at age 20. His passionate cries of 'C'mon!' have seen him take out the US Open in 2001, Wimbledon 2002 and Davis Cup challenges. Maintaining a dream to win the Australian Open, he was defeated in the final in 2005.

In summer, sports fans' focus quickly shifts and the hordes head for picturesque **Adelaide Oval** (Map p67; ☎ 08-8300 3800; www.cricketsa.com.au; King William Rd, North Adelaide) – where the most dramatic match of the Bodyline series was played – to catch the drama of one-day and test match cricket (the five-day international version of the game). The Redbacks are the state cricket team.

The states's National Basketball League (NBL) teams are the women's Adelaide Lightning and men's Adelaide 36ers (www.adelaide36ers.com).

Various sporting events take over the city and race through surrounding areas, including the inaugural six-day Jacob's Creek Tour Down Under (www.tourdownunder.com), an international cycling teams race in the style of the Tour de France, which is held annually in Adelaide and country areas.

## RELIGION

By far the most common religion is Christianity, with 64% of SA's population claiming affiliation (including Roman Catholic, Anglican, Uniting Church, Lutheran and evangelical forms). Non-Christian religions account for just over 2% of the population, with over half this number Buddhist. About 20% of the population describe themselves as having no religion.

## ARCHITECTURE

Central Adelaide retains fine stone buildings from the early days of settlement, many of which are now protected by the National Trust and by State Heritage legislation. Its gracious mansions and stately homes from the Victorian era were generally built for the colonial gentry.

Many towns sprang from the copper and wheat booms of the 1840s to 1870s. Buoyed by wealth and optimism, their founders tended to build solidly and grandly in stone, particularly when it came to churches, hotels and public buildings. You'll find some of the best examples at Burra, Kapunda, Mintaro, Moonta, Quorn and Robe.

Several country areas have architectural styles that reflect the culture of their first settlers. Fine examples of this are the distinctive Lutheran churches and German farmhouses of the Barossa Valley, the English country homes of the Adelaide Hills, the Scottish-heritage town of Strathalbyn, the 'Englishness' of Mintaro, and the Cornish cottages and sombre Methodist chapels of the copper towns such as Kapunda, Burra, Moonta and Kadina.

Many buildings show clever adaptation to the local climate and the lack of manufactured building materials. They include the miners' dugouts at Burra and Coober Pedy, the thatched farm sheds of the Mid-North and Barossa Valley, the pine-and-pug settlers' cottages in the Flinders Ranges, and the broad-veranda homesteads throughout the pastoral districts around the Flinders Ranges and outback.

## ARTS

South Australia, and particularly Adelaide, prides itself on its visual and performing arts scene which claims some of the best festivals in the country. The Art Gallery of South Australia features an impressive collection (p63), while the performing arts scene boasts an opera company, several good theatre companies, a dance company and a symphony orchestra.

Centre stage in the performing arts spotlight is the Adelaide Festival Centre. The main venue for the biennial Adelaide Festival of Arts, regarded as the nation's foremost performing arts and cultural event. Details on the Adelaide Festival of the Arts, Adelaide Fringe and Womadelaide are listed on p71.

Adelaide has a healthy live music scene, with a range of local and touring acts performing gigs. Adelaide's Governor Hindmarsh (The Gov, see p79) is one of Australia's best live-music venues, and classical and jazz music often accompanies food and wine at regional festivals. Several SA musicians and bands – including Paul Kelly, Cold Chisel, Ruby Hunter, Archie Roach and Guy Sebastian have achieved success on the international stage.

Adelaidian Anthony LaPaglia won the 2004 Golden Globe for his role in the TV series *Without a Trace*. He also starred in *Murder One*, *Frasier* and *Lantana*.

## Cinema

It's a little-known fact that *The Story of the Kelly Gang,* produced in Australia in 1906, was the world's first feature-length film. This auspicious beginning kicked off a cycle of boom and bust periods for Australian cinema that continues to this day.

Following decades of neglect leading to the industry's virtual extinction, the 1970s and '80s saw the beginning of a renaissance for Australian film. In the 1990s, films such as *Strictly Ballroom, Muriel's Wedding* and *The Adventures of Priscilla, Queen of the Desert* consolidated Australia's reputation for producing quirky comedies filled with local eccentrics and misfits.

Sydney has dominated big-budget film production over the last few years, but SA continues to be the 'quiet achiever' of Australian cinema. Established in 1972 to kick-start the local film industry, the South Australian Film Corporation has achieved commendable successes, encouraging and supporting the creation of acclaimed productions that not only showcase spectacular landscapes but explore local issues, culture and history. Indigenous stories have found a mainstream voice via films such as *The Tracker, Rabbit-Proof Fence* and *Australian Rules.* Portrayals of a nation beginning to come to terms with its racist past and present, all three films made extensive use of SA's unique scenery.

In *The Tracker* (2002, director Rolf de Heer), filmed entirely on location in the Arkaroola Wilderness Sanctuary in the northern Flinders Ranges, an Aboriginal tracker leads three white men in pursuit of another Aborigine accused of murder.

South Australia's most famous filmic landscape remains the desolate region around Coober Pedy. Contributing stunning backdrops for scenes in *Mad Max Beyond Thunderdome* and *The Adventures of Priscilla, Queen of the Desert,* it also provided otherworldly settings for films such as *Red Planet* and cult sci-fi flick *Pitch Black.*

Notable SA films include:

**Australian Rules** (2001, director Paul Goldman) Underlying racism is central to this tale of a teenage footballer in a small coastal town who falls in love with an Aboriginal girl from the local mission.

**Rabbit-Proof Fence** (2000, director Phillip Noyce) Powerful true story of three Aboriginal girls who set out on a 2400km journey home, having been removed from their families as part of government policy to train them as domestic staff for White families.

Geoffrey Rush and Noah Taylor both shine (sorry…) as the respectively older and younger incarnations of brilliant but traumatised pianist David Helfgott in the movie *Shine* (1996, director Scott Hicks).

**Holy Smoke** (1998, director Jane Campion) Kate Winslet is the young Australian under the influence of a charismatic guru. Harvey Keitel is the macho cult specialist hired to 'recondition' her at a remote outback location. A sometimes messy battle of both wills and sexes ensues.

**Gallipoli** (1980, director Peter Weir) A powerful antiwar statement infuses this story of mateship between two young Australians in the Lighthorse regiment who take part in the 1915 Gallipoli campaign.

**Breaker Morant** (1980, director Bruce Beresford) Based on true events, the British Army's need for political scapegoats sees three Australian soldiers court-martialled and found guilty of murdering civilian prisoners during the Boer War.

**Storm Boy** (1976, director Henri Safran) A scenic adaptation of Colin Thiele's much-loved children's book about a young boy's isolated existence with his reclusive father on a remote stretch of SA coast.

**Sunday Too Far Away** (1974, director Ken Hannam) Set on an outback shearing station, unionism and mateship under back-breaking work conditions infuse this slow-moving yet intense story.

## Literature

South Australia has been producing notable writers since colonial times. CJ Dennis (of *The Songs of a Sentimental Bloke* fame) is one of the country's most celebrated early poets, while early feminist and writer Catherine Helen Spence became a controversial figure 145 years ago when she wrote *Clara Morison.* The first novel written by a woman about Australia, it details the struggles of a young, educated Scottish woman who, after being jilted on arrival in 1850s SA, must make a new life among the working class.

For something more light-hearted try *Maisie: Her Life, Her Loves, Her Letters 1898-1902,* edited by Joan Willington. This collection of letters gives a fascinating view of colonial social life in SA through the eyes of the enthusiastic young Maisie Smith.

There are also some excellent local contemporary novelists and writers. Peter Goldsworthy's books have received critical acclaim; his most recent novel, *Three Dog Night,* was short-listed for the 2004 Miles Franklin Award. Garry Disher's work covers several genres, including literature, children's writing and nonfiction. His *The Sunken Road* charts one family's fortunes in the wheat and wool country of SA's Mid-North. Geraldine Halls is a thriller writer of international repute, sometimes using the pen name Charlotte Jay. Her acclaimed novel *This Is My Friend's Chair* is a beautifully paced saga of the disintegration of an Adelaide family over 50 years, beginning in the 1920s. Also worth a look is *Bringing the Water,* edited by Mary Costello and Barry Westburg. An anthology of stories based on the theme of clean water, it was inspired by the fact that Port Adelaide was the only major port in Australia where ships refused to take on drinking water (you need only taste it to know why).

Something in SA's water must encourage the development of award-winning children's authors. Mem Fox's *Possum Magic,* Australia's best-selling picture book, has sold more than two million copies, while the first volume of Gillian Rubinstein's *Otori* trilogy, *Across the Nightingale Floor,* out-polled JK Rowling to win the Youth Jury Prize in the German Children's Book Awards. Any discussion of SA writers would be incomplete without mention of Colin Thiele. Author of the multiaward-winning *Storm Boy* and *Blue Fin,* he is one of Australia's most distinguished writers for young people.

Culture vultures should check out the *Adelaide Review* (www.adelaidereview .com.au), Adelaide's fortnightly cultural publication, with listings on what's happening in and around town.

## Visual Arts

The South Australian Museum in Adelaide has a fine collection of Aboriginal art and cultural artefacts. Also in Adelaide, the Tandanya Indigenous Cultural Institute has a gallery featuring exhibitions of Aboriginal art from around Australia. Cultural sites featuring cave paintings and rock carvings are scattered through the northern Flinders Ranges, and several of them can be visited. Other well-known rock-carving sites are near Innamincka on Cooper Creek. In 1992 the world's oldest rock carvings (43,000 years) were found in the Olary region, 350km north of Adelaide.

South Australia's first professional European artists were the Chauncy sisters, Martha and Theresa, who arrived in the colony just six weeks after its proclamation. Each had trained as a miniature portraitist, with Martha painting in oil and watercolour and Theresa working in wax. Martha also painted landscapes and flower studies. Both artists exhibited at the Royal Academy in London, then the most prestigious exhibition venue in the British Empire.

Women dominated SA's visual-arts scene from the 1890s to the 1940s, when they were the most influential art teachers and the chief supporters of modernism. Significant painters during this period were Dorrit Black, Stella Bowen, the Hambidge sisters (Alice, Helen and Millicent), Margaret Preston and Nora Heysen. In 1938, Nora Heysen, the daughter of painter Hans Heysen, won the Archibald Prize, Australia's major award for portraiture.

In contrast, the only really notable male painters of the period were Hans Heysen and Horace Trenerry. Heysen became SA's best-known painter and one of Australia's most famous landscape artists; working in oil and watercolours, he successfully captured the atmosphere and beauty of SA's rural landscapes. The Art Gallery of South Australia holds a large collection of Heysen's work, while other paintings are on display at his studio and house, the Cedars, in Hahndorf (see p91), which hosts a festival in his honour.

See p63 for details on contemporary galleries in Adelaide.

South Australia is home to the most prestigious award in Australian Landscape Art – the Fleurieu Peninsula art prize has a generous purse of $50,000.

For insightful belly laughs from writers able to look at the amusing quirks of life in Adelaide, check out the *Encyclopaedia of SA Culture* at www .saculture.com.

# Environment Tim Flannery & Susannah Farfor

Tim Flannery is a naturalist, explorer and the author of award-winning books including *The Future Eaters* and *Throwim Way Leg,* and the landmark ecological history of North America, *The Eternal Frontier.* Tim Flannery lives in Adelaide where he is director of the South Australian Museum and a professor at the University of Adelaide.

Australia's plants and animals are just about the closest things to alien life you are likely to encounter on earth. That's because Australia has been isolated from the other continents for at least 45 million years. The other habitable continents have been able to exchange various species at different times because they've been linked by land bridges. Just 15,000 years ago it was possible to walk from the southern tip of Africa right through Asia and the Americas to Terra del Fuego. Not Australia, however. Its birds, mammals, reptiles and plants have taken their own separate and very different evolutionary journey, and the result today is the world's most distinct – and one of its most diverse – natural realms.

The first naturalists to investigate Australia were astonished by what they found. Here the swans were black – to Europeans this was a metaphor for the impossible – while mammals such as the platypus and echidna were discovered to lay eggs. It really was an upside-down world where many of the larger animals hopped and where each year the trees shed their bark rather than their leaves.

## A UNIQUE ENVIRONMENT

There are two big factors that go a long way towards explaining nature in Australia: its soils and its climate. Both are unique. Australian soils are the more subtle and difficult to notice of the two, but they have been fundamental in shaping life here. On the other continents, in recent geological times processes such as volcanism, mountain building and glacial activity have been busy creating new soil. Just think of the glacial-derived soils of North America, north Asia and Europe. They feed the world today, and were made by glaciers grinding up rock of differing chemical composition over the last two million years. The rich soils of India and parts of South America were made by rivers eroding mountains, while Java in Indonesia owes its extraordinary richness to volcanoes.

Tim Flannery's *The Future Eaters* is a 'big picture' overview of evolution in Australasia, covering the last 120 million years of history, with thoughts on how the environment has shaped Australasia's human cultures.

All of these soil-forming processes have been almost absent from Australia in more recent times. Only volcanoes have made a contribution, and they cover less than 2% of the continent's land area. In fact, for the last 90 million years, beginning deep in the age of dinosaurs, Australia has been geologically comatose. It was too flat, warm and dry to attract glaciers, its crust too ancient and thick to be punctured by volcanoes or folded into mountains.

Under conditions such as these no new soil is created and the old soil is leached of all its goodness by rain, and is blown and washed away. Even if just 30cm of rain falls each year, this adds up to a column of water 30 million kilometres high passing through the soil over 100 million years, and that can do a great deal of leaching. Almost all of Australia's mountain ranges are more than 90 million years old, so you will see quite a lot of sand here, and a lot of country where the rocky 'bones' of the land are sticking up through the soil. It is an old, infertile landscape, and life in Australia has been adapting to these conditions for aeons.

Australia's misfortune in respect to soils is echoed in its climate. In most parts of the world outside the wet tropics, life responds to the rhythm of the seasons – summer to winter, or wet to dry. Most of Australia experiences seasons – sometimes very severe ones – yet life does not respond solely to them. There are almost no trees that shed their leaves in winter, nor do any Australian animals hibernate. Instead there is a far more potent climatic force that Australian life must obey: El Niño.

The cycle of flood and drought that El Niño brings to Australia is profound. The rivers – even the mighty Murray River, the nation's largest, can be miles wide one year, while you can literally step over its flow the next. This is the power of El Niño, and its effect, when combined with Australia's poor soils, manifests itself compellingly.

So challenging are conditions in Australia that its birds have developed some extraordinary habits. Relatively few of Australia's birds are seasonal breeders, and few migrate. Instead, they breed when the rain comes, and a large percentage are nomads, following the rain across the breadth of the continent. The kookaburras, magpies and blue wrens you are likely to see – to name just a few – have developed a breeding system called 'helpers at the nest'. The helpers are the young adult birds of previous breedings, which stay with their parents to help bring up the new chicks. Just why they should do this was a mystery until it was realised that conditions in Australia can be so harsh that more than two adult birds are needed to feed the nestlings.

Over 80% of SA normally receives less than 250mm of rain annually, while nearly half has an annual evaporation rate exceeding 3000mm. This combination makes SA by far the driest Australian state.

## WILDLIFE
### Animals
Australia is, of course, famous as being the home of the kangaroo and other marsupials. Unless you visit a wildlife park, such creatures are not easy to see as most are nocturnal, although it is possible to see a kangaroo in rural areas in the daytime. Their lifestyles, however, are exquisitely attuned to Australia's harsh conditions. Have you ever wondered why kangaroos, alone among the world's larger mammals, hop? It turns out that hopping is the most efficient way of getting about at medium speeds. This is because the energy of the bounce is stored in the tendons of the legs – much like in a pogo stick – while the intestines bounce up and down like a piston, emptying and filling the lungs without needing to activate the chest muscles. When you travel long distances to find meagre feed, such efficiency is a must.

Marsupials are so efficient that they need to eat a fifth less food than equivalent-sized placental mammals (everything from bats to rats, whales and ourselves). But some marsupials have taken energy efficiency much further. If you get to visit a wildlife park or zoo you might notice that far-away look in a koala's eyes. It seems as if nobody is home – and this is near the truth. Several years ago biologists announced that koalas are the only living creatures that have brains that don't fit their skulls. Instead they have a shrivelled walnut of a brain that rattles around in a fluid-filled cranium. Other researchers have contested this finding, however, pointing out that the brains of the koalas examined for the study may have shrunk because these organs are so soft. Whether soft-brained or empty-headed, there is no doubt that the koala is not the Einstein of the animal world, and we now believe that it has sacrificed its brain to energy efficiency. Brains cost a lot to run – our brains typically weigh 2% of our bodyweight, but use 20% of the energy we consume. Koalas eat gum leaves, which are so toxic that they use 20% of their energy just detoxifying this food. This leaves little energy for the brain, and living in the tree tops where there are so few predators means that they can get by with few wits at all.

Despite anything an Australian tells you about koalas (aka 'dropbears'), there is no risk of one falling onto your head (deliberately or not) as you walk beneath their trees.

South Australia (SA) doesn't have many koalas, but you may see them in the Adelaide Hills, along the Murray River and on Kangaroo Island, where they're prone to eating themselves out of house and home if their numbers aren't controlled.

The peculiar constraints of the Australian environment have not made everything dumb. The koala's nearest relative, the wombat (of which there are three species), have large brains for a marsupial. These creatures live in complex burrows and can weigh up to 35kg, making them the largest herbivorous burrowers on earth. Because their burrows are effectively air-conditioned, they have the neat trick of turning down their metabolic activity when they are in residence. One physiologist who studied their thyroid hormones found that biological activity ceased to such an extent in sleeping wombats that, from a hormonal point of view, they appeared to be dead! Wombats can remain underground for

## WILDLIFE IN FLIGHT

South Australia (SA) has many different habitats, ranging from wetlands to arid gibber plains and from eucalypt forests to mulga scrub and saltbush plains. Throughout the state, 380 species of birds have been recorded including 35 migrants, eight introduced species, and a number of occasional visitors such as the albatross.

Almost half of the 70 species of waders are annual migrants from breeding grounds in the northern hemisphere. They range from tiny dotterels to cranes. Largest of the waders is the brolga, a crane with a wingspan up to 2m. You're most likely to see this bird stalking through the lignum on dried-up outback flood plains.

Parts of the Flinders Ranges, such as the Mt Remarkable, Flinders Ranges and Gammon Ranges National Parks, have large trees, dense scrub, massive rocky outcrops, open grassy areas, reedbeds and water holes virtually side by side. Many coastal areas, such as St Kilda and the Coorong, have shallows backed by scrub or mangroves. The Murray River has billabongs, lakes, grassy flats, large trees and extensive cane-grass thickets.

The best areas for seeing parrots and cockatoos are along the Murray and in timbered areas of the Southeast and the southern Mt Lofty Ranges.

In the arid outback, prime spots for bird-watching include Cooper Creek, near Innamincka, and Purnie Bore, in Witjira National Park. Flocks of cockatoos and pigeons come in to drink at such places, which also provide stepping stones for migratory water birds on their long journeys across Australia. The inland salt lakes are mainly dry, but when they fill after rare floods they can become major nesting areas.

Large areas of native bush in conservation parks in the Murraylands, the upper Southeast and Eyre Peninsula are fantastic for honeyeaters and insect-eaters when the mallee gums and banksia are in flower. Here you'll also find the elusive mallee fowl, which incubates its eggs in a huge pile of rotting vegetation.

On Kangaroo Island, you may see glossy black cockatoos and Cape Barren geese. The island's northern coastal shallows are excellent places to observe water birds such as gulls, ducks, pelicans, swans and waders. Elsewhere, you might spot an osprey or white-bellied sea-eagle patrolling the coastal cliffs.

The Southeast has major wetlands at the Coorong and Bool Lagoon, where water birds reign supreme. Other good spots to see nesting waders and other water birds are the mangrove swamps around both the Spencer Gulf and Gulf St Vincent.

There are penguin-watching tours on Kangaroo Island and Granite Island (off Victor Harbor), while several islands off the far west coast are breeding grounds for millions of short-tailed shearwaters.

South Australia has 21 species of raptor (birds of prey) including peregrine falcons, owls and nightjars. The largest is the wedge-tailed eagle, with a wingspan of up to 3m. While you'll see falcons, kites, hawks and eagles in (or above) all habitats, the only owl you're likely to come in contact with is the boobook owl. Found in a wide range of habitats, its mournful 'boo-book' call is a common nightly sound throughout rural SA.

a week at a time, and can get by on just a third of the food needed by an equivalent-sized sheep. One day perhaps, efficiency-minded farmers will keep wombats instead of sheep. You're likely to see them only at night as they cross the roads; they're quite common along the Eyre Highway (Hwy 1) west of Ceduna.

South Australia's native marsupials include koalas, platypuses, kangaroos, potoroos, bandicoots, water rats, marsupial moles, gliding possums, pygmy possums and various rats and mice. The state is home to four species of kangaroo: the red kangaroo, western and eastern grey kangaroos, and the euro, generally found in dry, hilly country. Rock wallabies, their smallish, agile relatives, live in colonies in the rocky ranges. The endangered yellow-footed rock wallaby inhabits the Flinders and Gawler Ranges. When camping in sandy areas of the outback, you'll often see tracks like those of tiny kangaroos around your swag in the morning. Most likely they will have been left by the spinifex hopping-mouse, which spends the daylight hours in deep burrows under vegetation. Similar tracks are left by Mitchell's hopping-mouse in southern mallee areas.

One of the more common marsupials you might catch a glimpse of in the national parks in SA's Southeast are the species of antechinus, or marsupial mouse. These nocturnal, rat-sized creatures lead an extraordinary life. The males live for just 11 months, the first 10 of which consist of a concentrated burst of eating and growing. And like teenage males, the day comes when their minds turn to sex, which then becomes an obsession. As they embark on their quest for females they forget to eat and sleep. Instead they gather in logs and woo passing females by serenading them with squeaks. Just two weeks after they reach 'puberty' – every single male is dead, exhausted by sex and burdened with swollen testes. This extraordinary life history may have evolved in response to Australia's trying environmental conditions. It seems likely that if the males survived mating, they would compete with the females as they tried to find enough food to feed their growing young. Basically, antechinus dads are disposable. They do better for antechinus posterity if they go down in a testosterone-fuelled blaze of glory.

Australia's deserts are a real hit-and-miss affair, as far as wildlife is concerned. If visiting in a drought year, all you might see are dusty plains, the odd mob of kangaroos and emus, and a few struggling trees. Return after big rains, however, and you'll encounter something close to a Garden of Eden. Fields of white and gold daisies stretch endlessly into the distance, perfuming the air. The salt lakes fill with fresh water, and millions of water birds – pelicans, stilts, shags and gulls – can be seen feeding on the superabundant fish and insect life of the waters. It all seems like a mirage, and like a mirage it will vanish as the land dries out, only to spring to life again in a few year's or a decade's time.

There's a fantastic diversity in Australia's southern waters, where the Great Australian Bight is home to more kinds of marine creatures than anywhere else on earth. The largest creatures found in the Australian region are marine mammals such as whales and seals, and there is no better place to see them than SA. In springtime southern right whales crowd into the head of the Great Australian Bight. You can observe them near the remote Aboriginal community of Yatala as they mate, frolic and suckle their young. Kangaroo Island is a fantastic place to see seals and sea lions (p117). There are well-developed visitors centres to facilitate viewing of wildlife, and nightly penguin parades occur at some places where the adult blue penguins make their nest burrows. Indeed, Kangaroo Island's beaches are magic places, where you're able to stroll

Pizzey and Knight's *Field Guide to Birds of Australia* is an indispensable guide for bird-watchers and anyone else even peripherally interested in Australia's feathered tribes. Knight's illustrations are both beautiful and helpful in identification.

Surprisingly, marine turtles that have strayed from northern breeding grounds are often sighted off the western and southern coasts of the Eyre Peninsula.

among fabulous shells, whale bones and even spot jewel-like leafy sea dragons amid the sea wrack.

Reptiles are abundant in SA, particularly snakes which include the most venomous species known – the fierce snake (or inland taipan) of the far northeast. Another dangerous snake to stay away from is the tiger snake.

Some visitors mistake lizards for snakes, and indeed some Australian lizards look bizarre. Some of the strangest are the Lake Eyre dragon, which lives on the lake's dry salt crust, and the thorny devil, with its deceptively ferocious appearance incorporating thorn-like protusions on its back. Largest of all is the perentie, which grows to over 2m.

## Plants

South Australia's Plant Diversity Centre publishes *Flora of South Australia* and administers a comprehensive website (www.flora.sa.gov.au) with fact sheets, identification tips, distribution maps and census data on SA's plants, fungi and algae.

Australia's plants can be irresistibly fascinating. Wild flowers range from delicate orchids to hardy paper daisies. The state's floral emblem is Sturt's desert pea, an annual ground creeper with large, vivid crimson blooms which flower in the north in winter and early spring.

The massed, rich purple flowers of Salvation Jane (also known as Patterson's curse) are a stunning feature of the Mid-North and Flinders Ranges in early spring. Although apiarists love them, they can be poisonous to stock. Wild hops, another weed of the Flinders, puts on a good springtime show with red, papery flowers.

In winter and spring, coastal SA and the mallee belt are transformed by flowers of every hue including magnificent heaths. After good autumn and winter rains in the outback, sandy plains explode with colour as daisies and other annuals hurry to set seed before the soil dries out again.

The Australian Arid Lands Botanic Garden in Port Augusta (p201) is a good place to learn about arid-zone flora, while the Adelaide Botanic Garden (p66) boasts a large collection of temperate-zone flora, including a mallee section.

The landscape is dominated by fire and drought-tolerant plants such as acacias, eucalypts and saltbush. Most obvious are the larger eucalypts –

---

### THE WILD SIDE

South Australia has 314 conservation areas covering 210,000 sq km (21.3% of the state's land area). The day-to-day management of public land conservation areas is carried out by the **Department for Environment & Heritage** (DEH; www.environment.sa.gov.au/parks).

The 20,000 sq km Great Australian Bight Marine Park includes a major breeding area of the southern right whale. This is more a multiuse area than a national park as commercial activities such as fishing are allowed within its boundaries.

Vast regional reserves in the remote arid regions of the state provide a measure of protection for important habitats and natural features, while allowing other land uses such as mining and pastoralism to take place.

The majority of SA's designated national park areas sit in arid regions including the Late Eyre, Lake Torrens and Lake Gairdner parks which consist of mainly dry saltpan beds. Many of the state's scenic and ecological highlights are protected in national parks. On Kangaroo Island, Flinders Chase National Park is best known for its coastal scenery and wildlife, including rare species of birds and mammals. The Flinders Ranges, Mt Remarkable and Gammon Ranges National Parks in the Flinders Ranges have stunning scenery, great bushwalks and colonies of yellow-footed rock wallabies. Canunda, Coffin Bay, Innes and Lincoln are popular coastal parks; Nullarbor National Park, on the far west coast, has massive cave systems; and Witjira in the far north has the fascinating Dalhousie Springs, a unique wetland habitat on the edge of the Simpson Desert.

You hardly need to travel far to get into nature, as parks such as Belair, Morialta and Kuitpo are all on Adelaide's doorstep.

called 'gum trees' – which include the river red gums that grow along watercourses throughout the state, the blue gums and candlebarks of the Mt Lofty Ranges and lower Southeast, sugar gums of Kangaroo Island and the southern Flinders Ranges, and the coolibah on flood plains throughout the outback. 'Mallees' in the drier, more infertile areas in the south are particularly resistant to fire and drought.

There's a distinct boundary between the eucalypt-dominated communities of the south and the acacia (wattle) communities further north. Distinctive and widespread outback acacias include myall (common around Port Augusta) and mulga, favoured by Aboriginal people for making boomerangs, spears, shields and digging sticks. Another common wattle with hard, narrow leaves is 'dead finish', so-called because when these tough plants start to die in a drought you know the country's finished!

The shrubby saltbush of the outback makes nutritious food for grazing animals such as kangaroos, sheep and cattle.

South Australia's mangrove forests, along the shores of Gulf St Vincent and Spencer Gulf are breeding areas for many water-bird species and marine creatures, including the King George whiting, SA's most popular table fish.

## ENVIRONMENTAL CHALLENGES

The European colonisation of Australia, commencing in 1788, heralded a period of catastrophic environmental upheaval, with the result that Australians today are struggling with some of the world's most severe environmental problems. It may seem strange that a population of just 20 million, living in a continent the size of the USA minus Alaska, could inflict such damage on its environment, but Australia's long isolation, its fragile soils and difficult climate have made it particularly vulnerable to human-induced change.

The destruction of forests has had a profound effect. Many Australian rangelands have been chronically overstocked for more than a century, the result being extreme vulnerability of both soils and rural economies to Australia's drought and flood cycle, as well as extinction of many native species. The development of agriculture has involved land clearance and the provision of irrigation, and here again the effect has been profound.

Due to habitat degradation, the escape of domestic cats into the Australian bush and the introduction of vermin such as rabbits, foxes, pigs, goats and wild camels, a third of SA's mammals have become extinct since settlement in 1836. Public concern over this tremendous loss of biological diversity resulted in the declaration of the Native Vegetation Act 1983, which places strict controls on further clearances. Although there have been successful reintroductions in small protected areas, large-scale recovery of threatened species is unlikely without the removal of foxes and feral cats.

In terms of financial value, just 1.5% of Australia's land surface provides over 95% of agricultural yield, and much of this land lies in the irrigated regions of the Murray–Darling Basin. This is Australia's agricultural heartland, yet it too is under severe threat from salting of soils and rivers. Irrigation water penetrates into the sediments laid down in an ancient sea, carrying salt into the catchments and fields. If nothing is done, the lower Murray River will become too salty to drink in a decade or two, threatening the water supply of Adelaide.

South Australia's low rainfall and lack of permanent streams have created a huge challenge in developing the state. Many towns in the Southeast and on the Eyre Peninsula rely on underground basins for

B Beale and P Fray's *The Vanishing Continent* gives an excellent overview of soil erosion across Australia. Fine colour photographs make the issue very graphic.

---

**SO LONG, SO MANY, SO HIGH...**

- South Australia covers 984,400 sq km – 12.8% of the entire country.
- South Australia's coastline stretches for 3,700km.
- Mt Woodroffe (1435m), in Musgrave Ranges, is SA's highest point.
- The Murray, Australia's largest river, meanders for 650km through SA.
- South Australia has around 100 islands, the largest by far being Kangaroo Island.
- Over 80% of SA is less than 300m above sea level.
- Around 80% of SA's land is classed as arid, or 'the outback'.
- The 5400km-long Dog Fence cuts through the Great Victorian Desert, Coober Pedy and Moon Plain, along its length from Surfers Paradise in Queensland to the Bight near the Western Australian border.

---

survival. In some areas, these resources are being exploited beyond the recharge rate.

Despite the enormity of the biological crisis engulfing Australia, governments and the community have been slow to respond. It was in the 1980s that coordinated action began to take place, but not until the '90s that major steps were taken. The establishment of **Landcare** (www.landcareaustralia.com.au), an organisation enabling people to effectively address local environmental issues, and the expenditure of $2.5 billion through the National Heritage Trust Fund have been important national initiatives. Yet so difficult are some of the issues the nation faces that, as yet, little has been achieved in terms of halting the destructive processes. Individuals are also banding together to help. Groups such as the **Australian Bush Heritage Fund** (www.bushheritage.asn.au) and the **Australian Wildlife Conservancy** (AWC; www.australianwildlife.org) allow people to donate funds and time to the conservation of native species. Some such groups have been spectacularly successful; the AWC, for example, already manages many endangered species over its 450,000-hectare holdings.

So severe are Australia's problems that it will take a revolution before they can be overcome: sustainable practices need to be implemented in every arena of life – from farms to suburbs and city centres. Renewable energy, sustainable agriculture and water use lie at the heart of these changes, and Australians are only now developing the road map to sustainability that they so desperately need if they are to have a long-term future on the continent.

# South Australia Outdoors

Seekers of wilderness experiences or an adrenaline rush will find a smorgasbord of choices in the rugged hills, wide open spaces and expansive coastline of South Australia (SA). While you could happily slurp up a surreal week of vineyard views and liquid lunches, discovering the perfect drop to stock your cellar with, there are plenty of opportunities for exploration outdoors. There are countless trails for hikers, riders and cyclists; rock walls to scale; wildlife to encounter; and waters to paddle, fish, surf and plunge into.

Useful contacts for more information include the outdoor gear shops in Adelaide (p80). Pick up a copy of the *Ultimate Experience* brochure for listings of adrenaline sports around the city.

## ABSEILING & ROCK-CLIMBING

Enthusiasts scale gorge walls and 10m- to 15m-high cliffs near Adelaide at the **Morialta Conservation Park** (www.environment.sa.gov.au/parks/morialta/rock.html) and Onkaparinga Gorge. Both areas have routes suitable for beginner and advanced grades. **Rock Solid Adventure** ( ☎ 08-8270 4244; www.rock-solid-adventure .com) organises climbs in these areas.

Tap into local climbing knowledge at www .thecrag.com.

The Flinders Ranges offers some scope for climbing around Warren Gorge (p208), near Quorn, while 120m cliffs elsewhere in the park challenge skilled climbers.

## BUSHWALKING

South Australia's extensive designated walking tracks weave a web over the state. Park tracks wend through leafy gorges jumping with wildlife, along remote and rugged coastlines, and through arid and ancient landscapes with craggy monoliths where you may find no trails at all apart from those formed by cattle, sheep and kangaroo pads. The legendary Heysen Trail, which links the Flinders Ranges to the coast of the Fleurieu Peninsula, can be experienced through individual day hikes or as a long-distance expedition.

Lonely Planet's *Bushwalking in Australia* provides detailed information about bushwalking, including in the Mt Remarkable and Wilpena Pound areas.

Conservation parks and state forests in the Adelaide Hills (p86) offer excellent walking on the city's doorstep. Further south Deep Creek Conservation Park (p105), near Cape Jervis on Fleurieu Peninsula, provides scenic yet challenging walks along exposed coastline, with possible whale sightings in season.

On Kangaroo Island, wilderness tracks through Flinders Chase National Park (p125) and Cape Gantheaume Conservation Park (p124) will take anywhere from one hour to two days to complete.

Vintage sleuths in the Barossa Ranges don't have to venture far from the cellar door to find some outdoor activities. Walking tracks wend past wineries and historic Lutheran churches, native bushland and wildlife in Para Wirra Recreation Park and Kaiser Stuhl Conservation Park (p166).

The 26km Riesling Trail (p175) in the Mid-North follows a dismantled railway through the Clare Valley between Auburn and Clare, and has plenty of excellent wineries en route where you can stop and quench your thirst.

Huge dunes and long, empty beaches are the highlights in the Coorong (p146) and Canunda National Parks (p149) in the lower Southeast. On the Eyre Peninsula, beach and scrubland walks near Lincoln National Park include the 109km Investigator Trail (p226), while nature lovers and

## THE HEYSEN TRAIL

The roughly 1200km-long Heysen Trail (named after Hans Heysen, the famous SA landscape artist) starts at Cape Jervis, south of Adelaide, winds along the ridge tops of the Mt Lofty and Flinders Ranges and finishes in Parachilna Gorge, north of Wilpena Pound. It passes through some of the state's major scenic and historical highlights, and traverses two of its finest conservation areas: the Mt Remarkable and Flinders Ranges National Parks.

From Cape Jervis the trail heads east along the coast, where you'll pass lookout points for seasonal sightings of southern right whales. Although designed as a long-distance route, the many access points along the way make it ideal for half- and full-day walks.

For the most part it's clearly marked and apart from a handful of very steep or rough areas the going is seldom difficult for fit and experienced walkers. Places to stay along the trail include campsites, huts and B&Bs in nearby towns, though they become fewer north of Quorn. A permit is required to camp in conservation areas and in some state forests, and the landholder's permission is required to camp on private property.

Each of the trail's 15 sections is described by its own foldout map-guide (available at map and outdoor specialist shops), which include an excellent 1:50,000 topographic strip map.

- **Cape Jervis to Newland Hill** (60km) Follows the rugged coastline with superb coastal views, sandy beaches and beautiful forest. A spectacular waterfall in Deep Creek Conservation Park is the only reliable water spot. This section is for the fit and well-equipped; have tough clothing (including gardening gloves) to protect against thorns.

- **Newland Hill to Mt Magnificent** (65km) A hilly section meandering through a mix of native forest and farmland, with stunning views from high points such as Mt Cone and Mt Magnificent.

- **Mt Magnificent to Mt Lofty** (50km) Traverses a hilly mosaic of farmland, native bush and pine forest including the Kuitpo Forest, Mt Lofty Botanic Gardens, Cleland Conservation Park and the old Bridgewater Mill.

- **Mt Lofty to the Barossa Range** (80km) High ridge tops through native bush, pine forest and farmland via the magnificent and steep Mt Lofty Ranges, Norton Summit and Cudlee Creek. This section finishes in beautiful hills on the edge of the Barossa Valley. For the fit.

- **Barossa Range to Hamilton** (85km) Crosses the Barossa Range through magnificent gums and Kaiser Stuhl Conservation Park, then leads into wine country at Tanunda, heading out to Greenock and tiny Hamilton, about 15km northwest of Kapunda.

- **Hamilton to Logans Gap** (75km) Follows a timbered ridge before climbing Peters Hill, with scenic views of the saw-toothed Tothill Range and plenty of wildlife. Crosses farmland and follows the range for the final 43km to Logans Gap. Some steep rugged sections.

For full Heysen Trail details, pick up Terry Lavender's series of books entitled *The Heysen Trail A Walkers Guide*, or look out for the Department for Environment & Heritage's published trail guides.

bushwalkers are discovering the Gawler Ranges National Park (p229), near Ceduna.

The ancient, remote landscape of the Flinders Ranges warrants a trip in itself for many lured by the network of tracks traversing through the Flinders Ranges (p210) and Mt Remarkable (p205) National Parks. The Gammon Ranges National Park (p214) has stacks of potential for walkers who don't need a track to follow.

Winter is the best time for walking in the north in order to avoid the searing heat, though maximums of around 10°C with light rain and a bitter wind are sometimes experienced. In the south, autumn and spring (which can be changeable) are more popular than summer (very hot) and winter (cold and sometimes wet). Always carry windproof clothing in the cooler months; hypothermia can be a real health risk during winter, particularly if you're poorly prepared and happen to get lost. Many tracks, particularly in forested areas, are closed during the fire danger period and on total fire ban days.

- **Logans Gap to Newickie Creek** (55km) Traverses hilly, mainly open country. Follows the ridge top into historic Burra, then enters a wide belt of jumbled, rounded hills. Some steep slopes.
- **Newickie Creek to Spalding** (85km) A sparsely populated section which leads through a varied landscape of rugged hills and gorges with fantastic sweeping panoramas from the higher points; highlights include Tourillie Gorge and abundant wildlife.
- **Spalding to Hughes Gap** (85km) Beautiful walking in a generally easy section (steep in parts) crossing the sparsely populated hills of the northern Mt Lofty Ranges, then heading into the Flinders Ranges at Crystal Brook.
- **Hughes Gap to Melrose** (75km) This mostly easy section climbs onto the main spine of the southern Flinders Ranges, with marvellous views over Spencer Gulf to the west, followed by remote timbered ridge tops, then descends the range to picturesque Melrose under Mt Remarkable. Features euros and plenty of birdlife.
- **Melrose to Woolshed Flat** (70km) A steep and rocky section which heads through the trees to Mt Remarkable summit, then descends along steep, rugged ridges to Wilmington. Continues up the Port Augusta road, followed by 30km of rough, timbered ridges to the Pichi Richi Pass. Provides outstanding views, wildlife, magnificent gums and solitude. Be fit and prepared.
- **Woolshed Flat to Buckaringa Gorge** (65km) A generally rugged, remote stretch passing through spectacular scenery (home of the rare yellow-footed rock wallaby) in Quorn and Dutchmans Stern Conservation Park. Isolated country from Quorn, with rock formations and plenty of wildlife. You can see to the edge of the world from Mt Arden, near the northern end. For the well-experienced walker.
- **Buckaringa Gorge to Hawker** (62km) Although rugged in parts, this section is more subdued and open with isolated homesteads en route.
- **Hawker to Wilpena** (50km) Passes through semiarid station country dominated by the spectacular Elder Range and Wilpena Pound's south wall, featuring abundant wildlife, beautiful gum-lined creeks and native pine forest. Crosses the Wilpena Pound Range at Bridle Gap with magnificent views at the entry to the pound. Water supplies are extremely limited in this remote section.
- **Wilpena to Parachilna Gorge** (65km) Traverses the dramatic landscapes for which the Flinders Ranges are famous, with historic ruins and abundant wildlife. Continues along the foot of the towering Wilpena Range, then north along deep, narrow valleys between the ABC and Heysen Ranges, leading to beautiful Parachilna Gorge. Some good short walks here.

## CANOEING & KAYAKING

Abundant wildlife, good fishing, magnificent river scenery and quiet places to camp make the Murray River and its associated wetlands great spots for canoeing adventurists. Other good spots include the Coorong, Eyre Peninsula and the mangrove inlets between Port Adelaide (take mozzie repellent!) and St Kilda, and the Onkaparinga River south of Adelaide.

Sea-kayakers should try Rapid Bay on the Fleurieu Peninsula, the northern coast of Kangaroo Island, Boston Bay at Port Lincoln, the bays of Spencer Gulf and Gulf St Vincent, and the islands off Victor Harbor, where gear hire is available.

**Canoe South Australia** ( ☎ 08-8240 3294; www.sa.canoe.org.au) can provide information on clubs and courses, and gear for sale.

Trade state walking secrets via Walking SA ( ☎ 08-8338 3099; www.walkingsa.org.au).

## CAVING

South Australia has extensive cave systems in the Southeast (p149), and in the far west at the Murrawijinie Caves (p232) under the Nullarbor Plain, an extraordinary feature of the barren landscape. Near Mt Gambier in the Southeast, you can visit show caves on guided tours at Tantanoola (p149) and the World Heritage–listed Naracoorte Caves (p157), where ancient fossilised marsupials were found between the stalactites and stalagmites. Accredited divers can also explore the world-class Piccaninnie Ponds (p149). At Kelly Hill on Kangaroo Island (p124), the dry limestone caves feature squiggly helictites and also offer adventure caving.

## CYCLING

Cyclists have staked their claim on Adelaide, which has a good network of cycling routes. One of these follows the path through the Torrens River Linear Park, taking you about 40km along the Torrens River from the sea into the foothills of the Mt Lofty Ranges.

Bicycle SA ( ☎ 08-8410 1406; www.bikesa.asn .au), the state's umbrella organisation for touring cyclists, provides information and organises endurance rides of 200km to 1200km, camping weekends and guided tours.

You can weave along bike trails between cellar doors in winery regions, or check out the variety in regions like the Fleurieu Peninsula, Mt Lofty Ranges, Barossa Valley and Flinders Ranges. Extreme enthusiasts can pedal 800km along the dedicated Mawson Trail (see below) from Adelaide to the Flinders Ranges. Cycling through the outback and Murray Mallee is often very monotonous (and requires serious advanced planning). The fact that 'it's there' is too great a pull for some (often called 'mad') who will head out under the scorching sun across the Nullarbor to Western Australia or up the Stuart Hwy into the Northern Territory.

For more details on cycling see p270.

## FISHING

You can cast a line in just about anywhere along the coast, where conditions range from pounding surf to millpond calm. There's good freshwater fishing in the Murray River, numerous lakes and freshwater streams, and even outback waterholes.

---

### THE MAWSON TRAIL

Like bushwalkers, cyclists have their own rugged long-distance challenge in SA: the 800km Mawson Trail from the Festival Centre, in the heart of Adelaide, to Blinman in the Flinders Ranges.

Named after Sir Douglas Mawson, a great Australian explorer and geologist who found inspiration in the Flinders Ranges, the trail traverses remote scenic back country along mainly dirt roads and 4WD tracks. A good dose of difficult cycling makes it an unforgettable experience.

The trail is marked at 1km intervals and intersections, and is broken into five sections, each with its own brochure complete with excellent strip maps.

Apart from the section north of Wilmington, which requires a bush camp or two, the Mawson Trail can be planned as a series of day rides between towns.

- **Adelaide to Marrabel** (170km) Follows the Torrens River Linear Park cycle path to Athelstone, on Gorge Rd, then north through the Adelaide Hills to the Barossa Valley wineries, and on to Kapunda.

- **Marrabel to Spalding** (220km) Heads through the bald hills around Burra, doing a major switch back along the way and passing close to tiny Hallett. Challenging hills.

- **Spalding to Wilmington** (170km) Through mainly rolling farmland and the townships of Laura and Melrose; climbs up onto the southern Flinders Ranges in the Wirrabara Forest.

- **Wilmington to Hawker** (140km) An extremely scenic stretch via picturesque Warren Gorge, with testing climbs between Quorn and Hawker.

- **Hawker to Blinman** (100km) An moderate section with terrific scenery and plenty of wildlife. Via Wonoka and the Moralana Scenic Drive to Rawnsley Park, and then on to the Wilpena Pound Resort. Follows vehicle tracks through the Flinders Ranges National Park.

On surf beaches the catch includes Australian salmon, mulloway, shark, tommy rough, trevally, bream, tailor and flathead. Popular spots include the ocean beaches between Port Lincoln and Ceduna on the west coast (p232), Browns Beach on the southern tip of Yorke Peninsula (p122), Waitpinga Beach near Victor Harbor (p105), Pennington Bay on Kangaroo Island (p121), and the Ninety Mile Beach (p146) near Kingston SE.

While the best sea fishing is generally from a boat, particularly in the gulfs, SA's long jetties allow you to fish in fairly deep water. There are some beauties on the Yorke Peninsula and Eyre peninsulas, and at Wallaroo and Ceduna, where you can catch a wide range of species. If the ink stains on the piers are anything to go by, squid makes for many a meal, and blue-swimmer crabs are also hauled in. The latter can be caught in shallow sheltered water in the northern coastal areas of the two gulfs and in suitable habitats along the west coast.

Rock fishing yields species such as sweep, groper, snapper, salmon trout and trevally. Salmon and mulloway lurk where the rocks are exposed to the Southern Ocean. However, watch out for extremely dangerous 'king waves' that occasionally roll in from the ocean. It's smart to wear lightweight clothing and a buoyancy vest if you're fishing close to the water, particularly where the rocks are exposed to swells.

The most popular eating fish in SA is the succulent King George whiting. You can catch them right along the coast, but the best spots are in sheltered waters with sandy bottoms, with most caught in the gulfs, Investigator Strait, and bays along the west coast.

Provided you have a SA or interstate boat licence you can hire dinghies with outboards in some areas.

South Australian Trails (www.southaustralian trails.com) has a wealth of information on activities in the great outdoors including horse riding, canoeing, hiking, cycling and diving with useful maps, safety tips and links to organisations.

## HORSE & CAMEL RIDING

Sadly, due to the huge costs of public liability insurance in Australia, riding ranches have closed down and there are few opportunities to ride horses or camels in SA.

You can get yourself in the saddle at Norman Bay on the Fleurieu Peninsula (p104), Naracoorte (p157), the Clare Valley (p173), and Rawnsley Park (p209) in the Flinders Ranges. Lurching camel treks are possible along the Murray River (p137), around Coober Pedy (p243) and William Creek (p237), and from Coward Springs (p248) to Lake Eyre.

## SCUBA DIVING & SNORKELLING

The state's underwater world hides a great diversity of dive spots on jetties, wrecks, drop-offs and caves, with reefs and sponge beds sporting fish, starfish, colourful sponges, nudibranchs and soft corals. Shore-diving off Adelaide's metropolitan beaches is limited, though boat divers can plunge to a sunken reef formed by the scuttled dredge, *South Australian,* which lies at a depth of 20m about 6km off Glenelg. It's now home to a staggering variety of marine life.

There's a whole other world to discover under SA's water; go to www .dive-southaustralia.com for inspiration.

The Fleurieu Peninsula (p98), south of Adelaide, has some cool little shore and boat dives including Port Noarlunga's reef marine reserve (which has a signposted underwater trail suitable for snorkellers), Aldinga and Snapper Point. The Rapid Bay jetty is renowned for its abundant marine life (including leafy sea dragons) and has been the location for underwater film shoots. Scuttled in 2002 the intact HMAS *Hobart* is the new 'burb for marine critters and is now regarded as one of the country's best wreck dives.

There are reefs, wrecks and drop-offs around Kangaroo Island (p116), and plenty of wrecks around Port MacDonnell (p153) and the Yorke

Peninsula including near Ardrossan (p185), Innes National Park (p189) and Edithburgh (p187). There's a jetty dive for every wind condition on the Yorke Peninsula – if one side is too rough, the other will usually be diveable. At Dangerous Reef, off Port Lincoln, those pushing the fear factor can look a white pointer shark in the eye – and teeth – from the safety (?) of a suspended diving cage (p224).

One of the best freshwater dives in the world is at Piccaninnie Ponds (p149), near Mt Gambier. Here, divers with cave-diving certificates can explore the legendary formations, huge caverns and deep sink holes in incredibly clear water. Also excellent is Ewens Ponds Conservation Park.

## SWIMMING & SURFING

Uncrowded, white and sandy swimming beaches stretch right along the coast, with the safest generally being on Gulf St Vincent and Spencer Gulf. Anywhere that's exposed to the Southern Ocean and Investigator Strait, which separates Kangaroo Island from the mainland, may have strong rips and undertows. Those seeking tan-line free bathing can head to the nudist beach at Maslin Beach on the Fleurieu Peninsula, 40km from Adelaide.

There's reasonable surf south of Adelaide in the right conditions – Seaford and Southport have reliable, if small, waves. Surfers descend on any area exposed to the Southern Ocean's rolling swells. The closest surf to Adelaide of any real consequence is near Victor Harbor at Waitpinga Beach, Middleton and Port Elliot. Pennington Bay (p121) has the most consistent surf on Kangaroo Island. Pondalowie (p189), on the 'foot' of Yorke Peninsula, has the state's most reliable strong breaks. Other notable sites are scattered between Port Lincoln, at the southern tip of Eyre Peninsula, and the famous Cactus Beach (p232) in the far west.

There's endless potential for sailboarding and kiteboarding along the coast and on many lakes. In summer Adelaide beaches have strong sea breezes. The windiest city beaches (from north to south; see p81) are Semaphore, Henley Beach, North Glenelg and Seacliff, and Sellicks Beach (p103). Each has its own set of hazards, so check with locals before plunging in. The state's most popular place for both advanced and novice windsurfers is Goolwa, with a range of conditions in a reasonably small area. Other top spots include Barmera (Lake Bonney; p135), Beachport (Lake George; p149), Meningie (Lake Albert; p145) and Milang (Lake Alexandrina; p111). Robe (p147), Port Lincoln and the beaches around Yorke Peninsula are good coastal spots.

## WHALE- & DOLPHIN-WATCHING

Migrating southern right whales often come within a few hundred metres of shore as they pass along the ocean coast to breeding grounds in the Bight between July and September. Hot spots for whale-watching include Victor Harbor (p105), the south coast of Kangaroo Island, Port Lincoln, Elliston and, the hottest and most reliable of them all, from the Aboriginal community of Yalata at Head of Bight (p232) on the far west coast. The recorded message service on ☎ 1900 931 223 provides information about recent whale sightings.

Bottlenose dolphins can be seen year-round along the coast, including at Adelaide's beaches, Middleton on the Fleurieu Peninsula and Blackfellows (p227) on the Eyre Peninsula.

Waxheads can get the scoop around the state with plenty of details on surf breaks at www.surfsouthoz.com.

The *Atlas of Australian Surfing: Travellers Edition*, by legendary Oz surfer Mark Warren, promises to reveal the biggest waves and the best-kept-secret surf in Australia.

# Food & Drink

A cosmopolitan mix has resulted in a very exciting food scene in South Australia (SA). The Greeks, Yugoslavs, Italians, Lebanese and many others who came to Australia from the late 1940s through to the 1960s brought their food to add to that of the early British and German settlers. The Chinese have been enlivening taste buds since the gold-rush days, while more recently Indian, Thai, Malaysian, Vietnamese and Middle Eastern tastes have added new dimensions. Modern Australian (Mod Oz) is used to describe the country's cuisine, often described as a melange of East and West. Dishes aren't usually too fussy and the flavours are often bold and interesting.

Australia's first espresso cafés opened in the 1950s – Lucia's Pizza & Spaghetti Bar (p75) in Adelaide is still in business.

## STAPLES & SPECIALITIES

Australia's best food comes from the sea. Nothing compares to this continent's seafood, including tommy-ruff, groper and the esteemed King George whiting harnessed from some of the purest waters you'll find anywhere, and usually cooked with care. Connoisseurs prize SA's fantastic crayfish (rock lobster), estuary scallops and home-grown oysters. Marron are prehistoric-looking freshwater crayfish from Kangaroo Island, while their freshwater cousins, yabbies, can be found throughout the Southeast. Barramundi are farmed in SA or transported from the Northern Territory. Carnivores prize the quality of Kangaroo Island beef, Maggie Beer's pheasants and venison from the Adelaide Hills.

Almost everything grown from the land (as opposed to the sea) was introduced to Australia. The fact that the country is huge (similar in size to continental USA) and varies so much in climate, from the tropical north to the temperate south, means that there's an enormous variety of produce on offer.

*The Market – Stories, History and Recipes from the Adelaide Central Market* by Catherine Murphy features delicious recipes by Rosa Matto, one of Adelaide's finest chefs. Cath Kerry's *The Haigh's Book of Chocolate* is a dangerous tome indeed!

A stroll through Adelaide's Central Market (p67) will give you a taste of the diversity of fresh produce, the nation's best tomatoes, and organics grown in the fertile hills and surrounds. South Australia seems to breed passionate small producers intent on perfecting their product – boutique vignerons, Haigh's fine chocolates, David Medlow's smooth fruit pectin gels and Maggie Beer's farmhouse pastes and tastes. You'll find liquid-gold honey produced by pure strains of Ligurian bees on Kangaroo Island.

There's a small but brilliant farmhouse cheese movement, hampered by the fact that all the milk must be pasteurised (unlike in Italy and France, home of the world's best cheeses). Despite that, the results can be great. Keep an eye out for Udder Delights, Woodside Cheese Wrights and Kangaroo Island products.

Australians' taste for the unusual typically kicks in only at dinner. Most people still eat cereal for breakfast, or perhaps eggs and bacon on weekends. They devour sandwiches for lunch with nearly the same verve as they do in the UK, and then eat anything and everything in the evening. *Yum cha* (the classic southern Chinese dumpling feast), however, has found huge popularity with urban locals in recent years, particularly for lunch on weekends, and nori rolls sit alongside focaccias in café cabinets.

## DRINKS

You're in the right place if you're after a drink. Once a nation of tea- and beer-swillers, Australia has now turned its attention to coffee and wine also.

With the exception of the desert regions, chances are that you'll be within slurping distance of one of SA's world-renowned wine regions. Most wineries have cellar doors for tastings; if you like the wine, you're generally expected to buy. See the wineries section (p48) for detailed coverage.

Plenty of good wine comes from big producers with economies of scale on their side, but the most interesting wines are usually made by 'boutique' vignerons where you pay a premium – but the gamble means the payoff, in terms of flavour, is often greater. Much of the cost of wine (nearly 42%) is due to a high taxing programme courtesy of the Australian government.

Beer in Australia has suffered from the bland, chilled-so-you-can-barely-taste-it variety. However, SA has the robust, full-bodied Coopers (brewed in Adelaide) on its side. It has a range of light and full-strength ales and beers for the connoisseur, including sparkling ale (Coopers red), pale ale (Coopers green) and the Extra Strong Vintage Ale. Coopers also produces an excellent stout; don't despair if you're desperate for a Guinness, as several pubs in Adelaide have it on tap. Some locals drink a mixture of stout and lemonade (called portagaff), or stout and beer (called black-and-tan). For boutique brews, head to Port Adelaide (p85).

An annual publication with lots of useful information on many readily available wines is the *Penguin Good Australian Wine Guide,* by Huon Hooke and Ralph Kyte-Powell.

In SA, you usually buy beer from the bottle shop in 'echoes' or 'stubbies' (375mL bottles), and beer is served across the counter in glasses of various sizes – see the boxed text below. As well, you might be asked if you want 'super', 'heavy' or 'draught' (that's full-strength beer) or 'light' (low-alcohol beer). Standard beers contain around 5% alcohol, while 'light' beers have between 2% and 3.5%.

In terms of coffee, Australia is leaping ahead, with Italian-style espresso machines in virtually every café. Boutique roasters are all the rage and, in urban areas, the qualified *barista* (coffee maker) is virtually the norm. Expect the best coffee in Adelaide and nearby gourmet regions, with the option of soy milk or *chai* (spicy milk tea).

## CELEBRATIONS

Celebrating in the Australian manner often includes equal amounts of food and alcohol. A birthday could well be a barbecue (barbie) of steak (or prawns), washed down with a beverage or two. Weddings are usually big slap-up dinners with far from memorable food, except at expensive affairs and those held at wineries.

Many regions now hold food festivals in keeping with SA's obsession. There are harvest festivals in wine regions such as the Barossa (p163),

---

**WHAT'RE YOU HAVIN', MATE?** *George Dunford*

In most places you can dodge the brand issue (West End and Coopers are the local brews) by just saying you want 'a beer', but then what size do you want? South Australia has the most obscure sizes in Oz, so here's a quick cheat sheet:

- Butcher: 200mL or 7oz glass. A glass in Victoria. Reserved for the older drinkers.
- Schooner: 285mL or 10oz glass. A pot in Victoria, but a full 142ml/5oz smaller than a New South Wales (NSW) schooner. The 'usual' size in SA.
- Pint: 425mL or 15oz. There's nothing like it in Victoria, but in NSW it's a schooner.
- Imperial Pint: 570mL or 20oz. The size of a pint you'd be given in an Irish pub anywhere else in Australia.

Confused? Add to this the fact that the measurement of a pint is different again (actually closer to 475mL) and you've got no idea how much you're drinking. Maybe you'd do better with a cheeky something from the Clare Valley?

Adelaide Hills (p86) and McLaren Vale (p101). Look for regular regional markets where a variety of producers – many organic – sell an array of interesting produce and foods.

For many an event, especially in the warmer months, Eskies (a portable, insulated ice chest to keep everything cool), tables, chairs, and a cricket set or a footy are loaded into cars for a barbie by the lake/river/beach. If there's a 'total fire ban' (which, increasingly, occurs each summer), the food is precooked and the barbie becomes more of a picnic, but the essence remains the same.

## WHERE TO EAT & DRINK

Typically, a restaurant meal is a relaxed affair. It may take 15 minutes to order, another 15 before the first course arrives, and maybe half an hour between entrées and mains. The upside of this is that any table you've booked in a restaurant (with the exception of Adelaide's fast-paced Asian places) is yours for the night, unless you're told otherwise. So sit, linger and live life in the slow lane.

A competitively priced place to eat is in a pub that offers a counter meal. This is where you order your meal (usually staples such as a fisherman's basket, steak, Vienna schnitzel or chicken *parmigiana* – a fried chicken, cheese and sauce delight that is an obsession in itself for some) at the kitchen, take a number, and wait until it's called out over the counter or intercom. Solo diners find that cafés and noodle bars are welcoming, good fine dining restaurants often treat you like a star, but sadly, some mid-range places may still make you feel a little ill at ease.

An interesting feature of the Australian dining scene is the 'bring your own' (BYO), a restaurant that allows you to bring your own alcohol. If the restaurant also sells alcohol, the BYO bit is usually limited to bottled wine only and a corkage charge is added to your bill. The cost is either per person, or per bottle, and ranges from nothing to $15 per bottle in fancy places; enquire when you book.

Most restaurants open at noon for lunch (sometimes referred to as 'dinner') and from 6pm for dinner (sometimes referred to as 'tea'). Locals usually eat lunch between noon and 2pm, and dinner bookings are usually made for 7.30pm or 8pm, though in Adelaide some restaurants stay open past 10pm. Be aware that pubs may only serve 'tea' from 6pm to 7.30pm.

**TRY A PIE FLOATER**

In Adelaide and a few country places you can really delve into local culture with a pie floater (a meat pie with tomato sauce floating in thick, green pea soup). It sounds horrible and doesn't look so hot either, but plenty swear by it.

### Quick Eats

There's not a huge culture of street vending in SA, though you may find a pie, wurst or coffee cart in some places. Most quick eats traditionally come from a deli (milk bar), which serves traditional hamburgers (with bacon, egg, pineapple and beetroot if you want) and other takeaway foods. Fish and chips is still hugely popular, most often eaten at the beach on a Friday night.

Bakeries are popular lunch spots – particularly where American-style fast food joints are lacking – with inexpensive pies, sausage rolls, sandwiches and pastries.

Pizza has become one of the most popular fast foods; most home-delivered pizzas are American-style (thick and with lots of toppings) rather than Italian-style. That said, wood-fired, thin Neapolitan-style *pizze* are often available, even in country towns.

## VEGETARIANS & VEGANS

Cafés almost always have vegetarian options, and some restaurants have complete vegetarian menus. Adelaide has a couple of dedicated restaurants, with the refreshing approach of treating 'vegetarian' as a cuisine rather than simply a lifestyle choice. Take care with risotto and soups, though, as meat stock is often used. Vegans will find the going tougher, but there are usually dishes that are vegan-adaptable at restaurants. The Australian Vegetarian Society's useful website (www.veg-soc.org) lists vegetarian-friendly places to eat throughout SA.

## WHINING & DINING

Dining with children in SA is relatively easy. Avoid the flashiest places and children are generally welcomed and catered for, particularly at Chinese, Greek or Italian restaurants. Kids are usually more than welcome at cafés, and pub bistros often see families dining early. Some places offer dedicated kids' menus while at others everything comes straight from the deep fryer – such as crumbed chicken and chips.

The best news for travelling families, weather permitting, is that there are plenty of free or coin-operated barbecues in parks. On weekends and public holidays fierce battles can erupt over who is next in line for the barbie. For more information on travelling with children, see p253.

## HABITS & CUSTOMS

At the table, it's good manners to use British knife and fork skills, keeping the fork in the left hand, tines down, and the knife in the right, though Americans may be forgiven for using their fork like a shovel. Talking with your mouth full is considered uncouth, and fingers should only be used for food that can't be tackled any other way.

If you're invited to someone's house for dinner, always take a gift such as a bottle of wine, flowers or a box of chocolates. 'Shouting' is a revered custom where people rotate paying for a round of drinks. Just don't leave before it's your turn to buy! At a toast, everyone should (gently) touch glasses.

Australians like to linger a bit over coffee. They like to linger a really long time while drinking beer. And they tend to take quite a bit of time if they're out to dinner.

Smoking is banned in restaurants, cafés and other eateries where food is consumed indoors, so sit outside if you love to puff.

Australians love to shorten everything, including people's names. See the Glossary (p281) for some definitions.

The Australian Food & Wine website, www .campionandcurtis.com, run by two food writers who trained as chefs, has information on cooking schools, restaurants, cook books plus plenty of their own modern Australian recipes. They'll email a monthly newsletter, too.

---

### AUTHORS' RECOMMENDATIONS

The team of authors who wrote this edition have an eclectic list of favourite places for a bite in SA.

**Good Life** (p76; ☎ 08-8223 2618; 170 Hutt St, Adelaide; pizzas $12.50-18.90; ☺ lunch Tue-Fri, dinner Tue-Sun) These sensational organic pizzas could be the best you've ever tasted.

**Maggie Beer's Farm Shop & Restaurant** (p168; ☎ 08-8562 4477; www.maggiebeer.com; Pheasant Farm Rd, Nuriootpa; mains $16-20; ☺ lunch & light meals) Feast from celebrity-gourmet Maggie's kitchen.

**Organic Market & Café** (p91; ☎ 08-8339 7131; 5 Druids Ave, Stirling; meals $3.50-12; ☺ breakfast & lunch) A vibrant and lively café with a great atmosphere.

**Rising Sun Hotel** (p175; ☎ 08-8849 2015; Main North Rd, Auburn; mains $6.50-15.50; ☺ lunch & dinner) Good solid food in a great country pub.

**Salopian Inn** (p102; ☎ 08-8323 8769; Main Rd, McLaren Vale; mains $16-30; ☺ lunch Thu-Tue, dinner Fri & Sat) A serious foodie haunt with a not-to-be-missed reputation.

**Star of Greece** (p103; ☎ 08-8557 7420; The Esplanade, Port Willunga; mains $20-35; ☺ lunch) Superb seafood in a funky boathouse-style cliff-top restaurant, on a stunning beach.

**BILLS & TIPPING**

The total at the bottom of a restaurant bill is all you really need to pay. Legally, it has to include Goods and Services Tax (GST), as do menu prices, and there is no 'optional' service charge added. Waiters are paid a reasonable salary, so they don't rely on tips to survive. Often, though, especially in cities, people tip a little in a café, while the tip for excellent service can go as high as 15% in whiz-bang establishments.

## COOKING COURSES

There are many good cooking classes with top chefs in Adelaide's fine produce stores, including **Bottega Rotolo** ( ☎ 08-8362 0455; www.bottegarotolo .com.au), **Outdoors on Parade** ( ☎ 08-8362 8822; www.outdoorsonparade.com.au) and **Pete & Peppa** (Adelaide Central Plaza); the latter hosts animated 20-minute cooking instructions during Friday lunch-time. Details on up-and-coming events on the Fleurieu Peninsula are listed on www.fleurieufood.com.au. Other excellent classes in foodie heaven include:

**Blessed Cheese** ( ☎ 08-8323 7958; www.blessedcheese.com.au) One-day cheese-making courses in McLaren Vale.

**Mt Lofty Country House** ( ☎ 08-8339 6777; www.mtloftyhouse.com.au) Closely observe expert kitchen practices on a big-bucks cooking retreat in the Adelaide Hills.

**Rosa Matto Cookery School** ( ☎ 08-8373 6106) Among Adelaide's finest chefs.

**Thorn Park Cooking School** ( ☎ 08-8843 4304; www.thornpark.com.au) Gourmet weekends with wine matching in the Clare Valley.

A 'Tim Tam shooter' is where the two diagonally opposite corners of this rectangular chocolate biscuit are nibbled off, and a hot drink (tea is the true aficionado's favourite) is sucked through the fast-melting biscuit as if through a straw.

# Wineries

South Australia (SA) is the heart, soul and belly of Australian winemaking. This is not just idle sentiment, either. The quantity of wine produced from South Australian grapes is huge: SA currently produces 49% of all Australian wines and over 60% of the nation's wine exports.

The life-blood of the South Australian wine industry

JOHN BANAGAN

The state's long and successful history of winemaking dates to the 1800s when settlers and refugees arrived from Europe clutching vine cuttings that loved SA's Mediterranean climate, its hot, dry summers and cool, wet winters. Luckily 80% of the land consists of vast plains, so there has been enough suitable land to create an economically viable industry. Luckily too, SA has avoided debilitating grape diseases, such as phylloxera. The state's first vintage was bottled in 1841 in the Adelaide Hills.

Johann Gramp planted the Barossa Valley's first vineyard on the banks of Jacob's Creek in 1847. The Barossa Valley is now Australia's major wine-producing region; Barossa winemakers produce 21% of all Australian wines, including full and fruity Shiraz and Cabernet Sauvignon and some very classy Riesling.

Meanwhile, around the same time, a certain Dr Penfold planted French vine cuttings outside 'the Grange', the little stone cottage he and his wife Mary built in Magill, on the outskirts of Adelaide, in 1845. Little did the good doctor know that many years hence a 1955 Grange would be voted as one of the 20th century's top 12 wines.

South Australia now has 21 wine regions supporting 432 wine producers, 268 of those with cellar doors (which means they open to the public for wine tasting and sales). Around 80% of these cellar doors lie within a two-hour radius of Adelaide. So what does that make South Australians, apart from just lucky? It means that winemaking and wine drinking are a major part of this state's economy and culture, and that visiting wineries for a tasting and lunch is a regular day out for many locals. Wineries often offer restaurants and accommodation, and are usually child friendly with disabled access.

---

### APPRECIATING WINE

The National Wine Centre of Australia is based, quite appropriately, in central Adelaide. As well as daily tasting sessions and a heap of info about winemaking, there are regular two-hour courses offering theme tastings on Australian wines. These classes are open to everyone, novices included, and cover topics such as 'The Many Faces of Chardonnay' and 'Shiraz Master Class'. Regional tastings include 'White Wines of the Adelaide Hills' and 'Best of the West'. School was never like this. Apply to the **National Wine Education & Training Centre** ( ☎ 08-8222 9277; www.winesa.asn .au/winecourses; National Wine Centre of Australia, cnr Botanic & Hackney Rds; from $55).

The following five major wine regions differ widely in their culture, landscapes and wines, but the regions are similar in that they are fairly compact and all contain villages with friendly pubs, some great restaurants and a hefty sprinkling of terrific B&Bs and self-contained cottages. This makes for some marvellous touring or short breaks. So gird your loins, gather up your spear and credit cards and go forth to fill up the car boot with SA's real liquid treasures…

## ADELAIDE HILLS

The hills, a labyrinth of winding roads, villages, and shady oases of lush vegetation and tall trees, are a 30-minute drive from Adelaide. Autumn, when vine leaves turn a fiery red and the rows of vines crossing these protected valleys and hillsides glow at sunset, is a beautiful time to visit. Summer's good too as the hills give relief from the dry heat of Adelaide. This is one of SA's cooler climates, with night mists and rainfalls that develop some complex and truly top-notch white wines, especially Chardonnay and Sauvignon Blanc. Out of around 20 cellar doors, the following are classic wineries.

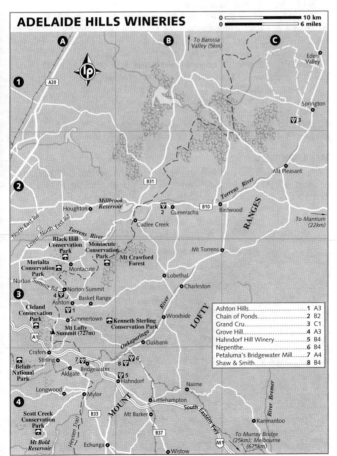

**ADELAIDE HILLS WINERIES**

| | |
|---|---|
| Ashton Hills | 1 A3 |
| Chain of Ponds | 2 B2 |
| Grand Cru | 3 C1 |
| Grove Hill | 4 A3 |
| Hahndorf Hill Winery | 5 B4 |
| Nepenthe | 6 B4 |
| Petaluma's Bridgewater Mill | 7 A4 |
| Shaw & Smith | 8 B4 |

'The hills, a labyrinth of winding roads, villages, and shady oases of lush vegetation and tall trees, are a 30-minute drive from Adelaide'

**Petaluma's Bridgewater Mill** ( ☎ 08-8339 3422; www.bridgewatermill.com.au; Mt Barker Rd, Bridgewater; ☽ 10am-5pm) One of the state's premier wineries and best restaurants, you would be mad not to book in here for a tasting followed by lunch. The Chardonnay is exquisite, the Riesling fabulous, Coonawarra reds succulent and the Bridgewater Mill Sauvignon classy.

**Ashton Hills** ( ☎ 08-8390 1243; ashtonhills@bigpond.com; Tregarthen Rd, Ashton; ☽ 11am-5.30pm Sat, Sun & public holidays) Overlooking the Piccadilly Valley, this winery has brilliantly flavoursome Chardonnay and some very classy Riesling and Pinot Noir.

> Australia's first exported wine was a case of Adelaide Hill's hock, sent as a gift in 1845 to England's Queen Victoria.

**Shaw & Smith** ( ☎ 08-8398 0500; www.shawandsmith.com; Lot 4 Jones Rd, Balhannah; ☽ 11am-4pm Sat & Sun) Fabulous views over the Mt Lofty Ranges are a feature of this modern winery, as are more outstanding whites; the elegant Vineyard Chardonnay and Sauvignon Blanc and joined by some grand Merlot.

**Nepenthe Wines** ( ☎ 08-8388 4439; www.nepenthe.com.au; Jones Rd, Balhannah; ☽ 10am-4pm) Nepenthe was described by Homer as a potion that eased grief and banished sorrow from the mind. Accordingly, Nepenthe Wines is the source of some great happiness, especially the Semillon, Chardonnay and, surprisingly, Cabernet Sauvignon.

**Chain of Ponds** ( ☎ 08-8389 1415; www.chainofponds.com.au; Main Adelaide Rd, Gumeracha; ☽ 9.30am-4.30pm Mon-Fri, 10am-4pm Sat & Sun) The Vineyard Balcony Restaurant and an 1800s vineyard B&B keeps wine tasters fed and bedded, while the Rosé Novello Nero and Riesling keeps them satisfied.

**Grove Hill** ( ☎ 08-8390 1437; marguerite@grovehill.com.au; 120 Old Norton Summit Rd, Norton Summit; ☽ 11am-5pm Sun) Traditional winemaking techniques are used by these descendants of the original 1846 winemakers. Don't miss their Sparkling Marguerite, a 100% barrel-fermented sparkling wine.

Also worth a visit:

**Grand Cru** ( ☎ 08-8568 2799; R Dewells Rd, Springton; ☽ 10am-5pm)

**Hahndorf Hill Winery** ( ☎ 08-8388 7512; Pains Rd, Hahndorf; ☽ 10am-5pm)

## MCLAREN VALE

Situated between the cool hills of the Mt Lofty Ranges and the long sandy beaches of the coastline, McLaren Vale is a playground for Adelaidians. The Vale is only a 45-minute drive from the city, perfect for lunch and some wine tasting after a morning on the beach or a walk in the hills.

The warm oceanside climate delivers a great variety of wines; try a full but slightly more refined McLaren Vale Shiraz, while lovers of a gutsy

> The McLaren Vale vineyards are a 45-minute drive from Adelaide
>
> RICHARD I'ANSON

Grenache can celebrate a few blended specials. White-wine drinkers should sample classic Chardonnay and Sauvignon Blanc, while locals enjoy a glass of chilled sparkling Shiraz with their Sunday brunch.

Around 30 cellar doors tucked away down little lanes often have accompanying gardens that welcome picnickers and hold many impromptu food and wine celebrations. The following selections are top local favourites.

**Fox Creek Wines** ( ☎ 08-8556 2403; www.foxcreekwines.com; Malpas Rd, Willunga; ⊙ 10am-5pm) Serious Shiraz connoisseurs rave about this little winery's Reserve Shiraz. Taste a range of the Reserve reds to really appreciate the subtle flavours in their make-up. The Vixen Sparkling Shiraz Cabernet Franc is also a cracker. Picnickers are welcome in the pretty garden.

**Wirra Wirra Vineyards** ( ☎ 08-8323 8414; www.wirrawirra.com; McMurtrie Rd, McLaren Vale; ⊙ 10am-5pm Mon-Sat, 11am-5pm Sun & public holidays) Consistently good and reasonably priced stickies (dessert wines), and whites include the citrus Scrubby Rise Viognier and aromatic Riesling. The Reserve Shiraz is very popular. This friendly and picturesque (1894) cellar door has a nice picnic area, and *pétanque* balls are also available.

'The Vixen Sparkling Shiraz Cabernet Franc is also a cracker'

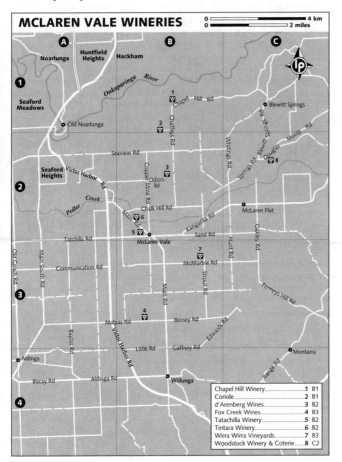

**MCLAREN VALE WINERIES**

| | |
|---|---|
| Chapel Hill Winery | **1** B1 |
| Coriole | **2** B1 |
| d'Arenberg Wines | **3** B2 |
| Fox Creek Wines | **4** B3 |
| Tatachilla Winery | **5** B2 |
| Tintara Winery | **6** B2 |
| Wirra Wirra Vineyards | **7** B3 |
| Woodstock Winery & Coterie | **8** C2 |

**Tatachilla Winery** ( ☎ 08-8323 8656; www.tatachillawinery.com.au; 151 Main Rd, McLaren Vale; ☻ 10am-5pm Mon-Fri, 11am-5pm Sun & public holidays) This winery sits in central McLaren Vale. A modern cellar door offers flagship red wines for tasting, including the Keystone Grenache-Shiraz and berry-flavoured Cabernet Sauvignon. However, the Sauvignon Blanc is also very good.

**d'Arenberg Wines** ( ☎ 08-8323 8710; www.darenberg.com.au; Osborn Rd, McLaren Vale; ☻ 10am-5pm) The award for most imaginative names goes to this winery, perched enticingly on a hillside. Stump Jump Grenache Shiraz, Dead Arm Shiraz, and the Broken Fishplate Sauvignon Blanc are all favourites. Do book ahead for a fabulous lunch (and lemon soufflé) in their adjacent restaurant. One sour note: the restaurant charges full price for their own wines, way above cellar-door rates.

**Coriole** ( ☎ 08-8323 8305; www.coriole.com; Chaffeys Rd, McLaren Vale; ☻ 10am-5pm Mon-Fri, 11am-5pm Sat, Sun & public holidays) This lovely (1860) cellar door also sells aromatic olive oils and sweet vinegars, as well as a range of great white wines. Try any of the super Semillon blends, perfect for summer drinking, and their Shiraz. The gardens are great for a picnic.

**Chapel Hill Winery** ( ☎ 08-8323 8429; www.chapelhillwine.com.au; Chapel Hill Rd, McLaren Vale; ☻ noon-5pm) This restored (1865) chapel and school has vineyard and ocean views. A picnic ground means fun for all the family. The wines are made for drinking now, and include some nice whites; the blended Chardonnay is a very pleasant surprise.

Also recommended:

**Tintara Winery** ( ☎ 08-8329 4124; www.hardys.com.au; Main Rd; ☻ 10am-4.30pm) This cellar door has Australia's oldest vintage wine bottle (1867) on show.

**Woodstock Winery & Coterie** ( ☎ 08-8323 0156; Douglas Gully Rd; ☻ 9am-5pm Mon-Fri, noon-5pm Sat, Sun & public holidays) Their reds are grand but hold out for the stickies and fortified; especially loved is the Tawny Port.

> 'A four-hour drive from Adelaide, the Coonawarra is the perfect excuse for a long weekend'

## COONAWARRA

This glorious wine region was established in the late 1800s and fully utilises the famous and unique *terra rossa* soil for the good of us all. Literally 'red earth', it is a section of old sea coast that now provides one of Australia's best wine-growing soils. A four-hour drive from Adelaide, the Coonawarra is the perfect excuse for a long weekend. Most of the region's 22 cellar doors are signposted off the Riddoch Hwy. The following wineries should not be missed for their world-class Shiraz, Cabernet Sauvignon and Merlot. Mind you, the Chardonnay is also pretty irresistible…

### TOP TEN WINERY RESTAURANTS

- Petaluma's Bridgewater Mill Winery & Restaurant, Adelaide Hills (p50)
- Skillogalee, Clare Valley (p57)
- d'Arrys Verandah Restaurant, at d'Arenberg McLaren Vale (p52)
- Kaesler Estate Restaurant & Cottages, Barossa Valley (p56)
- Hollick, Coonawarra (p54)
- Salters, at Saltram Wine Estates Barossa Valley (p56)
- Salt n Vines Bar & Bistro, at Kirrihill Estate Clare Valley (p57)
- Tateham's, Clare Valley (p58)
- Bonneyview, Riverlands (p136)
- Reilly's Wines, Clare Valley (p58)

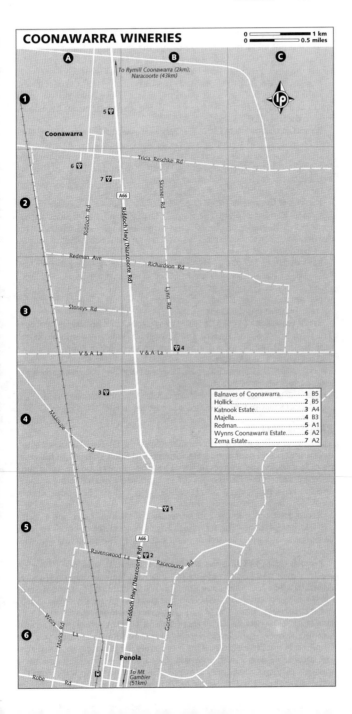

# COONAWARRA WINERIES

To Rymill Coonawarra (2km);
Naracoorte (43km)

Coonawarra

Tricia Reschke Rd

Stunner Rd

A66

Pb 'tchppry

Riddoch Hwy (Naracoorte Rd)

Redman Ave

Richardson Rd

Lynn Rd

Stoneys Rd

V & A La — V & A La

Mazoupe

Rd

Ravenswood La

A66

Racecourse Rd

Gordon St

Riddoch Hwy (Naracoorte Rd)

Weirs

La

Marks Rd

Penola

To Mt
Gambier
(51km)

Robe — Rd

| | | |
|---|---|---|
| Balnaves of Coonawarra | 1 | B5 |
| Hollick | 2 | B5 |
| Katnook Estate | 3 | A4 |
| Majella | 4 | B3 |
| Redman | 5 | A1 |
| Wynns Coonawarra Estate | 6 | A2 |
| Zema Estate | 7 | A2 |

**Zema Estate** ( ☎ 08-8736 3219; www.zema.com.au; Riddoch Hwy; ☽ 9am-5pm) This cellar door is not much more than a hut, but the wine epitomises the region's unbeatable reds; silken and peppery Shiraz and Cabernet Sauvignon that touch the soul. You only visit here for the wine, but what wine…

**Majella** ( ☎ 08-8736 3055; www.majellawines.com.au; Lynn Rd; ☽ 10am-4.30pm) If it were possible to liquefy Christmas pudding, it would taste like this winery's warm and spicy Cabernet Sauvignon. All the fruit comes from the estate's vineyards; truly homemade.

**Wynns Coonawarra Estate** ( ☎ 08-8736 2225; www.wynns.com.au; Memorial Dr; ☽ 10am-5pm) The oldest and founding winery of the Coonawarra, Wynns' cellar door is imbued with the scent of past great vintages. Renowned for their top-quality and truly peppery Shiraz, Wynns also produce fragrant Riesling and fantastic golden Chardonnay. Vertical tastings – tasting the same wine from a number of past vintages – are also possible.

'the Barossa produces immensely quaffable big smooth and full reds'

**Balnaves of Coonawarra** ( ☎ 08-8738 2946; www.balnaves.com.au; Riddoch Hwy; ☽ 9am-5pm Mon-Fri, 10am-5pm Sat & Sun) The friendly tasting area here includes a small trout pond. Balnaves produces some of the best reds and whites in the district; its Cabernet Sauvignon is worth trying but it is difficult to get past the Chardonnay.

**Katnook Estate** ( ☎ 08-8737 2394; www.katnookestate.com.au; Riddoch Hwy; ☽ 9am-4.30pm Mon-Fri, 10am-4.30pm Sat & Sun) Another cracker of a winery, with nice picnic grounds. There is a good variety of styles and prices. The Riddoch wines are reasonably cheap, while those under the Katnook brand are more expensive but delicious.

**Rymill Coonawarra** ( ☎ 08-8736 5001; www.rymill.com.au; Riddoch Hwy; ☽ 10am-5pm) The Bees Knees Sparkling Red and Sauvignon Blanc are a suitable match with their surroundings; a dramatic and modern cellar door.

Also worth a quick slurp:

**Hollick** ( ☎ 08-8737 2318; www.hollick.com; Ravenswood Lane; ☽ 9am-5pm) Has a popular restaurant, some nice whites and a smashing Riesling.

**Redman** ( ☎ 08-8736 3331; www.redman.com.au; Riddoch Hwy; ☽ 9am-5pm Mon-Fri, 10am-4pm Sat & Sun) Has some nicely priced smooth and easy reds.

## BAROSSA VALLEY

The fruitful valley has two major subregions, the Barossa Valley with hot, dry summers and cool, moderate winters, and Eden Valley with hills that provide a cooler and wetter climate. These two zones produce some quite different wines; the Barossa produces immensely quaffable big smooth and full reds, particularly Shiraz, while Eden Valley is becoming known for its fortified range and Rieslings.

Around 60 cellar doors can be reached within an hour and a half's drive from Adelaide. The wineries range from small boutiques to huge complexes; most are owned by multinationals. The following wineries are outstanding:

**Penfolds** ( ☎ 08-8568 9290; www.penfolds.com.au; Tanunda Rd, Nuriootpa; ☽ 10am-5pm Mon-Fri, 11am-5pm Sat & Sun) Penfolds produce Grange – widely regarded as Australia's best red wine – enough said. With notice and minimum numbers, a range of premium wine can be tasted ($110 per person).

**Peter Lehmann Wines** ( ☎ 08-8563 2100; www.peterlehmannwines.com.au; Para Rd, Tanunda; ☽ 9.30am-5pm Mon-Fri, 10.30am-4.30pm Sat & Sun) Another multiaward-winning winery, with classic Barossa Shiraz and Riesling. Mind you, the Semillon is equally fabulous. This is probably the best range of consistent and affordable wines in the Barossa. Buy a bottle of anything and enjoy it with a picnic in the winery grounds. There's a parkland walk from the cellar door along the Para River to Richmond Grove.

**Rockford Wines** ( ☎ 08-8563 2720; info@rockfordwines.com.au; Krondorf Rd, Tanunda; ⏰ 11am-5pm Mon-Sat) This 1850s winery uses traditional winemaking methods and produces a small range of superb wines. The Shiraz is a smooth and spicy killer, while their Alicante Bouchet is a fantastic example of how a Rosé should smell and taste on a hot summer's day. The intimate tasting room is in a historic stable.

**Grant Burge Wines** ( ☎ 08-8563 3700; admin@grantburgewines.com.au; Barossa Valley Way, Jacob's Creek, Tanunda; ⏰ 10am-5pm) A tranquil and attractive setting for

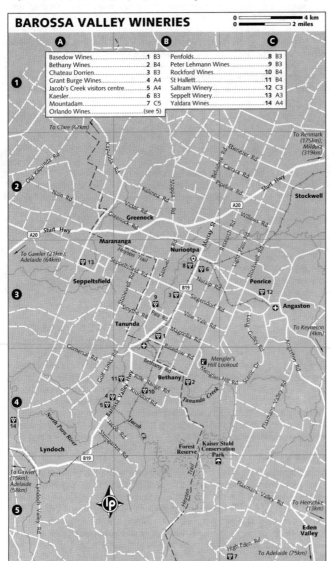

**BAROSSA VALLEY WINERIES**

| | | | |
|---|---|---|---|
| Basedow Wines | 1 B3 | Penfolds | 8 B3 |
| Bethany Wines | 2 B4 | Peter Lehmann Wines | 9 B3 |
| Chateau Dorrien | 3 B3 | Rockford Wines | 10 B4 |
| Grant Burge Wines | 4 A4 | St Hallett | 11 B4 |
| Jacob's Creek visitors centre | 5 A4 | Saltram Winery | 12 C3 |
| Kaesler | 6 B3 | Seppelt Winery | 13 A3 |
| Mountadam | 7 C5 | Yaldara Wines | 14 A4 |
| Orlando Wines | (see 5) | | |

'The Shiraz is a smooth and spicy killer'

producing landmark wines such as the Meschach Shiraz, and excellent fragrant full whites, with names inspired by pioneering ancestors. Try the Frontignac, Chardonnay, Semillon and sparkling whites.

**Orlando Wines** ( ☎ 08-8521 3000; www.jacobscreek.com.au; Barossa Valley Way, Rowland Flat; ✦ 10am-5pm) One of the oldest operations in the valley, now with one of the most modern cellar doors. The French-owned winery produces Jacob's Creek, arguably the world's favourite budget bottle. However, quantity does not necessarily mean lack of quality; the Riesling in particular is out-standing value. The cellar door has a restaurant and interactive displays.

**St Hallett** ( ☎ 08-8563 7000; www.sthallett.com.au; St Hallett's Rd, Tanunda; ✦ 10am-5pm) Using only Barossa grapes, this winery is known for their reasonably priced but consistently good whites; notably Eden Valley Riesling and Poacher's Blend. Similarly, the Faith Shiraz is great value, but order Old Block Shiraz when someone else is buying. There is also a nice outdoor area.

**Kaesler** ( ☎ 08-8562 4488; www.kaesler.com.au; Barossa Valley Way, Nuriootpa; ✦ 10am-5pm Mon-Sat, 11.30am-4pm Sun & public holidays) This estate has a fantastic restaurant and some great B&B accommodation, all perfect for a weekend of pure sloth and indulgence. The Shiraz blends are fine wines, and if you have a deep pocket and a love of red meat, try the Old Bastard Shiraz.

**Saltram Wine Estates** ( ☎ 08-8564 3355; www.saltramwines.com.au; Nuriootpa-Angaston Rd, Angaston; ✦ 9am-5pm Mon-Fri, 10am-5pm Sat, Sun & public holidays) Another old (1859) winery, this one is set in beautiful gardens. A first-rate restaurant and a selection of peppery Shiraz make this a very popular place.

**Bethany Wines** ( ☎ 08-8563 2086; www.bethany.com.au; Bethany Rd, Bethany; ✦ 10am-5pm Mon-Sat, 1-5pm Sun) The Bethany family produces classic wines and ports that are perfect for sipping under any circumstances.

**Basedow Wines** ( ☎ 08-8563 0333; 161 Murray St, Tanunda; ✦ 10am-5pm Mon-Fri, 11am-5pm Sat & Sun) An atmospheric and authentic tasting cellar on Tanunda's main street. It offers a great and affordable range of wines.

Other recommendations:

**Henschke** ( ☎ 08-8564 8223; www.henschke.com.au; Henschke Rd; ✦ 9am-4.30pm Mon-Fri, 9am-noon Sat) This winery is known for its iconic Hill of Grace red, but Henschke's other wines are also classics.

**Mountadam** ( ☎ 08-8564 1900; www.mountadam.com; High Eden Rd, Eden Valley; ✦ 11am-4pm) A small range of terrific wines includes a good earthy Cabernet Sauvignon.

**Seppelt Winery** ( ☎ 08-8568 6217; www.seppelt.com.au; Seppeltsfield Rd, Seppeltsfield; ✦ 10am-5pm Mon-Fri, 11am-5pm Sat & Sun) Has bluestone buildings dating from 1851, a dramatic family mausoleum, and lovely gardens with barbecues and date palms. Port and sherry lovers shouldn't miss out on these superb fortifieds; 100-year-old Para Tawny Port costs a measly $500.

**Chateau Dorrien** ( ☎ 08-8562 2850; dorrienwines@ozmail.com.au; cnr Seppeltsfield Rd & Barossa Valley Way, Tanunda; ✦ 10am-5pm) Has fantastic meads and a series of colourful murals painted on wine vats. A craft market is held four mornings a week (10am to 4pm Saturday to Tuesday).

**Yaldara Wines** ( ☎ 08-8524 0225; www.yaldara.com.au; Hermann Thumm Dr, Lyndoch; ✦ 9.30am-5pm) A refurbished 1947 winery on the North Para riverside, with a notable antiques collection, regular winery tours ($6.50) and café. Kids can really let off steam in these grounds.

## CLARE VALLEY

This charming region is a two-hour drive from Adelaide. Despite a consistent warm climate, wine-industry specialists say that cooler microclimates found here – in the region's rivers, creeks and valleys – noticeably affect the wines. This helps to explain why so many Clare Valley white wines can be laid down for long periods and still be so good. The valley produces some of the best Riesling available, as well as some grand Semillon and Shiraz. Major subregions include Polish Hill River and Watervale.

'The Bethany family produces classic wines and ports that are perfect for sipping under any circumstances'

The 35 winery cellar doors in the valley include the following classics.

**Jim Barry** ( ☎ 08-8842 2261, 08-8842 3752; Main North Rd, Clare; ☉ 9am-5pm Mon-Fri, 9am-4pm Sat & Sun) Given that this winery has garnered more than 50 gold medals and 10 trophies, calling it a local icon would not be amiss. The flagship Armagh Shiraz will be too pricey for most, but the superb Riesling and golden Chardonnay are very affordable.

**Grosset** ( ☎ 08-8849 2175; www.grosset.com; King St, Auburn; ☉ 10am-5pm Wed-Sun Sep until sold out) This winery normally sells out of wine within six weeks of opening. Jeffrey Grosset is a craftsman, and was once named as the international Riesling winemaker of the year. If you find their doors open, enter quickly…

**Leasingham** ( ☎ 08-8842 2785; www.leasingham-wines.com.au; 7 Dominic St, Clare; ☉ 8.30am-5pm Mon-Fri, 10am-4pm Sat & Sun) This range of wines is consistently good and affordable, with Riesling, Shiraz and some great Cabernet blends.

**Annie's Lane at Quelltaler** ( ☎ 08-8843 0003; www.annieslane.com.au; Quelltaler Rd, Watervale; ☉ 8.30am-5pm Mon-Fri, 11am-4pm Sat & Sun) This winery's flagship wines are Copper Trail Shiraz and Riesling. A winery museum and art gallery contain personal touches such as the VE Day closure notice from WWII.

**Skillogalee** ( ☎ 08-8843 4270; www.skillogalee.com.au; Trevarrick Rd, Sevenhill; ☉ 10am-5pm) This delightfully named small family winery is known for its top-range elegant Riesling, spicy Shiraz and fabulous food. Indulge your sensual self with a long lunch on their shady veranda.

**Taylors Wines** ( ☎ 08-8849 2008; www.taylorswines.com.au; Taylors Rd, Auburn; ☉ 9am-5pm Mon-Fri, 10am-4pm Sat & Sun) One of the region's largest wineries. Forgive the unfortunate mock-castle roof: this winery produces wines fit for royalty.

**Kirrihill Estate** ( ☎ 08-8842 4087; www.kirrihillwines.com.au; Wendouree Rd, Clare; ☉ 10am-4pm) Established in 1998, this young winery has already garnered awards,

South Australia has 66,654 hectares of vineyards, 42% of all Australian plantings

South Australia's 2003 grape crop was 647,000 tonnes, 46% of all Australian grape crushings

South Australian wine exports for 2003 were valued at $1.673 billion; 75% of SA wineries export wine

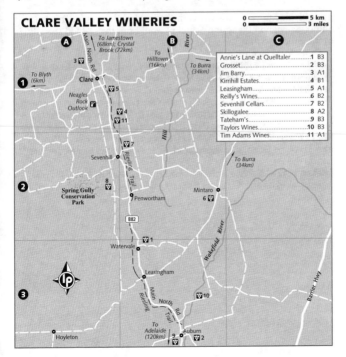

CLARE VALLEY WINERIES

| | |
|---|---|
| Annie's Lane at Quelltaler | 1 B3 |
| Grosset | 2 B3 |
| Jim Barry | 3 A1 |
| Kirrihill Estates | 4 B1 |
| Leasingham | 5 A1 |
| Reilly's Wines | 6 B2 |
| Sevenhill Cellars | 7 B2 |
| Skillogalee | 8 A2 |
| Tateham's | 9 B3 |
| Taylors Wines | 10 B3 |
| Tim Adams Wines | 11 A1 |

**WINE TASTING** *Adam Marks*

Whether seriously appraising or just tasting a wine, consider three elements: colour/appearance, nose and palate. Then trust your own taste buds – only *you* know whether you like it or not.

**Colour & Appearance**

Use a clean, clear glass in good light and examine the wine's colour and appearance by holding it against a white background. White wine varies in colour from water white to intense gold, depending on age, grape variety and winemaking techniques. It should not be brown. A red wine will generally progress from crimson through brick red to tawny as it ages. The colour should be brilliant and clear with no deposit.

**Nose**

When nosing a wine, preferably use a glass with a tapered mouth. This assists in concentrating the volatile aromas rising from the wine. Your nose is a particularly potent sensory organ – accordingly it is essential to remember that we smell much of what we would describe as 'taste'. Characteristics such as 'berries', 'spice' or 'wood' are not tasted in the mouth, but registered through the nose. The wine's nose should have several pleasant smells and be free of any obvious rank odours.

**Palate**

Your tongue and mouth can basically only detect four taste sensations: these are salt, sweetness, bitterness and acid, and they are apparent on different areas of the tongue. Your palate is used to qualify the expectations of the wine's colour and nose. When 'savouring' a wine in your mouth, consider the wine's balance. The amount of fruit must be in balance with the acids and tannins. Persistence of flavour is a major virtue of any wine. The longer it lasts, the greater the pleasure.

probably due to very experienced hands behind the scenes. Outstanding Shiraz, Sauvignon Blanc and Semillon would suit the seafood specialities of the enticing Salt n Vines Bar & Bistro upstairs.

Other local favourites:

**Tim Adams Wines** ( ☎ 08-8842 2429; www.timadamswines.com.au; Warenda Rd, Clare; ☽ 10.30am-5pm Mon-Fri, 11am-5pm Sat & Sun) Makes a yummy Riesling and Shiraz.

**Sevenhill Cellars** ( ☎ 08-8843 4222; www.sevenhillcellars.com.au; College Rd, Sevenhill; ☽ 9am-4.30pm Mon-Fri, 10am-4pm Sat) The valley's oldest winery, established by Jesuit priests in 1851. Priests still run the winery and produce very good Verdelho, Riesling and blended Cabernet Sauvignon. The marvellous St Aloysius Church (1875) and lovely grounds adjoin the winery.

**Reilly's Wines** ( ☎ 08-8843 9013, 0409-679 479; www.reillyswines.com; Burra St, Mintaro; mains $16-24; ☽ 10am-5pm) Some good, affordable chewy reds sit here alongside a fragrant Watervale Riesling.

**Tateham's** ( ☎ 08-8849 2030; tatehams@chariot.net.au; Main North Rd, Auburn) This small restaurant-winery is a beautiful old stone building. A relatively new winery, it produces a great clear Riesling.

# Adelaide

ADELAIDE

CONTENTS

| | |
|---|---|
| Orientation | 61 |
| Information | 62 |
| Sights | 63 |
| Activities | 68 |
| Walking Tour | 69 |
| Adelaide for Children | 70 |
| Tours | 70 |
| Sleeping | 72 |
| Eating | 75 |
| Drinking | 77 |
| Entertainment | 78 |
| Shopping | 80 |
| Getting There & Around | 80 |
| **Around Adelaide** | **81** |
| Glenelg | 81 |
| South of Glenelg | 84 |
| Glenelg to Port Adelaide | 84 |
| Port Adelaide | 85 |

Sophisticated and calm, Adelaide (population 1,467,300) is a big town with a big heart and a refined mind. Bordered by the hills of the Mt Lofty Ranges and the blue of the Gulf St Vincent, it offers a good and affordable quality of life. There's a healthy live music and arts scene, nearby conservation areas to explore, and sandy beaches on which to frolic. Adelaide makes an excellent base for trips to the Murray River, the historic towns and gardens of the Adelaide Hills, and the wineries of the Barossa Valley and McLaren Vale – all less than an hour's drive away.

The traditional owners of the Adelaide area are the Kaurna people; their territory extends south towards Cape Jervis and north towards Port Wakefield. Early European colonists (free settlers) began to arrive in 1836, building with stone, pride and plenty of style to create a capital with a European feel and encircled by green parklands. Successive settlers have provided a vibrant cosmopolitan mix, promoting a hedonistic spirit with varied cuisines, magnificent wines and numerous galas that celebrate a thriving arts community.

More major festivals and events are held in Adelaide than in any other city in Australia; the epicurean playground spans the cultured and cerebral, artistic and gastronomic, petrol-burning and sports crazed. During the Adelaide Fringe Festival, the city really shows its spark. Much of its artistic flair is due to the liberalism under the progressive premier Don Dunstan during the late '60s and '70s and its history as a city that boasts many firsts (the University of Adelaide was the first university in Australia to admit women into degree courses).

## HIGHLIGHTS

- Indulging in fresh produce at the **Central Market** (p67)
- Perusing master works and Rodin sculptures (and having an art-inspired lunch) at the **Art Gallery of South Australia** (p63)
- **Riding** (p68) along the Torrens River to the bay or hills
- Catching a vintage tram to **Glenelg** (p82) for sundowners
- **Drinking** (p77) Coopers pale ale and **eating** (p68) Haigh's chocolate
- Feasting alfresco at **restaurants** (p75) serving innovative dishes of SA produce and quality wines
- Exploring the gentrified historic town, art spaces and museums of **Port Adelaide** (p85)
- Delving headlong into hedonism at any of Adelaide's fabulous **festivals** (p71)

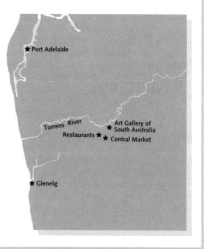

- TELEPHONE CODE: ☎ 08
- www.adelaidecitycouncil.com
- www.adelaidereview.com.au

## ORIENTATION

Adelaide's city centre is a grid bordered by North, East, South and West Tces. King William St, the main thoroughfare, dissects the city; most cross streets change their name here. Victoria Sq, the geographical centre, has bus stops and the Glenelg tram terminus. Franklin St, which runs off the square, contains Adelaide's central bus station.

Rundle St, lined with cafés, restaurants, bookshops, retro clothing shops and independent cinemas, is the social centre for all ages. Heading west the street becomes Rundle Mall, the main shopping strip. Across King William St, Rundle Mall turns into Hindley St, with its mix of bars, dance clubs and strip joints.

Elegant North Tce, north of Hindley and Rundle Sts, hosts a string of magnificent public buildings, including the art gallery, museum, state library and the University of Adelaide. Continue north and you're in the lush North Parklands, home to the Adelaide Festival Centre. King William Rd crosses into North Adelaide at the Torrens River, which has walking and cycling paths.

See Getting There & Around (p80) for details on getting to the city centre from the airport and train station.

### Maps

Central Adelaide maps from the South Australian Tourism Commission visitors centre (see Tourist Information on p63) should be

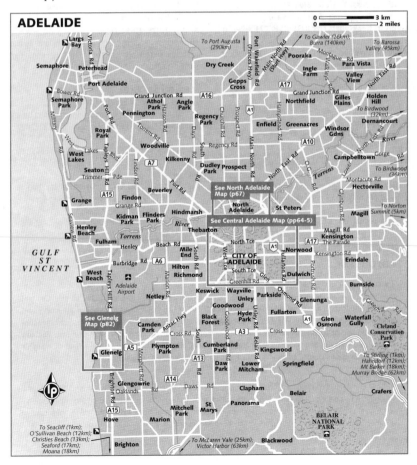

ample for navigating your way around central Adelaide. For something more in-depth, pick up a Royal Automobile Association (RAA), Hema or Westprint map, available from the RAA and bookshops. The **Map Shop** (Map pp64-5; ☎ 8231 2033; mercator@mapshop.net.au; 6 Peel St) stocks a range of maps, charts and guides for walking, hiking and touring in South Australia (SA).

# INFORMATION
## Bookshops                                Map pp64–5
**ABC Shop** ( ☎ 8410 0567; level 2, Myer Centre, Rundle Mall)

**Adelaide Booksellers** ( ☎ 8410 0216; www.adelaide booksellers.com.au; 6A Rundle Mall) Quality second-hand books.

**Borders Books, Music & Café** ( ☎ 8223 3333; 97 Rundle Mall) A vast collection of books and CDs.

**Imprints Booksellers** ( ☎ 8231 4454; 107 Hindley St) The booklover's bookshop.

**Mary Martin's Bookshop** ( ☎ 8359 3525; 249 Rundle St) An Adelaide institution.

**RAA** ( ☎ 8202 4600; www.raa.net; 55 Hindmarsh Sq) Publications on travel bushwalking, natural and social history, and Aboriginal culture.

## Emergency
**Ambulance** ( ☎ 000, 13 29 62)
**Fire** ( ☎ 000, 8204 3600)
**Lifeline** ( ☎ 13 11 14, 8202 5820) Provides 24-hour counselling.
**Police** (Map pp64-5; ☎ 000, 8303 0525; 26 Hindley St)
**RAA Emergency Roadside Assistance** ( ☎ 13 11 11, 8202 4600)
**Rape & Sexual Assault Service** (Map pp64-5; ☎ 8226 8777/87; 55 King William Rd, North Adelaide)

## Internet Access                          Map pp64–5
**Adelaide City Council** ( ☎ 8203 7203; 25 Pirie St; ☽ 8.30am-5.30pm) Free access.

**State Library of South Australia** ( ☎ 8207 7250, Internet bookings 8207 7248; North Tce near cnr Kintore Ave; ☽ 9.30am-8pm Mon-Wed & Fri, 9.30am-6pm Thu, noon-5pm Sat & Sun) Free access; book ahead.

**Zone Internet Café** ( ☎ 8223 1947; 238 Rundle St; per min $0.10; ☽ 9.30am-11pm)

## Media
Adelaide's daily tabloid paper is the parochial *Advertiser* (or 'Tiser'), though the *Age*, the *Australian* and the *Financial Review* newspapers are widely available – often in cafés. The *Adelaide Review* (www.adelaidereview .com.au), a free fortnightly publication, has highbrow articles, often covering the city's history and current social issues, and culture and arts sections. The weekly *Independent* comes out on Sunday; some articles originate in the UK paper of the same name.

## Medical Services
**Emergency Dental Service** ( ☎ 8272 8111; ☽ Sat, Sun & after hours) Provides dentist contact details.
**Royal Adelaide Hospital** (Map pp64-5; ☎ 8222 4000; North Tce)
**Simpsons Pharmacy** (Map pp64-5; ☎ 8231 6333; cnr West Tce & Waymouth St; ☽ 7am-midnight Mon-Sat, 9am-midnight Sun)
**Traveller's Medical & Vaccination Centre** (Map pp64-5; ☎ 8212 7522; 29 Gilbert Pl; ☽ 9am-5pm Mon-Fri, to 7pm Wed, 9am-12.30pm Sat)
**Women's & Children's Hospital** (Map p67; ☎ 8161 7000; 72 King William Rd, North Adelaide)

---

### ADELAIDE IN...

#### Two Days
If you're here at festival and fringe time, lap it up. Otherwise, start your day at the **Central Market** (p67) then head off on a **walking tour** (p69) of the city's sights, perusing art works and exhibitions along the way. Wind up at the **National Wine Centre** (68) for education and pleasure before dining at a (prebooked) restaurant on Gouger St (p75). Next day, visit the **Jam Factory Craft & Design Centre** (opposite) or the **Bradman Collection** (p65) and take a tour of **Haigh's Chocolates** (p68) before hopping on a tram for sundowners in **Glenelg** (p83).

#### Four Days
Follow the two-day itinerary, then put together a picnic basket from the Central Market and journey to the nearby **Adelaide Hills** (p86), **McLaren Vale** (p101) or **Barossa** (p159) wine regions. Next day, explore the museum trail and arty historic centre of **Port Adelaide** (p85), then take in a show back in the city – possibly at the **Weimar Room** (p78).

## Money
**Map pp64–5**

Banks and ATMs are prevalent throughout the city centre, particularly on and around Rundle Mall. Out of hours, head to the airport or casino.

**American Express** (Amex; ☎ 1300 139 060; Shop 32, Rundle Mall; ◷ 9am-5pm Mon-Fri, 9am-noon Sat) To exchange foreign currencies try here.

**Thomas Cook** ( ☎ 8231 6977; Shop 4, Rundle Mall; ◷ 9am-5pm Mon-Fri, 10am-4pm Sat) Or try here to exchange your foreign currency.

## Post
**Main post office** (Map pp64-5; ☎ 13 13 18; 141 King William St; ◷ 8am-5.30pm Mon-Fri, 9am-12.30pm Sat) Handles poste restante; have mail addressed to you c/o Poste Restante, Adelaide 5001.

## Tourist Information
**Arts SA** ( ☎ 8207 7100; artsa@sa.gov.au) Information on cultural attractions, venues, performing arts, festivals and special events; pick up a directory at SATC.

**Disability Information & Resource Centre** (DIRC; Map pp64-5; ☎ 8223 7522/79; www.dircsa.org.au; 195 Gilles St; ◷ 9am-5pm Mon-Fri) Provides information on accommodation, venues, tourist destinations and travel agencies for people with disabilities.

**Information kiosk** (Map pp64-5; Rundle Mall at King William St end; ◷ 10am-5pm Mon-Thu, 10am-8pm Fri, 10am-3pm Sat, 11am-4pm Sun) Provides Adelaide-specific information and free walking tours at 9.30am Monday to Friday.

**South Australian Tourism Commission visitors centre** (SATC; Map pp64-5; ☎ 1300 655 276, 8303 2033; www.southaustralia.com; 18 King William St; ◷ 8.30am-5pm Mon-Fri, 9am-2pm Sat & Sun) Abundantly stocked with leaflets and publications on Adelaide and SA. There's also a booking service and BASS ticket-selling outlet.

## SIGHTS
Most of Adelaide's sights are located within walking distance of the city centre, with many strung along North Tce, including the South Australian Museum, State Library, Art Gallery of South Australia, Botanic Gardens and National Wine Centre of Australia. Many visitors also stay in or take a day to explore beachside Glenelg (p81), and the nearby Barossa Valley (p159), Adelaide Hills (p86) and McLaren Vale (p101) regions.

The **Discover Adelaide Card** ( ☎ 8400 2222; www.adelaidecard.com.au; $48) can be an economical way of seeing the city's sights; check the appeal and book at BASS in the SATC.

## Art Galleries
**Map pp64–5**

The wonderful **Art Gallery of South Australia** ( ☎ 8207 7000; www.artgallery.sa.gov.au; North Tce; admission free; ◷ 10am-5pm) represents all the big names in Australian art through the eras. The early appeal of Australia's major cities is given pictorial perspective in the collection of colonial art. It also has an impressive international art collection boasting masters such as Van Dyck, Southeast Asian works and a significant collection of 20 bronze sculptures by Auguste Rodin. The temporary exhibitions are first rate. You could easily return here many times over a couple of days, but if you've got limited time, perhaps start with the Australian galleries, featuring southern Australian landscapes. The audio-tour (free) of the Australian collection is insightful, as are the guided tours (free) run at 11am and 2pm weekdays, 11am and 3pm weekends. Peruse the great bookshop and indulge your other senses at the top-notch **café** (sandwiches $7, mains $21.90), with a menu inspired by the current exhibition.

Discover **public art works** on a walk around the city and along Hindley St (maps available at the visitors centre). Adelaide's arts precinct oscillates around the West End (the area near West Tce). Galleries with quality contemporary exhibits include:

**Jam Factory Craft & Design Centre** ( ☎ 8410 0727; www.jamfactory.com.au; Lion Arts Centre, cnr Morphett St & North Tce) Quality local arts and crafts and a glass-blowing studio.

**Experimental Art Foundation** ( ☎ 8211 7505; www.eaf.asn.au; Lion Arts Centre, cnr Morphett St & North Tce) Focuses on innovation.

**Greenaway Art Gallery** ( ☎ 8362 6354; 39 Rundle St, Kent Town; ◷ 11am-6pm Tue-Sun)

## South Australian Museum
The enthralling exhibits of the **South Australian Museum** (Map pp64-5; ☎ 8207 7368; www.samuseum.sa.gov.au; North Tce; admission free; ◷ 10am-5pm) include Australia's natural history, whales and Antarctic explorer Sir Douglas Mawson (with expedition footage). The absorbing Aboriginal Cultures Gallery displays artefacts of the Ngarrindjeri people of the Coorong and lower Murray. Included in the display is the *story* of Dreamtime spirit ancestor Ngurunderi, and how the Murray was created. Keep your eyes on that lion as you pass through the taxidermal displays...

ADELAIDE

# CENTRAL ADELAIDE

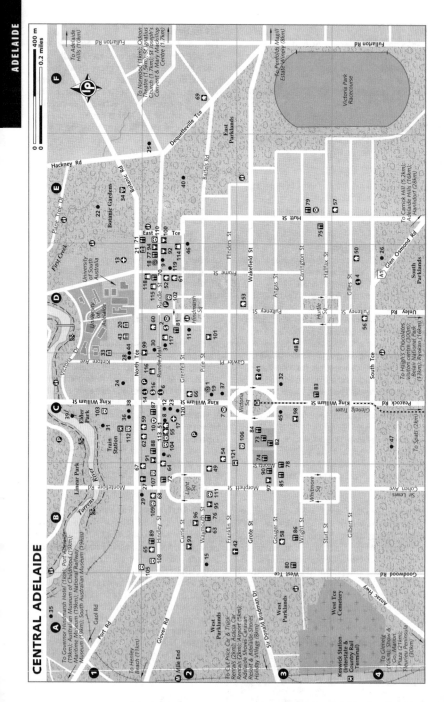

| INFORMATION | |
| --- | --- |
| ABC Shop | (see 116) |
| Adelaide Booksellers | (see 16) |
| Adelaide City Council | 1 C2 |
| American Express | 2 D2 |
| Borders Books, Music & Café | 3 D2 |
| Disability Information & Resource | |
| Centre | 4 D4 |
| Imprints Bookseller | 5 C2 |
| Information Kiosk | 6 C2 |
| Main post office | 7 C2 |
| Map Shop | 8 C2 |
| Mary Martin's Bookshop | 9 D2 |
| Police station | 10 C2 |
| RAA | 11 D2 |
| Rape & Sexual Assault Service | 12 C2 |
| Royal Adelaide Hospital | 13 D1 |
| SATC visitors centre | 14 C2 |
| Simpsons Pharmacy | 15 B2 |
| Thomas Cook | 16 C2 |
| Traveller's Medical & Vaccination | |
| Centre | 17 C2 |
| Youth Hostel Association | (see 49) |
| Zone Internet Café | 18 D2 |

| SIGHTS & ACTIVITIES | |
| --- | --- |
| Adelaide Town Hall | 19 C2 |
| Art Gallery of South Australia | 20 D1 |
| Australian Geographic Shop | (see 116) |
| Ayers Historic House | 21 D2 |
| Balaena Café | (see 43) |
| Botanic Gardens | 22 E1 |
| Bradman Collection | (see 28) |
| Edmund Wright's House | 23 C2 |
| Experimental Art Foundation | (see 29) |
| Government House | 24 C1 |
| Greenaway Art Gallery | 25 E2 |
| Himeji Gardens | 26 D2 |
| Holy Trinity Church | 27 B2 |
| Institute Building | 28 C1 |
| Jam Factory Craft & Design | |
| Centre | 29 B2 |
| Jurlique International Day Spa | 30 D2 |
| Linear Park Hire | 31 C1 |
| Magistrate's Court | 32 C3 |
| Migration Museum | 33 D1 |
| National Wine Centre of Australia | 34 E1 |
| Old Adelaide Gaol | 35 A1 |
| Old Parliament House | 36 C1 |
| Old Treasury Building | 37 C2 |
| Parliament House | 38 C1 |
| Popeye | 39 C1 |
| Rymill Park | 40 E2 |
| St Francis Xavier Cathedral | 41 C3 |
| St Mary's Convent | 42 B2 |
| South Australian Museum | 43 D1 |
| State Library of South Australia | 44 D1 |
| Supreme Court | 45 C3 |

| Tandanya Indigenous Cultural | |
| --- | --- |
| Institute | 46 D2 |
| Veale Gardens | 47 C4 |

| SLEEPING | |
| --- | --- |
| Adelaide Backpackers Inn | 48 D3 |
| Adelaide Central YHA | 49 B2 |
| Adelaide Old Terraces | 50 D4 |
| Adelaide Paringa Motel | 51 C2 |
| Austral Hotel | 52 D2 |
| Backpack Oz | 53 D3 |
| Cannon St Backpackers | 54 C2 |
| City Central Motel | 55 C2 |
| City Parklands Motel | 56 D4 |
| Clarice Motel | 57 E4 |
| Director's Studios & Suites | 58 B3 |
| Festival Lodge | 59 C2 |
| Hotel Richmond | 60 D2 |
| Majestic Roof Garden Hotel | 61 D2 |
| Mercure Grosvenor Hotel | 62 C2 |
| My Place | 63 B2 |
| Plaza Hotel | 64 B2 |
| Princes Arcade Motel | 65 B2 |
| Quest on King William | 66 C2 |
| Radisson Playford Hotel & Suites | 67 B2 |
| Rockford Adelaide | 68 B2 |
| Royal Coach Motor Inn | 69 F2 |
| Strathmore Hotel | (see 59) |

| EATING | |
| --- | --- |
| Amalfi Pizzeria Ristorante | 70 D2 |
| Botanic Café | 71 E2 |
| Café Tapas | 72 B2 |
| Central Market | 73 C3 |
| Chinatown | 74 C3 |
| Chinatown Café | (see 74) |
| Citrus | 75 E3 |
| Coles Supermarket | (see 73) |
| Cumberland Arms | 76 B2 |
| East Taste Continental | (see 71) |
| Exeter | 77 D2 |
| Felafel House | (see 77) |
| Gauchos | 78 B3 |
| Good Life | 79 E3 |
| Hawker's Corner | 80 B3 |
| Jasmin Indian Restaurant | 81 D2 |
| Ky Chow | 82 C3 |
| La Trattoria | 83 C3 |
| Lucia's Pizza & Spaghetti Bar | (see 73) |
| Malacca Corner | 84 C3 |
| Nu's Thai | 85 B3 |
| Pie Cart | (see 112) |
| Prince Albert | 86 B3 |
| Sprouts | (see 81) |
| T Bar | (see 73) |
| Thai in a Wok | (see 81) |
| Vego and Lovin' It | (see 18) |
| Wok-in-a-Box | 87 C2 |

| Woolworths | 88 C2 |
| --- | --- |
| Worldsend Hotel | 89 B2 |
| Ying Chow Chinese Restaurant | 90 B3 |
| Zuma Caffé | (see 73) |

| DRINKING | |
| --- | --- |
| Apothecary 1878 | 91 C2 |
| Belgian Beer Café | 92 D2 |
| Botanic Bar | (see 71) |
| Edinburgh Castle Hotel | 93 B2 |
| Fumo Blu | 94 D2 |
| Garage Bar | 95 B2 |
| Grace Emily Hotel | 96 B2 |
| Mars Bar | 97 B3 |
| Queen's Arms Hotel | 98 C3 |
| Short Black | (see 104) |
| Skin@Club199 | 99 D2 |
| Treasury | (see 37) |
| Universal Wine Bar | 100 E2 |
| Wine Underground | 101 D2 |

| ENTERTAINMENT | |
| --- | --- |
| Academy Cinema City | 102 D2 |
| Adelaide Festival Centre | 103 C1 |
| Adelaide Symphony Orchestra | 104 C2 |
| Bass | (see 14) |
| Heaven Nightclub Complex | 105 B2 |
| Her Majesty's Theatre | 106 C3 |
| Lion Theatre & Bar | (see 29) |
| Mercury Cinema | (see 29) |
| Minke Bar | 107 B2 |
| Mojo West | 108 B2 |
| Moonlight Cinema | (see 22) |
| Moskva Vodka Bar West | 109 B2 |
| Nova Cinema | (see 9) |
| Palace East End Cinemas | 110 E2 |
| PJ O'Brien's | (see 71) |
| Savvy | 111 B2 |
| Skycity Casino | 112 C1 |
| Weimar Room | 113 C2 |

| SHOPPING | |
| --- | --- |
| Annapurna | (see 115) |
| Haigh's Chocolates | (see 16) |
| Market East | 114 D2 |
| Mountain Designs | 115 D2 |
| Myer | 116 C2 |
| Opal Field Gems | (see 16) |
| Paddy Palin | (see 115) |
| T'Arts | 117 D2 |
| Urban Cow Studio | 118 D2 |

| TRANSPORT | |
| --- | --- |
| Access Rent-a-Car | 119 D2 |
| Adelaide Metro Information Centre | 120 C2 |
| Central Bus Station | 121 C2 |
| Explore | (see 121) |
| Hawk-Rent-A-Car | (see 121) |

The **Balaena Café** (kids meals $5-6, breakfast & lunch $5.50-12.50) runs the length of an enormous sperm whale skeleton and serves value-packed meals.

## Migration Museum

The fascinating **Migration Museum** (Map opposite; ☎ 8207 7580; www.history.sa.gov.au; 82 Kintore Ave; admission by donation; ☿ 10am-5pm Mon-Fri, 1-5pm Sat & Sun) is next door to the State Library, and tells the stories of migrants who came from all over the world to make their home in SA. The museum has information on more than a hundred nationalities in their database, along with some poignant personal stories.

## State Library of South Australia    Map opposite

The newspaper reading room inside the **State Library** (☎ 8207 7242; North Tce near cnr Kintore Ave; ☿ 9.30am-8pm Mon-Wed & Fri, 9.30am-6pm Thu, noon-5pm Sat & Sun) has publications from around the world – these come by surface mail, so don't expect yesterday's (or last week's) editions.

Cricket fans can pore over the personal items of cricketing legend Sir Donald Bradman next door in the Institute Building, which houses the **Bradman Collection** (☎ 8207 7271; Institute Bldg, cnr North Tce & Kintore Ave; admission free; ☿ 9.30am-6pm Mon-Thu, 9.30am-8pm Fri, noon-5pm Sat & Sun). Tours ($6.50) run at 11.30am and 12.30pm Monday to Friday.

ADELAIDE

## Aboriginal Cultural Centre

Visit **Tandanya Indigenous Cultural Institute** (Map pp64-5; ☎ 8224 3200; 253 Grenfell St; adult $4; ☉ 10am-5pm) to learn about the local Kaurna people. It has fun interactive displays on living with the land, offers free didgeridoo shows (noon Monday to Friday) and Torres Strait Islander dances (noon Saturday and Sunday), and contains galleries, a café, and art and crafts.

## Historic Buildings

Built in 1878 and decommissioned in 1988, the **Old Adelaide Gaol** (Map pp64-5; ☎ 8231 4062; Gaol Rd, Thebarton; adult/student $7/5.50; ☉ 11am-4pm Mon-Fri, 11am-3.30pm Sun) displays a range of home-made escape devices. Commentary tapes are provided for self-guided tours, or take a guided tour on Sunday. Spooky ghost tours by appointment.

Architect **Edmund Wright's house** (Map pp64-5; 59 King William St; admission free; ☉ 9am-4.30pm), built in 1876, was originally constructed for the Bank of SA in an elaborate Renaissance style with intricate decoration (you can view the historic foyer and reception area). His other buildings include the imposing 1863–66 **Adelaide Town Hall** (Map pp64-5; King William St btwn Flinders & Pirie Sts), built in 16th-century Renaissance style with the faces of Queen Victoria and Prince Albert carved into the façade, and the **Main Post Office**, opposite, commenced in 1867 and altered in 1891.

In Springfield, 7km southeast of the city, you'll find the wonderful Elizabethan manor house **Carrick Hill** ( ☎ 8379 3886; www.carrickhill.sa .gov.au; 46 Carrick Hill Drive; adult/child/family $9/6.50/23; ☉ 10am-4.30pm Wed-Sun & public holidays) set on 40 hectares of bushland, lawns and manicured English-style gardens. Tours run at 11.30am and 2.30pm. Catch bus No 171 from King William St and get off at stop 16.

## Botanic Gardens & Other Parks

The city and North Adelaide are surrounded in a green swath of attractive parkland, gardens and large trees.

Stroll, jog or find a grassy patch to read your book in the splendid, city-fringe **Botanic Gardens** (Map pp64-5; www.botanicgardens.sa .gov.au; North Tce; ☉ 7am-sunset Mon-Sat, 9am-sunset Sat, Sun & public holidays). Highlights include a unique prefabricated palm house (1877), the **Museum of Economic Botany** (check out its stencilled ceiling), and the 1988 **Bicentennial Conservatory** (adult/child/family $3.30/1.70/8; ☉ 10am-5pm), which recreates a tropical rainforest environment. Free 1½-hour guided walks depart from the kiosk at 10.30am on Monday, Tuesday, Friday and Sunday.

Old money **North Adelaide** (Map opposite) is an attractive suburb with bluestone cottages, pubs and alfresco restaurants. It's separated from the city by the Torrens River and the **North Parklands**. On Montefiore Hill stands the **statue of Colonel William Light**, Adelaide's disputed founder. In the afternoon there's a nice view of the city's gleaming office towers rising above the trees, with the Adelaide Hills making a scenic backdrop.

**Rymill Park** (Map pp64–5), in the East Parklands, has a boating lake, a 600m running track and possums in the trees that emerge at night. The South Parklands contain the **Veale Gardens** (Map pp64–5), with streams and flowerbeds. The restful Japanese **Himeji Gardens** (Map pp64-5; ☎ 8203 7483; South Tce) blends two styles of Japanese garden: *senzui* (lake and mountain) and *kare senzui* (dry garden). Sports grounds to the west complete Adelaide's ring of green.

## Adelaide Oval

To the north of the Torrens River, the **Adelaide Oval** (Map below; ☎ 8300 3800; www.cricketsa .com.au; King William Rd, North Adelaide) is the hallowed site of interstate and international cricket matches. A statue of 'the Don' (Donald Bradman) graces this most picturesque of test cricket grounds, which was established in the 1870s and hosted its first test match in 1884. It has the oldest scoreboard (1911) still in use for test matches in Australia. When there are no games on you can take a two-hour **Adelaide Oval/Museum Tour** (adult/student $10/5), departing at 10am Monday to Friday and 2pm Sunday from the south gate on War Memorial Dr.

## Adelaide Zoo

Around 1400 exotic and native mammals, birds and reptiles reside at the **zoo** (Map below; ☎ 8267 3255; www.adelaidezoo.com.au; Frome Rd; adult/ child/family $15/9/48; ☽ 9.30am-5pm). There are free tours and a children's petting zoo, but the major drawcard is the Southeast Asian rainforest exhibit.

You can take a water cruise to the zoo from Elder Park, out the front of the Adelaide Festival Centre, on **Popeye** (Map pp64-5; ☎ 8295 4747; adult/child return $8/4.50; ☽ departs hourly 11am-3pm Mon-Fri, every 20 min 10.30am-4.30pm Sat & Sun). Otherwise, catch bus No 272 or 273 from Currie St, or walk there from Elder Park or the Botanic Gardens.

## Markets

You can find just about everything at the 250-odd shops in the **Central Market** (Map pp64-5; btwn Grote & Gouger Sts; ☽ 7am-5.30pm Tue & Thu, 7am-9pm Fri, 7am-3pm Sat) – abundant and fresh vegetables, breads, cheeses, seafood and

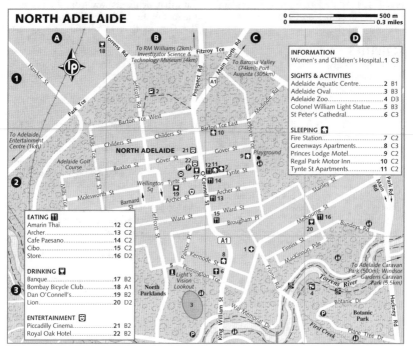

**NORTH ADELAIDE**

0 ____ 500 m
0 ____ 0.3 miles

**INFORMATION**
Women's and Children's Hospital..1 C3

**SIGHTS & ACTIVITIES**
Adelaide Aquatic Centre.............2 B1
Adelaide Oval............................3 B3
Adelaide Zoo.............................4 D3
Colonel William Light Statue........5 B3
St Peter's Cathedral....................6 C3

**SLEEPING**
Fire Station...............................7 C2
Greenways Apartments................8 C3
Princes Lodge Motel....................9 C2
Regal Park Motor Inn..................10 C2
Tynte St Apartments...................11 C2

**EATING**
Amarin Thai..............................12 C2
Archer.....................................13 C2
Cafe Paesano............................14 C2
Cibo.......................................15 C2
Store.......................................16 D2

**DRINKING**
Banque....................................17 B2
Bombay Bicycle Club..................18 A1
Dan O'Connell's.........................19 B2
Lion........................................20 D2

**ENTERTAINMENT**
Piccadilly Cinema.......................21 B2
Royal Oak Hotel........................22 B2

gourmet produce – you name it. Good luck making it out without succumbing to the temptation to eat here. There are a few hot eating spots (see p75), including Lucia's, T Bar and Chinatown. Bargain hunters should head down on Tuesday afternoon or after lunch on Saturday. For market tour details, see p71.

In the back lanes of East End Adelaide (towards East Tce), **MarketEast** (Map pp64-5; Ebenezer Pl; ☒ 11am-5pm Sat & Sun) has 'unique designs, art and funky finds'.

## Haigh's Chocolates

If you're craving chocolate, you need settle only for the best at the iconic **Haigh's Chocolates visitors centre** ( ☎ 8372 7077; www.haighschocolates.com; 154 Greenhill Rd, Parkside; admission free; ☒ 8.30am-5.30pm Mon-Fri, 9.30am-4.45pm Sat). Dedicated to fine chocolate production, Haigh's takes you through the life-cycle of chocolate from cacao nut to hand-dipped truffle on tours of the factory (1pm and 2pm Monday to Saturday, 20 minutes); samples are included, bookings are essential.

To get there from the city, take bus No 190, 191, 191B or 192 from King William St. Get off at stop 1 on Unley Rd just over Greenhill Rd.

# ACTIVITIES

There are plenty of ways to get out and enjoy Adelaide's mild climate – from cycling tracks and sunning at beaches, to sipping wines and munching at the market. When there's a festival on in town, get into it.

If you squint…no, it still doesn't look like Venice, but paddling along in an original **gondola** ( ☎ 8358 1800; www.adelaidegondola.com.au; 2 people 30 min $60) on the Torrens may still float your boat. Boats depart from Red Ochre Restaurant near the weir and golf course. You can order a bottle of wine and take up to four people for the ride.

Paddle, pedal or skate along side the Torrens River with hire equipment from **Linear Park Hire** (Map pp64-5; ☎ 8223 6271; Elder Park; ☒ 9am-5pm), just below the Adelaide Festival Centre.

Perched on the city's doorstep, the historic **Penfolds Magill Estate Winery** ( ☎ 8301 5569; 78 Penfolds Rd, Magill; ☒ 10.30am-4.30pm Mon-Fri, 11am-5pm Sat & Sun) is home to perhaps Australia's best known wine. Enjoy a tasting at the cellar door, indulge at the gourmet restaurant –

tailor-made to the wines and sporting great city views – or partake in the 'Great Grange Tour'. You can take a self-guided tour with tastings of Australian wines ($8.50) at the **National Wine Centre of Australia** (Map pp64-5; ☎ 8222 9222; www.wineaustralia.com.au; cnr Botanic & Hackney Rds; ☒ 10am-6pm). You'll get a good insight into all the issues winemakers contend with, and even have your own virtual vintage rated.

For a bit of pampering, head to the **Jurlique International Day Spa** (Map pp64-5; ☎ 8410 7180; www.jurlique.com.au; 22-38 Rundle Mall Plaza, Rundle Mall), where aromatherapy baths are spiced with certified organic and biodynamic herbs grown in the hills.

## Cycling & Walking

Free guided walks are on offer in the peaceful Botanic Gardens (Map pp64-5) and at the information kiosk, which also stocks free trail guides. Self-guided walks such as 'Historical Walking Trails' tell the story of Adelaide's many fine buildings, while others cover public art, and the wonderful riverside Linear Park – a 40km walking/cycling path that wends its way from the beach to the foot of the Adelaide Hills (mainly along the Torrens River). Adelaide is a cyclist-friendly city, with good cycling tracks and cycle lanes on some main city roads. You can take your bike on trains, but not trams or buses. Excellent cycling maps (free) are available from bike shops.

**Trails SA** (www.southaustraliantrails.com) details hiking and cycling trails in SA. Hire bikes from hostels or **Linear Park Hire** (Map pp64-5; ☎ 8223 6271; Elder Park; bikes & in-line skates per day/week $20/80; ☒ 9am-5pm), just below the Festival Centre. Tours, including bikes, to the Barossa Valley and coast (from $35) are organised by **Bikeabout** ( ☎ 0413-525 733; www.bikeabout.com.au).

## Water Sports

For details on Adelaide's beaches, see p81.

Aquatic centres with 25m or 50m pools are scattered around the suburbs; you'll find them listed under 'Swimming Pools' in the *Yellow Pages* telephone directory. Closest to the city is the **Adelaide Aquatic Centre** ( ☎ 8344 4411; Jeffcott Rd, North Adelaide), with swimming and diving pools, a gym and other facilities.

Wannabe waxheads can learn to **surf** on the Fleurieu Peninsula (see p109).

Contact **Adelaide Dive Centre** ( ☎ 8231 6144; www.adskin.com.au) for southern oceans diving at sites such as HMAS *Hobart*; see also Glenelg (p83).

## WALKING TOUR

North Tce, Adelaide's cultural boulevard, is lined with fine buildings constructed from 1830 to 1880 – a legacy of the copper, wheat and wool booms.

Starting at the grand old **Botanic Hotel (1)**, head west along North Tce to **Ayers Historic House (2**; ☎ 8223 1234; 288 North Tce; adult/child $8/5; ⏱ 10am-4pm Tue-Fri, 1-4pm Sat & Sun), which was built in 1845. This elegant residence of early South Australian premier Sir Henry Ayers, after whom Ayers Rock (Uluru) in the Northern Territory was named, now features period furnishings and costume displays.

Across the road is a small campus of the **University of South Australia (3)**. Next door is the more imposing façade of the **University of Adelaide (4)**, founded in 1874 – the first university in Australia to admit women to degree courses.

Further west along North Tce is the impressive **Art Gallery of South Australia (5**; p63) – an easy spot to lose a few hours. Next door, the **South Australian Museum (6**; p63) has fine Aboriginal and natural history displays, and a café alongside a giant whale skeleton.

Near the corner of Kintore Ave, is the **State Library of South Australia (7**; p65) and the 1836 **Institute Building (8)** – the oldest building on North Tce, housing Bradman's cricketing memorabilia. From here, head up Kintore Ave to the fascinating **Migration Museum (9**; p65).

Back on North Tce, pass the **National War Memorial (10)** and continue west, following the stone wall surrounding the grounds of the 1838 **Government House (11)** to the **South African War Memorial (12)** at King William Rd.

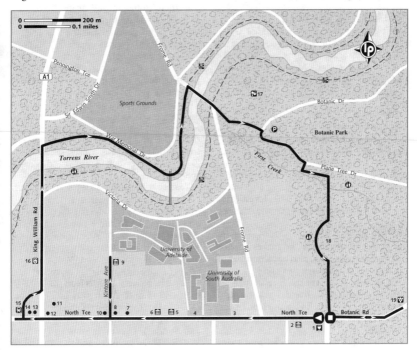

Opposite, you'll see the elegant façade of **Parliament House (13)**, featuring 10 marble Corinthian columns. It was built in two stages: the west wing was completed in 1889 and the east wing in 1939. Continue along North Tce to **Old Parliament House (14**; ☎ 8212 6881; 10am-5pm Mon-Fri, noon-5pm Sat & Sun), set up in its original state and boasting a restaurant, then on to grand **Railway Station (15)**, now home to the casino. Loop past intriguing street art to the **Adelaide Festival Centre (16**; p78), then across and down to the Torrens River. Meander east along the walking path to Frome Rd, and the entrance to the **Adelaide Zoo (17**; p67).

Head south along Frome Rd, turning left onto a footpath to follow the fence of the zoo. Take the right fork – Plane Tree Dr – and follow it to the gate of the stunning **Botanic Gardens (18**; p66). Continue generally south following the signs to the main gate on North Tce, then toast a hard-day's sightseeing back at the **Botanic Bar (1**; p78), or indulge at **Botanic Café (1**; p76). If you've got the time, detour via the **National Wine Centre (19**; p68).

## ADELAIDE FOR CHILDREN

The free monthly paper *Adelaide's Child* (www.adelaideschild.com.au), available at cafés and libraries, contains a comprehensive events calendar. *Adelaide for Kids: A Guide for Parents*, by James Muecke, has comprehensive details \ is available at bookshops.

**Dial-An-Angel** ( ☎ 8267 3700) provides nannies and babysitters to all areas.

During school holidays, the **South Australian Museum**, **State Library**, **Art Gallery of South Australia**, **Zoo** (p63) and **Botanic Gardens** (p66) run inspired kid- and family-oriented programmes to go with accessible and interactive general displays. The **Investigator Science & Technology Museum** ( ☎ 8410 1115; www .investigator.org.au; Regency Institute of TAFE, Days Rd, Regency Park; adult/child $8.50/5.50; 9am-5pm Mon-Fri) has live demonstrations and makes science fun. **Port Adelaide** (p85) also has a number of museums with kid-friendly exhibits.

At **Glenelg** (p83), you can hire all manner of water toys for an active day at the beach, or perhaps take drooling munchkins on a tour of **Haigh's Chocolates Visitor Centre** (p68).

Books on tape are perfect for keeping travelling kids happy. You can find them

---

**QUIRKY ADELAIDE**

At the **Australian Museum of Childhood** ( ☎ 8240 5200; 95 Dale St, Port Adelaide; admission $3.50; 11am-4pm Sat, Sun & public holidays), housed in an old school hall, a trip down memory lane will guarantee every sentence starts with 'I remember…' This overflowing toy box has toys from the 1890s through to Mouse Trap and today's faves. And the best part? You can actually play with them. Share, children.

West-bound bus Nos 151, 152 or 153 will get you to Port Adelaide from North Tce.

---

at the **ABC Shop** (Map pp64-5; ☎ 8410 0567) on the 3rd floor of Myer Shopping Complex on Rundle Mall. Also in the Myer complex, the **Australian Geographic Shop** (Map pp64-5; ☎ 8211 7700) stocks nature-based books, toys and activities (including bug-eye lenses, strap-on kangaroo tails and southern hemisphere night sky charts) for fun activities.

## TOURS

The many tours in and around Adelaide include gardens, bird-watching, historic buildings, art galleries and the usual sightseeing tours by various means of transport. You can travel between most city sights on the free city buses (see p81), or on the jump-on/jump-off tram-bus run by **Adelaide Explorer** ( ☎ 8364 1933; www.adelaideexplorer.com.au). Tickets cover the city and coast (adult/child $30/10) or city only ($25/10) and are valid for two days; there are three departures daily. Pick up a brochure at the visitors centre. For details on boat cruises, see Adelaide Zoo (p67), Port Adelaide (p86) and Glenelg (p83).

**Tourabout Adelaide Walking & Private Tours** ( ☎ 8333 1111; www.touraboutadelaide.com.au) brings to life Adelaide's founders, shakers, shapers and landmarks in three two-hour guided walks (around $25): Adelaide's Cultural Heritage (Friday), West Tce Cemetery (first Sunday in the month) and West End Arts walks (Thursday). Bookings essential.

**Tauondi Aboriginal Cultural Tours** ( ☎ 8341 2777) offers 45-minute Aboriginal guided tours ($10 to $15) covering plants and their uses in the Botanic Gardens (Wednesday to Friday and Sunday), Dreaming stories in Cleland Wildlife Park (see p89), and the Aboriginal

Cultures Gallery in the South Australian Museum. Bookings are essential.

**Adelaide's Top Food & Wine Tours** ( ☎ 8231 4144; www.food-fun-wine.com.au) uncovers SA's gastronomic soul with dawn tours of the buzzing Central Market, on which stallholders introduce their varied produce. **Susie's Boutique Tours** ( ☎ 0417-841 008; www.susiestours.com.au;

☾ 10am Tue, Thu-Sat) also runs two-hour market tours.

**Prime Mini Tours** ( ☎ 8276 1600; www.primemini tours.com; ☾ Tue-Thu) run a tour titled 'City & Brewery' ($50, 5½ hours), which combines the Rodney Fox Shark Experience in Glenelg, Haigh's Chocolates and the South Australian Brewing Company. It also runs excellent

---

### FESTIVALS & EVENTS

Adelaide is Australia's festival epicentre. A continuous high-calibre stream of fantastic international and local events attracts performers and audiences from around the world, particularly for the Glenelg Jazz Festival and the Adelaide Festival of the Arts. At the Adelaide Fringe Festival, Aussie stand-up comedians are joined by their European and American counterparts and other headline acts from the Edinburgh Fringe Festival.

#### January
**Jacob's Creek Tour Down Under** (www.tourdownunder.com.au) South Australia's six-stage version of the Tour de France.

#### March
**Adelaide Festival of Arts** (www.adelaidefestival.com.au) Culture vultures absorb international and Australian dance, drama, opera and theatre performances on even-numbered years.
**Adelaide Fringe** (www.adelaidefringe.com.au) A biennial independent arts festival (even-numbered years), second only to Edinburgh Fringe.
**Clipsal 500** (www.clipsal500.com.au) Rev heads rejoice as Adelaide's streets become a four-day Holden versus Ford racing track.
**Womadelaide** (www.womadelaide.com.au) One of the world's best live-music events with more than 400 musicians and performers from around the globe. Held in odd-numbered years.

#### April – July
**Medieval Festival** (April) Held at Carrick Hill, this celebration of Middle Ages culture includes jousting and other knightly activities, such as feasting.
**Adelaide Cabaret Festival** (www.cabaretfringe.com; mid-June) The only one of its kind in the country.
**Adelaide's Festival of Ideas** (www.adelaidefestival.com.au; July) The glorious, the good and the innovative from around the world descend on Adelaide for a biennial talkfest (odd-numbered years).

#### August
**Royal Adelaide Show** (www.adelaideshowground.com.au) Agricultural and horticultural displays and entertainment.
**South Australian Living Artists** (www.salafestival.com) Innovative exhibitions and displays across the city.

#### October
**Bartercard Glenelg Jazz Festival** First-class New Orleans and Australian jazz bands.
**Classic Adelaide Rally** (www.classicadelaide.com.au) Full of lovingly maintained machines.
**Feast** (www.feast.org.au) A three-week lesbian and gay cultural festival with a carnival, theatre performances, talks and dances.

#### November
**Credit Union Christmas Pageant** (www.cupageant.com.au) An Adelaide institution for more than 70 years – floats, bands and marching troupes take over the city streets for the day.
**Mitsubishi Horse Trials** (www.adelaidehorsetrials.com.au) An Olympic-level event held in the city-centre parklands.

#### December
**Bay Sports Festivals** A large sports fest held in Glenelg, including beach volleyball, aquathon, a surf carnival, hockey and gridiron.

tours incorporating the Barossa (from $65, including lunch); Hahndorf, Victor Harbor and McLaren Vale (from $54); winery-focussed McLaren Vale and Adelaide Hills ($95); Wildlife ($92), including dinner at Warrawong; and Murray River ($82), including a cruise and lunch.

Those drawn to the paranormal can get spooked with **Prismteam** ( ☎ 8234 3938; www.go.to /prism) on a haunted tour with three-course meal ($76) or weekend Haunted Kapunda tour ($395 including meals and accommodation). See also Old Adelaide Gaol (p66).

A huge variety of tours cover Adelaide, the Adelaide Hills, Fleurieu Peninsula and Barossa Valley. One-day trips to the southern Flinders Ranges and Kangaroo Island are very rushed and not recommended.

**Adelaide Eco Tours** ( ☎ 1800 639 933) One-day nature and wildlife tours ($149) to the Fleurieu Peninsula including wine tasting.

**Barossa Valley Tours** ( ☎ 8563 2233, 0417-852 453; www.barossavalleytours.com; full-day tours $39, with lunch $47) A local operator whisks you around the major sites in the area, including a selection of wineries, and stops for a two-course lunch (optional).

**Enjoy Adelaide** ( ☎ 8332 1401; www.enjoyadelaide .com.au) Tours include wine- and almond-tasting on the Fleurieu Peninsula with penguin viewing at Victor Harbor (adult/child $60/38); Victor Harbor, the Murray River and Hahndorf (adult/child $50/30), which can incorporate the Cockle Train; the Murray River including a cruise ($85); the Barossa Valley (adult/child $65/38, including lunch); and a half-day tour (adult/child $35/20) visiting Haigh's, Mt Lofty Summit and Hahndorf.

**Groovy Grape Getaways** ( ☎ 1800 661 177; www .groovygrape.com.au) Fun backpacker tours of the Barossa ($65) including the Whispering Wall, Big Rocking Horse, a few wineries and a barbecue lunch.

**Tour Delights** ( ☎ 8262 6900) Small-group tours of the Barossa ($50), including four wineries and Maggie Beer's Farm Shop.

A gamut of coach tours are run by **Premier Stateliner** ( ☎ 8415 5566; www.premierstateliner.com. au), **Adelaide Sightseeing** ( ☎ 8231 4144; www.adel aidesightseeing.com.au) and **Great Sights** ( ☎ 1300 850 850; www.greatsights.com.au).

## SLEEPING

Motels and hotels are dotted all over Adelaide, though there's also a 'motel alley' along Glen Osmond Rd, which leads into the city centre from the southeast. Bear in mind that this is a main arterial, so some places can be noisy. For extra calm, consider places in leafy North Adelaide, 2km north of the city centre. For beachside accommodation near the city, see Glenelg (p83).

### Budget
#### HOSTELS                              Map pp64–5
A couple of city pubs have rooms, but hostels offer the best value. Many hostels tempt with free apple pie or cheesecake for supper and most have dedicated TV rooms with a selection of movies, and a well-stocked guest kitchen. They generally offer a free service to/from the airport, bus and train stations, and have their own travel agencies or will book tours and car hire.

**Adelaide Central YHA** ( ☎ 8414 3010; www.yha .com.au; 135 Waymouth St; dm/d from $20/57, non-YHA members extra $5; P ☒ ☐ ) It may not be party central, but you will get plenty of sleep in the spacious and comfortable rooms (with luggage lockers), and it's surrounded by great bars and nightspots. Gleaming facilities, excellent communal areas with a pool table, TV rooms and free nightly movies. Daily bike hire $10.

**My Place** ( ☎ 8221 5299; www.adelaidehostel.com .au; 257 Waymouth St; dm $20, d with TV $54; P ☐ ) The wonderfully welcoming atmosphere will soon have you calling this relatively small and quiet hostel home. It's just a stumble away from pubs and Light Sq nightspots and has a cosy TV room, sauna and plant-rimmed terrace to laze on. Affable, multilingual staff will get you out on the town with evening adventures to local pubs – especially good for solo travellers. Rates include breakfast and daily bus to Glenelg. Bike hire $10 per day.

**Backpack Oz** ( ☎ 8223 3551; www.backpackoz.com .au; cnr Wakefield & Pulteney Sts; dm/s/d incl breakfast $22/55/60; ☒ ☐ ) This gleaming family-run hostel in a former hotel has spacious dorms and a guesthouse over the road (which is great for couples). Guests can still get a coldie and shoot some pool at the converted bar. There's a comfortable communal area and free dinner on Wednesday. Full linen provided.

Other backpacker hostels include:
**Adelaide Backpackers Inn** ( ☎ 8223 6635; 118 Carrington St; dm/s/tw/d incl breakfast & supper $20/44/50/55; ☒ ☐ ) A relaxed and ultraclean place with roomier dorms than most and an annex across the road (try to get a window).

**Cannon St Backpackers** ( ☎ 1800 069 731, 8410 1218; www.cannonst.com.au; 110 Franklin St; dm/tw $20/55; (P) (🖳) ) A frat house–style party place, with a popular backpackers' bar. Some bemoan the lack of sleep and the tattiness.

### HOTELS

**Princes Lodge Motel** (Map p67; ☎ 8267 5566; prin ceslodge@senet.com.au; 73 Lefevre Tce, North Adelaide; s with bathroom $48, d without/with bathroom incl breakfast $66/85, f $92; (P) (😡) ) In a grand old house overlooking parkland and the hills, this friendly but tired lodging is close to chichi North Adelaide's restaurants and within walking distance of the city.

**Austral Hotel** (Map pp64-5; ☎ 8223 4660; www .theaustral.com; 205 Rundle St; s $35, d & tw $55, tr/q $70/ 80) There's no heating or air-con in these basic pub rooms up a tight staircase, but it's just a few steps to everything in the East End. Lounge in the relaxed bar downstairs. Shared bathrooms.

**Plaza Hotel** (Map pp64-5; ☎ 8231 6371; www .plazahotel.com.au; 85 Hindley St; s/d $66/72; (😡) ) A colonial-style hotel with private bathrooms and laundry and kitchen facilities for guests.

### CAMPING

Adelaide has some excellent caravan parks in prized positions near the beach, with great facilities. Linen is generally supplied for more expensive cabins and units.

**Adelaide Shores Caravan Resort** ( ☎ 8356 7654; www.adelaideshores.com.au; 1 Military Rd, West Beach; sites per 2 people $25, on-site vans/cabins from $50/65; (P) (😡) (🖳) (🏊) ) Nestled behind dunes on a lovely beach with a walking/cycling track extending to Glenelg (3.4km) in one direction and Henley Beach (3.5km) in the other, this is a great spot to be in summer. There are lush sites, glistening amenities and passing dolphins.

**Adelaide Shores Holiday Village** ( ☎ 8355 7360; cabins from $85, units/villas from $120/150; (P) (😡) (🏊) ) Attached to the Caravan Resort, this place has comfortable self-contained family accommodation, playgrounds, pools and a communal leisure centre.

Other camping options:

**Adelaide Caravan Park** ( ☎ 8363 1566; www.adelaide caravanpark.com.au; Richmond St, Hackney; powered sites per 2 people $26, cabins/units from $75/95; (😡) ) An orderly park on the banks of the Torrens River, 2km northeast of the city centre.

**Windsor Gardens Caravan Park** ( ☎ 8261 1091; 78 Windsor Grove, Windsor Gardens; unpowered/powered sites per 2 people $19.50/22, units from $60; (😡) ) In a treed area by the Torrens, 7km northeast of the city centre.

## Mid-Range

Log onto www.needitnow.com to see the prices available for hotels in Adelaide with discounts in excess of 50% of the rack rate.

**Clarice Motel** (Map pp64-5; ☎ 8223 3560; 220 Hutt St; s/d $50/65, units from $80; (P) (😡) ) Steps away from great dining on Hutt St, Clarice has basic double rooms with shared facilities, and motel units. Rates include light breakfast.

**Festival Lodge** (Map pp64-5; ☎ 8212 7877; 140 North Tce; s/d incl breakfast $90/110; (P) $7.50; (😡) ) While its old-style (yet immaculate) rooms may not be of the boutique variety found elsewhere along this strip, Festival Lodge has affordable rooms in a prime position opposite the casino and a hop from the Adelaide Festival Centre.

**Majestic Roof Garden Hotel** (Map pp64-5; ☎ 8100 4400; www.majestichotels.com.au; 55 Frome St; d/tw from $130/145, extra person $30; (P) $12; (😡) ) This new city-centre motel has attractive, boutique-style minimalist rooms and a gym.

**Royal Coach Motor Inn** (Map pp64-5; ☎ 8362 5676; www.royalcoach.com.au; 24 Dacquetteville Tce, Kent Town; d from $145, extra adult/child $15/10; (P) (😡) (🏊) ) Just a stroll through Rymill Park from the East End and Central Business District (CBD), these bright rooms have a queen-sized bed and single sofa. There's a Grecianlike indoor pool and one child can stay for free.

**Regal Park Motor Inn** (Map p67; ☎ 8267 3222; www.regalpark.com.au; 44 Barton Tce East, North Adelaide; d from $100; (P) (😡) (🖳) (🏊) ) Overlooking parkland in quiet, elegant North Adelaide. There's a children's playground and swimming pool on site.

**Strathmore Hotel** (Map pp64-5; ☎ 8238 2900; www .strath.com.au; 129 North Tce; d incl breakfast from $115; (P) (😡) ) Huddled between larger entities, this traditional hotel with a wrought-iron balcony is directly opposite the train station and casino. Its attractive and good-value renovated rooms have all the mod cons.

Motels with standard, comfortable facilities in and around the city centre include:

**Adelaide Paringa Motel** (Map pp64-5; ☎ 8231 1000; www.macbitz.net.au/paringa; 15 Hindley St; s $99, d $125-150, extra adult/child $20/5; (P) (😡) (🖳) ) In a heritage building at the heart of hyper Hindley St. Rates include breakfast.

**City Parklands Motel** (Map pp64-5; ☎ 8223 1444; www.citypark.com.au; 471 Pulteney St; d without/with bathroom $73/88, tr $99, f $150; **P** **※** ) Overlooking the southern parklands, an easy walk to the market area and Hutt St and Grote St restaurants.

**Mercure Grosvenor Hotel** (Map pp64-5; ☎ 8407 8888; www.mercuregrosvenorhotel.com.au; 125 North Tce; economy/standard d $110/195; **P** **※** ) Opposite the casino, compact room configurations at this hotel feature a double or two single beds. Children under 16 stay free.

You'll find small but comfortable units at **City Central Motel** (Map pp64-5; ☎ 8231 4049; www .arta.com.au/ccentral.html; 23 Hindley St; s/d/tw $70/75/80; **P** ) and **Princes Arcade Motel** (Map pp64-5; ☎ 8231 9524; 262-66 Hindley St; d $60, with kitchenette $80; **P** ).

### APARTMENTS & COTTAGES

Holiday apartments in and around Adelaide are listed under Apartments & Flats and Apartments – Serviced in the *Yellow Pages*. Many apartments are just over the Torrens River in North Adelaide. Reduced monthly rates are generally available.

**Director's Studios** (Map pp64-5; ☎ 8213 2500; www .savillesuites.com.au; 259 Gouger St; d/studio $115/130; **P** **※** ) These warm and unfussy classically styled rooms are on the west business side of town. Studio rooms contain kitchenettes. Children under 14 stay free.

**Greenways Apartments** (Map p67; ☎ 8267 5903; www.greenwaysapartments.com; 45 King William Rd, North Adelaide; 1-/2-/3-bedroom apt $90/125/170; **P** **※** ) Within good strolling distance from the city centre, these standard apartments reduce rates by $10 for stays of more than three days.

**Quest on King William** (Map pp64-5; ☎ 8217 5000; www.questapartments.com.au; 82 King William St, North Adelaide; 1-/2-bedroom apt from $145/190; **P** $7; **※** ) These immaculate apartments right on the city's doorstep contain kitchenettes and some have DVD players. There are laundries on site.

**Tynte St Apartments** (Map p67; ☎ 1800 882 774, 8223 0582; www.majesticapartments.com.au; 82 Tynte St, North Adelaide; d $202, extra adult/child $17/6; **P** **※** ) These comfy self-contained studio apartments on a tree-lined street just off O'Connell St can sleep up to three people.

**Adelaide Old Terraces** (Map pp64-5; ☎ 8364 5437; www.adelaideoldterraces.com.au; various city locations, incl 26 Blackburn Street; d $140-200; **P** ) Asian antiques and provincial furniture give these heritage-listed cottages near Hutt St lots of character.

They can sleep up to seven and there's a minimum two-night stay. Continental breakfast provisions supplied.

**North Adelaide Heritage Group** ( ☎ 8272 1355; www.adelaideheritage.com; cottages $140-360; **※** ) manages a range of beautifully refurbished cottages around Adelaide. The 1866 bluestone **Fire Station** (Map p67; 80 Tynte St, North Adelaide) was operational during Victorian times – line up to book the Fire Engine Suite, outfitted with a genuine red and shiny fire engine.

## Top End

The following hotels are right in the city centre. Most offer package deals on weekends, when room prices are generally a fair bit cheaper than during the week. It's worth checking bargain hotel-booking websites for deals of over 50% off rack rates. Generally, children under 12 stay free.

**Rockford Adelaide** (Map pp64-5; ☎ 8211 8255; www.rockfordhotels.com.au; 164 Hindley St; standard/ refurbished d $155/165, spa ste $195-245, extra person $20; **P** $6; **※** **🖳** **🏊** ) Rooms in this contemporary, boutique-style hotel are decorated in warm, natural tones as smooth as chocolate. In all but the cheaper doubles, expect bathrobes, complimentary champagne and chocolates. Riverside rooms have balconies. Guests have use of the nearby gym.

**Radisson Playford Hotel & Suites** (Map pp64-5; ☎ 8213 8888; www.Radisson.com/adelaideau; 120 North Tce; midweek d from $205, weekend B&B d from $185; **P** $11; **※** **🖳** **🏊** ) Be sure to check for special deals at this award-winning five-star boutique hotel with opulent, luxurious rooms and a gym on premises.

**Ryokan** ( ☎ 8370 3507; maandini@adam.com.au; 16 Brightview Ave, Blackwood; B&B per person $175; 4-course Japanese meal $95) For a special occasion, stay in this unique five-star contemporary

Japanese-style house with a wonderful calm atmosphere in the southern hills.

# EATING

Dining out in Adelaide sits high on the social register – aided by inexpensive prices and high standards. Foodies flock to Gouger St, where you can sample from every continent and get some of the gutsiest Chinese food around. Choose from the market's delights, café quickies, and restaurant dining from Argentine to Vietnamese and everywhere in between. In Chinatown (by the Central Market), many Asian eateries serve cheap lunches and yum-cha brunches (all you can eat for around $10).

Pull up a people-watching pew at the lively Italian and Thai alfresco cafés and restaurants in Rundle Street, or relax at the quiet cluster of good restaurants on nearby Hindmarsh Sq. Diverse cafés sit alongside sleaze on Hindley St, while chic restaurants with gourmet accolades huddle on Hutt St.

Across the river in North Adelaide, Melbourne and O'Connell Sts have a wealth offering including Italian bistros, gourmet cuisine and cool pubs providing great food and live music.

## Restaurants & Cafés
### GOUGER ST &
### CENTRAL MARKET                    Map pp64–5
You can pretty much take your pick from any of the restaurants along this strip and be guaranteed a great meal. Listed here is just a sample.

**Chinatown Café** ( ☎ 8231 2230; Shop 38-41 Moonta St, Chinatown; meals $5.50-6.80; ☼ 10.30am-4.30pm daily, to 8.30pm Fri) Straight up mixed-Asian favourites served with the backdrop of a no-fuss décor. The massive laksa ($5.50) is a winner. Most dishes come with a vegetarian option.

**Lucia's Pizza & Spaghetti Bar** ( ☎ 8231 2303; 2 Western Mall, Central Market; meals $6-7.50; ☼ breakfast & lunch Mon-Thu & Sat, breakfast, lunch & dinner Fri) This little piece of Italy is an Adelaide institution (operating since 1957) renowned for some of the finest coffee in town. Breakfast and cheap tucker are served during market hours, and all sauces are home-made – try Friday's lasagne special or the home-made pizzas.

**T Bar** ( ☎ 8410 5522; 44 Gouger St; breakfast $2.50-7.50, lunch $6-7.50; ☼ breakfast & lunch) Take a sidestep out of the market and indulge at

---

this 140-variety tea emporium, also serving great coffee, cakes and tasty meals.

**Zuma Caffé** ( ☎ 8231 4410; 56 Gouger St; meals $2.20-8; ☼ market hr) On the edge of the market, Italian-style Zuma's big breakfast fry-up ($7.70) will keep you humming through the day. Voluptuous muffins ($2.20) and lunch dishes are also a good bet.

**Malacca Corner** ( ☎ 8231 5960; Western Mall, Central Market; mains $6-13; ☼ market hr) Sensational Malay Asian, including Singapore laksa, wet noodle dishes and *poh-piahs* (doughy parcels of sprouts and peanuts) in a tucked away corner of the market.

**Nu's Thai** ( ☎ 8470 2288; 117 Gouger St; mains $10-30; ☼ lunch Thu & Fri, dinner Tue-Sun) A contemporary Thai restaurant regarded as the best in town – despite a change in ownership serving dishes such as crispy chilli barramundi.

**Guacho's** ( ☎ 8231 2299; 91 Gouger St; mains $22.50-29.50; ☼ lunch Mon-Fri, dinner daily) Carnivore's only need apply – you'll get the finest dose in this Argentinean meat house.

Tacked on the Central Market's western end is **Chinatown**, with a collection of cafés doing fast and furious trade (especially on Friday night) and bursting with contented diners slurping soup and noodle dishes.

### EAST END                          Map pp64–5
The eastern end of Rundle St (off Rundle Mall) and its side streets burst with lively alfresco cafés and restaurants.

**East Taste Continental** (ETC; ☎ 8359 2255; 6 East Tce; breakfast $6.50-12; ☼ breakfast & lunch) The place to head for big breakfasts, served until 3.45pm.

**ADELAIDE**

**Vego and Lovin' It** ( ☎ 8223 7411; 1st fl, 240 Rundle St; burgers $8.20, wraps from $4.40; ☯ 10am-4.30pm Mon-Fri) Get a weekly vitamin dose disguised in a scrumptious veggie burger or wrap at this artsy, hippy sharehouselike kitchen.

**Amalfi Pizzeria Ristorante** ( ☎ 8223 1948; 29 Frome St; mains $12-22; ☯ lunch Mon-Fri, dinner Mon-Sat) Regulars swear by the pizza and pasta (made with the best ingredients available) at this buzzing Adelaide institution situated just off Rundle St. It's often difficult to get in, but hang around as it's definitely worth the wait.

**Botanic Café** ( ☎ 8224 0925; 4 East Tce; mains $17-25; ☯ lunch & dinner) Order from a seasonal menu styled from the best regional produce in this swish, contemporary hot spot opposite the Botanic Gardens. On Friday and Saturday nights it turns into a buzzing tapas bar.

**Sprouts** ( ☎ 8232 6977; 39 Hindmarsh Sq; meals $11-17; ☯ lunch & dinner) Vegetarians and vegans are in good company here. Famous herbivores are prominently named at the entry to this small, stylish dining room which serves dishes such as Cajun spiced tofu and mushroom crepe wraps.

**Jasmin Indian Restaurant** ( ☎ 8223 7837; 31 Hindmarsh Sq; mains $19.50; ☯ lunch Tue-Fri, dinner Tue-Sat) Mrs Singh's mouth-watering North Indian cuisine garners a full house and keeps Jasmin among Australia's top 100 restaurants. If you like it hot, try the vindaloo.

**Exeter** ( ☎ 8223 2623; 246 Rundle St; snacks $1.20-5.50, meals $10-17; ☯ lunch & dinner) This perennial favourite, old-style pub in the middle of the city serves inspired meals ranging from venison vindaloo and roo fillets to chicken laksa and tofu burgers. The **Austral Hotel** ( ☎ 8223 4660; 205 Rundle St; bar menu $7.50-15; ☯ lunch & dinner) also serves excellent pub food.

### WEST END

Adelaide's original 'sin strip' is the artsy-alternative side of town with plenty of good eateries among glittery bars.

**Worldsend Hotel** (Map pp64-5; ☎ 8231 9137; 208 Hindley St; bar meals $7-11, dining room $16-19; ☯ lunch & dinner) Enjoy great-value bar meals with a good casual vibe and mixed crowd. Upmarket meals are in a separate dining room.

**Café Tapas** ( ☎ 8211 7446; 147 Hindley St; ☯ lunch & dinner) Are you keen for food or a fruity margarita? Both are excellent. The entertainment comes for free from Thursday to Sunday night.

**Prince Albert** (Map pp64-5; ☎ 8212 7912; 154 Wright St; mains $10-18; ☯ lunch & dinner) A relaxed and reliable haunt for those seeking cheap pub grub that looms large. Schnitzels ($10.90) hang off the end of the plate, and there's live music too. The **Cumberland Arms** (Map pp64-5; ☎ 8231 3577; 205 Waymouth St; meals $8-18; ☯ lunch & dinner Mon-Fri) also serves cheap meals.

### AROUND TOWN                                 Map pp64–5
**Hawker's Corner** (cnr West Tce & Wright St; meals $6-12; ☯ lunch & dinner Tue-Sun) The place to pick up cheap Asian dishes.

**La Trattoria** ( ☎ 8212 3327; 346 King William St; mains from $12; ☯ lunch Mon-Fri, dinner daily) A tried and tested favourite for pizza and pasta.

There's great eating in buzzing cafés and restaurants on Hutt St.

**Good Life** ( ☎ 8223 2618; 170 Hutt St; pizzas $12.50-18.90; ☯ lunch Tue-Fri, dinner Tue-Sun) Sensational organic pizzas disappear in record time at this provincial-style restaurant. Fancy roast duck with *shitake* mushrooms and spring onion ginger jam? Book ahead.

**Citrus** ( ☎ 8224 0100; 199 Hutt St; mains $12-22; ☯ breakfast, lunch & dinner) A European-style boulevard café, with quality output and a drool-worthy antipasto window.

### NORTH ADELAIDE                              Map p67
Cafés and restaurants line Melbourne and O'Connell Sts, the main thoroughfares into the city.

**Store** ( ☎ 8361 6999; 157 Melbourne St; breakfast $5-12, lunch $8.50-15.50; ☯ breakfast, lunch & dinner) Gourmet gremlins champ at the bit to pile into this northside haunt for breakfast, lunch and dinner, and anything in between.

**Cafe Paesano** ( ☎ 8239 0655; cnr O'Connell & Tynte Sts; breakfast $4-11.50, mains $12-21; ☯ lunch & dinner) This jovial Italian bistro has alfresco dining on the footpath and huge portions. Entrées are ample.

**Royal Oak Hotel** ( ☎ 8267 2488; 123 O'Connell St; mains $16-23; ☯ lunch & dinner Wed-Sun) Relax on the back seat of an old car at this eclectic old stone pub. Order from the hearty menu, or share a meze platter ($17). There's live music, particularly jazz.

**Amarin Thai** ( ☎ 8239 0026; 106 Tynte St; mains $8.50-17.50; ☯ lunch Wed-Fri, dinner Mon-Sat) Off O'Connell St, intimate Amarin serves excellent Thai food to faithful locals.

**Archer** ( ☎ 8361 9300; 47 O'Connell St; bar menu $7.50-14.50, mains $20-26; ☯ lunch & dinner) Meaty Mod

Oz cuisine is served in the refined library of this deconstructionist-style pub, with a long accompanying list of fine SA wines. Burgers, curries and grills are served in the bar, which has Victorian and Western Australian microbrews on tap.

**Cibo** ( ☎ 8267 2444; 10 O'Connell St; mains $26.50-31; ⏱ lunch & dinner) Smart dining Italian style with attentive yet unfussed service, a refined atmosphere and a dedicated pizza oven. Two-course lunch meal-deals ($25) include a glass of wine.

### Quick Eats & Late Bites   Map pp64–5
**Pie Cart** (pies $2.50; ⏱ 6pm-midnight Mon-Fri, 4pm-4am Sat, 4-11pm Sun) Detour past this iconic place at Adelaide Railway Station for late night munchies on your stumble home, the perfect time to chow down on a pie floater (a meat pie with tomato sauce floating in thick, green pea soup).

**Falafel House** (258 Rundle St; dishes $5-7.50; ⏱ 11.30am-at least 2am) Try the felafels and kebabs bursting with fresh salad.

Noodle shops dotted around the city are great places to get filling, cheap and tasty meat and vegetarian meals fast. Try **Thai in a Wok** ( ☎ 8224 0969; 37 Hindmarsh Sq; mains $7.50-13.50; ⏱ lunch Mon-Fri, dinner Wed-Sat) and **Wok-in-a-Box** ( ☎ 8231 0121; cnr King William & Hindley Sts; meals $7-8; ⏱ lunch & dinner).

### Self-Catering Map pp64–5
**Central Market** (btwn Grote & Gouger Sts; ⏱ 7am-5.30pm Mon-Thu, 7am-9pm Fri, 7am-3pm Sat) You can find just about everything at the Central Market's 250-odd shops – abundant and fresh vegetables, breads, cheeses, seafood and gourmet produce – you name it. Don't miss the Providore and a sample from the Yoghurt Company. Bargain hunters should

head down on Tuesday afternoon or after lunch on Saturday. There's also a **Coles Supermarket** (Central Market Arcade, cnr King William & Gouger Sts; ⏱ daily) here.

**Woolworths** ( ☎ 8232 0787; 86 Rundle Mall) Has an attached liquor store.

## DRINKING
To get a true Adelaide experience, head for the bar and order a schooner (half pint) or pint of Coopers, the local brew, or a glass of SA's impressive wine. Most pubs feature a 'happy hour' with reduced-price drinks at some stage in the evening. In Hindley St, grunge and sleaze collides with student energy, and groovy bars sit amid adult bookshops and strip joints.

**Short Black** (Map pp64-5; ☎ 841 9390; 87 Hindley St) Pause at the streetside counter for a quickie coffee.

**Spats** (Map pp64-5; ☎ 8272 6170; 108 King William Rd; Hyde Park; dessert $7.50) Cosy up on a couch in a booth for wicked desserts, hot chocolates and liquor coffees.

**Grace Emily Hotel** (Map pp64-5; ☎ 8231 5500; 232 Waymouth St) There's live music most nights, featuring some great up-and-coming Australian bands and artists. If you're up for a bit of wildlife spotting, look out for the tiny native bats which feed on insects under the street lights near the beer garden.

**Worldsend Hotel** (Map pp64-5; ☎ 8231 9137; 208 Hindley St) A mixed crowd gathers here to soak up the casual vibe.

**Exeter** (Map pp64-5; ☎ 8223 2623; 246 Rundle St) This groovy, old-style inner-city pub attracts plenty of postwork and uni imbibers. Pull up a stool or claim a wooden table in the atriumlike beer garden and settle in for the evening. Music (most nights) ranges from acoustic to electronica.

**Garage Bar** (Map pp64-5; ☎ 8212 9577; 163 Waymouth St, Light Sq) Kick back at this groovy, converted-garage bar with darts, pool and table football. Thursday is bingo night.

**Botanic Bar** (Map pp64-5; ☎ 8227 0799; 309 North Tce) Cocktails sink to soulful beats and a ruby-red glow suffuses this retro barcum-stately manor in Adelaide's East End.

**Universal Wine Bar** (Map pp64-5; ☎ 8232 5000; 285 Rundle St) A hip crowd registers here to select from more than 450 South Australian, national and international wines. The menu is packed with dishes crafted from SA produce.

**Treasury** (Map pp64-5; ☎ 8212 0499; Treasury Bldg, 144 King William St) A refined bar catering to the 28- to 50-year-old professionals in the business end of town.

Other eclectic spots include:

**Apothecary 1878** (Map pp64-5; ☎ 8212 9099; 118 Hindley St) Get a dose from the old dispensary turned wine bar.

**Fumo Blu** (Map pp64-5; ☎ 8232 2533; Rundle St) A hip underground cigar bar/club with a tropical fish tank, superdry martinis and Moët by the glass.

**Belgian Beer Café** (Map pp64-5; ☎ 8359 2233; 27-29 Ebenezer Pl, off Rundle St) A European-style drinking hall with 26 imported Belgian superbrews and lots of noisy chatter.

**Wine Underground** (Map pp64-5; ☎ 8232 1222; 121 Pirie St) Allow the first half-hour to trawl through the list of some 450 wines.

There are also a few worthy spots north of Adelaide's CBD.

**Banque** (Map p67; ☎ 8267 6999; 107 O'Connell St, North Adelaide) A stylish, doof-free zone with classic films projected onto the walls and live music (from jazz to acoustic) five nights a week, and a monthly cotton club.

**Archer** (Map p67; ☎ 8361 9300; 47 O'Connell St, North Adelaide) A fantastic place for a drink with a room for every mood, from the jovial front bar (which has a sports screen), to the fireside lounge with chesterfields, snooker room and upbeat music room, with DJs on weekends.

**Bombay Bicycle Club** (Map p67; ☎ 8269 4455; 29 Torrens Rd, Ovingham) Appreciate the Rudyard Kipling–inspired décor and become a member of the 100-beer club.

**Lion** (Map p67; ☎ 8367 0222; 161 Melbourne St, North Adelaide) A range of punters keep the Lion busy throughout the week. There are plenty of beers on tap, live (rock) entertainment,

cheap burger and beer deals, and an upmarket restaurant attached.

Other North Adelaide options include the **Royal Oak** (opposite) and **Dan O'Connell's** (Map p67; ☎ 8267 4034; 165 Tynte St, North Adelaide), with a giant pepper tree in the beer garden.

## ENTERTAINMENT

Arts-connoisseur Adelaide has a phenomenal cultural life that compares favourably with much larger cities. The free monthly *Adelaide Review* (www.adelaidereview.com) features theatre and gallery listings, and the *Advertiser* (www.theadvertiser.news.com.au) newspaper lists events and cinema programmes and gallery details on Thursday and Saturday. The Theatre Association of South Australia compiles the **Adelaide Theatre Guide** ( ☎ 8272 6726; http://theatreguide.tripod.com), a comprehensive site listing dates, venues, booking details and reviews of comedy, drama and musical events and other performance arts.

Bookings for big events can be made through **BASS** (Map pp64-5; ☎ 13 12 46; www.bass.sa.com.au; SATC visitors centre, 18 King William St) and the riverside **Adelaide Festival Centre** (Map pp64-5; ☎ 8216 8600; www.afct.org.au; King William Rd). This hub of performing arts in SA hosts touring and local plays, festival events, concerts and musicals. The **State Theatre Company** (www.statetheatre.sa.com.au) is based here.

Other theatre venues include **Her Majesty's Theatre** (Map pp64-5; ☎ 8212 8600; 58 Grote St), the **Lion Theatre & Bar** (Map pp64-5; ☎ 8212 9200; Lion Arts Centre, 13 Morphett St) and **Odeon Theatre** ( ☎ 8333 0444; cnr Queen St & The Parade, Norwood).

The multipurpose **Adelaide Entertainment Centre** (Port Rd, Hindmarsh) hosts everything from ballet to opera to big-name concerts.

## Nightclubs                                    Map pp64–5

The scene is ever changing, though the West End and Light Sq are a pretty safe bet for

---

**THE AUTHOR'S CHOICE**

**Weimar Room** (Map pp64-5; ☎ 8410 4700; 27 Hindley St; entry $10-16; ☼ 8pm-2am Fri-Sun) This über-cool place is a European-style cabaret venue with a 'rough-around-the-edges, turn-of-the-century' chic and a range of shows including flamenco, tango, theatre sports, jazz, big bands and cabaret. You can also eat here, and the bar serves absinthe.

club activity. Pick up a copy of *Onion* from pubs, cafés and music shops for 'dance news and fat reviews'.

**Savvy** ( ☎ 8221 6030; 149 Waymouth St, Light Sq) Pumps with commercial house music, featuring DJs and guests. It's very popular with the 18 to 25 set.

**Heaven Nightclub Complex** ( ☎ 8216 5216; www .heaven.com.au; 7 West Tce; ☾ 8pm-6am) Nectar for clubbers – different bars play different music including retro, rhythm and blues, house and dance.

In other areas:

**Garage Bar** ( ☎ 8212 9577; 163 Waymouth St, Light Sq) Has a good vibe, and takes off with the resident DJ on weekends.

**Moskva Vodka Bar West** ( ☎ 8211 9007; 192 Hindley St; ☾ from 9pm Wed-Sun) A West End club with a packed, chandelier-decorated dance floor and watermelon martinis.

**Minke Bar** ( ☎ 8211 8088; 142 Hindley St; ☾ from 9pm Wed-Sun) A grungy-but-cool New York–style bar.

**Mojo West** (west end of Hindley St) Weekend nightclub popular with the 18- to 24-year-old uni crowd. There's a free barbecue on Sunday.

**Mars Bar** ( ☎ 8231 9639; 120 Gouger St; ☾ 10.30pm-late Wed-Sat) A popular dance club.

The massive Marion Plaza, 21km southwest of the city, includes various nightspots. Bus Nos 720, 243, 246, 247 and 263 head to Marion from the city centre; the Wandering Star (p81) will bring you home.

## Casino

**SkyCity Casino** (Map pp64-5; ☎ 8218 4100; North Tce ☾ 10am-4pm, to 6am Fri-Sun) Housed in the grand old train station, this casino has all the flashing lights, trilling machines, two-up games and psychedelic carpet you could ask for. There are two bars, two restaurants and a café. Smart casual dress is required (but clean jeans are OK).

## Cinemas

Check the entertainment pages in the *Advertiser* for what's on around town. Cinemas slash ticket prices on Tuesday.

**Mercury Cinema** (Map pp64-5; ☎ 8410 1934; Lion Arts Centre, 13 Morphett St) This cinema publishes a quarterly calendar detailing its upcoming art-house films and festival screenings. Pick one up at cafés or the SATC visitors centre.

**Academy Cinema City** (Map pp64-5; ☎ 8223 5000; Hindmarsh Sq; tickets $14) Screens new-release mainstream films.

**Moonlight Cinema** (Map pp64-5; ☎ 1900 933 899; www.moonlight.com.au; Botanic Gardens; adult/concession $14/10; ☾ mid-Dec–mid-Feb) In summer, pack a picnic and mosquito repellent, and spread out on the lawn to watch old and new classics under the stars.

**Nova & Palace East End Cinemas** (Map pp64-5; ☎ 8232 3434; 251 & 274 Rundle St; adult/concession $13.50/9.50) Both cinemas feature new-release art-house, foreign-language and independent films as well as some mainstream flicks. The wonderful old **Piccadilly Cinema** (Map p67; ☎ 8267 1500; 181 O'Connell St, North Adelaide; adult/concession $14/10) also screens independent films.

## Live Music

To get your finger on the pulse, grab a copy of free street press papers *Rip It Up* or *db* – available at record shops, hotels, cafés and nightspots – which have listings and reviews of bands and DJs playing around town. Dedicated websites provide up-to-date listings for Adelaide's jazz scene (www.jazz .adelaide.onau.net), the Adelaide Symphony Orchestra (www.aso.com.au), and general events at South Australian Music Online (www.musicsa.com.au).

**Elder Hall** (www.music.adelaide.edu.au/elderhall; University of Adelaide) Excellent acoustics make this one of Australia's finest concert halls; it hosts major concerts, often of the orchestral variety.

**Governor Hindmarsh Hotel** ( ☎ 8340 0744; www .thegov.com.au; 59 Port Rd, Hindmarsh; cover charge from $10) Live music fans should check out the line-up at 'The Gov' when heading into town. It received the Australian 'Live music venue of the year award' in 2003, among other awards, and features some legendary local and international acts. The atmospheric bars attract a mixed crowd of all ages (and flavours) – while the odd Irish fiddle band sits around in the bar, a back venue hosts folk, jazz, blues, salsa, reggae and dance music.

The **Royal Oak Hotel** (Map p67; ☎ 8267 2488; 123 O'Connell St, North Adelaide) is a great pub with a lively crowd and a variety of music including lounge and jazz. Other pubs offering good live music include the cosy **Grace Emily Hotel** (Map pp64-5; ☎ 8231 5500; 232 Waymouth St), **Austral Hotel** (Map pp64-5; ☎ 8223 4660; 205 Rundle St), on Friday and Saturday nights, **Exeter** (Map pp64-5; ☎ 8223 2623; 246 Rundle St) and

PJ O'Brien's (Map pp64-5; ☎ 8232 5111; 14 East Tce). Cover charges vary depending on the act.

## Sport

Sport plays a huge part in the city's daily life. Adelaide hosts a number of world-class international events that take over the city streets and turn into big parties, including tennis matches, car racing and one-day and test cricket matches.

Australian Football League (AFL) rules the city, with two local competitive teams: the Adelaide Crows and Port Power. The Redbacks are the state's cricket team and basketball has the Adelaide 36ers.

## SHOPPING

Shops and department stores (including Myer, David Jones and Harris Scarf) line Rundle Mall. The beautiful old arcades running between the mall and Grenfell St retain their original splendour and house plenty of eclectic little shops. Rundle St and the lanes running off it are home to boutique and retro clothing shops; you'll also find some on Norwood Pde in Norwood. The huge Marion Plaza, in Oaklands Park southwest of the city, is SA's largest shopping complex.

Tourist souvenir shops lurk around Rundle Mall and nearby King William St. For something more stylish, head to **Tandanya Indigenous Cultural Institute** (Map pp64-5; ☎ 8224 3200; 253 Grenfell St), or seek out local art and crafts at the **Jam Factory Craft & Design Centre** (Map pp64-5; ☎ 8410 0727; Lion Arts Centre, cnr Morphett St & North Tce). Other good spots selling textiles, artworks, and accessories by established and emerging artists and designers include **T'Arts** (Map pp64-5; ☎ 8232 0265; 10G Gays Arcade, Adelaide Arcade, Rundle Mall) and **Urban Cow Studio** (Map pp64-5; ☎ 8232 6126; 11 Frome St).

A collection of opal shops around King William St and the end of Rundle Mall sell opals mined out of Coober Pedy. **Opal Field Gems** (Map pp64-5; ☎ 8212 5300; 33 King William St) has a mock-up opal mine and a free museum attached to its shop.

**RM Williams** (☎ 8269 3752; 5 Percy St, Prospect) sells handmade boots (women/men $250/220) from one piece of leather, first crafted for Aussie stockmen in the early 1800s. June sales can halve the price.

Outdoor gear shops are grouped on Rundle St, including **Mountain Designs** (Map pp64-5; ☎ 8232 0690; 203 Rundle St), **Annapurna** (Map pp64-5;

☎ 8223 4633; 210 Rundle St) and **Paddy Palin** (Map pp64-5; ☎ 8232 3155; 228 Rundle St).

## GETTING THERE & AROUND

All international and interstate flights to and from Adelaide go via Adelaide airport. Many regional flights also depart from here. The international and domestic airports are 7km from the city centre (due to move into new terminal buildings in October 2005). Budget, Hertz, Avis and Thrifty have car rental desks at the airport.

The interstate **train terminal** (Map pp64-5; Railway Tce, Keswick) is just southwest of the centre of town. Adelaide's **central bus station** (Map pp64-5; 101-111 Franklin St) contains terminals and ticket offices for all major interstate and statewide services, and also has left-luggage lockers. For details on travelling to and from Adelaide see the Transport chapter (p265).

### Getting to/from the Airport & Train Station

**Skylink** (☎ 8332 0528; www.skylinkadelaide.com; adult/child one-way $7.50/2.50; ⏰ 7am-10pm) runs hourly shuttles between 5.30am and 9.30pm to/from Adelaide airport via the Keswick interstate train station (adult/child one-way $4/1.50), if prebooked. Most hostels will pick you up and drop you off if you're staying with them. Taxis charge around $17 between the airport and city centre.

### Car & Motorcycle

If you want to hitch a ride (sharing petrol costs) or buy a second-hand car, check out the hostel notice boards.

The *Yellow Pages* lists more than 20 vehicle rental companies in Adelaide, including all the major national companies. Some do not allow cars to be taken to Kangaroo Island. Expect to pay around $45 per day (less for longer rentals) for car hire with the cheaper companies:

**Acacia Car Rentals** (☎ 8234 0911; 91 Sir Donald Bradman Dve, Hilton) Cheap rentals for travel within a 100km radius.

**Access Rent-a-Car** (Map pp64-5; ☎ 1800 812 580, 8359 3200; 60 Frome St) Also rents Vespa motor scooters ($50 per day including helmet).

**Cut Price Car-&-Truck-Rentals** (☎ 8443 7788; cnr Sir Donald Bradman Dr & South Rd, Mile End South)

**Explore** (Map pp64-5; ☎ 8231 2223; explorecoachlines@ bigpond.com.au; 101 Franklin St)

**Hawk-Rent-A-Car** (Map pp64-5; ☎ 1800 004 295, 8371 2824; 101 Franklin St)
**Wicked Campers** ( ☎ 1800 246 869; 07-3257 2170; www.wickedcampers.com.au) Fitted-out vans for from $60/48 per day for one/eight weeks' rental.

**Show & Go** ( ☎ 8376 0333; 236 Brighton Rd, Somerton Park) has motor scooters (from $55 per day) and motorcycles from 250cc (from $69) to 1000cc (from $169). You need a car driving licence to rent a scooter, while a full motorcycle licence is required for the bikes – a motorcycle learner's licence is acceptable for 250cc bikes.

## Public Transport

The **Adelaide Metro Information Centre** (Map pp64-5; ☎ 8210 1000; www.adelaidemetro.com.au; cnr King William & Currie Sts; 8am-6pm Mon-Sat, 10.30am-5.30pm Sun) provides timetables and sells tickets for the integrated metropolitan buses, trains and Glenelg tram. Tickets can also be purchased on board, at staffed train stations, and in delis and newsagents. There are day-trip ($6.20), two-hour peak ($3.30) and off-peak ($2) tickets. Train tickets can be purchased from vending machines on board trains, or at staffed train stations. The peak travel time is before 9am and after 3pm. The Bee Line and City Loop buses are free.

**Bee Line (No 99B)** runs in a loop from the Glenelg tram terminus at Victoria Sq, up King William St and around the corner past the train station to the City West campus of the University of South Australia. It leaves the square every five minutes on weekdays from 7.40am to 6pm (9.20pm Friday), every 15 to 17 minutes on Saturday from 8.27am to 5.30pm, and every 15 minutes on Sunday from 10am to 5.30pm.

**City Loop (No 99C)** runs clockwise and anticlockwise around the margins of the CBD from the train station, passing the Central Market en route. It generally runs every 15 minutes on weekdays between 8am and 6pm (9pm Friday), and every 30 minutes on Saturday between 8.15am and 5.15pm, and Sunday between 10am and 5.15pm.

**Wandering Star Service** ( ☎ 8210 1000; tickets $6; 12.30-5am Fri & Sat) will pick you up from designated spots/nightclubs and deliver you to your front door within most city suburbs, including the Adelaide Hills, Glenelg and Marion (for the Marion Plaza nightclubs).

Vintage trams rattle between Moseley Sq (Glenelg) and Victoria Sq (City) approximately every 15 minutes from 6am to 11.50pm daily. See Getting There & Around (p84) for details.

Suburban trains depart from **Adelaide Railway Terminal** (Map pp64-5; ☎ 8210 1000; North Tce), by the Casino. The five metro routes are: Belair via Goodwood and Blackwood; Gawler via North Adelaide and Ovingham; Grange; Noarlunga via Goodwood, Marion, Brighton and Seacliff; and Outer Harbor via Port Adelaide, Glanville and Largs. Trains run between 6am and midnight, with (some services starting at 4.30am).

For complete timetables, checkout the Adelaide Metro Information Service website (www.adelaidemetro.com.au).

## Taxi

There are licensed taxi ranks all over town, or call **Adelaide Independent Taxis** ( ☎ 13 22 11, wheelchair users 1300 360 940) or **Suburban Taxis** ( ☎ 13 10 08).

# AROUND ADELAIDE

Adelaide's sandy beaches (www.coastaladelaide.com.au), stretching from Maslin Beach in the south through Glenelg to Semaphore and Largs Bay in the north, are excellent for swimming, bodyboarding and taking in the sunset, and often feature a few dolphins. Inland from Semaphore, Port Adelaide is a growing hive of activity midway through a gentrification of its historic centre.

## GLENELG

In the relaxed seaside town of Glenelg (www.glenelgholiday.com.au), or 'The Bay', leopard-print clad septgenarians cruise the streets with shopping carts, locals mingle happily with tourists to stroll the promenade, and weekend crowds plough faces and tongues into mountainous ice-cream cones. The tram trundles past beachy murals along the Jetty Rd shopping strip to the bustling alfresco cafés around Moseley Sq, which leads to a great swimming beach.

## Information

**Glenelg Book Exchange** ( ☎ 8294 6407; 2C Moseley St; 9am-5pm Mon-Sat, 10.30am-5pm Sun) You can pick up second-hand books between beach stops here.

**Glenelg visitors centre** ( ☎ 8294 5833; Glenelg foreshore; ☽ 9am-5pm Mon-Fri, 10am-3pm Sat & Sun) Behind the Town Hall, also provides Internet access.

**Kappy's Bettanet Internet Café** ( ☎ 8294 8977; 55 Jetty Rd, Glenelg; 15/60 min $2/5; ☽ 7.30am-10.30pm) For fast Internet connections, head to Kappy's, attached to a great café.

**Stephens Pharmacy** ( ☎ 8295 7466; cnr Jetty Rd & Gordon St; ☽ 8.30am-10pm) Keeps late hours and sunscreen.

**Toilets** Beachside behind the visitors centre; you'll also find a shower.

## Sights

Take a vintage **tram** from Victoria Sq in the city centre for Glenelg's sunset views.

Governor Hindmarsh, SA's first Governor, and the first colonists travelled from England on **HMS Buffalo**; a full-size replica sits on the Patawalonga, east of Holdfast Shores Marina. The proclamation of SA was read in 1836 at **Old Gum Tree** on MacFarlane St, near the beach where the European settlers landed. There's a full-costume re-enactment on the site every year on Proclamation Day.

Upon settlement, Glenelg quickly became a busy seaport and a favoured spot for wealthy squatters, who built their grand townhouses near the beach. The bluestone **Town Hall** (Moseley Sq), Gothic-style **St Andrews Church** (Jetty Rd), Tudor-style **Partridge House** (38 Partridge St) and numerous fine Victorian mansions and stately homes are imposing reminders of Glenelg's prosperous past.

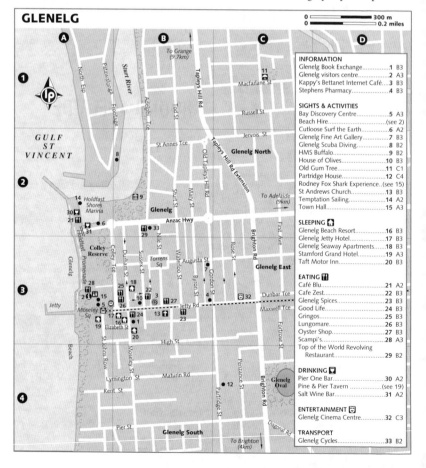

The **Bay Discovery Centre** ( ☎ 8179 9504; Moseley Sq, Glenelg; admission free; ☉ 10am-5pm) depicts life and the hardships experienced by the first European settlement and addresses the plight of the local Kaurna people, who lost both their land and voice.

Shark victim turned shark advocate Rodney Fox promotes understanding of the much-maligned creature and its position in the delicate ocean ecosystem at **Rodney Fox Shark Experience** ( ☎ 8376 3373; www.rodneyfox .com.au; Glenelg Town Hall, Moseley Sq, Glenelg; adult/child $6.50/4.50; ☉ 10am-5pm). It offers a fascinating insight into the 'smoke and mirrors' of the filming of *Jaws*.

You'll get oils, pure soaps, leaf extract, wood products, fruits, paintings and tastings at the **House of Olives** ( ☎ 8564 0141; 45 Jetty Rd, enter from Sussex St; ☉ 10am-5pm), all made with one thing in common in this den of olive mania.

**Glenelg Fine Art Gallery** ( ☎ 8294 0321; 26 Gordon St), inside the old fire station, features mostly local art.

## Activities

Glenelg's 215m jetty is a popular fishing spot where you can usually catch tommyruff, whiting and garfish. **Beach Hire** ( ☎ 8294 1477; ☉ sunny days Sep-Apr), near the visitors centre, hires out deck chairs, umbrellas, wave skis and bodyboards. This is a good spot for kiteboarding – contact **Cutloose Surf the Earth** ( ☎ 8294 3866; Holdfast Shores) for demos and lessons.

You can head out on a catamaran with **Temptation Sailing** ( ☎ 0412-811 838; www.dolphinboat .com.au; Holdfast Shores Marina, Glenelg) to swim with dolphins ($98, 3½ hours) or spot dolphins ($48, 3½ hours).

**Glenelg Scuba Diving** ( ☎ 8294 7744; www.glenelg scuba.com.au; Patawalonga Frontage) hires snorkelling and scuba gear and also offers scuba courses and dive charters.

## Sleeping

Glenelg has plentiful accommodation, including many holiday flats and serviced apartments which generally quote weekly rather than daily rates.

**Glenelg Beach Resort** ( ☎ 8376 0007; www.glenelg beachhostel.com.au; 7 Moseley St, Glenelg; dm $25, d/f from $60/70; ▢ ) With a fabulous beachside location, this charming terrace dating from 1879 is Adelaide's budget golden child. Fan-cooled

rooms sport period details and are bunk-free. There's nightly entertainment in the bar, open fireplaces and a large plasma TV screen in the lounge, a pool room with juke box, and a courtyard garden. Rates include linen, breakfast and airport pick-ups. If this is full, try **Glenelg Jetty Hotel** ( ☎ 8294 4377; 28 Jetty Rd).

**Glenelg Seaway Apartments** ( ☎ 8295 8503; 18 Durham St; dm/d from $20/70; ℗ ) This friendly place is just a minutes' walk from the tram stop. Its self-contained apartments can sleep up to five people, and the backpacker unit has a kitchen.

**Taft Motor Inn** ( ☎ 8376 1233; 18 Moseley St; motel d from $95, 1-/2-bedroom apt from $127/137; ℗ ⛏ ⛉ ) Comfortable motel rooms come with an obligatory Namatjira print on the wall; some rooms have kitchenettes, and there's a barbecue and playground on site. Transport from the airport, railway and bus stations is provided.

**Glenelg Holiday & Corporate Letting** ( ☎ 8376 1934; www.glenelgholiday.com.au; 1-bedroom apt $95; ℗ ⛏ ) Contact this agent for self-contained beachfront apartments ranging from one to five bedrooms.

**Stamford Grand Hotel** ( ☎ 8376 1222; www.stam ford.com.au; Moseley Sq; d city/ocean views from $180/220; ℗ ⛏ ) At the top of the comfort scale, this towering luxury hotel overlooks Gulf St Vincent. Packages available.

## Eating & Drinking

There are plenty of spots to pick up a good lamb spit, cheap pasta, Asian noodle or ice-cream takeaway on Jetty Rd, where alfresco cafés bustle in sunny weather.

**Cafe Zest** ( ☎ 8295 3599; 2A Sussex St; breakfast $4-8.90, meals $6.90-11.90; ☉ breakfast & lunch) This itty-bitty gallery-cum-café has a laid-back atmosphere and meals with a twist. Baguettes and bagels are crammed with taste-bud tingling combinations, and good coffee is served with a home-baked treat.

**Oyster Shop** ( ☎ 8376 7200; cnr Jetty Rd & Nile St; fish & chips $4.95; ☉ lunch & dinner) Grab the attention of staff – hidden behind a mountain of oysters ready to shuck – to order flipping fresh sushi, sashimi or a fisherman's basket ($9.95) to take away and scoff at the beach.

**Good Life** ( ☎ 8376 5900; Level 1, cnr Jetty Rd & Moseley St; pizzas $12.50-18.90; ☉ lunch Tue-Fri & Sun, dinner Tue-Sun) Mount the stairs from Jetty Rd to enter this casually stylish organic pizzeria which boasts a warm open fire in winter and flings back its doors for breezy terrace dining in summer. Thin crusts are piled high with tasty toppings such as spicy garlic venison *mettwurst* (German sausage) with Kalamata and green split olives.

**Glenelg Spices** ( ☎ 8376 1388; 111 Jetty Rd; meals $10-17; ⊙ lunch & dinner) Delightful spicy aromas waft from this very popular Malaysian/ Thai restaurant.

**Gringos** ( ☎ 8295 3524; Shop 1, Colley Tce; snacks $4-10.50; mains $14-18.50; ⊙ lunch & dinner) Grab a beer and chilli-up in the sun at this vibrant and colourful Mexican cantina opposite Moseley Sq, or take your bulging burrito down to the beach.

**Lungomare** ( ☎ 8376 1255; 1 Colley Tce; pizza & pasta $12-19; ⊙ lunch & dinner) This perennial favourite Italian café and bar overlooks Moseley Sq.

**Scampi's** ( ☎ 8376 6200; Foreshore; mains $20-30; ⊙ lunch & dinner) Book a table by the window and watch the sun go down over the bay while feasting on seafood.

**Top of the World Revolving Restaurant** ( ☎ 8376 0050; 760 Anzac Hwy; mains $12-22; ⊙ breakfast Sat & Sun, lunch Wed-Sun, dinner daily) The name says it all really. Choose from the flavours of the world menu and indulge in 360° views of Adelaide.

**Pier & Pine Tavern** ( ☎ 8376 1222; Moseley Sq; bar meals $9.50-12.50; ⊙ lunch & dinner) Inside the hard-to-miss monolithic Stamford Grand Hotel (see p83) at the pier. On warm days, grab a beer and catch the breeze at the overlooking the foreshore.

A short stroll north of the pier will lead you to **Holdfast Shores Marina** (www.holdfastshores .com.au), a towering development with some good restaurants and bars directly behind the beach. Sassy **Salt Wine Bar** ( ☎ 8376 6887; Holdfast Shores; mains $18-24; ⊙ 4-11.30pm Mon & Tue, 11am-11.30pm Wed, Thu & Sun, 11am-12.30am Fri & Sat) pulls punters in to dine or just for drinks, while **Café Blu** ( ☎ 8350 6688; Ramada Pier Hotel, 16 Holdfast Promenade; meals $12.50-21.50; ⊙ lunch & dinner) is enthusiastically reputed to have 'the best (bleep) margarita pizza on the planet'. The attached **Pier One Bar** is a good spot for sundowners – especially for sports fans. Acoustic sets and DJs spinning dance tracks keep it lively from Thursday to Sunday. Wednesday is burger and beer night ($9.50).

## Entertainment

**Glenelg Cinema Centre** ( ☎ 8294 3366; 119 Jetty Rd; adult/concession/child $14/10.50/9.50) Screens mainly mainstream films, and offers movie-and-meal deals with local restaurants.

## Getting There & Around

The vintage tram service between Victoria Sq, in the city, and Glenelg offers a scenic adventure through Adelaide's suburbs – verging on a thrill ride when it picks up speed to shoot over the bridge. Trams leave every 15 minutes from 6am to 11.50pm, and arrive at Moseley Sq about 25 minutes later.

You can also take bus Nos 263, 266, 275 and 278 from the city to the last stop on Anzac Hwy, about five minutes' walk from Jetty Rd.

Hire bikes from **Glenelg Cycles** ( ☎ 8294 4741; 754 Anzac Hwy; bikes per day $18; ⊙ 9am-5pm Mon-Fri, 9am-4pm Sat & Sun).

## SOUTH OF GLENELG

Heading south of Glenelg, the first of the 'old-time' metropolitan beaches is **Seacliff**, about 16km from the city centre, which includes **Brighton**, a popular swimming, sailboarding and sailing spot. There's a cliff-top monument to the Aboriginal Dreamtime ancestor Tjilbruke at Kingston Park, just south of Seacliff. Generally quiet **O'Sullivan Beach** has a concrete boat ramp leading off Galloway Rd, while larger **Christies Beach**, nearby, has a jetty and reef popular with scuba divers. Heading south, **Seaford** and adjoining **Moana** have a boat ramp and small beach that's popular with novice surfers. **Maslin Beach** (p103) about 40km south from the city centre, is Adelaide's only nudist beach.

## GLENELG TO PORT ADELAIDE

In winter, towns along this route resemble any other deserted seaside holiday locations, though in the summer the coast thrives with Adelaidians making the beachside pilgrimage. There's good swimming, often accompanied by dolphins. **West Beach**, the closest beach (10km) to the city, and **Henley Beach** have lovely stretches of sand. The square at Henley Beach is surrounded by hip restaurants and cafés and the best pub on the coast: the **Ramsgate Hotel** ( ☎ 8356 5411; 328 Seaview Rd, Henley Beach). To get there, take bus Nos 130 to 137 from Grenfell and Curry Sts.

In Grange, the popular **Grange Jetty Kiosk** ( ☎ 8235 0822; cnr Jetty Rd & Esplanade, Grange; mains $12-22; ⊙ breakfast Sun, lunch Wed-Mon, dinner Wed-Sat) has a seafood-heavy menu. Floodlit dunes and the lights of the jetty make it a romantic spot at night. Take bus No 130 or 137 from Grenfell St and get off at stop 29A.

North of here are the weed-free, shallow water beaches of chilled-out **Semaphore** and **Largs Bay**; the latter has a cool old hotel and heritage-listed jetty. Take bus No 152 to Semaphore from North Tce.

## PORT ADELAIDE

Port Adelaide, known to the Kaurna Aboriginal people as Yerti Bulti, is in the midst of a gentrification project which has turned its warehouses into art spaces, museums and antique shops.

The **Port Adelaide visitors centre** (☎ 8405 6560; www.portenf.sa.gov.au; 66 Commercial Rd) has brochures on everything you can do in town, including details on the Ship's Graveyard and Dolphin Trail, a shore-based walk that offers good vantage points for bottlenose dolphin viewing. The **Maritime Museum** (☎ 8207 6255; 126 Lipson St; adult/child/family $8.50/3.50/22; ⏰ 10am-5pm) has several vintage ships including the *Nelcebee*, the third-oldest ship on Lloyd's shipping register. There's also a computer register of early migrants. Combined tickets ($15/6/35) cover the next door **National Railway Museum** (☎ 8341 1690; www.natrailmuseum .org.au; Lipson St South; ⏰ 10am-5pm), which has a huge collection of railway memorabilia. The **South Australian Aviation Museum** (☎ 8240 1230; www.saam.org.au; cnr Ocean Steamers Rd & Honey St; adult/child/family $6/3/15; ⏰ 10.30am-4.30pm) has an impressive collection of old birds.

Dolphin cruises are run by **Port River Dolphin Cruises** (☎ 8447 2366) and **Falie Charters** (☎ 8341 2004; www.falie.com.au), in the tall ship *Falie*. Tours of the brewery and cellar at **Port Dock Brewery Hotel** (☎ 8240 0187; www.portdock breweryhotel.com.au; 10 Todd St) can be arranged; the pub brews its own distinctive beers.

Follow the lighthouse to the **Fisherman's Wharf Market** (☎ 8341 2040; ⏰ 9am-5pm Sun) to peruse a range of antiques and bric-a-brac.

In a converted warehouse opposite the Maritime Museum, **Lipson Café** (☎ 8341 0880; 117 Lipson St; breakfast $2-8.50, lunch $4-14; ⏰ breakfast & lunch) keeps the arty community ticking over with great food in generous proportions.

West-bound bus Nos 151, 152 or 153 will get you there from North Tce, or you can take the train. **Lipson Bike Hire** (☎ 8240 0463; 118 Lipson St) hires bicycles.

# Adelaide Hills

**CONTENTS**

| | |
|---|---|
| Stirling Area | 90 |
| Mylor | 91 |
| Hahndorf | 91 |
| Nairne to Woodside | 93 |
| Mt Barker to Strathalbyn | 94 |
| Strathalbyn | 94 |
| Clarendon | 95 |
| Norton Summit Area | 96 |
| Lobethal | 96 |
| Birdwood Area | 96 |

ADELAIDE HILLS

Even in the driest summer months the Adelaide Hills, a 30-minute drive from the city, offer crisper air, lush woodland shade and the delicious scent of eucalyptus from stands of gum trees. In autumn this is reinforced by the glorious colours of introduced deciduous trees, particularly in the wetter central area around Mt Lofty. Travelling along picturesque narrow roads you'll pass carts of fresh produce for sale, stone cottages, olive groves and vineyards. Locals wear grins from ear to ear, happy with the good life.

German settlers escaping religious persecution were on the scene early, establishing several villages, including Hahndorf, in 1839. Mixed in with these are typically British places such as Strathalbyn (established by the Scots), Stirling (by the English) and Callington (by the Cornish). Many buildings of the initial boom period, from 1837 to the 1860s, have survived, giving the hills a distinctive European heritage. The colony's first highway, from Adelaide to Mt Barker, opened in 1845. And by the 1850s, Adelaide's colonial gentry were beginning to build grand summer houses, many with stunning gardens that are now open for viewing.

The Adelaide Hills encompass the region bordered by Clarendon and Strathalbyn to the south, Mt Barker and Nairne to the east, and Mt Pleasant to the north. Numerous conservation and wildlife parks contain stunning views and the chance to interact with native fauna. There are also plenty of bushwalking options: the region is criss-crossed by hundreds of kilometres of tracks, including the Heysen Trail.

**ADELAIDE HILLS**

## HIGHLIGHTS

- Eating apple strudel in the German-heritage town of **Hahndorf** (p91)
- Tasting the region's wonderful cold-climate **wines** (p49)
- Surveying the view over Adelaide and the sea from **Mt Lofty Summit** (p89)
- Getting up close and personal with the furred and feathered locals at **Cleland Wildlife Park** (p89)
- Whiling away an afternoon over a pint or three at Macclesfield's **Three Brothers Arms** (p94)
- Walking among the trees on the **Heysen Trail** (p38) or in any of the region's national parks (p88)
- Taking a scenic drive and exploring the picturesque town of **Strathalbyn** (p94)
- Scaling the surprisingly nontacky **Big Rocking Horse** (p96)

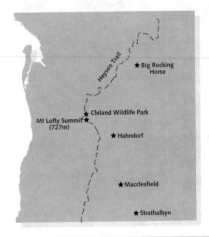

★ Big Rocking Horse

★ Cleland Wildlife Park

Mt Lofty Summit ★ (727m)

Heysen Trail

★ Hahndorf

★ Macclesfield

★ Strathalbyn

- TELEPHONE CODE: ☎ 08
- www.visitadelaidehills.com.au
- www.adhills.com.au

## National Parks & Gardens

Contact the **Department for Environment & Heritage** (DEH; www.environment.sa.gov.au/parks) offices at Belair National Park and Cleland Conservation Park for information on parks within the Adelaide Hills.

Outstanding private gardens in the central hills area participate in the seasonal 'Open Garden Scheme'. For details, contact the visitors centres in Hahndorf (p91) or Mt Lofty Summit (opposite).

### BELAIR NATIONAL PARK

Popular with fitness enthusiasts, **Belair National Park** ( ☎ 08-8278 5477; Upper Sturt Rd, Belair; entry per car $6.50; ☼ 8am-sunset), with its ornamental lake,

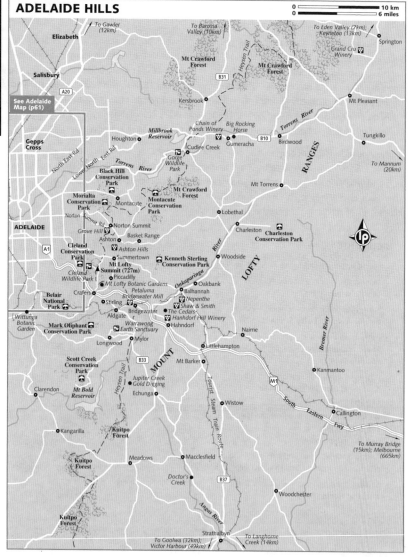

**ADELAIDE HILLS**

0 _____ 10 km
0 _____ 6 miles

ADELAIDE HILLS

picnic facilities and tennis courts, seems an odd choice for the National Park label. Declared in 1891, it is in fact Australia's second oldest. Only 9km south of the city centre, it also has some lovely walking tracks and **Old Government House** (☼ 1-4pm Sun), built in 1859 as a summer residence for governors of South Australia (SA), where the grand lifestyle of SA's colonial gentry is on display.

At the edge of the national park is **Belair Caravan Park** ( ☎ 08-8278 3540; Upper St Rd; unpowered/powered sites per 2 people $16/19, cabins $50-65). Nearby, **Nunyara Holiday Units** ( ☎ 08-8278 1673; 5 Burnell Dve, Belair; d/f $70/85, extra person $7.50) offer excellent-value self-contained units with million-dollar views of the city and coast.

From Adelaide, drive south along Unley Rd (which becomes Belair Rd), take bus No 195 from King William St to stop 27, or take the train through tunnels and valleys to Belair station.

### MORIALTA CONSERVATION PARK
This rugged **park** (☼ 8am-5pm Mon-Fri, later on weekends) on the western escarpment 10km east of the city centre has spectacular views and waterfalls. From the entrance, it's 2km (a 35-minute walk) to the first waterfall, or you can take a testing 2½-hour return walk past a series of **waterfalls** on Fourth Creek, which usually flows from late autumn to early summer. The most impressive falls are the second set, about 45 minutes from the car park.

From Adelaide, drive northeast on Payneham Rd, veer right onto Montacute Rd and turn right onto Stradbroke Rd. Bus No 105 from Grenfell and Currie Sts stops at the entrance on Stradbroke Rd.

### GLELAND CONSERVATION PARK
Stretching from the western foothills up to Mt Lofty, this steep park 7.5km southeast of the city centre has excellent bushwalking through tall eucalypt forest and moist gullies. There are picnic areas and a restaurant at popular **Waterfall Gully**.

Make like Dr Doolittle and walk with the animals at **Cleland Wildlife Park** ( ☎ 08-8339 2444; www.environment.sa.gov.au/parks/cleland; Summit Rd, Cleland; adult/student $12/9; ☼ 9.30am-5pm). You can get up close and interact with many species of Australian fauna, feed kangaroos and emus, and even have your photo taken with a koala ($12, 2pm to 4pm). The hissing Tasmanian devils are particularly fascinating to

watch when active at feeding time, while the koalas and wombats are generally catching some zzzs. You could easily spend a good few hours here. Dusk **wildlife** and **Aboriginal tours** (adult $20), which bring Dreaming *stories* to life, run with minimum numbers only, so call ahead. A café here sells light lunches and snacks.

Public transport is limited; take bus No 163F from Grenfell St at 9.52am, 10.52am or 12.52pm and get off at Crafers for a connecting No 823 service to the wildlife park.

From Cleland Wildlife Park, walk through the bush (2km) or drive up to **Mt Lofty Summit** (727m), which has beautiful views over Adelaide and Gulf St Vincent. **Mount Lofty Summit visitors centre** ( ☎ 08-8370 1054; Mt Lofty Summit Rd; ☼ 9am-5pm) has plenty of literature on local attractions and walking tracks; the video of the Ash Wednesday bushfires on 16 February 1983 is harrowing. There's a **restaurant** (mains $9.50-15; breakfast, lunch & dinner) in the same building.

**Bikeabout** ( ☎ 0413-525 733; www.bikeabout.com.au) offers downhill cycling tours ($45) from Mt Lofty Summit to Hahndorf.

### MT LOFTY BOTANIC GARDEN
From Mt Lofty, continue south for about 1.5km to the stunning **Mt Lofty Botanic Garden** ( ☎ 08-8370 8370; www.dehaa.sa.gov.au/botanic gardens/mtlofty.html; gates on Mawson Dr & Lampert Rd; ☼ 8.30am-4pm Mon-Fri, 10am-6pm Sat & Sun; P $2.20). Nature tracks wind past a lake, exotic temperate plants, native stringybark forest and, in season, spectacular camellia, magnolia and rhododendron displays.

### OTHER PARKS & GARDENS
The **National Trust** ( ☎ 08-8223 1655) has a number of small nature reserves in the Adelaide Hills, several of which are dedicated to preserving rare remnants of native forest.

Some good parks for bushwalking and wildlife are: **Charleston Conservation Park**, 8km east of Lobethal; **Black Hill Conservation Park**, 10km northeast of the city centre; **Kenneth Stirling Conservation Park**, 5km northwest of Oakbank; **Mark Oliphant Conservation Park**, 4km south of Stirling; and **Scott Creek Conservation Park**, between Mylor and Clarendon.

## Getting There & Around
For a taxi service, contact **Hilltop Taxis & Hire Cars** ( ☎ 08-8388 2211).

ADELAIDE HILLS

**ADELAIDE HILLS**

---

**DETOUR: ADELAIDE HILLS SCENIC DRIVE**

The Adelaide Hills themselves are one big scenic drive. For something more specific, head out early to catch morning views and breakfast at **Mt Lofty Summit** (p89). Wend through the hills to **Lobethal** (p96), then north via Cudlee Creek to **Chain of Ponds Wines** (p50) or the Big Rocking Horse – your choice. Continue to **Birdwood** (p96) before heading south to Woodside and Hahndorf. Eat some apple strudel, then head to **Cleland Conservation Park** (p89) or to **Warrawong Sanctuary** (p91) for a guided walk before returning to Adelaide via the Southeastern Fwy. Take a good map.

Another picturesque option heads south to **Strathalbyn** (p94) via **Macclesfield** and **Meadows** (see p94).

---

**BUS**

**Transit Plus** ( ☎ 08-8339 7544; www.transitplus.com.au), has regular daily services to various towns along its routes from Mt Barker to Adelaide, Lobethal and Strathalbyn. Its Adelaide to Mt Barker service visits Crafers (28 minutes), Stirling (31 minutes), Aldgate (38 minutes), Bridgewater (40 minutes) and Hahndorf (50 minutes), while the Lobethal and Nairne services also call in at Hahndorf (one hour). There are a few No 823 buses from Crafers to Mt Lofty Summit and Cleland Wildlife Park (10 minutes). Bus Nos 840 and 164F depart each hour from Adelaide for Hahndorf (70 minutes). It's advisable to pick up a timetable at a newsagent as bus numbers vary; single trip tickets cost $3.40.

**Premier Stateliner** ( ☎ 08-8415 5563; www.premierstateliner.com.au) runs a daily service from Adelaide south to Victor Harbor via Goolwa, Clarendon ($5.50, one hour) and Meadows ($7, 1½ hours).

See p70 for details on sightseeing tours to the Adelaide Hills from Adelaide.

**TRAIN**

**SteamRanger** ( ☎ 1300 655 991, 08-8391 1223; www.steamranger.org.au; Gawler St, Mt Barker) operates two tourist trains, which run from Mt Barker station on most Sundays. The trains operate on alternative weeks. The **Highlander** (adult/child/family return $26/16/68) takes a scenic journey to Strathalbyn, while the **Southern Encounter** (adult/child/family return $52/31/135) goes to Victor Harbor via Strathalbyn, Goolwa and Port Elliot – you can get on and off at any of these places. The **Strathlink** ( ☎ 08-8555 2691 in Strathalbyn; adult/child/family return $30/18/78), a classic railcar, runs between Goolwa and Strathalbyn, connecting with the Cockle Train (see p109).

## STIRLING AREA

☎ 08

The pretty little townships of **Aldgate**, **Crafers**, **Piccadilly** and **Stirling** are noted for their stunning autumn colour, thanks to extensive plantations of exotic deciduous trees. While there's not a great deal to do in these towns, they offer excellent cafés and restaurants, atmospheric (generally pricey) accommodation and make a good base.

You'll find some glorious old English-style gardens in each of the four towns; most notable are those of **Stangate House** at Aldgate, **Mt Lofty Botanic Garden** (see p89), near tiny Piccadilly and **Beechwood Heritage Garden** ( ☎ 8228 2311; Snows Rd; ⚘ spring & autumn), in Stirling, which surrounds one of the early summer residences of Adelaide's colonial gentry. It features the state's oldest conservatory, an old-fashioned rose garden, a Victorian rock garden and beautiful rhododendron hybrids.

The **Autumn Leaves Festival** ( ⚘ biennially in May, even-numbered years) is held in Aldgate.

### Sleeping & Eating

The rustic and basic YHA cottages in national parks along the Heysen Trail at **Mt Lofty**, **Norton Summit**, **Mylor** and **Kuitpo Forest** offer a fantastic opportunity to get out into nature. Make bookings at the **Adelaide Central YHA** (Map pp64-5; ☎ 8414 3000; www.yha.com.au; 135 Waymouth St, Adelaide; cottages Mon-Thu $60, Fri-Sun $80). Bring your own linen.

**Mount Lofty Railway Station** ( ☎ 8339 7400; www.mlrs.com.au; 2 Sturt Valley Rd, Stirling; d B&B with/without bathroom $95/65, f from $110) Trainspotters rejoice. The *Overland* whooshes through this converted heritage-listed train station (with simple self-contained accommodation) in otherwise quiet and lush Stirling. Breakfast provisions are included.

Plenty of B&Bs dot the hills, ranging from boutique to homely, and from $120 to $210, and are invariably more expensive on weekends. Pick up a **South Australian B&B** (www.sabnb .org.au) brochure or contact the visitors centre in Hahndorf (p92) for bookings. Atmospheric and doily-free options include:

**Adelaide Hills B&B** ( ☎ 8339 1898; metzger@arcom .com.au; 35 Garrod Cres, Stirling; d $120; ✿ ) Take your pick of rooms with ferny outlooks and a king-sized bed or twin beds. Breakfast provisions are provided, and the owners speak German and Afrikaans.

**Eagle on the Hill Hotel** ( ☎ 8339 2211; Mt Barker Rd; d incl breakfast $75; mains $14-25; ✿ ) About 3km west of Crafers, this famous spot burned down in the 1983 bushfires, but has been resurrected like a phoenix from its ashes to offer self-contained rooms. The pub serves hearty fare and has great city-light views.

**Mt Lofty House** ( ☎ 8339 6777; www.mtloftyhouse .com.au; 74 Summit Rd, Crafers; d incl breakfast from $200; ✿ 🖳 🖳 ) Overlooking the Mt Lofty Botanic Garden, this baronial mansion was built as a family home in the 1850s. There's a range of beautifully decorated heritage rooms and garden suites equipped for business or luxuriating.

There are plenty of takeaway places in Stirling and Aldgate, while the region's appreciation for fine, often organic, foods guarantees you won't be stuck for quality choices.

**Rennies Café** ( ☎ 8339 7333; 4 Mt Barker Rd, Stirling; mains $10-13; ✦ lunch & dinner) You might find light jazz wafting through this stylish little café where serves tasty mixed cuisine.

**Jimmies** ( ☎ 8339 1534; 6 Main St, Crafers; mains $10.50-18; ✦ breakfast & lunch Sat & Sun, dinner daily) A lively evening spot loved for its wood-fired oven pizzas. Live jazz on Thursday night.

---

**THE AUTHOR'S CHOICE**

**Organic Market & Café** ( ☎ 8339 7131; 5 Druids Ave, Stirling; meals $3.50-12; ✦ breakfast & lunch) Hill-types flock to this vibrant and lively café off Mt Barker Rd. It's perhaps the busiest spot in town – and rightly so; the food's delicious and everything's made with love. Gorge on plump savoury or sweet muffins and great coffee, and leave feeling virtuous and healthy. The Portuguese custard tarts are wicked.

---

**Stirling Pub** ( ☎ 8339 2345; 52 Mt Barker Rd, Stirling; bar meals $10-20; ✦ lunch & dinner) The bar meals are great deals if you can handle the smoke, otherwise nab a spot in the sun for lunch.

**Aldgate Café** ( ☎ 8339 2530; 6 Strathalbyn Rd, Aldgate; pizza $6.50-10, pasta $10, meat dishes $12.50; ✦ lunch & dinner) Tasty meals are served up opposite the pub. Featured specials from Monday to Wednesday cost $8.

**Aldgate Pump Hotel** ( ☎ 8339 2015; 1 Strathalbyn Rd, Aldgate; mains $13-24; ✦ lunch & dinner) A charming pub with an unconventional menu packed with surprises.

**Bistro 49** ( ☎ 8339 4416; 49 Mt Barker Rd, Stirling; mains $18-25) Relaxed elegance and great food, including herb-roasted venison or mushroom ragout.

**Petaluma's Bridgewater Mill Winery & Restaurant** ( ☎ 8339 3422; www.bridgewatermill.com.au; Mt Barker Rd, Bridgewater; mains around $30; ✦ lunch Thu-Mon) In a restored 200-year-old flour mill, with an award-winning restaurant overlooking Cox's Creek and the Old Rumbler waterwheel.

## MYLOR
☎ 08 / pop 100

The main attraction of leafy Mylor is **Warrawong Sanctuary** ( ☎ 8370 9422; www.warrawong .com; Stock Rd, Mylor), about 3km from town, the first of the feral-free, privately run Earth Sanctuaries. Book ahead for the excellent 1½-hour guided walks (adult/child/family $22/17.50/59) at dawn (Friday to Sunday) and sunset (nightly). Accommodation/walk/ dinner packages in luxury tents are available (adults $150); accommodation per child is $12, not including tours and meals. The windows in the **restaurant** (mains around $19; ✦ breakfast, lunch & dinner) give close-up views of many native birds, including rainbow lorikeets.

From Adelaide, turn off the freeway at Stirling and follow the signs from the Stirling roundabout. A taxi from Stirling is about $12.

**Burnslea Log Cabin** ( ☎ 8388 5803; burnslealc@yahoo .com; Leslie Creek Rd, Mylor; d $85) has a fantastic self-contained log cabin which comes with breakfast provisions and alpaca petting.

See p90 for details on the YHA cottage. There's a general store and café in town.

## HAHNDORF
☎ 08 / pop 1660

You could be forgiven for thinking you've arrived slap-bang in the centre of a German

## GOURMET GARDEN

Make sure you arrive in the Adelaide Hills with a decent hunger for fine foods and a thirst for excellent wines. Hills producers thrive on passion for their produce and it seems only right to indulge in the fruits of their labour.

South Australia's fruit salad bowl overflows with cherries, apples, pears and so many strawberries you'll need to pick your own! On a drive through the hills you'll find plenty of roadside honesty-box stalls with bursting fresh goods.

For a true hills picnic experience head to Stirling's **Organic Market** (p91) and put together your own feast from crusty Matisse bread, a range of Woodside and Udder Delights cheeses, olives, perhaps some fig paste, a pear and a cluster of muscatels, then head off to sample a few wines.

The Adelaide Hills had a thriving wine industry between 1840 and 1900, but Australia's fond ness for beer and big reds put it on the backburner. In fact, the first wine ever exported from Australia was the Adelaide Hills–grown Echunga hock, sent to Queen Victoria in 1845. The wine region is set to boil again with its cool climate providing ideal conditions for the production of high quality Riesling, Chardonnay, Sauvignon Blanc, Sangiovese, Pinot Noir and other elegant reds. There are now many local wineries dotted around Hahndorf and Birdwood, including award-winning, celebrated wineries such as **Shaw & Smith** (p50) and **Chain of Ponds Wines** (p50).

The Adelaide Hills Harvest Festival (March) celebrates the hills' food and wines.

Find out more info on the wineries of the Adelaide Hills on p49.

theme park at Hahndorf, 28km southeast of Adelaide. European trees flirt with gums, and cascades of colourful flowers flow from half wine-barrels along the main street, which is lined with antique and knick-knack shops, German-themed cafés, and the cellar doors of some quality wineries. This is the oldest surviving German settlement in Australia, settled in 1839 by about 50 Lutheran families who left Prussia to escape religious persecution; the town took its name from the ship's captain, Hahn; and *dorf* is German for village. It's a hive of activity on weekends and holidays.

The town was placed under martial law during WWI; its Lutheran school was closed and, in 1917, its name was changed to Ambleside. It was renamed Hahndorf in 1935. Hahndorf still has an honorary Burgermeister, who acts as the town's goodwill ambassador. The town celebrates its artistic heritage during the **Heysen Festival** (September).

The **Adelaide Hills visitors centre** ( ☎ 8388 1185; 41 Main St; ⏲ 9am-5pm) stocks plenty of brochures, reserves B&B accommodation and has Internet access.

### Sights & Activities

The 1857 **Hahndorf Academy** ( ☎ 8388 7250; 68 Main St; ⏲ 10am-5pm Mon-Sat, noon-5pm Sun) houses an art gallery with rotating exhibitions and several original sketches by Sir Hans Hey-

sen, the famed landscape artist and resident of Hahndorf. A visit to the attached **German Immigration Museum** is worth the gold coin donation. It illustrates the early life of German settlement in the Adelaide Hills and has an extensive collection of bizarrely carved pipes.

You'll see more than 300 of Sir Hans' original works on a tour through his studio and house, the **Cedars** ( ☎ 8388 7277; Heysen Rd; tours $8; ⏲ 11am, 1pm & 3pm Sun-Fri), about 2km northwest of Hahndorf.

If tourist tat isn't your thing, check out the fine local and Australian crafts including woodwork, ceramics and jewellery at **Bamfurlong Fine Crafts** ( ☎ 8388 1195; 34 Main St; ⏲ 11am-5pm).

Distinctive German architecture is evident in old Main St buildings, including the first **butcher's shop** (1839), **Thiele Cottage** (1842), the former Australian Arms Hotel (1854), now home to a leathersmith and **bush gallery** ( ☎ 8388 1095; 46 Main St), and the still-licensed **German Arms Hotel** (1862). Most form part of a heritage walk documented in a brochure available from the visitors centre.

There are old photographs and insightful displays at the **Adelaide Hills Settlement Museum**, housed inside **Mawson Ridge Wines** ( ☎ 8388 1288; 24 Main St), where you can also taste and buy produce.

You can reach some quality wineries in the Hahndorf area from Balhannah Rd, off Main St in the centre of town, including: **Shaw & Smith** ( ☎ 8398 0500; Lot 4 Jones Rd, Balhannah; ☽ 10am-4pm Sat & Sun), **Nepenthe Wines** ( ☎ 8388 4439; Jones Rd, Balhannah; ☽ 10am-4pm) and **Hahndorf Hill Winery** ( ☎ 8388 7512; Pains Rd, Hahndorf; ☽ 10am-5pm).

Pick your own strawberries between November and May from the famous **Beerenberg Strawberry Farm** ( ☎ 8388 7272; Mount Barker Rd; ☽ 9am-5pm), also renowned for its plethora of jams, chutneys and sauces.

## Sleeping & Eating

Bed and Breakfast accommodation in Hahndorf and its surrounds can be booked through the Adelaide Hills visitors centre (p92).

**Hahndorf Resort** ( ☎ 1800 350 143; www.hahndorfresort.com.au; 145 Main St, Hahndorf; unpowered/powered sites per 2 people $15/16.50, basic cabins from $49, motel d $95, chalets $95-145; ✖ ▣ ⛟ ) In keeping with the local theme, Bavarian-style chalets encircle this sprawling verdant resort. It is well supplied with tennis courts, a swimming pool and a fauna park, a supervised kids' club and **Hans Heysen Restaurant** (mains from $10; ☽ lunch & dinner). Located 1.5km from town, bus Nos 840 and 164F stop at the gate. Half-/full-day bike hire costs $7.50/15.

**Old Mill Motel** ( ☎ 8388 7888; 98 Main St; d without/with spa Mon-Thu $65/105, Fri-Sun $90/120; buffet lunch/dinner from $14/15; ☽ lunch & dinner; ✖ ) You can pick up good-value Main St motel rooms and buffet meals.

**Stables Inn** ( ☎ 8388 7988; www.stablesinn.com.au; 74 Main St; d without/with spa from $100/120, f $150; lunches $5-8.50, mains $9.50-18.90; ☽ lunch & dinner; ✖ ) Comfy bottle-green rooms boast a TV and microwave behind this cosy saddle-club restaurant with an extensive café-style menu.

**Hahndorf Inn Motor Lodge** ( ☎ 8388 1000; 35 Main St; tw/d/f $95/100/130, Sat night extra $10; ✖ ⛟ ) Behind the Hahndorf Inn you'll find comfortable, exposed brick motel rooms, an indoor pool, barbecue and laundry facilities.

**Motel Zorro's** ( ☎ 8388 1309; 60 Main St; d without/with spa $100/153; ✖ ) Murals of angels, hearts and the like dominate these tiled rooms, some with palatial bathrooms fit for Cleopatra's entourage.

Wurst, sauerkraut, pretzels, strudel and German beer abound in Hahndorf.

**Café Dalila** ( ☎ 8388 1072; 23 Main St; dishes $8-14; ☽ breakfast & lunch) Delightful results come out of a French, Israeli and Middle Eastern mix in a scrumptious range of baguettes, platters and supreme soups.

**Casalinga** ( ☎ 8388 7877; 49 Main St; pizza & pasta $10-17, mains $18-20; ☽ dinner) This friendly local haunt pumps out pizza and pasta made from the best ingredients. Live acoustic music on Friday.

**Hahndorf Inn** ( ☎ 8388 1000; 35a Main St; breakfast $4.50-15, mains $10-22; ☽ breakfast, lunch & dinner) Fancy a meal of cheese Krasky, Vienna sausage, sauerkraut and apple strudel? There's a friendly buzz in this rustic place – perhaps it's the lack of pokies chinking and chiming in the background. Gather around a wine barrel with a stein of German beer (on tap).

**German Arms Hotel** ( ☎ 8388 7013; 50 Main St; mains $9.50-16; ☽ lunch & dinner) Lively and packed on weekends, the pub's bratwurst, pies and economical old favourites are popular.

## NAIRNE TO WOODSIDE
☎ 08

Only 10 minutes down the Southeastern Fwy and the old Princes Hwy from Hahndorf, **Nairne** was founded by a Scottish sheep farmer in 1839. Originally a wheat-growing centre, it grew rapidly after the railway arrived in 1883 and many old stone buildings remain. As with neighbouring **Littlehampton** and Mt Barker, the historic town's quiet charm is under threat from encroaching housing estates. The **Albert Mill** ( ☎ 8388 6858; albertmill@optusnet.com.au; 4 Junction St; garden/courtyard d $120/160; ✖ ) was built as a steam-driven flour mill in 1857. It ran until 1906, and now offers beautifully atmospheric B&B rooms.

Turn off Main Rd and follow signs to the communications towers at the summit of **Mt Barker**, about 4km from town. It's a five-minute walk from here to a superb panoramic view of the west and down towards Lake Alexandrina in the southeast.

For an interesting detour from Nairne, continue 15km west along the Murray Bridge road to the tiny township of **Kanmantoo**, and 5km further to the quietly decaying town of **Callington**. Established by Cornish miners in 1850, it has loads of character – if you're an artist or photographer, don't miss it!

North of Nairne, **Woodside** is home to **Melba's Chocolate Factory** ( ☎ 8389 7868; Henry St; entry free; ☽ 10am-4.30pm). Along with all your milk-bar favourites is a collection of cow pats, horse cakes and sheep nuts, that are – you guessed it – disgustingly delicious chocolate replicas of the real thing and which bring a whole new meaning to eating crap.

A worthwhile detour is to follow the signs to the old wooden swing bridge between Woodside and **Oakbank**. The small village of Oakbank is fattening up on antique and craft shops, such as the **Oakbank Weaver** (9 Elizabeth St), in the old Pike's Brewery, where you can pick up a walking guide listing historical sites. Each Easter the town hosts the hugely popular **Oakbank Easter Racing Carnival**, said to be the greatest picnic race meeting in the world.

## MT BARKER TO STRATHALBYN

The largest town in the Adelaide Hills, **Mt Barker** is stretching at its seams and booming estate housing is storming its hills. The **visitors centre** (☎ 08-8391 1633; 23 Mann St; ☺ 9am-5pm Mon-Fri) has brochures covering 11 rural walks from 3km to 9.5km, and another taking in sites in the town. **Tourist trains** (see p109) run from here to Strathalbyn and Victor Harbor on Sundays.

The most scenic route to **Strathalbyn** heads south via **Echunga**, **Meadows** and **Macclesfield**, meandering through hills of grazing land alongside the gum-lined Angas River, making it a popular route for motorcyclists.

At Echunga, you can explore the walking tracks and fossick at **Jupiter Creek Gold Diggings**, about 5km out of town on Fields Rd. Gold was discovered in 1852 and the field was worked at various times until 1930.

The attractive villages of Meadows and Macclesfield retain their quiet charm with interesting heritage buildings and some great little galleries. Near Meadows is the **Kuitpo Forest** (forest headquarters ☎ 08-8388 3267; Willunga Rd; camping permits per person Apr–Nov $3), a popular spot for bird-watching, cycling and walking. See p90 for details on the YHA cottage.

Meadows' bakery is a winner, as is Macclesfield's 1841 Tudor-style **Three Brothers Arms** (☎ 08-8388 9265; 40 Venables St; mains $19.50-22.90; ☺ lunch & dinner), with a wonderfully rustic ambience, great food and creamy pots of Old Speckled Hen to go with it. Check out the penny-encrusted bar. The willows by the Angas River in town are said to have grown from cuttings brought from near Napoleon's grave. There's a beautiful roadside stop at Doctor's Creek between here and Strathalbyn.

## STRATHALBYN
☎ 08 / pop 2600

Strathalbyn is one of the jewels in the crown of the hills region. Manicured gardens flank the Angas River as it flows through this picturesque 'heritage town', overlooked by the turreted **St Andrew's Church**. Established in 1839 by Scottish immigrants, much of its old streetscapes and impressive buildings have been preserved. You can easily spend a few hours wandering through the historic High St, perusing its many antique and bric-a-brac shops, and New Age shops housed in 'ye olde worlde' buildings. Cyclists and motorcyclists descend on the town on weekends providing plenty of glittering 'bike-candy'.

History buffs can bone up on the town's Celtic heritage at the **Old Courthouse Museum** (cnr South Tce & Rankine St; admission $2; ☺ 2-5pm Wed, Thu, Sat & Sun), which includes the old police station and cells.

**Strathalbyn visitors centre** (☎ 8536 3212; South Tce; ☺ 9am-5pm Mon-Fri, 10am-4pm Sat, Sun & public holidays), in the train station, has oodles of information on Strathalbyn and its surrounds, and walking-tour maps with detailed heritage information. While here, duck into the attached **Stationmasters' Gallery** (☎ 8536 3452; ☺ 10am-4pm Wed-Sun), which hosts changing exhibitions.

Strathalbyn is about 12 minutes' drive from the wineries at **Langhorne Creek** (see p112).

### Sleeping & Eating

**Strathalbyn Caravan Park** (☎ 8536 3681; Ashbourne Rd; unpowered/powered sites per 2 people $10/16.50, cabins with bathroom $60) This modest spot off West Tce has shady sites, a couple of cabins, disabled facilities, barbecues and tennis courts.

**Robin Hood Hotel** (☎ 8536 2608; 18 High St; s/d incl breakfast $35/60) Basic rooms at this 1867 hotel on historic High St share bathrooms and a guest lounge.

**Victoria Hotel** (☎ 8536 2202; 16 Albyn Tce; d incl breakfast without/with spa Mon-Thu $95/105, Fri-Sun $110/135; mains $8.50-18.50; ☺ lunch & dinner; ☒ ) This stylish country hotel opposite the Angas River parkland has comfortable rooms and a great veranda for lunch, a beer and watching the slowly passing parade.

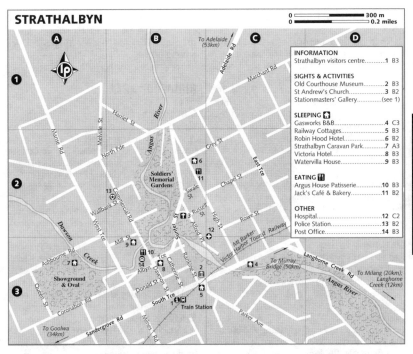

STRATHALBYN

0 ——— 300 m
0 ——— 0.2 miles

| INFORMATION | |
|---|---|
| Strathalbyn visitors centre | **1** B3 |

| SIGHTS & ACTIVITIES | |
|---|---|
| Old Courthouse Museum | **2** B3 |
| St Andrew's Church | **3** B2 |
| Stationmasters' Gallery | (see 1) |

| SLEEPING | |
|---|---|
| Gasworks B&B | **4** C3 |
| Railway Cottages | **5** B3 |
| Robin Hood Hotel | **6** B2 |
| Strathalbyn Caravan Park | **7** A3 |
| Victoria Hotel | **8** B3 |
| Watervilla House | **9** B3 |

| EATING | |
|---|---|
| Argus House Patisserie | **10** B3 |
| Jack's Café & Bakery | **11** B3 |

| OTHER | |
|---|---|
| Hospital | **12** C2 |
| Police Station | **13** B2 |
| Post Office | **14** B3 |

**ADELAIDE HILLS**

**Watervilla House** (☎ 8536 4099; 2 Mill St; d $140) This grand 1840s residence in the heart of Strathalbyn will transport you back in time with its antique Victorian décor. Full cooked breakfast included.

**Gasworks B&B** (☎ 8536 4291; 12 South Tce; d $140, extra person $50; ☒) Stay in one of the beautifully restored residences of the old gasworks, with terraced gardens overlooking a sweep of trickling river. Each cottage has a spa and kitchen for cooking up bumper breakfast provisions.

**Railway Cottages** (☎ 8536 4910; www.railway cottages.com.au; 3-5 Parker Ave; s/d $120/130) These self-contained three bedroom country-style cottages have doily details, open fires and breakfast provisions.

**Argus House Patisserie** (Dawson St; meals $6.50-8.50; ☉ breakfast & lunch) Locals huddle over papers and occasionally watch the bikies roar by at this wholesome café in the old Argus press building. There's a good mix including pizzas, laksa, *pad thai* and home-made cakes.

**Jack's Café & Bakery** (☎ 8536 4147; 24 High St; sandwiches $4-7.50; ☉ daily) Tasty cakes, pies and

gourmet fare are the go at this large spot in the centre of historic High St. Nab a kerbside table.

### Getting There & Away
See the Getting There & Around section on p90 for information on bus services from Mt Barker and the SteamRanger's scenic steam train rides departing from **Strathalbyn station** (☎ 8555 2691).

## CLARENDON
☎ 08 / pop 300
Scenically set in a valley at a major crossing point on the Onkaparinga River, pretty Clarendon has its share of historic buildings, and is dominated by the **Old Clarendon Winery Complex** (☎ 8383 6166). Originally part of the original Clarendon Vineyard Estate, the winery was established with vines brought from Spain in the late 1840s, and now has a cellar door, craft shop, restaurant and comfortable rooms with views over the township.

The bus service between Adelaide and Victor Harbor stops at Clarendon (p90).

## NORTON SUMMIT AREA
☎ 08

Perched on the edge of the western scarp, the pretty township of **Norton Summit** was the birthplace of Sir Thomas Playford, SA's longest-serving state premier.

You can explore the ruins of **Marble Hill** (◔ 11am-5pm Sun), the state governor's former summer residence, about 6km away off the Lobethal road. The mansion was destroyed in the 1955 bushfires, but its hilltop setting is an impressive sight with superb views.

At Norton Summit you're within easy striking distance from Adelaide's main apple, pear, cherry and vegetable-growing area around **Ashton**, **Summertown** and **Basket Range**. There are also several vineyards and wineries.

### Sleeping & Eating
**Fuzzies Farm** ( ☎ 8390 1111; fuzzyt@ozemail.com.au; Norton Summit; cabins per week around $90) In a great setting at the edge of Morialta Conservation Reserve 15km east of Adelaide, this friendly organic farm has self-contained bushland cabins and a café. You can also pick up tips on animal care, organic gardening and building construction. Weekly rates for helpers include meals. Bookings are essential.

See p90 for details on the YHA cottage.

**Scenic Hotel** ( ☎ 8390 1705; Old Norton Summit Rd; dishes $12-24; ◔ lunch & dinner) Views over Adelaide make the veranda at this lovely cosy restaurant the top spot to be to enjoy contemporary Australian meals or just a drink.

## LOBETHAL
☎ 08 / pop 1500

Established by Lutheran settlers in 1842, attractive Lobethal has many interesting old buildings including **German-style cottages** and houses from the 1840s. During December, the town is ablaze with **Christmas lights**, luring swarms of sightseers from the city.

The tourist precinct centres on the **Old Woollen Mills** (1 Adelaide–Lobethal Rd), which houses the **Heart of the Hills Market** ( ◔ 10am-4pm Sat, Sun & public holidays), with local crafts and tasty concoctions; the cellar door of **Tilbrook Estate** ( ◔ 10am-5pm Sat, Sun & public holidays); and the excellent **National Costume Museum** (adult/child $3.50/ free; ◔ 10am-4pm Tue-Sun), with original gowns and menswear from 1812 to 2000.

Young kids can experience a fairytale existence through the life-sized **Fairyland Village**

( ☎ 8389 6200; 21 Adelaide–Lobethal Rd; adult/child $6/4; ◔ 10am-5.30pm Sat, Sun & public holidays); home to Cinderella and the Cottingley Fairies among others.

See p93 for towns south of Lobethal.

## BIRDWOOD AREA
☎ 08
### Gumeracha
pop 645

A scenic drive from Adelaide to Birdwood leads through the **Torrens River Gorge** and Gumeracha. Among the wineries here is the highly celebrated **Chain of Ponds Wines** ( ☎ 8389 1415; www.chainofponds.com.au; Main Adelaide Rd; lunch $17-24; ◔ 11am-4pm Mon-Fri, 10.30am-4.30pm Sat & Sun), about 1km before town, with scenic views from its restaurant–cellar door (book ahead for lunch).

Turn right at Gorge Rd to reach the west end of Cudlee Creek, where the **Gorge Wildlife Park** ( ☎ 8568 2206; Redden Dve, Cudlee Creek; adult/child $10/5; ◔ 8am-5pm) offers koala cuddling.

The **Big Rocking Horse**, which doesn't rock, looms over the road here but is unusually tasteful as far as 'big' tourist attractions go. It's attached to the **Toy Factory** ( ☎ 8389 1085; Main Adelaide Rd; ◔ 9am-5pm), where quality handmade wooden toys are sold at factory prices.

### Birdwood
pop 724

National Trust–classified buildings and quality craft and antique shops line Birdwood's attractive main street. Originally called Blumberg (the hill of flowers), this pretty town was founded by German settlers in 1848. During WWI it was renamed after the commander of the Australian forces, Field Marshall Lord Birdwood.

In the 1850s Birdwood was a busy gold-mining and agricultural centre. An impressive reminder of those days is its old flour mill (1852), now inhabited by the impressive collection of immaculate vintage and classic cars and motorcycles of the **National Motor Museum** ( ☎ 8568 5006; Shannon St; www.history.sa.gov.au; adult $9; ◔ 9am-5pm). Rev heads can get a double dose at the **Motorcycle & Heritage Museum** (26 Shannon St).

The **Bay to Birdwood Classic** (www.baytobirdwood.com.au) in September sees a cavalcade of pre-1950 automobiles streaming into town, while the **Rock 'n' Roll Rendezvous**, held in November, features aged rockers as well as cars.

## Sleeping & Eating

**Birdwood Inn B&B** ( ☎ 8568 5212; 31 Shannon St, Birdwood; d $100, spa access $40) This well-restored cottage has tasteful home-style rooms and a lounge with garden views and plenty of comforts.

**Birdwood B&B Cottages** ( ☎ 8568 5444, 38 Olivedale Rd; d $145-160) Three separate cottages present different variations on the B&B theme, from the colourfully rustic mud-brick studio to the chintzy homestead with two four-poster beds.

**Sunnybrook B&B** ( ☎ 8568 2159; www.sunnybrookbnb.com.au; Mannum Rd, Tungkillo; d $120-160) In nearby Tungkillo, Sunnybrook has a couple of cottages in a rural setting – complimentary Devonshire tea inclusive.

**Mt Crawford Forest** ( ☎ 8524 6004; sites per person Apr-Nov $3), 13km from Birdwood on the Williamstown road, has native forest and plantations of eucalypt and *Pinus radiata*. The Heysen Trail (www.heysentrail.asn .au) passes through the forest; bush camping permits are available from the forest headquarters.

In Mt Pleasant, 10km past Birdwood towards Springton, **Talunga Hotel/Motel** ( ☎ 8568 2015; 43 Melrose St; d $72; mains $7-15; ☺ lunch & dinner) has simple motel-style rooms and cheap bar specials; the more atmospheric dining room at the **Totness Inn Hotel** ( ☎ 8568 2346; 148 Melrose St; dishes $12-20; ☺ lunch & dinner) is separated from the bar.

**Blumberg Tavern** ( ☎ 8568 5243; 24 Shannon St, Birdwood; mains $12-18) A popular pub with an old truck jutting out of its 2nd-floor veranda.

**Birdwood Wine & Cheese Centre** ( ☎ 8568 5067; 22 Shannon St, Birdwood) Pick up a picnic hamper (two/four people $25/45), or order a cheese platter with olives and crackers (three/six cheeses $3/6) to eat while tasting wines (three/six wines $3/6); half of the boutique producers featured don't have their own cellar door.

# Fleurieu Peninsula

CONTENTS

**Southern Vales**     **101**
McLaren Vale     101
Willunga     102
**Gulf St Vincent Coast**     **103**
Maslin Beach to Sellicks Beach     103
Yankalilla     104
Normanville to Rapid Bay     104
Cape Jervis     104
**Encounter Coast**     **105**
Victor Harbor     105
Port Elliot     109
Middleton     109
Goolwa     110
Currency Creek     111
Milang & Clayton     111
Langhorne Creek Wineries     112

Stunning beaches rim the scenic coastline of the Fleurieu (*floo*-ree-o) Peninsula, south of Adelaide. The protected beaches of Gulf St Vincent offer good swimming and plenty of water-based activities, while there's popular boating around Goolwa and the Murray River Mouth, and crisp surf on the south's rugged Encounter Coast. The Heysen Trail traverses the coast, meandering from Cape Jervis through to the Adelaide Hills. A few conservation parks provide camping and bushwalking opportunities.

Boutique wineries dotted like liquid gems in the hills of the lower Mt Lofty Ranges – particularly around McLaren Vale – create a vivid landscape. Gentrified stone cottages retain their rustic charm amid a patchwork of vineyards, orchards and verdant valleys.

The peninsula was named in 1802 by the French explorer Nicholas Baudin after Napoleon's minister for the navy. Smuggling businesses, which ran rife in the early days of settlement, were replaced by whaling near Encounter Bay in 1837. The Foundation Inn, built in 1838, quickly became a rendezvous for desperadoes, such as the escaped convicts from Tasmania who lived in the central ranges. By the middle of the next decade things quietened down due to settlements all along the Adelaide road. Agricultural development of the peninsula was rapid. Goolwa, at the mouth of the Murray River, had become a busy river port by the 1850s, and grand summer retreats began to appear at Port Elliot and Victor Harbor soon after.

Today, protected baby whales and their mothers can be seen off the southern beaches.

**FLEURIEU PENINSULA**

## HIGHLIGHTS

- Quaffing wines and hitting the gourmet trail around **Willunga** (p102) and **McLaren Vale** (p101)
- Taking a trip on the majestic **Murray River Mouth** (p110) – Australia's largest river and the lifeblood for three states
- Surfing, swimming and sunning on the beaches between **Port Elliot** (p109) and **Goolwa** (p110)
- Searching for whales on their migration path in **Encounter Bay** (p109)
- Snorkelling and diving **Rapid Bay** (p104) or **HMAS Hobart** (p105)
- Hiking a section of the **Heysen Trail** (p38)
- Riding back in time on the coastal steam **Cockle Train** (p109)
- Tasting world-first wines at **Langhorne Creek** (p112)

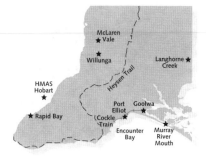

TELEPHONE CODE: ☎ 08

- www.fleurieupeninsula.com.au
- www.fleurieufood.com.au

## National Parks

For information on the peninsula's conservation areas, contact the **DEH** ( ☎ 08-8552 3677; 57 Ocean St, Victor Harbor) for the southern region and **Belair National Park** ( ☎ 08-8278 5477; Upper Sturt Rd, Belair) for the north, or check out the website www.environment.sa.gov.au/parks.

## Getting There & Around

**Premier Stateliner** ( ☎ 08-8415 5555) runs up to four buses daily from Adelaide to McLaren Vale ($6.70, one hour), Willunga ($7.10, 70 minutes), Victor Harbor ($15.60, two hours), Port Elliot ($15.60, two hours) and Goolwa ($15.60, two hours).

Regular suburban trains run between Adelaide and Noarlunga Centre. Several **Southlink** ( ☎ 08-8186 2888; www.southlink.com.au) buses (Nos 751 and 752) run from here to Aldinga or Sellicks Beach via McLaren Vale and Willunga, while Bus No 750 goes to Port Willunga.

A few ferry lines run passenger/vehicle services to Kangaroo Island. **Kangaroo Island Ferries** ( ☎ 13 22 33; www.kiferries.com.au) operates two ferries each way daily from Marina St Vincent at Wirrina, 12km south of Normanville, to Kingscote. **Sealink** ( ☎ 131301, 08-8202 8688; www.sealink.com.au) operates at least four ferries each way daily between Cape Jervis and Penneshaw on Kangaroo Island. Both companies have connecting bus services to the port from Adelaide, Goolwa and Victor Harbor, stopping in towns on the way. See p118 for details.

Bicycle hire is available in McLaren Vale (p102) and Victor Harbor (p109).

> **DETOUR: ENCOUNTER COAST & MCLAREN VALE**
>
> When summer temperatures are soaring, indulge in water activities along the **Encounter Coast** (p105), visit the **Murray River Mouth** (p110) and perve on penguins on **Granite Island** (p107). In winter, check whale sightings on the Encounter Coast and cruise down to **Victor Harbor** (p105). If your timing is right, then soak up a liquid lunch at one of **McLaren Vale's wineries** (p50) on your return.

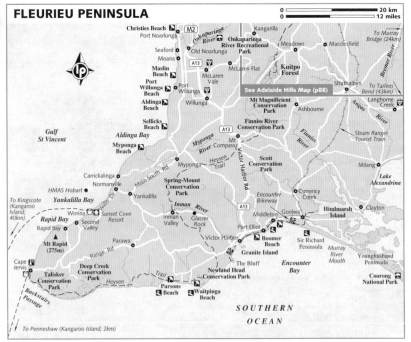

FLEURIEU PENINSULA

**Steam trains** ply scenic routes on Sundays from Mt Barker to Victor Harbor via Goolwa (p90), along the coast between Victor Harbor and Goolwa (p109) and between Goolwa and Strathalbyn (p111). They're an experience rather than a mode of transport.

For details on tours to the Fleurieu Peninsula from Adelaide, see (p70).

# SOUTHERN VALES

The scenic rolling hills of the vales are dotted with a patchwork of vineyards and olive groves, and blossoming almond groves in season. The region is particularly noted for its consistently fine reds. Most of the peninsula's 70 or so wineries are concentrated around McLaren Vale and nearby McLaren Flat.

Strenuous walks can be found through the gorge at Onkaparinga River Recreation Park, which extends up the river nearby Old Noarlunga, and cyclists can explore the area along the old railway siding.

Though now an outer suburb of Adelaide, the historic precinct of Old Noarlunga is largely intact and includes numerous interesting buildings.

## MCLAREN VALE

☎ 08 / pop 2000

Infiltrated by worshippers of the gourmet gods, McLaren Vale (37km from Adelaide) has plenty of ways to delight the senses. Most of the 48 wineries with cellar-door sales are within a few minutes drive or satisfying ride from the town centre, and there are plenty of places to potently mix rambling Mt Lofty Ranges views with fine wine and foods.

McLaren Vale's main event is the **Wine Bushing Festival** (late Oct or early Nov), a grand feast of wine, food, art and music to celebrate the new vintage. The **Sea & the Vines Festival** (Jun long weekend) is a celebration of wine and seafood.

## Information

**McLaren Vale & Fleurieu visitors centre** (☎ 8323 9944; www.mclarenvale.info; Main Rd, McLaren Vale; 9am-5pm Mon-Fri, 10am-5pm Sat & Sun), at the northern end of McLaren Vale, can assist with accommodation and shares space with **Stump Hill Café & Wine Bar** (☎ 8323 8999), which offers tastings from local wineries with no cellar door. If you can't bear to leave,

contact **Boston Recruitment** (☎ 8323 9935) for vineyard work in the area.

## Sights & Activities

Most people come to McLaren Vale to cruise the wineries, and while you could easily spend a couple of days doing nothing else, there are a few ways to break it up (and sober up) between tastings. You can pick up a *McLaren Vale Heritage Trail* brochure from the visitors centre for a guided stroll through town, stopping along the way at **Dridan Fine Arts** (☎ 8323 9866; www.dridanfinearts.com.au; Hardy's Tintara, Main Rd; 10am-5pm), which displays fine local artisans' work, including items constructed from wine barrels, and has curated exhibitions. Nearby is the **Tintara Winery Cellar Door** (☎ 8329 4124; www.hardys.com.au; Main Rd; 10am-4.30pm), with tastings and Australia's oldest vintage wine bottle (1867) on show.

Smooth is the word at **David Medlow Chocolates** (☎ 8323 8818; McLaren on the Lake, Kangarilla Rd), from the Belgian chocolates to the soft pectin fruit gels, but you won't get away from wines here – a vintage Shiraz in dark Belgian chocolate perhaps?

All things olive-related are covered at the **Olive Grove** (☎ 8323 8792; www.olivegroves.com.au; Warners Rd), which has tastings of the fruit and pressings from its 100-year-old groves.

A great way to see the area and sample its delights is to follow the **walking & cycling track** along the old railway line from McLaren Vale to Willunga, 6km south.

## Tours

For details of tours departing from Adelaide, see p70.

**McLaren Vale** (☎ 0414-784 666; www.mclarenvale tours.com.au) allows you to invent your own tour (3½ hours, $50 per person) aided with suggestions from boutique wineries and gourmet producers in the vale. Tours can also be arranged through **Southern Spirit** (☎ 0407-223 361), which has a limousine and

### MCLAREN VALE TASTINGS

Most local wineries are open daily for tastings; the visitors centre has details and maps. See p50 for a few recommendations. A few are within easy walking distance of the town centre, though for many you'll need your own wheels.

minibus for hire, and **Integrity Tours & Charter** (☎ 8382 9755, 0402-120 361); this company also covers Goolwa and Victor Harbor.

## Sleeping & Eating

There are numerous B&Bs in the McLaren Vale region (see also Willunga, opposite) with doubles starting at $120; the visitors centre can arrange bookings.

**McLaren Vale Lakeside Caravan Park** (☎ 8323 9255; www.mclarenvale.net; Field St; unpowered/powered sites per 2 people $18/22, vans/cabins with bathroom from $50/75; 🏊 ) In a pretty rural setting by a creek close to town, this pristine place provides the only budget accommodation in McLaren Vale. There's ample amenities, a pool, spa and tennis court.

**McLaren Vale Motel** (☎ 1800 631 817; 8323 8265; www.mclarenvalemotel.com.au; Caffrey St; s/d from $90/ 105, child extra $10; 🅿 🖥 🏊 ) Near the visitors centre, this friendly motel has spacious units and complimentary laundry facilities.

Several wineries have café-restaurants, matching Mod Oz cuisine with their fine drop; see Tastings & Feasting (below) for details.

**Blessed Cheese** (☎ 8323 7958; www.blessedcheese .com.au; 150 Main St; dishes around $8; 🕑 breakfast & lunch) This spot cranks out great coffee, rich Cocoloco hot chocolate, good-value nosh and murderous cakes. Join the Cheese & Wine Trail (from $10) and pick up mini-Eskies containing a selection of cheeses, crackers, olives and muscatels; bike hire is available ($30/21 per day/three hours). Enthusiasts can book for the cheese-making course, held on Sunday.

**Oscar's Diner** (☎ 8323 8707; 201 Main Rd; dishes $10.50-14.50; 🕑 lunch & dinner) A reliable favourite with delicious gourmet pizza, a sunny courtyard and a crackling open fire in winter.

**Marienberg Limeburners** (☎ 8323 8599; Main Rd; mains $14.50-23; 🕑 lunch & dinner) Blondewood brightens this bastion of fine European-based Mod Oz cuisine on even the woolliest of days.

**Salopian Inn** (☎ 8323 8769; Main Rd; mains $16-30; 🕑 lunch Thu-Tue, dinner Fri & Sat) Just out of town, this serious foodie haunt has a not-to-be-missed reputation. Head down the stone stairs to the cellar to choose your own bottle of wine.

**Brian's Olive Shop** (☎ 8323 9231; 142 Main Rd; 🕑 10am-5pm Mon-Sat, 11am-5pm Sun) Duck in here for the vale's best plump olives.

For superb coffee and meals with plenty of local and regional ingredients, head to **Market 190** (☎ 8323 8558; www.market190.com.au; 190 Main Rd; meals $6-14; 🕑 8am-6pm) or **Tin Shed Café** (☎ 8323 7343; 225 Main Rd; meals $3.90-10.90; 🕑 breakfast & lunch), the cosiest tin shed in town.

## WILLUNGA
☎ 08 / pop 1200

Intriguing, arty Willunga took off in 1840 when high-quality slate was mined nearby and exported all around Australia. Today, the restored old buildings in this quiet, pretty little town house gourmet eateries and galleries showcasing the work of established and emerging fine artists. The town comes into full bloom during its **Almond Blossom Festival** in July.

The lack of development in Willunga since its boom years has preserved numerous heritage buildings dating from the 1850s. You can visit them with the *Willunga Walk* brochure, available around town. On High St, the old Court House and Police station (1855) is now a small **museum** (admission $2; 🕑 10am-4pm Tue, 1-5pm Sat & Sun).

Green fingers will enjoy the fragrant display garden at **Ross Roses** (☎ 9556 2555; www .rossroses.com.au; St Andrews Tce).

Willunga is central to the **Kuitpo Forest** to the northeast and small conservation parks to the southeast including **Mt Magnificent Conservation Park**, 13km from Willunga. There

---

**TASTINGS & FEASTING**

You can cover all bases by teaming your tastings with perfectly matched dishes and good atmosphere at some great cellar door–restaurant combos. D'Arry's Verandah restaurant at **d'Arenberg Wines** (☎ 08-8323 8710; www.darenberg.com.au; Osborne Rd) has fine valley views, while the gardens surrounding **Woodstock Winery & Coterie** (☎ 08-8323 0156; Douglas Gully Rd) are a tranquil haven for birds. **Coriole** (☎ 08-8323 8305; www.coriole.com; Chaffeys Rd) has beautiful cottage gardens in which to enjoy cheese platters and great olives. Add in an active component with Blessed Cheese's (see above) fun **wine & cheese trail**; it hires out bikes but is good for drivers, too.

are outstanding views from the summit of Mt Magnificent, which can be reached by a steep 150m walking track off a dirt road from Mt Compass. You'll also find beautiful native forest, plenty of wildlife and an access point for the Heysen Trail. From here it's an hour's walk down to the 103-hectare **Finniss River Conservation Park**.

On Victor Harbor Rd, 9km south of Willunga, tiny **Mt Compass** is best known for the annual **Compass Cup**, a fun day of cow racing and other activities in February.

## Sleeping & Eating

There are plenty of B&Bs in and around Willunga; book through the visitors centre in McLaren Vale (p101). For further options see McLaren Vale (opposite) and Maslin Beach to Sellicks Beach (right).

**Willunga Hotel** ( ☎ 8556 2135; High St; s/d $30/60; dishes $16-20; ☽ lunch & dinner) Straight-up rooms, with shared bathrooms and a TV lounge, and simple pub meals are the go here.

**Citrus & Sea & Vines Cottages** ( ☎ 8295 8659; www.seavinescottage.com; d $150; ☷ ) These beautifully restored stone cottages have the perfect proportions of cosiness and style.

**Willunga House** ( ☎ 8556 2467; www.willunga house.com.au; 1 St Peters Tce; d $160-220; ☷ ) If you're looking for a real treat, this graceful old mansion off the main street with a feast for breakfast might be the place.

**Compass Country Cabins** ( ☎ 8556 8425; Cleland Gully Rd; cabins per 2 people 1st/2nd night $80/75, extra adult/child $10/8; ☷ ) The self-contained pine cabins overlook a gum-fringed lake on this property about 3km southeast of Mt Compass and 1.5km east of Main South Rd.

**Fleurieu Resort Caravan Park** ( ☎ 8556 8600; Heysen Blvd, Mt Compass; unpowered/powered sites per 2 people $15/19, cabins from $72) A compact new park 2km from Mt Compass and central to all Fleurieu sights.

**Willie Hill Café** ( ☎ 8556 2379; 27 High St; breakfast $3.90-10.50, mains $8.50-14.50; ☽ breakfast, lunch & dinner) All your prayers will be answered at this eclectic café-cum–art space in a decommissioned stone church. Cleanse your palate with tangy, freshly pressed juices and there'll be no room for guilt. Order at the counter and take a stone.

**Russell's** ( ☎ 8556 2571; pizzas $12-16; ☽ Friday night) It may resemble a ramshackle chicken coup, but it's the place to be on Friday evening for wood-fired pizza. No-one minds

the wait for a meal (which could be hours) – it's all about the atmosphere.

For food on the go, head to the **bakery** or **Willunga Farmers Market** ( ☽ 8am-12.30pm Sat), next to the Alma Hotel for local produce, food stalls and more.

# GULF ST VINCENT COAST

Popular, sandy swimming beaches line the coast from Maslin Beach to Sellicks Beach, 50km from the city; conditions are generally quiet unless there's a strong westerly blowing.

## MASLIN BEACH TO SELLICKS BEACH

The suburbs have gobbled up all the old coastal resorts as far south as Maslin Beach, where you can legally skinny dip between beautiful cliffs burnished with orange and white at sunset. South of Maslin Beach, the old coastal resorts of **Port Willunga** and **Aldinga Beach** are good spots to snorkel, with a lovely white ribbon of sand stretching the entire 6km from here to **Sellicks Beach**, a popular sailboarding spot. Beyond here the coast is rocky virtually all the way to Cape Jervis, although there's a good stretch of sand at Carrickalinga and Normanville.

## Sleeping & Eating

**Port Willunga Cottages** ( ☎ 08-8557 8516; www.portwillcott.com.au; 22 Ozone Ave, Port Willunga; d 1st/2nd night $180/160; ☷ ) Antique furnishings abound in these self-contained cottages with private gardens. Weekly rates available.

The following resorts are close to beaches.

**Beachwoods Eco Tourist Park** ( ☎ 08-8556 6113; www.beachwoods.com.au; 2 Tuart Rd, Aldinga; unpowered/powered sites per 2 people $14/19, dm $16, vans/cabins from $40/60; ☷ ) A bushy site.

**Aldinga Bay Holiday Village** ( ☎ 08-8556 5019; www.aldingabayholiday.com.au; Esplanade; 2-bedroom villas $95)

**Aldinga Holiday Park** ( ☎ 08-8556 3444; www.aldingaholiday.com.au; Cox Rd, Aldinga Beach; unpowered/powered sites per 2 people $13/17, cabins from $55, 2-bedroom cottages $90) Cottages are yurts here.

## Eating

**Star of Greece** ( ☎ 08-8557 7420; The Esplanade, Port Willunga; mains $20-35; ☽ lunch) Seafood is done so well at this acclaimed cliff-top restaurant,

**FLEURIEU PENINSULA**

in a boathouse-style old kiosk with funky thrift-shop décor, that diners make it their first booking in town. Adelaidians stake their worthiness on reports that Kylie eats here when she's in town.

## YANKALILLA
☎ 08 / pop 550

Past Sellicks Beach, Main South Rd leaves the coast and passes through some beautiful gum-lined country and lots of quaint stone cottages to Yankalilla. Just in from the bay near Normanville, this valley town has gained fame thanks to the image of Jesus and the Virgin Mary that has mysteriously appeared on the wall of the **Anglican church**. Cynics may tell you it's just salt damp.

The small house at 48 Main St (the road to Victor Harbor), was the first country school established by the Sisters of St Joseph, the teaching order founded by Mary MacKillop and Father Julian Woods.

**Yankalilla Bay Tourism** ( ☎ 8558 2999; 106 Main Rd; ☺ 9am-5pm Mon-Fri, 10am-4pm Sat & Sun) has tips on local sights and can book accommodation.

From Yankalilla you can head along the coast to Cape Jervis or to Victor Harbor via **Inman Valley**, an access point for the Heysen Trail. Along the way, check out the 250-million-year-old gouge marks left by a glacier at **Glacier Rock**, 20km from Yankalilla.

## NORMANVILLE TO RAPID BAY
☎ 08

Just to the west of Yankalilla, the swimming beaches of Normanville and Carrickalinga have the only decent stretch of sand between Sellicks Beach and Cape Jervis. The Main South Rd returns to the sea here before heading back into scenic hill country to Cape Jervis, via the small hamlet of Second Valley and a detour to Rapid Bay.

See opposite for details of diving and snorkelling along this stretch. **High Country**

**Trails** ( ☎ 8558 2507; Main South Rd, Normanville), 1km south of the Normanville turn-off, offers one hour horse walk-trot trail rides ($40) through the sand dunes and along Normanville beach. Bookings are essential.

**Normanville Beach Caravan Park** ( ☎ 8558 2038; Jetty Rd; unpowered/powered sites per 2 people $17/20, bunkhouse $40, cabins/cottage with bathroom $73/90) and **Beachside Caravan Park** ( ☎ 8558 2458; Cape Jervis Rd; unpowered/powered sites per 2 people $17/20, cabins & villas $52-81), about 2km towards Cape Jervis from Normanville, are on the beachfront.

For self-contained cabins and counter meals, head to the **Normanville Hotel** ( ☎ 8558 3200; 46 Main Rd, Normanville; d $80; mains $12-23; ☺ lunch & dinner). The **beach kiosk**, by the jetty, offers big breakfasts, café fare and great views.

Twelve kilometres south of Normanville, you'll hardly need to leave **Sunset Cove Resort** ( ☎ 1800 083 111; www.sunset-cove.com.au; Willis Dr; unpowered/powered sites per 2 people $20/25, cabins $75, motel d from $125; ☒ ☒ ), which comes complete with a café, restaurant and almost any type of activity you could wish for. The jetty area in sleepy **Second Valley**, 16km from Normanville and 21km from Cape Jervis, is a great spot for photographers and artists due to the colourful fishing shacks (best in morning light) and folds of grey slate and buff marble in the cliff. **Second Valley Caravan Park** ( ☎ 8598 4054; 2 Park Ave; unpowered/powered sites per 2 people $14.50/18, vans/cabins $35/55) is a small, well-shaded spot; or for something more upmarket, head to the historic **Leonards Mill** ( ☎ 8598 4184; leaonardsmillhotel@bigpond.com; Cape Jervis Rd; unit/cottage d $98/120; mains $14-19; ☺ lunch & dinner).

Rolling hills end abruptly in cliffs which drop into azure water at **Rapid Bay**, reminiscent of a small coastal town of 30 years ago. Its jetty is a famed **diving** site – home of plenty of leafy sea-dragons among other critters – and offers good fishing. The basic, exposed **camping ground** (adult/child $5/2.50), on the foreshore in front of the gravely beach, is popular with fisherfolk.

## CAPE JERVIS
☎ 08 / pop 100

This little fishing and holiday centre at the end of Main South Rd, 107km from Adelaide, is the terminal for ferry services to Kangaroo Island and the starting point for the Heysen Trail (see p38). From here you can look across Backstairs Passage to Kangaroo Island, 13km away. There's a **swim-**

**SURF, DIVE & SNORKEL**

The Fleurieu Peninsula's diversity of marine life, including leafy and weedy sea-dragons, seals, nudibranchs and some endemic species, can be explored in a range of shore and boat dives. Top spots include Aldinga drop-off, Second Valley, Rapid Bay jetty, Cape Jervis and the destroyer **ex-HMAS Hobart**, which was scuttled off Yankalilla Bay in 2002 and now entertains scuba divers – its deck and all the fixtures are at 14m to 20m. Obtain permits (single/double dives $50/95) from **Dolphin Dive** ( ☎ 08-8558 2733; www.diveexhmashobart.com; 52 Main St, Normanville), which also rents gear and runs dive certification courses.

Port Elliot has the most powerful waves, with swells often holding at 3m; other good breaks for experienced riders are at Waitpinga Beach and Parsons Beach, about 12km southwest of Victor Harbor. The best months for surfing are March to June inclusive, when northerly winds prevail. Pick up a copy of the Fleurieu Peninsula surf guide, *Surfing Secrets* (also available on www.fleurieupeninsula.com.au), which lists all the top spots along the Mid-Coast and Encounter Coast, along with a difficulty rating and optimal wind direction for each break. The **surf report** (Gulf St Vincent Coast ☎ 1902 241 018; Encounter Coast ☎ 1900 931 543) is updated regularly.

You can learn to surf (around $40 including gear) with: **Red Sun Safaris** ( ☎ 08-8276 3620; www.redsunsafaris.com.au), **South Coast Surf Academy** ( ☎ 0414-341 545; www.danosurf.com.au) or **Surf & Sun Safaris** ( ☎ 1800 786 386; www.surfnsun.com.au).

ming beach 2km north of the ferry terminal. **Fishing trips** (snapper and whiting) are run by **Cape Jervis Charter Services** ( ☎ 8598 0222).

A popular rural experience is the **Cape Jervis Station** ( ☎ 1800 805 288, 8598 0288; www.capejervisstation.com.au; Main South Rd; unpowered/powered sites per 2 people $14/17, dm $50, d $70-150, mains $10-17), a working sheep station 3.5km from the ferry terminal with camps and cottages to suit any budget. Other ultraclean motel rooms are alongside the **Cape Jervis Tavern** ( ☎ 8598 0276; Main South Rd; d/f $66/77, extra person $6; mains $11-18; ⏰ lunch & dinner; ⛖ ), 1.5km from the ferry terminal. Counter meals are served in the psychedelic-carpeted dining room.

There's some rugged walking options in nearby **Talisker Conservation Park**, with the interesting remains of a historic (1862) silver-lead mine, and **Deep Creek Conservation Park** (headquarters ☎ 8598 0263; www.environment.sa.gov.au/parks/deepcreek; sites per car $4-16), with testing walking tracks, expansive coastal views, a spectacular waterfall and sandy beaches. Within the park are five bush camping areas, two cottages and a homestead.

# ENCOUNTER COAST

The stunning coastline between Victor Harbor and Goolwa has some beautiful swimming beaches and great surf. This coast is hyper-popular in summer; between June and October you might be lucky enough to see a southern right whale on its migratory path.

Steam-driven tourist trains shunt along this coast (see p109 and p111), or you can push under your own steam along the Encounter Bikeway Trail (23km); maps are available from visitors centres.

## VICTOR HARBOR
☎ 08 / pop 8650
A row of towering pines lines the foreshore of this magnet for holiday-makers and retirees seeking the sun, water sports and golf courses. Victor Harbor (www.victor.sa.gov.au), 84km south of Adelaide, overlooks Granite Island and Encounter Bay, where Flinders and Baudin had their historic meeting in 1802 (p18). There's a memorial to the event up on the steep headland known as the Bluff, about 4km south of town, below which Victor Harbor's first whaling station was established in 1837 with another following soon after on Granite Island. The unrestrained slaughter of southern right whales, on which the industry was based, eventually made operations unfeasible, and they ceased in 1864. Today, Victor Harbor is a good place from which to spot these creatures.

## Information
Banks and the post office line Ocean St; most places in town have Eftpos and credit card facilities. There are three pharmacies on Ocean St.

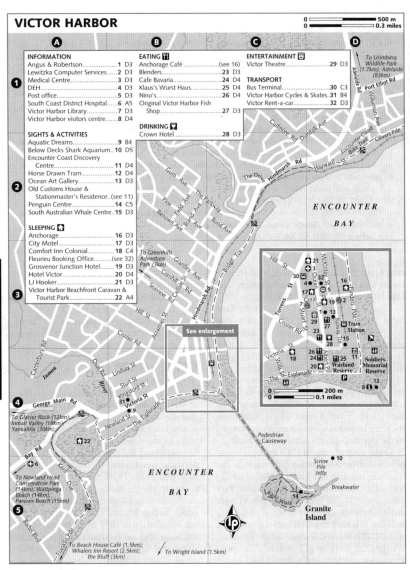

# VICTOR HARBOR

0 _____ 500 m
0 _____ 0.3 miles

### INFORMATION
Angus & Robertson.................**1** D3
Lewitzka Computer Services......**2** D3
Medical Centre.......................**3** D3
DEH.....................................**4** D3
Post office............................**5** D3
South Coast District Hospital......**6** A5
Victor Harbor Library................**7** D3
Victor Harbor visitors centre......**8** D4

### SIGHTS & ACTIVITIES
Aquatic Dreams......................**9** B4
Below Decks Shark Aquarium..**10** D5
Encounter Coast Discovery
   Centre..............................**11** D4
Horse Drawn Tram..................**12** D4
Ocean Art Gallery...................**13** D3
Old Customs House &
   Stationmaster's Residence..(see 11)
Penguin Centre......................**14** C5
South Australian Whale Centre..**15** D3

### SLEEPING
Anchorage.............................**16** D3
City Motel..............................**17** D3
Comfort Inn Colonial..............**18** C4
Fleurieu Booking Office..........(see 32)
Grosvenor Junction Hotel........**19** D3
Hotel Victor...........................**20** D4
LJ Hooker..............................**21** D3
Victor Harbor Beachfront Caravan &
   Tourist Park........................**22** A4

### EATING
Anchorage Café ...................(see 16)
Blenders................................**23** D3
Cafe Bavaria..........................**24** D4
Klaas's Wurst Haus.................**25** D4
Nino's...................................**26** D4
Original Victor Harbor Fish
   Shop.................................**27** D3

### DRINKING
Crown Hotel...........................**28** D3

### ENTERTAINMENT
Victor Theatre.......................**29** D3

### TRANSPORT
Bus Terminal.........................**30** C3
Victor Harbor Cycles & Skates..**31** B4
Victor Rent-a-car...................**32** D3

---

*FLEURIEU PENINSULA*

---

**Angus & Robertson** ( ☎ 8552 2799; 32 Ocean St)
Generalist bookshop stocking new titles and Lonely Planet
guides.

**DEH** ( ☎ 8552 3677; 57 Ocean St)

**Lewitzka Computer Services** ( ☎ 8552 6269; 2 Coral
St; Internet access per 10 min/1hr $2/6; ☻9am-5pm
Mon-Sat) Near the train station.

**Medical Centre** ( ☎ 8552 1444; 65 Ocean St)

**South Coast District Hospital** ( ☎ 8552 0650; Bay St)

**Victor Harbor Library** ( ☎ 8552 3009; 10 Coral St;
☻10am-5.30pm Tue-Thu, 10am-6pm Fri, 10am-1pm
Sat) Offers free Internet access; prebooking a computer is
recommended.

**Victor Harbor visitors centre** ( ☎ 8552 5738; www
.tourismvictorharbor.com.au; causeway; ☻9am-5pm;
🖵 ) Can book accommodation and tours.

## Sights

The **Encounter Coast Discovery Centre** ( ☎ 8552 5388; 2 Flinders Pde; adult/concession $4/3, child/family $2/10; ◷ 1-4pm), opposite the causeway, has interesting displays exploring local history from pre-European times to around 1900 and includes the **Old Customs House & Station Master's Residence** (1866), set up in its original state.

Leading local artists exhibit and sell their works at the artists co-op, **Ocean Art Gallery** ( ☎ 8552 1316; 7 Railway Tce; ◷ 10am-4pm), in an old railway cottage behind the station.

Between June and October you might be lucky enough to see a southern right whale swimming near the causeway. Victor Harbor is on the migratory path of these splendid animals. Head to the Bluff for a good lookout point. The **South Australian Whale Centre** ( ☎ 8552 5644; www.sawhalecentre.com; 2 Railway Tce; adult/student $6/4.50; ◷ 11am-4.30pm), opposite the causeway, has awe-inspiring displays of Victor's largest visitors. Engaging kid's programs ($6) are run during holidays.

Victor Harbor is protected from the angry Southern Ocean by lichen-covered, boulder-strewn **Granite Island**, connected to the mainland by a causeway; you can ride out there on the 1894 double-decker **horse-drawn tram** (one-way adult/child/family $4/3/12; ◷ every 40 min 10am-4pm).

The island has the Kaiki Walk (1.5km circuit, 40 minutes) and is a rookery for penguins. The **Granite Island Nature Park** ( ☎ 8852 7555; www.graniteisland.com.au) runs the **Penguin Centre** (adult/child/family $4/2/10; ◷ 12.30-3.30pm Sat, Sun & holidays), which details the little penguins' breeding, life habits and behaviour. You can watch sharks being fed through underwater windows, depending upon visibility, at the **Below Decks Shark Aquarium** (adult $15; ◷ 11am-5pm). Contact **Regardless** ( ☎ 0413-854 511) about whale and dolphin cruises.

Mingle with the land mammals at the **Urimbirra Wildlife Park** ( ☎ 8554 6554; Adelaide Rd; adult/concession/child $9/7.50/4.50; ◷ 9am-6pm), 5km from town. Much of the Australian fauna range freely, including 'roos (feed bag $0.50), while you can pat a furry koala at feeding times. Free barbecues and tables make it a good picnic spot.

**Greenhills Adventure Park** ( ☎ 8552 5999; www .greenhills.com.au; Waggon Rd; adult/child $20/15; ◷ 10am-5pm) has plenty of activities, particularly for those travelling with kids, including waterslides, minigolf, archery and canoeing on the Hindmarsh River.

## Activities

The **Encounter Coast Bike Trail** extends 29.5km from the Bluff to Laffin Point, past Goolwa. Sample distances from Victor Harbor are: Rosetta Head (5.5km), Port Elliot (8.5km) and Goolwa (16.5km). The visitors centre stocks maps. For bike hire, see p109; the SteamRanger accepts bikes.

Short **walking trails** at the Bluff provide elevated panoramic coastal views from the old whale lookout station.

Waitpinga Beach and Parsons Beach in **Newland Head Conservation Park**, about 12km southwest of town, are good for **surf fishing**, with salmon, mullet, mulloway, tailor and flathead being common catches.

**Surf & Sun Safaris** ( ☎ 1800 786 386; www.surf nsun.com.au) runs half-day sea-kayaking adventures ($50) to the bird mecca of Wright Island, in addition to an organised surf school. **Aquatic Dreams** ( ☎ 8552 2094; www.surf diveskate.com.au; 68 Victoria St; ◷ daily) rents out surf gear (surfboards/bodyboards/wetsuits $20/15/10), snorkelling and diving gear, and can organise shore **scuba dives**. Victor Harbor's major attraction for divers is its diversity of marine life including sea lions (in winter), dolphins, eagle rays and leafy sea dragons. Visibility is variable, but averages around 15m.

**Victor Harbor Boat Charters** ( ☎ 8552 3142) offers fishing charters (half/full day $65/100 including bait, tackle extra) and runs dive charters.

**Granite Island Eco Tours** ( ☎ 8552 7555) runs various dolphin and seal cruises (adult/child $40/28), and one-hour guided walks (adult/child/family $12.50/9/36; tours depart 6pm/9pm in winter/summer) to witness the penguins haul out of the water along the north shore between the causeway and jetty after sunset. These leave from the centre at dusk (leave your camera flash behind).

## Sleeping

Victor Harbor has the full gamut of holiday accommodation. Holiday apartments are a particularly good option for longer stays; contact **LJ Hooker** ( ☎ 8552 1944; www.ljhooker.com.au; 73 Ocean St) or **Fleurieu Booking Office** ( ☎ 1800 241 033, 8552 1033; fpbo.com.au; 66 Ocean St). Book B&Bs through the visitors centre (see p108).

**Grosvenor Junction Hotel** ( ☎ 8552 1011; 40 Ocean St; dm $30, s/d/f $35/70/80) Reasonable rooms – some with balconies – share sex-segregated bathrooms. The backpacker rooms are twin share. Continental breakfast is included.

**Anchorage** ( ☎ 8552 5970; anchoragevh@ozemail .com.au; cnr Coral St & Flinders Pde; s/d from $40/70, d with bathroom from $85/120; ❄ ) This heritage-listed grand villa on the seafront is the pick of the bunch. Most of its comfortable rooms face the beach, some with a balcony overlooking the bay (which you'd pay through the teeth for in Sydney!). The spa rooms are pretty swish. Rates include breakfast, and the café-bar downstairs is a winner too.

**Whalers Inn Resort** ( ☎ 8552 4400; www.whalers innresort.com.au; 121 Franklin Pde; d without/with balcony $100/170; ❄ ▣ ) Out under the Bluff, this upmarket spot has sublime views, a restaurant, cocktail bar, a croquet lawn and tennis courts.

Motel-style units are available at:

**Hotel Victor** ( ☎ 8552 1288; www.victorhotels.com.au; cnr The Esplanade & Albert Pl; s/d from $95/105, extra $12 on Sat) There are often attractive packages for standard, compact motel rooms. Book ahead for rooms overlooking the bay and Granite Island.

**Comfort Inn Colonial** ( ☎ 8552 1822; www.comfort colonial.com.au; 2 Victoria St; d $95, with kitchenette $105, extra person $10; ❄ ) Clean motel rooms of the exposed-brick-wall era. Laundry available.

**City Motel** ( ☎ 8552 2455; 51 Ocean St; d $77; ❄ ) Standard but cheap motel units with microwave.

**Victor Harbor Beachfront Caravan & Tourist Park** ( ☎ 8552 1111; 114 Victoria St; powered sites per 2 people from $26, cabins without/with bathroom $56/68, villas $80) This grassy, treed spot has a playground and barbecues but is a bit of a hike from town on the grottier end of Victor's beach. It's not advised to eat the fish from the river nearby.

There's an attractive **bush camping ground** (sites per car $6.50) near Waitpinga Beach.

## Eating & Drinking

Grab a steaming paper package from one of Victor Harbor's plethora of takeaway shops, just a stroll away from the beach, and calve out your patch under the large Norfolk Island pines on the grassy foreshore. **Klaus's Wurst Haus** (hotdogs $5-7; ❄ Sat & Sun) crafts German hot dogs from his tiny van near the causeway, while the **Original Victor Harbor Fish Shop** ( ☎ 8552 1273; 20 Ocean St; fish & chips $6; ❄ lunch & dinner) was runner-up for the

2003 best fish and chips in South Australia award, but covers all bases with schnitzels, hamburgers, kebabs and roast chicken.

**Blender's** (cnr Ocean St & Albert Pl; smoothies $4; ❄ 9am-6pm) A quick stop for fresh smoothies and juices, ice-cream and loaded baked potatoes ($5).

**Cafe Bavaria** ( ☎ 8552 7505; 11 Albert Place; meals $4.50-10.50; ❄ breakfast & lunch) Buckle up your lederhosen and lash down a onion-topped bratwurst roll before cruising the German tortes at this café overlooking the park.

**Nino's** ( ☎ 8552 3501; 17 Albert Pl; pizzas from $7, mains $7-12.50; ❄ lunch & dinner) Italian comfort standards are the go, along with gourmet pizzas including the kebabs, with marinated lamb and onion.

**Anchorage Café** ( ☎ 8552 5970; cnr Coral St & Flinders Pde; mains $14.50-22.50; ❄ breakfast, lunch & dinner) This salties' lair, with fishing nets trawling from the ceiling and a bar hewn from the hull of an old wooden whaling boat, has a great atmosphere and a Mediterranean-Greek meets Mod Oz menu. It serves breakfast, lunch and dinner, and Devonshire tea or coffee and cake ($6.50) in between. The beachside terrace benches are the perfect spot for sundowners year-round.

**Beach House Café** ( ☎ 8552 4417; 62 Franklin Rd, Encounter Bay; pizzas $9-14, curries around $12; ❄ dinner) Is it Italian-style Indian or the other way around? You decide over your own butter chicken 'pizza with personality'. The beachside position overlooking Wright Island and the Bluff is spot on.

**Grosvenor Junction Hotel** ( ☎ 8552 1011; 40 Ocean St; bar specials $5, meals $10-12; ❄ breakfast, lunch & dinner) has a bistro and ultracheap daily specials ($5), which may feature rissoles or lambs fry at the bar/TAB double act. **Hotel Victor** ( ☎ 8552 1288; cnr The Esplanade & Albert Pl; meals $11-24; ❄ breakfast, lunch & dinner) and **Crown Hotel** ( ☎ 8552 1022; 2 Ocean St; meals $9-24; ❄ lunch & dinner) also have bistros, the latter with a popular breezy corner for a beer in the sun.

## Entertainment

**Victor Cinemas** ( ☎ 8552 1325; Ocean St; adult/child $11/8) Screens films daily during school holidays and four days a week at other times.

## Getting There & Around

For details on bus services, including ferry connections to Cape Jervis and Wirrina, near Yankalilla, see p100.

**Victor Harbor Cycles & Skates** ( ☎ 8552 1417; 73 Victoria St; ☻ 9am-5.30pm Mon-Fri, 9am-noon Sat) rents out bikes for $10/25 per hour/day ($15 per day for rentals of more than three days). Helmets and locks are included, and baby seats ($5) are available. Book within office hours for weekend delivery.

You can rent cars through **Victor Rent-a-car** ( ☎ 8552 1033; 66 Ocean St). For taxi service, call the **Peninsular Taxi Group** ( ☎ 131 008, 8552 2622).

More scenic train rides than an actual mode of transport, **SteamRanger Tourist Railway** ( ☎ 8552 2782; www.steamranger.org.au; Victor Harbor Station) runs the **Cockle Train** (one way/return $16/23) along the scenic Encounter Coast between Victor Harbor and Goolwa via Port Elliot every Sunday. **Southern Encounter** (Victor Harbor Station; adult/child/family return $52/31/135) does a return trip from Mt Barker (see p90) to Victor Harbor via Strathalbyn, Goolwa and Port Elliot on alternate Sundays.

## PORT ELLIOT
☎ 08 / pop 1200
On Encounter Bay, just 8km east of Victor Harbor, Port Elliot is the most charming of the towns along this stretch. Its historic heart synchronises with a bohemian verve and the picturesque **Horseshoe Bay** offers a sheltered swimming beach and a cliff-top walk – great for spying whales in season. There's a surf life-saving club, and well-maintained showers beside the Bowls Club. **Commodore Point**, at the eastern end, is a good surf spot for experienced surfers, but there are better ones at nearby **Boomer Beach** and **Knights Beach**.

For surf-gear hire, head to **Southern Surf Shop** ( ☎ 8554 2376; 36 North Tce). Those feeling less energetic can pick up a second-hand book at the **Bargain Barn** ( ☎ 8554 2103; 43 The Strand).

### Sleeping & Eating
Holiday rentals can be organised through **Dodd & Paige** ( ☎ 8554 2029; 51 The Strand).

**Royal Family Hotel** ( ☎ 8554 2219; rfhotel@chariot .net.au; 32 North Tce; s/d $30/40; mains $9-16; ☷ ) Basic old-style pub rooms and shared bathrooms, with a lounge that'll take you back in time.

**Arnella by the Sea** ( ☎ 8554 3611; narnu@bigpond .com; 28 North Tce; dm/s/d $25/30/60) Fans of shabby-chic will love Arnella's cosy rooms in Port Elliot's oldest building. There's a communal lounge and the kitchen has the works, or cook on the garden barbecue.

**Thomas Henry B&B** ( ☎ 8554 3388, 8 Charteris St; s/d $120/150) This lovely, doily-free old guesthouse has spacious fan-cooled rooms. You can eat the large cooked breakfast outside under the grapevines in warm weather.

**Trafalgar House B&B** ( ☎ 8554 3888; www.trafalgar house.com.au; cnr The Strand & Freeling St; d B&B from $125, cottage from $120) At the top of the hill near the whale-spotting cliff, this serene cottage has a log fire and lovely garden.

**Port Elliot Tourist Park** ( ☎ 8554 2134; www .portelliotcaravanpark.com.au; Middleton Rd, Port Elliot; unpowered/powered sites per 2 people $24/28, cabins/units/cottages from $75/98/120, extra person $7) In an unbeatable position nestled behind the sand dunes on Horseshoe Bay, this grassy park has a laundry and sporting facilities, including a tennis court. It can be a touch on the windy side. Prices quoted are for high season.

**Flying Fish** (1 The Foreshore; takeaway $9-14.50; ☻ lunch & dinner) Sit down for lunch and you'll be here all day – the views are sublime. Otherwise grab a quality takeaway of Coopers-battered flathead (a fish) and chips and head back to the sand.

**Café Saté** ( ☎ 8554 2622; 40 North Tce; mains $11.50-16.90; ☻ lunch Thu-Sun, dinner Tue-Sun) Rice, curry and Asian noodle dishes are served at this hut-style place with alfresco garden tables.

There's a **supermarket**, some **takeaway** joints and the uber-popular **Port Elliot Bakery** on North Tce, the main street through town.

## MIDDLETON
☎ 08 / pop 400
A laid-back vibe permeates this little holiday town with a few arts and crafts shops and a good beach for novice surfers.

'The Boardroom' is an open-sided lean-to decked out with graffiti-covered surfboards. You can read the ongoing debate arguing why 'surfers rule' or 'bodyboarders rule'.

**Big Surf Australia** ( ☎ 8554 2399; Main Rd), near the Strathalbyn turn-off, hires surfboards/ bodyboards/wetsuits ($20/10/10) and can arrange surfing lessons.

**Middleton Caravan Park** ( ☎ 8554 2383; www .middletoncaravanpark.com.au; 21 Goolwa Rd; unpowered/ powered sites per 2 people $16/18, cabins from $60; ☷ ) Gardenlike, this park has ample facilities and is a short walk from the beach.

A grand turn-of-the-century limestone building, **Sea Change B&B** ( ☎ 8554 5213; www .citrus-seachange.com; 48 Goolwa Rd; B&B $195; ☷ ☗ )

has four stately bedrooms with bathrooms and king-size beds, a library, and games and TV room.

**Blues Restaurant** ( ☎ 8552 1551; Goolwa Rd; mains around $28; ☽ dinner) serves delicious food is, or you can head to the pub or chow down on your choc-full pie at **Heritage Pies & Pastries** ( ☎ 8554 2666; Goolwa Rd; pies $2.60; 10am-6pm).

## GOOLWA

☎ 08 / pop 3000

A restful and unassuming place, Goolwa has a generous expanse of sand upon which locals and visitors alike indulge in simple beach pleasures. At the point where Australia's largest river meets the ocean, Goolwa initially grew with the developing trade along the river. As large sea-going vessels were unable to get through the sandbars at the Murray Mouth, the state's first railway line was built in 1854 to nearby Port Elliot, which became Goolwa's sea port. In the 1880s a new railway to Adelaide from Murray Bridge spelt the end for Goolwa as a port town. However, boat building is a continuing art, celebrated in the biennial **Wooden Boat Festival** (March, odd-numbered years).

### Information

**Alexandrina Library Centre** ( ☎ 8555 7000; cnr Cadell & Dawson Sts; ☽ 9am-5pm Mon-Fri, 9am-noon Sat) Free Internet access.

**Signal Point visitors centre** ( ☎ 8555 3488; The Wharf; ☽ 9am-5pm) Plenty of literature and an interpretive centre (adult/child/family $5.50/2.75/13.20) with interactive displays on the life and ecology of the Murray River.

### Sights & Activities

Goolwa's gentrified centre has a number of heritage buildings dating from the 1850s and '60s, including the **Goolwa Hotel** (1853), the **Corio Hotel** (1857), and the former **Customs House** (1859); pick up a self-guided walking tour brochure from the visitors centre.

**Goolwa Museum** ( ☎ 8555 2221; 11 Porter St; adult/child $2.50/0.50; ☽ 2-4.30pm Tue-Thu, Sat & Sun, daily school holidays) sheds light on the town's past, early settlement and farming, the Murray River and ships that have come to grief nearby.

Local art works are displayed at the **South Coast Regional Art Centre** ( ☎ 8555 1500; Goolwa Tce; ☽ 1-5pm Wed-Fri, 10am-4pm Sat & Sun) in the Old Goolwa Police Station.

On the waterfront a short walk upstream from the main wharf, is the **Goolwa Maritime Gallery**, which includes an art gallery in a WWII barge, and a riverboat museum in an 1882 stone building.

There are toilets and a kiosk at **Goolwa Beach**, and a **boardwalk** which traverses the dunes and offers an expansive view down the coast. Head to **Barrell Surf & Skate** ( ☎ 8555 5422; 10C Cadell St) for gear hire (long-board/bodyboard/wetsuit $20/10/15). You can hire jet skis, catamarans and sailboards on the waterfront between the wharf and the barrage. A bird-watching hide towards the **Goolwa Barrage** ( ☽ 8am-5pm) spies on activity where fresh water meets the sea.

Hindmarsh Island Bridge links the mainland with **Hindmarsh Island**. Development and sacred sites collided here, and disputes over the building of this aesthetically bland bridge continued for years, dividing local opinion, Aboriginal communities and the state's academic and political powerhouses. You can drive down to the Murray River Mouth to see dredges working 24/7 to prevent the mouth from silting up. Tip: slather on mosquito repellent – they're voracious!

**Spirit Australia Cruises** ( ☎ 1800 442 203, 8555 2203; www.coorongcruises.com.au; Main Wharf) runs eco-cruises on the Murray and Coorong including lunch and guided walks. The MV *Aroona* takes cruises on the lower Murray (adult/child $35/20), while you can explore the Murray Mouth and Coorong on MV *Wetlands Explorer*, on a day cruise (adult/child $75/45), a 4½-hour Coorong Discovery Cruise (adult/child $70/52), or a six-hour Coorong Adventure Cruise (adult/child $84/57). The five-day Great Murray River Run cruise to/from Border Cliffs costs $940 per person with a coach return. Bookings are essential.

### Sleeping

Holiday rentals in and around Goolwa and Hindmarsh Island are managed by **LJ Hooker** ( ☎ 8555 1785; www.ljhooker.com.au/Goolwa; 25 Cadell St) and the **Professionals** ( ☎ 8555 2122; www.professionalsgoolwa.com.au; 1 Cadell St), which has a good range at the budget end. Off-peak rates are about half those charged during December, January and Easter. Houses accommodating six people range from $250 to $700 per week in the off-season ($450 to $1500 in peak times). Linen required.

**Goolwa Riverport Motel** ( ☎ 1800 155 033, 8555 5033; Noble Ave; d/f from $100/120; 🏊 🖭 ) These ample single-level units, 4km from town, have disabled facilities.

**Goolwa Central Motel** ( ☎ 8555 1155; www.goolwa central.bestwestern.com.au; 30 Cadell St; s/d from $110/120; 🏊 🖭 ) Standard sparse motel rooms in the centre of town, with an attached Irish pub serving Kilkenny and Guinness.

**Narnu Farm** ( ☎ 8555 2002; Monument Rd; cottages from $95; 🏊 ) On Hindmarsh Island, this family-oriented pioneer-style farm has rustic cottages and plenty of animal activity.

Contact the visitors centre (opposite) for details on Goolwa's B&Bs, many in beautifully refurbished cottages.

**Rivershack** ( ☎ 8296 3859; www.rivershack.com.au; 228 Liverpool Rd; d from $80; 🏊 ) This gorgeous two-bedroom shack on the riverfront has fine river-life views. Breakfast available.

**Boathouse** ( ☎ 8555 0338; 138 Liverpool Rd; 2-night d incl breakfast $350) Tranquillity doesn't come better than at this stylishly rustic waterfront boathouse. A complimentary bottle of wine will help you ease in. There's a two-night minimum stay.

Goolwa's caravan parks feature barbecues and laundry facilities.

**Goolwa Caravan Park** ( ☎ 1800 130 353, 8555 2737; www.goolwacaravanpark.com.au; Noble Ave, Goolwa; unpowered/powered sites per 2 people from $16/20, cabins from $70; 🏊 🖭 ) A swish park close to the river, 3.5km from town, with boat access to the river and canoes, aquabikes and bicycle hire for guests.

**Goolwa Camping & Tourist Park** ( ☎ 8555 2144; 40 Kessell Rd; unpowered/powered sites per 2 people $15/20, on-site vans $36-48, self-contained cabins $70-85, extra adult/child $5.50/3.50; 🏊 ) A simple camping ground about 15 minutes' walk from the town centre.

**Hindmarsh Island Caravan Park** ( ☎ 8555 2234; Madsen St; unpowered/powered sites per 2 people $14/16, cabins $40-60) Sites scattered throughout treed surrounds about 100m from the river.

## Eating

Goolwa boasts three bakeries and plenty of fast food joints for surf-starved stomachs to stodge up at.

**Café Lime** ( ☎ 8555 5522; 1/11 Goolwa Tce; dishes $8-14; 🕙 breakfast & lunch, closed Thu) Pick up heat-and-eat gourmet goodies or a takeaway cone of salt and pepper squid with lime salted fries ($9.50), or nab a table to indulge in corn bread, baguettes and lip-smacking hot dishes. Espresso perfecto.

**Hector's** ( ☎ 8555 5885; Main Wharf; breakfast $4.50-10.50, mains $13.50-16; 🕙 breakfast, lunch & dinner Tue-Sun) A breezy wharf-side haven for relaxed snacks and mixed café fare.

**Woks 2 Eat** ( ☎ 8555 1491; 9 Cadell St; mains $9.50-15; 🕙 lunch & dinner) All your favourite Asian comfort foods – that's wok! Lunch specials are a steal, and the serves aplenty.

**Beach House Café** ( ☎ 8555 5055; Cadell St; pizzas $9.60-14.50, curries $11.50-13; 🕙 dinner Thu-Sun) Wood-fired 'pizzas with a difference'-sister of the Victor Harbor operation serving up treats such as tandoori lamb pizza with mozzarella and mango chutney.

Pub meals are served at Goolwa's two 1850s hotels: **Goolwa Hotel** ( ☎ 8555 2012; 7 Cadell St; mains $10-18; 🕙 lunch & dinner), adorned with the figurehead from the *Mozambique*, wrecked at the Murray Mouth in 1864, and nearby **Corio Hotel** ( ☎ 8555 2011; Railway Tce; mains $11-26; 🕙 lunch & dinner), with slightly more upmarket meals.

## Getting There & Around

For connections to Goolwa see p100.

**Goolwa Taxi Service** ( ☎ 131 008, 8552 8222) charges approximately $22/60 to Port Elliot/ Strathalbyn.

The **Strathlink** ( ☎ 8552 2782; www.steamranger .org.au; adult/child/family return $30/18/78) classic railcar runs between Goolwa and Strathalbyn on Sundays. See p109 for details of the Cockle Train.

## CURRENCY CREEK
☎ 08

Once slated as the capital of SA, this hamlet 10km from Goolwa now seems content with producing award-winning wines. **Currency Creek Winery** ( ☎ 8555 4013; www.currency creekwines.com.au; Winery Rd; d $115-130; mains $20-25; 🕙 lunch & dinner) has a restaurant, cellar-door tastings and the Black Swamp walking trail (3km) past a historic railway bridge. Keep an eye out for Aboriginal canoe trees.

## MILANG & CLAYTON

Sleepy Milang, on Lake Alexandrina about 33km from Goolwa, was established in 1853 as a river port, with bullock wagons carrying goods overland to and from Adelaide. In its heyday Milang handled more than half the total Murray River exports from SA. It comes alive in late January during the **Freshwater Yachting Classic**. Further south, tiny

Clayton is noted for **yabby fishing**, water-skiing and sailing. **Backwater Boats** ( ☎ 08-8537 0372; www.backwaterboats.com.au) hires out kayaks (three hours $25), sailing boats and catamarans ($50) and motor boats ($60), and runs sailing courses.

## LANGHORNE CREEK WINERIES

On flood plains between the Angas and Bremer Rivers 16km east of Strathalbyn, Langhorne Creek (www.langhornewine .com.au) is one of Australia's oldest wine-growing regions, producing Shiraz, Cabernet Sauvignon, Chardonnay and some world-first varieties.

Along Wellington Rd on the east side of the Bremer River, a cellar door cooperative includes **Cleggett Wines** ( ☎ 08-8537 3133; www .cleggettwines.com.au), a fascinating winery which discovered Malian and Shalistin grapes (bronze/pink and golden white mutated Cabernet Sauvignon grapes, respectively).

**Bleasdale Winery** ( ☎ 08-8537 3001; Wellington Rd; ☺ 9am-5pm Mon-Fri, 11am-5pm Sat & Sun), the district's first winery, has a large range, historic cellars and an old lever press made from red gum. The small **Lake Breeze Winery** ( ☎ 08-8537 3017; Step Rd; ☺ 10am-5pm) has some acclaimed reds and sits in magnificent red gum country by the Bremer River. The most recent of the Aboriginal canoe trees in this area dates from the 1930s.

See Goolwa (p110) for nearby sleeping options.

FLEURIEU PENINSULA

# Kangaroo Island

CONTENTS

| | |
|---|---|
| Kingscote | 118 |
| American River | 120 |
| Penneshaw & Dudley Peninsula | 121 |
| Playford Highway | 123 |
| North Coast Road | 123 |
| South Coast Road | 124 |
| Flinders Chase National Park | 125 |

Kangaroo Island (KI), 13km off the coast of South Australia (SA), is part wildlife wonderland of birds, native animals and ocean-based creatures, and part significant agricultural region. Its wild and rugged coastline shelters beaches edged with turquoise seas, while the interior contains native forest and bush, 30% of which is maintained as either conservation or national parks. Kangaroo Island's isolation from European diseases and feral species greatly protected the island's native flora and fauna.

Many island place names are French named by explorer Nicholas Baudin, who surveyed the coast in 1802–03. He found the island uninhabited, though archaeologists have since found evidence of Aboriginal habitation about 2250 years ago. Baudin's English counterpart Matthew Flinders named the island after his crew enjoyed a feast of kangaroo meat here.

A motley collection of whalers, sealers, escaped convicts and ship deserters began to make their homes on the island in the early 1800s. They brought Aboriginal women from Tasmania, and abducted others from the mainland. Before long, KI had a reputation as one of the most lawless and vicious places in the British Empire. The worst scoundrels were rounded up in 1827, and thereafter a rough sort of respectability was achieved.

South Australia's first official settlement was established on KI at Reeves Point (near Kingscote) in 1836. It struggled on for two years, but the lack of fresh water lead most of the colonists to move to Adelaide. Those who were left embarked on a semisubsistence lifestyle.

While here, be sure to try the island's local produce, including fresh seafood and marron (a freshwater crayfish), honey produced by a pure strain of Ligurian bees, jams from indigenous fruits, sheep-milk cheeses, local wines and eucalyptus oil.

## HIGHLIGHTS

- Studying animal behaviour and hiking the rugged bush and coast at **Flinders Chase National Park** (p125)
- Marvelling at the **little penguins** in Penneshaw (p121)
- Learning the history of the **lightstation** at Cape Willoughby (p121)
- Caving in the fairies' playground at the dry **Kelly Hill Caves** (p124)
- Sighting a leafy sea dragon and other diverse sea life on a **scuba dive** (p116)
- Sampling the island's fine produce, including **honey** (p124), **sheep's cheese** (p123) and **eucalyptus drops** (p124)

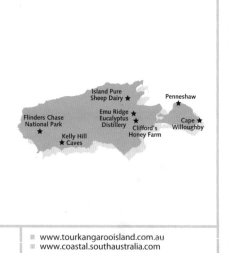

- TELEPHONE CODE: ☎ 08
- www.tourkangarooisland.com.au
- www.coastal.southaustralia.com

# Information

The Royal Society of South Australia's *Natural History of Kangaroo Island* gives comprehensive (though densely scientific) coverage of the island's natural history. *The Southern Land – Kangaroo Island*, by Jean M Nunn, gives a historical account of the island.

**Kangaroo Island Gateway visitors centre** ( ☎ 08-8553 1185; www.tourkangarooisland.com.au; ☿ 9am-5pm Mon-Fri, 10am-4pm Sat & Sun) Well stocked and manned by knowledgeable and helpful staff, this rich asset provides good maps, books accommodation and sells park entry tickets and Island Parks Passes. You'll find it just outside Penneshaw, on the road to Kingscote.

**Department for Environment & Heritage** (DEH; Map p119; ☎ 08-8553 2381; www.environment.sa.gov.au /parks; 37 Dauncey St, Kingscote) stocks Island Parks Passes (adult/student/child/family $42/31/ 25/110), which cover entry fees for all conservation areas and ranger-guided tours, except the penguin walks. Passes can also be purchased at most sights. Complimentary passes are given if you stay five nights in heritage accommodation.

There are **bank** facilities in Kingscote and Penneshaw. Bear in mind that mobile **phone reception** is only available in Kingscote, Penneshaw, American River, the airport and some areas of Emu Bay.

For **medical assistance**, contact the **Kangaroo Island Medical Clinic** (Map p119; ☎ 08-8553 2037; 64 Murray St, Kingscote) or **Kangaroo Island Hospital** (Map p119; ☎ 08-8553 4200; The Esplanade).

**Fire restrictions** are in place from 1 December through to 30 April.

## Accommodation

There are basic camping grounds within Flinders Chase National Park and at American

# KANGAROO ISLAND

0 ————— 20 km
0 ————— 12 miles

**SIGHTS & ACTIVITIES**
Clifford's Honey Farm........................1 C2
Emu Ridge Eucalyptus Distillery........2 C2
Island Pure Sheep Dairy....................3 C2
KI Outdoor Actions............................4 B3
Parndana Wildlife Park.......................5 B2
Paul's Place......................................6 B2
Stokes Bay Bush Garden...................7 B2

**SLEEPING** 🏠
Blue Hills Farm Stay..........................8 B3
Flinders Chase Farm..........................9 A3
Kaiwarra Food Barn.........................10 B3
Kangaroo Island Wilderness Resort......11 A3
Western Kangaroo Island Caravan Park..12 A3

**TRANSPORT**
Airport...........................................13 C2

*Investigator Strait*

To Wirrina (8km)

To Victor Harbor (50km); Adelaide (103km)

Rapid Head

King George Beach
Cape Cassini
Emu Bay
Point Marsden
Backstairs Passage
Cape Jervis

Western River Conservation Park
Snelling Beach
Stokes Bay
Emu Bay
Bay of Shoals
Nepean Bay
Cape Jervis

Cape Torrens Conservation Park
Western River Cove
Lathami Conservation Park
Kingscote
Browns Beach
Hog Bay
Penneshaw

Harvey's Return
Snug Cove
Cygnet River
Western Cove
Eastern Cove
Antechamber Bay

Cape Borda
Ravine des Casoars
Parndana Conservation Park
Playford Hwy
Parndana
American River
Baudin Beach
Dudley Peninsula
Chapman River

West Bay
Flinders Chase National Park
West End Hwy
White Lagoon
Hog Bay Rd
Prospect Hill Lookout (Mt Thisby)
Pelican Lagoon
Dudley Conservation Park
Cape Willoughby

Snake Lagoon
Rocky River
Karatta
Little Sahara
Lake Ada
Murray Lagoon
Pennington Bay
Cape Hart Conservation Park

Cape Bedout
Maupertuis Bay
Hanson Bay Sanctuary
Kelly Hill Conservation Park
South Coast Rd
Vivonne Bay
Vivonne Bay Conservation Park
Seal Bay
Cape Gantheaume Conservation Park
D'Estrees Bay
Point Tinline

Admirals Arch
Cape du Couedic
Remarkable Rocks
Seal Bay Conservation Park
Cape Gantheaume
Cape Linois

*SOUTHERN OCEAN*

Casuarina Islets

**KANGAROO ISLAND**

River, Antechamber Bay, Stokes Bay, Vivonne Bay, Western River Cove and Browns Beach.

The main settlements of Kingscote and Penneshaw offer a range of accommodation including caravan parks, hostels, hotels, motels and guesthouses, while American River has several motels and rental apartments. Just outside Flinders Chase National Park, you'll also find the full range (p125). Packages can offer good value, particularly through the less frequented winter months.

Some of the most atmospheric accommodation can be found in the remote historic cottages for rent through **DEH** ( ☎ 08-8559 7235; www.environment.sa.gov.au/parks; basic huts per person $15-20, cottages for 2 people $75-120). These range from basic huts to the lightkeepers' cottages at Cape Willoughby, Cape Borda and Cape du Couedic. Six-bed Mays Homestead and the basic Postmans Cottage are at Rocky River. Each has heating and basic cooking facilities.

Bed and Breakfasts abound on KI, with plenty in the four-star range. These can be booked through the **Kangaroo Island Gateway visitors centre** ( ☎ 08-8553 1185; www.tourkangaroo island.com.au) and **Ferry Island Connections** ( ☎ 1800 618 484; www.ki-ferryconnections.com). For stays of over a few nights, the best value can be found in holiday house rentals (doubles from $70 a night) around the island, including the beach settlements of Emu Bay and Vivonne Bay. For listings, contact the visitors centre or **Century 21** (Map p119; ☎ 08-8553 2688; www.cen tury21.com.au/kangarooisland; 66 Dauncey St, Kingscote).

## Activities
### ADRENALINE SPORTS
Seeking an adrenaline rush? **KI Outdoor Action** (Map p115; ☎ 08-8559 4295; South Coast Rd, Vivonne Bay) rents out surfboards, bodyboards, sandboards to surf down some dunes, kayaks and sailboards – along with a guide if required. Quad-bike tours explore the outfit's 202 hectares; night wildlife-spotting tours see plenty of 'roo action.

### BOAT HIRE & FISHING
There's plenty of good fishing around the island, including at jetties in Kingscote, Penneshaw, Emu Bay and Vivonne Bay. Common catches are garfish, tommy-ruff and squid, while the Kingscote jetty also has gummy shark and snook.

Rock fishing right around the coast can yield trevally and 'sweep', but you have to watch out for 'king waves', particularly on the south coast.

Good, accessible surf beaches are Pennington Bay, the mouth of South West River at Hanson Bay, and West Bay in Flinders Chase National Park. Salmon, flathead, tommies and whiting are common catches here.

In March and April, most beaches yield good catches of mullet. The best places for King George whiting are the southern end of D'Estrees Bay, near Point Tinline, and King George Beach, between Snelling Beach and Stokes Bay on the north coast.

**Country Cottage** (Map p119; ☎ 08-8553 2148; Centenary Ave, Kingscote) hires out tinnies (to fit three people) with trailer and with outboard motors, but you need a licence. The daily hire rate is $65.

Fishing tours (half-/full-day around $75/ 130) run out of Kingscote, Emu Bay and American River; bait, tackle and refreshments are included and you can keep your catch. Operators include:

**American River Fishing Charters** ( ☎ 08-8553 7456) Half- and full-day tours.

**Jag Fishing Tours** ( ☎ 08-8553 7202; jagfishingchar ters@bigpond.com) Full- and half-day tours include lunch.

**KI Fishing Charters** ( ☎ 08-8242 0352; www.kifish chart.com.au) Lunch can be organised.

**Mark West Fishing Charters** ( ☎ 08-8553 2043; www.markwestfishingcharters.com.au) North and south coast.

**MV Cooinda Fishing Services** ( ☎ 08-8553 1072; www.kidiving.com) Half-day tours.

### HEALTH
Well you may not think this is an activity, but **KI Health Retreat** ( ☎ 08-8553 5374; www.ki-health retreat.com; Emu Bay; weekend/week package $490/1990) will definitely get your body back into action. *Harper's Abroad* has even rated it as one of the world's 100 best retreats. Lose weight, de-stress and quit unhealthy habits with a cleanse of the body and lots of exercise in a beautiful location away from it all. Rates include transport from Adelaide (flights on week packages), all meals, massages and daily activities such as yoga and pilates.

### SCUBA DIVING & SNORKELLING
Kangaroo Island hosts a huge variety of marine creatures and plant life around the coast, including soft and hard corals. There

are something like 230 species of fish here, including colourful blue groper and blue devil fish. The island's marine pride is the elusive leafy sea dragon. A number of the island's 60 known shipwrecks have been located and these make interesting, but not spectacular, dive sites.

The best diving sites are off the east and north coasts, which are well sheltered and hence the water is clearer: visibility is 10m to 20m on average. The east coast has sheer drop-offs covered in invertebrates and corals – some of the caves have rare black tree corals; waters of the north coast are shallower and have numerous rocky reefs, with drop-offs and chasms. You can expect to meet seals, sea lions or dolphins on most dives.

The island's two operators cater for novice and experienced divers.

**KI Diving Safaris** ( ☎ 08-8559 3225; www.kidiving safaris.com) Charter operators offering double dives from Western River Cove ($250, including equipment) and various multiday packages with land- or boat-based accommodation. Hire gear available ($65).

**KI Diving Services** ( ☎ 08-8553 1072; www.kidiving .com) Offers 'discover scuba' half-day dives for novices ($89, including all gear), double boat dives ($138 including tank and weights, $30 extra for gear hire), and 3-day PADI open-water certification courses ($415, including full gear).

### SWIMMING & SURFING

The safest swimming is along the north coast, where the beautiful, clear water is warmer and the rips generally less savage than in the south. There are a number of good beaches, but access can be a problem; those you can get to include Emu Bay, Stokes Bay, Snelling Beach and Western River Cove.

For surfing, head to the south coast. Pennington Bay has the strongest and most reliable waves, while Vivonne Bay and Hanson Bay in the southwest can also be good, but be aware of rips – Hanson Bay is only for experienced surfers. 'The Sewer' is a popular break near Point Tinline in D'Estrees Bay.

### WALKING

There's plenty to see under your own foot power on KI. The DEH publish an excellent and comprehensive *Bushwalking in Kangaroo Island Parks* brochure, which lists the track notes and highlights of island walks and hikes. *Kangaroo Island on Foot*, by Jody Gates, is good for longer hikes.

## Tours

The DEH operates guided tours and walks at the sea lion colony at Seal Bay, the show cave at Kelly Hill Caves, the historic lighthouses at Cape Borda and Cape Willoughby, and the penguin rookeries at Kingscote and Penneshaw.

### PACKAGE TOURS

The ferry operators (see p118) and various Adelaide-based tour operators offer packages ex-Adelaide with coach and ferry passage; competition is fierce, so shop around to pick up a good deal. A plethora of one- to three-day coach tours (generally including accommodation and meals) are run by:

**Adelaide Sightseeing** ( ☎ 08-8231 4144; www .adelaidesightseeing.com.au/ki.htm) Some small-group tours visiting the main sights.

**Adventure Tours** ( ☎ 1300 654 604; www.adventure tours.com.au) Popular two-/three-day ex-Adelaide tours (from $320/445).

**Camp Wild Adventures** ( ☎ 08-8132 1333; www .campwild.com.au) Two-/three-day small-group wildlife safaris ($320/370) ex-Penneshaw including sand-boarding, swimming, surfing and all the main sights. Discounts for hostel memberships.

**Kangaroo Island Ferry Connections** ( ☎ 13 13 01, 08-8202 8688; www.sealink.com.au; 440 King William St, Adelaide) This range of day tours (from KI/Adelaide $99/181) can also be picked up on the island. The one-day tour from Adelaide is only for those extremely short on time. Overnight trips with two-day tours cost $302.

**Wayward Bus** ( ☎ 1300 653 510; www.waywardbus .com.au) Backpacker oriented two-day tours ($310) covering all the major sights; stays can be extended.

### DAY TOURS

See the visitors centre or tourism website (www.tourkangarooisland.com.au) for details of coach tours to Seal Bay and Flinders Chase National Park. Several operators specialise in luxury 4WD tours. The following operators run small-group tours:

**Alkirna Nocturnal Tours** ( ☎ 08-8553 7464; www .alkirna.com.au) Well, it's a night tour really. These naturalist-led tours view nocturnal creatures around American River (adult/child $52/34, two hours).

**Adventure Charters of Kangaroo Island** ( ☎ 08-8553 9119; www.adventurecharters.com.au) Small group off-the-beaten-track 4WD tours (adult/child per day $295/200) exploring the various habitats and landscapes of KI. Great lunch spread.

**Kangaroo Island Discovery Tours** ( ☎ 1800 228 212; www.austdreaming.com.au) Personalised 4WD tours (adult/child including lunch $198/148) to private areas just outside the national park from the Kangaroo Island Wilderness Resort. Special-interest tours can be arranged.

**KI Ferries** ( ☎ 13 22 33; www.kiferries.com) Day tours ($93) to Seal Bay and Flinders Chase National Park, or central sights (eucalyptus distillery, sheep dairy, beehives and wildlife park).

**Surf 'n' Sun** ( ☒ 1800 786 386; www.surfnsun.com.au) Three-day 4WD tours ($340) with a strong focus on wildlife include snorkelling and a surfing lesson. Tours depart from Adelaide.

You can be as active or lazy as you like on a skippered yacht with **Kangaroo Island Sailing** ( ☎ 08-8553 2111; www.picknowl.com.au/homepages /kisail; Kingscote jetty), which cruises along the northern coast, on Nepean Bay and past the Redbanks' beautiful burnished cliffs. Swim, fish and help to sail on half-day cruises (adult/child $50/35 including morning tea) and full-day adventures ($80/50 including lunch), or stay aboard for longer cruises ($120 per person per day including linen and meals).

## Getting There & Away

For flights (around $125) between Adelaide and Kingscote, contact **Emu Airways** ( ☎ 08-8234 3711; www.emuairways.com.au) or **Regional Express Airlines** (Rex; ☎ 13 17 13; www.regionalexpress.com.au).

If you don't have your own vehicle, catch the bus to Cape Jervis or Wirrina, 10km south of Normanville, and ferry across to the island, then hire a car booked for collection at the ferry terminus at Penneshaw or Kingscote. Bookings are essential.

**Kangaroo Island Sealink** ( ☎ 13 13 01; www.sea link.com.au) operates three vehicular ferries between Cape Jervis and Penneshaw daily (adult/child/infant $32/16/free, bicycles/ motorcycles/cars $5.50/22/70, 45 minutes). One driver is included with the vehicle price (cars only, not bikes). It operates a bus service connecting with ferry departures at Port Jervis from Adelaide's central bus station (adult/student $18/15, two hours), Goolwa and Victor Harbor ($12, 40 minutes).

**Kangaroo Island Ferries** ( ☎ 13 22 33; www.kifer ries.com) operates at least two daily ferries each way between Wirrina (10km south of Normanville), and Kingscote (one-way adult/ child/bicycle/car $30/14/5/64, two hours). Bus services to/from Adelaide (adult/child $14.50/8, 1¾ hours) and Goolwa/Victor Harbor ($9.50/5) are timed for each ferry.

## Getting Around

Kangaroo Island is a big place and there is no public transport. Unless you're taking a tour, the only feasible way to get around is to bring or hire your own transport.

The island's main roads are sealed; some gravel roads can give you a wild ride if it's been a while since grading, including those to Cape Willoughby, Cape Borda and smaller coastal areas. To avoid coming to grief, overturning or 'going bush' on corners, take it slowly. 'Roos and wallabies often leap onto roads, particularly from dusk to dawn; keep your speed under 70km/h at these times.

Petrol is available in Kingscote, Penneshaw, American River, Parndana, and on the west of the island at Vivonne Bay and Kangaroo Island Wilderness Resort (though this can be intermittent).

### TO/FROM THE AIRPORT

The airport is 14km from Kingscote; a **shuttle bus** ( ☎ 08-8553 2390; $12) connects the airport and Kingscote.

### TO/FROM THE FERRY LANDINGS

The **Sealink Shuttle** ( ☎ 13 13 01) connects with most ferries, linking Kingscote and American River with Penneshaw ($11). Bookings are essential.

### CAR & MOTORCYCLE HIRE

Not all Adelaide car-rental companies will rent cars for KI trips; with ferry prices it's cheaper to hire on the island – but book ahead. Cars can be hired from:

**Budget** ( ☎ 08-8553 3133; www.budget.com.au; Kingscote airport)

**Hertz** ( ☎ 1800 088 296, 08-8553 2390; Kingscote airport)

**Kirks Car Rentals** ( ☎ 08-8598; 0011; thebookingoffic e@Yankalilla.net.au) Late-model vehicles from Penneshaw and American River.

## KINGSCOTE

☎ 08 / pop 1440

The quite seaside town of Kingscote, the main town on the island, dates from 1836 when it became the first official colonial settlement in SA. Most services are based here and there are a few sights to see.

## Information

Branches of the ANZ and Bank SA on Dauncey St have ATMs, and the post office is the CBA bank agent.

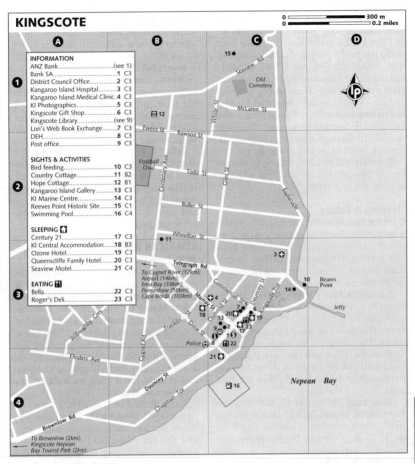

## KINGSCOTE

**INFORMATION**
ANZ Bank..............................(see 1)
Bank SA....................................**1** C3
District Council Office................**2** C3
Kangaroo Island Hospital..........**3** C3
Kangaroo Island Medical Clinic..**4** C3
KI Photographics......................**5** C3
Kingscote Gift Shop..................**6** C3
Kingscote Library.....................(see 9)
Lori's Web Book Exchange........**7** C3
DEH.........................................**8** C3
Post office...............................**9** C3

**SIGHTS & ACTIVITIES**
Bird feeding...........................**10** C3
Country Cottage.....................**11** B2
Hope Cottage.........................**12** B1
Kangaroo Island Gallery..........**13** C3
KI Marine Centre.....................**14** C3
Reeves Point Historic Site........**15** C1
Swimming Pool.......................**16** C4

**SLEEPING**
Century 21..............................**17** C3
KI Central Accommodation......**18** B3
Ozone Hotel............................**19** C3
Queenscliffe Family Hotel........**20** C3
Seaview Motel.........................**21** C4

**EATING**
Bella......................................**22** C3
Roger's Deli............................**23** C3

**District council office** (Dauncey St) Issues camping permits for Western River Cove in the island's northwest.

**KI Photographics** ( ☎ 8553 2599; Dauncy St) For film, camera batteries and one-hour processing.

**Kingscote Gift Shop** ( ☎ 8553 2165; cnr Dauncey & Commercial Sts) The official visitors centre is in Penneshaw (p115), but you'll pick up plenty of information brochures here.

**Kingscote Library** ( ☎ 8553 2015; Dauncey St) Check your emails here and at the Ozone Hotel (p120).

**Lori's Web Book Exchange** ( ☎ 8553 9093; Dauncy St; ⏱ 10am-5.30pm Wed-Fri, from 9.30am Sat) Stock up on reading material here.

## Sights & Activities

The site of the first settlement is at **Reeves Point Historic Site**, within walking distance of the town centre. It's very picturesque, with lawns and shady trees, but there's not much left apart from the cemetery, a well and a few bits and pieces. The point itself has shallows and sand bars, making it a good spot to observe water birds. **Hope Cottage** ( ☎ 8553 3141; Centenary Ave; adult/child $5/1; ⏱ 1-4pm) overlooks Reeves Point from the top of the hill. Built in 1857, it's now a National Trust museum furnished in period style, and has a reconstructed lighthouse and a eucalyptus-oil distillery.

As Kingscote doesn't have a good swimming beach most locals head out to **Emu Bay**, 18km northwest of town. The best swimming spot in town is the **tidal swimming pool**, about 500m south of the jetty.

The **KI Marine Centre** ( ☎ 8553 3112; Kingscote Wharf; adult/child \$10/5; ⊙ tours 7.30pm & 8.30pm winter, 8.30pm & 9.30pm summer) runs one-hour tours of the penguin colony and saltwater aquariums, which will give you a taste of what's lurking in the waters around KI (seahorses, giant cuttlefish etc). Wear sturdy footwear and leave your camera flash behind. Nearby, **bird feeding** (Kingscote Wharf; requested donation adult/child \$2/free; ⊙ 5pm) attracts around 40 of those majestic (if somewhat comical) beaked battleships, pelicans, as well as Pacific gulls.

**KI Gallery** ( ☎ 8553 2868; 1 Murray St; admission free; ⊙ 10am-5pm) has an excellent selection of local arts and crafts.

## Sleeping & Eating

**KI Central Accommodation** ( ☎ 8553 2787; 19 Murray St; dm/d \$20/50) Nearby Kingscote's main strip, this small and well-maintained hostel has a cosy communal lounge and kitchen. Rooms share bathrooms and dorms can be used as family rooms.

**Queenscliffe Family Hotel** ( ☎ 8553 2254; 57 Dauncey St; s/d with bathroom & breakfast \$70/80; lunch \$6.50-12.50, mains \$10-19.50; ⊙ breakfast, lunch & dinner) This pub has older but comfortable rooms. Those over the bar can be noisy, particularly on Friday and Saturday night. The traditional pub bistro serves dishes ranging from grills and island seafood to stir-fries and a curry of the day.

**Ozone Hotel** ( ☎ 1800 083 133, 8553 2249; www .ozonehotel.com; Kingscote Tce; d/tr/f with bathroom from \$114/127/165; mains \$11-27; ⊙ breakfast, lunch & dinner; ✉ ▯ ⌨ ) Opposite the foreshore with million-dollar waterfront views, the more upmarket Ozone has modern rooms, a pool and spa. The bistro menu features some of the best food in town (mostly grills and seafood) and there are plenty of KI wines to try at the bar. It gets packed on weekends. Lunch-time bar snacks run \$7.50 to \$8.50.

**Seaview Motel** ( ☎ 8553 2368; www.seaview.net .au; 51 Chapman Tce; s/d/f \$120/135/180) Sit back and soak up the views at this charming old-style guesthouse overlooking the bay and tidal pool. Choose from comfortable rooms with shared facilities or motel units (some with kitchen facilities).

**Kingscote Nepean Bay Tourist Park** ( ☎ 8553 2394; www.kingscotetourist.citysearch.com.au; Third Ave; unpowered/powered sites per 2 people \$17/20; vans & cabins \$40-45, cabins with bathroom from \$75) In Brownlow, about 3km southwest of Kingscote,

you'll find the full camping-resort range of accommodation and good facilities. There's a breezy coastal walking trail from here to Kingscote.

**Roger's Deli** ( ☎ 8553 2053; Dauncey St; meals \$4-16; ⊙ breakfast & lunch) You can get all manner of tasty burgers, salads, sweet things, coffee, hot food and daily specials (such as large pasta and salt and pepper squid) at Roger's bakery-deli-newsagency. There are also deli foods to take away.

**Bella** ( ☎ 8553 0400; 54 Dauncey St; lunch \$7-15, small pizzas \$11-13.50, mains \$15-25; ⊙ lunch & dinner) Dine indoors or alfresco at Bella's popular Italian café-restaurant–pizza bar. There are lunch-time baguettes, dinner time lasagne and grills, and takeaway pizza and hot barbecue chickens.

## AMERICAN RIVER
☎ 08 / pop 300

On the coast between Kingscote and Penneshaw, this tranquil town on a small peninsula shelters a calm inner bay, named **Pelican Lagoon** by Flinders. The town was named after the American sealers who built a trading schooner here in 1804. There's excellent bird-watching and plenty of Tammar wallabies in this area. Pelicans provide a daily feeding frenzy down on the wharf and at night you'll often see **wallabies** hopping around in town.

From the end of Scenic Dr, a moss- and fern-fringed **coastal walk** (2km one way) passes through natural scrub, sugar gums and she-oak (the island's last remaining habitat of the Glossy Black Cockatoo) to the rock wall remains of the old fish cannery. The return along the beach features picturesque lichen-covered rocks.

## Sleeping & Eating

There's a packed general store with plenty of provisions, bait and tackle and a bottle shop. A few motels in town have attached café-restaurants.

**Island Coastal Units** ( ☎ 8553 7010; www.kangaroo -island-au.com/coastalunits; d cabins from \$66, self-contained units from \$95) Nestled amongst trees opposite the foreshore, these new lodgings are equipped with TVs, fans and heating; the units also contain kitchens. Barbecues and meatpacks are available.

**Matthew Flinders Terraces** ( ☎ 0427-772 646; www.kangaroo-island-au.com/matthewflinders; Bayview

Rd; self-contained 2-bedroom units from $125) Perched on a steep hillside with gardens and native trees, these contemporary-styled rooms have balconies to chill out on overlooking Eastern Cove.

**River Valley Gallery & Café** (cnr Scenic Dr & Redbanks Rd; ☺ lunch) Serves home-baked cakes and light meals.

The visitors centre in Penneshaw organises permits for the **American River Campsite** ($3.85), a grassy site on the foreshore with showers and toilets.

Other options include:

**Ulonga Lodge** ( ☎ 8553 7171; www.ulonga.com.au; cabins $105, 2-bedroom units $135, breakfast per 2 people $25; ☺ breakfast year round, lunch Oct-May) Sit on your balcony and watch the birds on Eastern Cove. There's a café and row boats.

**Kangaroo Island Lodge** ( ☎ 8553 7053; www.kilodge .com.au; The Esplanade; d $140-180, extra person $23; breakfast buffet from $14, mains $21-25; ☺ breakfast & dinner; ☒ ☒ ) Comfortable motel suites with fridge and TV overlook the pool or American River. The restaurant serves island specialties and seafood, and there's a bar.

**Wanderer's Rest of Kangaroo Island** ( ☎ 8553 7140; www.wanderersrest.com.au; Bayview Rd; d incl breakfast $208; mains $17-22; ☺ dinner; ☒ ☒ ) Kidfree suite with balconies; it's restaurant serves countrystyle cuisine.

## PENNESHAW & DUDLEY PENINSULA

☎ 08 / pop 300

Looking across Backstairs Passage to the Fleurieu Peninsula, Penneshaw is the arrival point for ferries from Cape Jervis. This quiet resort town nestling under scenic hills at Hog Bay has several points of minor interest; there are not many places where locals can boast fairies in the bottom of their gardens – let alone fairy penguins. You'll hear their clacking safety call, a cross between a duck and dog yap, all over town at night.

The **Kangaroo Island Gateway visitors centre** ( ☎ 8553 1185; www.tourkangarooisland.com.au; ☺ 9am-5pm Mon-Fri, 10am-4pm Sat & Sun) is well stocked and manned by knowledgeable staff. It also books accommodation and sells park entry tickets and Island Parks Passes. It is located just outside Penneshaw on the road to Kingscote. **Grimshaw's Corner Store & Cafe** (cnr Third St & North Tce) has an ATM and the **post office** (Nat Thomas St; ☺ 9am-5pm Mon-Fri, 9-11am Sat) acts as a bank agency, with Eftpos cash-withdrawal facilities.

## Sights & Activities

Right by the vehicle ferry termi. Bay. The small white dome at the la. protects a replica of **Frenchman's Rock**, a bou. der carved by a member of Baudin's expedition. The Fireball Bates walking track sheds light on the days when old Penneshaw was an enclave of outcasts; pick up a brochure from the visitors centre.

**Penneshaw Penguin Centre** ( ☎ 8553 1103; tours adult/child/family $8/6.50/20; ☺ tours 7.30pm & 8.30pm winter, 8.30pm & 9.30pm summer), on the foreshore near the ferry terminal, allows you to get a close-up, unobtrusive view of the **little penguins** that nest along the shore as they ply the penguin highway. This is possibly the best place to see them in Australia, and the interpretive centre will shed further light on their life cycle and habits. Book ahead and leave camera flashes behind.

Artefacts from local shipwrecks and early settlement memorabilia is on display at **Penneshaw Maritime & Folk Museum** (Howard Dr; adult/child/family $3/2/7; ☺ 10am-noon & 3-5pm Mon, Wed & Sat, but hours fluctuate), which also has detailed models of both Flinders' *Investigator* and Baudin's *Geographe* ships.

The **Cape Willoughby Lightstation** ( ☎ 8553 1191; Willoughby Rd), 28km southeast of town, first operated in 1852 and is now used as a weather station. Tours (adult/child/family $10.50/6.50/28) run at 11.30am, 12.30pm and 2pm, also 3.15pm and 4pm in holiday periods. You can get a bucket of prawns to go with a bottle of wine from nearby **Dudley Wines** ( ☎ 8553 1333; ☺ 11am-5pm).

About 24km out towards Kingscote you come to a steep staircase leading up to the summit of **Prospect Hill (Mt Thisby)**. Used by Flinders as a lookout while mapping the coast, this large sand hill offers panoramic views north towards American River and south over **Pennington Bay**, one of the island's best surfing and surf-fishing spots.

## Sleeping & Eating

Most of Penneshaw's accommodation is near the ferry terminal. See Accommodation (p116) for details on the old lighthouse keeper's quarters at Cape Willoughby.

**Penguin Walk YHA Hostel** ( ☎ 8553 1344; www .yha.com.au; 33 Middle Tce; dm/d $23/60, d/tr with bathroom $75/90; ☒ ☒ ) The YHA's spacious, modern rooms have linen, an en suite bathroom, table and large luggage lockers. There's a small communal kitchen and lounge, a laundry and resident penguins in the garden, which overlooks Hog Bay.

**Marty's** ( ☎ 8553 1227; www.martysoasis.com.au; North Tce; dm/tw $25/55; 🖳 ) Sunshine yellow and blue, this place is basic but clean with a TV lounge, table tennis and a grassy communal garden. It's behind the café-pizzeria.

**Kangaroo Island Seafront** ( ☎ 8553 1028; www .seafront.com.au; 49 North Tce; d/tr $120/145, ocean view $210, chalets $195, cottages $175; 🏊 🖳 ) This hilltop hotel has a range of accommodation. Standard motel-style rooms are in the original guesthouse, and slightly more modern and spacious ones come with ocean-view rooms. Nestled behind native trees, the secluded self-contained chalets and cottages are serviced and sleep up to three and six respectively. The attached, beachy **Sorrento's Restaurant** (mains $16.50-24.50; 🕑 breakfast & dinner) serves KI produce and local seafood, including squid and oven-baked octopus.

**Seaview Lodge** ( ☎ 8553 1132; www.seaviewlodge .com.au; Willoughby Rd; tw or d with bathroom $155; 3-course meals $55) This gracious B&B is in a

beautifully restored 1860 farm homestead with cottage gardens and lovely views. It's at the Kingscote end of town.

**Beach House** ( ☎ 8331 1841; Browns Beach; d $160, extra person $25) A secluded three-bedroom shack on the beachfront with plenty of resident penguins to keep you company. It sleeps up to six and is 13km west of Penneshaw.

The visitors centre issues **camping permits** ($3.85) for bush sites at **Chapmans River** (on Antechamber Bay) and **Browns Beach** (12km from town on the Kingscote road). The sites are attractive, but facilities are rudimentary.

**Penguin Stop Café** ( ☎ 8553 1211; Middle Tce; dishes $7-12; 🕑 10am-5pm Mon-Fri, 9am-4pm Sat) Kangaroo Island's gourmet specialists serve up local produce in snapping fresh lunches and mouth-watering cakes. Pre-order picnic hampers to sample the island's fare on the go.

The popular, basic family bistro at **Penneshaw Hotel** (North Tce; mains $9-19; 🕑 lunch & dinner) serves grills and seafood, while **Marty's** ( ☎ 8553 1227; North Tce; pizzas $11-16; 🕑 lunch & dinner) does a roaring pizza trade.

## MINGLING WITH THE LOCALS

Kangaroo Island was originally covered by mallee and tea-tree scrub, with large trees generally confined to the wetter western end. Although most of the island is farmed, there's quite a bit of native bush remaining in road reserves and conservation areas. From July to November it's obvious why KI is referred to as a **wild flower** garden.

One of the island's most common eucalypts – the narrow-leafed mallee – is an excellent source of **eucalyptus oil**; it once supported a thriving industry and is still distilled on the island.

Wildlife tends to be more of a feature here than on the mainland due to the lack of dingoes, foxes and rabbits, though feral cats, which you'll occasionally find nailed to trees, and wild pigs wreak havoc for some species and their environment. **Grey kangaroos**, **wallabies**, **bandicoots** and **possums** are fairly common and particularly visible at dawn and dusk. Animals abound in wilderness areas, particularly the Rocky River area of Flinders Chase National Park. **Tammar wallabies** are a serious pest to many farmers (some say due to the loss of their habitat) and thousands are shot each year.

**Koalas** and the **platypus** were introduced to Flinders Chase National Park many years ago when it was feared they might become extinct on the mainland. Ironically, koala numbers on the island have increased to the point where they are at risk of starvation, and heated debate rages over whether to cull or relocate them to the mainland. **Echidnas** are native to the island, but, like the platypus, they are shy and rarely seen. Around the southern coast are colonies of **New Zealand fur seals** and **Australian sea lions**, and **dolphins** and **southern right whales** are often seen offshore.

Of the 243 **bird species** recorded on the island, several are either rare or endangered on the mainland. One species – the dwarf emu – has become extinct since European settlement, and there are fears the **glossy black cockatoo** may soon join it. Only a few hundred of these large, noisy birds are left due to the widespread destruction of coastal she-oak woodlands both here and on the mainland (she-oak seeds are their exclusive diet). Bird-watchers benefit from an expert's eye and knowledge on tours with ornithologist **Chris Baxter** ( ☎ 08-8553 5303; baxterfarm@bigpond.com).

## PLAYFORD HIGHWAY

The bitumen Playford Hwy traverses the centre of the island, veering away from Birchmore Rd (which turns into South Coast Rd) near Cygnet River, 12km from Kingscote. Here, **Island Pure Sheep Dairy** (Map p115; ☎ 08-8553 9110; Gum Creek Rd, Cygnet River; adult/child $5/4; ❧ 1-5pm) will take you on a journey through cheese production. You can also taste their highly regarded yoghurts and cheeses (in Spanish, Greek, Italian and Cypriot styles) and watch sheep being milked (from 3pm).

The inland to the small farming community of **Parndana**, 39km from Kingscote, has a well-stocked general store, hotel, fuel sales, Internet access, a launderette, and the **Parndana Wildlife Park** (Map p115; ☎ 08-8559 6050; ❧ 9am-5pm), where you can catch up on wildlife if you've had your eyes closed while travelling around the island. From here you can travel along Stokes Bay Rd to Stokes Bay (22km), along Hickman's Rd to the south, or continue along Playford Hwy, which leads 36km to the West End Hwy then becomes a dirt road for the 30km to Cape Borda.

## NORTH COAST ROAD

Stunning beaches, cliffs, bushland and rolling farmland line the North Coast Rd from Kingscote along the coast to meet the Playford Hwy about 85km from town (the bitumen only stretches as far as Emu Bay). Apart from small shops at Emu Bay and Stokes Bay there are no facilities along this road.

### Sights & Activities

The 5km-long sandy beach at **Emu Bay**, 18km from Kingscote, is one of the island's best swimming spots. It's very popular in summer and is one of the few beaches onto which you can drive a car.

About 36km further west, **Stokes Bay** has a beautiful beach, a penguin rookery and a large rock pool suitable for swimming; walk through a natural tunnel among huge boulders just east of the car park. There's a dangerous rip outside the pool.

On the way in you'll pass **Stokes Bay Bush Garden** (Map p115; ☎ 08-8559 2244; adult/child $5/ free), where you can take a stroll through the native bush protecting rare and endangered plants. Nearby, you can feed kangaroos and hold a koala on a tour of **Paul's Place** (Map p115; ☎ 08-8559 2232; ❧ call for opening times).

Stunning **Snelling Beach** looks ⸮ magnificent from North Coast Rd a⸮ climb onto the plateau to the west. Con tinue 7km west and you'll come to the turnoff to **Western River Cove**, where a pleasant beach is crowded by sombre cliffs at either end. The mouth of the river is quite pretty, with jagged grey rocks decorated with vivid splashes of green algae and orange lichen. The road to the cove is extremely scenic as it winds about on the ridge tops, with big gums, deep gullies and fine views most of the way. However, steep slopes make it unsuitable for caravans – the same applies to the southern access, which turns off North Coast Rd 6km further on.

About 3km west as the crow flies, but 26km by road, is **Western River Conservation Park**. Its major scenic highlight (in winter and early spring) is a picturesque waterfall that tumbles into a deep, dark gully. Don't try to get to the bottom of the hill in a conventional vehicle if the track is anything but dry.

### Sleeping & Eating

**Kangaroo Island Experience & Rock Pool Cafe** ( ☎ 08-8559 2277; www.kiexperience.com; Stokes Bay; unpowered sites per 2 people $10; luxury tents d $130) You can dine alfresco on seafood with a glass of local wine at this place in Stokes Bay. It also has a small, grassed campsite with rainwater for drinking (but no showers) and basic provisions. The self-contained luxury tents are between Stokes Bay and Snelling.

**Western River Cove** ( ☎ 08-8553 1185; campsites $3.85) Although uninspiring in itself, the camping area is only a short walk from a nice beach. It has toilets and a picnic shelter but no showers. Get permits from the Kangaroo Island Gateway visitors centre.

Also in Emu Bay is the much-talkedabout **KI Health Retreat** (see p116).

Plenty of fully-equipped holiday rentals are available in Emu Bay – many of which are built on the hill and maximise stunning views of the bay. You'll need to bring your own supplies. For details, see Accommodation (p115) or try:

**Loverings Beach Houses** ( ☎ 08-8553 8261; Emu Bay; PO Box 155, Kingscote 5223; d from $75, extra person $10) Houses sleep up to 10 people.

**Wintersun** ( ☎ 08-8553 5163; www.emubayholidays .com.au; Emu Bay; d from $100, extra person $15; ❧ ) Neat and modern 2-bedroom beachside units and 3-bedroom houses.

**Emu Bay Holiday Homes** ( ☎ 08-8553 5241; www
.emubaysuperviews.com.au; r per person from $35) Cosy
(and a bit frilly) cabins and holiday homes on a property
set back a bit from the beach, but with expansive views.
Cot and highchair available.

## SOUTH COAST ROAD

South Coast Rd (as Birchmore Rd) turns off
Hog Bay Rd (the Kingscote to Penneshaw
road) about 15km from Kingscote and ter-
minates 105km further on at West Bay, in
Flinders Chase National Park. Apart from
the coast and the wild flowers in spring,
the scenery along the road itself is nothing
startling until you get to the tall timber at
Kelly Hill Caves, but there are plenty of
sights along the way.

Kangaroo Island's south coast is exposed
to the Southern Ocean and is a wild contrast to the sheltered north. Given any sort
of blow from the south the shore is awash
with booming breakers and great clouds
of spray. It's easy to see why some of the
island's worst shipwrecks occurred here.

### Sights & Activities

A detour off either Hog Bay or Birchmore
Rds will take you past the **Emu Ridge Eucalyptus Distillery** ( ☎ 08-8553 8228; Willsons Rd; MacGillivary; ☺ 9am-2pm), a self-sufficient operation
extracting eucalyptus oil from the KI narrow leaf mallee. The attached craft gallery
sells plenty of eucalyptus oil products, including chemical-free beauty products and
delicious eucalyptus drops.

It's almost worth swimming the Backstairs Passage for the honey ice cream at
nearby **Clifford's Honey Farm** ( ☎ 08-8553 8295;
Elsegood Rd, MacGillivary; ☺ 9am-5pm), and to taste
a few of the honeys made by the last remaining colony of pure Ligurian bees – the
mallee variety is like liquid gold!

The turn-off to **Cape Gantheaume Conservation Park** is 24km from Kingscote, followed
by a rough 16km to **Murray Lagoon** and the
**ranger's office** ( ☎ 08-8553 8233). This is KI's
largest wetland and you'll usually see hundreds of swans, ducks, waders and other
water birds (the Bald Hill walk will reveal its
delights). Ospreys and sea eagles nest along
the coastal cliffs of Cape Gantheaume, a
wilderness protection area.

From the ranger's office it's 23km to **Point
Tinline**, a popular surfing and surf-fishing
spot on the stunning **D'Estrees Bay**. If you're

feeling fit you can walk around the coast
to Seal Bay, seeing spectacular cliffs and
colonies of New Zealand fur seals and Australian sea lions en route. It's mostly an
easy and enjoyable walk, but it takes two
days and there's no drinking water; check
with the ranger at Murray Lagoon before
setting out.

At **Seal Bay Conservation Park** ( ☎ 08-8559
4207), ranger-guided tours stroll the beach
alongside a large colony of (mostly sleeping) Australian sea lions. About 500 sea
lions live here, but you'll only see around
200 basking along the water's edge, even
on a warm day. You'll get close enough
for good photos, but don't expect exciting
action unless it's the breeding season. The
**information centre** has displays on issues af-
fecting sea life, including a disturbing one
on the effects of plastic rubbish on sea birds
and mammals. Tours (beach and boardwalk
adult/child/family $12.50/7.50/24) depart
from here between 9am and 4.15pm daily
(and also at 7pm during summer holidays).
The nearby **lookout** ($9/5.50/24) offers fine
views along the beach.

Back on South Coast Rd, the next turn-
off on your left (just before the Eleanor
River, about 7km from the Seal Bay road)
will take you to **Little Sahara**, a vast expanse
of white sand hills rising above the surrounding mallee scrub.

Further towards the west, **Vivonne Bay** has
a quiet settlement and beautiful sweeping
beach. This is a good surfing spot with some
of the strongest waves on the coast, but seek
local advice before plunging in as there are
some fierce undertows. Just east of town,
KI Outdoor Action has plenty of activities
(see p116).

Nearby to Flinders Chase National Park
is **Kelly Hill Conservation Park** ( ☎ 08-8559 7231),
where a series of dry limestone caves dates
back 80,000 years and has gravity-defying
helictites. The story goes that these caves
were 'discovered' in the 1880s by a horse
named Kelly, which fell into them through
a hole. There's a pleasant picnic area among
tall gums and some interesting short walks
over the tops of the caves.

Guided tours of the **show cave** (adult/child/
family $10.50/6.50/28) leave every 45 minutes be-
tween 10am and 4.15pm daily, more regularly during school holidays. Adventure
**caving tours** (adult/child/family $26.50/16/71) depart

at 2pm; book ahead. The **Hanson Bay Walk** (9km) takes you from the caves through mallee scrub and past freshwater wetlands, with fine coastal views at the mouth of Southwest River at Hanson Bay.

You're pretty much guaranteed to see a few koalas on a self-guided 'koala walk' at **Hanson Bay Sanctuary** ( ☎ 08-8559 7344; www.esl .com.au/hansonbay.htm; gold coin donation).

## Sleeping & Eating

Whether you're camping at a basic site or staying in motel-style rooms, 'roos, wallabies and other wildlife will never be far from view. There's basic **bush camping** (Cape Gantheaume Conservation Park; per person $4, per car & up to 5 people $6.50) at Murray Lagoon and D'Estrees Bay.

**Kaiwarra Food Barn** (Map p115; ☎ 08-8559 6115; South Coast Rd; dm $22, cottages from $60) Opposite the Seal Bay turn-off, the self-contained wooden cabins here sleep up to six people. Light meals (including marron) and Devonshire teas are served in the licensed Food Barn.

**Blue Hills Farm Stay** (Map p115; ☎ 08-8559 4204; http://bluehills_farmstay.tripod.com; Crabbs Rd; d $90, extra person over 3 $10) Comfy accommodation, friendly residents and an excellent family experience (including cow milking) are the go on this mixed farm, 6km from South Coast Rd. Breakfast provisions provided; country meals available.

**Vivonne Bay Camping Ground** ( ☎ 08-8559 4287; camp/van sites per 2 people $4.40/8.80, power $2.20, extra person $1.10) Rough and ready sites are pleasantly situated in bushland off the road to the jetty. There are barbecues and toilets but no showers.

**Vivonne Bay Store** ( ☎ 08-8559 4285; meals $6.50-13; ☺ breakfast & lunch; ☐ ) This friendly general store–cum-café has an exhaustive list of takeaway meals, all-day breakfasts, deli foods and meat. It also stocks fuel, fishing bait and tackle, liquor and offers postal services.

**Western Kangaroo Island Caravan Park** (Map p115; ☎ 08-8559 7201; www.westernki.com.au; South Coast Rd; unpowered/powered sites per 2 people $17/21, self-contained cabins $90-120 ☒ ) Just a few minutes' drive east of Rocky River, this ultrafriendly and relaxed farm-based caravan park has good facilities, including a camp kitchen with plenty of covered tables and laundry amenities. Check out the koala walk and the very cool telephone cabin in an old bakery truck. The shop sells limited groceries, fruit and vegetables, meat, tasty home-

made heat-and-eat meals (such as curries) and (for guests only) beer and wine.

**Kangaroo Island Wilderness Resort** (Map p115; ☎ 08-8559 7275; www.austdreaming.com.au; South Coast Rd; dm $40, d $120-180; bar meals $10-20, restaurant mains $29-28; ☒ ☐ ) This well-planned ecoresort on the national park's boundary provides its guests with an overwhelming wildlife experience. Typical counter meals (such as schnitzel and grills) are available at the wall-less Bushman's Bar, while the restaurant serves Mod Oz cuisine with plenty of local ingredients. Limited groceries, local food products, takeaway foods and petrol are available at the shop. Kangaroo Island Discovery Tours run from here (see Tours p117).

**Flinders Chase Farm** ( ☎ 08-8559 7223; chillers@ internode.on.net; West End Hwy; dm/cabins $20/50, d & tw with bathroom $70) There's a casual charm to this farm, about 10 minutes' drive from Rocky River, with cosy 'love shacks', dorms in wooden buildings and tropical bathrooms. There's a good outdoor kitchen, a campfire area and roaming kangaroos.

## FLINDERS CHASE NATIONAL PARK

Occupying the western end of the island, Flinders Chase is one of SA's most significant national parks. Much of the park is mallee scrub, but there are some beautiful, tall sugar-gum forests, particularly around Rocky River and the Ravine des Casoars, 5km south of Cape Borda. There's wild, often spectacular scenery right around the coast, which you can reach from roads and walking tracks.

The **Flinders Chase visitors centre** ( ☎ 08-8559 7235; Rocky River; ☺ 10am-5pm, from 9am in summer) supplies useful information and park maps, and has displays on the changing landscape of the island, prehistoric animals, current ecosystems and a fossil sandpit for budding archaeologists. It also stocks plenty of souvenirs and books on the island's nature and ecology, and has a good café and toilets.

## Sights & Activities

Once a farm, **Rocky River** is an excellent spot to see wildlife with plenty of 'roos, wallabies and Cape Barren geese lining the road in. Kangaroos at Rocky River have become so brazen that they'll badger you for food (parks officers request that you don't succumb to their demands). Plenty of good walks start from behind the visitors centre, including one to potentially view the platypus (4.5km return).

From Rocky River a road leads south to a 1906 lighthouse perched atop wild and remote **Cape du Couedic**. A boardwalk leads down to **Admirals Arch**, a spectacular archway formed by pounding seas, and passes through a colony of New Zealand fur seals which are fascinating to watch (once you get used to the ripe smell).

At Kirkpatrick Point, a few kilometres east of Cape du Couedic, the **Remarkable Rocks** are a cluster of huge, weather-sculpted granite boulders perched on a dome that swoops 75m down to the sea. En route you pass **Weirs Cove**, where a flying fox once brought supplies up the cliffs from the small landing far below.

Another road will take you from Rocky River to picturesque **West Bay**, a good surf-fishing spot. Behind the beach, a wooden cross marks the grave of an unknown sailor from the windjammer *Loch Vennachar,* lost nearby with all hands in 1905.

This road passes the starting points of three short walking tracks that lead down to the sea: the longest, and arguably the most interesting, is the 6km return walk to **Breakneck River**. It features beautiful gums, chuckling tea-coloured water and spectacular coastal scenery.

To get to **Cape Borda** ( ☎ 08-8559 3257), which features a lighthouse (1858) atop soaring cliffs, you can take either the dirt Shackle Rd (pick up a driving tour brochure from the national park office) or West End Hwy and Playford Hwy. Guided lighthouse **tours** (adult/child/student $10.50/6.50/28) are run at 11am, 12.30pm and 2pm, with extra tours

at 3.15pm and 4pm during summer holidays. The cannons are fired on the 12.30pm tour.

Nearby, at **Harvey's Return**, a poignant cemetery speaks volumes about the reality of isolation in the early days. It's a long scramble down to the stony beach, which has unusual striped rocks and the remains of a haulage way. This is where supplies for the lighthouse staff were landed. You have to wonder how they managed to get the cargo out of the boat without losing half of it, not to mention the work involved in getting it up the hill.

From Harvey's Return you can drive to **Ravine des Casoars** (literally 'Ravine of the Cassowaries', referring to the now-extinct dwarf emus seen here by Baudin's expedition). There's a beautiful walk down to the coast, with tall gums beside a gurgling stream. It's a great spot for bird-watching and listening to the sounds of nature.

## Sleeping & Eating

Within Flinders Chase National Park the main campsite is at **Rocky River** (kiparksaccom@saugov.sa.gov.au; sites with car & up to five people $19.50, per person $5.50), with shower facilities, roaming wildlife, walking tracks and the luxury of the visitors centre's **Chase café** (dishes $5.50-12.50; ☺ 9am-5pm). There are also basic sites at **Snake Lagoon**, **West Bay** and **Harvey's Return** (sites with car & up to five people $6.50, per person $4). Keep all food secured in your car if you have one. The **DEH** has some beautiful refurbished heritage accommodation at Rocky River, Cape du Couedic and Cape Borda; see Accommodation (p115) for details.

See p125 for options just outside the national park.

# Murray River

CONTENTS

| | |
|---|---|
| **Murraylands** | **130** |
| Murray Bridge | 130 |
| Mannum | 133 |
| **The Riverland** | **135** |
| Blanchetown | 135 |
| Barmera | 135 |
| Loxton | 137 |
| Berri | 138 |
| Renmark | 140 |

Australia's greatest river starts in the Snowy Mountains of New South Wales (NSW), and for most of its length forms the boundary between NSW and Victoria. Meandering for 650km through South Australia (SA), it is wide and serene often lined with shimmering yellow cliffs.

The Murray is a bolt hole for many Adelaidians, where the dreamy waters act as a soothing ointment for the pressures of city life. Whether pottering about in a dinghy pretending to fish, cruising in a houseboat, hanging off the back of a ski-boat for dear life or gliding through backwater reserves in a canoe, this river is a mecca for modest hedonists and nature lovers.

The Murray is lined almost throughout with huge river red gums, and is home to flora and fauna reliant on riverside habitats. The Murray River National Park and Chowilla Game Reserve and Regional Reserve form part of the renowned Unesco Bookmark Biosphere Reserve. These are major breeding grounds for the state's waterfowl and other birds.

The Murray is certainly a river of life for South Australians, many of whom rely wholly or partly on it for their livelihood or their domestic water supplies. However, there is an unfortunate tendency to take the river for granted. As a result, deteriorating water levels have become a major conservation issue, especially in SA. Native birds, fish and wetland habitats are suffering considerably. This dire situation has resulted in ongoing 'negotiations' between federal and state political bodies to agree on what levels of water flow are required to keep the river healthy.

## HIGHLIGHTS

- Looking up at lanky giraffes and down at scurrying bilbies at **Monarto Zoological Park** (p131)
- Luxuriating on a **floating mansion** hired in pretty Mannum (p130)
- Tickling a hairy-nosed wombat at **Brookfield Conservation Park** (p135)
- Sipping chilled pink Shiraz on the deck of winery & bird reserve **Banrock Station** (p136)
- Paddling a canoe along the serene creek in **Chowilla Game Reserve** and **Chowilla Regional Reserve** (p140)
- Exploring vast **Gluepot Reserve** (p136) revelling in the bird, reptile and bat species
- Cruising and partying on the splendid paddle-wheeler **Murray River Princess** (p134)
- Whirling your partner to the sounds of the **South Australian Country Music Festival** (p131)

- TELEPHONE CODE: ☎ 08
- murraylands.info
- www.riverland.info

## National Parks

The **Department for Environment & Heritage** (DEH; ☎ 08-8595 2111; www.environment.sa.gov.au/parks; 28 Vaughan St, Berri; 🕑9am-4pm Mon-Fri) has information, trail maps, park and camping passes. Visitors centres can also help with permits. Parks and reserves include Chowilla Game Reserve and Regional Reserve, Bookmark Biosphere Reserve and Gluepot Reserve as well as Danggali, Billiatt, Brookfield, Big Bend and Swan Reach Conservation Parks.

## Information

There are many places along the Murray where the road crosses the river by vehicle ferry. The ferries are free and usually run 24 hours a day.

**Canoe SA** (☎ 8240 3294; www.sa.canoe.org.au) publishes a series of canoe trail guides to the Murray and associated wetlands. Pick up these free guides from the outdoor shops in Adelaide (p80).

## Tours

Locally operated tours tend to be better than those operating ex-Adelaide. Check with visitors centres and read the individual town information for recommended local tours.

Adelaide coach tour operators **Premier Stateliner** (☎ 8415 5566; www.premierstateliner.com; Adelaide central bus station, 111 Franklin St, Adelaide) and **Adelaide Sightseeing** (☎ 8231 4144; www.adel aidesightseeing.com.au; Adelaide central bus station, 111 Franklin St, Adelaide) offer a day trip to Mannum,

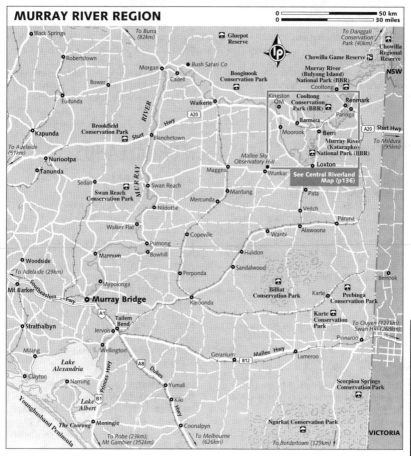

MURRAY RIVER REGION

---

### HOUSEBOATS

One thing that most South Australians would agree on is that the Murray River has a special aura and mystique. Therefore sailing serenely along this gentle waterway for a few days is the best way to restore anyone's equilibrium. To add to this, South Australians usually wish to travel in surroundings that are more than just comfortable, and conducive to much merriment and sensual fun.

A range of truly superb houseboats can be hired by anyone with these requirements and a driving licence. Standard facilities are modern, very comfortable and spacious. Facilities normally include two-way radios, air-con, fabulous fitted kitchens (with dishwasher and microwave), TV/ video, barbecue and canopied sundecks. Not bad, when 'normal season' rates for a week average out to $33 per person, per night for a four-berth. Berths can accommodate two to 12 people.

Even the floating mansions are affordable. Worth around $3 to $4 million each, these boats are two- or three-storeys high, with glass walls, Jacuzzis, cocktail bars, home theatres and vast living areas. Twelve people over a 'normal season' week will only pay $60 per night each.

Mannum, where quality boats are built, is the real centre of activity, although houseboats can be hired from Adelaide and most riverside towns. Around Mannum the scenery is attractive, although the waterway is a little busier than upstream of Renmark, where the cliffs are also more prominent.

Book well ahead, especially for the months from October to April. The very friendly **Houseboat Hirers Association** ( ☎ 08-8395 0999; www.houseboat-centre.com.au; 7 Gollop Crescent, Redwood Park, Adelaide) have a houseboat holiday brochure detailing each boat and can make free bookings on your behalf.

Prices are the cheapest in winter or the off-peak season, which is from the beginning of June until the end of August. 'Normal' season is from the beginning of September to 12 December, and then from 27 January to 31 May. 'Peak' season covers the main holiday breaks: 12 December to 27 January and 8 April to 13 April. Minimum bookings can apply.

---

a short cruise on the MV *Proud Mary* and lunch or tea at a local hotel ($99).

### Getting There & Away
**Premier Stateliner** ( ☎ 08-8415 5555; www.premier stateliner.com; Adelaide central bus station, 111 Franklin St, Adelaide) has daily services from Adelaide to the Riverland; Waikerie ($30, 2½ hours), Kingston-on-Murray (Kingston OM; $35, three hours), Berri ($38, 3½ hours) Loxton, Barmera and Renmark ($38, four hours).

**Murray Bridge Passenger Service** ( ☎ 08-8415 5579; www.premierstateliner.com.au; Adelaide central bus station, 111 Franklin St, Adelaide) runs from Adelaide to Murray Bridge ($15, 1¼ hours) and, Monday to Friday, to Mannum ($20, 2½ hours).

**Overland** (Great Southern Railway; ☎ 13 21 47, 08-8213 4444; www.trainways.com.au; Adelaide–Murray Bridge $7; ☺ Thu-Sun) passes through Murray Bridge from Adelaide to Melbourne.

**Greyhound Australia** ( ☎ 13 20 30; greyhound.com. au; ☺ daily) passes through Barmera ($36, four hours), Berri ($41, 4¼ hours) and Renmark ($46, 4¾ hours) on the way from Adelaide to Sydney.

# MURRAYLANDS

## MURRAY BRIDGE
☎ 08 / pop 13,017
South Australia's largest river town is very much a working town with little of interest for many visitors. However, there are some great children's adventure and wildlife parks nearby, which makes this town a super stop for families. Many South Australians also use the town as a base for fishing trips or stop here for river-holiday supplies and to pick up hired boats.

Dairying is a major industry, with cows being grazed on reclaimed swamp right along the river. Milk factories at Murray Bridge and nearby Jervois process most of SA's dairy products.

### Information
**Murray Bridge visitors centre** ( ☎ 8539 1142; mbvc@rcmb.sa.gov.au; 3 South Tce; ☺ 8.30am-5.30pm Mon-Fri, 10am-4pm Sat, Sun & public holidays) A little gold mine with comprehensive information and knowledge on the region and beyond.

## Sights & Activities

Attractions include the **Anglican Cathedral of St John the Baptist** ( ☎ 8532 2270; Mannum Rd) built in 1887. It is claimed to be the smallest cathedral in the world, with the shortest prayers, perhaps? Call at the Registry (4 Clara St) for access.

**Captain's Cottage Museum** ( ☎ 8531 0049; 12 Thomas St; adult/child $3.50/1; ☼ 10am-4pm weekends & public holidays) has exhibits on the town's early farming and riverboat days.

**Dundee's Wildlife Park** ( ☎ 8532 3666; dundees @lm.net.au; 3166 Jervois Rd; adult/child $8/5; ☼ 10am-5pm) is 4km out of town just beyond the Southeastern Fwy. Children really love this place, and saltie and freshwater crocs are a big drawcard. Additionally there are native birds (including many gorgeous parrots), snakes, a kiddies' zoo and various furry mammals, some of which can be cuddled. All-you-can-eat meals ($8 to $15) and a beer garden keep mum and dad happy.

Next door, **Puzzle Park** ( ☎ 8532 3709; Jervois Rd; adult/child $14/7; ☼ 10am-5pm) is another children's paradise. More than 30 rides include a 90m waterslide, toddlers' and puzzle pool, fort, maze, paddleboats, minigolf and a flying fox – whee! Who has time for the barbecue or licensed café?

**Sturt Reserve** is the point of departure for riverboat cruises, and has been well developed as another fun place for the family. There's a BMX track, two pipe-skate ramps, a Rage Cage (multi-use sporting complex),

free playground, coin-operated barbecues and Bertha the Bunyip. Bertha is an Aboriginal Dreamtime monster who lives in the water. This wonderful animatronic model will surprise her audience; anyone with a sense of humour and a dollar to spare.

**Murray Bridge Drive-in Cinema** ( ☎ 8532 3666, 8532 1836; Swanport Rd; per legal car load $18; ☼ 7.30pm Wed, Sat & Sun) is one of the state's last two drive-in cinemas (the other is in Barmera, p136, so enjoy a film under the stars, with a blanket and popcorn.

On 1000 hectares, 20km west of town, the fabulous **Monarto Zoological Park** ( ☎ 8534 4100; www.monartozp.com.au; Old Princes Hwy, Monarto; adult/child/family $16/10/52; ☼ 10am-3.30pm) is certainly worth a detour. See free-range cheetahs, lions, rhinos, African painted dogs, zebras, giraffes, meerkats and the endangered and very cute bilby. A host of native creatures makes up a big list! A one-hour guided safari bus tour and a walk with a guide are included in the price. There are also walking tracks, hot air balloon flights, a bistro and disabled facilities. The **Murray Bridge Passenger Service** ( ☎ 8415 5533; Adelaide central bus station, 111 Franklin St, Adelaide; adult/child $30/15; ☼ departs Adelaide 9am & returns from Monarto at 12.45pm Mon-Fri, departs Adelaide noon & returns from Monarto at 3.45pm Sat) offers the only public transport to the park.

### RIVER CRUISES

The following operators run short cruises that welcome families or wining and dining

---

**FESTIVALS & EVENTS**

Check with local visitors centres for possible date changes for this selection of events.

**Riverland Rodeo** ( ☎ 08-8582 5511; Jan) Berri hosts the bucking broncos, and gals and guys of the rodeo circuit – Yeeha!

**Easter Sailing Regatta** ( ☎ 08-8588 2289; Apr) Serene Lake Bonney is made for this elegant racing spectacle.

**Riverland Balloon Fiesta** ( ☎ 08-8586 6704; May) Renmark bursts with hot air and colour this month.

**South Australian Country Music Festival & Awards** ( ☎ 08-8341 0979; www.riverlandcountrymusic .com; Jun) Line up for some grand dancing and music in Barmera.

**South Australian Stumpy Awards** ( ☎ 08-8539 1142; Aug) The Murraylands Bush Poetry Competition is a two-day play with words. All single and rhyming couplets welcome in Murray Bridge!

**Australian International Pedal Prix** ( ☎ 08-8539 1142; Sep) Boys and girls of all ages head for Murray Bridge with their home-made pedal or box carts to join in hilarious street races; tremendous fun.

**Barmera Sheepdog Trials** ( ☎ 08-8588 2559; Oct) Canines show us all up, yet again…

**Murray Bridge Gold Cup Races** ( ☎ 08-8539 1142; Oct) A dress-up fiesta of fun, horse races and, hopefully, many winning tickets.

**Riverland Food & Wine Festival** ( ☎ 08-8582 3321; Oct) Sip and savour some regional goodies in Berri.

**Loxton Christmas Lights** ( ☎ 08-8584 7919; Dec) Loxton lights up with more than a hundred sparkling and flashing houses.

**MURRAY RIVER**

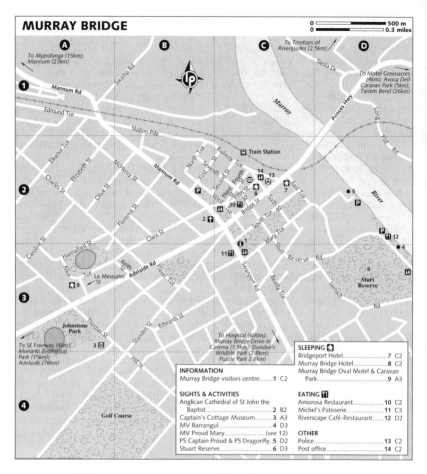

## MURRAY BRIDGE

0 ————— 500 m
0 ————— 0.3 miles

To Treetops of Riverglades (2.5km)

To Mypolonga (15km); Mannum (23km)

To Motel Greenacres (4km); Avoca Dell Caravan Park (5km); Tailem Bend (26km)

Train Station

To Treetops of Riverglades (2.5km)

To Hospital (600m); Murray Bridge Drive-In Cinema (1.5km); Dundee's Wildlife Park (2.8km); Puzzle Park 2.8km)

To SE Freeway (4km); Monarto Zoological Park (15km); Adelaide (78km)

Johnstone Park

Golf Course

Sturt Reserve

**INFORMATION**
Murray Bridge visitors centre.......1 C2

**SIGHTS & ACTIVITIES**
Anglican Cathedral of St John the
  Baptist.......................................2 B2
Captain's Cottage Museum.........3 A3
MV Barrangul................................4 D3
MV Proud Mary.....................(see 12)
PS Captain Proud & PS Dragonfly..5 D2
Stuart Reserve.............................6 D3

**SLEEPING**
Bridgeport Hotel..........................7 C2
Murray Bridge Hotel....................8 C2
Murray Bridge Oval Motel & Caravan
  Park........................................9 A3

**EATING**
Amorosa Restaurant..................10 C2
Michel's Patisserie......................11 C3
Riverscape Café-Restaurant.......12 D2

**OTHER**
Police.........................................13 C2
Post office..................................14 C2

enthusiasts of the Murray River. Dining rates depend on a number of factors, so check with the visitors centre for cruises to suit your mood. The **MV Barrangul** ( ☎ 0407-395 385; adult/family $12/30) departs daily from the Sturt Reserve and offers lunch and dinner cruises. The **PS Captain Proud & Dragonfly** ( ☎ 8532 2292; www.captainproud.com; adult $12; Wed, Fri-Mon) offers lunch and dinner cruises (PS *Captain Proud*), or short cruises (PS *Dragonfly*) which depart from the Murray Bridge Wharf. The **MV Proud Mary** ( ☎ 8231 9472; www.proudmary.com.au; Proud Australia Nature Cruises, Level 4, 18-20 Grenfell St, Adelaide; adult/child $24/14; 11am Fri) also has a choice of cruises. Booking is essential for all three options.

## Sleeping

**Treetops of Riverglades** ( ☎ 8532 6483; 32 Torrens Rd; 2-person 2-night $200; ) This modern double-storey retreat overlooks bird-filled wetlands, and offers secluded views from a wide balcony. Other facilities include a wood heater, barbecue and canoes. Not one for the kids.

**Avoca Dell Caravan Park** ( ☎ 8532 2095; 199 Murray Dr; unpowered sites per 2 people/vans/cabins with bathroom $22/50/70; ) Roughly 6km out of town, this cheerful and small park sits on tiered levels overlooking the river. Facilities include a camp kitchen, barbecue and minigolf.

**Motel Greenacres** ( ☎ 8532 1090; 140 Princes Hwy; s/d $70/82; ) Five kilometres east of the town centre and without a doubt the best

MURRAY RIVER

of the motels. The rooms are small, but immaculate, cheerful and bright. Family units, a barbecue and lawn add to the welcoming facilities.

**Murray Bridge Oval Motel & Caravan Park** ( ☎ 8532 2388; 4 Le Messurier St; cabins with bathroom $55/60, motel d $85; 🔀 ) With spotless and colourful motel rooms, and good deals on cabins.

Many of the town's central lodgings are a little dated, although welcoming enough. If you are in the market, it may be worth checking up with the visitors centre for additional B&Bs that lie just out of town. For budget rooms in town, the **Murray Bridge Hotel** ( ☎ 8532 2024; mbchotel@lm.com.au; 20 Sixth St; s/d $35/55; 🔀 ) and **Bridgeport Hotel** ( ☎ 8532 2002; bridgeport.hotel@lhgroup.com.au; 2 Bridge St; s/d $30/58; 🔀 ) both have rooms with basic facilities, although the Bridgeport has a small common room with a TV.

### Eating
The Bridgeport and Murray Bridge Hotels (above) have the usual good-value counter meals.

**Riverscape Café-Restaurant** ( ☎ 8531 0855; Sturt Reserve; mains $18-25; 🕙 lunch & dinner) Sit on the balcony and watch the river and people drift by. A combination of friendly service and meals of weight-gaining proportions keep this place busy. Monday and Tuesday nights are $8-schnitzel nights. Save space for the desserts; you could sleep in the chocolate cake.

**Amorosa Restaurant** ( ☎ 8531 0559; 55 Bridge St; mains $13-22; 🕙 lunch Mon-Fri, dinner Mon-Sat) This little restaurant sits in a shopfront among the streets takeaways, and is very popular. Amorosa's chef declares an Italian preference and specials include imaginative dishes such as the pan-fried sirloin served with olive croissants.

**Michel's Patisserie** ( ☎ 8531 0249; Woolworths complex, Swanport Rd; light meals $7; 🕙 breakfast & lunch) Cakes and filled savoury rolls are the speciality here. The coffee is good and the cakes are wicked, the creme anglaise and chocolate in particular. Coffee and cake is $9.

### Getting Around
**Murray Bridge Taxis** ( ☎ 8531 0555) operate 24 hours a day.

The visitors centre has route maps and timetables for the local bus service.

## MANNUM
☎ 08 / pop 2195
A thriving port until Murray Bridge took all its trade, picturesque Mannum found itself a new identity as the houseboat capital of SA. Houseboats are actually made here, and this is also the main centre from which to hire these luxurious floating penthouses (see p130). This neat and pretty little town sits on a wide section of the Murray River, alongside tall river gums and clusters of pelicans and waterfowl. It is a great spot for pottering about on a boat, walking or fishing.

### Information
The **visitors centre** ( ☎ 8569 1303; www.psmarion.com; 6 Randell St; 🕙 9am-5pm Mon-Fri, 10am-4pm Sat, Sun & public holidays) can make bookings for river cruises and houseboats. The centre also incorporates the **Mannum Dock Museum of River History** (adult/child $5/2) featuring the river, the Ngarrindjeri Aboriginal communities and the region's first paddle-wheelers, including the adjacent 1898 PS *Marion*. An art gallery displays travelling exhibitions.

### Sights & Activities
The free **Bird Sanctuary** is home to a number of waterfowl, while **Cascade Waterfalls**, 9km from town off the main road to Murray Bridge, are worth a visit for their picturesque and rugged scenery. Although the falls only flow during winter, the beautiful river red gums in the creek downstream of the gorge can be enjoyed at any time.

For houseboat hire see p130.

If you fancy water-skiing, fishing, canoeing or sailboarding, drop into **Breeze Holidays** ( ☎ 8569 2223; Main St, Mannum) for a range of equipment; canoes ($10 per hour), fishing gear including rod, tackle, yabby nets ($5 per hour), ski boat, driver and lessons ($120 per hour). Also ask about sailboards, catamarans, kneeboards and dinghies, which may be available.

Using his experience of building movie sets, Michael Chorney creates stunning garden and house sculptures that are designed from archaeological artefacts. **Chorney Studios Garden Art** ( ☎ 8569 2336; www.chorney-studios.com.au; East Front Rd) is 16km upstream from Mannum towards Younghusband.

Seventeen kilometres to the northwest of Swan Reach, vermin-proof fencing encloses

**THE AUTHOR'S CHOICE**

**PS Murray River Princess** ( ☎ 08-8569 2522; www.captaincookcruises.com.au; Captain Cook Cruises, 96 Randell St; d per 2 nights $414) This grand and ornate paddle-wheeler is a party boat, make no bones about it. The lovely old boat has three floors with chandeliers and rich furnishings. Shared spas, saunas, bars and a dining saloon mean that everyone mixes in together and has fun. Regular stops include guided nature and heritage walks, while the tranquil green water and shimmering yellow cliffs of the river valley dominate the scenery. Take a two-, three-, four- or five-night cruise; rates include everything except drinks. Three nights cost the same as two, and prices rise according to room type. Transfers from Adelaide are available.

more than 1000 hectares of virgin mallee at the **Yookamurra Sanctuary** ( ☎ 8562 5011; yookamurra@australianwildlife.org; adult/child $15/12). It holds guided nocturnal walks on the last Friday of every month and offers camping and walk packages (adult/child $50/45). See brush-tailed burrowing bettongs, stick-nest rats, bilbies, Mallee fowls and western grey 'roos. It's also home to around 100 species of birds, and the occasional orphaned hairy-nosed wombat baby. Book all visits in advance.

The **PS Marion** ( ☎ 8569 1303; Mary Ann Reserve; $11; ☽ 11am, 12.30pm, 2pm Fri, Sat & Sun) has been recommissioned since her birth in 1897, and takes occasional short trips. Check at the visitors centre about her schedule.

## Sleeping & Eating

**Mannum House B&B** ( ☎ 8569 2631; www.mannumhouse.com.au; 33 River Lane; d $135; ☒ ) This B&B is a little cracker, and one for couples who want cheerful surroundings, spick-and-span comfort, huge and tasty cooked breakfasts and great river views. A cosy guest sitting room looks over the river (shared only with fresh flowers, the other guest couple and the cat).

**Heritage Centre B&B** ( ☎ 8569 1987; 49 Randell St; s/d $95/120; ☒ ) A cute and petite cottage was built at the back of the old Mannum bank, up against a 20-million-year-old fossil wall. To the trained eye, markings depict global catastrophes such as the Ice Age. These extraordinary surroundings incorporate a

lovely four-poster bed and modern facilities. Definitely couples only, and basketball players are advised to look elsewhere.

**Mannum Motel** ( ☎ 8569 1808; www.mannummotel.com.au; 76 Cliff St; s/d/d with river view $75/80/90; mains $18-23; ☽ dinner Tue-Sun; ☒ ☒ ) This red-brick motel sits above the ferry landing and is also just a hop away from the centre of town. The rooms and holiday apartments are comfortable, if a little tired. Unit six has the best river view. There are also disabled facilities, a half-tennis court and some good deals available.

**Mannum Caravan Park** ( ☎ 8569 1402; mannpark@lm.net.au; Purnong Rd; unpowered/powered sites per 2 people $15/17, cabins d $58; ☒ ) Old fashioned by most standards, the facilities include a barbecue, showers and a kiosk. However, the park is set right on the riverside, is a five-minute walk to the main street, and has some small but well-equipped cabins (linen $10 per person).

**Pretoria Hotel** ( ☎ 8569 1109; www.pretoriahotel.com.au; Randell St; mains $15-20; ☽ lunch, dinner) The hotel has a vast and bland bistro, but attractive outside deck and riverside views. An indoor cubbyhole provides videos and amusements for kids and teens.

**Mannum Community Club** ( ☎ 8569 1010; Randell St; mains $8-17; ☽ lunch & dinner) A cheerful and relaxed atmosphere makes this club a great prospect for visitors and locals alike. A gleaming wooden bar leads to the dining room, where children are as welcome as adults.

**DETOUR: BIG BEND & SWAN REACH CONSERVATION PARK**

Take the eastern riverside route from Mannum to Swan Reach, via Bowhill, Purnong and Nildottie. This is a lovely section of the Murray River. Around 9km from Swan Reach the Murray makes a tight meander known as **Big Bend**; artists and photographers love this spot, with the sweeping curves of the river and glowing ochre-coloured cliffs.

Once you reach Swan Reach take the free ferry across the river and head west for 14km towards Sedan. The road leads to the 2017-hectare **Swan Reach Conservation Park**, a home to furry and feathered creatures including the rare hairy-nosed wombat, emus and kangaroos.

**Mannum Hotel** ( ☎ 8569 1808, 8569 1453; 76 Cliff St; mains $10-20; ☺ lunch & dinner) A traditional pub, nevertheless the cheaper bar food and more sophisticated dining menu are very popular. Check out the extensive wine list.

## Getting Around
**Mannum Taxis** ( ☎ 0428-834 861) runs limited hours (around 6am to 6pm) but it's worth asking about out-of-hours trips.

# THE RIVERLAND

The area between Blanchetown and Renmark is known as the Riverland. Through intensive irrigation this area has been turned into a major agricultural area, where hundreds of kilometres of dry, dusty bush and farmlands are interrupted by lush green citrus orchards, fruit farms and armies of vineyards and olive trees.

The Riverland is generally known for cask wines, and great value they are too. There are also a few cracking little wineries such as Bonneyview in Barmera, with Australia's oldest Petit Verdot vines, and the larger Angoves known for their St Agnes Brandy.

## BLANCHETOWN
☎ 08 / pop 211
**Brookfield Conservation Park** (5500 hectares) is about 9km west of the town on the Sturt Hwy. The park was originally purchased by the Chicago Zoological Society as a wombat reserve, and a 10km nature drive takes you through the haunts of southern hairy-nosed wombats, emus and kangaroos.

For a touch of Aussie sheep-station living, stay overnight at **Portee Station** ( ☎ 8540 5211; portee@portee.com.au; signposted 10km south of Blanchetown; s/d $135/190), B&B guests stay in the family's 1870s colonial-style homestead, with lawn sweeping down to the water's edge. The rooms are spotless and nicely furnished and there are expensive local tours on offer (from $70). Lambing occurs over three days in July and shearing in early June.

## BARMERA
☎ 08 / pop 1946
Barmera was once on the overland stock route from NSW and sits on the shores of the serene Lake Bonney. This wide and attractive freshwater lake is a great holiday

---

---

spot with safe swimming and small, sandy beaches.

Barmera is a corruption of Barmeedji, the name of the Aboriginal group that lived in this area at the time of white settlement. World land-speed record holder Donald Campbell failed in an attempted to break his water-speed record on this lake in 1964.

## Information
**Barmera visitors centre** ( ☎ 8588 2289; barmera vic@hotkey.net.au; Barwell Ave; 9am-5.15pm Mon-Fri, 9am-noon Sat, 10am-1pm Sun) A travel agent and booking service for coach companies at the Barmera Travel Centre.

## Sights & Activities
Lake Bonney is very popular for swimming and water sports, and even has a nudist beach at Pelican Point Nudist Resort (abandon all modesty ye who enters there) on the lake's western shore. The lake is ringed by large, dead red gums, whose stark branches are often festooned with cormorants.

On the road to Morgan, 19km northwest of town, the evocative 1859 **Overland Corner Hotel** ( ☎ 8588 7021; Old Coach Rd; ☺ 11am-10pm Mon-Sat, 11am-8pm Sun) is named after a bend in the Murray River where drovers and travellers once camped. It is a great pub serving bar food (meals $11 to $17), and has a resident ghost, a museum and a beer garden. An 8km self-guided **nature trail** leads down to the river from the pub past an ochre quarry and fossils. Pick up a map (50c) at the bar.

Throw your 10-gallon hat in the air with glee; the **South Australian Country Music Festival**

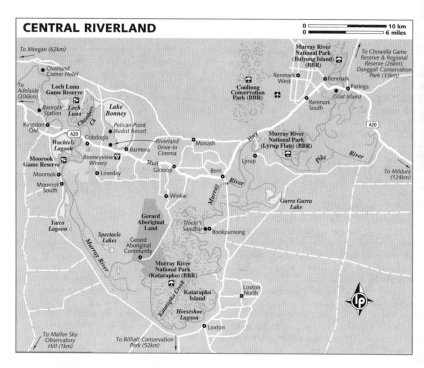

**CENTRAL RIVERLAND**

**& Awards** ( ☎ 8341 0979; www.riverlandcountrymusic .com) are celebrated with much merriment over 10 days in June.

The **Country Music Hall of Fame** ( ☎ 8588 1463; Barwell Ave; adult/child $2/1) is a tiny museum for die-hard fans; ask at the visitors centre about access.

**Riverland Drive-In Cinema** ( ☎ 8588 1188; www .riverlanddrivein.com; Sturt Hwy; per legal car load $18) has screenings most weekends. Take your sweetie for a snuggle under the stars; this is one of the few remaining drive-ins in the country.

The small and friendly **Bonneyview Winery** ( ☎ 8588 2279; bonneyview_wines@hotkey.net.au; Sturt Hwy; ☽ 10am-5pm) is famous for their current liqueur and Australia's oldest Petit Verdot vines. Local artist Gary Duncan's mosaic-style works are hung on the wall of the cellar door and super little restaurant.

Wildlife reserves with walking trails can be found at **Moorook Game Reserve** (on the road to Loxton) and at **Loch Luna** across the Murray from **Kingston-on-Murray** (Kingston OM); the latter backs onto the Overland Corner Hotel.

Twitchers should not miss **Gluepot Reserve** ( ☎ 8892 9600; gluepot@riverland.net.au; Gluepot Rd, off Lunn Rd, 64km north of Waikerie; per vehicle $6.50; per campers vehicle $12; ☽ 8am-6pm), Australia's largest community-owned and -managed conservation area. This huge (54,390 hectares) protected mallee scrub was set up by Birds Australia, and is part of Unesco's international Bookmark Biosphere Reserve. Dozens of different native birds are seen here, including 17 threatened species. There are also 50 reptile and 12 bat species.

Another one for fans of feathers or the grape; **Banrock Station** ( ☎ 8583 0299; www.banrock station.com.au; Holmes Rd off Sturt Hwy, Kingston OM; ☽ 10am-5pm) is an ecofriendly winery that produces really good, cheap wine. Try the fabulous sparkling Shiraz (chilled, of course); it will pop your corks! An outdoor deck overlooks a bird-filled wetland, and is a perfect setting for a light lunch or some supping. The 2.5km and 9km boarded wetland walks are massively popular with twitchers and are wheelchair friendly; bookings essential.

Hire canoes, kayaks and other gear from **Riverland Leisure Canoe Tours** ( ☎ 8588 2053; Thelma

Rd, Barmera; canoe/kayak per day $30/20); they will deliver to all towns around the river (incurring reasonable mileage costs) and offer guided canoe tours for an evening, half-day and full day with meals ($15/25/50).

**Eco Cruises** ( ☎ /fax 8583 0223; Kingston OM; adult $30; ⏰ 9am-noon, 2-5pm & 6-9pm) are very popular, and children under 12 are free if accompanied by two adults. The three-hour cruise describes local indigenous history and backwater habitats.

Old Rex and his **Bush Safari Co** ( ☎ 8543 2280; www.safarico.com.au; Murray River Camel Farm, btwn Morgan & Waikerie; adult $40) have been around for a long time offering very popular boat tours of the Murray and wetlands as well as some great camel tours. A 1½-hour camel tour ($40) and a 2½-hour boat trip ($25, October to April) can be combined. Longer versions of these tours explore the region more thoroughly.

## Sleeping & Eating
**Barmera Backpackers** ( ☎ 8588 3007, 0417-883 055; backpack@riverland.net.au; 6 Bice St; dm/t/dm per week for workers $17/22/115; 🖳 ) This small, bright and cheerful YHA is centrally based, and takes up to 25 international (or card-holding) backpackers. The manager also acts as a labour contractor (see also p135). A grassed backyard with seating is a nice place to relax, while the dorms and facilities are pleasant and clean.

**Barmera Lake Resort-Motel** ( ☎ 8588 2555; lake resort@riverland.net.au; Lakeside Dr; s/d $60/70; mains $10-20; ⏰ lunch & dinner; 🍴🍷 ) Right on the lake and complete with a small swimming pool, this motel is good value, although 'resort' is a bit of a stretch. Facilities include a barbecue, laundry, tennis court and on-site **Café Mudz**.

**Barmera Country Club** ( ☎ 8588 2888; counbarm@ ozemail.com.au; Hawdon St; s/d/d with spa $94/112/142; mains $15-25; ⏰ dinner; 🍴🍷 ) The town's most exclusive accommodation is a little faded, but is being gradually updated. A golf course backs onto the rooms and creates a nice setting. The facilities are grand and include floodlit tennis courts, heated spas and pool, barbecue, laundry and dining room. Negotiated rates are possible for longer stays.

**Lake Bonney Holiday Park** ( ☎ 8588 2234; fax 8588 1974; Lakeside Dr; unpowered sites per 2 people/camp cabins/park cabins $15/38/60; 🍴 ) The spacious and popular lakeside park is fabulous for families, with plenty of legroom for the kids. Facilities include small beaches for on-site swimming, an electric barbecue and a laundry. The park is also walking distance from town.

**Bonneyview Winery** ( ☎ 8588 2279; bonneyview _wines@hotkey.net.au; Sturt Hwy; mains $15-20 ⏰ lunch Thu-Sun, dinner Thu-Sat) For atmosphere and fine food you cannot beat this attractive white-washed cottage restaurant and cellar door. The food is unpretentious, tasty and satisfying. Try a yummy ploughman's lunch or oven-baked barramundi and bottle of Petit Verdot – perfect!

**Barmera Hotel-Motel** ( ☎ 8588 2111, 8588 1077; Barwell Ave; bar mains $9-10; bistro $12-20; ⏰ lunch & dinner) This large and busy hotel sits in the middle of town and serves schnitzels, calamari and steak dishes.

## Getting Around
**Barmera Taxi Service** ( ☎ 0409-839 387) operates 24 hours a day.

## LOXTON
☎ 08 / pop 3358
Loxton is an appealing town on the Murray River loop. You can canoe from here across to the Katarapko Creek section of the Murray River National Park (a major breeding ground for waterfowl), or simply meander by the river. The hospitality here is excellent for all wallet sizes. Golf fans will also relish golf and accommodation packages.

## Information
**Loxton visitors centre** ( ☎ 8584 7919; www.loxton tourism.com.au; Bookpurnong Terrace; ⏰ 9am-5pm Mon-Fri, 9.30am-12.30pm Sat, 1-4pm Sun) Has national park information, Internet access, a small art gallery and crafts shop on the premises.

## Sights & Activities
The town's major attraction is **Loxton Historical Village & Heritage Walk** ( ☎ 8584 7194; www .loxtonhistoricalvillage.com.au; Scenic Dr; adult/child/ family $8/4/21; ⏰ 10am-4pm Mon-Fri, 10am-5pm Sat, Sun & school holidays), with more than 35 fully furnished buildings from the days of the early settlers, including a pine-and-pug settler's hut, a pine-slab shearing shed, blacksmiths and dairy house. Ask about Village Alive days when the townsfolk dress up and inhabit the village – spooky but fun!

MURRAY RIVER

Find the **Tree of Knowledge** by the caravan park – it's marked with flood levels from previous years.

Slurp some winners at the five-year-old winery **Salena Estate** ( ☎ 8584 1333; www.salena estate.com.au; Bookpurnong Rd; 🕑 9am-4.30pm Mon-Fri, 11am-3pm Sat). The Salena family have won awards at local, national and international wine shows.

We all love the glitter and sparkle of Christmas, and Loxton puts on a real show of **Christmas lights** during December, when more than 350 homes put on decorative displays.

Two other great spots for messing around on the river are **Bookpurnong Cliffs and Lookout**, great for picnics and camping, with access to the sandbar on the opposite bank, while **Thiele's Sandbar** (Bookpurnong Rd) has houseboat moorings, good fishing and an enclosed swimming area.

The **Katarapko Game Reserve** section of the Murray River National Park is the real star of the area, and loved by bird and nature-lovers. Only accessible by water, you can easily canoe across from town and walk along the park's timbered banks.

**Canoes** can be hired from Loxton River-front Caravan Park ($7 an hour or $30 per day).

A 30-minute drive from Loxton takes you to the private and self-built **Mallee Sky Observatory Hill** ( ☎ 8587 6242; www.malleesky.com; nr Wunkar; donation adult/child/family $5/2/13; 🕑 6pm-7.30pm). The owners are members of the Astronomical Society of South Australia and will welcome you to share their passion. Recommended donation includes a cuppa.

### Sleeping & Eating

**Harvest Trail Lodge** ( ☎ 8584 5646; www.harvest trail.com; 1 Kokoda Tce; dm/d/dm per week for workers/d $27/45/140; 🔀 🖳 ) All dorms at this hostel are four-person (with TV and fridge), and there is a great balcony-barbecue area. The owner/managers will find you work, and transport to and from jobs is free. The hostel is not solely for backpackers, with itinerant workers also in residence.

**Loxton Community Hotel-Motel** ( ☎ 1800 656 686, 8584 7266; www.loxtonhotel.com.au; East Tce; hotel s/d $57/77, motel $80/90; bar meals $8-10; bistro meals $12-20; 🕑 lunch & dinner; 🔀 🖳 🍸 ) This excellent hotel has immaculate rooms for very good rates and helpful staff. Disabled access, a

barbecue, special family units, and some very good weekend and golf deals make this a great place to rest awhile.

**Mill Cottage** ( ☎ 0439-866 990; www.millcottage .com.au; 2 Mill Rd; d $120; 🔀 ) This is a lovely little cottage. The cosy living room has glowing yellow walls, polished floors and a wood fire. There is a nice garden, and breakfast provisions are supplied. The cottage is 1km from the Loxton roundabout by the rail tracks; not the prettiest part of town.

**Loxton Riverfront Caravan Park** ( ☎ 8584 7862; loxtoncp@sa.ozland.net.au; Riverfront Rd; unpowered sites per 2 people/cabins/en suite cabins $13/40/55; 🔀 ) About 2km from town, this park is peaceful, planted with many beautiful red gums and sits right on the Murray. There are well-maintained grounds and good cabins. Canoes can be hired ($7 an hour or $30 per day) and there is a free 9-hole par-3 golf course.

**Loxton Community Club** ( ☎ 8584 7353; loxclub@ riverland.net.au; Bookpurnong Tce; mains $8-20; 🕑 breakfast, lunch & dinner) With the kitchen open daily, you can always get a good feed here. Specials include lunches and a schooner on Friday ($6), schnitzel night on Wednesday ($8), and weekday lunch specials ($6.50). An underground playground keeps the kids occupied and DJ parties on a Friday night liven up town a little.

### Getting Around

**Loxton Taxis** ( ☎ 8584 5400, 0418-839 289) offers a 24-hour service around Loxton and further afield.

## BERRI

☎ 08 / pop 4241

Berri sits on a wide, attractive bend on the river (the Aboriginal name *berri berri* means 'big bend in the river'). This country town has few obvious amusements, but it is a nice place from which to explore the river and go bushwalking. Berri is the regional centre both for state government and agricultural casual labour agencies.

The **visitors centre** ( ☎ 8582 5511; bbtour@inter node.on.net; Riverview Dr; 🕑 9am-5pm Mon-Fri, 10am-4pm Sat & Sun) has a ton of information, sells national park passes and will make Premier Stateliner bookings.

### Sights & Activities

As well as any water-based activities such as boating, water-skiing and fishing there are some great bushwalks to be had. For general fishing information, mud maps and equipment try **Hook, Line & Sinker** ( ☎ 8582 2488; hlsinker@riverland.net.ay; 8 Denny St, Berri; ☼ 9am-5pm Mon-Fri, 9am-1.30pm Sat, 10am-2pm Sun).

Road access to beautiful Katarapko Creek section of Murray River National Park is through Berri, Loxton or Winkie (near Glossop). This beautiful stretch of river and Katarapko Island are great areas for bushwalking and camping, canoeing and bird-watching.

Visitors are always welcome to join the **Bookmark Biosphere Bushwalking Club** ( ☎ 8588 1017, 8582 2843), which every other Sunday explores a different part of Unesco's vast Bookmark Biosphere Reserve. The walks are of different lengths and terrains, and confirmations are required by Thursday prior to the walk.

**Berri Estates** ( ☎ 8582 0340; Old Sturt Hwy, Glossop; ☼ 9am-5pm Mon-Fri, 9am-4pm Sat, 10am-4pm Sun) are believed to be one of Australia's biggest wineries; unfortunately they are not one of the most attractive cellar doors. Tastings and cellar-door sales are located 7km west of Berri.

**Country Arts SA** ( ☎ 8584 5807; 23 Wilson St; admission free; ☼ 9.30am-4.30pm Mon-Fri) is worth checking out. Some of the local and travelling exhibitions are really good.

Golf is hugely popular in the Riverland, and **Big River Golf & Country Club** ( ☎ 1800 801 516, 8582 3666; www.bigrivergolf.com; Sturt Hwy; adult/child $25/15) has quite a following. Consider a lessons package or green fees and accommodation package (right). Rates here are for 18 holes, and Wednesday and weekends may be busy, but visitors are still welcome.

A goodie for children is **Monash Adventure Park** ( ☎ 8582 5511; Madison Ave; admission free; ☼ 10am-5pm) which has many delights: a crazy leaning tower, Burmese rope bridge, wave bridge, maze, flying fox and mini–basketball court – and who could resist a slippery dip?

Apart from the fact that **Cobb Webb Leadlight Studios** ( ☎ 8583 7883; Dalziel Rd, Winkie; admission free; ☼ 10am-4pm Mon-Fri, weekends by appointment) is based in a town with a wonderful name, these nature-based designs are really lovely and well worth a look.

Check out the fantastic murals and totem poles on and around the base of **Berri Bridge**, created by local artist Gary Duncan and friends.

## Sleeping & Eating

**Berri Backpackers** ( ☎ 8582 3144; need@email.com; Sturt Hwy; dm/dm per week for workers $20/120; 🖳 ) Book ahead to try and get a bed here; international backpackers revel in the Balinese surroundings and hippy environment, and just won't leave! Among other facilities in the large grounds are a sauna, soccer field, tennis court, bicycles and canoes. An elaborate tree house, tropical gardens and meditation hut all aid relaxation. The atmosphere is really cool and there's seasonal work in local orchards and vineyards.

**Berri Resort Hotel** ( ☎ 1800 088 226, 8582 1411; www.berriresorthotel.com; Riverview Dr; hotel s/d $55/70, motel s/d/d with spa $110/120/130; meals $11-18; ☼ breakfast, lunch & dinner; 🕮 🖳 🛒 ) This hotel-motel has cornered the market for mid-range accommodation. The motel rooms are overpriced, but children under 13 are free, there is disabled access, a gym, barbecue, three bars, a nightclub and an excellent licensed bistro. This community-owned and -managed hotel is hugely popular with the locals and always brimming with life.

**Big River Motor Inn** ( ☎ 1800 801 516, 8582 2688; www.bigrivergolf.com; Sturt Hwy: s/d $95/104, dinner with B&B s/d $129/185; meals $20-26; ☼ dinner Mon-Sat) With a golf course right outside their door, many guests will take up the excellent golf-B&B packages that can include tuition. However, the dinner-B&B packages are most popular because the motel has long held the local crown for fine dining and comfortable accommodation.

**Berri Riverside Caravan Park** ( ☎ 8582 3723; www.berricaravanpark.com.au; Riverview Dr; unpowered sites per 2 people/dm/cabins $16/27/50; 🕮 🖳 🛒 ) It is easy to see why this park has won numerous awards and is always packed. Sitting just over the road from the river, this green park and facilities are spotless and beautifully maintained. Facilities include a tennis court, playground, good camp kitchen and laundry.

**Hamley House** ( ☎ 8582 2583, 8582 2292; mains $22-28; ☼ dinner Tue-Sat) Just mentioning dishes like curried prawns, beef fillet tornados, jaffa profiteroles, and apple and pear cake should have you slavering and ringing for a table right away. The elegant dining rooms and bar have disabled access and are simply but comfortably furnished.

**Mallee Fowl** ( ☎ 8582 2096; Sturt Hwy; mains $22-28; ☼ lunch & dinner Thu, Fri & Sat) For a bit of fun

MURRAY RIVER

take the family out to this bush restaurant. You don't have to eat the emu and duck dishes, but you may have to dance! The surroundings make it easy; corrugated-steel and wood barns full of bric-a-brac and lots of lively folk toe-tapping away. The menu has steak and veggie choices, and kids' choices include cow pat pies.

**Red Gum Café** ( ☎ 8582 5344; Riverview Dr; mains $15; ☻ brunch Sat & Sun, lunch Thu-Sun, dinner Sat) Stroll down to the riverside for your weekend brunch, sip champagne and read the papers alfresco. Adjacent to the visitors centre, this café serves all-day breakfasts and great coffee.

## Getting Around

**Berri Taxis** ( ☎ 131 008) operate a round-the-clock service.

## RENMARK

☎ 08 / pop 4470

Renmark is more a country town than a tourist destination, as there's little to do. However, it is a great jumping point into some of the large parks and river conservation areas. Many people pick up their houseboats here and head to some of the loveliest stretches of the Murray. Renmark is also the first major river town across from the NSW border; it sits 254km from Adelaide.

## Information

**Renmark visitors centre** ( ☎ 8586 6704; www.ren markparinga.sa.gov.au; 84 Murray Ave; ☻ 9am-5pm Mon-Fri, 9am-4pm Sat, 10am-4pm Sun) Also the booking office for Premier Stateliner. There is a free interpretive centre and the recommissioned 1911 paddle-wheeler PS *Industry* sits alongside and cruises the river occasionally.

## Sights & Activities

**Olivewood Homestead** ( ☎ 8586 6175, 8586 5796; cnr Renmark Ave & 21st St; adult/child $4/1; ☻ 10am-4pm Thu-Mon, 2-4pm Tue) would only appeal to those interested in local history. A small museum and old-style log cabin has a lovely restful garden with rows of palm, citrus and olive trees. Afternoon teas are served to coach parties and those partial to a drop.

Turn off Renmark Ave at the Renmano Winery and follow the signs for **Ruston's Rose Gardens** ( ☎ 8586 6191; rustrose@riverland.net.au; adult $4; ☻ 9am-5pm 15th Sep-1st Jul) to wander among 50,000 roses (4000 varieties). The gardens are a bit overgrown and wild but real rose

lovers will delight in the shades and scents of the blooms.

Well known for their St Agnes Brandy and ginger wine, **Angoves** ( ☎ 8580 3148; www .angoves.com.au; Bookmark Rd; ☻ 9am-5pm Mon-Sat, 10am-4pm Sun) is a winery with a full range of wines to mull over and enjoy.

**Chaffey Theatre** ( ☎ 8586 1800; 8586 1899; 17th St) has films or live theatre most weeks, usually on Friday and Saturday nights. Events to look out for are the Melbourne Comedy Roadshow in May – always a sell-out – and regular tours by the Bangarra Dance show.

**Bredls Wonderland of Wildlife** ( ☎ 8595 1431; cnr Sturt Hwy & 28th St; adult/child/family $8/4/22; ☻ 10am-6pm Thu-Sat summer; 10am-5pm Sat-Thu winter) has live animal shows that the children will love. At 11am and 1pm daily there are monkey-handling, goanna and snake shows. Ring ahead to avoid disappointment, as these shows depend on audience numbers.

Ask at the visitors centre for free local walking track maps. Five walking tracks range in length: the Ranger's Walk runs along the river from the visitors centre for 6km. Goat Island, on the Sturt Hwy has walking tracks among gums trees, where you may see koalas. These lovely sleepy creatures may also be found near the caravan park on the other side of the road.

Don't miss the huge 17,508-hectare **Chowilla Game Reserve** and **Regional Reserve**. Just upstream from Renmark (part of the sprawling Unesco Bookmark Biosphere Reserve), is a great area for bush camping, canoeing and bushwalking. Access is along the north bank from Renmark.

Other notable parks include the 253,660-hectare **Danggali Conservation Park** and the 59,148-hectare **Billiatt Conservation Park**, home to rare western whipbirds, red-lored whistlers and mallee fowls.

**Rivermate Boat Hire** ( ☎ 8586 6928, 8586 5480; Speight Engineering, 91 16th St; per day $75) hire out 25-horsepower 14-foot punts that take four people. Rates improve with longer bookings; a boat and trailer are $350 per week. You will need a boat licence and a $150 cash bond.

**Canoes** are available for hire ($5 per hour) from the Renmark Riverfront Caravan Park (opposite), which is 1km out of town on the river.

**Renmark River Cruises** ( ☎ 8595 1862; www.ren markrivercruises.com.au; adult/child/family $28/12/60; ☻ closed Mon) depart each day from the main wharf. The MV *Big River Rambler* takes a two-hour, 7km cruise with commentary past the Murray River cliffs. The company also conducts guided tours by motorised dinghy ($59 per person, minimum two people).

## Sleeping & Eating

**Renmark Hotel-Motel** ( ☎ 8586 6755; www.renmark hotel.com.au; Murray Ave; hotel s/d $60/70, motel $80/90; bistro mains $14.50-22; ☺ bistro breakfast, lunch & dinner; ⊠ ⊡ ) The clean hotel rooms are good value in this huge century-old place, which has been extensively renovated. Children under 12 are free and good meals are served in the front bar, bistro and dining room.

**Liba Liba Houseboats** ( ☎ 1800 810 252, 8586 6734; www.libaliba.com.au; Jane Eliza Landing, Renmark; 3 nights per 4 people $353) A great alternative to land-based accommodation, the paddle-wheel houseboats come with a fitted galley and microwave, barbecue, video and large living area. There's also a dinghy and free parking.

**Renmark Riverfront Caravan Park** ( ☎ 8584 6315; renrivcarapk@riverland.net.au; Sturt Hwy; unpowered sites per 2 people $19, cabins $35-60; ⊠ ) This park is nice and neat, and sits idyllically on the river 1km east of town. Roaming ducks, water birds and pelicans have tree-based koalas and possums as upstairs tenants. Facilities include older vans, a playground, barbecue, camp kitchen, petrol and laundry. A shared bike and walking track goes along the river into town.

**Caffé Sorelle's** ( ☎ 8586 4888; 179 Murray Dr; mains $12.50-16.50; ☺ lunch & dinner) Boasting the best coffee in town, locals say that when Mama is around you can also expect an authentic plate of pasta. Well, we all love our mamas.

**Renmark Club Inc** ( ☎ 8586 6611; Murray Ave; mains $13-22; ☺ lunch & dinner) Across from the Renmark Hotel-Motel, the club has huge $8 specials on Tuesday and Thursday night.

There are also plenty of takeaways, pizza delivery services and fast-food outlets.

## Getting Around

**Renmark Taxis** ( ☎ 0408-851 155) operates a 24-hour service.

# The Southeast

CONTENTS

| | |
|---|---|
| **Princes Highway** | **145** |
| Coorong National Park | 146 |
| Robe | 147 |
| Beachport | 148 |
| Mt Gambier | 150 |
| Port MacDonnell | 153 |
| **Coonawarra Wine Region** | **153** |
| Coonawarra Wineries | 154 |
| Penola | 154 |
| Naracoorte | 156 |
| Naracoorte Caves National Park | 157 |
| Dukes Highway | 158 |

Long surf beaches, sheltered sandy bays and rugged cliffs shape the Southeastern coastline. The sea ranges from an angelic blue, beloved by swimmers, to rougher aquamarine waters that keep fishermen and surfers happy. The Princes Hwy runs along this coast, adjacent to the Coorong (an extensive coastal lagoon system), and encompasses some pretty fishing villages.

Exploring Coonawarra's renowned *terra rossa* (red earth) wine region will uncover atmospheric wineries producing full, silky wines, some of Australia's best reds. Surrounded by these vineyards is Penola, the spiritual birthplace of Australia's saint-in-waiting, Mary MacKillop.

The World Heritage–listed Naracoorte Caves contain ancient marsupial fossils and communities of bats that darken the skies at dusk. Migrating and breeding water birds return each year to Bool and Hacks Lagoons, while the peaceful crater lakes of Mt Gambier remind us how this volcanic region was created.

Underground caves in the lower Southeast enjoy visits from walkers and scuba divers who see Mt Gambier's subterranean vista, while those who prefer fresh air can walk up and around extinct volcanic vents and craters, and through rugged and beautiful coastline parks.

Aboriginal communities welcome those to the Coorong who want to learn a little about different habitats. Here nature and the Ngarrindjeri culture share an ancient heritage.

Throughout all of this are a myriad of sandy beaches just made for lazy days or picnics with rock lobster salad, and a bottle or two of peppery Coonawarra Shiraz – enjoy!

## HIGHLIGHTS

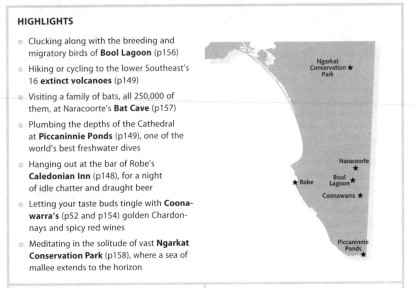

- Clucking along with the breeding and migratory birds of **Bool Lagoon** (p156)
- Hiking or cycling to the lower Southeast's 16 **extinct volcanoes** (p149)
- Visiting a family of bats, all 250,000 of them, at Naracoorte's **Bat Cave** (p157)
- Plumbing the depths of the Cathedral at **Piccaninnie Ponds** (p149), one of the world's best freshwater dives
- Hanging out at the bar of Robe's **Caledonian Inn** (p148), for a night of idle chatter and draught beer
- Letting your taste buds tingle with **Coonawarra's** (p52 and p154) golden Chardonnays and spicy red wines
- Meditating in the solitude of vast **Ngarkat Conservation Park** (p158), where a sea of mallee extends to the horizon

- TELEPHONE CODE: ☎ 08
- www.thelimestonecoast.com

# THE SOUTHEAST

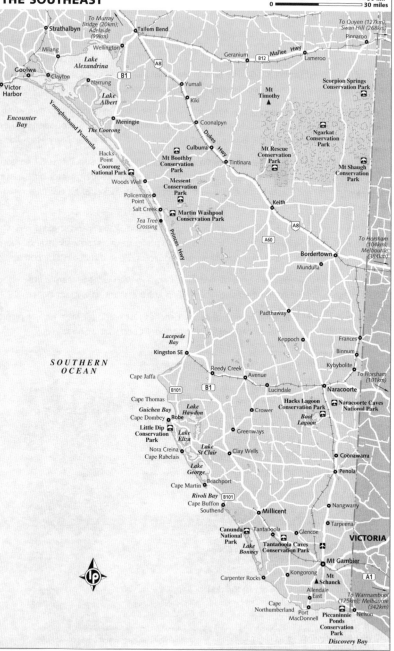

0 — 50 km
0 — 30 miles

To Murray Bridge (20km); Adelaide (99km)
Strathalbyn
Tailem Bend
To Ouyen (127km); Swan Hill (268km)
Pinnaroo
Milang
Wellington
Geranium
B12
Mallee Hwy
Lameroo
Goolwa
Clayton
A8
Scorpion Springs Conservation Park
Victor Harbor
Lake Alexandrina
B1
Narrung
Yumali
Kiki
Mt Timothy
Encounter Bay
Lake Albert
Meningie
Coonalpyn
Ngarkat Conservation Park
The Coorong
Younghusband Peninsula
Hacks Point
Culburra
Dukes Hwy
Mt Rescue Conservation Park
Coorong National Park
Mt Boothby Conservation Park
Tintinara
Mt Shaugh Conservation Park
Woods Well
Messent Conservation Park
Policemans Point
Salt Creek
Tea Tree Crossing
Martin Washpool Conservation Park
Keith
Princes Hwy
A8
A60
Bordertown
To Horsham (104km); Melbourne (384km)
Mundulla
Padthaway
SOUTHERN OCEAN
Lacepede Bay
Kingston SE
Reedy Creek
Avenue
Keppoch
Frances
Binnum
Cape Jaffa
B101
B1
Lucindale
Kybybolite
Naracoorte
To Horsham (101km)
Cape Thomas
Guichen Bay
Lake Hawdon
Crower
Hacks Lagoon Conservation Park
Naracoorte Caves National Park
Cape Dombey
Robe
Bool Lagoon
Little Dip Conservation Park
Lake Eliza
Greenways
Nora Creina
Lake St Clair
Clay Wells
Coonawarra
Cape Rabelais
Lake George
Penola
Cape Martin
Beachport
Rivoli Bay
Cape Buffon
B101
Nangwarry
Southend
Millicent
Tarpeena
Canunda National Park
Tantanoola
Glencoe
VICTORIA
Lake Bonney
Tantanoola Caves Conservation Park
Mt Gambier
A1
Carpenter Rocks
Kongorong
Mt Schanck
Allendale East
To Warrnambool (175km); Melbourne (342km)
Cape Northumberland
Port MacDonnell
Piccaninnie Ponds Conservation Park
Nelson
Discovery Bay

## National Parks

There are more than 15 conservation and national parks in the Southeast, including the 47,000-hectare Coorong and the World Heritage–listed Naracoorte Caves. Ask for a copy of the free and very informative *Tattler* and *National Parks* brochures from either Mt Gambier's **Department for Environment & Heritage** (DEH; ☎ 08-8735 1111; www.environment .sa.gov.au/parks; 11 Helen St, Mt Gambier; 8.45am-5pm Mon-Fri) or from their **Meningie office** (☎ 08-8575 1200; 32-34 Princes Hwy, Meningie; 9am-5pm Mon-Fri).

## Getting There & Away

### AIR

**Regional Express** (Rex; ☎ 13 17 13; www.regionalex press.com.au) and **O'Connor Airlines** (☎ 13 13 13, 08-8723 0666; www.oconnor-airlines.com.au) fly daily between Adelaide and Mt Gambier ($225).

### BUS

The bus station for Mt Gambier is the **Shell Blue Lake service station** (☎ 08-8725 5037; 100 Commercial St West).

**Premier Stateliner** (☎ 08-8415 5555; www.premier stateliner.com.au; Adelaide central bus station, 111 Franklin St, Adelaide) runs two routes between Adelaide and Mt Gambier ($55, 6½ hours).

You can either go along the coast Sunday to Friday via the Coorong and stopping at Meningie ($26, two hours), Kingston SE ($41, four hours), Robe ($46, 4½ hours) and Beachport ($50, five hours). Or you can travel inland daily via Bordertown ($40,

four hours), Naracoorte ($50, five hours), and Penola ($50, six hours). Premier also run services between Mt Gambier and Penola ($11, 30 minutes).

**V/Line** (☎ 1800 817 037, 13 61 96) run a weekday service between Mt Gambier and Melbourne ($60, 6½ hours) – you take the bus from Mt Gambier to Ballarat or Warrnambool (Friday only), where you can hop on a train for Melbourne.

# PRINCES HIGHWAY

From Murray Bridge the Princes Hwy (B1) follows the coast southwards to Kingston Southeast (Kingston SE), where it veers inland to Millicent and Mt Gambier. If you want to continue along the coast take the B101 from Kingston down to the picturesque fishing and holiday ports of Robe and Beachport before rejoining B1 at Millicent.

Meningie on Lake Albert (a large arm of Lake Alexandrina), was established as a minor port in 1866. It's a popular sailboarding spot, which isn't surprising, as the wind here always seems to be blowing.

Covering 12,250 hectares, **Messent Conservation Park** has plenty of wildlife and diverse vegetation, which includes statuesque pink gums and, in spring, spectacular wild flowers. There is good bushwalking and camping here, but vehicle access is 4WD only. The park is 6km from Salt Creek on the Coorong.

---

**FESTIVALS & EVENTS**

There's a heap of events on around the year, check with local visitors centres for further details.

**Robe Easter Classic** (☎ 08-8768 2465; Apr) The longest-running surf contest in South Australia (SA) began in 1968, and still wipes the competition.

**Mt Gambier Racing Club Gold Cup Carnival** (☎ 08-8274 9750; May) Mt Gambians celebrate winners, losers and their horses.

**Penola Festival** (☎ 08-8737 2855; May) This festival promotes the cultural aspect of the town, along with the odd glass of wine…

**Naracoorte Sheepdog Trials** (☎ 08-8762 1518; Jun) Bordertown is the setting for some mutts to show us and the sheep who is really in control.

**Coonawarra Cellar Doors** (☎ 08-8737 2855; Aug) If you need an excuse to visit the Coonawarra and drink their fabulous silky wines, take this one!

**Shakespeare in the Caves** (☎ 08-8762 1518; Sep) The World Heritage–listed wonder caves host the world's greatest plays; very appropriate.

**Coonawarra Cabernet Celebrations & Barrel Series Auction** (☎ 08-8737 2855; Oct) Meet winemakers, drink fabulous, full reds and bid for your own barrel of newly released wine.

**Blue Lake Carols** (☎ 08-8274 9750; Dec) Mt Gambier knows how to belt out a good carol, and in a fabulous setting.

En route to Messent you pass the 1880-hectare **Martin Washpool Conservation Park** (again 4WD access only), which has winter wetlands surrounded by vegetated dunes.

The mallee habitats in 4050-hectare **Mt Boothby Conservation Park** also feature walks and wildlife; this secluded park is 40km east of Meningie and is best reached from Woods Well on the Coorong, or from the Dukes Hwy to the north.

## COORONG NATIONAL PARK

The Coorong is a narrow lagoon curving along the coast for 145km from Lake Alexandrina to near Kingston SE. A complex series of saltpans, it is separated from the sea by the huge sand dunes of the Younghusband Peninsula. Take the old and unsealed Coorong Rd south of Salt Creek to view the Coorong from the inside. There is road access across the Coorong at Tea Tree Crossing (summer only) near Salt Creek, and the 42-Mile Crossing further south. With a 4WD you can continue on from both crossings to **Ninety Mile Beach**, a popular surf-fishing spot (with mulloway, flathead, salmon and shark).

This area is home to vast numbers of water birds. *Storm Boy*, a film about a young boy's friendship with a pelican, based on the novel of the same name by Colin Thiele, was shot on the Coorong. Pelicans are especially evident at Jack Point and elsewhere in the park, as are ducks, waders and swans.

Among the best places to watch birds are the freshwater soaks on the coastal side of the lagoon. The endangered hooded plover breeds on the beach, so if you're going to drive along the sand make sure to keep below the high-water mark. To protect the plovers' nests, the beach is closed north of Tea Tree Crossing from 24 October to 24 December. There's plenty of other wildlife here, including kangaroos and wombats, so be careful driving at night.

In 1836 the rich resources of the Coorong supported a large population of Ngarrindjeri Aborigines. Today many of their descendants still live in the district, and stonefish traps and middens remain as evidence of a vanished way of life. You can learn more about the Ngarrindjeri at their **Cultural Museum** at Camp Coorong, 10km south of Meningie and off the Princes Hwy. Cultural walks (from $35 per hour) are run

by an informed and passionate Ngarrindjeri curator and guide.

### Tours

**Adelaide Sightseeing** ( ☎ 08-8231 4144; www.adelaidesightseeing.com.au; 101 Franklin St, Adelaide; adult/child $135/80; ☺ Wed & Sat, closed Jun-Sep) Along with their Coorong Pelican Feeding Cruise (adult/child $95/50), this Adelaide-based company offer two of the better Coorong cruises. They include guided walks and information about the region, including aspects of the Ngarrindjeri Aboriginal communities.

**Coorong Nature Tours** ( ☎ 08-8574 0037, 0428-714 793; www.coorongnaturetours.com; adult/child $150/110) Based in Meningie, this renowned operator has run excellent tours to the Coorong and Southeastern conservation areas for 10 years. Tours include one- to three-day tag-along, overnight bushwalks and special bird-watching and nature-study trips. Tours can depart ex-Adelaide, and two-adult family trips take one child for free.

**Spirit of the Coorong Cruises** ( ☎ 08-8555 2203; www.coorongcruises.com.au; The Wharf, Goolwa; adult/child $70/52; ☺ Mon, Wed, Thu & Sun) These very popular cruises depart from Goolwa (p110) and explore the Coorong National Park. Take either a 4½-hour or six-hour cruise. Ex-Adelaide connections are available and meals are provided.

### Sleeping

The park has plenty of bush **campsites**, but you need a permit ($6.50 per car). These can be purchased from **DEH** ( ☎ 08-8735 1177; www.environment.sa.gov.au/parks; 11 Helen St, Mt Gambier; ☺ 8.45am-5pm Mon-Fri) and the roadhouse at Salt Creek.

**Camp Coorong** ( ☎ 08-8575 1557; www.ngarrindjeri.net; Princes Hwy; powered sites per 2 people/dm/cabins $12/24/60; 🏊 ) Run by the Ngarrindjeri Lands and Progress Association, this is a great place to learn about local Aboriginal history and the Coorong habitat. You need to book in advance and rates are cheaper for groups. The cabins are modern, well maintained and good value. Ask about linen hire, and bring your own food.

**Lake Albert Caravan Park** ( ☎ /fax 08-8575 1411; lacp@lm.net.au; 25 Narrung Rd, Meningie; unpowered sites per 2 people/cabins/cabins with bathroom $17/50/65) An old park with few facilities, but it sits right on the lake, is shaded by large gums and has some disabled access.

**Coorong Wilderness Lodge** ( ☎ 08-8575 6001; off the Princes Hwy, about 25km south of Meningie; unpowered/powered sites per 2 people $10/20, 4-person cabins $65; meals $13; ☺ lunch Mon-Fri) Situated at Hack Point, this fish-shaped centre is owned by members of the Ngarrindjeri community. There is good-value accommodation. The lodge also offers popular guided bush-tucker walks (per hour $7) and kayak tours (per hour $20). Kayaking equipment can also be hired (per half-day/day $30/50) if you don't want to take a tour. Book ahead for all facilities, including meals.

## ROBE
☎ 08 / pop 965

Robe is a charming fishing port and one of the nicest places to stay on this coastline. There are lovely beaches and the town pubs are welcoming. To the delight of local businesses, and the despair of anyone seeking solitude, Robe is an extremely popular holiday destination, with thousands of people descending on the town during Christmas and Easter holidays.

### Information
**Robe visitors centre** ( ☎ 8768 2465; www.robe.sa.gov .au; Mundy Tce; ☺ 9am-5pm Mon-Fri, 10am-4pm Sat & Sun) In the public library. It offers free Internet access.

### Sights & Activities
There are numerous heritage-listed buildings in Robe dating from the late 1840s to 1870s. The leaflet *Robe Walking Tours* includes the **Customs House** (1863) on Royal

---

**ROBE'S RICHES** *Denis O'Byrne*

Robe was established as a small fishing port and holiday town in 1846, making it one of the state's first settlements. Robe's citizens made a fortune in the late 1850s when the Victorian government instituted a $10-per-head tax on Chinese gold miners. Many Chinese miners circumvented this by landing at Robe and walking hundreds of kilometres to the Victorian goldfields; 10,000 arrived in 1857 alone. However, the flood stopped as quickly as it started when the SA government slapped its own tax on the Chinese. The **Chinamen's Wells** along their route (including one in the Coorong) are a reminder of that time.

---

Circus, which is now a nautical museum. Ask the visitors centre about access. Nearby is a **memorial** to the 16,500 Chinese diggers who landed at the port from 1856 to 1858.

Make some time to wander through **Wilsons at Robe** ( ☎ 8768 2459; Victoria St); it is full of witty and clever art and craft works that are all for sale.

The nice little town beach is safe for swimming, while **Long Beach** (2km from town off the Kingston SE road), is good for sailboarding and lazy days.

The **Little Dip Conservation Park** runs along the coast for about 13km south of town. It features a variety of habitats including lakes, wetlands and dunes. It is a lovely spot with some nice beaches, walks and camping spots. **Bishops Pate**, **Long Gully** and **Little Dip** are also popular with fishing folk. Access is via Nora Creina Rd.

**South Coast Cinema** ( ☎ 8768 2772; 37 Victoria St; $9; ☺ Wed, Fri-Sun) has two screens and shows contemporary hits.

Wave to giant **Larry the Big Lobster** in Kingston SE as you pass him by, with your optimism and fishing gear in hand. Kingston SE is a major centre for crayfishing and holds an annual Lobsterfest in the second week of January.

For no reason other than to taste a peppery and smooth Shiraz that will knock your socks off, stop at this attractive cellar door, **Cape Jaffa Wines** ( ☎ 8768 5053; www.capejaffawines .com.au; Limestone Coast Rd; ☺ 10am-5pm).

### Sleeping
There is plenty of accommodation, but you will be lucky to find any vacancies in peak periods. Motel rooms are around $95 per night, and if you are in the market, ask at the visitors centre about self-contained units and up-market B&Bs (some in historic homes). Prices jump off the graph for all lodgings during December and January.

**Weston, Raine & Horne** ( ☎ 8768 2028, 1800 672 028; www.raineandhorne.com.au/robe; 25 Victoria St) There is a lot of holiday rental properties on the books from $50 per night off-season.

**Caledonian Inn** ( ☎ 8768 2029; caled@seol.net .au; Victoria St; s/d $45/60, unit d $120) This delightful and historic inn has it all under one roof. The few hotel rooms upstairs share bathroom facilities, and are light and cosy, while simply furnished but attractive two-storey units nestle between the hotel and

---

**THE AUTHOR'S CHOICE**

**Robe Longbeach Caravan Park** ( ☎ 08-8768 2237; www.robelongbeach.com.au; 70 The Esplanade; unpowered sites per 2 people/cabins/cabins with bathroom/deluxe chalets $21/44/70/88; 🞐 🖥 🞐 ) This fabulous park is as close to the beach as you can get, and beats much of the town's accommodation hands down for sheer outstanding value. The cabins and chalets are very comfortable, and are for seekers of self-contained budget and mid-range accommodation. An extraordinary amount of amusements should make all the family grin with anticipation: a heated indoor pool, basketball and tennis courts, arcade machines and games room, playground, covered barbecue area and crayfish boiler! Need it be said; book well ahead?!

---

adjacent beach (rates include continental breakfast).

**Robe Cricklewood** ( ☎ 8768 2137; www.robe.sa .gov.au/cricklewood; 24 Wollundry Rd; d $150; 🞐 ) This appealing cottage has been beautifully refurbished, with split level floors, cathedral ceilings and exposed beams, while modern fittings make life easy. Views over Robe's lake can be toasted with a glass of grape juice on the balcony.

**Lake View Motel & Flats** ( ☎ 8768 2100; apt s/d 85/95, motel s/d $95/105; 🞐 ) Although the motel looks a little dated from the outside, there are surprisingly spacious and cheerful rooms here that overlook Lake Fellmongery. Some rooms also have basic cooking facilities, but all are very good value nevertheless. There is also a guest laundry and barbecue.

**Beachside** ( ☎ 1800 067 447, 0418-554 664; d $210; 🞐 ) This cute cottage is painted a jovial blue and yellow, and has a light-filled open-plan living area. The house is blessed with an amazing view straight out over the ocean. With only a short walk down to the beach this is a pretty special spot. Rates are reduced for second and subsequent nights, which make them a little more reasonable.

## Eating

**Caledonian Inn** ( ☎ 8768 2029; Victoria St; bar meals $13-20; 🞐 lunch & dinner) The hotel bar has retained its Scottish heritage and has a great atmosphere. There's a beer garden and live music in summer, and an extra bonus; no

pokie machines or TAB outlets. Bar meals service mainly carnivores and seafood fans. The winter specials are among the best-value meals in town.

**Gallerie** ( ☎ 8768 2256; cnr Victoria & Davenport Sts; mains $22-30; 🞐 breakfast, lunch & dinner, closed Tue & Wed in winter) Home of Dawson Estate wines, this is a trendy place with lots of polished wood and glass. A three-course fireside dinner is great value ($28), while pasta and ocean platters are fairly priced. An outdoor deck is perfect for alfresco munching.

**Wild Mulberry Café & Espresso Bar** ( ☎ 8768 5276, 46 Victoria St, mains $10-15; 🞐 breakfast, lunch & dinner in summer, breakfast & lunch in winter) Meals are served all day in this relaxed café. Artworks hang on the walls, and there is a nice shady garden with tables. If you're on a diet try to resist the enticements of moist cakes and fruit-filled crepes.

**Imaj Café** ( ☎ 8768 2081; 6 Victoria St; meals $12-18; 🞐 breakfast, lunch & dinner) Really a takeaway/delivery pizza joint, Imaj also serves filled lunch rolls and all-day breakfasts ($9.50).

Some of the best-value meals in town are the counter meals at the **Robe Hotel**. Robe locals buy their fresh fish and cooked seafood from **Robe Seafood & Takeaway** (Victoria St; fish & chips $6; 🞐 lunch & dinner Mon-Sat, hours vary in winter).

# BEACHPORT
☎ 08 / pop 407

If you have a yen for peace and solitude, you'll love this quiet seaside town. A long beach attracts lounging hedonists, while walkers who love a good view head for the coastal parks. The coastline has spectacular limestone cliffs and sandy bays shaped by wild and frothing aquamarine seas.

The **visitors centre** ( ☎ 8735 8029; www.wattle range.sa.gov.au; Millicent Rd; 🞐 9am-5pm Mon-Fri year-round, 10am-4pm Sat & Sun summer, 11am-2pm Sat & Sun winter) is centrally placed and offers Internet access. For more information on walking, 4WD and biking tracks check out www .southaustraliantrails.com or ask at the visitors centre.

## Sights & Activities

**Old Wool & Grain Store Museum** ( ☎ 8735 8313; 5 Railway Tce; adult/child $5/2; 🞐 10am-1pm Mon-Fri) is in a National Trust building on the main street. It has relics of Beachport's whaling days and rooms furnished in 1870s style.

For access outside these hours ask at the visitors centre.

There's good board surfing, and sailboarding is popular at **Lake George**, 5km north of the township.

There are good walking tracks in the attractive 710-hectare **Beachport Conservation Park**, which is sandwiched between the coast and Lake George 2km north of town. Look out for Aboriginal shell middens and enjoy the bird life, sheltered coves and bush camping.

**Canunda National Park**, with its giant sand dunes, lies 22km south of town (see the Coastline & Caves boxed text, below).

The hypersaline **Pool of Siloam** is a pretty lake among sand hills on the outskirts of town, and is perfect for young children, providing a safe and shallow swimming environment.

The 800m-long town **jetty** occasionally provides memorable fishing for pelicans and fishermen (with whiting, school shark, mullet, squid and many more). Lake George mullet are apparently excellent tucker.

**Penguin Island**, a rookery for little penguins, is in Rivoli Bay, 200m offshore. Each summer the parent birds take their young on swimming lessons between the island and the groyne opposite the Beachport Caravan Park, an unmissable sight!

On the Robe road, the impressive **Woakwine Cutting** through the Woakwine Range illustrates the lengths to which one determined farmer will go to drain a swamp.

In tiny Tantanoola, a *Pinus radiata* centre 15km southeast of Millicent, the Tantanoola Tiger Hotel has a special display; the stuffed **Tantanoola Tiger**. This poor beast, actually an Assyrian wolf, was shot in 1895 after creating havoc among local sheep flocks. It was presumed to have escaped from a shipwreck, although why a ship would have a wolf on board isn't clear!

## Sleeping & Eating

It is worth booking all Beachport accommodation in advance especially during the summer months. **John Cavanagh Real Estate** ( ☎ 8733 3388; www.jcavrealestate.com.au; 5 Davenport St, Millicent) has a brochure and website listing holiday homes for rent, from $65 per night.

**Bompas** ( ☎ 8735 8333; bompas@bipond.com; 3 Railway Tce; dm/d $25/95, cottage without/with spa $120/170; mains $11-24; ☼ breakfast, lunch & dinner; ✦ ) Bompas is an all-in-one licensed restaurant-café and small hotel. There are budget dorms with

---

**COASTLINE & CAVES**

This lower Southeast had a stormy birth that is still apparent in the volcanic craters of Mt Gambier (see p152). There's also a wealth of rugged coastline parks, water-filled pools and caves to explore along the Southeast coast that offer some truly striking and gorgeous views.

A footpath leads to the top of **Mt Schank**, an extinct volcano on the Mt Gambier road 13km north of Port MacDonnell. **Little Blue Lake**, about 3km west of Mt Schank, is a popular swimming place; it's icy cold even on the hottest day. Nearby is the **Mt Schank Fish Farm**, where you can catch your own rainbow trout.

On the coast adjacent to the Victorian border the 547-hectare **Piccaninnie Ponds Conservation Park** has walks, camping and reputedly the world's best freshwater dive feature: **the Cathedral**, a large underwater cavern with 40m visibility. The water is so clear that flowering plants grow 6m down. Permits and cave-diving qualifications are required before you dive or snorkel either here, or further west at tiny **Ewens Ponds Conservation Park** – check with the visitors centre in Mt Gambier for information or contact **DEH** ( ☎ 08-8735 1111).

Heading back up the coast is the fabulous 9300-hectare **Canunda National Park** which lies 13km southwest of Millicent. The elongated park has a number of attractions including giant shifting sand dunes, rocky coastal scenery, wombats, walks, bush camping areas and 4WD tracks. Experienced surfers love the seas here, and in summer you can drive along the beach and through the dunes from Southend to Carpenter Rocks. Contact DEH for information.

Formed as coastal caves in dolomite, and part of a 2000-hectare conservation park, the decorative **Tantanoola Caves** ( ☎ 08-8734 4153; admission $8; ☼ hourly 10.15am-4pm) are on the Princes Hwy another 6km to the southeast. Tours give access to the cave, and it's the only cave in SA suitable for wheelchairs.

TV, a few hotel rooms and two beachside cottages; 'Harbourmasters' has a spa ($170). Book ahead to beat the tour groups.

**Beachport Holiday Units** ( ☎ 8735 8388; www .beachportholidayunits.com; 24 McCourt St; 4-person/ 5-person units/8-person house $85/95/130; ⊠ ) These units offer modern and comfortable accommodation and are only a five-minute drive to the beach. Set in Beachport's 'suburbs' they offer great value all round. Unit one has full disabled facilities.

**Beachport Motor Inn** ( ☎ 8735 8070; beachport motel@bigpond.com; cnr Railway Tce & Lanky St; double/ unit $70/85; ⊠ ) Within two minutes' walk of the town beach, this little motel has neat and compact rooms and is good value (prices are for two).

**Beachfront B&B** ( ☎ 8735 8340, 0419-842 401; triz@seol.net.au; d $130; ⊠ ) There is a choice of continental or cooked breakfast for one or two lucky couples at this nice little beachfront B&B.

**Beachport's Southern Ocean Tourist Park** ( ☎ 8735 8153; sotp@seol.net.au; Somerville St; unpowered sites/cabins per 2 people $15/55; ⊠ ) This grassy, pleasant and well-maintained park is behind a slope in the town centre. The facilities include a laundry, ice, fuel, covered barbecues and a great little playground.

## MT GAMBIER
☎ 08 / pop 22,751

Built on the slopes of the extinct volcano from which it takes its name, Mt Gambier

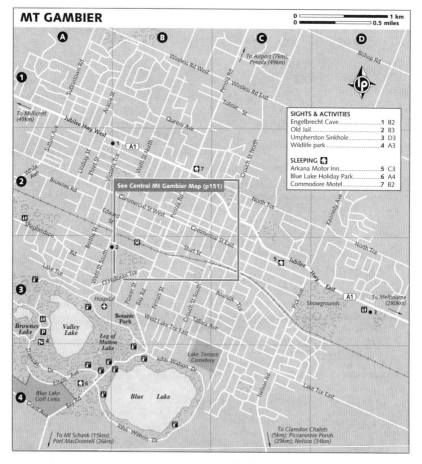

**MT GAMBIER**

SIGHTS & ACTIVITIES
| | | |
|---|---|---|
| Engelbrecht Cave | 1 | B2 |
| Old Jail | 2 | B3 |
| Umpherston Sinkhole | 3 | D3 |
| Wildlife park | 4 | A3 |

SLEEPING
| | | |
|---|---|---|
| Arkana Motor Inn | 5 | C3 |
| Blue Lake Holiday Park | 6 | A4 |
| Commodore Motel | 7 | B2 |

See Central Mt Gambier Map (p151)

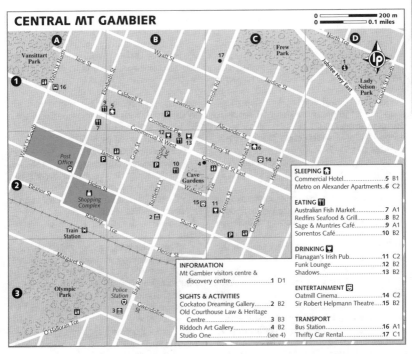

**CENTRAL MT GAMBIER**

0 ——— 200 m
0 ——— 0.1 miles

**INFORMATION**
Mt Gambier visitors centre &
  discovery centre.......................**1** D1

**SIGHTS & ACTIVITIES**
Cockatoo Dreaming Gallery.........**2** B2
Old Courthouse Law & Heritage
  Centre.....................................**3** B3
Riddoch Art Gallery....................**4** B2
Studio One................................(see 4)

**SLEEPING**
Commercial Hotel........................**5** B1
Metro on Alexander Apartments..**6** C2

**EATING**
Australian Fish Market.................**7** A1
Redfins Seafood & Grill...............**8** B2
Sage & Muntries Café..................**9** A1
Sorrentos Café...........................**10** B2

**DRINKING**
Flanagan's Irish Pub...................**11** C2
Funk Lounge..............................**12** B2
Shadows...................................**13** B2

**ENTERTAINMENT**
Oatmill Cinema..........................**14** C2
Sir Robert Helpmann Theatre.....**15** B2

**TRANSPORT**
Bus Station...............................**16** A1
Thrifty Car Rental......................**17** C1

is the region's major town and commercial centre; it lies 486km from Adelaide.

Although Mt Gambier is not much to look at, it is a friendly place, and a good base from which to go exploring. There are some excellent walking and biking tracks around the Crater Lakes.

Underground caves are a huge attraction for cave divers who can venture under Mt Gambier itself, while fishing fans head for Valley Lake, Glenelg River or the seas off Port MacDonnell.

## Information

The excellent **Mt Gambier visitors centre** (Map above; ☎ 1800 087 187, 8724 9750; www.mountgambier tourism.com.au; Jubilee Hwy East; ☑ 9am-5pm) is the biggest and most comprehensive in the region, and leaves out information packs overnight for late and weary travellers. It also provides heaps of info about tours to Glenelg National Park (in Victoria), Port MacDonnell for fishing, and the Coonawarra wineries for pure liquid joy.

Allow time to look through the **discovery centre** (Map above; adult/child $10/5; inside visitors

centre), which features a replica of the historic brig *Lady Nelson*. An audio-visual display acknowledges the devastating impact of European settlement on local Aboriginal people, and the work of Christina Smith, who attempted to mediate between the settlers and local Aborigines.

## Sights & Activities

History buffs may enjoy the **National Trust Old Court House Law & Heritage Centre** (Map above; ☎ 8725 7011; 42A Bay Rd; adult/child $4/2; ☑ 11am-3pm, closed Sep) and the **Old Jail** (Map opposite; ☎ 1800 626 844, 8723 0032; www.jailbackpackers.com; Langlois Dr; admission free; ☑ ring ahead), which was an operating jail until 1995.

Art fanatics and culture vultures will be happy: the **Riddoch Art Gallery** (Map above; ☎ 8723 9566; Commercial St East; admission free; ☑ 10am-5pm Tue-Fri, Sat 10am-2pm, closed Sun & public holidays) is one of SA's best regional galleries. Next door, **Studio One** (Map above; ☎ 8725 1788; Commercial St East; admission free; ☑ 11am-3pm Wed-Sun, closed public holidays) has some fine work by local painters, potters and porcelain painters. **Cockatoo Dreaming Gallery** (Map above; ☎ 8725

THE SOUTHEAST

6200; 22 Bay Rd; admission free; ☺ 9am-3pm Mon-Fri) displays and sells Aboriginal artworks.

There are three volcanic craters, two with lakes. The lakes are popular recreation spots and have been developed with boardwalks (over Valley Lake), a wildlife park, picnic areas, scenic drive and bike and walking tracks. The beautiful **Blue Lake** (Map p150) is an almost implausible shade of sapphire during summer, and is 204m deep at its deepest point. **Acquifer Tours** ( ☎ /fax 8723 1199; adult/child $6/3; ☺ 9am-2pm) run hourly tours here during September and October. The 45-minute tour takes you through the lake's aquifer system in a glass-panelled lift.

The Mt Gambier district is well known for its numerous caves. There are pretty floodlit sunken gardens in the **Umpherston Sinkhole** (Map p150; Jubilee Hwy East), and volunteers take tours, on the hour, down to the water table in the **Engelbrecht Cave** (Map p150; ☎ 8725 5493; Jubilee Hwy West; adult/child $6/3; ☺ summer), a popular cave-diving spot. Scuba divers can attain cave-diving qualifications, over three days, in Mt Gambier; book at the visitors centre.

The surrounding region has some fine walking, cave-diving and snorkelling opportunities. See p149 for details. Hire bicycles from **Bats Bike Hire** ( ☎ 0418 133 407; ☺ 7am-6pm Nov-Mar, 8am-5pm Apr-Oct) who will drop off and pick up at tourism spots, and cater for families (half-day $10, full day $20).

## Tours

**Lake City Tours** ( ☎ 8723 2991, 0412-838 765; ☎ closed Wed) This long-established company visits local attractions in Mt Gambier on its half-day (adult/child $36/21) and full-day tours (adult/child $75/43).

**Lake Terrace Cemetery Tours** ( ☎ 8725 3617, 8725 6617; $4; ☺ upon bookings) For history with an interesting perspective, take a daytime or twilight tour of this Mt Gambier cemetery with chatty members of the local history society.

## Sleeping

There are a heap of motel rooms along Jubilee Hwy, but many of these have overpriced and musty rooms. Unfortunately the case is the same with some of the caravan park cabins. It is worth checking rooms and cabins before booking.

**Commercial Hotel** (Map p151; ☎ 8725 3006; www .commersh.com.au; 76 Commercial St West; s/d $20/40) The budget rooms are brighter than alternative hotel rooms. Additionally, a small common room has a microwave, fridge and TV. Bathrooms are old, but clean and bearable.

**Clarendon Chalets** ( ☎ 8726 8306, 0418-838 926; www.clarendonchalets.com; Clarke Rd; d $120; ☒ ) A stack of awards have been won for these four stunning chalets set in a lovely garden and walnut orchard 7km south of town. Well fitted with combustion fires, spas, barbecue and bikes for hire; couples and families will be happy here.

**Commodore Motel** (Map p150; ☎ 1800 088 196, 8724 6400; www.commodoremotel.com.au; 1 Jubilee Hwy East; s/d $94/108; ☒ ☒ ) Very nice overall, this excellent motel has cheerful, well-maintained rooms and a large garden. Facilities include a guest laundry, playground, barbecue, indoor pool and spa and a licensed restaurant. Book ahead.

**Arkana Motor Inn** (Map p150; ☎ 8725 5433; www .users.bigpond.com/arkanamotorinn; 201 Commercial St East; s/d/units $80/85/120; ☒ ☐ ☒ ) One of the best in town, this inn has bright, clean and modern rooms with friendly touches, such as real milk, and mugs (instead of cups) for tea and coffee, yippee! A barbecue, cable TV, heated pool and spa, and great family rates keep us all happy. It's wise to book ahead, though.

**Metro on Alexander Apartments** (Map p151; ☎ 8723 9617, 0419-853 485; www.users.bigpond.com /metroonalexander; 33A Alexander St; d $160; ☒ ) These modern, stylish and comfortable self-contained apartments are perfect for couples or business people needing privacy or instant communications; a phone and Internet connection (for those with a laptop) are supplied.

**Blue Lake Holiday Park** (Map p150; ☎ 1800 676 028, 8725 9856; www.bluelakeholidaypark.com.au; Bay Rd; unpowered sites per 2 people/cabins/units/bungalows $19/65/75/96; ☒ ☒ ) Adjacent to a golf course and walking and cycling tracks, this amiable park is also close to the Blue Lake. The bonus is great facilities for kids and those with disabilities.

## Eating

**Australian Fish Market** (Map p151; ☎ 8725 2637; 85 Commercial St West; fish & chips $5; ☺ closed Tue) Opposite the Commercial Hotel, this is a favourite takeaway outlet serving chips with battered prawns, calamari or scallops.

**Sage & Muntries Café** (Map p151; ☎ 8724 8400; 78 Commercial St West; mains $19-26; ☺ breakfast, lunch

& dinner) This award-winning licensed café is very popular, and understandably so. Enticing daily specials include spicy sausages with mash and caramelised onions, or bowls of steaming homemade pasta that melts in the mouth. Let the waiting staff know if you're in a hurry, otherwise you can wait awhile for your food.

**Redfins Seafood & Grill** (Map p151; ☎ 8725 0611; 2 Commercial St West; mains $18-25; ☺ lunch daily, dinner Mon-Sat) Mt Gambians relish the seafood dinners in this attractive and upmarket dining room. Coffin Bay oysters are a speciality, and lunch-time specials run Monday to Friday (from $5).

**Sorrentos Café** (Map p151; ☎ 8723 0900; 6 Bay Rd; mains $14-24; ☺ breakfast, lunch & dinner) All-day brekkies ($8.50) are served along with pastas and risottos in this attractive old stone building. The glass-roofed alfresco area is a perfect spot for diving into a deep Baileys or passionfruit cheesecake.

For good-value pub-grub (lunch and dinner mains for around $9 to $14) try **Flanagan's Irish Pub** (Map p151; ☎ 8725 1671; 6 Ferrers St) and the **Commercial Hotel** (Map p151; ☎ 8725 3006; 76 Commercial St West).

## Drinking & Entertainment

**Flanagan's Irish Pub** (Map p151; ☎ 8725 1671; 6 Ferrers St; admission free) The first Irish pub in SA, Flanagan's has an authentic Irish flavour, as well as a dance floor, snooker tables and open fires. It's lively, and on Friday and Saturday nights you'll find bands playing contemporary, '70s and Irish music.

**Funk Lounge** (Map p151; ☎ 8725 4570; 216 Commercial St West; admission free; ☺ noon-2am Wed-Sat) Daytime and late-night fun can be had in this bar and eatery. The décor and finger food pay homage to the '70s, and please a crowd who cannot know how bad the '70s fashions really were. Imported beer and wine are more current.

**Shadows** (Map p151; ☎ 8723 9777; 5 Penola Rd; admission free Wed & Thu, $7 after midnight Fri & Sat; ☺ 9pm-4.30am Wed-Sat) This nightclub welcomes all, but is ruled mainly by those in their 20s. The music takes in the '80s, techno and dance, with DJs and live bands on alternate Saturday nights.

**Oatmill Cinema** (Map p151; ☎ 8724 9150, 1902 241 060; www.oatmill.com.au; 7 Percy St) This three-screen cinema shows contemporary, top-selling films on most days.

**Sir Robert Helpmann Theatre** (Map p151; ☎ 8723 8741; www.countryarts.org.au/helpmann; Civic Centre, 10 Watson Tce; ☺ box office 9.30am-4.30pm Mon-Fri) The Southeast's major entertainment venue has something on fairly regularly, but check with the centre's box office.

## Getting Around

**Lake City Taxis Co-op** (☎ 8723 0000) run to the airport.

Local car-hire agents are **Budget** (☎ 13 27 27; Mt Gambier Airport), **Hertz** (☎ 8723 0870; Mt Gambier Airport) and **Thrifty** (Map p151; ☎ 8723 2488, 0418-838 731; Penola Rd).

**McCormick's Bus Service** (☎ 8724 9778; ☺ Mon-Fri) serves four city routes; the visitors centre has timetables.

## PORT MACDONNELL
☎ 08 / pop 606

Only 28km south of Mt Gambier, this quiet fishing and holiday village has the state's largest crayfishing fleet, and now attracts day-visitors from Mt Gambier. It was once a busy port, hence the surprisingly large and handsome **customs house** (1863).

Twenty-five ships have been wrecked along the coast near here since 1844, which makes Port MacDonnell a popular dive site. For details ask at the Mt Gambier visitors centre (p151). The **Port MacDonnell & District Maritime Museum** (☎ 8738 7259; 49 Meylin St; adult/child $3/1; ☺ 12.30pm-4.30pm Wed, Fri, Sun & some holidays) holds various artefacts recovered from the shipwrecks.

The flamboyant colonial poet Adam Lindsay Gordon's little 1860 cottage home **Dingley Dell** (☎ 8738 2221; admission $8; 10am-4pm Wed-Fri) has some of his works and belongings on display.

# COONAWARRA WINE REGION

This lovely, peaceful region is just perfect for a few days of pottering around the wineries, and 'saintly' Penola, watching the protected birds of the Bool Lagoon and exploring the unique Naracoorte Caves. A heap of B&Bs are dotted around; take advantage of their reasonable rates, stay for a few days and amass a fine collection of glowing wines for your future delectation!

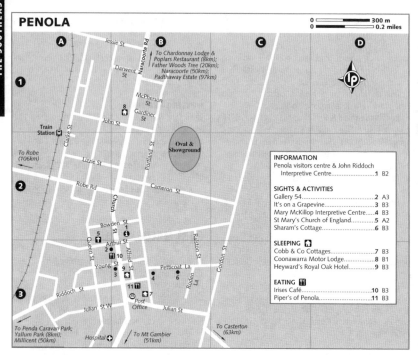

**PENOLA**

0 — 300 m
0 — 0.2 miles

Jessie St
Darwent St
McPherson St
Gardiner St
John St
Train Station
To Robe (106km)
Lizzie St
Robe Rd
Cameron St
Portland St
Oval & Showground
Bowden St
Church St
Queen St
Arthur St
Young St
Alfred St
Ralston St
Petticoat La
Roden La
Gordon St
Riddoch St
Post Office
Julian St W
Julian St
To Penda Caravan Park;
Yallum Park (8km);
Millicent (50km)
Hospital
To Mt Gambier (51km)
To Casterton (63km)

To Chardonnay Lodge &
Poplars Restaurant (8km);
Father Woods Tree (20km);
Naracoorte (50km);
Padthaway Estate (97km)

| INFORMATION | |
|---|---|
| Penola visitors centre & John Riddoch Interpretive Centre | 1 B2 |

| SIGHTS & ACTIVITIES | |
|---|---|
| Gallery 54 | 2 A3 |
| It's on a Grapevine | 3 B3 |
| Mary McKillop Interpretive Centre | 4 B3 |
| St Mary's Church of England | 5 A2 |
| Sharam's Cottage | 6 B3 |

| SLEEPING | |
|---|---|
| Cobb & Co Cottages | 7 B3 |
| Coonawarra Motor Lodge | 8 B1 |
| Heyward's Royal Oak Hotel | 9 B3 |

| EATING | |
|---|---|
| Irises Café | 10 B3 |
| Piper's of Penola | 11 B3 |

The red-gum country between Mt Gambier and Bordertown has some of the richest fodder-growing land and sheep and cattle grazing in SA, while the wine industry is around Coonawarra and Padthaway.

## COONAWARRA WINERIES

Not many could argue against the supremacy of the Coonawarra's glorious peppery Shiraz and spicy Cabernet Sauvignons. 'Terra Rossa' is the cry from the rooftops because more awards for the prestigious Jimmy Watson Trophy (for Australia's best one-year-old red wine) have been garnered here than by any other Australian wine region. The climate also produces some very special Chardonnays and Rieslings that also do not go without accolades.

The Coonawarra region starts at Penola's northern outskirts and straddles the road to Naracoorte for 14km. The first vines were planted in 1891, and although there are more wineries in the area, around 22 have cellar doors offering tastings and sales.

## PENOLA

☎ 08 / pop 1222

Penola has won fame for two things, the first of which is the town's association with the Sisters of St Joseph of the Sacred Heart. This was the order cofounded in 1867 by Mother Mary MacKillop, who has been beatified by the Vatican while they investigate her case for canonisation.

Secondly, Penola sits right in the middle of the Coonawarra wine district, which make it a prime base for those seeking a few days of relaxed wine tasting (see p52).

### Information

**Penola visitors centre** ( ☎ 8737 2855; www.wattleranger .sa.gov.au; 27 Arthur St; 🕙 8.30-5pm Mon-Fri, 10am-5pm Sat, 9.30am-4pm Sun) services the Coonawarra region as well as Penola.

In the same building the **John Riddoch Interpretative Centre** (admission free) has a history

---

**COONAWARRA TASTINGS**

See the Wineries chapter (p52) for a selection of cellar doors you may enjoy visiting.

of the district that dates from the 1850s, and an interactive display of natural gas technology.

## Sights & Activities

The **Mary MacKillop Interpretative Centre** ( ☎ 8737 2092; www.mackillop-penola.com; cnr Portland St & Petticoat Lane; $3.50; 10am-4pm) features the Woods-MacKillop Schoolhouse, and has information on the first school in Australia to welcome children from lower socioeconomic backgrounds. The school was cofounded by Mary MacKillop and Father Julian Woods in 1866.

You'll love **Petticoat Lane** and its quaint, old, slab cottages, several of which are open to the public, including the 1850 **Sharam's Cottage** (ask at the John Riddoch Interpretative Centre for admission times), the first dwelling in Penola. Duck if you're tall, otherwise the door lintel may take your head off as you walk in!

The magnificent **St Mary's Church of England** (1873) on Arthur Street, was designed by an accountant. Who said this profession has no soul?

**Yallum Park** ( ☎ 8737 2435, 8737 3414; Millicent Rd; admission $5; 2pm) is an opulent Italian-style two-storey mansion (1880), built by the district's first pastoralist, John Riddoch. The house, which is in original condition right down to the William Morris wallpaper, is a showpiece of how the wealthier Victorian-era squattocracy lived. It's about 8km from town, and the mansion's guide is the property's current owner.

About 20km north of Penola on Naracoorte Rd is **Father Woods Tree** a huge and old red gum, which was used as an outdoor church by Father Julian Woods for the region's first settlers.

**Gallery 54** ( ☎ 8737 2895; 54 Church St; admission free; 10am-4pm Thu-Sat & Mon, 11am-4pm Sun) is a very small gallery displaying the heart and soul of local knitters, metal workers, painters, sculptors and ceramic artists.

Bikes can be hired from the shop and accommodation booking service **It's on a Grapevine** ( ☎ 8737 2101, 0418-651 291; Shop 42A, Church St; half day $10, full day $20; 10am-5pm Mon-Fri;  ), which also opens for a few hours in the morning on busy weekends.

## Sleeping & Eating

There are many little historic cottages in the Penola district that have been nicely refurbished as self-contained B&Bs. Some of these are within walking distance of wineries, always a bonus! **Coonawarra Discovery** ( ☎ 1800 600 262; www.coonawarradiscovery.com) is a

THE SOUTHEAST

---

**DETOUR: BOOL LAGOON GAME RESERVE & HACKS LAGOON CONSERVATION PARK**

From Penola take the northbound Naracoorte Rd. After about 35km turn west onto Bool Lagoon Rd and follow for 7km.

Here an acknowledged Wetland of International Importance, the 3103-hectare **Bool Lagoon Game Reserve** and 195-hectare **Hacks Lagoon Conservation Park** welcome around 155 migrating and breeding bird species, including 79 water birds per year. A diminishing number of brolgas, once widespread in the region, spend the summer at Bool Lagoon along with many other endangered and rare species.

Be careful driving around in October, particularly on the Big Hill Rd, as this is when long-necked tortoises come out to breed. They're often seen crossing the roads, and they don't speed up to accommodate anyone in a hurry.

There are self-guided walks, and boardwalks give access to all. Guided tours are on offer with notice (☎ 08-8672 2340).

---

free online accommodation booking service, listing 60 B&Bs in the area.

**Heyward's Royal Oak Hotel** ( ☎ 8737 2322; fax 8737 2825; 31 Church Street; s/tw/d $44/77/88; meals $13-18; ☺ lunch & dinner; ☷ ) A busy and cosy hotel that is State Heritage– and National Trust–listed, this is a great community pub. Nice bedrooms upstairs have wonderful wooden four-poster beds and shared bathroom facilities. Locals pack in the bar to chomp great schnitzels and seafood. Ignore the pokies room; there are also boutique beers on tap and open wood fires in the bar.

**Cobb & Co Cottages** ( ☎ 8737 2526; www.cobbnco.com; 2 Portland St; d $125; ☷ ) These three cottages are bright and attractive, and each of them contains two bedrooms, a spa, and everything else that make life restful and easy. Their location is perfect; tucked away out of the main street they are still only a five-minute walk from Penola's restaurants and pub.

**Chardonnay Lodge & Poplars Restaurant** ( ☎ 8736 3309; www.chardonnaylodge.com.au; Riddoch Hwy; s/d $120/140; breakfast & lunch $9, dinner mains $24-28; ☺ breakfast, lunch & dinner; ☷ ☐ ) This is a top-notch motel with lovely gardens. Two disabled suites, five wineries within walking distance and an on-site restaurant and café make this a highly favoured option.

**Coonawarra Motor Lodge** ( ☎ 8737 2364; fax 8737 2543; 114 Church Street; d/f $105/125; ☷ ) This friendly motel on the winery strip is child friendly and has a room with disabled access. At the time of writing, refurbishments include building an attached licensed café.

**Penola Caravan Park** ( ☎ 8737 2381; cnr Riddoch Hwy & South Tce; unpowered sites per 2 people/cabins $16/50) This small but friendly park offers basic budget facilities. There are sites with

access to shower blocks ($19), and small and dated cabins.

**Pipers of Penola** ( ☎ 8737 3999; www.pipersof penola.com.au; 58 Riddoch St; mains $13-26; ☺ dinner Mon-Sat, closed Sun) This place is a little smasher: a classy but intimate dining room with friendly staff and tasty fare. The inventive menu produces goodies such as cheese soufflés and spicy kangaroo vindaloo. The prices are very good, as is the wine list.

**Irises Café** ( ☎ 8737 2967; 48 Church Street; mains $9.50-16.50; ☺ breakfast & lunch) This bring-your-own (BYO) and licensed café serves homemade soups and crusty-topped pies, pastas, and a filling, juicy apple crumble.

# NARACOORTE
☎ 08 / pop 4785
Settled in the 1840s, Naracoorte is one of the oldest towns in the state and really acts as a service town to the surrounding agricultural areas. It is nice enough, and proximity to the Victorian border and the World Heritage–listed Naracoorte Caves makes it an obvious practical stop.

**Naracoorte visitors centre** ( ☎ 1800 244 421, 8762 1518; www.naracoortetourism.com.au; MacDonnell St; ☺ 9am-4pm) is housed in an old flour mill.

## Sights
In the visitors centre, the **Sheep's Back Museum** ( ☎ 8762 1518, 8762 0745; MacDonnell St; adult/child $5/2; ☺ 9am-4pm) follows the history of the SA wool industry from the 1840s to today. For serious wool industry fetishists only.

**Naracoorte Art Gallery's** ( ☎ 8762 3390; 91 Ormerod St; admission free; ☺ 11.30am-4.30pm Tue-Fri, 10am-noon Sat) collection of traditional and contemporary artworks will both surprise and delight.

**Yulgilbar Wood Gallery** ( ☎ 8762 3246; yulgilbar@ rbm.com.au; opposite Naracoorte Caves; admission free; ⏰ 10am-5pm) has displays for sale of light furniture and household objects that have been finely crafted from native and glowing red-gum woods.

Stop to taste the sultry red wines at **Padthaway Estate Winery** ( ☎ 8765 5555; www.padthawayhomestead.com.au; Riddoch Hwy; d $175; dinner $55; ⏰ lunch & dinner), and then contemplate lunch or dinner and staying at the B&B. This gem is a dignified and fine-looking old historic homestead (1882) set in private and lush gardens, 47km from Naracoorte on the Riddoch Hwy. Padthaway vineyards surround the house. A three-course dinner includes mains such as homemade tortellini of chicken and gibson blue cheese, sage and pinenut butter ($55). The rooms are sumptuous and cosy and the original settler's cottage is great for families ($120).

With their forests and scrubland the Naracoorte Ranges are made for exploration by horse. **Limestone Coast Adventures** ( ☎ 8764 7457, 0427-647 457; Riddoch Hwy, Straun, near Naracoorte; $30) runs horse-riding tours. Three trail rides are available; the longest lasts half a day. Tuition and pony rides are also available.

### Sleeping & Eating
**Naracoorte Backpackers** ( ☎ 8762 3835; www.naracoortebackpackers.com.au; 4 Jones St; dm per week $130; 🖳 ) The manager of this hostel acts as a casual-labour contractor for local vineyards, and provides transport for working travellers. The facilities are enough to get by with for a few weeks or so.

**Handyside Cottage** ( ☎ 8762 2906, 0408-810 645; http://home.rbm.com.au/peake; 15 Handyside St; d $120; 🔀 ) This nice little pink and white stone cottage has pretty lawned gardens. Children are welcome and there's a barbecue, wood fire and breakfast provisions. The cottage is very neat and well maintained and rates reduce ($105 per double room) for stays of two or more nights.

**William MacIntosh Motor Lodge** ( ☎ 8762 1644; willnara@bigpond.com; Adelaide Rd; d/tw $105/120; mains $17-22; ⏰ lunch & dinner; 🔀 🔊 ) This lodge is on the right side of town, and has neat and pleasant rooms. An on-site licensed restaurant also provides room service.

**Naracoorte Hotel/Motel** ( ☎ 8762 2400; 8762 0022; 73 Ormerod St; D $70, mains $14-18; ⏰ lunch &

dinner) With daily specials ($7.50) and good-value bistro-style food, this is a popular pub in the centre of town. The hotel has older but clean and neat motel rooms.

**Naracoorte Holiday Park** ( ☎ 8762 2128; www.naracoorteholidaypark.com.au; 81 Park Tce; powered sites per 2 people/vans/cabins $21/62/73) This immaculate and modern park sits by a creek and offers great family accommodation and amusements; a miniature train, minigolf course and swimming lake.

**Country Roads Motor Inn** ( ☎ 8762 3900; www.countryroadsnaracoorte.com.au; 20 Smith St; s/d $87/97; 🔀 ) Within walking distance of the town centre, and has pleasant, clean and spacious rooms.

**Blue Wattle Café** ( ☎ 8762 3565; 31 Robertson St; mains $15-22; ⏰ lunch & dinner) This licensed and colourful café has happy customers. The bright surroundings are perfect for tucking into bowls of tasty pasta, gourmet pizzas and crisp, fresh salads.

## NARACOORTE CAVES NATIONAL PARK
Roughly 12km to the southeast of Naracoorte, off the Penola road, is the only World Heritage–listed site in SA. The discovery of an ancient fossilised marsupial in these limestone caves made history and featured in the BBC David Attenborough series *Life on Earth*. The signage is sporadic so take a good map.

The excellent **Wonambi Fossil Centre** ( ☎ 08-8762 2340; naracoortecaves@saugov.sa.gov.au; Hynam-Caves Rd; ⏰ 9am-5pm winter, 9am-sunset summer), houses a re-creation of the rainforest environment that covered this area 200,000 years ago. Life-size models of extinct animals and their habitats have been lovingly reconstructed and, like couch potatoes, some models grunt and move; children of all ages will enjoy them.

The limestone caves have bizarre formations of stalactites and stalagmites. The caves include **Victoria Fossil Cave**, **Alexandra Cave**, **Blanche Cave** and **Wet Cave**; the latter can be seen on a self-guided tour. For the others, ranger-guided tours run from 9.30am to 3.30pm.

It is worth visiting the **Bat Cave** at dusk during summer, to see thousands of bats depart en masse to find their tucker. Although the cave is not open to the public, infrared TV cameras allow you to see where the endangered southern bentwing

THE SOUTHEAST

bats huddle. They return each spring to give birth.

All the above options, including the Bat Cave and Wonambi Fossil Centre, are priced as follows: single-cave tours adult/child $11/$6.50; two-cave tours $17.50/10.50. For further price details check out www.environment.sa.gov.au/parks/nara coorte.

Adventure tours to undeveloped caves in the area with the rangers acting as guides (wear sneakers or trainers and old clothes) start at $28 for novices and $60 for a minimum of four advanced explorers. These tours need to be booked well ahead.

## DUKES HIGHWAY

The last town on the SA side of the border is **Bordertown** (population 2455). The town is the birthplace of former Labor prime minister Bob Hawke, and there's a bust of Bob outside the town hall. On the left as you enter from Victoria is a wildlife park, with various species of Australian fauna, including rare white kangaroos snoozing behind a wire fence.

The 207,941-hectare **Ngarkat Group of Conservation Parks** consists of four parks (Scorpion Springs, Mt Shaugh, Mt Rescue and Ngarkat) near the Victorian border. The parks contain a wonderful range of wildlife: echidnas, pygmy possums, dunnarts, kangaroos, lizards and birds. Walking tracks range from 10-minute strolls to five-hour hikes, and there is a good network of 4WD tracks. Please drive slowly, especially during dusk and dawn, when the wildlife feeds and roams.

# Barossa Valley

**CONTENTS**

| | |
|---|---|
| Lyndoch | 163 |
| Bethany | 164 |
| Tanunda | 164 |
| Nuriootpa | 167 |
| Angaston | 168 |
| Eden Valley | 169 |

**BAROSSA VALLEY**

The Barossa Valley is a treat that should be savoured slowly, like the famous and fabulous wines that are produced in this region. Despite the compact size of the area, the gentle hills and bountiful 25km-long valley produce huge amounts of big, luscious and fruity wines. The Barossa Valley alone accounts for 21% of Australia's wine output.

The Barossa's 80 wineries all lie within easy reach of each other, around 65km northeast of Adelaide. The wineries also provide the lifeblood of the region's small towns, whose distinctly German heritage dates back to 1842. Fleeing religious persecution in Prussia and Silesia, settlers created a Lutheran heartland where German traditions persist today.

The physical signs of this early settlement are everywhere. The valley is dotted with the steeples of distinctive Lutheran churches, and many town streets are lined with tiny cottages. Cultural legacies of the early settlers include a dubious passion for marching oompah bands, and an appetite for wurst, pastries, festivals and superb wines.

Take a few days and immerse yourself in the valley's gentle and relaxing atmosphere. There are some super walks to be had through the lovely rolling countryside. It is also easy enough to avoid day-tours from Adelaide by meandering along back roads; try the palm-fringed road to Seppeltsfield, the Marananga route to the sleepy historic hamlet of Bethany and the back roads between Angaston and Tanunda.

## HIGHLIGHTS

- Hopping on a **bicycle** (p162) and discovering vine-lined back roads, historic Lutheran churches and old German farmhouses
- Savouring the valley's **flavours** (p167); Bavarian *brezel* (similar to a prezel), pastries baked in a wood-fired oven, pheasant pâté and quandong mead
- Boarding a **hot-air balloon** (p162) in Tanunda and looking down over the rolling hills of Australia's most famous wine region
- Learning how to nose a Pinot Noir, swirl a Shiraz and savour a Semillon at a few **Barossa wineries** (p54)
- Luxuriating with your beloved in a **weekend cottage** (opposite) with bubbling spa and champagne
- Striding the walking tracks of the **Kaiser Stuhl Conservation Park** (p166), spotting kestrels and hawks
- Dancing around a maypole at the colourful **Barossa Vintage Festival** (p163)

Tanunda ★

Kaiser Stuhl Conservation Park ★

- TELEPHONE CODE: ☎ 08
- www.barossa-region.org

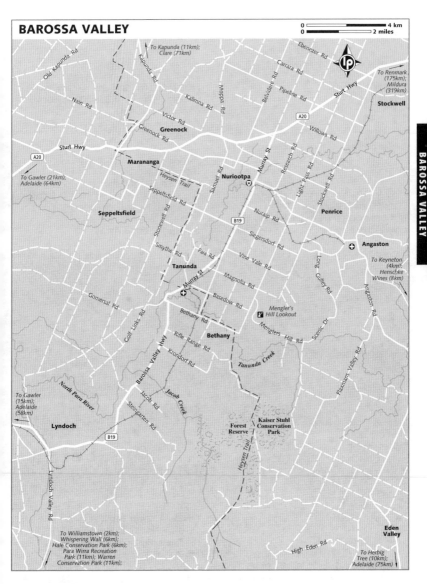

BAROSSA VALLEY

## Accommodation

The Barossa has numerous self-contained cottages and romantic hideaways, which offer the complete spa-bath and champagne package. These weekenders are worth the price for a few days of self-indulgence. Book ahead during public holidays and festivals, and be warned, rates become ugly at these times. The Tanunda visitors centre (p164) has details of a huge selection of cottages, as does **Barossa BnB Booking Service** ( ☎ 1800 227 677, 08-8524 5353; www.bnbbookings.com;  8am-8pm).

## Tours

There are a huge number of day tours operating from Adelaide that will take in the

**BAROSSA VALLEY**

**WINERIES**

From the moment that Johann Gramp planted the valley's first grapes on his property at Jacob's Creek in 1847, the Barossa Valley was destined to become a major Australian wine region. The valley is best known for Shiraz, with the most important of its whites.

Today the valley has around 80 wineries from boutiques to huge complexes, the latter mostly owned by multinationals; more than 60 of these have cellar doors offering public tastings. These are listed in tourism guides, which also detail disabled facilities. The Wineries chapter (p54) lists a mix of popular wineries that also produce top-notch wines. For those who wish to maintain the illusion of healthy pursuits, take the **Para Road Trail**, an informal cycling and walking path that runs between Nuriootpa and Tanunda and follows the river to a number of cellar doors.

main tourist sights as well as a few wineries. For those more interested in wine tasting, stick with smaller Adelaide companies and tour operators based in the valley. They visit more wineries and gain access to smaller cellar doors that do not always welcome coach parties. Barossa Valley tour operators also offer Adelaide pick-ups. Rates given here are per person and are for local departures.

**Balloon Adventures** ( ☎ 08-8389 3195; www.balloon adventures.com.au; $260; ☽ daily, weather permitting) Fly the sky in a hot-air balloon and sail serenely over the valley. The one-hour flight departs from Tanunda and includes a champagne breakfast.

**Barossa Daimler Tours** ( ☎ 08-8524 9047; www .barossadaimlertours.com.au) With seats polished by royal posteriors, these ex-royal vehicles transport up to four passengers around wineries, sights and gourmet outlets (from $195). They collect from and return to your accommodation.

**Barossa Valley Day Tour** ( ☎ 08-8262 6900; $60; ☽ Sat) This tour departs Adelaide and takes in five wineries and Maggie Beer's Farm Shop & Restaurant – a good mixture.

**Barossa Valley Tours** ( ☎ 08-8563 2233; www .barossavalleytours.com) Personalised winery tours are now affordable for us all; the Heritage & Wine Tours is for between two and seven people and will visit your choice of sights and wineries for a great price (per person $60).

**Ecotrek** ( ☎ 08-8383 7198; www.ecotrek.com.au) Deluxe cycling adventures are on offer with departures from

Adelaide. Tours include two-day all-inclusive wine tasting and gourmet trips ($560).

**Groovy Grape Getaways** ( ☎ 1800 66 11 77, 08-8371 4000; www.groovygrape.com.au) These tours depart from Adelaide and are popular with backpackers ($65).

**Prime Mini Tours** ( ☎ 08-8293 4900; www.primemini tours.com; ☽ Tue, Thu, Sat & Sun) This Adelaide-based company offers a number of winery tours. The Barossa Valley Supreme tour ($72) is one of the best valley tours on offer.

Adelaide coach tour operators offering day trips that incorporate lunch (from $90) include **Premier Stateliner** ( ☎ 08-8415 5566; www .premierstateliner.com.au) and **Adelaide Sightseeing** ( ☎ 08-8231 4144; www.adelaidesightseeing.com.au).

## Getting There & Away

There are several routes from Adelaide, with the most direct being the Main North Rd through Elizabeth and Gawler. If you're coming from the east and want to tour the wineries before hitting Adelaide, the scenic route via Springton and Eden Valley to Angaston is the best bet.

**Barossa Valley Coaches** ( ☎ 08-8564 3022; bvcoach@ bvcoach.com) has twice-daily return services from Adelaide (once on Sunday) to Lyndoch ($11, 1½ hours), Tanunda ($13, 1½ hours), Nuriootpa ($14, two hours) and Angaston ($15, two hours).

## Getting Around

The Barossa is pretty good for **cycling**, with routes that can take in a few wineries. Ask at the Tanunda visitors centre (p164) or cycle-hire outlets for the best directions. The **Para Road Trail** is a rough bike path which runs between Nuriootpa and Tanunda and passes several wineries.

Bicycles can be rented from the **Tanunda Caravan & Tourist Park** ( ☎ 08-8563 2784; Barossa Valley Way, Tanunda; adult/child per day $20/12), and the **Barossa Bunkhaus Travellers Hostel & Cottage** ( ☎ 08-8562 2260; Barossa Valley Way; per day $10) in Nuriootpa.

**Barossa Valley Taxis** ( ☎ 1800 288 294, 08-8563 3600) have a 24-hour daily service that runs throughout the valley. From Tanunda the cost is around $20 to Angaston and $15 to Nuriootpa.

Alternatively, you can rent a car from the **Caltex service station** ( ☎ 08-8563 2677; 212 Murray St, Tanunda) from $55 per day for the first 150km.

## FESTIVALS & EVENTS

The Barossa celebrates anything and everything from marching oompah bands to lavender harvesting, as well as a host of events rejoicing in the region's fruitful grapes. Check with the Tanunda visitors centre (p164) or South Australian Tourism Commission (p263) for specific dates as these often change from year to year.

### January

**Jacob's Tour Down Under** ( ☎ 1300 852 982, 08-8563 0600; www.tourdownunder.com.au/index.php ) The Barossa leg of the Tour Down Under sees international cyclists battling for supremacy in a truly exciting race.
**Valley Hot Rodders 'Cruise On'** ( ☎ 08-8524 5170; www.barossa-region.org/calendar.asp) The Hot Rodders celebrate their customised cars with rock 'n' roll dancing and just a little posturing.

### February

**Barossa Under the Stars** ( ☎ 1300 852 982, 08-8563 0600; www.barossaunderthestars.com.au) Spare tickets for this event are as rare as hen's teeth. Rocking entertainers such as Rod Stewart, Cliff Richards and John Farnham shake up the night for wine-slurping picnickers.
**German Oompah Fest** ( ☎ 1300 852 982, 08-8563 0600; www.barossa-region.org) Yet another event worthy of note, heralding much bystander frivolity.

### March

**Barossa Vintage Festival** ( ☎ 1300 852 982, 08-8563 0600; www.barossa-region.org/vintagefestival) The biggest and most colourful of the valley festivals takes place in odd-numbered years starting on Easter Monday. The week is a heap of ungainly and daft fun; brass bands and processions, maypole dancing, winery tug-of-war contests. All of these events are enjoyed with much mirth and grape juice.

### May

**Barossa Hot Air Balloon Regatta** ( ☎ 1300 852 982, 08-8563 0600; www.barossa-region.org) The rolling green valley makes a beautiful backdrop for this spectacle.

### July

**Shiraz Alliance Barossa** ( ☎ 08-8563 3668; www.barossa-region.org) A big wine party showcasing the wine that many believe is the true star of the valley.

### August

**Barossa Jazz Weekend** ( ☎ 1300 852 982, 08-8563 0600; www.barossa-region.org) August trumpets an excuse to indulge in the music of the soul as well as gourmet food and wine at a number of Barossa cellar doors.
**Cooper's Rally SA** ( ☎ 08-8340 4899; www.barossa-region.org) The first leg of the Australian Rally Championship Super Series has definite appeal for rev heads of all ages.

### September

**Barossa Wine Show** ( ☎ 1300 852 982, 08-8563 0600; www.barossa-region.org) A presentation dinner and lip-smacking public tastings yet again celebrate the wonderful grape.

### October

**Barossa Music Festival** ( ☎ 08-8564 2511; www.barossa.org) Picnics, wine (naturally), theatre and big-name bands playing mainly classical, chamber and jazz music. The intimate venues include wineries, barrel halls and historic churches.

### November

**Lyndoch Lavender Festival** ( ☎ 08-8524 4538; www.barossa-region.org) This harvest celebration is one for bees and those with a preference for delicate nasal delights.

# LYNDOCH

☎ 08 / pop 1251

Lyndoch is a quiet working town. There's not much here for marauding visitors, but it is worth a pit stop at the hugely popular and licensed **Lyndoch Bakery & Restaurant** ( ☎ 8524 4424; Barossa Valley Hwy; meals $8-18; ☒ lunch), one of the valley's German-style bakeries. Try

---

**DETOUR: BAROSSA GOLD FIELDS**

Take the road south from Lyndoch for 8km towards Williamstown. Turn west for 5km, and then take the Goldfields Rd for 4km to the **Para Wirra Recreation Park**. Here you will find the **Barossa Gold Fields**, which in the late 1860s were found to contain enough gold to set 4000 diggers chasing mainly unfulfilled dreams. Small amounts of gold were found up to the 1930s. There's a walking track around the diggings at Victoria Hill and at the North Tunnel, which was partially excavated in 1895.

---

handcrafted German rye bread, pretzels or pastries. Daily specials always include German cuisine.

About 7km southwest of Lyndoch, the Barossa Reservoir has the famous **Whispering Wall**, a concrete dam wall with amazing acoustics; conversations held at one end can be heard clearly 150m away at the far end of the wall.

Free Internet access is available at **Lyndoch public library** ( ☎ 8524 4009; 29 Barossa Valley Way, Lyndoch).

## BETHANY

☎ 08 / pop 70

The site of the first German settlement in the Barossa, this sleepy but attractive hamlet is about 5km from Tanunda. A tree-lined avenue contains a number of old cottages, including the tiny **Landhaus**. Built of stone, mud and straw in the 1840s, the first resident was a shepherd and, judging by the height of the lintels, not a very tall one.

Also worth a visit is the little **cemetery**, which has headstones in Gothic script dating from the 1860s. The depressing number of children's graves illustrates the hardships faced by the early settlers.

**Bethany Wines** ( ☎ 8563 2086; www.bethany.com .au; Bethany Rd; 10am-5pm Mon-Sat, 1-5pm Sun) is a marvellous cellar door, which sits on a hill above the large and attractive Bethany Reserve. The Bethany family produces classic wines and ports that are perfect for sipping under any circumstances (see p54 for other winery suggestions).

**Sonntag House** ( ☎ 8563 0775; www.sonntaghouse .com.au; Bethany Rd; d $140; ), an 1840s stone

cottage that has been gently and prettily refurbished (also providing disabled access) is placed perfectly for those seeking a quiet getaway, although children are also welcome. The colourful cottage garden, wood fire, claw-footed bath and close proximity to Bethany Wines are other enticing attractions.

## TANUNDA

☎ 08 / pop 3865

Sitting in the centre of the valley both geographically and socially, Tanunda is the Barossa township that is the most geared towards visitors. Despite an incredibly high number of visitors each year, the town still maintains a surprisingly low-key character. Most attractions lie within an easy stroll of each other on Murray St, the main road through town.

The region's **Tanunda visitors centre** ( ☎ 8563 0600; www.barossa-region.org; 66-68 Murray St, Tanunda: 9am-5pm Mon-Fri, 9am-4pm Sat & Sun) includes the **Barossa Wine Centre** an interpretive educational centre ($2.50). The **Tanunda public library** ( ☎ 8563 2729; 83 Murray St, Tanunda) has free Internet access.

### Sights & Activities

Tanunda has numerous historic buildings including the early cottages around Goat Sq, on John St. This was the *ziegenmarkt*, a meeting and market place laid out in 1842 as the original centre of Tanunda.

There are fine old Lutheran churches in all the valley towns but Tanunda has some of the most interesting, including the 1849 **Tabor Church** (79 Murray St) and 1868 **St John's Church** (Jane Place), which had life-size wooden statues of Christ, Moses and the apostles Peter, Paul and John donated in 1892. The **Langmeil Lutheran Church** (Maria St), is associated with Pastor Kavel, who arrived in South Australia (SA) in 1838 and was the state's first Lutheran minister.

**Barossa Valley Historical Museum** ( ☎ 8563 0507; 47 Murray St; admission $4; 11am-5pm Mon-Sat, 1-5pm Sun) has exhibits on the valley's early settlement and a crammed antique shop in the 1866 telegraph station.

The **Barossa Regional Gallery** (3 Basedow Rd; admission free; 11am-4pm Tue-Sun) has an eclectic collection of paintings and crafts. The upstairs gallery houses a small memorial of photos of WWI and WWII veterans.

Confirm the gallery's opening hours at the Tanunda visitors centre.

Artisans make kegs and other wooden items at the **Keg Factory** ( ☎ 8563 3012; St Halletts Rd; admission free; ☺ 8am-4.30pm Mon-Sat, 10am-4.30pm Sun), 4km south of town.

About 3km from Tanunda, **Norm's Coolies** ( ☎ 8563 2198; off Gomersal Rd; adult/child $8/4; ☺ 2pm Mon, Wed & Sat) go through their paces at the Breezy Gully Farm. This show is unmissable, especially once you realise that this army of trained sheepdogs may be smarter and more alluring than their audience.

Families with young children might want to head for **Storybook Cottage & Whacky Wood** ( ☎ 8563 2910; Oak St; adult/child $6/2.50-4.50; ☺ 10am-5pm, closed Tue & Thu outside school holidays) off the highway towards Lyndoch. There are hands-on models, rides, games and a picnic ground. A rabbit warren allows Junior to play at being Peter the Rabbit.

**Basedow Wines** ( ☎ 8563 0333; 161 Murray St, Tanunda; ☺ 10am-5pm Mon-Fri, 11am-5pm Sat & Sun) is an atmospheric and authentic tasting cellar sitting on Tanunda's main street. It offers a great and affordable range of wines (see p54 for other winery suggestions).

From Tanunda, take the scenic route to Angaston through Bethany and via **Mengler's Hill**. It runs through beautiful rural country featuring huge gums; the view over the valley from Mengler's Hill is superb as long as you ignore the dreadful sculptures in the foreground.

En route is the 390-hectare **Kaiser Stuhl Conservation Park** with some great views and walking tracks (see p166).

## Sleeping

Much of the accommodation in the valley centres on Tanunda.

**Tanunda Hotel** ( ☎ 8563 2030; www.sahotels.com.au /tanunda/index.asp; 51 Murray St; s/d $50/60) Rates rise for rooms with bathroom facilities, but this family-run hotel is comfortable, friendly and sits in the centre of town. Opened in 1846, the hotel is a real community centre and holds an annual yabby sandwich contest (December to February) that all keen fisherfolk are welcome to enter. The pub grub is also popular.

**Lanzerac Country Estate B&B** ( ☎ 8563 0499; www.lanzerac.com.au; Menge Rd; d $150; ☒ ) An ornamental 'lake' and vineyards frame the estate. Units are furnished with comfortable

beds and draped curtains. The décor also includes a selection of stone horses, cupids and other depictions of a past, more louche era. Although the glory is now a little faded, the little private patios, spas and atmosphere do signal that fun can be had. When in Rome…

**Langmeil Cottages** ( ☎ 8563 2987; www.langmeil cottages.com; 89 Langmeil Rd; d $150; ☒ ☒ ) These cottage units share some luxurious furniture. A sauna and hot, therapeutic spa are just what is required after hill walking or a little too much tippling, and make this an attractive prospect. A barbecue, laundry and bicycles are also provided for guests.

**Valley Motel** ( ☎ 8563 2039; 73 Murray St; s/d $75/95, d with spa $100; ☒ ) There are only a few rooms at this central motel so book ahead. Apart from sitting on Murray St, the motel has spotless and good-quality rooms (and great showers). The good-value bistro is family-friendly and always busy (see p166).

**Merlot Cottages** ( ☎ 8563 0577; 20 Elizabeth St; www.merlotcottage.com.au; d $250; ☒ ) Just a five-minute walk into Tanunda and a view that encompasses the Barossa Ranges means that this 1850s cottage and adjacent suites are always in demand. A large and very pretty garden is lined with aromatic lavender bushes and rosemary hedges. Bicycles are also provided; minimum bookings apply.

**Tanunda Caravan & Tourist Park** ( ☎ 8563 2784; www.tanundacaravantouristpark.com.au; Barossa Valley

**BAROSSA VALLEY** (sidebar)

Way; sites per 2 people/vans/cabins/cabins with bathrooms $17/48/58/75; 😢 ) This spacious green park is walking distance to central Tanunda, and is dotted with mature trees offering shade and character. The great facilities include a good playground, barbecues, laundry, bike hire (adult/child per day $20/12) and separate bathrooms for children and the disabled. A welcoming picture.

## Eating

Avoid the bland tourist traps – there are some nice little cafés and bakeries that supply atmosphere and a satisfying chunk of cake or German goodies.

**Tanunda Hotel** ( ☎ 8563 2030; www.sahotels.com.au/tanunda/index.asp; 51 Murray St; mains $9-18; 😊 lunch & dinner) This hotel offers specials on weekdays ($8) and has counter meals for children ($5).

**Tanunda Apex Bakery** ( ☎ 8563 2483; Elizabeth St; meals $4-10 😊 breakfast & lunch) A wood-fired oven, traditional recipes and dedication are the keys to the long-standing success of this German-style bakery. Take your pick and

relish the breads, cakes (especially the *bienenstich*), pies and pasties.

**Barossa Wurst Haus & Bakery** ( ☎ 8563 3598; 86A Murray St; meals $6-11; 😊 breakfast & lunch) Locals pack this bakery for all-day breakfasts ($9), pies and quiches, traditional German *mettwurst* sausage rolls, wonderful crusty bread, home-made soups and other goodies. Smart travellers will follow in their footsteps.

**Valley Motel** ( ☎ 8563 2039; 73 Murray St; mains $13-17; 😊 lunch & dinner) The motel's bistro is really good value and child-friendly. Daily specials include meals such as chicken curry and peppercorn-crusted rump steak. Lunch and dinner menus include a children's selection.

**Zinfandel Tea Rooms** ( ☎ 8563 2822; 34 Murray St; meals $5-15; 😊 breakfast & lunch) This tearoom is tucked away in a little cottage. Small rooms with tablecloths and doilies highlight mouth-watering buttery shortbread tarts, apple strudels and excellent savoury German lunches.

**1918 Bistro & Grill** ( ☎ 8563 0405; 94 Murray St; mains $19-26; 😊 lunch & dinner) A local institution,

---

### ESCAPING THE MADDING CROWDS

For a little solitude and tranquillity you cannot beat the region's parks. They contain a range of walking tracks that should satisfy everyone, from Sunday strollers to more energetic bushwalkers. Feathered and furry wildlife is also abundant. Ask at the Tanunda visitors centre (p164) for track maps, although many paths are delineated. The **Heysen Trail** (see p38) also passes through this region.

The beautiful 1417-hectare **Para Wirra Recreation Park** (Humbug Scrub Rd, One Tree Hill) sits in the northern Mt Lofty Ranges and offers a choice of hill and valley views. There are good family facilities with disabled access, barbecues, sporting ovals and tennis courts. Walking tracks and scenic drives give a greater access to the 100 native birds that flutter around the trees, while emus hang hopefully around picnic areas. Western grey 'roos graze at dawn and dusk.

Photographers, naturalists and twitchers love the hilly and steep rocky ridges of the 191-hectare **Hale Conservation Park**. The walking tracks here are more challenging, although well worth the effort. Keep your eyes open for the short-beaked echidna and extremely shy yellow-footed antechinus (a mouse-sized marsupial).

The nearby **Warren Conservation Park** (363 hectares) is a tranquil paradise for lovers of nature, with forests, reservoirs and a host of native flora that should delight naturalists. Eucalypts, wattles, banksias, heaths and hakeas all flower in spring, while species of eucalypt include the pink, blue and statuesque river red gum. The park is also traversed by the **Heysen Trail**.

En route from Mengler's Hill to Angaston is the turn-off for the 390-hectare **Kaiser Stuhl Conservation Park**, known for some excellent walks. The Stringybark Loop Trail (2.4km) and Wallowa Loop Trail (6.5km) commence at the park entrance. Fantastic views exist from the top of the Barossa Ranges. Abundant native flora, such as banksias, acacias and grevilleas, and birdlife can also be enjoyed. In particular, look out for Nankeen kestrels and brown hawks. Western grey 'roos also bound through this park.

For park information contact the **Department for Environment & Heritage** (DEH; ☎ 08-8336 0901; www.environment.sa.gov.au/parks; Main St, Athelstone; 😊 9am-5pm Mon-Fri).

though not one for vegetarians or those with picky appetites. Long-lunching carnivores and steamed-pudding lovers will rejoice with this hearty celebration of the stomach.

**Avanti Pizza Pasta** ( ☎ 8563 0722; cnr Murray & Julius Sts; meals $4.50-16; ☽ dinner Mon-Fri, lunch & dinner Sat & Sun) This takeaway place also has a few tables for diners. A fresh, clean and bright interior and an extensive menu should satisfy most pizza lovers.

## Shopping

There are a few little gems tucked away on Murray St. Browse your way through **bric-a-brac** and **bookshops** as well as **arts & crafts** outlets.

**Old Mill Gallery & Café** ( ☎ 8563 0222; www.old millgallery.com; 34 Murray St; admission free) Displays of vibrant art and woodwork decorate the old mill, and talented local artists, such as Brian Wadsworth, create a great ambience. The artworks are worth a browse, even if just as an excuse for a cup of tea or organic coffee and some home-made cake (around $8).

**Raven's Parlour Bookshop** ( ☎ 8563 3455; 32A Murray St) The bookshop is housed in the old mill and is a true delight. Browsers can mooch through comprehensive shelves of new books covering the full gamut of subjects, as well as thousands of second-hand (not so) dusty bargains.

**Mortuary Collectables Diecast Model Specialists** ( ☎ 8563 0485; 76 Murray St; ☽ 10am-5pm closed Wed) With this name you could be forgiven for thinking that Frankenstein's creation was inspired at this location, rather than diehard car model junkies. The shop is stacked from top to bottom with every type and size of car model; everything from V8 super car collectables to replica James Bond cars.

**Kathy's Old-Fashioned Sweetshop** ( ☎ 8563 1166; 86D Murray St) A real trip down memory lane is waiting for any grown-up kids who enter this sugary paradise. Sherbet fountains, sugar mice, space ships and gobstoppers (huge enough to silence a politician) are all stocked. These genuine articles are imported from overseas with loving care.

## NURIOOTPA

☎ 08 / pop 3865
At the northern end of the valley, Nuriootpa is the commercial centre of the Barossa.

**Nuriootpa public library** ( ☎ 8562 1107; 10 Murray St, Nuriootpa) offers free Internet access.

There are pleasant picnic areas and river walks along the **North Para River**, which winds through town.

**Luhrs Cottage** ( ☎ 8562 1407, 8562 3886; Immanuel Way, Light Pass Rd; admission by donation; ☽ 9.30am-3.30pm Mon-Fri, 10am-4pm Sat, Sun & public holidays) is a delightful little dwelling in the hamlet of Lights Pass, about 3km east of Nuriootpa. Built in 1846 of mud and straw as a residence for schoolteacher Mr Luhrs, the cottage is now a museum. The schoolroom displays are amusing.

**Quilt & Craft Cottage** ( ☎ 8562 3212; Main Rd, Angaston to Nuriootpa Rd; admission free; ☽ 10-4.30pm Mon-Sat) is stuffed full of craft fabrics and quilting supplies. The display by local quilters may thrill those with a love of the thread and needle.

## Sleeping & Eating

**Barossa Bunkhaus Travellers Hostel** ( ☎ 8562 2260; Barossa Valley Way; dm $17, cottage d $50) This pleasant and clean accommodation is about 1km from town and there are great views over the surrounding vineyards. However, there is no heating or air-con, and the dorms are a bit basic. Bicycles can also be hired here ($10 per day).

**Kaesler Estate Restaurant & Cottages** ( ☎ 8562 2711; www.kaeslerrestaurantcottages.com; d $160; mains $20, desserts $10; ☽ lunch & dinner; ☒ ) To really score a winner, book yourself a comfortable suite with spa (breakfast and fresh flowers inclusive). Then indulge in the wines and superb food of the adjacent restaurant, dining either in an old hayloft or outdoors by a small waterway. The atmosphere in the restaurant is nearly as good as the food, which is super. You are sincerely advised not to miss out on the light and fluffy sticky date pudding and caramel sauce.

**Treetops B&B** ( ☎ 8562 2522; www.bnbbookings.com /treetops.htm; Seppeltsfield Rd, Maranaga; d $170; ☒ ) Set high on a hill among trees (the name is a clue), the views from this light-filled property are great. The rooms have polished wooden floors and are tastefully furnished. Breakfast is included, while dinner and picnic hampers can be supplied. An en suite spa, open log fire and inviting two-night dinner package all combine to shout 'book me!'

**Nuriootpa Vine Inn & Vine Court** ( ☎ 8562 2133; www.vineinn.com.au; 14 & 49 Murray St; s/d $97/115 & s/d

$78/91; mains $8-20; (🕐 lunch & dinner; 🗙 🖵 ) These standard motels have two plus points: they are central to Nuriootpa and also within walking distance of a couple of wineries. The cheaper Vine Court has disabled access and also welcomes families, and the Vine Inn has a restaurant and serves counter meals in their bar.

**Whirlwind Farm** ( ☎ 8562 2637; www.whirlwindbb .com; Samuel Rd; d $140; 🗙 ) This farmhouse B&B has a private guest wing with wooden beams and attractive airy rooms. A large veranda and pepper tree offer sheltered spots for contemplating life or snoozing with the papers after breakfast. As the farm sits next to Maggie Beer's restaurant, a great lunch is also guaranteed.

**Peppers Hermitage Barossa Valley** ( ☎ 8562 2722; www.peppers.com.au; Seppeltsfield Rd, Marananga; d $270, d with spa $340, 2-4–course meals $48; 🗙 🖵 🖵 ) A number of very classy suites have been carefully designed as intimate and relaxing retreats. Rates vary according to which additional indulgence you wish to enjoy. A licensed restaurant is on the grounds; delicate Asian- and Mediterranean-inspired dishes include Thai seafood curry – with SA Hiramasa kingfish and king prawns. There is also a guest library (with books, CDs and DVDs), hot spa, sauna and outdoor pool. Some very good packages make this a weekend winner.

**Barossa Valley SA Tourist Park** ( ☎ 8562 2615; Penrice Rd; sites per 2 people/cabin/cabin with bathroom/ family $17/38/49/65; 🖵 ) This friendly park is green, peaceful and shady and sits close to the river. There are walking tracks, tennis courts, barbecue areas, playgrounds and an Internet kiosk. The cabins have small balconies and a central grassed oval that just calls out for cricket and baseball stars.

**Maggie Beer's Farm Shop & Restaurant** ( ☎ 8562 4477; www.maggiebeer.com.au; Pheasant Farm Rd; mains $16-20; 🕐 lunch) Celebrity-gourmet Maggie has been very successful with her range of condiments, preserves and pâtés; delicious vegetarian versions included. It is highly recommended that you stop here for a mouth-watering lunch or to pick up a picnic hamper (order in advance).

**Linke's Nuriootpa Bakery & Tearooms** ( ☎ 8562 1129; 40 Murray St; light meals $5-10; 🕐 breakfast & lunch Mon-Sat) The bakery welcomes children and serves the 'Nuriootpa Pasty'; a winning formula. You can also enjoy rolls, baguettes, sandwiches and afternoon teas.

# ANGASTON
☎ 08 / pop 1933

This picturesque town was named after George Fife Angas, one of the area's pioneers. A rural feel to the town is exemplified by the surrounding hills of the Barossa Ranges. There are a few places to wander around, while a classic restaurant and other good places to eat certainly make it worth a stop. There are some lovely B&Bs here too and these provide the town's main accommodation.

Magnificent **Collingrove Homestead** ( ☎ 8564 2061; Eden Valley-Angaston Rd; $8; 🕐 1-4.30pm Mon-Fri, 11am-4.30pm Sat & Sun) was built by Angas' son John in 1856. Now owned by the National Trust, the property is still furnished with the family's original antiques. Devonshire teas are served daily and formal banquets upon request. Situated about 7km from town, the grounds are also delightful and worth a visit.

Open daily, **Timeless Books** ( ☎ 8564 2222; 48 Murray St) has 85 categories of books to sell. Book lovers can wander and dream their way through these laden shelves to literary bliss.

## Sleeping & Eating
Angaston is normally much quieter than Tanunda, so in busy times check here for accommodation before going further afield.

**Vineyards Motel** ( ☎ 8564 2404; vineyardsmotel1@ ihug.com.au; cnr Stockwell & Nuriootpa Rd; s/d $60/66; 🗙 🖵 ) Across the road from the renowned Vintners Bar Grill, this motel is in a prime spot to catch the custom of those who do not want to drink and drive. Courtesy cars for guests to other local restaurants are also on offer. A good-value stop.

**Caithness Manor B&B** ( ☎ 8564 2761; www .caithness.com.au; 12 Hill St West; d $170; 🗙 🖵 🖵 ) This B&B is set in a beautifully refurbished girls' school with not an ink stain in sight. Friendly hosts and top-quality furnishings make this an exceedingly comfortable and cosy place to stay. The hillside location gives a great view over the town, especially from the pool, hot spa and barbecue deck. Ask about their excellent weekly rates.

**Treasured Memories** ( ☎ 8524 6380; www.treas uredmemories.com.au; Lot 6 Gawler Park Rd; d $160; 🗙 ) This property was once an old art studio, and celebrates open views across the Barossa Ranges. An open deck looks down over 9 hectares of fields while a hot spa bubbles enticingly. What are you waiting for?

**Angaston Roaring 40s** ( ☎ 8564 2901; 30 Murray St; mains $10-15; ☺ breakfast, lunch & dinner) Here is the living proof that the simple things in life are often the most satisfying. This café–licensed restaurant has friendly staff and the food is fresh and tasty. Light and crusty pizzas are made with fresh dough and well worth the extra calories, and the wine list is also very good.

**Rendezvous Organic Café & Restaurant** ( ☎ 8564 3533; 22 Murray St; mains $8-18; ☺ breakfast & lunch Thu-Sun) Both carnivores and their vegetarian friends will love the cooked breakfasts and tasty, imaginative lunches. Homemade soups, chicken and sweet potato curry, and yummy pumpkin, prune and pineapple cake are all recommended.

**barr-vinum** ( ☎ 8564 3688; 6-8 Washington St; mains $30; ☺ lunch Tue-Fri & Sun, dinner Tue-Sat) A small restaurant offers fine dining and Barossa wines by the glass. Enjoy dishes such as beef sirloin with roast celeriac, candied shallot, roast garlic and olive tapenade.

**Vintners Bar Grill** ( ☎ 8564 2488; Nuriootpa Rd; mains $18-25; ☺ lunch & dinner) One of the Barossa's landmark restaurants, Vintners stresses simple elegance in both their food and atmosphere. There are views across surrounding vineyards, and the dining room has an open fire and swathes of crisp white linen. Lunch and dinner menus concentrate on local produce, and the prices are not exorbitant. Additionally, the great wine list naturally promotes the region. Enjoy!

## EDEN VALLEY

Tucked quietly between the Adelaide Hills and the Barossa Valley, this valley includes the charming hamlets of Springton, Eden Valley (the town shares the same name as the valley) and Kyneton, and is famous for its looming red gums and high-altitude wines (with particularly good Rieslings). Named the Rhine Valley by Johann Menge in 1838, its quality stable includes **Mountadam** ( ☎ 08-8564 1900; www.mountadam.com; High Eden Rd; ☺ 11am-4pm); **Henschke** ( ☎ 08-8564 8223; www.henschke.com.au; Henschke Rd; ☺ 9am-4.30pm Mon-Fri, 9am-noon Sat), home of grand old vines and the famed Hill of Grace Shiraz; and **Grand Cru** ( ☎ 08-8568 2799; R Dewells Rd, Springton; ☺ 10am-5pm).

### Springton
☎ 08 / pop 278
On the Mt Pleasant side of Springton stands a gnarled river red gum known as the **Herbig Tree**. In the late 1850s, its hollow trunk was home to immigrants Friedrich and Caroline Herbig, who bore the first two of their 16 children here.

Good quality arts and crafts are exhibited at **Springton Gallery and B&B** ( ☎ 8568 2839; 10 Miller St; d $140; gallery ☺ 11am-5pm Sat & Sun), which has B&B rooms inside a renovated hay loft. In the 1892 blacksmith's shop nearby, **Cat's Face Hammer Restaurant** ( ☎ 8568 2633; 14 Miller St; mains $16-18; ☺ generally lunch Sat & Sun, dinner Wed-Sun, call ahead) is the place to go for provincial charm and deliciously fresh food.

# The Mid-North

**CONTENTS**

| | |
|---|---|
| **Highway 1** | **174** |
| Port Pirie | 174 |
| **Clare Valley** | **174** |
| Auburn | 175 |
| Mintaro | 175 |
| Clare | 176 |
| Jamestown | 178 |
| **Barrier Highway** | **178** |
| Kapunda | 178 |
| Tarlee | 180 |
| Burra | 180 |
| Hallett to Broken Hill | 182 |

THE MID-NORTH

This is a landscape of rolling hills and plains almost entirely covered by a patchwork of tilled fields, ranging sheep and vast armies of vineyards. There are some beautiful timbered areas, but often the countryside is entirely treeless. Much of the Mid-North was open grassland at the time of European settlement, and farmers and miners created more open land.

The 1840s saw Australia's first mining rush that helped put the infant colony of South Australia (SA) on its feet. From Kapunda in the south to Port Pirie and Jamestown in the north, this region contains many charismatic townships that date from this early copper-mining era. The cottages and streetscapes of Auburn, Mintaro, Burra and Kapunda have changed little over the past 150 years. These are still strong and friendly communities that welcome visitors.

Fragrant green-gold Rieslings and velvety Shiraz and Cabernet Sauvignons are regional specialities. These stunning wines can be tasted at boutique wineries dotted throughout the Clare Valley, the region's heartland. The winemakers are often descended from families with purple blood running through their veins, which makes for great tales at the cellar doors over a glass of something special.

No trip here is complete without touching base with any of the regional communities. Take time to enjoy the enthusiasm and talent of the artists who flock to Clare or Kapunda, or to listen to anecdotes over a pint in any of the town pubs.

**THE MID-NORTH**

## HIGHLIGHTS

- Camping out under the stars on a **horse trail ride** (p173) from Burra
- Celebrating your good taste with a fabulous lunch and bottle of chilled Riesling at **Skillogalee** (p57)
- Wandering through an **artist's studio** (p178) and exploring their imaginations
- Gazing into your beloved's eyes and staying overnight in a romantic cottage in **Mintaro** (p176)
- Going for gold; hiring bikes and taking the **Riesling Trail** (p174), stopping to sniff 'n' sip at liquid landmarks along the way
- Exploring the evocative **Kapunda Museum** (p179) with the past brought alive through folks' everyday paraphernalia
- Revelling in the Clare Valley's magnificent **boutique wineries** (p56) and sipping away, without fear of tomorrow

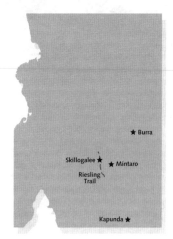

★ Burra

Skillogalee ★   ★ Mintaro

Riesling Trail

Kapunda ★

- TELEPHONE CODE: ☎ 08
- www.clarevalley.com.au

THE MID-NORTH

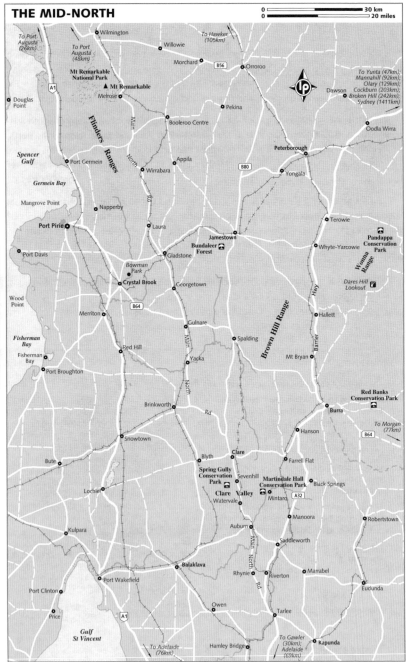

# THE MID-NORTH

0 _____ 30 km
0 _____ 20 miles

To Port Augusta (26km)
To Hawker (105km)
Wilmington
Willowie
Morchard
B56
Orroroo
To Port Augusta (48km)
Mt Remarkable National Park
▲ Mt Remarkable
Melrose
Pekina
Dawson
To Yunta (47km); Mannahill (92km); Olary (129km); Cockburn (203km); Broken Hill (242km); Sydney (1411km)
Douglas Point
A1
Booleroo Centre
Oodla Wirra
Flinders Ranges
Main
Appila
Peterborough
Spencer Gulf
North
Port Germein
Wirrabara
B80
Yongala
Germein Bay
Rd
Mangrove Point
Napperby
Laura
Terowie
Pandappa Conservation Park
Port Pirie
Jamestown
Whyte-Yarcowie
Womma Range
Bundaleer Forest
Port Davis
Gladstone
Dares Hill Lookout
Wood Point
Bowman Park
Georgetown
Crystal Brook
Hallett
Merriton
B64
Hwy
Fisherman Bay
Gulnare
Brown Hill Range
Fisherman Bay
Red Hill
Main
Spalding
Barrier
Port Broughton
Yacka
Mt Bryan
North
Red Banks Conservation Park
Brinkworth
Rd
Bute
Snowtown
Burra
Hanson
To Morgan (77km)
B64
Blyth
Clare
Lochiel
Spring Gully Conservation Park
Sevenhill
Farrell Flat
Martindale Hall Conservation Park
Black Springs
Clare Valley
Watervale
Mintaro
A32
Manoora
Robertstown
Kulpara
Auburn
Main
Saddleworth
Balaklava
North
Rhynie
Riverton
Marrabel
Eudunda
Port Wakefield
Rd
Port Clinton
Owen
Tarlee
Price
Gulf St Vincent
A1
To Gawler (30km); Adelaide (69km)
Kapunda
To Adelaide (76km)
Hamley Bridge

## National Parks

About 3km southwest of Sevenhill, the 400-hectare **Spring Gully Conservation Park** features blue-gum forest and red stringy barks, and 18m-high water cascades in winter. The wildlife includes curious kangaroos and around 50 species of birds, and there are 4WD and walking tracks.

The 1024-hectare **Red Banks Conservation Park** originally supplied wood and water to Aboriginal communities and Burra's nearby mines. A disused mine and dugouts still exist, while this habitat now supports reptiles, birdlife, western grey 'roos, short-beaked echidnas and some rare, and very cute, hairy-nosed wombats.

The 19-hectare **Martindale Hall Conservation Park** in Mintaro was initially established in the 1840s as a sheep station and dwelling for the Bowman family; landed gentry with pretensions. Their personal downfall, due to the Depression and a drop in wool prices, resulted in the necessary selling of their land, which along with the hall, is now open to the public.

For regional park information get in touch with the **Department for Environment & Heritage** (DEH; ☎ 08-8892 3025, 08-8204 1910; www .environment.sa.gov.au/parks; 77 Grenfell St, Adelaide; ⊙ 9am-5pm Mon-Fri).

## Accommodation

There are numerous refurbished properties that offer self-contained accommodation and hosted B&Bs. The cottages around Auburn, Mintaro and Clare are lovely, and worth paying the price for a few special days of indulgence. However, unless you get a good package try and avoid staying here on weekends; many Friday and Saturday night rates are verging on greedy.

## Tours

Check with the Adelaide visitors centre for specialist winery tours to the Clare Valley that are ex-Adelaide. Local operators include the following selection.

**Burra Trail Rides** ( ☎ 08-8892 2627, 0427-808 402; burratrailrides@bigpond.com; Basin Farm, Burra) Rides available include one-hour ($35) full-day ($90) and two- or three-day rides ($220/315) following the old stock routes. This experienced operator offers tuition, friendly horses, good family rates and a lot of 'Yeehaaing' if you so wish.

**Clare Valley Experiences** ( ☎ 08-8843 4169; david@jspace.net; Clare Valley; per person $180) Private tours in a flash motor are offered for those who wish to stretch their hedonistic muscles. Choose where you want to go; a maximum of four passengers ensures some intimate fun.

**Clare Valley Tours** ( ☎ 08-8843 8066, 0418-832 812; www.cvtours.com.au; 4-/6-/8- hr tours $58/78/100) A mix of attractions and wineries are visited. The buses take two to six people and the day includes lunch, one free attraction and transport to and from any Clare Valley location.

**Grant's South Oz Eco 4WD Tours** ( ☎ 08-8566 2339, 0407-605 914; www.grantssouthoztours.com.au; Kapunda; per person $165) Full-day tours offer a private itinerary and the comfort of a 4WD. Grant will tour the Clare Valley, Mintaro and Burra, among other places.

---

### FESTIVALS & EVENTS

**Jailhouse Rock** ( ☎ 08-8892 2154; Feb) If you can, get locked up in Burra for this hop.

**Jazz in the Monster Mine** ( ☎ 08-8892 2154; Mar) There are no monsters, no miners, and there's certainly no gold here. However the mine is still jumping in Burra.

**Kapunda Celtic Festival** ( ☎ 08-8892 2154; Mar/Apr) The weekend before Easter Kapunda celebrates Paddies Day with pub parades, green beer and lots of merriment.

**Romeria del Rocio Spanish Festival** ( ☎ 08-8842 2131; Apr) A great event in Clare that takes place over four days, with much clicking of heels and fingers.

**Clare Valley Gourmet Weekend** ( ☎ 08-8842 2131; May) One of the valley's major events; a festival of wine, food and music hosted by local wineries over the long weekend. Cheers!

**CJ Dennis Weekend** ( ☎ 08-8849 2112; Sep) Poets gather in Auburn to celebrate a great ex-resident.

**Clare Show** ( ☎ 08-8842 2374; Sep) The largest one-day show in SA. It's celebrated with concert bands, Irish dancers, Bavarian dancers, performing dogs and bell ringers. Says it all, really.

**Kapunda Show** ( ☎ 08-8892 2154; Oct) Country celebrations mean sustenance and merriment; fun for the kids and the grown-ups.

**Christmas Street Party** ( ☎ 08-8892 2154; Dec) Kapunda do it again, in public… yup, they party!

THE MID-NORTH

## Getting There & Away

**Premier Stateliner** ( ☎ 08-8415 5555) run daily buses from Adelaide to Port Wakefield ($17, 1½ hours) and Port Pirie ($31, three hours).

**Mid-North Passenger Service** ( ☎ 08-8823 2375) departs Adelaide daily for Auburn ($15, 2¼ hours), Clare ($22, 2½ hours) and Peterborough ($27.50, five hours). Buses depart for Burra ($22, 3½ hours) on Monday and Friday, Jamestown ($26, 4½ hours) Tuesday to Sunday, and Orroroo ($32, five hours) on Wednesday, Friday and Sunday.

**Barossa Valley Coaches** ( ☎ 08-8564 3022) depart for Kapunda ($16, 4½ hours) Monday to Friday, involving a 3¾-hour stopover in Gawler.

# HIGHWAY 1

There's not much on this route to grab your attention, but Hwy 1 is by far the best bet if you're in a hurry to get to the north. A plethora of ugly roadhouses, motels and fast-food joints make **Port Wakefield** a useful pit stop, but not much more than that.

The site of one of the district's earliest homesteads, **Bowman Park** is in an attractive valley 5km northeast of Crystal Brook. It's a popular recreation area and an access point for the **Heysen Trail** (see p38).

## PORT PIRIE

☎ 08 / pop 13,263

Huge lead- and zinc-smelting complexes and grain terminals dominate this town's skyline, economy, culture and environment. If this does not appeal much, the best suggestion is to keep your foot down…

However, if you are interested in the smelting industry ask about industry tours at the **visitors centre** ( ☎ 8633 8700; 3 Mary Elie St; 9am-5pm Mon-Fri, 9am-4pm Sat & 10am-3pm Sun), which shares space with the **arts centre**.

For a coffee break or something to eat on your journey, head to the Pirie Plaza on Grey Tce or Main St.

# CLARE VALLEY

The Clare Valley is compact, stretching just from Auburn in the south to Jamestown in the north, but still delivering a hefty amount of the South Australia's grape juice. It is wonderfully scenic countryside with high, round hills and pockets of large gums that overshadow the stone-clad farms. Vineyards and farmlands fill and colour the slopes of the valley with changing seasonal hues.

Around Auburn, Watervale, Mintaro (a declared heritage town) and Clare are attractive buildings and wineries dating from the 1840s. In their early days, these towns helped with supplies for miners working at the Burra copper mines.

## Getting There & Around

For the Clare Valley wine region take the Main North Rd from Adelaide, heading towards Gawler.

---

### WINERIES

God bless them, the Jesuits established the region's first winery, **Sevenhill Cellars** ( ☎ 08-8843 4222; www.sevenhillcellars.com.au; College Rd, Sevenhill; 9am-4.30pm Mon-Fri, 10am-4pm Sat) in 1851, three years after arriving from Vienna. They named it after the Seven Hills of Rome, and wanted to produce altar wine for their Catholic brethren in the colony and overseas; they did so with great success. In fact, a Jesuit brother still oversees wine production.

The old stone buildings are lovely, especially **St Aloysius Church** (1875). A religious retreat operates adjacent to the cellar door (sup quietly) and bike and walking tracks pass through the peaceful and pretty grounds. The winery produces some powerful Shiraz from their own grapes and exports a successful range of wines.

Today the valley – which has more than 35 wineries – is noted mainly for its Riesling and Shiraz. You can walk or ride past some of the district's finest wineries on the **Riesling Trail**, a 25km path that follows the old railway alignment between Auburn and Clare and contains three loops to take in other wineries and sights. This is a great way to enjoy the valley. The Clare visitors centre has trail maps detailing all the important liquid stops.

See the Wineries chapter (p56) for a list of top-notch cellar doors.

Clare Valley Taxis ( ☎ 131 008; ⊗ 8am-6pm Sun-Thu & 24hr Fri & Sat with bookings) operates throughout the valley and can also drop you off or pick you up along the Riesling Trail.

Clare Valley Cycle Hire ( ☎ 08-8842 2782, 0418-802 077; cvcycle@capri.net.au; 32 Victoria Rd, Clare; ⊗ 8am-8pm) has rates for a half/full day ($17/25). The operators will also collect any wine you buy along the way, bless them!

# AUBURN

☎ 08 / pop 334

This 1849 township has a timeless, sleepy quality reminiscent of an old European village. The streets are lined with some beautifully preserved hand-built stone buildings, and cottage gardens overflow with bright, untidy and fragrant blooms. This lovely little place is perfect for a romantic weekend or as a base from which to tour the Clare Valley wineries. Only 24km south of Clare, Auburn also has one of the state's best pubs and a classic French restaurant, snails et al.

Now on the main route to the valley's wineries, Auburn initially serviced bullockies and South American muleteers whose wagons, up to 100 a day, trundled between Burra's copper mines and Port Wakefield.

Clare Valley's largest winery **Taylors Wines** (see p57) sits on the edge of town, while the brilliant 25km **Riesling Trail** starts (or ends) at the restored Auburn Train Station, now a café and cellar door.

## Sleeping & Eating

Auburn BnB Hotline ( ☎ 0400 257 597, 0419-824 488) is a free accommodation booking service. Bear in mind that rates are generally raised on Friday and Saturday nights, but there may be some weekend deals.

Auburn Shiraz Motel ( ☎ 8849 2125; auburn.shiraz@bigpond.com; Main North Rd; s/d $55/65; ⊠ ) This small motel has been proudly renovated and is now an excellent-value option. The Shiraz-coloured exterior contains nine bright and spotless units with friendly hosts.

Tateham's ( ☎ 8849 2030; tatehams@chariot.net.au; Main North Rd; d $165, 2-courses $44; ⊗ lunch & dinner Wed-Sun) A gourmet restaurant–winery produces classical wines and French-Swiss cuisine (including, eeek, snails in champagne) for your delight. Dining rates are offered on a two- to five- course basis, with recommended wines per course at higher rates.

Casual light meals such as savoury crepes and coffee and cakes can also be taken alfresco. Charming self-contained B&B cottages offer beautifully furnished rooms, complete with discreetly placed condoms.

Lavender Blue Country Apartments ( ☎ 1800 227 677, 8566 2056; www.lavenderblue.com.au; d $120 ⊠ ) These are cheerful, modern and well-equipped apartments, built for privacy and self-contained fun. The gardens have an outdoor sauna, and mountain bikes are available for guests. Wood fires and great little kitchens complete a cosy picture.

Dennis Cottage ( ☎ 8277 8177; www.denniscottage.com.au; St Vincent St; d $200; ⊠ ) This historic cottage has been beautifully renovated, and it has an enchanting secluded garden complete with cascading greenery, wafting jasmine, a creek and a tiny wooden bridge. The cottage's Tuscan-style décor and modern furniture are comfortable and designed for a very special few days.

## MINTARO

☎ 08 / pop 80

A few kilometres up the road from Auburn, Mintaro (1848) is another stunning old village that could have been lifted out of the English countryside and plonked into the Australian bush. The whole village is

THE MID-NORTH

**DETOUR: RIVERTON**

Head 12km south from Auburn on the B82 to Rhynie. Then head east for 4km to Riverton, and follow the signs for the train station, now a tiny museum (admission $3).

Originally a camping place for the wagon teams carting copper ore from Burra to Port Adelaide in the 1840s, Riverton was the scene of a shoot-out in 1921. It happened at the train station, when a crazed passenger on the Broken Hill Express fired numerous shots into the busy dining room. Several people were wounded and Broken Hill MP Percy Brookfield was killed trying to disarm the gunman. Some describe this as Australia's first political assassination, hmm…

a declared heritage site. Lovingly tendered stone buildings with pretty and lush shady gardens help give Mintaro a fabulous character and ambience.

There are swathes of cottages in the bush perfectly equipped for short breaks. The places to rent in Mintaro itself are pretty fab, and sit just over the road from the historic pub and two other super restaurants in which to celebrate your stomach. The visitors centre in Clare (right) has historic walk pamphlets and lists B&Bs. A small fact of no consequence: Mintaro slate is used internationally in the manufacture of billiard tables.

**Martindale Hall** ( ☎ 8843 9088; www.martindale hall.com; adult/child $7/2.50; ◷ 11am-4pm Mon-Fri, noon-4pm Sat & Sun) is a spectacular 1880 Georgian Mansion with period furnishings, a magnificent blackwood staircase and Italian-marble fireplaces. Its grandeur certainly makes a totally unexpected sight among the gum trees. The hall is clearly signposted from town (3km). Bed-and-breakfast packages start from $95 per person. Formal dinner B&B packages for two nights are $145 per person and employ traditional upstairs and downstairs 'servants'.

**Mintaro Garden Maze** ( ☎ /fax 8843 9012; adult/child $5/3; ◷ 10am-4pm Mon, Wed & Thu, 10am-5pm Sat & Sun, closed Tue except school holidays) is really one for the kids, and serves tea and coffee to quench your thirst.

### Sleeping & Eating

**Devonshire Mews** ( ☎ 8843 9058, 0429-441 954; devon@ neonet.com.au; Burra St; d $140; ⚌ ) The 150-year-

old community hall and cottages are surrounded by a lovely garden filled with flowers, and old almond and claret-ash trees whose white blossoms fill the air and make this a very popular wedding venue. Accommodation includes spa baths and all mod cons. Overall, a splendid place to stay and enjoy Mintaro.

**Mintaro Mews** ( ☎ 8843 9001, 0400-484 242; http://users.chariot.net.au/~minmews; Burra St; 2-night B&B per person $60, dinner & B&B per 2 people on weeknights $130, mains $20-24; ◷ lunch & dinner) Probably the first place here to get booked up, this quaint and attractive Mews accommodation (with indoor heated pool and spa) has an award-winning restaurant and self-select wine cellar.

**Magpie & Stump Hotel** ( ☎ 8843 9014, 8843 9191; Burra St; mains $15-19; ◷ lunch daily, dinner Mon-Sat) As with Auburn, there is a fantastic village pub (1851). However, this one has more history, jazz playing in the background, and sticky-date pudding on the menu. Friendly hosts, log fires, pool table, slate floors (naturally) and a beer garden make this a pub to savour.

**Reilly's Wines** ( ☎ 8843 9013, 0409-679 479; www .reillyswines.com; Burra St; mains $16-24; ◷ lunch daily, dinner Mon, Wed, Fri & Sat) A popular place to just sit and relax, Reilly's has a great little restaurant serving traditional and Mediterranean food. They're directly over the road from the pub.

## CLARE

☎ 08 / pop 2930

Named after County Clare in Ireland, this 1842 town is very much the centre of the valley and regional wineries. Clare is surprisingly undeveloped and feels more like a small country town than a tourism centre, which is something of a blessing.

The **Clare visitors centre** ( ☎ 1800 242 131, 8842 2131; www.clarevalley.com.au; 229 Main St; ◷ 9am-5pm Mon-Sat, 10am-4pm Sun & public holidays) has Internet available.

For casual work during March and April, contact the wineries directly.

### Sights & Activities

There are great views over vineyards from Quarry and Billy Goat Hill.

Clare has some heritage-listed buildings, which are covered by the free visitors centre *Clare Historic Walk* pamphlet. This includes

**St Michael's Church** (1849), the valley's first substantial building.

The old police station and courthouse (1850) is now **Clare National Trust Museum** (☎ 8842 2376, 8842 2374; adult/child $6/2; ☼ 10am-noon & 2-4pm Sat, Sun & public holidays), featuring displays of Victorian clothing, furniture and household effects.

Young kids will love **Geralka Farm** (☎ 8845 8081, 8845 3318; Spalding Rd; adult/child $8/4; ☼ 1.30-5pm Sun, public holidays, daily school holidays), a modern farm with an underground mine train (the Wheal Sarah mine), Clydesdale horses that can be patted and fed, Shetland pony rides, farmyard animals, wagon rides and walks.

## Sleeping

**Taminga Hotel** (☎ 8842 2808, 8842 2461; 302 Main St; s/d $23/45) The rooms are pretty basic, but the pub is friendly enough. There is a garden grill and bar during the summer.

**Riesling Trail Country Cottages** (☎ 0412-265 031; www.rieslingcottages.com.au; d $130; ☒ ) A choice of locations offers proximity to Clare's centre or the lovely views of Polish Hill River Valley, and the Riesling Trail. These award-winning and luxurious self-contained cottages come complete with spa baths, wood fires, barbecues, breakfast provisions and sighs of contentment.

**Clare Country Golf Club** (☎ 8842 1060; clare@ countryclubs.com.au; White Hut Rd off Main North Rd; d $145, mains $20-26; ☼ lunch & dinner; ☒ ▯ ▨ ) The country club has top-quality rooms. Book the double spa-bath option and you'll be happy bunnies. A gym, greens, billiard table, pool, sauna and tennis courts should keep you amused. If all that fails, the cocktail bar and excellent restaurant, serving modern Australian cuisine, should do the trick.

**Clare Valley Cabins** (☎ 8842 1155; www.clare valleycabins.com.au; Hubbe Rd; d $100; ☒ ) The 52-acre setting offers seclusion and feathered and furry neighbours at this park, 6km from Clare. The two-bedroom cabins are comfortable and have been well equipped. Extra bodies are $25 per person, and breakfast and barbecue provisions are provided. Mountain bikes, a games hut and massages (normal/full-body $45/65) can also help the fun.

**Mundawora Mews** (☎ 8842 3762; www.munda woramews.com; d $120; ☒ ) Five minutes from Clare, the self-contained Mews suites are surrounded by a 50-hectare vineyard and grazing property, bird and wildlife and blue sky. A tennis court, breakfast provisions and barbecue complete a very welcoming picture.

**Clare Caravan Park** (☎ 8842 2724; www.clare -caravan-park.com.au; Main North Rd; unpowered sites per 2 people/cabins/en suite cabins/$17/49/65; ☒ ) Sitting 4km south of town, this very attractive park has secluded spots among parklands, a creek and giant gum trees. There are family cabins and one cabin has disabled facilities. Bikes can be hired (per half-day/full day $9/15).

Also recommended is the **Clare Central Motel** (☎ 8842 2277; www.weblogic.com.au/central; 325 Main North Rd, Clare; d $105; ☒ ▨ ) with spacious and neat rooms and great refreshing showers. A light breakfast and saltwater swimming pool are welcome additions.

## Eating

There are a few takeaway places in town, but the better restaurants are either at the wineries or on Clare's outskirts. See the menus at Clare's visitors centre.

**Salt n Vines Bar & Bistro** (☎ 8842 1796; saltn vines@bigpond.com; Kirrihill Estate, Wendouree Rd; mains $18-25; ☼ lunch & dinner Thu-Sun) The setting should be enough to enjoy this light and airy hillside bar-restaurant. Grab a balcony table and sit back with a bottle of excellent Kirrihill Estate Shiraz or Riesling. The food is consistently good and seafood is a speciality.

**Citadel** (☎ 8842 1453; 187 Main North Rd; mains $12-18; ☼ lunch Fri & Sat, dinner Thu-Mon) Housed in the old Salvation Army hall, this small and cheerful restaurant serves some good and tasty pasta, pizzas and meat main dishes. Takeaways welcome.

**Coffee & Cork** (☎ 8842 3477; 12 Main North Rd; mains $19-24; ☼ breakfast Sat & Sun, lunch Wed-Sun, dinner Wed, Fri & Sat) Clare locals love to sit on the balcony or in the modern restaurant and enjoy the excellent coffee or a long and lazy meal with friends. Great artworks cover the walls and an adjacent cellar door increases the sensual delights on offer. This place is popular; bookings are essential for dinner.

The **Clare Hotel** (☎ 8842 3477; Main St; mains $12-20; ☼ lunch & dinner) has the best pub food in town.

**NORTHERN ARTS**

A number of excellent artists have opened their studios in this region, and it is fascinating to see how they work. Far from being intimidating, many of the artists are modest and unassuming; they just happen to have a gift. Many enjoy a chat and a joke, and will happily tell you about their work and techniques.

Numerous wineries, little galleries and restaurants display craft and artworks, but don't miss out on the following.

**Corella Hill Studio** ( ☎ 08-8843 0036; signposted from Watervale; admission free; ☻ 10am-5pm) at Watervale features the distinctive work of well-known local artist Murray Edwards. This amiable and humorous man has a powerful way of expressing emotion through colour and light. His landscapes are vibrant and glorious, and his skies capture the dreaminess of a summer day. The mud-brick gallery is on a ridge with fine views.

At Blyth, a small township 11km west of Clare, is the **Medika Gallery** ( ☎ 08-8844 5175; www .medikagallery.com.au; 16 Moore St, Blyth; admission free; ☻ 10am-5pm Mon-Fri, 2-5pm Sat & Sun). Artist Ian Roberts produces finely detailed watercolours of birds and plants that are both delicate and ac-curate. The gallery is in the photogenic 1886 **St Petrie Kirche Lutheran Church.**

Kapunda's love of informal art and caricature can be seen everywhere. **Murals** of past heroes and present characters grinning away can be found outside the post office, on the corner of Main and Crase Sts and inside the Sir John Franklin and Kidman Hotel bars.

The **Kapunda Gallery** ( ☎ 08-8566 3368; kapundatourisinfo@bigpond.com; 7 Hill St; ☻ 9am-4pm) sits upstairs from the visitors centre and is an informal meeting place for local amateur and profes-sional artists. The energy and enthusiasm is infectious and artworks at all levels of ability can be thoroughly enjoyed. Look out for Christian Vocke's affectionate depictions of voluptuous ladies and richly coloured sketches of the region. Christian's art and pottery work is also displayed in Clare galleries.

## JAMESTOWN
☎ 08 / pop 1352

Jamestown was established during the wheat boom of the 1870s, and is still very much a service town for the area; it was never designed with aesthetic priorities in mind. However, there are a number of attractive stone buildings dating from those heady days. These include the town's four pubs and its courthouse; you could assume that the former provided customers for the latter.

Jamestown is a cheaper option than stay-ing around Clare. It is friendly enough with a fair bit of budget hotel accommodation, some reasonable motel units and honest pub food.

Ten kilometres out on Spalding Rd is the headquarters of **Bundaleer Forest**. Turn west to a pleasant bush-picnic area, from where you can do scenic walks of up to 5km.

Right in the town centre, the **Belalie Hotel-Motel** ( ☎ /fax 8664 1065; 36 Ayre St; hotel s/d $30/60, motel s/d $55/70; ☻ ) has basic rooms, some with air-con. Across the street, the **Commercial Hotel** ( ☎ 8664 1013; 35 Ayre St; s/d $30/55; ☻ ) room rates include a light breakfast. Counter meals are served at both pubs ($10 to 18).

**Railway Hotel-Motel** ( ☎ 8664 1035, 8664 1375; 32 Alexandra Ave; s/d $58/68; dining-room mains $10-15; ☻ lunch & dinner; ☻ ) has some of the bet-ter motel rooms in town, and serves both counter food and dining room meals, with fish and steaks the speciality.

# BARRIER HIGHWAY

Running mainly through open sheep and wheat country, the Barrier Hwy is the most direct route from Adelaide to Burra, the old copper-mining town. You can go this way to the Flinders Ranges by turning off at Te-rowie, or continue northeast from Terowie to Sydney via Broken Hill.

## KAPUNDA
☎ 08 / pop 2303

This very special place should be thoroughly enjoyed for its friendliness, great and innova-tive displays of local history and art, as well as for its very healthy love of street parties. Look out for the superb **murals** (see above).

Kapunda was also home to Sir Sidney Kidman (the famous 'Cattle King') whose properties covered 340,000km of land and whose horse sales were reputed to be the largest in the world. Kidman apparently thought England would make a good horse paddock.

## Information

**Kapunda visitors centre** ( ☎ 8566 2902; kapundato urisinfo@bigpond.com; 7 Hill St; ☼ 9am-4pm) Centrally located, this enthusiastic centre has a heap of information and a surprise in the cellar: a witty display depicting Kapunda life, past and present. Don't miss the videos – very funny stories told by some real old raconteurs. These characters also pop up in the community mural on the corner of Main and Crase Sts. Internet access is available.

## Sights

The heritage-listed Baptist church (1866) houses **Kapunda Museum** ( ☎/fax 8566 2286; 11 Hill St; adult/child $5/2; ☼ 1-4pm), truly one of the state's best folk museums. All sorts of things are bundled in here, including ancient hospital equipment and rooms decked out in different eras of Kapunda's history. Take a look at the towers on the museum roof; during the war mad Tiger Moth pilots would fly sideways through this narrow gap.

Entry to **Bagot's Fortune** ( ☎ 8566 2286; 5 Hill St), in the old *Herald* printing office, is included in the price for the museum. This mining interpretation centre has displays on the Cornish, Welsh, Irish and German pioneers and the different roles they played in the town's development.

**Map Kernow** (or, in old Cornish, 'Son of Cornwall'), an 8m-high bronze statue, stands at the Adelaide end of town as a tribute to pioneering miners. The town's Cornish

---

### KAPUNDA'S COPPER

Kapunda is modest about its heritage; a rich deposit of highest-grade copper was found here in 1842 and it became the first copper-mining town in Australia. By 1861 Kapunda was the colony's major commercial centre outside Adelaide. Large-scale operations ceased in 1878 and the mines closed altogether in 1912. Many of the solid stone buildings erected during the boom years have survived intact, although most of the miners' chalk cottages have had to be rebuilt.

---

heritage is celebrated at the annual Kapunda Celtic Festival (see p173).

At the old mine site there is a **lookout** with views over the open cuts and stone chimneys. A 1.5km walking track has information signs to guide you through the area.

Many of Kapunda's fine old buildings can be viewed on a 10km **heritage trail** around the streets and mine site, and on a much shorter walk or bike ride through the town centre. Both are described in the booklet *Discovering Historic Kapunda*, available at the visitors centre.

The **Kapunda Gallery** ( ☎ 8566 3368; kapundatour isinfo@bigpond.com; 7 Hill St; ☼ 9am-4pm) is upstairs from the visitors centre, and is always a thoroughly colourful and enlivening experience (see opposite).

## Sleeping & Eating

The visitors centre has details on other B&B accommodation, some within the town, others further afield.

**Sir John Franklin Hotel** ( ☎ 8566 3233; fax 8566 3873; 63 Main St; s/d $25/55; bar meals $8-15; ☼ lunch & dinner) This 1849 hotel has budget rooms, cheap bar meals and a great front bar, although it can be a little feral at weekends. Check out the brilliant caricatures of past and present locals on the bar walls.

**Peppertrees B&B** ( ☎ 8566 2776; www.peptrees .mtx.net; 47 Clare Rd, Kapunda; s/d $95/120; ☒ ) You can't get much better than this: your own suite of beautifully decorated rooms in a classic Australian bluestone set in pretty gardens. The rates include sparkling wine and a full breakfast. Booking is essential, and it is not for children.

**Ford House** ( ☎ 8566 3341, 0419-856 998; tj.scholes@ bigpond.com; 80 Main St; d $80; ☒ ) This attractive two-storey building (1860) was Kapunda's original general store. The family room ($120) has a balcony, which overlooks Main St, perfect for one of Kapunda's many street celebrations. The rooms are neat, comfortable and clean, if a little sombre, although friendly hosts add some cheer. Hearty cooked breakfasts are an extra $10.

**Kapunda Tourist & Leisure Park** ( ☎ 8566 2094; www.kapundatouristpark.com; Dutton Park; unpowered sites per 2 people/cabins/2-bed cabins $18/65/75; ☒ ) There are plenty of trees, birds and shade, if few facilities, other than showers, at this amiable park. Within walking distance of

THE MID-NORTH

the town centre, the golf course and trotting circuit offer adjacent fun.

**Wheatsheaf Hotel** ( ☎ 8566 2198; www.wheatsheaf1855.com; Allendale North; mains $12-22; ✆ brunch, lunch & dinner) The hotel serves very good unpretentious bistro-style food, using local produce. The brunches are popular, as is the art displayed on the walls. Only 5km from Kapunda, this is where the locals go to dine out for an evening.

**Fresh Fields** ( ☎ 8566 3222; 39 Main St; mains $10-14; ✆ breakfast, lunch & dinner) A Kapunda institution, this cosy café serves massive all-day breakfasts ($10) and their speciality is pan-fried whiting with mushroom risotto and basil. Yum!

**Kapunda Bakery Café** ( ☎ 8566 2739; cnr Smedley & Main Sts; $3; ✆ breakfast & lunch) Follow the constant stream of locals to this bakery. Not only does the baker have an exuberant humour (even better than the brewed coffee) but the pasties, German breads and cakes are freshly baked every day. The original bakery (1860) downstairs is equipped from that era and open as a free display.

Although all the hotels in town serve meals, the **Sir Sydney Kidman Hotel** ( ☎ /fax 8566 2205; 50 Main St; mains $8-20; ✆ lunch & dinner Wed-Sat) does the best pub food in town.

## TARLEE
☎ 08 / pop 100

Halfway between the Barossa and Clare Valleys is Tarlee, whose main attraction is **Tarlee Antiques** ( ☎ 8528 5328; Main St; ✆ 10am-4pm). If you're into browsing bric-a-brac and glassware, you'll love this; seven rooms crammed to the ceilings. Next-door **Tarlee Country Treasures** ( ☎ 8528 5355; ✆ 10am-4pm) has another collection at the more cutesy-pie end of the range.

## BURRA
☎ 08 / pop 1106

This nice little town was a copper-mining centre in the 1800s and lives today on those dusty memories. A pretty creek runs through Burra, and a choice of pubs keeps visitors well lubricated. History buffs will enjoy wandering around well-preserved relics of the mining days; stone buildings and tall chimneys, engine houses, massive churches, pubs and tiny cottages.

It was hard living. Hundreds of miners and their families lived initially underground in rooms they dug out of the red earth. The bare, grassy hills around town remain decimated of trees – they fed the smelter furnaces.

The town was divided geographically and culturally between the miners who formed their own suburbs: Llwchwr, Redruth, Aberdeen and Hampton – Redruth is the only one that still officially exists today. The district, Burra Burra, was named by Afghan cameleers and takes its name from the Hindi word for 'great' by one account, and from the Aboriginal name for the creek by another.

### Information

**Burra visitors centre** ( ☎ 8892 2154; www.visitburra.com; 2 Market Sq; ✆ 9am-5pm) Sells the Burra Passport ($25), which includes the *Discovering Historic Burra* booklet (describing 49 sites on an 11km heritage trail) entry to eight sites and four museums, or an eight-site passport minus museum entry ($15). Children have free entry to sites.

### Sights & Activities

Many visiting exhibitions rest at the **Burra Art Gallery** ( ☎ 8892 2154; Old Kooringa Telegraph Station & Post Office; admission free; ✆ 1-4pm) alongside a great collection of work by ST Gill, a painter who depicted the region's mining industry from the late 1800s until he followed the gold rush to Victoria in 1847.

The following attractions are included in the Burra Passport or have free admission.

**Market Sq Museum** (Market Sq; adult/child $4.50/2.50; ✆ 1-3pm Mon-Wed, 11.30am-1.30pm Thu, 2.15pm-

---

**BURRA'S BIRTH**   *Denis O'Byrne*

Thomas Pickett, a shepherd, discovered copper at Burra in 1845. The deposit proved to be phenomenally rich, and by 1850 it was supporting the largest metalliferous mine in Australia. In 1851 Burra had a population of 5000, which made it Australia's seventh largest town at that time. By then Pickett had met a terrible fate; he'd fallen into his lonely campfire while drunk and had burned to death.

By 1860 the mine was producing 5% of the world's copper; more than 1000 men and boys, most of them Cornish, were employed there at that time. It closed 17 years later, mainly because of flooding problems and falling ore grades, but reopened for 10 years from 1971.

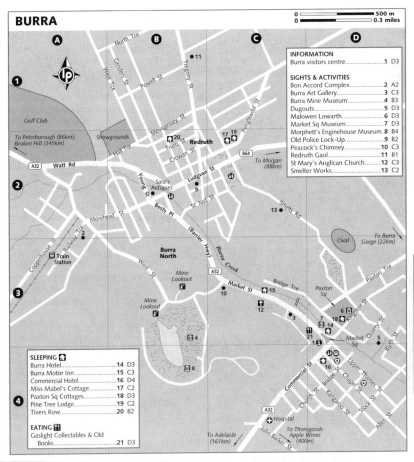

**BURRA**

**INFORMATION**
Burra visitors centre....................**1** D3

**SIGHTS & ACTIVITIES**
Bon Accord Complex................**2** A2
Burra Art Gallery.......................**3** C3
Burra Mine Museum..................**4** B3
Dugouts.....................................**5** D3
Malowen Lowarth.....................**6** D3
Market Sq Museum....................**7** D3
Morphett's Enginehouse Museum.**8** B4
Old Police Lock-Up....................**9** B2
Peacock's Chimney...................**10** C3
Redruth Gaol............................**11** B1
St Mary's Anglican Church........**12** C3
Smelter Works...........................**13** C2

**SLEEPING**
Burra Hotel..............................**14** D3
Burra Motor Inn........................**15** C3
Commercial Hotel.....................**16** D4
Miss Mabel's Cottage................**17** C2
Paxton Sq Cottages...................**18** D3
Pine Tree Lodge........................**19** C2
Tivers Row................................**20** B2

**EATING**
Gaslight Collectables & Old
  Books.....................................**21** D3

THE MID-NORTH

3.30pm Sat) has a shop, post office and a house as they might have looked between 1880 and 1930.

The 33 attached cottages at **Paxton Sq** were built for Cornish miners in the 1850s as an alternative to the dugouts, and are available for accommodation (see p182). One cottage; **Malowen Lowarth** ( ☎ 8892 2577, Kingston St; adult/child $4.50/2.50; ⏰ 2-4pm Sat, 9.30-12.30am Sun-Fri), has been furnished in 1850s style and provides a fascinating glimpse of how a mine manager (or mine captain) lived in those days.

**Morphett's Enginehouse Museum** ( ☎ 8892 2244; off Market St; adult/child $4.50/2.50; ⏰ 11am-1pm Mon, Wed & Fri, 11am-2pm Sat, Sun & holidays) is a reconstructed three-storey Cornish engine house

that once pumped water from the mine. The engine house is on the grounds of the original mine site, now converted into the open-air **Burra Mine Museum**. Information boards detail the history of the mine.

The **Bon Accord Complex** ( ☎ 8892 2056; Railway Tce; adult/child $4.50/2.50; ⏰ 1-3pm Mon-Fri, 1-4pm Sat & Sun) came about when a Scottish mining enterprise discovered underground water here instead of copper. Not to be deterred, the canny Scots sold the site to the town, and the property supplied water for Burra until 1966.

In Burra's early days nearly 1500 people lived in **dugouts** along the creek. A couple of these survived floods but are empty of furnishings.

Other interesting old buildings accessed with the Burra Passport are **Redruth Gaol** (Tregony St), 1849 **St Mary's Anglican Church** (Market St), **Peacock's Chimney** (Market St), the **Old Police Lock-Up** (Tregony St) and the old **Smelter Works** (Smelts Rd).

Having worked up a thirst, head for **Thorogoods Apple Wines** ( ☎ 8892 2669; www.thorogoods .com.au; signposted from John Barker St; admission free; ☺ noon-4.30pm), which turns out a range of truly scrumptious light and delicate drinks: wine, liqueur, sparkling, cider and beer, all made out of apples.

## Sleeping & Eating

A number of old cottages have been converted into nice-and-simple B&B accommodation. The rates are around $120 with breakfast, $100 without.

**Paxton Sq Cottages** ( ☎ 8892 2622; paxtoncot tages@bigpond.com.au; Kingston St; d $65) These pristine cottages are great value for backpackers, families and friends. There is not much of the solid wood furniture, but it is good quality, and the cooking facilities are fine for a short while. One cottage has disabled fittings.

**Tivers Row** ( ☎ 8892 2461; www.burraheritagecot tages.com.au; 8-18 Truro St; d $120) A row of historic Cornish cottages has been lovingly restored and fitted out with period furnishings. The pretty courtyard gardens are equally pretty and well maintained. Book through Sara's Antiques at 1 Young Street.

**Burra Motor Inn** ( ☎ 8892 2777; fax 8892 2707; Market St; s/d $80/90; ☒ ☎ ) This motel is the most modern accommodation in town and has large rooms overlooking the creek. The motel gets booked out at weekends.

**Gaslight Collectable & Old Books** ( ☎ 8892 3003; 20 Market Sq; ☺ 10am-5pm) This bookshop serves happy browsers coffees and yummy cakes. Relax into the wafting coffee aromas and soothing classical music.

Four out of five of the town's hotels have budget accommodation. Try the **Commercial Hotel** ( ☎ 8892 2010; 22 Commercial St; s/d $35/55, mains $8-15; ☺ lunch & dinner), which also offers reasonable pub food, and the **Burra Hotel** ( ☎ 8892 2389; 5 Market Sq; s/d $28/50). The visitors centre acts as a booking agent for all accommodation.

Recommended for couples is **Miss Mabel's Cottage** ( ☎ 8892 2758, 0438-195 358; Penglawdd St Llwchwr; d $115) set on half a hectare with fruit trees, an open fire and home-made jam. More modern-style, and with slightly larger grounds, **Pine Tree Lodge** ( ☎ 8892 2758; 0438-195 358; Penglawdd St; d $120) is perfect for lively families.

## HALLETT TO BROKEN HILL

Noted for fine Merino wool, Hallett is at the start of the 91km **Dares Hill Scenic Drive**, which takes you the roundabout way to Terowie.

There is good variety in the landscapes along the way, including a panoramic outlook towards the Murray River from **Dares Hill**, 27km from Hallett. About 43km further on, in the Wonna Range, the 1056-hectare **Pandappa Conservation Park** has attractive hill scenery and is home to plenty of wildlife, including euros (hills kangaroos) and red and grey kangaroos.

From the old railhead of **Terowie** you can either head northwest to **Peterborough** (24km) and **Orroroo** (61km), or northeast along the sealed Barrier Hwy to **Broken Hill** (296km). The Barrier Hwy passes through semiarid station country, with small service centres at **Oodles Wirra** (35km), **Yunta** (94km), **Mannahill** (139km), **Olary** (176km) and **Cockburn** (243km and right on the SA/New South Wales border). Each has a pub and sells fuel.

Please remember to discard fresh fruit and vegetables at state borders.

# Yorke Peninsula

CONTENTS

| | |
|---|---|
| **East Coast** | **185** |
| Port Wakefield to Ardrossan | 185 |
| Port Vincent | 186 |
| Port Vincent to Edithburgh | 186 |
| Edithburgh | 187 |
| Yorketown | 188 |
| Warooka | 188 |
| Marion Bay | 188 |
| Innes National Park | 189 |
| **West Coast** | **190** |
| Minlaton | 190 |
| Maitland | 190 |
| **The Copper Triangle** | **191** |
| Moonta & Around | 191 |
| Kadina | 193 |
| Wallaroo | 193 |
| Port Broughton | 194 |

YORKE PENINSULA

Shimmering with the Copper Coast and blessed with rugged heathlands in the south, the Yorke Peninsula is the weekender of choice for Adelaide's more adventurous families. Sure there's no big landmarks to conquer or wild party towns, but there are several charming fishing villages along the eastern coast, and the heritage of Kadina, Moonta and Wallaroo forges the unique Copper Triangle, once the financial boon of the state.

Early 19th-century explorer Matthew Flinders described the Yorke Peninsula as an 'ill-shaped leg', which was probably the sentiment of a disgruntled sailor. True the inland area is rather dull, now given over to wheat-farming, but the coastline is actually quite attractive with loads of opportunities to fish, dive or swim from the upper thigh of Ardrossan and Port Broughton to the tip of the toe at Innes National Park. This park is a magnet for surfers who love the variety of breaks buried in bushland and the chance to camp right on the beach. Fisherfolk also like the chance to chase snapper and King George whiting from Marion Bay or one of the ports along the east coast.

There's some good eating to be found with oysters farmed around the region and a few burgeoning wineries producing new drops. Then there's the Cornish pasty, the unofficial dish of the Copper Triangle, which made a wholesome meal to fuel the region's miners during the 19th century. Visitors come from across the globe for Lowender Kernewek, a festival of Cornish heritage that includes folk dancing, feasting and a fair whack of beer swilling.

## HIGHLIGHTS

- Camping out (or chickening out in a self-contained lodge) at **Innes National Park** (p189), known for its wind-ravaged beaches
- Tucking into a meal at **Edithburgh's eateries** (p187), famous for their cuisine all along the peninsula
- Enjoying a few beers and a pasty during **Lowender Kernewek** (p191), the festival of all that is Cornish in the Copper Triangle
- Checking the colour of a two-cent coin at the copper capital of **Kadina** (p193), which has its very own currency museum
- Doing absolutely nothing in chilled-out **Port Broughton** (p194)
- Wandering through yesteryear at **Moonta** (p191), a former mining town known for its National Trust–listed buildings
- Surfing the basic breaks at **Pondalowie Bay** (p189)

★ Port Broughton

★ Kadina
★ Moonta

Pondalowie Bay
★
Innes
★ National Park

★ Edithburgh

- TELEPHONE CODE: ☎ 08
- www.yorkeregion.on.net
- www.yorkepeninsula.com.au

YORKE PENINSULA

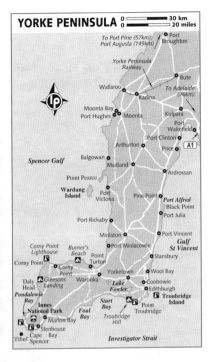

**YORKE PENINSULA**

To Port Pirie (57km);
Port Augusta (149km)
Port Broughton
Yorke Peninsula Railway
Bute
Wallaroo
To Adelaide (96km)
Kadina
Moonta Bay
Port Hughes  Moonta
Kulpara
Port Wakefield
Port Clinton
Arthurton
Price  A1
Spencer Gulf
Balgowan
Maitland
Point Pearce
Ardrossan
Wardang Island
Port Victoria
Pine Point  Port Alfred
Black Point
Port Julia
Port Rickaby
Minlaton
Port Vincent
Gulf St Vincent
Corny Point Lighthouse
Burner's Beach
Port Minlacowie
Corny Point
Point Turton
Stansbury
Corny Point
Daly Head
Gleesons Landing  Warooka
Yorketown
Wool Bay
Lake Fowler
Coobowie
Pondalowie Bay
Edithburgh
Innes National Park
Sturt Bay
Point Troubridge
Troubridge Island
Marion Bay
Foul Bay
Troubridge Hill
Stenhouse Bay
'Ethel'  Cape Spencer
Investigator Strait

## National Parks

The big natural drawcard is **Innes National Park**, a thick patch of Mallee scrub broken up with some pleasant beaches. There are several excellent surfing spots in the park and fishing is popular around Marion Bay. Admission to the park is $6.50 per carload and payable at the entrance.

Small Conservation Parks such as **Leven Beach** and **Troubridge Island** are well-preserved pockets of wilderness.

## Accommodation

Unused holiday homes are definitely the go for accommodation on the peninsula. Owners often rent out their properties through agencies with prices starting at $60 per night, usually with full kitchen, laundry and linen. Here's a selection of rental agencies operating throughout the peninsula:

**Bottom End Accommodation** ( ☎ 08-8854 5172; www.bottomend-accommodation.com) Books for Marion Bay, Point Turton, Edithburgh and other more hidden spots.

**Country Getaways** ( ☎ 08-8832 2623; www.country getaways.info) Has houses around Port Vincent.

**Elders** ( ☎ 08-8825 3055; www.elders.com.au/moonta; cnr George & Ellen Sts, Moonta) Has properties in Moonta Bay, Port Hughes and Wallaroo.

**LJ Hooker** ( ☎ 08-8825 2007; www.ljhooker.com.au /moontawallaroo; cnr George & Ellen Sts, Moonta) Also looks after Moonta Bay, Port Hughes and Wallaroo.

**Professionals Real Estate** ( ☎ 08-8823 3422; www .sa.professionals.com.au; 43 Owen Tce, Wallaroo; houses per night $85-200)

There's also good **bush camping** (per site $7) available all over the peninsula – including Burners Beach, Corny Point Lighthouse, Gleesons Landing and Troubridge Hill – through the District Council of Yorke, with offices at:

**Maitland** ( ☎ 08-8832 2701; 8 Elizabeth St)
**Minlaton** ( ☎ 08-8853 3800; 18 Main St)
**Warooka** ( ☎ 08-8854 5055; Player St)
**Yorketown** ( ☎ 08-8852 0200; 15 Edithburgh Rd)

## Getting There & Away

There are no commercial flights to the Yorke Peninsula, but **Premier Stateliner** ( ☎ 08-8645 9911; www.premierstateliner.com.au; 23 Darling Tce) does have daily buses from Adelaide to Kadina, Wallaroo and Moonta ($21, all 2½ hours). Another service from Adelaide stops at Port Broughton ($28, two hours) before heading on to Port Augusta (to Port Broughton $37, three hours).

# EAST COAST

The sealed road from the top of Gulf St Vincent down to Stenhouse Bay near Cape Spencer is never far from the sea. En route, tracks lead to sandy beaches and secluded coves with small fishing towns dotting the coast.

## PORT WAKEFIELD TO ARDROSSAN

Turning off Hwy 1 just north of Port Wakefield, you pass the **Clinton Conservation Park**, noted for its tidal shallows and mangroves that are the perfect habitat for migratory wading birds and colonies of cormorants.

**Price** is a small salt-mining centre 18km further on. Between Price and Ardrossan, dirt roads turn off to **Macs Beach** and **Tiddy Widdy Beach**.

Grain-exporting port **Ardrossan** (population 1000) is dominated by leviathan silos to the south. It was the birthplace of the **stump-jump plough**, created to hop over the

YORKE PENINSULA

---

**DETOUR: BUTE**

Short but sweet, Bute makes a good spot for a family to spend a day browsing crafts or visiting animals. If you're coming from Port Wakefield, turn north at Kulpara, or alternatively turn off Hwy 1 at Snowtown to get to this historic town. There are plenty of well-preserved buildings to explore including **Gunner Bill's Museum & Gallery** ( ☎ 08-8826 2208; Railway Tce; 11am-4pm Wed, Fri & Sun), a former police station that sells local handicrafts. Elsewhere there's a small but free fauna park featuring wallabies, peacocks and black swans. **Bute Hotel** ( ☎ 08-8826 2005; Railway Tce; s $55) has a dependable B&B option. Yorke Peninsula Railway (p191) also visits every second Sunday.

---

mallee stumps and rocks that were a nightmare for the early farmers of South Australia (SA). A sample plough is displayed at the waterfront, though nearby Arthurton also claims to have invented the plough (and also display their prototype).

The **National Trust Museum** ( ☎ 08-8837 3213, 8837 3939; Fifth St; adult/child $2/1; 2.30-4.30pm Sun & public holidays) features agricultural and maritime history exhibits, including yet another stump-jump plough.

The wreck of the barque *Zanoni* is a popular local **dive site**. It lies in 20m of water about 16km southeast of town, but you need permission from the **Department for Environment & Heritage** (DEH; ☎ 08-8336 0926; www.environment.sa.gov.au/parks).

You can stay at the town's best caravan park, **High View Holiday Village** ( ☎ 08-8837 3399; Highview Rd; powered sites per 2 people $20, cabins $55-60, chalets $60.50-65.50; ), a shady spot on the north side of town with extra facilities including a medium-sized pool and tennis courts. Otherwise there's **Ardrossan Hotel** ( ☎ 08-8837 3008; cnr First & Fifth Sts; s/d $60/70; ) with excellent motel rooms including queen-sized beds, TVs and fridges.

South of Ardrossan the main road passes the tiny coastal resort of **Pine Point**, where there's a small friendly **caravan park** ( ☎ 08-8838 2239; powered sites per 2 people $20, on-site vans $50). From here you can drive to **Black Point**, which has bush camping. Along the way you pass a long, sandy beach and numerous holiday shacks at **Port Alfred**.

## PORT VINCENT
☎ 08 / pop 500

This endearing resort town is set on a sweeping bay making for a good family holiday destination. There's a safe **swimming beach**, good fishing off the **jetty** and an interesting 2km **nature trail** along the coast.

### Sleeping & Eating

For good holiday houses in Port Vincent and the surrounding area try **Country Getaways** ( ☎ 8832 2623; www.countrygetaways.info).

**Tuckerway** ( ☎ 8853 7285; 14 Lime Kiln Rd; powered/unpowered sites per 2 people $7/5, dm/tw $14.50/29) This hostel has basic facilities with bunk-bed dorms, though for the same price you and your travelling partner can have a self-contained twin room. They occasionally book out with school trips.

**Port Vincent Foreshore Caravan Park** ( ☎ 8853 7073; Marine Pde; powered sites per 2 people $19-22, cabin $76-95, on-site van $35) With a waterfront location, this bait-selling place is helpful for fishing tips and has some cabins with spas.

**Hotel Ventnor** ( ☎ 8853 7036; cnr Marine & Main St; mains $10-20) Meals at this beachside pub have typical carnivorous leanings (seafood, schnitzel, steak and chicken), with a very pricey salad plate for vegetarians ($10).

## PORT VINCENT TO EDITHBURGH

About 13km further along from Port Vincent is picturesque **Stansbury**, a township with sweeping views that was the first European settlement on Yorke Peninsula. If you get tired of the beautiful **swimming beach**, the town's tiny **museum** ( ☎ 08-8852 4291, 08-8852 5020; North Tce; adult/child $2/$0.50; 2-4pm Sun & Wed) has local history including exhibits on the town's long-running RSL.

The town has a well-developed oyster industry, so bivalves can be bought cheaply ($6 a dozen) from several shops in town. Stansbury's **visitors centre** ( ☎ 08-8852 4577; cnr Towler & Weavers Sts; 9am-5pm Mon-Fri) has the *Coastal Walking Trails* brochure for paths around town.

You can stay at **Stansbury Foreshore Caravan Park** ( ☎ 08-8852 4171; powered sites per 2 people $19-21, cabins $63-87), a pleasant green park on the coast. Also on the waterfront, **Dalrymple Hotel** ( ☎ 08-8852 4188; Anzac Pde; d $40-60) has decent rooms including a cooked breakfast.

There's another jetty and swimming beach at **Wool Bay**, which has a large lime kiln built into the cliff and a **lookout** affording views along colourful coastal cliffs and across to **Coobowie**. The safe swimming beach in Coobowie makes this another good family spot.

You can stay in the pleasant **Coobowie Caravan Park** ( ☎ 08-8852 8132; Beach Rd; unpowered/powered sites per 2 people $13/16, units $50, cabins $60-80) with good-sized kids' playground and classy cabins.

Just north of town, **Barachel Alpacas** ( ☎ 08-8852 8029; Coobowie–Wool Bay Rd; ☼ by appointment) has a working alpaca farm, selling various handicrafts made from their wool.

# EDITHBURGH

☎ 08 / pop 500

Once a thriving port exporting salt, grains and wool, this attractive service town has a great seaside atmosphere and some of the best eateries on the peninsula. Edithburgh recently captured national headlines with the building of a windfarm approximately 3km south at Wattle Point (see Blowing in the Wind, below).

## Sights

The clifftop lookout above the town jetty looks down on the town's **tidal pool** and across to **Troubridge Island**, about 6km offshore. The island is a conservation park with important rookeries of little penguins, black-faced shags and crested terns.

The **museum** ( ☎ 8852 6187; Edith St; adult/child $3/$0.50; ☼ 2-4pm Sun) has a fascinating collection of memorabilia, including displays on local shipwrecks and a big, red fire engine.

There are some pleasant nature walks in **Edithburgh Flora Park** and along the coast from Edithburgh to **Sultana Point** (one hour, 4km) and **Coobowie** (1½ hours, 6km).

## Activities & Tours

There's good **scuba diving** on nearby wrecks and reefs that are known for soft corals,

fish, drop-offs and caves. The most popular wreck is the 3600 tonne cargo steamer *Clan Ranald*. For beginners, the bottom of the jetty is known for its attractive leafy sea dragons. **Edithburgh Surf & Tackle** ( ☎ 8852 6161; 28 Blanch St; ☼ Mon-Sat) stocks diving and fishing gear and can give you **fishing** tips.

**Troubridge Island Charters** ( ☎ 8852 6290; 4 Blanche St; half-/full day $90/120) does diving and fishing trips for a minimum of four people. They can also do a half-day tour out to Troubridge, where you can see the cast-iron **lighthouse** (1856) and keepers' cottages.

## Sleeping & Eating

Edithburgh is the tourist centre of the south, so you can expect some good eating and several accommodation options.

**Edithburgh House** ( ☎ 8852 6373; Edith St; s/d $75/85) This quaintly decorated place is a good blend of character and luxury, with 1950s ads decorating the walls, velvety bedspreads, and a delicious breakfast included. And with Faversham's Restaurant (p188) on the premises, there's no need to ever leave.

**Tippers B&B** ( ☎ 8852 4091; 35 Blanche St; www .tippersedithburgh.com.au; d $120) This expertly renovated B&B was the town's last blacksmith's shop, but has become two properties – a suite (sleeps two) and stables (sleeps four). Queen-sized beds, continental breakfasts and stylish decoration make this a perfect romantic weekender.

**Edithburgh Seaside Motel** ( ☎ 8852 6172; Blanche St; s/d/tr $68/78/88) It may seem like just another beachfront place, but this motel distinguishes itself with queen-sized beds, ornate light fittings, roomy en suites and massive TVs.

**Troubridge Hotel/Motel** ( ☎ 8852 6013; cnr Edith & Blanche Sts; s/d $60/72, mains $12-18; ☼ ) This plain-looking two-storey place has dependable rooms with fridges, TVs and new linen. Meals are popular with locals, especially the

**YORKE PENINSULA**

---

### BLOWING IN THE WIND

As late as 2004, you could drive past Wattle Point, just 3km south of Edithburgh, without missing anything. Today there are almost 60 large wind turbines catching the bluster, each one powering about 900 homes. Building of the complex was delayed as local environmentalists were concerned that birds would fly into the silently turning rotor blades, but eventually in 2004 work began. Each tower stretches to 68m – roughly the length of the Bayeux Tapestry. With another plant at Starfish Hill on the Fleurieu Peninsula, these slow-turning blades represent the future of SA's energy industry.

---

**THE AUTHOR'S CHOICE**

**Faversham's Restaurant** ( ☎ 08-8852 6373; Edithburgh House, Edith St; mains $22-24; ⏲ 11am-10pm) This is the place you've been working up an appetite for. Expect first-class meals such as rack of lamb stuffed with feta or 'roo fillet with sweet potato mash and roasted beetroot. Chef Mike Goodlet has cooked at the Hyatt, so even regular Wednesday night Taste of Asia feasts promise superb dining.

---

Sails Seafood, a massive platter of butterfish, whiting, prawns and calamari.

**Edithburgh Caravan Park** ( ☎ 8852 6056; O'Halloran Pde; unpowered/powered sites per 2 people $17/20, on-site vans $38, cabins $60-120) This beachside park offers a range of accommodation, from executive cabins with spas to basic unpowered campsites.

**Lighthouse keepers' cottages** ( ☎ 8852 6290; q $320) You can stay in these cottages on Troubridge Island for a minimum of two nights with four adults; rates include a 15-minute boat ride to and from the island.

**Location Cafe** ( ☎ 8852 6023; cnr Blanche & Edith Sts; entree $7-9.50, mains $9-17; ⏲ lunch & dinner Mon, Thu, Fri, breakfast, lunch & dinner Sat) A snazzy newcomer on the main street, the Location has big-city dining with country prices. A good wine list complements tasty casual food such as vegetarian lasagne and yummy burgers with zippy salsa.

## YORKETOWN

☎ 08 / pop 750

With roads coming from every direction, Yorketown is the region's business and administrative hub and has two classic 1870s pubs to slake a traveller's thirst. About 200 small **salt lakes** in the immediate area once supported a thriving salt-mining industry.

The **Southern Yorke Peninsula Community Telecentre** ( ☎ 8852 1820; www.sypctc.on.net; 33 Stansbury Rd) stocks a range of tourist brochures, and has an Internet café.

### Sleeping & Eating

**Yorke Hotel** ( ☎ 8852 1221; 1 Warooka Rd; s/d $30/45, meals $6-8; ⏲ lunch & dinner) Right in the centre of town, this pub offers modest rooms which include light breakfast. You can also grab a good pub meal at the hotel's uniquely Y-shaped bar.

**Melville Hotel/Motel** ( ☎ 8852 1019; www.melvillehotel.com; 1 Minlaton Rd; s $44, d & tw $52; meals $6-20; ✗ ) The other pub in town has better rooms with TVs, saggy beds and 1970s décor. Their meals are terrific with á la carte lunches and seafood-heavy dinners (expect local specialities: garfish, whiting, oysters).

**Peesey Park** ( ☎ 8242 1220; www.peeseypark.com; 6 Kirra Rd; s/d $67/107) This top farmstay on the road to Warooka is the definition of country hospitality with wood fires, a garden for relaxing strolls, period furniture and menagerie of geese, sheep and a friendly dog.

**Yorketown Caravan Park** ( ☎ 8852 1731; Memorial Dr; unpowered/powered sites per 2 people $11/15, on-site vans $21, cabins $77) This very basic park has a toilet block and few other facilities.

## WAROOKA

☎ 08 / pop 250

This unspectacular country town was named for the Aboriginal word *wiruka* (muddy waterhole). A few heritage buildings are worth a look, including the former police station (1879), now housing a **folk museum** ( ☎ 8854 5003; Brentwood Rd; ⏲ 10am-3pm Fri or by appointment). There's an interesting recycled-paper shop, **Paper Nymph** ( ☎ 8854 4137; 48 Warooka Rd; www.papernymph.com; tours $5; ⏲ noon-5.30pm Tue-Fri) which does tours of its paper-making facilities that are ideal for kids.

The **Warooka Hotel/Motel** ( ☎ 8854 5001; Main St; s/d $50/65) has clean motel units with new fittings, or you can book bush campsites at **Warooka Council Office** ( ☎ 8854 5055; Player St; per car $7.50).

## MARION BAY

☎ 08 / pop 120

Originally the port for nearby gypsum mines, Marion Bay was almost abandoned when the present shipping facility was developed at Stenhouse Bay. Today it's a booming resort centre beloved for its proximity to Innes National Park.

The **Marion Bay Store** ( ☎ 8854 4008) provides information on fishing, diving and surfing in the area. It also sells provisions, takeaway food and ice, fills scuba tanks and can arrange boat hire.

To get out catching the big fish, **Yorke Peninsula Fishing Charters** ( ☎ 8854 4044; yorkecharters@hotmail.com; per day $150) takes off from Marion Bay with a minimum of four people (five on weekends). Another good outfit is **Reef Encounters** (☎ 8349 4271; Pondalowie Bay; 1-day/weekend fishing $130/250), which has a great weekend package that includes accommodation and cooked breakfast.

## Sleeping & Eating
**Marion Bay Seaside Apartments** (☎ 8339 1909, 8854 4066; s $80-100, d $90-120) Opposite the store, these roomy self-contained units sleep five and have Austar TV and pricier places with sea views.

**Marion Bay Holiday Villas** (☎ 8278 5635; www .marionbayvillas.com.au; Waratah Ave; units $110-140) These slick new units have full kitchens and limited space, so they're better for couples than large families.

**Yorke's Holiday Units** (☎ 8552 1753; www.yorkes .com.au; cnr Waratah Ave & Templetonia Dr; $90-100) With full kitchens, CD stereos and videos, these tricked-up units are designed for younger partying groups of five.

**Marion Bay Caravan Park** (☎ 8854 4094; 20 Willyama Dr; unpowered/powered sites per 2 people $16/19, cabins $64-71) This friendly park is located close to the beach with bushy environs not far from Innes National Park.

**Marion Bay Tavern** (☎ 8854 4141; Main Rd; mains $9-15; lunch & dinner) This well-renovated joint is a great venue for a cheeky schooner or twenty, plus there are well-presented meals with all the old favourites (fish and chips, steaks etc) on the table.

## INNES NATIONAL PARK
At the southwestern tip of Yorke Peninsula, the popular Innes National Park comprises mainly coastal heath and rolling mallee country bounded by a spectacular coastline. The unique geology of the area saw large deposits of gypsum mined here in the 1890s. Today an impressive chain of salt lakes and rugged headlands makes this park a real original. Some roads remain unsealed, so take it easy on blind corners.

### Information
Entry permits ($6.50 per car) are available at the self-registration station or **DEH office** (☎ 08-8854 3200; Stenhouse Bay; 9am-4.30pm Mon-Fri, 10.30am-2pm Sat & Sun), which has brochures on camping, walking, fishing and surfing.

### Sights & Activities
There's plenty of **wildlife** including the endangered mallee fowl and western whipbird,

but emus and big western grey kangaroos are more commonly spotted. To protect native fauna, pets aren't allowed in the park. The park includes the abandoned gypsum-mining settlement of **Inneston**, best explored on the signposted walk (45 minutes, 700m).

Most of the **walking** around Innes is limited to short strolls of less than an hour. From **Browns Beach** to **Gym Beach** (two hours, 3km) is a longer walk passing through tall sand dunes, and can be relatively sheltered. Walking out to Cape Spencer's **lighthouse** takes less than ten minutes and offers absolutely stunning views of Althorpe and Kangaroo Islands.

The rough seas around the peninsula have left several **shipwrecks**; the *Ethel* and *Ferret* are both visible from land and you may be able to see the masts of the *Willyama* sticking out; this makes it an easy dive to find. To try **diving** in the park, ask at the **Marion Bay Store** (☎ 8854 4008), though rugged conditions can mean it's only for the experienced.

The **surfing** at Innes is challenging, though beginners can take a dumping at **Pondalowie Bay**, which combines beach and reef breaks. **Chinaman's** is definitely for experienced waxheads, with strong left-hand reef breaks. Tucked up closer to Marion Bay, **Rhino Head** is an average left-hand reef break.

There's good **fishing** with **Browns Beach**, the southern end of **Pondalowie Bay**, **Cape Spencer** and **Stenhouse Bay** all proving to be good spots. Grab a charter from Marion Bay (opposite) to get the local tips.

### Sleeping & Eating
There are a number of sheltered **bush campsites** (per car $6.50-16) close to nice beaches. The camps at Pondalowie Bay, Surfers Beach and Casuarina Beach are the best appointed with showers and good beach positions. Drinking water is limited, so bring your own in summer.

Alternatively, there are comfortable **lodges** (per night $80-110) with showers and cooking facilities at Inneston and Stenhouse Bay. **Shepherd's hut** (Shell Beach; per night $30) at has no showers.

**Rhino's Tavern** (☎ 08-8854 4066; Stenhouse Bay; lunch & dinner) serves a good 'curry of the moment' as well as steaks and whiting. The attached general store sells camping supplies, fuel and groceries.

# WEST COAST

The west coast is more sparsely settled than the east, with fewer and smaller towns. Unlike the east, it misses out on the sea breezes in summer, and as a result is generally hotter. There are plenty of good fishing and surfing beaches in the southwest.

## MINLATON

☎ 08 / pop 750

This attractive service town ostentatiously describes itself as the 'barley capital of the world', but it is central enough to use as a base from which to explore the peninsula. The visitors centre at **Harvest Corner Information & Craft** ( ☎ 8853 2600; 29 Main St; ☺ 10am-5.30pm Mon-Fri, 10am-4pm Sat & Sun) is a useful resource that also sells pretty handicrafts.

Main St has a **memorial** to WWI ace Captain Harry Butler. To see the 'Red Devil'

---

**DETOUR: CORNY POINT & POINT TURTON**

Heading north on the dirt road from Marion Bay takes you to **Corny Point**, with rough tracks leading off to remote surfing, fishing and bush camping.

**Trespassers** on Formby Bay, with right-hand reef breaks up to 3m, is strictly for experienced surfers; the turn-off is 17km from Marion Bay. Further north, **Daly Head** has similarly big waves.

You'll pass **Gleesons Landing** camping ground on the way to rugged Corny Point, which features a lighthouse and **caravan park** ( ☎ 08-8855 3368; cornypointcaravanpark .com; unpowered/powered sites per 2 people $13.50/16.50, on-site vans $35, d cottage $90).

The coast road from Corny Point to Point Turton passes **Leven Beach Conservation Park**, which offers attractive **Burners Beach** campsite. You can book campsites through **Yorke Peninsula Council** ( ☎ 08-8853 3800; per car $7.50). **Point Turton** has a **caravan park** ( ☎ 08-8854 5222; www.pointturton.com; unpowered/powered sites per 2 people $14/17.50, cabins $55-100) and general store.

Dirt roads lead along the coast from Point Turton to **Port Victoria**, hiding fishing spots and tiny resort towns on a coastal track suitable only for 4WDs.

---

**DETOUR: PORT VICTORIA**

To get to this small fishing town from Maitland take the clearly signposted route 21km or turn off the Minlaton–Maitland Rd. Either way, you'll arrive at a quiet town that was once the state's fourth-largest shipping terminal. The jetty has a quaint **Maritime Museum** ( ☎ 08-8834 2202; adult $3; ☺ 2-4pm Sat, Sun & public holidays) with displays detailing the windjammer era. There are top swimming beaches south of town at **Rifle Butts Beach** and **Second Beach**, with a cliff-top walk (30 minutes, 1km) to Rifle Butts; grab a brochure from the hotel.

There's diving with sea lions at **White Rock** and the **Goose Islands**, plus shipwrecks in the waters off **Wardang Island**. **Hutchy's Charters** ( ☎ 0429-413 414, 08-8252 9515; 1-day charter $120) has a 7m vessel to get you diving or fishing.

You can refill air tanks and stay at the leafy **Gulfhaven Caravan Park** ( ☎ 08-8834 2012; Port Victoria; unpowered/powered sites per 2 people $18/21, cabins $65-110), or at **Port Victoria Hotel/Motel** ( ☎ 08-8834 2069; Main St; s/d $55/70), which has plain motel units.

---

fighter Harry flew head for the **Minlaton Museum** ( ☎ 8853 2027; Main St; adult/child $3/$0.50; ☺ 9.30am-1pm Tue-Fri, 9.30am-noon Sat). The result of years of beachcombing, **Seashells Museum** ( ☎ 8853 2518; 17 Maitland Rd; adult/child $2/1; ☺ 10am-5pm) has large shark jaws, whales' teeth and sea turtle shells.

The relaxed **Minlaton Caravan Park** ( ☎ 8853 2345; Maitland Rd; unpowered/powered sites per 2 people $15/17, cabins $50-70; ☺ ) is an older park with pleasant gum trees. Alternatively, the **Hotel Minlaton** ( ☎ 8853 2014; 26 Main St; s/d $50/60) has budget motel units.

## MAITLAND

☎ 08 / pop 1100

Established in 1872, Maitland is the commercial centre for the middle peninsula. The National Trust **museum** ( ☎ 8832 2220; Gardiner Tce; adult/child $3/1 ☺ 2-4pm Sun & public holidays) in the old school has displays on local Aborigines and early German settlers.

You can stay at **Hotel Maitland** ( ☎ 8832 2431; Robert St; s/d $37/59, meals $10-15; ☺ breakfast, lunch & dinner), which has basic pub rooms with breakfast at the restaurant included.

# THE COPPER TRIANGLE

In 1859 a shepherd on Wallaroo Station found traces of copper, which heralded the discovery of the wealthiest copper lode in Australia. The Wallaroo mine was thriving within a year, and soon another appeared at Moonta, attracting Cornish miners and their families. The seaside towns have remained healthy since the mines dwindled, with holiday homes and villas sprawling from Wallaroo to Moonta Bay (the latter is virtually part of Moonta). Catching the recent seachange swell, Port Broughton (to the north of the triangle proper) has become a lazy holiday destination.

## Getting Around

**Copper Triangle Cabs** ( ☎ 08-8821 3444) of Kadina provides a 24-hour taxi service. For those who prefer to drive themselves, **Excel Rent-a-Car** ( ☎ 08-8821 2777; Adelaide Rd, Kadina) is located at Kadina Gateway Motor Inn.

For a daytrip, **York Peninsula Railway** (YPR; ☎ 8821 2333; train station, Wallaroo; ☽ 11am every 2nd Sun) runs from Wallaroo to Kadina (return adult/concession/child $10/8/6) and Bute (adult/concession/child $25/18/13) aboard the 'Super Chook' railcars chugged along by a diesel engine. The trip takes about four hours, collecting passengers at Kadina and dropping them off for two hours to explore Bute; listen out for the departure whistle.

## MOONTA & AROUND

☎ 08 / pop 3084

Developed around a copper mine, Moonta was once the second-largest town in SA. A real-estate boom has buoyed the town's fortunes with two residential suburbs, Patrick's View and Simms Cove, virtually linking Moonta Bay and Port Hughes. Now well developed, it's a far cry from the original Aboriginal word *moonterra* (impenetrable scrub)

that gave the town its name. The **Moonta visitors centre** ( ☎ 8825 1891; Kadina–Moonta Rd; ☽ 9am-5pm) has a selection of history pamphlets.

## Sights

Local mining history is unearthed at the **Moonta Heritage Site** (Arthurton Rd), 1km from town, where you'll find rustic ruins including stone chimneys and engine houses. Several sites have been developed with walking tracks and information signs. You can get here on the **Tourist Train** ( ☎ 8825 1891; Moonta Mines Museum; adult/child $5/2; ☽ departs 1pm, 2pm & 3pm Sat & Sun), a small tram that makes 50-minute town tour on the way to the mines.

**Moonta Mines Museum** ( ☎ 8251 1891; Verco St; adult $5/2; ☽ 1.30-4pm Wed & Fri-Sun) is in the impressive **Moonta Mines School**, and houses some interesting displays, including the dramatic story of Elizabeth Woodcock, SA's only executed woman.

Other historic buildings include the austere **Moonta Mines Methodist Church** (Verco St; admission by donation; ☽ 1.30-4pm daily Sep-Apr, 1.30-4pm Wed, Sat & Sun May-Aug) and the **Miners Cottage** ( ☎ 8251 1891; Verco St; adult/child $2.50/1; ☽ 1.30-4pm Wed, Sat & Sun), a romantic Cornish dwelling with period furnishings. Many of Moonta's finest historic buildings are featured in *Up Street Moonta*, a walking tour brochure available from Moonta visitors centre.

Off the road to Moonta Bay, there's something for (almost) everyone at **Moonta Lavender Farm** ( ☎ 8825 3025; 24 Kitto Rd; adult/child $4/2; ☽ 10am-4.30pm Wed-Mon), where mums can delight in organic cosmetics, kids can take the Nursery Rhyme Trail, and dads will just have to be patient.

**Port Hughes** and **Moonta Bay** are quiet seaside resorts with sandy beaches; there's good swimming south of the Port Hughes jetty, while Moonta Bay's sandy flat beach is perfect for kids or sandcastle kings.

Just 3km from Moonta on the Wallaroo Rd, a section of the 1980s **Wheal Hughes**

---

### FESTIVALS & EVENTS

**Kernewek Lowender Festival** ( ☎ 1800 654 991, 08-8821 2333; www.kernewek.org; May) A celebration of the Copper Triangle's Cornish heritage. Kadina, Moonta and Wallaroo erupt with Celtic games, Cornish fairs and feasting. Expect plenty of pasties and beer. Held in odd-numbered years.

**Farm Festival** ( ☎ 1800 654 991, 08-8821 2333; first week of Oct) The National Dryland Farm, Heritage & Information Centre hosts a weekend celebration of agriculture including cook-ups, horse rides and farming demonstrations that draws cockies from across the state.

**Copper Mine** (☎ 8825 1892; Moonta–Wallaroo Rd; adult/concession/child $22/18/11) has been reopened. There are daily one-hour tours.

## Activities

There's plenty of local fisherfolk who'll take you out to secret spots. Most require a minimum of two people and will supply free soft drinks. Here are a few good operators that depart from Moonta Bay or Port Hughes:

**Wildfish'n Charters** (☎ 8825 3603, 0428-253 603; www.wildfishin.com.au; Port Hughes; 1-day autumn-spring/summer $120/150) Charges extra in summer to chase snapper.

**A1 Fishing Charters** (☎ 8825 1810, 0428-251 810; www.a1fishing.com.au; per day $135)

**Copper Triangle Charters** (☎ 8825 3814; Port Hughes; $120) Can handle a maximum of five.

**Port Hughes Fishing Charters** (☎ 8825 3388, 0418-859 431; Port Hughes; 1-day $120) Can do overnight trips and lunches on request.

## Sleeping

The big real estate agents in Moonta have holiday homes to rent, ranging from $60 to $180 per night. They're conveniently on opposite corners in the main street, so check out **Elders** (☎ 8825 3055; www.elders.com.au/moonta; cnr George & Ellen Sts), then head across to **LJ Hooker** (☎ 8825 2007; www.ljhooker.com.au/moonta wallaroo; cnr George & Ellen Sts).

### BUDGET

**Cornwall Hotel** (☎ 8825 2304; cnr Ryan & Ellen Sts, Moonta; s/d $29/49) This boozer has simple pub rooms with sweet common areas and plump new mattresses.

**Moonta Bay Top Tourist Park** (☎ 8825 2406; Foreshore, Moonta Bay; unpowered/powered sites per 2 people $21/23, cabins $66-73, cabins with spa $109) Close to the jetty, this family-friendly park has some good luxury cabins that include spas.

**Port Hughes Tourist Park** (☎ 8825 2106; South Tce, Port Hughes; unpowered/powered sites per 2 people $21/23, units $70-93) There are two great sites in this park with the West Tce overlooking the jetty, and the reception in South Tce. The South Tce site has better facilities, though, including a good children's park.

### MID-RANGE

**Moonta Bay Patio Motel** (☎ 8825 2473; 196 Bay Rd, Moonta Bay; s/d/tr $78/89/100) You should opt for a spectacular sea-view room at the Patio,

---

> **THE AUTHOR'S CHOICE**
>
> **Peppertree Cottage** (☎ 8825 2680; 85 Wallaroo Rd, Moonta; s/d $90/120; ⚅) Looking for a quiet weekend away? Peppertree has plenty to keep you cosily inside, like a claw-foot bath, massive bed and chilled lounge area. There's no TV so you can catch up on reading by your very own pool. Huge cooked breakfasts are standard, but if you get too lazy evening meals are available.

which has comfy units handy to the beach. Their restaurant (below) also has impressive vistas.

**Cabarita B&B** (☎ 8825 2981; 47 South Tce, Port Hughes; d $130) Packed with features including a four-poster bed and spa, this is a good getaway spot with a busy garden (even the gnomes look exhausted). The cooked breakfast is an extra treat.

### TOP END

**Cliff House** (☎ 8821 3900; Hughes Ave, Moonta Bay; apt $200) These beach-front villas are an excellent self-contained option with spas, full kitchens and everything you'd need for a great beach escape.

## Eating

**Moonta Bay Patio Motel Restaurant** (☎ 8825 2473; 196 Bay Rd, Moonta Bay; mains $16-26; ☽ lunch & dinner) As well as excellent views, this restaurant has a complex menu of baked barramundi, bush lamb and seafood filo, plus an extensive vegetarian selection.

**La Cantina Cafe** (☎ 8825 3253; 16-18 Ellen St, Moonta; mains $8-17; ☽ 3pm-late Tue-Wed, 10am-late Thu-Fri, 3pm-late Sat, 5pm-8.30pm Sun) This place excels at pasta, pizza and some kick-arse desserts (tiramisu, sticky date pudding).

**Bayview Cafe** (☎ 8825 3399; 167 Bay Rd, ☽ 7am-10pm) For penny-pinching breakfasts, pizza, fish and chips, and other seaside favourites, the jetty views at this place will satisfy.

In the Copper Triangle, the Cornish pasty is close to a religion. Locals are divided between the **Cornish Kitchen** (12 Ellen St, Moonta) and **Cousin Jack's Bakery** (☎ 8825 3377; 37 George St, Moonta; ☽ 8.30am-5pm Mon-Fri, 8.30am-12.30pm Sat) – both do great pasties along with breads, cakes and coffee. Others prefer the **Moonta Bakery** (☎ 8825 2115; 8 George St, Moonta; ☽ 7am-6pm) which also serves yummy breakfasts.

# KADINA

☎ 08 / pop 3745

The capital of Yorke Peninsula was founded in 1860 to service nearby copper mines, with the town's name taken from the Aboriginal words *kaddy-yeena* (lizard plain). While the population has plummeted since its mining heyday, Kadina endures as an agricultural and administrative centre. The **National Dryland Farm, Heritage & Information Centre** (NDFHIC; ☎ 1800 654 991, 8821 2333; off Kadina–Moonta Rd; ☺ 9am-5pm Mon-Fri, 10am-3.30pm Sat & Sun) is the peninsula's best-stocked visitors centre.

## Sights & Activities

While not as historically rich as Moonta, Kadina does have some noteworthy reminders of yesteryear. The booklet *A Look At The Heritage of Kadina*, available at the NDFHIC complex, is a self-guided walk around more than 30 historic buildings.

Just off the Kadina–Moonta Rd in the NDFHIC complex is **Kadina Heritage Museum** ( ☎ 8821 2333; adult/concession/child $8/6/2; ☺ 9am-5pm Mon-Fri, 10am-2pm Sat & Sun) which showcases the magnificently restored Matta House (1863), old farming machinery and a blacksmith's shop.

Budding billionaires will enjoy the **Banking & Currency Museum** ( ☎ 8821 2906; www.yp-connect.net/~vortronald; 3 Graves St; adult/concession/child $5/4/2; ☺ 10am-4.30pm Sun-Thu, closed Jun) in the old Bank of SA building (1873) which has comprehensive displays all about moolah. Staff are happy to do tours as well as trade in rare coins.

The **Wallaroo Mine**, 1km west of town, takes half an hour to stroll around, and includes numerous shafts and the stone ruin of **Harvey's Enginehouse**, now a home for pigeons.

## Sleeping

**Ironhorse Junction** ( ☎ 8821 3886; www.yp-connect.net/~ironhorse/; Frances Tce; dm/s/d $30/40/65) Set in the old train station this is an exceptional hostel with DVDs, satellite TV, spa and even the odd Harley ride ($30, one hour). The cheerful owner, Reg Holliday, is a vacationer by name and nature, happily sorting out local activities.

**Kadina Hotel** ( ☎ 8821 1008; 29 Taylor St; s/d $45/60) Accommodation here is great for pub rooms, though each has a strange built-in private bathroom that's like a separate shack. Big TVs and continental breakfasts are good touches.

**Kadina Gateway Motor Inn** ( ☎ 8821 2777; Adelaide Rd; s/d/tw $92/102/104; ☒ ) The town's best motel makes for a pleasant stay amid the gum-treed garden in quality rooms.

**Kadina Caravan Park** ( ☎ 8821 2259; Lindsay Tce; unpowered/powered sites per 2 people $19/21, cabins $59) This predominantly residential park has lawned campsites and newer cabins for an economical stay.

## Eating & Drinking

Like many regional towns, Kadina has pub dining in spades with a few interesting venues outside of the hotels.

**Kahuna Cafe** ( ☎ 8821 1144; 4 Goyder St; mains $10-18; ☺ lunch & dinner) Surf's up at this casual spot doing seafood, flavoursome pastas and hefty Kahuna burgers. The feel is beachy with quick meals served effortlessly.

**Emperors Dragon Inn & Kadina Pizza Bar** ( ☎ 8821 2525; 31-33 Taylor St; mains $6-14; ☺ dinner Wed-Sun) Italian-Chinese relations haven't been this good since Marco Polo. This kooky joint straddling East-West divides has takeaway or eat-in food ranging from Four Treasure Steamed Duck ($12) to the tried-and-true Hawaiian ($8).

**Royal Exchange Hotel** ( ☎ 8821 1084; 7 Digby St; meals $8-14; ☺ lunch & dinner) This historic hotel has the town's largest gaming room and a big dining room that does good meal deals.

**Wombat Hotel** ( ☎ 8821 1108; 19 Taylor St; mains $6-12; ☺ lunch & dinner) This marsupial marvel dishes up bargain specials ($6) including snags and curries. The front bar is good for a quiet schooner.

**Bakery Cafe** ( ☺ 7.30am-5pm) This bustling little bakehouse is a good spot to try yet another variation on the Cornish pasty and sip well-brewed coffee.

# WALLAROO

☎ 08 / pop 2720

This coastal corner of the Copper Triangle once served as the mining port for Moonta and Kadina with a huge copper smelter that seared with 30 furnaces. Wallaroo gets the crown for strangest name in the Triangle, taken from the Aboriginal word *wadla-waru* (wallaby's urine). Dwarfed by huge silos and a large loading chute, Wallaroo's economic woes have been relieved by the grain that now passes through the port. The **post office**

YORKE PENINSULA

( ☎ 8823 2020; cnr Irwin St & Owen Tce; ⏱ 9am-5pm Mon-Fri) keeps a few tourist brochures.

## Sights & Activities

The solid ex–post office holds the **Heritage & Nautical Museum** ( ☎ 8823 2015; Jetty Rd; adult/child $5/2; ⏱ 2-4pm Tue, Thu, Sat & Sun, 10.30am-4pm Wed) which has displays on windjammers that sailed here from England, as well as George the giant squid. This is the starting point for a 9km heritage drive and much shorter **walking trail** through town. Both are described in *Discovering Historic Wallaroo*, which covers places of historical interest.

For a daytrip **York Peninsula Railway** (YPR; ☎ 8821 2333, train station, return to Kadina adult/concession/child $10/8/6, return to Bute adult/concession/child $25/18/13, ⏱ 11am every second Sunday) goes to Kadina and Bute aboard the 'Super Chook' railcars chugged along by a diesel engine.

To see kangaroos, emus and black swans in a reserve environment you can visit **Wallaroo Fauna Park** ( ☎ 8823 3069; Ernest St; admission by donation; ⏱ 9.30am-2pm Mon, Wed & Thu or by appointment), a small locally run park.

There's plenty of fishing or just boat-based sightseeing to be had around the area. Most boats come with tackle, a skipper and soft drinks, but may need a minimum of four to get you out on the water. Here's a selection of operators:

**Captain Cook Charters** ( ☎ 8862 1557; 1-day $120)
**Copper Cove Charters** ( ☎ 0417-873 359; 1-day $110)
**Wallaroo Fishing Charters & Tours** ( ☎ 0428-233 792; 1-day $120)

## Sleeping & Eating

Several holiday homes are rented out by the **Professionals Real Estate** ( ☎ 8823 3422; www.sa.professionals.com.au; 43 Owen Tce; houses $85-200). Many places book out well in advance during Kernewek.

**Office Beach Holiday Cabins & Caravan Park** ( ☎ 8823 2722; 11 Jetty Rd; unpowered/powered sites per 2 people $17/19-21, units $80-105, cabins $55) You pay for the jettyside position with rather cramped sites, though the more expensive units do come with redeeming spas and some great views.

**Sonbern Lodge Motel** ( ☎ 8823 2291; 18 John Tce; s $28-67, d $44-84) This former-temperance hotel (relax – they're licensed now) is an old-fashioned charmer right down to the pool table, antique wind-up phone and grand-

father clock. Out the back there are private motel units, while upstairs has basic pub-style rooms.

**Mac's Beachfront Villas** ( ☎ 8823 2137; 9 Jetty Rd; apt $130) For a family spot, Mac's is hard to beat, with beachside location, portable barbecues and self-contained units that sleep up to five. Higher-end rooms throw in extra features such as spas, and champers and chocolates on arrival.

**Skinner's Jetty Fish Cafe** ( ☎ 8823 3455; Jetty Rd; mains $6-20; ⏱ lunch daily, dinner Fri & Sat) This café hooks patrons with its beachside location, and different dining options here – from the sophisticated upstairs dinner watching the sunset to the ice cream from the kiosk downstairs. The seafood is highly regarded and the platters are huge.

**Jetty Road Bakehouse** ( ☎ 8823 3600; Jetty Rd; snacks $3-7; ⏱ 8am-6pm) Down by the sea, this bakery does a roaring trade with beachgoers who love their cakes, pies, and good coffee.

## PORT BROUGHTON

☎ 08 / pop 1400

If you find it hard to relax, then kicking back in this mellow holiday town will cure even the acutest workaholic. Apart from swimming or fishing, the only real activity comes in the form of the town's large prawn fleet.

The best swimming is off the jetty, but to get more involved with the water **Stress Relief Charters** ( ☎ 8381 9543; www.stressreliefcharters.com.au; 1-day fishing $110) can take you out to net a few whoppers. The Port Broughton Hotel has basic visitor information if you must find something to do.

### Sleeping & Eating

**Hotel Broughton** ( ☎ 8635 2004; Bay St; s/d $30/45, meals $10-14; ⏱ lunch & dinner; 🚺 ) This waterside classic does pub rooms with comfy beds, TVs and good views. Their counter meals are generous.

**Port Broughton Caravan Park** ( ☎ 8635 2188; 2 Barker St; powered sites per 2 people $21, on-site van $38, cabins $50) Popular for its foreshore location, this is a well-appointed and friendly park.

**Bay St Cafe** ( ☎ 8635 2552; Bay St; mains $10-19; ⏱ 10am-late Thu-Sun) Definitely the place to eat in town, you can grab anything from brunch to dinner here, with a terrific menu that includes innovatively presented Eyre Peninsula oysters, risottos and salmon.

# Flinders Ranges

CONTENTS

| Southern Ranges | 199 |
|---|---|
| Port Augusta | 199 |
| Port Germein | 203 |
| Wirrabara & Around | 204 |
| Melrose | 204 |
| Mt Remarkable National Park | 205 |
| Wilmington | 205 |
| Quorn | 206 |
| Around Quorn | 207 |
| Kanyaka | 208 |
| **Northern Ranges** | **208** |
| Hawker | 208 |
| Hawker to Wilpena | 209 |
| Flinders Ranges National Park | 210 |
| Blinman | 212 |
| Around Blinman | 213 |
| Hawker to Leigh Creek | 213 |
| Parachilna to Blinman | 214 |
| Leigh Creek | 214 |
| Copley to Gammon Ranges National Park | 214 |
| Gammon Ranges National Park | 214 |
| Arkaroola Wildlife Sanctuary | 215 |

Simply known to most as 'the Flinders', this soaring series of mountains is one of the great outdoor drawcards of South Australia (SA). The region was once a vital way station on trade routes so ruins, archaeological sites and abandoned mines remain dotted through the hills and gullies. Before Europeans arrived, the area was prized by the local Adnyamathanha (or 'Hill People') for its red ochre deposits that were important for medicinal and ritual uses. You'll still see the rich ochre colours, brought out by vivid sunsets that stretch over the landscape.

The ranges themselves are a continuation of the Mt Lofty Ranges, which begin near Crystal Brook and run north for 400km to Mt Hopeless, before petering out in the Strzelecki Desert. At the northern fringes scenery is stark, semiarid with rugged purple ridges, dramatic bluffs and gum-lined creeks. As well as bushwalks and great views, there are numerous sites of cultural interest such as abandoned mines and settlements, and Aboriginal rock paintings and rock carvings. In the south, sweet country towns remain while hamlets are fading into ghost towns, but all have an enduring country hospitality.

As in many other dry mountain regions of Australia, the vegetation is surprisingly diverse and colourful; tall river red gums are a feature throughout, while dark stands of native pine are more obvious in the north. The western flanks are in a rain shadow, so the vegetation is much sparser than on the eastern side. In the south the hills are covered with large gums, while beyond Quorn the vegetation generally becomes scrubbier.

## HIGHLIGHTS

- Chugging through the bush from Port Augusta to Quorn on the **Pichi Richi Railway** (p206)
- Admiring the panorama after climbing to the top of **Mt Remarkable** (p205)
- Enjoying the pleasant village atmosphere of historic **Melrose** (p204), reputedly the oldest town in the Flinders
- Wrapping your laughing gear around a quandong slice in Copley's famous **bakery** (p214)
- Bushwalking up to the rim of **Wilpena Pound** (p210)
- Examining the sacred Aboriginal paintings etched into **Arkaroo Rock** (p210)
- Spotting yellow-footed rock wallabies, emus and loads of kangaroos in **Flinders Ranges National Park** (p210)
- Learning timeless Adnyamathanha lore at Aboriginal-run **Iga Warta** (p214)

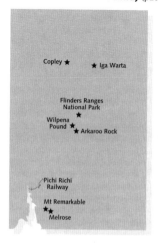

- TELEPHONE CODE: ☎ 08
- www.flindersranges.com

**FLINDERS RANGES**

# FLINDERS RANGES

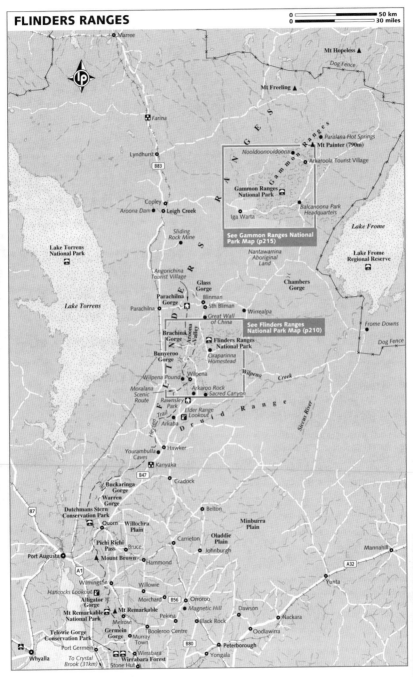

0 ____ 50 km
0 ____ 30 miles

Marree

Mt Hopeless ▲

Dog Fence

Mt Freeling ▲

Farina

R A N G E S

Paralana Hot Springs
Nooldoonooldoona
Mt Painter (790m)

Lyndhurst
B83

Arkaroola Tourist Village

Gammon Ranges
National Park

Copley
Aroona Dam    Leigh Creek
Balcanoona Park
Headquarters

Iga Warta

**See Gammon Ranges National Park Map (p215)**

Lake Frome

Sliding
Rock Mine

Lake Torrens
National Park

Nantawarrina
Aboriginal
Land

Lake Frome
Regional Reserve

Angorichina
Tourist Village

Glass
Gorge

Chambers
Gorge

Parachilna
Gorge

Blinman
Sth Bliman

Lake Torrens

Parachilna

Wirrealpa

Great Wall
of China

**See Flinders Ranges National Park Map (p210)**

Frome Downs

Brachina
Gorge

Aroona
Valley

Flinders Ranges
National Park

Dog Fence

Bunyeroo
Gorge

Oraparinna
Homestead

Wilpena Pound

Wilpena

Wilpena    Creek

Moralana
Scenic
Route

Arkaroo Rock
Sacred Canyon

Siccus River

Rawnsley
Park

R a n g e

Heysen    Trail

Elder Range
Lookout

D r u i d

Arkaba

Yourambulla
Caves

Hawker

Kanyaka

B47

Cradock

Buckaringa
Gorge

Warren
Gorge

Belton

Minburra
Plain

Dutchmans Stern
Conservation Park

87

Quorn

Willochra
Plain

Carrieton

Oladdie
Plain

Pichi Richi
Pass

Bruce

Johnburgh

Mannahill

Port Augusta

Mount Brown

Hammond

A32

A1

Yunta

Wilmington

Willowie

Hancocks Lookout

Morchard
B56

Orroroo

Alligator
Gorge

Magnetic Hill

Dawson

Mt Remarkable
National Park

Mt Remarkable

Pekina

Black Rock

Nackara

Melrose

Oodlawirra

Telowie Gorge
Conservation Park

Germein
Gorge

Booleroo Centre

Murray
Town

Port Germein

Wirrabara Forest

B880

Peterborough

Whyalla

To Crystal
Brook (31km)

Stone Hut

Wirrabara

Yongala

## National Parks

There's plenty of good bushwalking and nature-spotting to be had throughout the Flinders. If you're planning to visit all the parks the Flinders Parks Pass (four-weeks/annual $21/77) represents good value (as it includes up to five nights camping in any one spot), and is available at rangers stations and other Department for Environment & Heritage (DEH) representatives (see p236 for a full listing). Alternatively, you can visit with a day pass ($6.50), available from park rangers or at self-registration centres as you enter the parks. There's camping at Mt Remarkable (p205), Gammon Ranges (p215) and Flinders Ranges National Parks (p212), with bush camping at several other spots too. You don't have to rough it, though, as there are cabins at Alligator Gorge (p205), Mambray Creek (p205) and Wilpena Pound Resort (p212) – the latter has motel-style rooms as well.

## Tours

There are lots of tours from Adelaide to the Flinders Ranges, with others mainly leaving from Port Augusta, Quorn, Hawker and Wilpena Pound. You should definitely book ahead as tours are very popular, though some (particularly flights) require minimum numbers to run.

**Mulpa Tours** ( ☎ 08-8520 2808; www.mulpatours.com.au) Tours (per four/five days $710 to $800/$1320 to $1340) with indigenous insight into the region take in Brachina Gorge, Copley and the Flinders Ranges with a chance to make music sticks and hear Aboriginal Dreaming *stories*.

**Iga Warta** ( ☎ 08-8648 3737; www.igawarta.com; Arkaroola) Provides a number of interesting, Aboriginal-run day trips (walks/tours $29/63).

**Swagabout Tours** ( ☎ 0408-845-378; www.swagabout tours.com.au) Run tours throughout SA. Their Adelaide to Alice Springs trip (five-/seven-/nine-/10-day tours $810 to $1125/$1320 to $1575/$1650 to $2025/$1800 to $2250) is a good trek passing through the Flinders Ranges, the Oodnadatta Track and Dalhousie Springs, before heading on to Uluru. Their Flinders Ranges trips (per three/four days $550/710) include the Ridgetop Tour and Wilpena, and can be extended to include Coober Pedy (see p237).

**Aussie Bush Tracks Tours** ( ☎ 08-86486567; www .aboutozzietours.com) Operates from Quorn and does trips (per half-/one day $78/140) of the area around town including Dutchman's Stern, as well as heading out on longer trips (three-/five-day tours $480/890) of Wilpena and Arkaroola.

**Wallaby Tracks Adventure Tours** ( ☎ 1800 639 933, 08-8648 6655; www.users.bigpond.com/headbush) These

tour operators also run Andu Lodge youth hostel in Quorn so they have good tours for backpackers, from a trip to Wilpena Pound (one day $119) to longer trips across to Coober Pedy (four days $800).

**Rawnsley Park** ( ☎ 08-8648 0008, 08-8648 0030; www.rawnsleypark.com.au) From near Wilpena there's plenty of tours from the Skytrek rough road (half-/one-day tour $85/130) to horse-riding (one-/two-hours $45/60).

**Central Air Services** ( ☎ 08-8648 0008) Offers several different scenic flights over Wilpena Pound (20 minutes/five hours $75/650); bookings are through Wilpena visitors centre (p210).

**Derek's 4WD Tours** ( ☎ 0417-475 770; www.dereks 4wdtours.com) For off-road action this company does several good trips (half-/one day tour $70 to $80/$125 to $135) including the Skytrek drive out of Hawker.

**Arkaroola Wilderness Sanctuary** ( ☎ 1800 676 042, 08-8648 4848; www.arkaroola.com.au) Books the famous Ridgetop Tour across Arkaroola.

The following tour companies run routes that include a number of Flinders Ranges destinations:

**Adventure Tours Australia** ( ☎ 1300 654 604, 08-8309 2299; www.adventuretours.com.au)

**Groovy Grape Getaways** ( ☎ 1800 661 177; www .groovygrape.com.au)

**Wayward Bus** ( ☎ 1800 882 823, 08-8410 8833; www .waywardbus.com.au)

## Getting There & Around

Port Augusta is the main transport hub for travel to and from the Flinders Ranges with air, bus and train services.

**Bute Buses' Mid-North Passenger Service** ( ☎ 08-8826 2346) visits Orroroo and Peterborough from Adelaide. **Yorke Peninsula Coaches** ( ☎ 08-8823 2375) head north from Adelaide to Peterborough ($27.50, five hours) once from Sunday to Friday, and to Orroroo ($30.50, 5½ hours) on Monday, Wednesday and Friday. At the time of research, no other bus companies served the Flinders Ranges. Check visitors centre for local operators.

The Flinders Ranges are well served by sealed roads off Hwy 1 and Main North Rd, both from Adelaide and the Barrier Hwy from New South Wales (NSW). As an alternative if you're coming from NSW, you can turn off the Barrier Hwy at Yunta and take gravel-surfaced back roads to Wilpena Pound, the Gammon Ranges National Park and Arkaroola.

Anyone planning to travel off the main roads, particularly in the north, should always be prepared for the shortage of drinking water, shops and service stations. If you're heading much further north than Leigh Creek, read Driving in the Outback (p238) for advice on the more extreme conditions, including where to ring for road condition updates.

Most points of interest in the south are accessible, with good sealed roads from Port Augusta and Melrose to Wilpena Pound via Quorn and Hawker. Further on the roads are gravel or dirt. The road from Hawker via Parachilna and Leigh Creek is sealed as far as Lyndhurst.

The restored **Pichi Richi Railway** ( ☎ 08-8633 0380; www.prr.org.au) connects Quorn to Port Augusta ($34, 2½ hours) on Saturdays from April to October on a scenic trip. See Quorn (p206) for more details.

# SOUTHERN RANGES

The southern Flinders Ranges district extends from just north of Crystal Brook to Hawker, and eastwards as far as Peterborough. It includes the Mt Remarkable National Park and several conservation parks, many just south of Quorn.

## PORT AUGUSTA
☎ 08 / pop 13,194
The Aboriginal name *kurdnatta* (heaps of sand) aptly describes this transport hub. Shipping booms in the 1880s made this a centre for trade, which was reinforced when it was made the headquarters for the Transcontinental Railway to Perth. Today the town remains a major crossroads for travellers. From here, main roads head west across the Nullarbor to Western Australia, north to Alice Springs and Darwin, south to Adelaide and east to Broken Hill and Sydney. The recent establishment of Baxter Detention Centre threw Port Augusta into a politically charged controversy.

### Orientation
To get to the town centre, you need to turn southwest off Victoria Pde. The main street is Commercial Rd, with most of the pubs and eating options. Victoria Pde continues northwest across the gulf (on the other side of which there are several accommodation options) before becoming the Stuart Hwy.

## Information
### INTERNET ACCESS
**Services SA** ( ☎ 132 324; 9 Mackay St; ☺ 9am-6pm) Offers free email.

### MEDICAL SERVICES
**Carlton Medical Centre** ( ☎ 8641 0411; cnr Main St & Carlton Pde) A healthcare option close to the centre of town.

### MONEY
The Commonwealth Bank, Bank SA, National Bank and Westpac are all on Commercial Rd in the town centre.

### POST
**Post office** ( ☎ 131 318; 50 Commercial Rd; ☺ 9am-5pm Mon-Fri)

### TOURIST INFORMATION
**DEH office** ( ☎ 8648 5020; Upstairs, 9 MacKay St; ☺ 9am-5.30pm Mon-Fri, 10am-4pm Sat & Sun) For information on the southern Flinders Ranges and far north with maps, road conditions and a huge old carpet python.
**Port Augusta visitors centre** ( ☎ 1800 633 060, 8641 0793; www.portaugusta.sa.gov.au; 41 Flinders Tce; ☺ 9am-5.30pm Mon-Fri, 10am-4pm Sat & Sun) Set in the Wadlata Outback Centre, this place acts as the major information outlet for the Flinders Ranges, outback and Eyre Peninsula.

### TRAVEL AGENCIES
**Harvey World Travel** ( ☎ 8642 3344; Commercial Rd; ☺ 9am-5pm Mon-Fri, 9am-11pm Sat) Books plane and bus tickets.

## Dangers & Annoyances
There's no doubt that Port Augusta has problems with alcoholism, with the centre of town designated as a dry area. Generally there are few problems, though readers have been irritated or saddened by constant requests for spare change.

## Sights & Activities
The acclaimed **Wadlata Outback Centre** ( ☎ 8642 4511; 41 Flinders Tce; adult/child $8.50/5.50; ☺ 9am-5.30pm Mon-Fri, 10am-4pm Sat & Sun) has many excellent exhibits, particularly the Flinders Range and Outback Tunnel of Time, tracing the Aboriginal and European past using audiovisual displays, interactive exhibits and a spooky giant snake. If you're overwhelmed on your first visit, there's a pass-out valid for 12 months. Right next door is the **Fountain Gallery** ( ☎ 8642 4557; 43 Flinders Tce; admission free;

**FLINDERS RANGES**

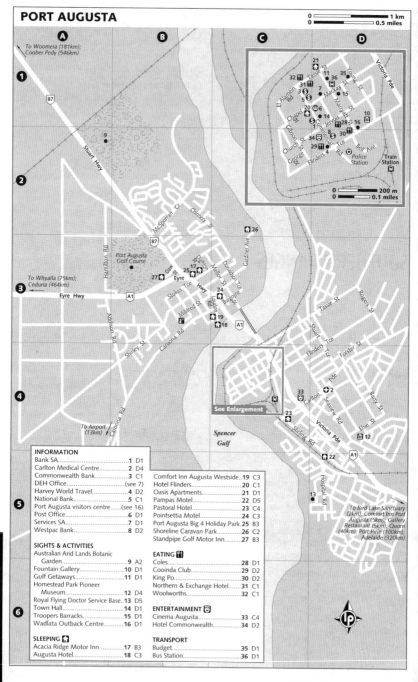

# PORT AUGUSTA

0 — 1 km
0 — 0.5 miles

To Woomera (181km);
Coober Pedy (546km)

To Whyalla (75km);
Ceduna (464km)

Eyre Hwy

Port Augusta
Golf Course

To Airport
(13km)

Spencer
Gulf

See Enlargement

Police
Station

Train
Station

0 — 200 m
0 — 0.1 miles

To Bird Lake Sanctuary
(2km); Comfort Inn Port
Augusta (5km); Gallery
Restaurant (5km); Quorn
(40km); Port Pirie (100km);
Adelaide (320km)

**INFORMATION**
Bank SA..............................................**1** D1
Carlton Medical Centre....................**2** D4
Commonwealth Bank........................**3** C1
DEH Office...................................(see 7)
Harvey World Travel.........................**4** D2
National Bank....................................**5** C1
Port Augusta visitors centre......(see 16)
Post Office........................................**6** D1
Services SA........................................**7** D1
Westpac Bank....................................**8** D2

**SIGHTS & ACTIVITIES**
Australian Arid Lands Botanic
  Garden............................................**9** A2
Fountain Gallery..............................**10** D1
Gulf Getaways..................................**11** D1
Homestead Park Pioneer
  Museum...........................................**12** D4
Royal Flying Doctor Service Base..**13** D5
Town Hall.........................................**14** D1
Troopers Barracks............................**15** D1
Wadlata Outback Centre.................**16** D1

**SLEEPING**
Acacia Ridge Motor Inn..................**17** B3
Augusta Hotel..................................**18** C3

Comfort Inn Augusta Westside...**19** C3
Hotel Flinders..................................**20** C1
Oasis Apartments.............................**21** D1
Pampas Motel...................................**22** D5
Pastoral Hotel...................................**23** C4
Pointsettia Motel..............................**24** C3
Port Augusta Big 4 Holiday Park...**25** B3
Shoreline Caravan Park....................**26** C2
Standpipe Golf Motor Inn..............**27** B3

**EATING**
Coles.................................................**28** D1
Cooinda Club....................................**29** D1
King Po..............................................**30** D2
Northern & Exchange Hotel...........**31** C1
Woolworths......................................**32** C1

**ENTERTAINMENT**
Cinema Augusta...............................**33** C4
Hotel Commonwealth......................**34** D2

**TRANSPORT**
Budget...............................................**35** D1
Bus Station........................................**36** D1

10am-4pm Mon-Fri), an intimate space with works by local and indigenous artists.

The **Homestead Park Pioneer Museum** ( ☎ 8642 2035; Elsie St; adult/child $2.50/1.50; ☺ 9am-noon Mon-Fri, 1-4pm Sat & Sun) features an original pine-log homestead (1850s) furnished in period style and a well-preserved rail carriage among its exhibits. For more local history, grab a two-hour **heritage walk** brochure from the visitors centre, which takes in numerous historic sites, including **Troopers Barracks** (1860) and the Corinthian-columned **Town Hall** (1887).

At **Royal Flying Doctor Service base** ( ☎ 8642 2044; 4 Vincent St; admission by donation; ☺ 10am-3pm Mon-Fri) you can find out more about the aerial medical service that goes to SA's remote areas with a short video and several displays. The base was in the process of relocating to the hangar at the airport when we visited.

The **Australian Arid Lands Botanic Garden** ( ☎ 8641 1049; Stuart Hwy; admission free; ☺ 9am-5pm Mon-Fri, 10am-4pm Sat & Sun, tours 11am Apr-Oct & 9.30am Nov-Mar) covers 250 hectares of sand hills and clay flats with the area's unique fauna. Walking the trails you'll learn about local plant life thanks to some good interpretative information, and you'll definitely see Sturts Desert Pea, the state's floral emblem. There's also a bush café doing snacks – creative roll ups, scones and brandy snaps – and a pricey gift shop.

**Bird Lake Sanctuary** is an eerie landscaping project that has created a bird-life habitat near the coal-burning power station. There is a picnic area and barbecue here.

## Tours

**Gulf Getaways** ( ☎ 1800 170 170; Augusta Fisheries, Marryatt St; 3hr cruise $77, full-day fishing charter $120) Hidden in the fish shop, this operator can take you out on a cruise that includes all drinks and food, or if you prefer to catch your own they do fishing trips for snapper, flathead and king fish.

**Augusta Water Cruises** ( ☎ 0438-857 001; 2½hr tour & cruise $75) Runs a cruise around the gulf with a short tour of town that includes morning tea at the Australian Arid Lands Botanic Garden.

## Sleeping

There are a several motels – most of the uninspiring transit variety – lining Hwy 1 on the way into and out of town. The pubs are a good cheaper option and many have better-appointed motel rooms attached.

### BUDGET

**Hotel Flinders** ( ☎ 8642 2544; 39 Commercial Rd; motel dm/s/d/tr $16.50/50/66/77) For a variety of pub rooms it's hard to beat the Flinders. If you don't like the luxury of two-bed (not bunks mind you) backpackers' room, then the larger rooms will do the trick. Some rooms have private bathrooms, TVs and bar fridges.

**Shoreline Caravan Park** ( ☎ 8642 2965; Gardiner Ave; unpowered/powered sites per 2 people $11/16, on-site vans $33, cabins $55, units $65) This well-positioned park near the water has loads of good facilities, including TV and games rooms, plus a great barbecue area. The luxury units are more like little motel rooms.

**Port Augusta Big 4 Holiday Park** ( ☎ 8642 2974; Hwy 1; unpowered/powered sites per 2 people $12/22, cabins $50-65, units $77-110) A leafy park like this attracts a friendly mob of 'roos around dusk, while you're setting up for dinner in the well-appointed campers kitchen.

Also recommended:

**Augusta Hotel** ( ☎ 8642 2701; 11 Loudon Rd; s/d $35/45) Renovated pub rooms with town views.
**Northern & Exchange Hotel** ( ☎ 8642 3906; 4 Tassie St; s $28-50, d $39-61) Has disabled facilities.
**Pampas Motel** ( ☎ 8642 3795; 76 Stirling Rd; s/d $35/40, motel s/d $65/75; ) Offers backpackers' rooms with a shared kitchen or self-contained motel rooms with microwaves and fridges.

### MID-RANGE

Unless otherwise stated the following rates are for rooms with shared facilities.

**Standpipe Golf Motor Inn** ( ☎ 8642 4033; cnr Stuart Hwy & Hwy 1; s $67-100, d $74-110; ) Attracting government employees and business types with its comfortable 1970s-ish units, this must be the only accommodation in SA that charges less on weekends. Staff are professional and friendly, and the two restaurant menus are a treat (see p202).

**Pointsettia Motel** ( ☎ 8642 2411; 24 Burgoyne St; s/d $55/60) The bargain status of this hotel is down to the competitiveness of this strip, but they do try harder at the Poinsettia, with new microwaves and TVs, a guest laundry and a restaurant.

**Pastoral Hotel** ( ☎ 8642 2818; cnr Stirling Rd & Carlton Pde; hotel s/d $38/48, motel s/d 75/80; ) The daggy pub accommodation here is fairly basic, but motel rooms have recently been renovated with big TVs, good bathrooms, and nearly silent air-con.

**Acacia Ridge Motor Inn** (☎ 8642 3377; 33 Stokes Tce; s/d $60/70) In a secluded but central location, this motel has old-style rooms featuring TVs, bar fridges and some kitchsy shower decorations. Their interconnecting rooms are a good bet for older families.

### TOP END

**Oasis Apartments** (☎ 8648 9000; Maryatt St; apt $99-149; ✂ 🖳 🖴 ) Luxury right by the water with washing machines and dryers in all rooms, *huge* TVs, fridges, microwaves, and sculpted grounds.

**Comfort Inn Port Augusta** (☎ 8642 2755; www .comfortpa.com.au; Hwy 1; d $96-120, f $134; ✂ ) Winner of the 2004 Comfort Inn of the Year, this highway-located place gets no traffic noise in its rooms which include king-sized beds, couches and well-stocked minibars. The on-site Gallery Restaurant (below) is superior dining.

**Comfort Inn Augusta Westside** (☎ 8642 2488; 3 Loudon St; s $98-160, d $106-160; ✂ 🖴 ) Handy to the gulf and the town centre, this excellently appointed hotel has all the mod cons including spas in the better rooms.

## Eating

Cuisine in town has improved with diners moving away from the traditional pub culture and keen to experiment (although the scene is hardly cosmopolitan).

**Gallery Restaurant** (☎ 8642 2755; Comfort Inn Port Augusta, Hwy 1; mains $16-25; ✺ lunch & dinner) This out-of-the-way spot is worth the trip as they give the usual suspects an unusual twist – *wasabi* oysters, emu satays, and the shareable drovers feast – croc steak, emu satay, buffalo steak and camel ragout with bush tomato relish ($45).

**Standpipe Golf Motor Inn** (☎ 8642 4033; cnr Stuart Hwy & Hwy 1; mains $9-19; ✺ lunch & dinner) With two menus, you get the best of both worlds at this motel eatery – the European-style menu has pastas, steaks and the ubiquitous whiting, while the terrific Indian menu has all the favourites from *aloo* to *sabji*. Both will serve the delicious quandong pie with spiced mascarpone for afters.

**King Po** (☎ 8642 5851; cnr Flinders Tce & Marryatt St; mains $12-16; ✺ lunch Mon-Fri, dinner daily) For all the usual Sino-treats, the King will not let you down, though the décor is tacky and the muzak odd. The addition of some 'Australian' dishes (steak or fish, mostly)

means there's something for even the tamest palette.

**Cooinda Club** (☎ 8641 0166; Commercial Rd; mains $7.50-17; ✺ lunch & dinner Mon-Sat) Specialising in pub-style dishes, the Cooinda loves a good theme night (schnitzel, seafood etc). But there's also a few gourmet surprises including the feral mixed grill with venison, emu and 'roo fillet.

**Hotel Flinders** (☎ 8642 2544; 39 Commercial Rd; ✺ lunch Mon-Fri, dinner Mon-Sun) The Flinders has one of the more innovative pub menus with dishes including Atlantic salmon, baked duck breast and chargrilled veggie stacks.

**Northern & Exchange Hotel** (☎ 8642 3906; 4 Tassie St; ✺ lunch & dinner) Joining these two old pubs has created a dining juggernaut. In this rambling space there's **Maxi's Pizza Bar** (pizzas $5.50-14) producing pizzas with kooky local names (Brachina Gorge Hawaiian) but familiar flavours; and **Wharfies Bistro** (entrées $3-9, mains $14-17) does oysters, steaks and hickory chicken and has an average salad bar. The bar also does counter meals ($10 to $16).

If you can't find something for your tastebuds, then self-catering from **Woolworths** (25 Tassie St; ✺ 7am-10pm) or **Coles** (Cnr Jervis & Maryatt Sts) are both easy options.

## Entertainment

The local weekly newspaper, the *Transcontinental*, will tell you where bands are playing and what films are on at **Cinema Augusta** (Brian Evans Theatre; ☎ 8648 9999; cnr Carlton & Victoria Pdes; ✺ Thu-Mon), which shows all the big flicks. For music the **Hotel Flinders** (☎ 8642 2544; 39 Commercial Rd) has bands on Saturday night and DJs on Thursdays, while **Hotel Commonwealth** (☎ 8642 2844; 73 Commercial Rd) have a disco every Saturday, and Friday night bands.

## Getting There & Away

### AIR

**Airlines of SA** (☎ 13 13 13; www.airlinesofsa.com.au) flies twice each Monday to Friday to/from Adelaide ($140).

### BUS

The **bus station** (☎ 8642 5055; 23 Mackay St) for Premier Stateliner and Greyhound Australia is central – you can book with Premier Stateliner here, but not Greyhound. **Premier Stateliner** (☎ 8642 5055; www.premierstateliner.com .au) runs daily to Adelaide ($39, four hours), Whyalla ($16, one hour) and Port Lincoln

($55, 4½ hours) with stops along the eastern side of the Eyre Peninsula, and at Ceduna ($75, 6½ hours). **Greyhound Australia** (☎ 13 14 99; www.greyhound.com.au) travels daily to Perth ($290, 30 hours), and Alice Springs ($210, 14 hours) via Glendambo and Coober Pedy, and Darwin ($440, 35 hours).

**Gulf Getaways** (☎ 1800 170 170; Augusta Fisheries, Marryatt St) runs a to Broken Hill ($44, 5½ hours) on Wednesday, which returns on Thursday. **Yorke Peninsula Coaches** (☎ 1800 625 099, 8666 2255; adult/child $5/2.50) head north to Quorn, Wilmington and a few smaller towns in the southern Flinders on Friday.

### TRAIN
From Port Augusta you can get to all mainland capitals by **train** (☎ 13 21 47). The *Indian Pacific* heads over to Perth (economy seat/economy sleeper/gold-class sleeper $272/844/1055, 33 hours) on Thursday and Sunday, while the *Ghan* now heads north all the way to Darwin (economy seat/economy sleeper/gold-class sleeper $403/1277/1598, 43 hours) via Alice Springs (economy seat/economy sleeper/gold-class sleeper $171/542/677, 16 hours) on Friday and Sunday.

For a more scenic trip, **Pichi Richi Railway** (☎ 8633 0380; www.prr.org.au) goes to Quorn ($34, 2½ hours) and back on Saturday.

### Getting Around
There is no bus service to the airport, but you can ring **Des's Cabs** (☎ 131 008) – it costs about $10 to the centre of town.

A town bus service operates daily except Sunday. Ask at the visitors centre for a route map and timetable.

Hire cars are available from **Budget** (☎ 8642 6040; 16 Young St), and **Gulf Getaways** (☎ 1800 170 170; Augusta Fisheries, 6 Marryatt St) also hire out a good range of campers, 4WDs and boats.

## PORT GERMEIN
☎ 08 / pop 279
The big claim to fame of this sleepy seaside town is that it has Australia's longest jetty, which means tractors drag boats back from the end of the jetty when the tide is out. It's a good spot for fishing, especially for nabbing the blue swimmer crabs that inspire the Festival of the Crab every New Year's Day.

Yellow-footed rock wallabies and euros (hills kangaroos) inhabit the steep hills and

crags of **Telowie Gorge Conservation Park**, 10km east of town. The access road ends at a car park, from where a 20-minute stroll takes you up an attractive rocky creek into the gorge.

Basic **Port Germein Caravan Park** (☎ 8634 5266; Esplanade; unpowered/powered sites per 2 people $15/19, cabins $53-66) has places by the sea, while the refurbished **Port Germein Hotel** (☎ 8634 5244; High St; s/d $30/60) has generous-sized rooms with continental breakfast included. They also do counter meals.

---

### DETOUR: PETERBOROUGH

For an interesting detour, take B56 east from Wilmington to Orroroo then head southeast on the B56/80 and on to Peterborough. Alternatively, if you're coming from NSW on the Barrier Hwy, take a right off the highway 11km after Oodlawirra.

Peterborough is a must for train buffs as it once had 100 trains a week passing through the area. The interstate gauges were standardised in the mid-1990s, leaving an impressive legacy at **Steamtown** (☎ 08-9651 2708; cnr West & Railway Tces; admission $5; ☻ 8.30am-4pm Mon-Tue, 9.30am-3pm Wed-Sun), a working railway museum with W-class steam locomotives, numerous freight and passenger vehicles, and an enormous railway roundhouse complete with a drop table for fixing trains.

Another reminder of the glory days is **St Cecilia** (☎ 08-8651 2654, 08-8651 3246; Callary St; s $58, tours by arrangement $5), an impressive two-storey Edwardian mansion (1912). The former bishop's residence is richly furnished with antiques, and filled with Roman Catholic history and memorabilia. You can stay in this unique heritage-listed setting, which hosts banquets in the Medieval Hall, including the 'Murder Mystery'.

Peterborough is the state's only operating government **gold battery**; it's used to treat ore from goldfields to the northeast, and is only visitable by tour from the caravan park.

Friendly **Peterborough Caravan Park** (☎ 08-8651 2545; 36 Grove St; unpowered/powered sites per 2 people $15/18, on-site vans $28, cabins $28-48, 1hr/2hr tours $7.50/15) is a pleasant park that also does town tours with the two-hour tour including the gold battery.

There are a couple of bush campsites without facilities on the road into Telowie Gorge, about 1km before the car park.

## WIRRABARA & AROUND

Heading north from Adelaide along Main North Rd you officially enter the Flinders Ranges region at **Stone Hut**, 10km north of Laura.

Nine kilometres further on is **Wirrabara**, a friendly town showing the faded prosperity of former times. **Wirrabara Heritage B&B** ( ☎ 08-8668 4018; Main North Rd; s/d $55/75) is a large 1895 house at the northern end of town. The owners, David and Angela Turvey, have a background in alternative medicine, so they offer massage ($35 per hour), meditation and reflexology to relax guests that little bit more.

About 7km to the west, the **Wirrabara Forest** was once noted for its huge river red gums – for a time a valuable source of jetty timbers and railway sleepers – and the majestic **King Tree** has been preserved. There are some good walks here, including part of the Heysen Trail. About 3.5km into the forest is **Ippinitchie Campground** ( ☎ 08-8668 4163; camping per 2 people $12), a basic camping ground near the Heysen Trail that you can pay for at the ranger's station on your way in. Also in the forest, and 7.5km from Wirrabara township, the **Wirrabara YHA Hostel** ( ☎ 08-8414 3001; dm $20) has basic facilities in an old hostel; they'll tell you where to collect the key from when you telephone to book. A little further on the road is **Taralee Orchards** ( ☎ 08-8668 4343;

---

### THE AUTHOR'S CHOICE

**Wheatley's Old Bakery** ( ☎ 08-8668 4225; 52-56 West Tce, Wirrabara; pies $4, slices $2.50-3; ⏱ 8am-6pm) 'Good old-fashioned country value' is almost a brand name, but this fantastic bakery really delivers just that. Innovative pies – try satay, buffalo or chunky steak – compete for stomach space with Appla Road (a Rocky Road, named for the region's roughest track) slices, quandong tart, lemon myrtle biscuits and monolithic lamingtons. Wash it down with a local soft drink (sarsaparilla is a winner) as you browse the collection of antiques, though beware as the sign advises: 'Unsupervised children will be sold as slaves'.

---

taraleeorch@dodo.com; Forest Rd; d $88), where you can stay amid biodynamic groves of stone fruit in a solar powered cottage that includes full kitchen and an unlimited supply of apricot jam, made from fruit grown right outside your window.

About 10km north of Wirrabara you can turn left and travel through the scenic **Germein Gorge** towards Port Germein.

## MELROSE

☎ 08 / pop 200

Established in 1853 when a copper mine was opened nearby, this pretty little town is the oldest settlement in the Flinders Ranges. Set right at the foot of **Mt Remarkable** (960m) and just outside Mt Remarkable National Park, it's a great location.

### Sights & Activities

There are several interesting old buildings including a few pug-and-pine settlers' cottages, two photogenic hotels and several other impressive old buildings. The 1860s police station now houses the National Trust **Melrose Courthouse Heritage Centre** ( ☎ 8666 2141; adult/concession $3/2, tours by appointment $5; ⏱ 2-5pm) featuring photos of yesteryear, gaol cells and an old-style kitchen.

You can explore Mt Remarkable's lower slopes on a pleasant 3km marked track which starts at the caravan park. It leads up to a **war memorial**, from where there's a panoramic view, then back via the abandoned **copper mine**, the reason for Melrose's existence. The town is a good base for longer walks in **Mt Remarkable National Park**. About 14km north of Melrose, a turn-off on the left will take you to the old **Spring Creek Mine**, crumbling stone ruins left after the copper boom ended.

### Sleeping & Eating

Melrose has some excellent accommodation options, including cottages and weekenders aimed at holiday-makers from Adelaide.

**North Star Inn-Hotel** ( ☎ 8666 2110; www.northstarhotel.com.au; Stuart St; ste $120, trucks $110; wheelie house $110) Refurbishing this 150-year-old hotel has created luxury suites that include claw-foot baths, wide verandas and light breakfasts. For a boutique mobile home, book into a truck – surprisingly plush self-contained units built onto the back of large road vehicles that sleep four. Pub meals are gourmet takes on usual fare such as chicken parma with stringy mozzarella or a punchy kangaroo salad.

**Mt Remarkable Cottage** ( ☎ 8666 2171; off Melrose–Wilmington Rd; d $60) This pleasant cottage just 4km north of Melrose is set in pleasant bush, and includes full kitchen and lounge so you can make yourself at home.

**Melrose Caravan Park** ( ☎ 8666 2060; Joe's Rd; dm $15, unpowered/powered sites per 2 people $17/23, on-site vans $35, cabins $50-80) Down by a babbling brook with huge river red gums, this small park has bush campsites and a range of self-contained cabins (all come with TVs and cooking facilities). They're helpful with advice and stock a good range of tourist brochures.

You can also stay at the **showgrounds** (caretaker ☎ 8666 2158, 8666 2140; off Melrose–Wilmington Rd; unpowered/powered sites per 2 people $6/12), which has good campsites scattered among gum trees, though facilities are basic.

## MT REMARKABLE NATIONAL PARK

Walkers and bush-lovers prize this steep and rugged park straddling the ranges between Melrose and Wilmington. You can bushwalk through secluded gorges and dramatic scenery on walks including the Heysen Trail or on shorter tracks where you'll spot euros, yellow-footed rock wallabies and plenty of bird life, such as kookaburras or brightly coloured corellas.

**Park headquarters** ( ☎ 08-8634 7068; ☺ 8.30am-4.30pm) is at Mambray Creek, where you can pay the entry fee ($6.50 per car). If coming from the north there's an honour box

at Alligator Gorge. Both stations also have brochures detailing camping and walking in the park.

### Sights & Activities

Located in the park's north, **Alligator Gorge** is an 11km rattle across from Wilmington. From this car park, you can take a short, steep walk (one to two hours, 1km to 2km) down into the picturesque gorge, or continue on a ring route (four hours, 9km) which has two camping spots en route. Some other walks include **Hidden Gorge** (four hours, 18km) and **Mambray Creek** (seven hours, 13km).

From a car park 3km north of Melrose, you can access a walking track (five hours, 12km) that climbs the summit of 960m **Mt Remarkable**, with stunning views from the top. The Heysen Trail (see p38) descends along the Mt Remarkable Range from the summit to Wilmington.

The other main base to explore from is **Mambray Creek**, which is a right turn off Hwy 1 about 21km north of Port Germein. A number of **walking tracks** head off into the ranges from here – the return walk to Alligator Gorge (10 hours, 26km) is the most ambitious, but Davey's Gully (one hour, 2.5km) is an easy stroll.

### Sleeping

There are two **lodges** ( ☎ 08-8634 7068; lodges $35-60) in the park – Mambray Creek (sleeping eight) and Alligator Gorge (sleeping six) – both are solar powered and self-contained.

There's plenty of **bush camping** (per car $16) including Longhill Camp, just 10-minutes' walk from the Alligator Gorge car park, or you can drive north on a bumpy dirt road to Stony Creek Camp. Mambray Creek camping ground has the best facilities including wheelchair access and water.

## WILMINGTON

☎ 08 / pop 250

Originally called Beautiful Valley, Wilmington is a somewhat stark and dusty contrast to its near neighbour, Melrose. It grew around the historic **Wilmington Hotel**, a Cobb & Co staging post in the 19th century and soon became a key agricultural centre. These days the town acts as an excellent base for bushwalkers on the Heysen Trail and other walks in the area.

**FLINDERS RANGES**

## Sights & Activities

From here it's an easy drive to the **Alligator Gorge** section of Mt Remarkable National Park.

The **Model Train & Toy Museum** ( ☎ 8667 5276; cnr Second & Main Sts; adult/child $2/free; ⏰ 9.30am-5.30pm) features a huge collection of toys including old favourites such as Meccano, toy cars and a charming model railway.

On the road to Port Augusta, the 7km detour to **Hancocks Lookout** turns off 3.5km from town. The views en route, and the expansive panorama over the western foothills to Spencer Gulf once you get there, make it worthwhile.

If you're heading for Quorn, the **Gunyah Rd scenic route** is an excellent if winding and dusty alternative to the bitumen road further east. It takes you through the eastern foothills of **Mt Brown**, with many beautiful views along the way.

## Sleeping

**Wilmington Tourist Park** ( ☎ 8667 5002; Stony Rd; unpowered/powered sites per 2 people $15/17.50, dm $17, cabins s/d $40/52) You will need to take a left on Second St and then head for Stony Rd to find this tourist park, but this secluded bush spot makes it worth the trip. There's goats and ponies for children to pat and a playground to frolic in; a communal barbecue area that hosts occasional damper bakings; plus it's an excellent base for bushwalking groups.

**Wilmington Hotel** ( ☎ 8667 5154; Main St; s/d $28/50, meals $9-14; ⏰ lunch) For a long time this 1879-constructed hotel has been the centre of town, offering basic accommodation and plain pub fare.

## QUORN

☎ 08 / pop 1005

This endearing little town at the edge of the outback has a rich and well-preserved history, thanks to some fairly active locals. Wheat farming began here in 1875, and the town prospered with the arrival of the Great Northern Railway from Port Augusta. Quorn became an important railroad junction until trains to rural areas were cut in the late 20th century.

Locals have tenaciously kept their Pichi Richi Railway running; it acts as a popular tourist route to the town. The well-preserved buildings have featured in some iconic

Australian films such as *Gallipoli* and *Robbery Under Arms*.

Quorn has plenty of day-tripping possibilities to places such as Dutchmans Stern, Mt Remarkable National Park and the Kanyaka ruins.

## Information

**Flinders Ranges visitors centre** ( ☎ 8648 6419; www.flindersrangescouncil.sa.gov.au; 3 Seventh St; ⏰ 9am-5pm Mon-Fri, 9am-4pm Sat & Sun) Well-stocked with maps and brochures.

**Post office** ( ☎ 8648 6170; 21 Railway Tce; ⏰ 9am-5pm Mon-Fri)

## Sights & Activities

The streetscape of Quorn is a real history lesson, especially the evocative **Railway Tce** – once a busy street near the train station but now a quiet, yet enduringly grand, thoroughfare. The old **flour mill** (now a motel), built in 1878, and an elaborate stone **town hall** (1891) are reminders of how significant this town once was. The visitors centre has a brochure detailing a self-guided walk past these and other sites.

### PICHI RICHI TOURIST TRAIN

A fragment of the long-defunct Great Northern Railway line has reopened as the **Pichi Richi Railway** ( ☎ 8633 0380; www.prr.org.au; train station, Railway Tce; one-way to Port Augusta adult/child $34/12, tours $8). The train runs through the Pichi Richi Pass and on to Port Augusta on Saturdays from April to October. Other same-day return trains run to Woolshed Flat and to the Old Willows Brewery Restaurant. Train buffs should ask at the station about a tour of the **workshop/museum** to see trains being restored and displays about steam history.

### ART GALLERIES

The town has a thriving artistic community with several art galleries. The **Carine Turner Studio Gallery** ( ☎ 8648 6355; 35 First St; ⏰ 10am-5pm Mon-Fri) has a good selection of fine arts including leadlight, batik, antiques and bric-a-brac. **Outback Colours** ( ☎ 8648 6765; 5 Seventh St; ⏰ 10am-4pm) has some beautiful paintings, as well as impressive pieces of red-gum furniture. Artist Val Francis displays many of her paintings of wildlife and landscapes at **Junction Art Gallery** ( ☎ 8648 6470; 11 Railway Tce; ⏰ 10am-3pm Wed-Sun or by appointment), which also has leather work and wood-turning.

FLINDERS RANGES

## Tours

There are some good small operators offering 4WD trips that go off-road and let you see the more remote spots of the Flinders.

**Ozzie's Bush Track Tours** ( ☎ 8648 6567; www.about ozzietours.com; 22 Pool St; ½-/1-/3-/5-day tours $78/140/480/890) Run by a volunteer fire-fighter who really knows the bush. Ozzie offers a range of tours from a popular half-day tour to nearby Dutchman Stern Conservation Park to five-day tours to Arkaroola and Wilpena Pound.

**Wallaby Tracks Adventure Tours** ( ☎ 1800 639 933, 8648 6655; www.users.bigpond.com/headbush; 1-/4-day tours $119/800) Good-value tours run out of Andu Lodge. Their popular Wilpena Pound trek is a one-day wonder that gives you a good look at this magnificent area, though they also run longer four-day trips across to Coober Pedy.

## Sleeping

**Willows State Bank** ( ☎ 8648 6391; 37 First St; d $120) Set in a two-storey restored bank, this magnificent building retains its period charm (including an old bank glass window featured downstairs) without sacrificing luxury. Four bedrooms are available with a huge living area downstairs, plus a kitchen and full laundry. More intimate rooms are upstairs including a charming sitting room and veranda.

**Old Willows Country Estate** ( ☎ 08-8648 6391; 39 Eighth St; d $140) Owned by the same people as Willows State Bank, the Country Estate has a similarly sophisticated fit out and sleeps up to eight people.

**Flinders Ranges Motel** ( ☎ 8648 6016; cnr West & Railway Tces; s/d $80/85) This restored mill holds comfortable motel units that have small fridges and TVs.

**Transcontinental Hotel** ( ☎ 8648 6076; 15 Railway Tce; s $29-32, d $45-55; ⚡ ) The pick of the town's four hotels for accommodation. It's a friendly place and includes a light breakfast.

**Andu Lodge** ( ☎ 1800 639 933, 8648 6655; www.users .bigpond.com/headbush; 12 First St; dm/s/d/f $20/30/50/75) A former hospital serves as the town's YHA, with clean rooms and a help-yourself attitude to videos and cereal for breakfasts. They hire out mountain bikes and run Wallaby Tracks Adventure Tours, so they have good tips for exploring the area.

**Austral Inn** ( ☎ 8648 6017; 16 Railway Tce, motel s/d $70/80, pub s/d $20/35) The flash front bar belies the rooms upstairs which are still very basic, though the motel rooms have 1970s kitschy appeal. A refit was in the works when we visited so rooms will soon suit the upmarket feel of the bar.

**Quorn Caravan Park** ( ☎ 8648 6206; Silo Rd; on-site vans $38, unpowered/powered sites per 2 people $17/20, cabins $45-62; ⚡ ) This large, shaded park is just behind the train station and is a wildlife haven for kookaburras, galahs and the odd kangaroo.

## Eating

Quorn's four hotels offer a choice of counter or dining-room meals, and a few other eateries around town provide good snack options.

**Austral Inn** ( ☎ 8648 6017; 16 Railway Tce; meals $10-24; ✆ lunch Sat & Sun, dinner daily) Easily the pick of Quorn's pubs, locals love the Austral for its innovative pizzas – which include a gutsy steak and a punchy 'roo – but you can also sit in for top-notch grub including steaks and Vietnamese spring rolls.

**Quandong Cafe** ( ☎ 8648 6155; cnr First & Sixth Sts; ✆ breakfast & lunch) A cosy café serving light lunches including soups and railways sleepers (pizza subs), or traditional afternoon teas – think scones and, of course, quandong slices.

**Old Willows Brewery Restaurant** ( ☎ 8648 6391; Pichi Richi Pass; mains $15; ✆ lunch Sat & Sun, dinner Thu-Sun) Offering a dash of bush tucker in everything they do – kangaroo Wellington, damper and quandong pie are old favourites – has made this place one of the best bites in town. It's wise to book ahead as they often have functions that shut out general customers.

**Transcontinental Hotel** ( ☎ 8648 6076; 15 Railway Tce; mains $8-15; ✆ lunch & dinner) Specialising in no-fuss pub grub, this is a good place for a low-key, low-budget feed.

## Getting There & Away

**Pichi Richi Railway** ( ☎ 8633 0380; www.prr.org.au; train station, Railway Tce) runs to Port Augusta on Saturday, April to October.

## AROUND QUORN
### Buckaringa Scenic Drive

The 56km unsealed road heading north from Quorn along the eastern foothills has plenty of interest. First up (7km from Quorn) is **Dutchmans Stern Conservation Park**, featuring a bold bluff shaped like the back of an 18th-century Dutch ship. The Heysen Trail runs through the park, and you climb the bluff via a walking ring route (four hours, 8.2km) that ascends through bush lined with native cranberries and fragrant saltbush.

Continuing on you'll pass **Warren Gorge**, **Buckaringa Gorge** and **Middle Gorge** – all of which are small but picturesque. There's a pleasant bush camping area at Warren Gorge, with a good rock-climbing spot.

**Buckaringa Sanctuary**, which encompasses Buckaringa and Middle Gorges, lies 30km north of Quorn. An ecotourism venture in the style of Warrawong Sanctuary in the Adelaide Hills is planned for the area – contact the Flinders Ranges visitors centre in Quorn for an update.

The scenic route continues on past the **grave** of Hugh Proby, founder of the settlement of Kanyaka, before meeting the main road to Hawker about 34km from Quorn.

## South of Quorn

Taking the Richman's Valley Rd from Railway Tce in Quorn makes a pleasant daytrip. Just 15km south of Quorn, you can stay in **Olive Grove** ( ☎ 08-8648 6245; Richman's Valley Rd; cabins $60), a basic cabin with kitchen facilities, but no linen. From here it's another 4km to rugged **Mt Brown Conservation Park** where you can take the walk to the summit (five hours, 12km).

Starting at Woolshed Flat, the **Waukarie Creek Trail** (five hours, 9km) meets the Heysen Trail near Olive Grove and passes through red gum and wattle trees, plus you may spot hollow trees burnt out for use as shelters by the Adnyamathanha people.

## KANYAKA

The ruins of several early settlements are scattered along the Quorn–Hawker road, but the most impressive is Kanyaka, 41km from Quorn. The remains of the 16-room **Kanyaka Homestead** and various stone outbuildings are all that survives of the once thriving station that was founded in 1851. There's a small, sad graveyard marking the resting spot of several of the Proby clan, Scottish settlers who built the homestead.

From the ruins you can take a 10-minute walk to the old woolshed. The track continues about 1.5km to a beautiful waterhole, which is overlooked by a massive boulder known locally as **Death Rock**. According to one story, local Aborigines once placed their dying kinsfolk here to see out their last hours.

# NORTHERN RANGES

A world away from the quaintness of the Southern Ranges, the lonely area between Hawker and the Strzelecki Desert contains three of the state's finest conservation areas: the Flinders Ranges and Gammon Ranges National Parks (see p198 for details of passes) and the Arkaroola Wildlife Sanctuary. Each of these parks has immense importance to local Aboriginal people and you can find out more at Iga Warta (p214), an education centre run to pass on Adnyamathanha lore to other Australians.

From Hawker to Marree, the road is sealed only as far as Lyndhurst. To get to the Gammon Ranges National Park and Arkaroola you take the gravel road from Copley, just north of Leigh Creek. Alternatively, you can go from Wilpena Pound via Wirrealpa Homestead and Chambers Gorge.

## HAWKER

☎ 08 / pop 298

Only 55km to the south of Wilpena Pound, Hawker is the last outpost of civilisation for many on their way out to the Strzelecki Track. If it wasn't for the buzz of flies the town might nod off, though there are a few attractions around it and it serves as a good pit stop for those heading further north. Much like Quorn, it is a town that was once a stop on the Great Northern Railway.

## Information

The town's main tourist information outlet is in **Teague Hawker Motors** ( ☎ 8648 4014; fax 8648 4283; www.hawkermotors.com.au; cnr Wilpena & Craddock Rds; 🖳 ), which sells books and DVDs on the outback and Flinders Ranges. Across the road, **Range View Motors** ( ☎ 8648 4049; 12 Wilpena Rd) has a laundry and does spare tyres and repairs.

## Sights & Activities

Teague Hawker Motors stocks a brochure which takes you on a **self-guided walk** around the town's oldest buildings and past several Aboriginal and historical murals painted around town.

If you like your great outdoors inside, **Wilpena Panorama & Jeff Morgan Gallery** ( ☎ 8648 4299; adult/child $5/2; 🕑 8am-5.30pm Mon-Sat, noon-5.30pm Sun) has a large round room with a depiction of Wilpena Pound that surrounds you. Jeff's other works – landscape and nature-inspired paintings mostly – are on display and for sale here.

**Yourambulla Caves**, 12km south of Hawker, has detailed Aboriginal rock paintings (including emu tracks), with three sites open to visitors. **Yourambulla Peak**, a half-hour walk from the car park, is the easiest spot to see paintings.

## Sleeping

**Outback Chapmanton Motel** ( ☎ 8648 4100; Wilpena Rd; s/d/units $80/86/90; ❄ ) This well-established motel offers the best rooms in town with the two-bedroom units making for a good family stay.

**Hawker Hotel/Motel** ( ☎ 8648 4102; Elder Tce; s/d $30/55, motel s/d $70/80) This budget-conscious hotel has no-frills hotel rooms as well as self-contained motel rooms.

**Hawker Caravan Park** ( ☎ 8648 4006; www.hawker sa.info/hcpark.htm; Chanceview Tce; unpowered/powered sites per 2 people $18/21, cabins $75-115; ❄ ) At the Wilpena end of town is this plush park with generous sites and a range of cabins that include, at the top end, an executive suite with spa bath.

**Flinders Ranges Caravan Park** ( ☎ 8648 4266; Leigh Creek Rd; unpowered/powered sites per 2 people $18/21, cabins $45-75, ½-/1-day tours $80/115) About 1km out on the Leigh Creek road, this friendly place had similar facilities for similar prices as the Hawker Caravan Park – it has a good campers' kitchen, and lots of trees. They also do exclusive 4WD tours up to Wilpena and into the bush.

Teague Hawker Motors also acts as the **Flinders Ranges Accommodation Booking Service** ( ☎ 1800 777 880, 8648 4022; www.frabs.com.au), with several stations and cottages in the northern Flinders.

## Eating

**Old Ghan Restaurant** ( ☎ 8648 4176; Leigh Creek Rd; mains $19-22; ☽ 10.30am-late Wed-Sun) Expect first-rate tucker such as kangaroo medallions with wattleseed and mustard ($20) or barramundi with quince and orange glaze ($22) at this old train station that makes for atmospheric and flavoursome dining.

**Hawker General Store** ( ☎ 8648 4005; cnr Cradock & Wilpena Rds; lunches $4-10; ☽ 8am-5.30pm Mon-Fri, 9am-5pm Sat & Sun) For many this will be the last chance to get city fare, including the

likes of roast veggie doorstops, focaccias and soy lattes, but there's also terrific quandong smoothies ($4), and you can stock up on groceries, both gourmet and standard.

**Sightseer's Café** ( ☎ 8648 4101; Elder Tce; mains $3-7; ☽ lunch & dinner Thu-Tue) For a quick-grab meal (including burgers and sandwiches) on your way through town, this takeaway place is the best bet.

## HAWKER TO WILPENA

There are inspiring views of the **Elder Range** and **Rawnsley Bluff** as you head towards Wilpena Pound. **Rawnsley Lookout**, about 41km from Hawker, has magnificent views of bold bluffs and soaring cliffs to the northwest and the **Chace Range** to the south. Rawnsley Bluff marks the southern end of the Flinders Ranges National Park.

**Arkaba Station** (Wilpena visitors centre ☎ 08-8648 0048; unpowered sites per 2 people $16, B&B d $150, cottage d $160), 21km north of Hawker, offers 4WD tours into the Elder Range (see p212). You can stay at the station either in the two bedroom cottage that sleeps seven, or in B&B accommodation in the homestead itself. There is bush camping near the homestead.

Friendly **Rawnsley Park** ( ☎ 08-8648 0008, 08-8648 0030; www.rawnsleypark.com.au; on-site vans $48, unpowered/powered sites per 2 people $17/24, units $83-103; ❄ 🖳 ), 35km from Hawker, has great accommodation and offers a range of activities including sheep-shearing demonstrations ($10), horse rides (one hour $45, two hours $60), 4WD tours (per half-/one day $80/120), mountain bikes to hire and good bushwalking (tracks range from half an hour to four hours). Their **Woolshed Restaurant** ( ☎ 08-8648 0126; www.woolshed-restaurant .com; meals $6-21, ☽ lunch & dinner, closed Feb) does good bush tucker with quirky names (the mixed grill is renamed Drover's Mix); take a peek inside the glassed woolshed that is used for shearing.

### DETOUR: MORALANA SCENIC ROUTE

This unsealed 28km route runs between the Wilpena and Leigh Creek roads. It takes in magnificent scenery between the Elder and Wilpena Pound Ranges, and is well worth doing. The turn-off is 24km from Hawker on the Wilpena road (46km on the Leigh Creek road).

FLINDERS RANGES

**Arkaroo Rock**, 40km from Hawker, is a sacred Aboriginal art site. It features reptile and human figures executed in yellow and red ochre, charcoal and bird-lime on the underside of a huge fallen boulder. This is one of the Flinders' most significant Aboriginal cultural sites, once used for initiation ceremonies. The return walk (one hour, 2km) from the car park (where there's a picnic area) has views of towering Chace Range.

## FLINDERS RANGES NATIONAL PARK

One of SA's most treasured parks, Flinders Ranges National Park has rugged gorges, saw-toothed ranges, abandoned homesteads, Aboriginal sites, abundant wildlife and, after rains, carpets of wildflowers. The park's most famous feature is the huge natural basin known as **Wilpena Pound** that covers about 80 sq km and is ringed by steep ridges.

Thanks to a conservation effort by the park, this the perfect place to spot grey kangaroos, euros and large families of emus, which are visible from the road. Rosellas, galahs and wedge-tailed eagles are easily spotted, but keep your eyes peeled for the cute nocturnal dunnart (marsupial mouse) or rare yellow-footed rock wallaby (recognisable by its spotted tail).

The **Wilpena visitors centre** ( ☎ 08-8648 0048; fax 08-8648 0092; 🕐 8am-5pm) is on the entrance road into the Wilpena Pound Resort. It

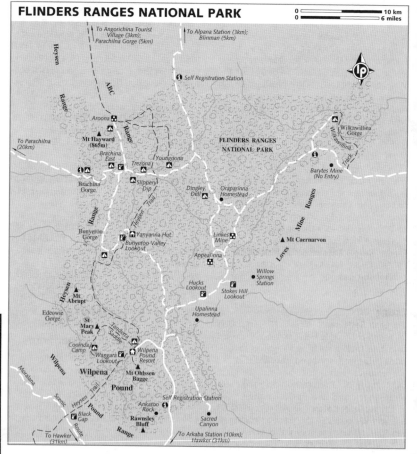

FLINDERS RANGES NATIONAL PARK

has a wealth of information on the park and its surrounding district. It also sells the Flinders Parks Pass (four-weeks/annual $21/77) though these can also be obtained at several self-service booths as you enter the park.

## Sights & Activities

The unmissable **Wilpena Pound** is accessible from the Wilpena Pound Resort via a shuttle bus ($3.50 return) that will take you to within 1km of the **Wilpena Wall**, which soars 500m high. From the rim you can see why the Adnyamathanha people believe it to be the joined bodies of two *akurra* (giant snakes), with St Mary Peak the head of one. *Wilpena* (or 'bent fingers') describes the shape of two ridges twisting together.

Natural history enthusiasts can drive the 20km **Brachina Gorge Geological Trail**, an outstanding layering of exposed sedimentary rock, covering 120 million years of the earth's history. Grab the excellent brochure at the visitors centre.

The Bunyeroo–Brachina–Aroona Scenic Drive is a 110km round trip, taking in the scenic **Bunyeroo Valley**, **Brachina Gorge**, **Aroona Valley** and **Stokes Hill Lookout**. The trail starts at the junction of the Brachina Gorge and Blinman roads, so head anticlockwise if you want to take in the whole round trip. Short walks along the way can make this a rigorous day trip, and a stop at **Bunyeroo Valley Lookout** is a must for its spectacular views.

Just outside the park's southeast corner, **Sacred Canyon** has galleries of Aboriginal rock drawings dotted along the rocks that feature animal tracks and designs.

### BUSHWALKS

Before heading out on any track make sure you've got enough water and sunscreen; leaving details of your plans and when you expect to be back is strongly recommended as search parties are only sent out in emergencies. That said, walking tracks are usually well marked by blue triangles; Heysen Trail sections are indicated by red markers. The DEH has a leaflet with brief descriptions of around 20 walks. In addition, the Royal Geographic Society of South Australia (RGSSA) has excellent pamphlets on several walks; these are available in the Wilpena visitors centre.

The shuttle bus ($3.50 return) from the Wilpena Pound Resort will deliver you to

---

### ADNYAMATHANHA DREAMING

Land and nature are integral to the culture of the traditional owners of the Flinders Ranges. The people collectively called Adnyamathanha (or 'Hill People') are actually a collection of the Wailpi, Kuyani, Jadliaura, Piladappa and Pangkala tribes, who exchanged and elaborated on *stories* to explain their spectacular local geography.

The walls of Ikara (Wilpena Pound), for example, are the bodies of two *akurra* (giant snakes), who coiled around Ikara during an initiation ceremony, gobbling up most of the participants. The snakes were so full after their feast they could not move and willed themselves to die, creating the landmark. Because of its traditional significance, the Adnyamathanha prefer that visitors don't climb St Mary Peak, which is reputed to be the head of the female snake.

In another *story* another *akurra* drank Lake Frome dry, then wove his way across the land creating creeks and gorges. Wherever he stopped, he created a large waterhole, including Arkaroola Springs. The sun warmed the salty water in his stomach causing it to rumble, a noise which can still be heard today in the form of underground springwater flowing.

Colour is essential to the Adnyamathanha as they use the area's red ochre in traditional ceremonies and medicine. Traditional *stories* purport that the vivid orange colour is from Marrukurli, dangerous dogs who were killed by Adnu, the bearded dragon. When Adnu killed the black Marrukurli the sun went out and he was forced to throw his boomerang in every direction to reawaken the sun. It was only when he threw it to the east that the sun returned. Meanwhile the blood of the Marrukurli had seeped into the earth to create sacred ochre deposits.

You can find out more about Adnyamathanha legends by following one of the Dreaming Trails, which are explained in the helpful brochure *South Australian Aboriginal Dreaming of the Flinders Ranges*, available at the region's visitors centres. The trails themselves take in Iga Warta, Arkaroola and other sacred sites in the Flinders.

the trailhead for most walks, though you can lengthen the stroll by walking from the campsite. Walks vary from short walks suitable for families to longer multiple-day treks.

For a good look at Wilpena the walk up to the ridge of **St Mary Peak** along the pound's rim is a good option, though the final climb up from **Tanderra Saddle** is a demanding scramble. The Adnyamathanha people request that you restrict your climbing to the ridge and don't climb the peak due to its traditional significance to them (see p211). The return walk (six hours, 15km) from the shuttle drop-off point climbs to a peak that gives good views of the ABC Ranges and Wilpena. If you have the time, take the longer outside track for better vistas of the area. You can keep going on a round trip (nine hours, 22km), camping overnight at **Cooinda Camp** before heading back via Hills Homestead the next day.

The track up to **Mt Ohlssen Bagge** (four hours, 6½km) is a quick but tough hike that yields a stunning panorama after the steep and rugged walk. Good short walks include the stroll to Hills Homestead (two hours, 6.6km) or the quick jaunt up to the Wilpena Solar Power Station (30 minutes, 500m), which powers the Wilpena Resort.

In the park's north, the **Aroona Ruins** – including a restored pug-and-pine hut – has a few less-travelled walks. The Yuluna Hike (four hours, 8km) weaves through a pretty stretch of the ABC Ranges that inspired the South Australian landscape artist, Hans Heysen. The challenging **Aroona–Youngoona track** (seven hours, 16km) follows the routes of early shepherds, with views of the Trezona and Heysen Ranges, before finishing at the Youngoona camping ground.

## Tours

**Arkaba Station** (Wilpena visitors centre ☎ 08-8648 0048; ½-/1-day tours $55/75) can be explored on a **4WD tour**, or there's a tag-along option if you have a 4WD. Tours include a barbecue/vegetarian lunch and sweeping panoramas from high ridge tops. Book through the Wilpena visitors centre (p210). Scenic flights over the pound and surrounding ranges are conducted by **Central Air Services** (☎ 08-8648 0008; 20min/5hr $75/650), who have a comprehensive five-hour flight that covers Lake Eyre and the Tirari Desert. Again,

bookings are through the Wilpena visitors centre (p210). **Sky Trek** (self-drive bookings ☎ 08-8648 0016; 6hr tour $45) is an rip-snorting 4WD route on Willow Springs Station, 21km northeast of Wilpena. You can drive yourself or jump aboard **Derek's 4WD Tours** (☎ 0417-475 770; www.dereks4wdtours.com; 1-day $135). Whether self-guided or not, the trip usually takes six hours including Mt Caernarvon (923m), the highest vehicle access point in the ranges.

## Sleeping & Eating

Unless you have a tent there is little cheap accommodation at Wilpena Pound itself.

**Wilpena Pound Resort** (☎ 1800 805 802, 08-8648 0004; wilpena@adelaide.on.net; unpowered/powered sites per 2 people $16/22; dm/s/d $25/120/130, permanent tents $75; ⬛ ▢) The resort has rooms with TVs, en suites and 1980s decor. The camping ground is set in pleasant bush with good facilities. If you didn't bring your own gear, the permanent tents make a good option, sleeping up to four. You purchase your permit at the visitors centre, which has a store selling essential grocery lines and takeaway food.

Within the national park (ie outside the resort) **bush camping areas** (per car $11) have basic facilities; permits are available from either the visitors centre or self-service booths along the way. **Trezona**, **Aroona** and **Brachina East** have creek-bank sites among big gum trees, while **Youngoona**, in the park's north, is a good base for walks and remote **Wilkawillina** is certainly the quietest.

## BLINMAN

☎ 08 / pop 50

This quaint hamlet owes its existence to the discovery of copper and the consequent building of a smelter in 1903. Today, the copper boom has busted and Blinman's claim to fame is as SA's highest town: 610m above sea level. Most of the structures at the **old copper mine** – it's on a small hill about 1km to the north – have been developed with lookouts and information boards. The **Blinman Mine Trail** (one hour, 1km) shows how ore was formed, mined and treated.

**Blinman Scenic Tours** (☎ 8648 4863; 20min/2hr flights $85/190) operate out of the nearby airfield with a 20-minute flight over the town or a longer sweep over Lake Torrens, Wilpena and surrounding stations.

## Sleeping & Eating

**Blinman Hotel** ( ☎ 8648 4867; www.blinmanhotel
.com.au; Main St; dm/s/d $20/90/100, mains $12-20; ⊠ )
Chunky cobblestones, historic photos and
capacious luxury rooms are combined in
this excellently renovated old classic. There
are basic bunkhouse rooms across the road
in a simpler building. The kitchen serves
up bush-flavoured dishes such as saltbush-
wrapped chicken breast ($18) or chargrilled
eucalyptus lamb ($19).

**Wild Lime Café & Gallery** ( ☎ 8648 4679; Mine Rd;
mains $7-10; ☑ 9am-5pm Tue-Sun) Run by a jewel-
lery maker and a painter, there are some
good souvenirs here, as well as tasty home-
made slices and cakes, sushi and darn good
coffee.

## AROUND BLINMAN

There are several day trips you can do on
the network of generally good dirt roads
around Blinman. These include a loop
through the Flinders Ranges National Park
via Aroona Valley and Brachina Gorge.
About 7km further on is the **Great Wall of
China**, a low ridge topped with a wall-like
layer of sandstone.

The rough track to **Chambers Gorge** turns
off the Arkaroola road about 64km northeast from Blinman. The gorge is surrounded
by huge gum trees and tan-coloured dolomite cliffs, with small rockpools and galleries of **Aboriginal rock carvings**. To reach the
carvings from the car park, walk 8.3km
up the gorge on your left from the main

road – the first major gallery is 350m upstream and on your left just before a small
waterfall.

A 2WD will get you to the carvings, but
you'll need a 4WD with good clearance to
get to the main gorge. It's a scramble to the
top of **Mt Chambers**, the highest point in SA,
affording stunning views of **Lake Frome** and
all the way along the ranges to **Mt Painter**
and Wilpena in the south.

## HAWKER TO LEIGH CREEK

From Hawker the road follows the rail
route that ferries coal from Leigh Creek
Coal Field to Port Augusta to fuel their
power station. Around 46km along the
road, you can turn off to stay at **Merna Mora
Station** ( ☎ 08-8648 4717; s/d $66/77), a beautiful
property with plenty of wildlife. The turn-
off is at the intersection for the Moralana
Scenic Route.

Another 36km from Merna Mora Station, Parachilna provides the next stop.
The **Prairie Hotel** ( ☎ 08-8648 4844; www.prairie
hotel.com.au; Parachilna; cabins $60-80, ste $195, meals
$9-15; ☑ lunch & dinner; ⊠ 🖵 ) is a world-class
stay with impressively remodelled suites,
though across the road the Overflow has
basic cabins (the cheaper ones are rooms,
the more pricey variety are self contained).
Wherever you stay, don't miss a meal in the
hotel – an imaginative menu features gourmet bush tucker (emu pâté on damper or
croc steaks are just two examples). They can
also organise flights over Wilpena Pound

---

**STAYING AT THE STATION**

Bunking down in a station can be an authentic way to experience rural SA. The accommodation
is generally basic and was probably once used by shearers, but now makes good beds for groups,
particularly walkers. Around Blinman there are loads of properties that take visitors and might
even let you help out with the farm chores.

**Alpana Station** ( ☎ 08-8648 4864; 5km south of Blinman; quarters $200) Has beds in the self-contained
shearers' quarters (sleeps 14) including stove, fridge and outside barbecue. If you're a bushwalker, they also do
drop off and car storage for the Heysen Trail.

**Angorichina Station** ( ☎ 08-8648 4863; 9km east of Blinman) The booking agent for several places near
town. All have beds for $15, with a minimum booking of $80. Angorichina in particular has excellent walks near the
homestead.

**Gum Creek Station** ( ☎ 08-8648 4883; 15km south of Blinman; woolshed $60, shearers' quarters $100) Both
the woolshed and the shearers' quarters sleep a minimum of five, in fairly basic share accommodation.

**Nilpena Station** (Prairie Hotel ☎ 08-8648 4844; 39km northwest off Parachilna–Leigh Creek Rd; shearers'
quarters $30, d cottage $100; ⊠ ) Near Parachilna, this place offers self-contained shearers' quarters (minimum of
6) or a small cottage. The natural spring also makes for good bird-watching.

with **Blinman Scenic Tours** (see p212). Just 10km before the Leigh Creek turn-off is the road to **Aroona Dam**, the town's water supply, which has a pleasant picnic spot and a self-guided walk (three hours, 5.5km).

## PARACHILNA TO BLINMAN

The 31km drive to Blinman passes through spectacular scenery of **Parachilna Gorge**, but check conditions before you leave – the road is impassable in the wet. As well as beautiful views, you'll find good camping and picnic spots along the creek.

The northern end of the Heysen Trail finishes at Parachilna Gorge and 2.6km further on is the **Angorichina Tourist Village** ( ☎ 08-8648 4842; Parachilna Gorge; unpowered sites per 2 people $18, on-site vans s/d $25/36, dm $13, units d $65), which has a variety of accommodation, though backpacker beds require a minimum of six guests. The store sells tyres and fuel, and hires mountain bikes.

From Angorichina, you can take the **Blinman Pools walk** (five hours, 6km) which follows a spring-fed creek passing abandoned dugouts through river red gums and cypress pines.

## LEIGH CREEK

☎ 08 / pop 690

The discovery of coal created this artificial oasis of leafy landscaping, owned almost entirely by NRG Flinders. From the nearby open-cut mine, NRG Flinders sends daily trainloads of hard brown coal down to Port Augusta power station. The **Leigh Creek visitors centre** ( ☎ 8675 2723; town centre; 2-hr tour free; ☻ 9am-5pm Mon-Fri, 10am-2pm Sat & Sun) schedules tours of the mine. Most businesses in town are in the main shopping centre.

Activities in the area are organised by **Barking Gecko** ( ☎ 8675 2366; www.barkinggecko-mtb tours.com.au; bike hire 1hr/1 day $12/35, kayaking 2 days $40) who have mountain bikes in good condition and also take kayaking trips to Aroona Dam.

The central **Leigh Creek Tavern** ( ☎ 8675 2025; Leigh Creek Town Shopping Centre; s/d $110/135, cabins $80, meals $8-20; ☒ ☒ ) offers luxury cabins and motel rooms, including use of the swimming pool and a good restaurant. Call at the service station for the **caravan park** ( ☎ 8675 2016; unpowered/powered sites per 2 people $12/18, cabins $60-70), which has a good shared kitchen and clean cabins.

## COPLEY TO GAMMON RANGES NATIONAL PARK

Take the Arkaroola Rd from Leigh Creek and you'll soon hit the sweet little township of Copley. The big attraction in town is the **Quandong Café & Bush Bakery** ( ☎ 08-8675 2683; Railway Tce; ☻ 8.30am-5pm Easter-Nov), home of great quandong pies and other bakery goodies popular with both passing greenies and grey nomads.

The pleasant old **Leigh Creek Hotel** ( ☎ 08-8675 2281; Railway Tce, Copley; s/d $40/60; ☒ ) has clean (if thinly mattressed) beds that come with breakfast. **Copley Caravan Park** ( ☎ 08-8675 2288; www.copleycaravan.com.au; Railway Tce West; unpowered sites per 2 people $18, cabins from $60; ☒ ) is a small park that does a good bonfire cook-up for guests.

Approximately 60km beyond Copley the indigenous-run **Iga Warta** ( ☎ 08-8648 3737; www.igawarta.com; Arkaroola Rd, via Copley; unpowered sites per 2 people $15, walks/tours $29/63) offers 4WD cultural tours focusing on the surrounding country and Aboriginal history. Bush-tucker walks and campfire stories are conducted by members of the Coulthard family, who founded this centre based on their father's vision to share their Adnyamathanha culture with all Australians. Anyone can use the campsites, with tents and swags for hire.

Immediately after Iga Warta is **Nepabunna**, an Adnyamathanha community which manages the land just before the park.

## GAMMON RANGES NATIONAL PARK

Covering 128,200 hectares, this remote park has deep gorges, rugged ranges and beautiful gum-lined creeks. Most of the park is difficult to get to, has limited facilities and will require a 4WD. The ranger's office is at **Balcanoona Park HQ** ( ☎ 08-8648 4829), 99km from Copley. Clued-up rangers will give walking tours of the area.

### Sights & Activities

From the park's entrance it's 22km to scenic **Italowie Gorge**, which has two campsites with self-registration. At Balcanoona, information signs in the big old shearing shed detail the park's cultural and natural history.

**Grindells Hut** is in a strikingly scenic area with commanding views and stark ridges all around. You can reach it on a 4WD track off

**FLINDERS RANGES**

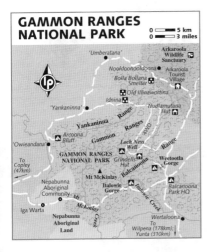

**GAMMON RANGES NATIONAL PARK**

0 — 5 km
0 — 3 miles

'Umberatana'
Arkaroola Wildlife Sanctuary
Nooldoonooldoona
Arkaroola Tourist Village
Bolla Bollana Smelter
Old Illinawortina
'Yankaninna'
Idnina
Nudlamutana Hut
Yankaninna Range
Ranges
Arcoona Bluff
Gammon
Loch Ness Well
'Owieandana'
To Copley (47km)
GAMMON RANGES NATIONAL PARK
Grindells Hut
Balcanoona
Weetootla Gorge
Range
Mt McKinlay
Nepabunna Aboriginal Community
Italowie Gorge
Balcanoona Park HQ
Iga Warta
Nepabunna Aboriginal Land
McKinlay
Wertaloona
Wilpena (178km); Yunta (310km)

the Arkaroola road or by walking through **Weetootla Gorge**. The hike is worthwhile, but it's 13km return; if you leave early in the morning you've a good chance of seeing yellow-footed rock wallabies. Check with the ranger before attempting to drive or walk in this area.

### Sleeping

There are **bush camping areas** (per car $6.50) at Italowie Gorge, Grindells Hut, Weetootla Gorge and Arcoona Bluff. You can purchase camping permits at Balcanoona Park HQ or use the Flinders Parks Pass (see p198). There are a few huts throughout the park that can be booked at the ranger's office: **Grindells Hut** (up to 4 $85) sleeping a maximum of eight and **Nudlamutana Hut**, (up to 5 $65). There are basic twin rooms in the shearers' quarters at **Balcanoona** (s $26) or the self-contained **manager's quarters** (up to 3 $42).

## ARKAROOLA WILDLIFE SANCTUARY

Once a sheep station and now a privately operated wildlife sanctuary, complete with a self-contained tourist village, Arkaroola is a remote and scenically spectacular part of the Flinders Ranges. The sanctuary was established in 1968 by Reg and Griselda Sprigg, through the introduction of strict conservation measures including hunting down feral goats.

The resort has a fascinating **visitors centre** ( ☎ 1800 676 042, 08-8648 4848; www.arkaroola.com .au) with displays on the area's natural history, including a scientific explanation of the frequent earth tremors that occur here; there's a seismological recording station in the centre.

From the visitors centre you can book guided or tag-along **tours**, or do your own thing on over 100km of graded, generally single-lane tracks. Most places of interest are accessible to conventional vehicles, with some hiking involved. For something more physical there are a number of excellent **bushwalks**; brochures are available from the information centre.

One of Arkaroola's highlights is the four-hour **Ridgetop Tour** ($85), along a 4WD track through wild mountain country, complete with adrenaline-pumping climbs and descents that climax at the freakish Sillers Lookout. Apart from the sweeping panoramas you may see wedge-tailed eagles, euros and yellow-footed rock wallabies. Another excellent tour allows you to do a little stargazing through high-powered telescopes at Arkaroola's **Dodwell and Oliphant Astronomical Observatories** ($30).

You can do **scenic flights** (30min/1hr flights $88/166) that are tailored to individual visitors, but can swoop over the Lake Frome or go as far afield as Innamincka's Dig Tree.

The **resort** ( ☎ 1800 676 042, 08-8648 4848; www .arkaroola.com.au; Arkaroola Rd Camp; unpowered/powered sites per 2 people $15/20, cabins $40, lodges $65-145; 🅿 ) includes a motel complex and caravan park. Campsites range from the dusty hilltop to the creekside spots. Comfortable cabins are a good budget bet, while air-con lodges are a self-contained paradise. Other facilities include a cosy bar-restaurant, small supermarket and service station.

EYRE PENINSULA &
WEST COAST

# Eyre Peninsula & West Coast

CONTENTS

**Eastern Eyre Peninsula**   **218**
Whyalla   218
Whyalla to Port Lincoln   221
Port Lincoln   222
Around Port Lincoln   225
**Western Eyre Peninsula**   **226**
Port Lincoln to Streaky Bay   226
Streaky Bay   228
**Eyre Highway & West Coast**   **228**
Port Augusta to Ceduna   228
Ceduna   229
Ceduna to Yalata   232

From the barren Nullarbor to the tuna-fishing burg of Port Lincoln, there's a fascinating array of experiences on the Eyre Peninsula and across to the border with Western Australia (WA). It's all about the seaside atmosphere with rugged cliffs and brooding heathlands around the Spencer Gulf to the east and stretching along the Great Australian Bight to the west.

Gourmands reckon Eyre is the Barossa Valley of seafood with beds of oysters scattered around the peninsula, prodigious tuna farms at Port Lincoln, and King George whiting biting off the end of every other pier. Still not full? How about rock lobster, abalone or prawns? Fishing fans pull off the highway to secret spots, just like the surfers who adore the rough breaks and high waves that the peninsula offers.

Then there's unique wildlife, from emus wandering the streets of Coffin Bay to basking sea lions off Point Labatt. The real standout is the southern right whales who migrate from Antarctica to mate near the Head of Bight from July to September. There are even dolphins popping out of the waves, but before you think about swimming with them remember that some scenes from *Jaws* were filmed by 'communing' with the great white sharks of this region.

And if all that wasn't enough there's Lincoln National Park to hike through, Whyalla's industry to test your mettle, beaches to lie on and, well, that seafood isn't going to eat itself…

## HIGHLIGHTS

- Bushwalking the Investigator Trail through scrubland and along beaches to end up in **Lincoln National Park** (p226)
- Waving to the rare oncoming car on the long barren plains of the **Nullarbor National Park** (p232)
- Hooking the mighty King George whiting off a jetty anywhere from **Whyalla** (p218) to **Streaky Bay** (p228) – but don't tell anyone where
- Enjoying the seafood spoils of the Eyre at **Ceduna** (p229) by going on a tour or slurping down an oyster
- Building a boat or tossing a tuna all for the sake of competition at **Port Lincoln's Tunarama Festival** (p219)
- Catching the curl at a near-deserted beaches around **Elliston** (p227)
- Peeking into the boudoir of mating whales off the **Head of Bight** (p232)
- Puzzling over two of Australia's largest (some might say tackiest) beasts – the **Big Galah** (p229) in Kimba and Border Village's **Big Kangaroo** (p233)

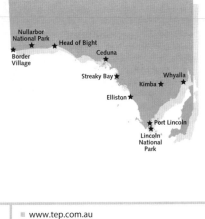

- TELEPHONE CODE: ☎ 08
- www.tep.com.au

# EASTERN EYRE PENINSULA

Travelling the coast from Whyalla to Port Lincoln you'll pass spectacular scenery as well as the popular resort towns of Cowell and Tumby Bay. These small ports were frantically shipping grain in the days before motor transport, but today they're a good place to put in a boat and chase King George whiting, tommy rough and other fish.

## National Parks

The Eyre Peninsula is blessed with some very different national parks – from cool and coastal Lincoln National Park to rugged Gawler Ranges National Park. The annual **Eyre Parks Pass** (per car $65), allows unlimited entry and camping (up to five nights in the same place) in all of Eyre Peninsula's conservation areas. You can buy it from the Department for Environment & Heritage (DEH) office in Port Lincoln (p222) and from other DEH outlets.

## WHYALLA
☎ 08 / pop 21,271

Hard-working Whyalla is the second-largest city in the state, grown from mining in nearby Iron Hill and shipbuilding. The shipbuilding may have ended, but One-Steel's smelter was refurbished in 2004 and

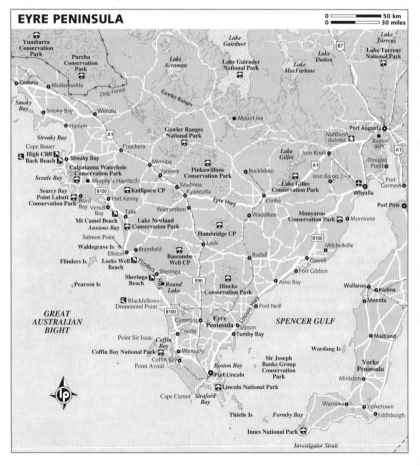

EYRE PENINSULA

the city is back in business, recently forging the tracks for the railway line up to Darwin. From Whyalla's large port, steel is shipped around the world.

Whyalla's other claim to fame is as cuttlefish capital. Thousands of **giant cuttlefish** flock here to spawn between May and August. They gather around Point Lowly and Black Point for their graceful courtship, which attracts divers.

**Whyalla visitors centre** ( ☎ 8645 7900; www.whyalla.com; Lincoln Hwy; ☒ 10am-4pm) is unmissable, marked by the large unfinished aqua ship out the front.

## Sights & Activities

First stop is the **Maritime Museum** ( ☎ 8645 7900; Lincoln Hwy; ☒ 10am-4pm, tours 11am-3pm on the hr) on the way into town. The museum features the 650-tonne WWII corvette HMAS *Whyalla* and an educational look into shipbuilding.

The historic **Mt Laura Homestead** ( ☎ 8645 3565; Ekblom St; adult/child $4/1; ☒ 10am-noon Mon-Fri, 2-4pm Sun) has a variety of displays including a blacksmith's shop, an old locomotive and a fragrant rose garden.

**Hummock Hill Lookout** gives a good view of the town, OneSteel complex and Spencer Gulf. The concrete fortifications housed a WWII anti-aircraft battery to protect the shipyards from Japanese attack; there were only four guns (one remains), so it's lucky there were no air raids.

**Point Lowly Lighthouse** is a popular day trip with the new **Freycinet Trail** (three hours, 8km) making for a leisurely coastal walk through dunes and bushland to Fitzgerald Bay, where you can camp or stay in the cottages at Point Lowly (right).

## Tours

**OneSteel works** ( ☎ 1800 088 589; www.cuttlefishcapital.com.au; 2½hr tour adult/concession/child $17/15.30/8; ☒ tours 1pm) takes you through the hot and sweaty iron-smelting industry, with daily excursions from

the visitors centre requiring close-toed footwear and clothes that cover arms and legs.

**Fish'n'Trips** ( ☎ 8645 4599; 31A Playford Ave, 8/4/2hr trips $160/75/40) Hook up with this tour company, which chases for whiting, squid and blue swimmer crabs, supplying tackle and gear.

## Sleeping

The accommodation options in town are uninspiring with only a few good spots by the beach.

### BUDGET

**Hotel Spencer** ( ☎ 8645 8411; Forsyth St; s/d/tw $30/50/40; ☒ ) This no-frills, quiet place has well-used beds, fridges, as well as tea and coffee facilities.

**Hillview Caravan Park** ( ☎ 8645 9357; http://home.austarnet.com.au/hillview; Mullaquana Rd, off Lincoln Hwy; unpowered/powered sites per 2 people $17/20, on-site vans $30, units $46) The friendly Finnish couple who owns Hillview love this desert patch where venerable buses come to die (see their large collection while here). The simple garden and dependable facilities make the 5km trip out of town worthwhile.

**Whyalla Foreshore Caravan Park** ( ☎ 8645 7474; www.whyalla-foreshore-caravan-park.com; Broadbent Tce; powered sites per 2 people $21, on-site vans $34, cabins $40) With a lovely beach frontage, this place doesn't have to try too hard to impress. There's wheelchair access and hire TVs, but otherwise facilities are fairly basic.

**Point Lowly Lighthouse Cottages** ( ☎ 8645 0436; 40km off Port Augusta Rd; dm $18) Isolated and perfect for land-based fishing and swimming this pair of cottages is a bargain at a scenic location. Facilities are basic so bring along bedding and cookware.

There's also free bush camping at Fitzgerald Bay and Point Lowly.

### MID-RANGE

**Eyre Hotel** ( ☎ 8645 7188; cnr Playford & Eyre Sts; s/d $60/75; ☒ ) The recent refit introduced big TVs and en suites, but this place keeps its grungy period fittings. Saturday's nightclub can interfere with sleep.

**Airport Whyalla Motel** ( ☎ 8645 2122; cnr Lincoln Hwy & Racecourse Rd; s/d/tw $75/80/85; 🕮 ) This family place has good-sized rooms, cable TV and chintzy decorations (gardenware includes a disturbing koala fountain and a startled wallaby).

**Alexander Motor Inn** ( ☎ 8645 9488; 99 Playford Ave; d $85; 🕮 ) With loads of facilities – electric blankets, TVs and en suites (one room has a spa) – this is a comfortable option in the city centre.

### TOP-END

**B&B on the Beach** ( ☎ 0428 262 326; www.band bonthebeach.com.au; 6 Neagle Tce; d/tr/q $150/165/180; 🕮 ) You can have this charming weatherboard house all to yourself; it includes soft mattresses on generously sized beds and a full kitchen. There's even a hot brekkie on request and a fire to curl around in bad weather.

**Derham's Foreshore Motor Inn** ( ☎ 1800 07 107, 8645 8877; www.derhamsforeshore.com.au; Watson Tce; s/d $120/130; 🕮 🖳 ) This efficient place has zippy modems, room service and first-class facilities, appealing to business travellers who love the beachside location. Beware of draining the minibar which might tip off the Finance Department.

## Eating

Eating options in Whyalla are fairly conservative; takeaway prevails, with a few forays into more exotic dishes.

**Derham's** ( ☎ 1800 07 107, 8645 8877; www.derhams foreshore.com.au; Watson Tce; mains $6.50-10.50; ☺ lunch Mon-Fri, dinner daily) The beach-cottage vibe at Derham's has a refreshing ease, and there's good views of the beach. The menu includes tasty curries, noodles, pastas and, of course, seafood.

**Spagg's** ( ☎ 8645 2088; www.whyallashoppinghub .com/spaggs; 26 Patterson St; mains $4.50-12; ☺ lunch Mon-Fri, dinner Wed-Sat) Vaguely Italian-influenced food is the go at this popular spot which also throws quiches and nachos into the multinational mix. The $8.50 meal nights (schnitzel, steak, Mexican and seafood) are top value.

**Eyre Hotel** ( ☎ 8645 7188; cnr Playford & Eyre Sts; mains $8-14; ☺ lunch & dinner) This hotel excels

---

### AUSTRALIA'S MOST UNWANTED

On the disused Port Augusta–Whyalla Rd lies one of Australia's most controversial government buildings, Baxter Immigration Reception and Processing Centre (Baxter IRPC), better known as Baxter Detention Centre. With the closing of Woomera Detention Centre in 2002, Australia opened its fourth facility to detain people for 'illegally' entering or staying in the country. It's the nation's largest facility, able to hold up to 660 detainees, although at the time of writing it had fewer than 200.

You can drive to the gatehouse of Baxter. Many tourists take photos of the sign regularly used by TV news reports to illustrate stories of alleged mistreatment at Baxter. The $40 million facility, however, is well protected to prevent escapes such as that of the 50 refugees who broke out of Woomera in 2002. As well as razor wire and motion sensors, an electrified fence with 9000 volts passing through it encircles the complex – this is four times the voltage of most cattle fences, but within international regulations of 10,000 volts. Guards discourage photos of fences or the facility itself for security reasons.

While some locals praised the centre's job creation in an economically depressed area, other Port Augustans strongly oppose detention. **Rural Australians for Refugees** (RAR; www.gulfviews .com/rar) is an active group of local volunteers who stage various activities to support detainees including visits, letter-writing campaigns and a release of balloons over the centre to symbolise freedom. Another group, **Baxterwatch** (www.baxterwatch.net), watches over the centre's conditions, investigating and publicising allegations of mistreatment.

It's possible to visit individual detainees, though it does require permission from the **Department of Immigration and Multicultural and Indigenous Affairs** (DIMIA; www.minister.immi.gov.au). Groups such as Rural Australians for Refugees and Baxterwatch have names of detainees to visit and also have letter-writing campaigns to communicate with detainees. If you are planning to go into the facility you should definitely organise it well in advance as Baxter is surrounded by as much red tape as razor wire.

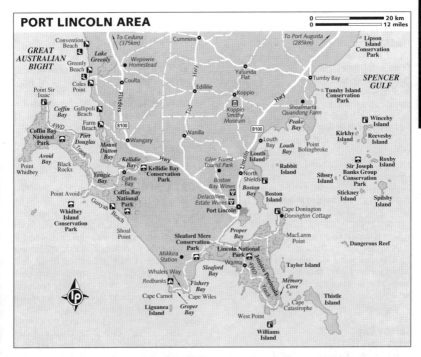

**PORT LINCOLN AREA**

with better than usual pub grub including veggie lasagne, salt and pepper squid, and walloping steaks.

**Flossy's Coffee Baa** ( ☎ 8644 3000; 53 Playford St; snacks $4-8; ☺ 11am-5pm Sun-Tue, 11am-11pm Wed-Sat) For a quick caffeine hit or a graze on some delicious cake or slice, this place should do the trick, with a flock of sheep puns.

The **Westland Hotel/Motel** ( ☎ 8645 0066; www .westlandhotel.com.au; 100 McDouall Stuart Ave) complex includes **Vega's Bar & Bistro** (meals $8-14; ☺ lunch & dinner), with a good salad bar and hearty specials. Outside, the gamey **Bottle & Bird** (meals $4.50-7.90; ☺ 10.30am-9pm Sun-Wed, 10.30am-10pm Thu-Sat) is very popular with locals; line up on one side for booze, and on the other for takeaway chicken, deep-fried banana fritters or burgers.

### Getting There & Around

**Premier Stateliner** ( ☎ 8645 9911; www.premierstate liner.com.au; 23 Darling Tce) has daily buses from Adelaide (six hours, $45) and Port Augusta (one hour, $16), and three buses a week to Port Lincoln (3½ hours, $48).

**O'Connor Airlines** ( ☎ 13 13 13; www.oconnor-air lines.com.au) flies daily to Adelaide (45 minutes,

$102), and **Regional Express** (Rex; ☎ 13 17 13; www.regionalexpress.com.au) flies daily to Adelaide (40 minutes, $79) too.

There's no bus service to the airport, but **Des's Cabs** ( ☎ 131 008) charges approximately $15 to the town centre. Hire cars are available from **Avis** ( ☎ 8645 9331), **Budget** ( ☎ 8645 5333) and **Hertz** ( ☎ 8645 3354). **Steel City Coaches** ( ☎ 8645 8414) operates bus services around town with timetables available at the visitors centre.

## WHYALLA TO PORT LINCOLN

On Franklin Harbour, mangrove-fringed **Cowell** is the first port of call for holidaying fisherfolk. The discovery of jade in the Minbrie Ranges to the town's north created Australia's only mine for the gemstone. Local jade products are sold at the **Cowell Jade Motel** ( ☎ 08-8629 2002; Lincoln Hwy; s $75-82, d $78-95, tr $89-106), which also does quality rooms. Close to the town centre, **Cowell Foreshore Caravan Park** ( ☎ 08-8629 2307; The Esplanade; powered sites per 2 people $19, on-site vans $35, cabins $45) offers beachside spots for parking caravans and does a good trade in local oysters for $5.50 per dozen.

The main street has two venerable pubs: **Franklin Harbour Hotel** ( ☎ 08-8629 2015; 1 Main St; s/d $37.50/50, mains $5.50-16; 🕑 lunch & dinner) and **Commercial Hotel** ( ☎ 08-8629 2181; 25 Main St; mains $10-20; 🕑 lunch & dinner) – both do rooms and meals, though the Franklin has better rooms and the Commercial has a more diverse menu. There is a small but interesting **folk museum** (4 Main St; adult $2) next door to the post office and **Mangrove Café** (2 Main St; snacks $4-6), which does good coffee, doorstops (chunky toasted sandwiches) and oyster shashliks.

Forty-three kilometres from Cowell, **Arno Bay** has a safe **swimming beach** and a fishing jetty. You can stay at the grand **Hotel Arno** ( ☎ 08-8628 0001; s $30, tw & d $50, motel s/d $70/80), which has pub and motel rooms.

Another 33km further on, pretty Port Neill boasts two good **swimming beaches**, **Port Neill Caravan Park** ( ☎ 08-8688 9067; unpowered/powered sites per 2 people $15/18, on-site vans $35, cabins $45-66) and the basic **Port Neill Hotel** ( ☎ 08-8688 9006; s/d $25/50).

## Tumby Bay
☎ 08 / pop 1100

Long curves of white sand beaches make for magnificent coastal stretches in this small town. Tumby Bay has several interesting old buildings that are worth a look, including the original schoolhouse, which today houses the National Trust's **CL Alexander Memorial Museum** ( ☎ 8688 2198; Lipsom Rd; adults $2; 🕑 2.30-4.30pm Fri & Sat).

**Hales Mini Mart** ( ☎ 8688 2584; 1 Bratten Way) has tourist information and hires outboard-powered tinnies from $35 per day (you'll need a boating licence).

From **Ski Beach**, 5km southeast of town, you can wade out at low tide to **Tumby Island Conservation Park**, a rookery for several bird species, including Cape Barren geese. The **Sir Joseph Banks Group of Islands**, 25km southeast, form a marine conservation park, with bird rookeries, sea-lion colonies and excellent scuba diving.

On the foreshore, **Tumby Bay Caravan Park** ( ☎ 8688 2208; Tumby Tce; unpowered/powered sites per 2 people $12/14, on-site vans $30, cabins $45) has good sites and even better cabins. The grand old classic **Tumby Bay Hotel** ( ☎ 8688 2005; North Tce; s/d/apt $25/35/120) has basic pub rooms upstairs or self-contained apartments handy to the beach.

---

> **DETOUR: KOPPIO**
>
> Just after Tumby Bay take the turn-off to get to the farming centre of **Koppio** in picturesque hills, 25km southwest of Tumby Bay. The National Trust's excellent **Koppio Smithy Museum** ( ☎ 08-8684 4243; adult/child $3/$0.50; 🕑 10am-5pm Tue-Sun) has an extensive collection of memorabilia, including a pioneer hut and numerous restored vintage tractors.

## PORT LINCOLN
☎ 08 / pop 12,664

At the southern tip of the Eyre Peninsula, Port Lincoln is 662km from Adelaide by road but only 250km as the crow flies. It was named by homesick Matthew Flinders for his home county of Lincolnshire.

Port Lincoln is a prosperous town with the state's largest grain-exporting terminal and most of its tuna fleet, allegedly worth more than $80 million. Fishing is big business with numerous **tuna farms** in Boston Bay and several seafood-processing factories. The industry's growth has created a new marina development in the south and an atmosphere of affluence.

### Orientation

The Lincoln Hwy becomes Hallett Pl, then Liverpool St. You take a right turn to get to the town jetty and Tasman Tce, which has most of the accommodation and eating options. The bus station is on Lewis St.

### Information

Banks are easily found on Tasman Tce or Liverpool St.

**DEH** ( ☎ 8688 3111; 75 Liverpool St; 🕑 9am-6pm Mon-Fri)

**Port Lincoln Hospital** ( ☎ 8683 2200; Oxford Tce) Has an accident and emergency department.

**Port Lincoln visitors centre** ( ☎ 1300 788 378; ☎ /fax 8683 3544; www.visitportlincoln.net; 3 Adelaide Pl; Internet per hr $5; 🕑 9am-5pm)

**Post office** ( ☎ 8682 1102; 68 Tasman Tce; 🕑 9am-5pm Mon-Fri)

**RAA** ( ☎ 8682 2934; 15 Adelaide Pl; 🕑 9am-5pm Mon-Fri) Has good information on road conditions and maps.

### Sights & Activities

The **Old Mill** on Dorset Pl was built in 1846 as the tower for a flour mill that was never completed. You can climb to the lookout for nice views out over the bay.

Set in an attractive park, **Mill Cottage** (Flinders Hwy; adult/child $4/$0.50; 2-4.30pm Mon, Wed & Sat) is a historic homestead (1866) housing many artefacts belonging to the Bishop family, who came to Port Lincoln in 1839. At the front and rear is a pleasant expanse of park usually busy with footy-kicking kids.

Next door, the **Rose-Wal Memorial Shell Museum** ( 8682 4416; Eyre Peninsula Old Folks Home, 26 Flinders Hwy; adult/child $2/$0.20; 2-4.30pm) has a collection of seashells valued at $100,000 including shell crafts and jewellery.

The **Axel Stenross Maritime Museum** ( 8682 1291; 97 Lincoln Hwy; adult/concession/child $4/3/1; 1-5pm Tue, Thu & Sun May-Aug, also 1-5pm Sat Sep-Apr)

commemorates the life of a colourful Finn-turned-local, who served as one of the region's most famous shipbuilders. Impressive displays include many of his unfinished boats and tools.

The **Seahorse Farm** ( 8683 4866; 5 Mallee Cr; adult/concession/child $10/8.50/7; tours 3pm) was Australia's first breeding centre for seahorses, supplying the cute critters to the pet market. The 40-minute tour shows off leafy sea dragons, the state marine emblem of South Australia (SA). Book at the visitors centre.

An easy way to explore the town is by following the **Parnkalla Walking Trail** (three to four hours, 14km) which clings to the coastline from Boston Bay to Proper Bay

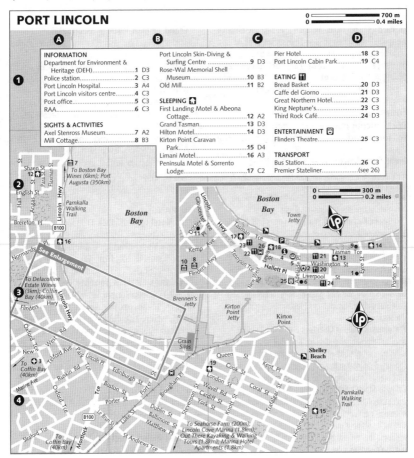

taking in the town's highlights, including the Axel Stenross Maritime Museum, Moreton Bay fig trees and pretty **Shelley Beach**. There's swimming in the protected netting off **Kirton Point Jetty**, but winter temperatures are prohibitive.

For a tipple, **Boston Bay Wines** ( ☎ 8684 3600; Lincoln Hwy; www.bostonbaywines.com.au; ⏱ tastings 11.30am-4.30pm Sat & Sun Feb-Nov, 11.30am-4.30pm daily Dec-Jan) is a small friendly winery with most major grape varieties, but particularly good is the Baudin's Blend. **Delacolline Estate Wines** ( ☎ 8682 4571; 31 Whillas Rd; ⏱ 1.30-4pm Sat & Sun) is another small local winery with a solid selection of up-and-coming whites.

Thirty-one kilometres offshore is **Dangerous Reef**, an important breeding area for the white pointer or great white shark. Shark sightings are rare, but there are normally heaps of Australian sea lions. Several of the charter companies (see below) will take you out there. To get among it, **Port Lincoln Skin-Diving & Surfing Centre** ( ☎ 8682 4428; 1 King St; 1-day hire $80) hires scuba equipment.

## Tours

Port Lincoln has a good variety of land and sea tours, and all can be booked through the visitors centre.

**Great Australian Bight Safaris** ( ☎ 1800 352 750; www.greatsafaris.com.au; ½-/1-/5-day tours $25/65/750) Has an excellent range, including a town tour plus Whalers Way, 4WD day tours to Memory Cove and the Coffin Bay Peninsula, a five-day sail-and-4WD safari.

**Out There Kayaking & Walking Tours** ( ☎ 8682 6853; www.outtheretours.com.au; 3/10 South Quay Blvd; 2hr/4hr/full-day walking tours $30/55/110, kayak hire 1hr/full-day $20/60, fleet tour adult/child $8/4) Offers a combination of walks and kayaking exploring Coffin Bay and Lincoln National Parks including some training for beginners. They also do a good walking tour of the fishing fleet that includes the chance to taste prawns and other seasonal seafood.

**Watermark Sailing Charters** ( ☎ 0427-831 916; www.southernhorizons.com.au; 1-/2-/full-day sail $70/180) Luxury sightseeing tours aboard their well-appointed catamaran to areas including Dangerous Reef. Longer trips (including meals) can be arranged.

**Calypso Star Charter** ( ☎ 8364 4428; www.calypso starcharter.com.au; 1-day dive $517) For the ultimate waterborne adventure this outfit offer the chance to cage dive with notorious great white sharks or less threatening sea lions. The can also hire out wetsuits (and bandages) if you don't have your own.

## Sleeping

Places to sleep in Port Lincoln are geared towards the school-holiday crowd, so call early if you're planning to stay during this season; book before your littlies are born to get a place here at Christmas.

### BUDGET

**Port Lincoln Cabin Park** ( ☎ 8683 4884; www.portlin coln.net/cabinpark/cabinmain.htm; 15 Stevenson St; d & tw $58) These self-contained homes are tightly packed but well-appointed (including spa, videos and full kitchens) and have room enough for a family of five.

**Pier Hotel** ( ☎ 8682 1322; Tasman Tce; s/d $35/60) This is typical pub accommodation – tea- and coffee-making facilities, tired furniture and TVs – that is a cheaper option in pricey Port Lincoln.

**Grand Tasman Hotel** ( ☎ 8682 2133; 94 Tasman Tce; s/d $50/60) The swanky refit downstairs didn't make it upstairs, but there are clean rooms, worn beds and big TVs. On disco nights (Thursday to Saturday) earplugs are provided for noisier rooms.

**Kirton Point Caravan Park** ( ☎ 8682 2537; Hindmarsh St; unpowered/powered sites per 2 people $16/21, camp cabins $35, on-site vans $51, cabins $64) Close to the town centre and on the water, this roomy place has excellent facilities, boat-launching jetties and a green pleasant park with pelicans. Camp cabins have four single bunks in each cabin.

### MID-RANGE

**Hilton Motel** ( ☎ 8682 1144; 11-13 King St; d $107-117) Showing its age a little, this competent hotel has big TVs (including cable), soft beds and the occasional dolphin view as it's right on the water. Some rooms come with spas.

**Peninsula Motel & Sorrento Lodge** ( ☎ 8682 2222; 12-14 Tasman Tce; s/d $80/90) You check in to both these properties at the Peninsula Motel, where the clean motel rooms afford excellent ocean views. Sorrento Lodge is the preferred option for travelling workers as it has self-contained units.

**Limani Motel** ( ☎ 8682 2200; www.limanimotel.com .au; 50 Lincoln Hwy; d $95) Don't be confused by the two-level parking complex at the entrance, oceanfront rooms in this great little spot are excellently appointed. Staff are cheery, and helpful with local itineraries.

**First Landing Motel** ( ☎ 8682 2919; 11 Shaen St; s $62-68, d & tw $69-85) Rooms in this sweet motel are romantically enhanced with four-poster beds and other accoutrements like big TVs and a beautifully flowered garden. They also run the **Abeona Cottage** (s $95-115, d $115-135), a well-appointed B&B right next door.

**TOP END**

**Marina Hotel Apartments** ( ☎ 8682 6141; 13 Jubilee Dr, Lincoln Cove; d $130-180) The picturesque cove-side locale justifies the premium for these fully self-contained apartments that include scenic balconies, spas and modish furniture.

## Eating

It's quality not quantity in the limited dining scene of Port Lincoln, with several great little eateries available.

**Caffe del Giorno** ( ☎ 8683 0577; 80 Tasman Tce; mains $11-23; ⏰ 7.30am-10pm Mon-Sat, 8.30am-9pm Sun) Redolent with aromas of coffee and rich tomato sauces, the snazzy Italian menu here includes gourmet pizzas, creative pastas and a whopping serve of whiting ($20). Counter service is the only disappointment.

**King Neptune's** ( ☎ 8682 6655; 5 Light St; mains $6-12) Right next door to the huge chicken-frying multinational, this plucky takeaway serves up damn good seafood that has townsfolk loyally queuing up at the takeaway side or packing into the low-key dining area.

**Grand Tasman Hotel** ( ☎ 8682 2133; 94 Tasman Tce) is definitely the best of the boozers, with two great dining options. The well-heeled opt for **Moorings** (mains $17-30; ⏰ dinner) for opulent meals such as roast quail ($21) or expertly cooked whiting. The **bistro** ( mains $6-14;

### THE AUTHOR'S CHOICE

**Third Rock Café** ( ☎ 8682 2849; 42 Liverpool St; mains $7-12; ⏰ 9am-6pm Sun, 8am-6pm Mon-Wed, 8am-8pm Thu-Sat) This is the perfect place for a little babycino parenting. Thanks to the large and, more importantly, sealed-off kids' play area out the back, you can peacefully enjoy a juice, decadent cheesecake or a slab of lasagne. There are monster nachos and several 'rockstops' – doorstop sandwiches topped with chicken and asparagus – as well as other gourmet treats. The only downside is closing time when the ankle biters are all yours again.

lunch & dinner) does the standard pasta-or-parma pub drill with a few bargain nights featuring roasts or smorgasbords.

**Bread Basket** ( ☎ 8682 5722; 21 Liverpool St; pies & pastries $3-5, sandwiches $4-6; ⏰ 7am-6pm Mon-Fri, 7am-2pm Sat) This is the top local choice for bakery treats.

**Great Northern Hotel** ( ☎ 8682 3350; 34 Hallett Pl; mains $8-15; ⏰ lunch & dinner) The Northern does no-fuss grub, such as gutsy steaks and huge plates of pasta. Their all-you-can-eat salad bar is a good option.

## Drinking

Grab a flavoursome cuppa at **Third Rock Café** ( ☎ 8682 2849; 42 Liverpool St) before a night out at the range of pubs. The **Great Northern** ( ☎ 8682 3350; 34 Hallett Pl) is the best place to meet locals, while tourists tend to drink at the **Grand Tasman Hotel** ( ☎ 8682 2133; 94 Tasman Tce). Check out the **Pier Hotel** ( ☎ 8682 1322; Tasman Tce) for live music.

## Entertainment

For details of entertainment check the *Port Lincoln Times*. The **Flinders Theatre** ( ☎ 8683 1199; 3 Hallett Pl; ⏰ Wed-Sun) shows all the big movie blockbusters. Pier Hotel has bands, even on laid-back acoustic Sunday, while the **Grand Tasman Hotel** ( ☎ 8682 2133; 94 Tasman Tce) has a rump-shaking disco from Thursday to Saturday.

## Getting There & Around

**Airlines of SA** ( ☎ 131 313) fly to Adelaide (45 minutes, $225) four times a day on weekdays and twice a day on weekends. **Premier Stateliner** ( ☎ 8645 9911; www.premierstateliner.com.au; 24 Lewis St) buses run daily from Adelaide (9½ hours, $78) stopping along the coast at Port Augusta (3½ hours, $48).

There's no bus service from the airport, but **Lincoln City Taxis** ( ☎ 8682 1222) do the trip for around $15. The local hire-car agencies are **Avis** ( ☎ 8682 1072), **Budget** ( ☎ 8684 3668), **Hertz** ( ☎ 8682 1933) and **No Frills Car Rentals** ( ☎ 1800 551 909; www.nofrillscarent.com.au).

**City of Port Lincoln Bus Services** ( ☎ 0427-616 261; single/day/week pass $1.50/3/12) operates two routes that take in most of the town.

## AROUND PORT LINCOLN

At the entrance to Boston Bay, **Boston Island** is a sheep-grazing property. You can have the entire island to yourself for $200 per person per week (minimum five people). Contact the Port Lincoln visitors centre for details.

Cape Carnot – better known as **Whalers Way** – features rugged coastal scenery with 120m cliffs. At **Fishery Bay** you can visit whaling station ruins, abandoned in 1842, or spot fur seals at **Cape Wiles**. The area is privately owned, but you can visit with a one-day permit ($25 plus $10 key deposit) from most petrol stations or Port Lincoln visitors centre. The permit includes camping at Redbanks or Groper Bay.

En route to Whalers Way is **Mikkira Station** ( ☎ 08-8685 6020; Fishery Bay Rd; day pass/camping $12/17), the first sheep station on Eyre Peninsula, which was recently used on the US TV series *Survivor* and has an excellent **koala sanctuary**. Visitors require a permit, available from the visitors centre.

Off the road to Coffin Bay, **Glen Forest Tourist Park** ( ☎ 08-8684 5053; www.visitglenforest .com; Greenpatch, Port Lincoln; adult/child $10/8, minigolf $4; ☺ 10am-5pm) has an array of fauna including dingoes, koalas, wombats and camels. Feeding of the cuddlesome koalas is at 1pm, and while you're waiting, have a quick round of putt-putt golf.

### Lincoln National Park

South of Port Lincoln, this magnificent stretch of coastline is all quiet coves, sheltered beaches and sheer cliffs. Apart from some barren patches from past farming activity, most of the park is dense with mallee scrub.

You can enter the park with an Eyre Parks Pass (p218) or purchase a permit ($6.50 per car including a night's camping) at the self-registration station on the way in. There's a good network of unsealed roads and tracks; most are suitable for conventional vehicles.

You'll need a 4WD to get from **Wanna** dunes, in the southwest, to tranquil **Memory Cove** (grab a gate key from Port Lincoln visitors centre for $20 deposit plus another $16 to camp) in the southeast, about 50km from Port Lincoln. Memory Cove is a **memorial** to the eight men who drowned off Cape Catastrophe during Matthew Flinders' 1802 expedition. Flinders named eight of the rugged islands off the coast after the missing men.

The lengthy **Investigator Trail** (six days, 109km) goes from Port Lincoln to end on Sleaford Bay after a figure-eight loop that includes Pillie Lake, Cape Donington and Taylors Landing. The trail follows the coast about 15km north of Port Lincoln and can be lengthened by taking the Parnkalla Trail (p223), to go south through Port Lincoln. Grab a map at the visitors centre.

There's a fully furnished **Donington Cottage** (s $33-35) and several **bush campsites** (per car $6.50), some with caravan access.

# WESTERN EYRE PENINSULA

The Flinders Hwy from Port Lincoln to Ceduna passes a number of popular summer holiday destinations, including Coffin Bay and Streaky Bay. Scattered between them are smaller resorts and beautiful surf beaches where you can ride the waves or fish.

## PORT LINCOLN TO STREAKY BAY
### Coffin Bay & Around
☎ 08

If Port Lincoln – with its tuna exports and wheat trade – is the industrial fat cat, then Coffin Bay is definitely the peninsula's glamourpuss. It basks languidly in the warm sun and calm bay waters, but by January the feline turns feral with holiday-makers. Oysters from the nearby beds are exported the world over, but you won't pay more than $6 a dozen around town. Don't let the Gothic name frighten you – it's another Matthew Flinders moniker to honour Sir Isaac Coffin, a Lord of the Admiralty.

The **Oyster Walk** – following the beach past quandong trees and the town jetty – is a good way to orientate yourself. To explore further out you can rent **tinnies** and **runabouts** at **Hire Boat Haven** ( ☎ 8685 4277; canoes & paddleboats $10, 1hr boat hire $20-50; ☺ 8am-5.30pm); 3.7m tinnies, canoes and paddleboats require no licence, but half-cabin fishing boats need a licensed skipper, which can be provided. Fuel is extra.

Just south of town is the wild coastal scenery of the **Coffin Bay National Park** . Entry ($6.50 per car) can be payed at the self-registration station or the **ranger's station** ( ☎ 8685 4047). Access for conventional vehicles has improved with sealed roads to scenic **Point Avoid** (20km) and **Yangie Bay** (the latter has bush camping), though you'll need a 4WD to take on the sandy 50km track to **Point Sir Isaac**. You can try a number of challenging walks through thick heathland including the **Boarding House Bay Hike** (eight hours, 23km) or **Sudden Jerk Lookout** (40 minutes, 2km).

### SLEEPING & EATING

A 1990s real-estate boom saw people buying up big in Coffin Bay, but owners are keen to share their properties (or pay off mortgages) by renting out unused holiday properties. **Century 21 Real Estate** ( ☎ 8685 4063; www.century21.com.au/coffinbay; 61 Esplanade; cottages $45-180) rents out properties ranging from beach 'shacks' (smaller homes) to larger self-contained townhouses.

**Coffin Bay Caravan Park** ( ☎ 8685 4170; Shepperd Ave; unpowered/powered sites per 2 people $15/20, on-site vans $37, cabins $50, cottages $60) There are plenty of good sites nestled among she-oaks and tea trees, with well-kept amenities and golf clubs ($5) for hire.

**Coffin Bay Motel** ( ☎ 8685 4111; Shepperd Ave; d $85; ✷ ) This motel has roomy units and also does standard counter meals.

**Bush camping** (per car $6.50) is allowed at several places in the national park; there's no drinking water and access is difficult.

The best dining is at **Oysterbeds Restaurant** ( ☎ 8685 4000; Shepperd Ave; mains $19-25; ✷ lunch & dinner Wed-Sat), which serves the finest local seafood.

## Coffin Bay to Elliston

At **Wangary**, on the Flinders Hwy, a gravel road leads to **Farm Beach**, a popular boat-launching spot. Further north is the rugged stretch of coastline known as **Gallipoli Beach**, once used as a location for Peter Weir's film *Gallipoli*. Near **Coulta**, 18km from Wangary, gravel roads lead to **Convention Beach**, **Greenly Beach** and **Coles Beach**, all popular surfing and surf-fishing spots.

You can admire the magnifcent coast at **Cummings Lookout**, 47km northeast from Coulta. Turning off 67km past Coulta, the road to Sheringa Beach will take you past some huge white dunes and **Round Lake**, which has excellent sailboarding and sheltered campsites.

The famous salmon-fishing spot at **Locks Well Beach** is 23km past the Sheringa turn-off. A long steep stairway – called **Staircase**

**to Heaven** – leads from the car park down to the gorgeous beach.

## Elliston & Around

☎ 08 / pop 240

On tranquil Waterloo Bay, 167km from Port Lincoln, Elliston has a beautiful swimming beach and a well-regarded fishing jetty (best for tommy rough or whiting). The **visitors centre** ( ☎ 8687 9200; www.ellistoninfocentre .com; tours $5; ✷ 8.30am-5pm Mon-Fri, 1-4pm Sat & Sun) has plenty of information and can organise tours of local lobster fisheries (see Hitting the Seafood Trail, p231).

Just to the north of town, take the unsealed 7km loop road to **Salmon Point** and **Anxious Bay** for some dramatic ocean scenery. En route you'll pass **Blackfellows**, with some of the west coast's best surfing breaks.

### SLEEPING & EATING

**Elliston Waterloo Bay Caravan Park** ( ☎ 8687 9076; Beach Tce; unpowered/powered sites per 2 people $15/18, cabins $25, en suite cabins $55; ✷ ) The beach is just over the hedge of this well-positioned park, which has good facilities and plenty of insider fishing tips.

**Elliston Hotel Motel** ( ☎ 8687 9009; Beach Tce; d $55, mains $7-12) A classic old sandstone pub offering plain rooms with en suites and serving big meals such as ham steak and pineapple or garfish and chips.

**Discovaus** ( ☎ 8687 9290; www.discovaus.com.au; d $60) This sun- and wind-powered restored train carriage 3km south of Elliston makes for an ecologically sound stay in a secluded location.

## North of Elliston

About 20km north of Elliston is **Lake Newland Conservation Park** with huge white dunes, wetlands and a long surf beach. You can explore the 20km beach up the coast to **Talia Caves**, which include colourful low cliffs, collapsed crevices and sinkholes.

Seven kilometres beyond the Talia Caves turn-off a road will take you to **Mt Camel Beach**, another good salmon spot. To the north are the sleepy townships of **Venus Bay** and **Port Kenny**.

## Baird Bay Area

Between Port Kenny and Streaky Bay, a network of gravel roads lead to **Point Labatt**, where there's a large colony of Australian sea lions that can be seen from cliff-top viewing platforms. The sea lions usually laze just 100m away on the rocks. En route you can visit **Murphy's Haystacks** (admission by donation), tall, colourful weather-sculpted granite tors standing on a hilltop 2km from the highway.

A further 12km towards Point Labatt is the southeast corner of the **Calpatanna Waterhole Conservation Park** with camping ($6.50 per car) at Wedina Well.

## STREAKY BAY
☎ 08 / pop 1081

This endearing little fishing and agricultural centre gets its name from the 'streaks' of seaweed Matthew Flinders spotted in the sea. Still visible at low tide, the seagrass attracts ocean critters, making for some first-class fishing.

Tourist information is available at **Stewarts Roadhouse** ( ☎ 8626 1126; www.streakybay.sa .gov.au; 15 Alfred Tce; ⊙ 6.30am-9pm).

### Sights & Activities
Housed in an old schoolhouse, the **Streaky Bay Museum** ( ☎ 8626 1142; Montgomery Tce; adult/child $3.50/$0.50; ⊙ 2-4pm Tue & Fri or by appointment) has interesting exhibits, including an iron lung and a pug-and-pine hut complete with period furnishings. The **Powerhouse Restored Engine Centre** ( ☎ 8626 1628; Alfred Tce; admission by donation; ⊙ 2-4pm Tue & Fri) has several working engines for rail buffs.

The scenic coast around Streaky Bay is perfect for surfing and fishing. To the south, **Back Beach** is good for surfing and salmon fishing, as is **High Cliff** further on. **Yanerbie**, at the northern end of Sceale Bay, has white Sahara-like dunes and a swimming beach. **Cape Bauer**, 5km northwest of town, has high, colourful cliffs.

Gourmet **oysters** are farmed in Streaky Bay, and you can buy a dozen for $6 from various outlets, including the caravan park. For more seafood, you can tour the **Abalone Farm** (1hr tour adult/child $10/5; ⊙ tours 10.30am) or check out what happens to the catch of the day at **Streaky Bay Marine Products** (40min tour adult/child $12/9; ⊙ 9am) – both are booked at **West Coast Trading Post** ( ☎ 8626 1377; 14-16 Bay Rd).

### Sleeping & Eating
**Foreshore Tourist Park** ( ☎ 8626 1666; unpowered/powered sites per 2 people $18/20, units $45-75, cabins $65-70) A friendly caravan park is a real find, but add a safe swimming beach, bunks aplenty in units and good kitchen facilities and you've got the perfect equation for family stays. The adjoining kiosk also does good takeaway.

**Streaky Bay Community Hotel/Motel** ( ☎ 8626 1008; 35 Alfred Tce; dm $20-24, hotel s/d $60/75, motel s/d $80/95, meals $8-16; ⊙ lunch & dinner) This comfortable classic has good-value hotel rooms, some with 'dolphin-side views' from balconies. Backpacker rooms are the best value with motel-style touches (including breakfast) and a maximum of four beds per room, though staff try their best to let you have a room to yourself. Their bistro does impressive *bain-marie*-based cuisine.

**Headland House** ( ☎ 8626 1315; 5 Flinders Dr; s/d $85/95; ⚡ ) Scenic Headland is a plush place with charming hosts, a full-sized pool table, large continental breakfasts and a fan collection from across the globe.

# EYRE HIGHWAY & WEST COAST

## PORT AUGUSTA TO CEDUNA
This 468km stretch of road is an unspectacular route to Ceduna, though the Gawler Ranges National Park (see Detour, opposite) is becoming an outdoorsy destination and the mining history of Iron Knob is interesting. Mostly the landscape is semiarid station country, becoming wheat paddocks after Kimba.

Off the highway 40km from Port Augusta, **Nuttbush Retreat** ( ☎ 08-8643 8941; www.nuttbush .com.au; Pandurra Station; powered sites $15 per 2 people, dm/s/cottages $33/55/95, mains $11-18; ⊙ dinner; ⚡ ), offers a good variety of accommodation on a former sheep station with goats, ponies and a very cheerful dog. Their restaurant is set in a restored woolshed with a hearty menu including steaks and pork chops.

A little further on, 62km from Port Augusta, **Iron Knob** is the porn-star named town that was once an iron-ore mine that supplied Whyalla with ore for smelting. **Guided tours** of the huge open-cut mine leave from the **visitors centre** ( ☎ 08-8646 2129; 1hr tour adult/child $3/1; ⊙ 9.30am-11.30am & 1.30-3.30pm Mon-Fri, tours 10am & 2pm Mon-Fri) and require closed footwear.

After another 88km you pass through **Kimba**, the largest of the peninsula's northern wheat towns. Apart from grain silos, its most obvious feature is the **Big Galah**. This 8m-high local icon stands guard over the **Halfway Across Australia Giftshop** ( ☎ 08-8627 2766; Eyre Hwy; ☼ 8am-5pm Mon-Fri, 8am-4pm Sat & Sun) which sells opals, jade and other semiprecious stones. To stay under the galah's watchful eye, the **Kimba Motel/Caravan Park** ( ☎ 08-8627 2040; Eyre Hwy; unpowered sites per 2 people $17, on-site vans $35, d $65) has a caravan park and motel units.

The main drawcard of attractive **Wudinna** is the Gawler Ranges National Park (see below). The **Gawler Ranges Information Outlet** ( ☎ 08-86802969; 44 Eyre Hwy) is the best resource for information on camping and walking in the park. You can stay in town at the well-equipped **Gawler Ranges Motel & Caravan Park** ( ☎ 08-8680 2090; www.gawlerrangesmotel.com; Eyre Hwy; unpowered/powered sites per 2 people $9/14.50, on-site vans $36, s $60-85, d $70-93; ▨ ).

---

### DETOUR: PINKAWILLINIE CONSERVATION PARK & GAWLER RANGES NATIONAL PARK

About 55km west of Kimba, Stringer Rd heads into Pinkawillinie Conservation Park, a rambling park of sand dunes fuzzed with mallee scrub and dotted with bush camping spots and 4WD tracks. Grab a brochure from the DEH offices for more information.

Accessible from marked roads heading north from Wudinna, Minnipa or Poochera, the new Gawler Ranges National Park is slowly being discovered by bushwalkers and nature-lovers alike. It's known for the spectacular **Organ Pipes** – shafts of granite projecting spectacularly out of cliffs – and **Mt Wudinna**, SA's largest exposed monolith. The **Granite Trail**, a 25km self-drive tour, is a quick way to see the mountain from Wudinna. You can enter the park with the Eyre Parks Pass (p218) or by getting a day permit ($6.50 per car), available at self-registration stations. There's bush camping at several sites and you can get more information (including maps and directions) from the Gawler Ranges Information Outlet in Wudinna. Some trails are suitable only for 4WD cars, but a 2WD with good clearance should be fine on trails into the park.

---

At Minnipa, 37km west, the **Minnipa Hotel/Motel** ( ☎ 08-8680 5005; motel d $70, hotel s/tw $25/48) has rudimentary rooms. Tiny **Poochera** and **Wirrulla** are little more than refuelling stops on the way to Ceduna.

## CEDUNA
☎ 08 / pop 2588

Depending on your journey, Ceduna is the last outpost of civilisation or the first oasis after the Nullarbor Plain. Ceduna is the west coast's last significant service centre, so it's aptly named from the Aboriginal word *cheedoona* (a place to rest). Ceduna's alter ego is as a major export terminal for cereal grains, salt and gypsum with a deepwater port at nearby Thevenard. Ceduna's fishing fleet keeps the town's three seafood-processing factories in business.

### Orientation
Turn off the Eyre Hwy onto McKenzie St, which leads to the town centre and foreshore (along O'Loughlin Tce). The cross street Poynton St has several dining options. Buses stop at the Shell Roadhouse and the airport is 3km east along the Eyre Hwy.

### Information
The visitors centre is located in Traveland Ceduna. The Commonwealth bank is in the post office and there's an ANZ ATM on the corner of Poynton and McKenzie Sts. The Bank of SA has a branch on McKenzie St.
**DEH** ( ☎ 8625 3144; 11 McKenzie St; ☼ 9am-5pm Mon-Fri) Has more information on Yumbarra Conservation Park.
**Post office** ( ☎ 8625 2020; 18 McKenzie St; ☼ 9am-5pm Mon-Sat)
**Traveland Ceduna** ( ☎ 1800 639 413; 8625 2780; 58 Poynton St; ☼ 9am-5.30pm Mon-Fri, 9am-noon Sat) As well as the visitors centre, there is Internet access for $5 per hour.

### Sights & Activities
The region's rich history is on display at **Ceduna Museum** ( ☎ 8625 2210; Park Tce; adult/child $3.50/2; ☼ 10am-noon Mon-Tue, Fri & Sat, 2-4pm Wed, 10am-noon & 2-4pm Thu). The Maralinga Room features articles and oddments about the British atomic tests that occurred northwest of here. A small collection of Aboriginal artefacts is displayed, along with a cast of a huge basking shark and a whale's skull.

Local indigenous artists from along the coast are featured at **Ceduna Aboriginal Arts & Culture Centre** ( ☎ 8625 2487; cnr Eyre Hwy & Kuhlmann

EYRE PENINSULA & WEST COAST

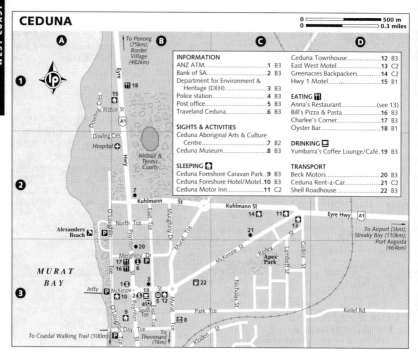

# CEDUNA

0 — 500 m
0 — 0.3 miles

To Penong (75km); Border Village (482km)

**INFORMATION**
ANZ ATM.................................1 B3
Bank of SA..............................2 B3
Department for Environment & Heritage (DEH)....................3 B3
Police station..........................4 B3
Post office..............................5 B3
Traveland Ceduna..................6 B3

**SIGHTS & ACTIVITIES**
Ceduna Aboriginal Arts & Culture Centre...............................7 B2
Ceduna Museum......................8 B3

**SLEEPING**
Ceduna Foreshore Caravan Park..9 B3
Ceduna Foreshore Hotel/Motel..10 B3
Ceduna Motor Inn..................11 C2

Ceduna Townhouse................12 B3
East West Motel....................13 C2
Greenacres Backpackers.......14 C2
Hwy 1 Motel..........................15 B1

**EATING**
Anna's Restaurant...............(see 13)
Bill's Pizza & Pasta...............16 B3
Charlee's Corner...................17 B3
Oyster Bar............................18 B1

**DRINKING**
Yumbarra's Coffee Lounge/Café.19 B3

**TRANSPORT**
Beck Motors..........................20 B3
Ceduna Rent-a-Car...............21 C2
Shell Roadhouse....................22 B3

To Airport (3km); Streaky Bay (110km); Port Augusta (464km)

*MURAT BAY*

To Coastal Walking Trail (100m)

To Thevenard (1km)

---

St; admission free; 9am-5pm Mon-Fri), a gallery space that includes painted emu eggs, didgeridoos and sea-inspired works.

Off the coast between Ceduna and Smoky Bay, the **Nuyts Archipelago** and **Isles of St Francis** are home to sea lions and little penguins. **Denial Bay**, 14km west of town, is a name synonymous with oysters. Several farms are open to the public with oysters selling for as little as $5 a dozen. Check Hitting the Seafood Trail (opposite) for aquaculture tours.

Just 28km north of town, **Yumbarra Conservation Park** is crossed by the extremely difficult **Goog's Track**. This vast area is strictly for experienced outback travellers with 4WD vehicles and crosses private property, so discuss any plans with the DEH office before heading into this area.

## Tours
There are several reliable charter outfits around town that can take you out to see the wildlife or maybe even hook some.
**Ceduna Boat Charter** ( 8625 2654, 0428- 643 519; www.cedunaboatcharter.com.au; 1-day fishing $95, whale tours $110) Runs fishing and diving charters in the area.

From July to September they also do whale tours (minimum of two people).
**Swagabout Tours** ( 0408-845 378; www.swagabout tours.com.au; 5-day tour $1450) Offers tours from Adelaide that explore the Eyre Peninsula before finishing with whale watching.

## Sleeping
### BUDGET
**Greenacres Backpackers** ( 8625 3811, 0427-339 722; 12 Kuhlmann St; dm $17) The town's only backpackers has hubcaps nailed to trees in the yard. The serviceable beds include breakfast, and staff sometimes run tours of the town.

**Ceduna Foreshore Hotel/Motel** ( 8625 2008; O'Loughlin Tce; unpowered/powered sites per 2 people $17/20, cabins $50-70, hotel s/d $30/40, motel s/d $75/85; ) Its coastal position has allowed this hotel to expand into a decent caravan park. Their motel rooms are showing their age, but include cable TV and big beds. The caravan park affords good views across the ocean.

### MID-RANGE
**East West Motel** ( 8625 2101; 66-76 McKenzie St; www .eastwestceduna.com.au; s $55-98, d $65-103; )

Definitely one of the slicker places in town, the East West has basic rooms (simple motel rooms with older bedding) through to deluxe apartments including DVDs, well-stocked bar fridges and air-conditioning. Anna's Restaurant (below) is another great feature.

**Highway 1 Motel** ( ☎ 8625 2208; Eyre Hwy; s $70-90, d $75-95) Out on the highway outside of town, this place is a good transit motel with executive rooms at the upper end of the price range. You can check-in 24 hours a day and it has disabled facilities.

**Ceduna Townhouse** ( ☎ 8625 2780; 22 McKenzie St; house $110; 🕱 ) This small house is a good spot for a group of up to six with TV/video and linen included. Its central location makes it a good spot from which to explore the town.

**Ceduna Motor Inn** ( ☎ 8625 2201; cnr McKenzie & Kuhlman Sts; s/d $66/77) Behind the SAFF petrol station, the rooms here have big TVs, soft mattresses and fridges – perfect for the end of a long drive. Fuelling up in the morning is convenient and staff will happily give you directions for the next leg of your trip.

## Eating

Ceduna has a simple dining scene, though experiencing seafood from the nearby Eyre Peninsula is a must.

**Anna's Restaurant** ( ☎ 8626 2101; East West Motel, 66-76 McKenzie St; mains $13-26; 🕑 lunch & dinner) You can tell this is the fancy place in town; their parma has 'a duo of cheeses'. There's a good children's menu and grown-ups

can tuck into expertly cooked whiting or gourmet snags in gravy.

**Ceduna Foreshore Hotel/Motel** ( ☎ 8625 2008; O'Loughlin Tce; mains $9-14; 🕑 lunch & dinner) Bistro meals at the Foreshore represent the best value in town, with a few interesting flourishes – deep-fried camembert, laksa and crepes to name a few. Seafood is simply prepared, but fresh.

**Charlee's Corner** ( ☎ 8626 9027; cnr Merghiny Dr & Poynton St; mains $11-19; 🕑 lunch Tue-Sat, dinner Tue-Sun) Greedy guts love the all-you-can-eat deal ($14.90) here on Thursday night, but other nights have plenty to offer too, including mussels in black bean, great satays and culinary-cringing 'Aussie' dishes such as tuna mornay.

**Bill's Pizza & Pasta** ( ☎ 8625 3590; 43 Poynton St; 🕑 9am-11pm Mon-Fri, Sat & Sun 4-10pm) Specialising in continental and Australian fare, Bill dishes up good pizzas, pastas and a great dessert selection including tiramisu and cannoli.

**Oyster Bar** ( ☎ 8626 9086; Eyre Hwy; meals $8; 🕑 9.30am-6pm Mon-Sat, 1-6pm Sun) If you missed seafood in town, here's your last chance to slurp down a few molluscs and enjoy a glass of wine near the (not very) Big Oyster.

## Drinking

Most of the town gathers at **Ceduna Foreshore Hotel/Motel** ( ☎ 8625 2008; O'Loughlin Tce) after sunset. For a caffeine jolt on your way through town, **Yumbarra's Coffee Lounge/Café** ( ☎ 8625 3399; 16 McKenzie St; snacks $5-7; 🕑 8am-5.30pm Mon-Fri, 8am-3pm Sat) does strong coffee with slices, sandwiches and yiros.

---

### HITTING THE SEAFOOD TRAIL

Ceduna represents the perfect place for exploring the many fishy delights of the Eyre Peninsula. Oysters are exceptional – there's even a festival celebrating them (see Festivals & Events, p219) – but other seafood is well worth sampling too. Visitors centres usually have the comprehensive *Seafood & Aquaculture Trail* brochure detailing more places to see (and if you're lucky) taste some great ocean produce. Here are our favourite picks:

**Elliston Crayfish Tours** ( ☎ 08-8687 9200; Elliston; adult/child $7/2; 🕑 2pm Mon, Wed & Fri) Walk through the art of craypots and learn how to capture the clawed critters.

**Smoky Bay Oyster Tour & Marine Aquariums** ( ☎ 8625 7077; 6-8 Sandy Creek Dr, Smoky Bay; admission $5.50; 🕑 3pm Mon-Fri) This is a brilliant tour of their aquariums which hold sharks and puffer fish, plus an oyster tasting at the end.

**Thevenard Fish Processors** ( ☎ 08-8625 2780; Thevenard; adult/child $5.50/2.20; 🕑 10am Mon, Wed & Fri) Select and package a vast selection of local fish.

**Astrid Oysters** ( ☎ 08-8625 3554; Denial Bay; 1hr tour $5.50; 🕑 by appointment) Will take you through the farming and harvesting of the tasty little bivalves.

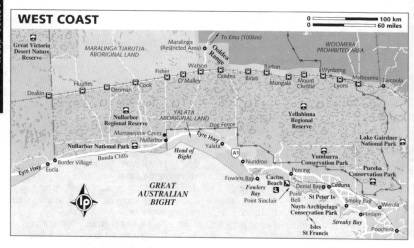

## Getting There & Around

**Regional Express** (Rex; ☎ 13 17 13; www.regionalex press.com.au) flies daily to Adelaide (1½ hours, $129). **Premier Stateliner** (☎ 8415 5555; www .premierstateliner.com.au) runs daily buses from/to Adelaide (11 hours, $90) and Port Augusta (6¼ hours, $72), while **Greyhound Australia** (☎ 13 14 99; www.greyhound.com.au) passes through Ceduna daily on their way to Perth (26 hours, $287).

There is no bus service from town to the airport, but **West Coast Taxis** (☎ 0428-253 791) charges $10 for an airport fare.

You can rent a car from the Budget outlet at **Beck Motors** (☎ 1800 654 730, 8625 2616; 54 Poynton St). **Ceduna Rent-a-Car** (☎ 8625 2085; 47 McKenzie St) specialises in campers and off-road vehicles.

## CEDUNA TO YALATA

The exhausting 482km from Ceduna to Border Village takes in several sites along the way, so stop for regular breaks. From Penong, 72km from Ceduna, you can turn-off for legendary surf at **Cactus Beach** with strong breaks, as well as beginner's waves. There's **bush camping** (per person $8) on private property close to the breaks.

Another 34km on is the turn-off to **Fowlers Bay**, an almost ghost town that has several heritage buildings, good fishing and impressive coastal dunes. **Fowlers Bay Caravan Park** (☎ 08-8625 6143; unpowered/powered sites per 2 people $14/17, on-site vans $35-40) has basic accommodation with a shop and takeaway food.

Continuing west on the Eyre Hwy there are pub rooms at **Nundroo Hotel/Motel** (☎ 08-8625 6120; dm/d/tr $10/77/90; ⊠) which also has a 24-hour fuel stop and restaurant.

## Yalata & Head of Bight

About 200km from Ceduna, the township of Yalata is an Aboriginal community of 400 people managing **Yalata Roadhouse** (☎ 08-8625 6807; www.wangkawilurrara.com/yalata; d $65, whale-watching permits $8; ☉ 8am-8pm) and the nearby Head of Bight whale-watching platforms. The roadhouse offers basic motel-style rooms and sells a huge range of Aboriginal art. It's also a good place to get a permit and directions to **Head of Bight**.

The whale-watching platforms at Head of Bight, 78km west of Yalata, afford spectacular views of a breeding ground for **southern right whales**, which migrate here from Antarctica in June. You can see them from July to September. The breeding area is protected by the 20,000 sq km **Great Australian Bight Marine Park**, which is the world's second-largest marine park after the Great Barrier Reef.

## Head of Bight to Border Village

From the **Nullarbor Hotel/Motel** (☎ 08-8625 6271; sites per 2 people $11, dm/s/d/tr $19/80/100/115; ☉ 7am-11pm), 94km after Yalata, you enter the **Nullarbor National Park**, which follows the coast to the WA border. Beneath the dry plains is a limestone cave system that can be seen at **Murrawijinie Caves**, an overhang behind the Nullarbor Hotel/Motel.

From signposted **lookouts** along the 80m-high **Bunda Cliffs** you can see where the plain spectacularly falls away into the Great Australian Bight.

**Border Village** marks the SA–WA border with a **caravan park** ( ☎ 08-9039 3474), motel, restaurant, petrol station and the **Big Kangaroo**, a giant marsupial statue that once offered passers-by a beer, but has now watered down to soft drink.

There's a fruit and vegetable quarantine checkpoint just beyond Border Village for vehicles entering WA and another before Ceduna for vehicles coming from WA. Be sure to throw away (or gobble quickly) all your fruit and vegetables before the checkpoints.

234

# Outback

OUTBACK

CONTENTS

| | |
|---|---|
| **Stuart Highway** | **239** |
| Woomera | 239 |
| Woomera to Coober Pedy | 239 |
| Coober Pedy | 240 |
| Around Coober Pedy | 246 |
| North to the Northern Territory | 246 |
| **Outback Tracks** | **246** |
| Marree | 247 |
| Oodnadatta Track | 247 |
| Oodnadatta | 248 |
| Birdsville Track | 248 |
| Strzelecki Track | 249 |
| Innamincka | 250 |

Red desert, gun-barrel straight roads and all those flies – few places are as evocatively Australian as the outback. It's a land of the unexpected, of constant contradiction: a region that covers 80% of South Australia (SA) yet has only 1% of the population; an Australian icon peopled by more than 50 different nationalities, and a dry area that has the world's sixth largest lake, Lake Eyre. Today much of the western area is owned by Aboriginal peoples and special permission is required to enter the country.

It's an area that has been making headlines for decades, firstly with controversial nuclear testing at Maralinga, then uranium mining at Roxby Downs and more recently with an immigration detention centre at Woomera. Conservation is a hot issue in the area with a planned uranium dump overthrown in the High Court in 2004 and debate about mining in national parks always fierce.

The tourist industry catch-cry is 'the accessible outback', which is true of the Stuart Hwy, a sealed road that runs up to Coober Pedy and beyond. Many prefer the rougher roads and take on the tracks – Oodnadatta, Birdsville and Strzelecki – which include Australia's most spectacular scenery. Others keep on driving to the Northern Territory (NT). If you're driving bear in mind that accommodation, petrol stations and food suppliers are extremely limited in the outback; you'll need to plan your stops carefully and drive safely. With the completion of the Ghan rail line all the way up to Darwin, it's easier to sit back, let someone else do the driving and watch the long flat plains unfold.

**OUTBACK**

## HIGHLIGHTS

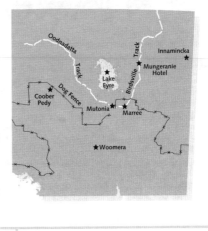

- Soaring over the scenic expanse of **Lake Eyre** and pondering the remains of **Marree Man** (p247)
- Getting down and dirty in the mines of **Coober Pedy** (p241)
- Checking out **Woomera's** collection of leftover military paraphernalia (p239) or better yet see the artistic interpretation at **Mutonia** (p247)
- Following the rough and tumble of the **Oodnadatta Track** (p247) to trace out the old Great Northern Railway line
- Sinking schooners and soaking in the natural spa at Mungeranie Hotel after tackling half of the **Birdsville Track** (p248)
- Admiring the vast stretch of the **Dog Fence** (p249) outside Coober Pedy or crossing it on the Strzelecki Track
- Digging into **Innamincka** (p250), the last isolated camp of Burke and Wills, Australia's most tragic explorers

- TELEPHONE CODE: ☎ 08

- www.pinkroadhouse.com.au
- www.opalcapitaloftheworld.com.au

OUTBACK

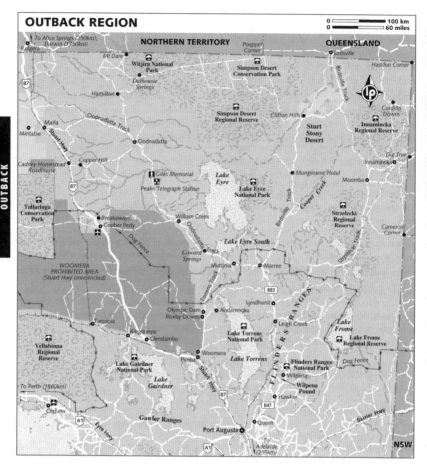

**OUTBACK REGION**

## National Parks

In the outback there are several unique environments – the dry salt pan of Lake Eyre, and the majestic Simpson Desert spreading from SA into Queensland (Qld) and the NT. The best way to explore all of this is to purchase a Desert Parks Pass ($90 per car), which allows access to all the parks with a map and handbook for using the park included. A Department for Environment & Heritage (DEH) ranger is based permanently at Innamincka, and there are seasonal rangers at Dalhousie Springs in Witjira National Park. Some areas are jointly managed by Aboriginal groups – including Witjira National Park – while others have traditional importance and are closed to the general public.

Desert Parks Passes are available from the following outlets:

**DEH regional offices** (Department for Environment & Heritage; ☎ 1800 816 078; www.environment.sa.gov.au/parks)

**Hawker Motors** ( ☎ 08-8648 4014; Wilpena Rd, Hawker)

**Mobil service station & police station** (Birdsville)

**Mt Dare Homestead** ( ☎ 08-8670 7835; Witjira National Park)

**Oodnadatta Hotel** ( ☎ /fax 08-8670 7804; Main St, Oodnadatta)

**Outback Roadhouse** ( ☎ 08-8675 9900; Railway Tce, North Marree)

**Pink Roadhouse** ( ☎ 08-8670 7822; Main St, Oodnadatta; ⏰ 8am-5.30pm)

**Royal Automobile Association** (RAA; ☎ 08-8202 4600; www.raa.net; 55 Hindmarsh Sq, Adelaide)

**FESTIVALS & EVENTS**

**Opal Festival** (www.opalfestival.com; adult/child $5/2; Easter) A fun day held every Easter Saturday in Coober Pedy featuring great food, music and a street parade. Visitors can get together and form their own teams for events such as the sausage-throwing competition, or sit on the sidelines and watch mine rescue and noodling demonstrations.

**Marree Australian Camel Cup** (Marree; 1st Sat in Jul, odd-numbered years) A celebration of the days when Marree was a post for camel trains carrying supplies to remote areas.

**Coober Pedy Races** (Labour Day weekend, October) Transforms Coober Pedy's residents into mad punters.

**Shell Mt Gillen service station** (☎ 08-8952 2347; Larapinta Dr, Alice Springs)

**Trading Post** (☎ 08-8675 9900; fax 08-8675 9920; Innamincka)

**Underground Books** (☎ 08-8672 5558; Lot 4, Post Office Hill Rd, Coober Pedy; ☽ 8.30am-5pm Mon-Fri, 10am-4pm Sat)

**Wadlata Outback Centre** (☎ 1800 633 060, 08-8641 0793; www.portaugusta.sa.gov.au; 41 Flinders Tce, Port Augusta; ☽ 9am-5.30pm Mon-Fri, 10am-4pm Sat & Sun)

**William Creek Store & Campground** (☎ 08-8670 7746; www.williamcreekcampground.com; Oodnadatta Track; William Creek)

## Tours

Tour companies are often a safe way to explore the outback, particularly if you're not used to driving in such conditions. Knowledgeable guides and fully-catered experiences can make it a well-informed and fun experience as well.

**Mulpa Tours** (☎ 08-8520 2808; www.mulpatours.com.au) An indigenous-run outfit, Mulpa Tours can take you into the Simpson Desert (eight-/10-day tour $1180/1325) and out onto the Strzelecki, Birdsville and Oodnadatta tracks. With good indigenous contacts, they can also take you onto lands that would require permits, such as their Pitjantjatjara tour, which includes sacred sites and bush medicine and tucker. Their outback loop (12-/22-day tour $2360/4182) samples the northern Flinders Ranges before heading out on the Strzelecki and other tracks. If you're not keen on restrictive tours you can take a 'tag-along' option where you drive yourself and camp or stay wherever you like.

**Reg Dodd's Arabunna Tours** (☎ 08-8675 8351; 1-day $90) Another good indigenous tour; it offers tours around Marree.

**Swagabout Tours** (☎ 0408-845 378; www.swagabouttours.com.au) A dependable outfit who run tours throughout SA, including the Flinders Ranges (p198) and along the Nullarbor (p230). Most of their tours offer the option of staying in local hotels or camping out under the stars. Their Adelaide to Alice Springs trip (five-/seven-/nine-/10-day tours $810 to $1125/$1320 to $1575/$1650 to $2025/$1800 to $2250) is a good trek passing through the Flinders Ranges, the Oodnadatta Track and Dalhousie Springs, before heading on to Uluru (Ayers Rock). The Flinders Ranges to Coober Pedy trip (seven-day tour $1100 to $1550) takes in Woomera and Wilpena Pound as well as fair swathes of the Oodnadatta Track.

**Big Country Safaris** (☎ 08-8538 7105; www.bigcountrysafaris.com.au; 10-day tour $1450) Readers recommend Big Country who do return tours from Adelaide that include the Simpson Desert, Coober Pedy and the Birdsville Track. Their one-way tour to Alice Springs follows 'the footsteps of John Flynn', the Royal Flying Doctors pioneer.

**Explore the Outback** (☎ 1800 064 244, 08-8672 3968; www.austcamel.com.au/explore.htm; 4-day trek $1025) Runs one of the most reliable camel treks and specialised conservation-based tours of the desert from north of William Creek. Can arrange transport from Coober Pedy.

**Desert Diversity Tours** (☎ 1800 069 911, 08-8672 5226; www.desertdiversity.com; 24hr tour $200-375) Operating out of Coober Pedy, this outfit follows the mail-run routes from Coober Pedy to Oodnadatta to William Creek. For other mail-run tours, see p243.

Also running from Coober Pedy, **Wrightsair** (☎ 08-8670 7962, 08-8670 6080; www.wrightsair.com.au; 1hr/2hr flight $135/260) and **Opal Air** (☎ 08-8672 3067, 0427-304 599; 1hr/3hr flight $65/390) both offer flights over Lake Eyre.

The following tours do large routes that include several outback destinations:

**Adventure Tours Australia** (☎ 1300 654 604, 08-8309 2299; www.adventuretours.com.au)

**Groovy Grape Getaways** (☎ 1800 661 177; www.groovygrape.com.au)

**Wayward Bus** (☎ 1800 882 823, 08-8410 8833; www.waywardbus.com.au)

OUTBACK

## Getting There & Away

### AIR

The only carrier that flies regular commercial flights into the outback is **Regional Express** (Rex; ☎ 13 17 13; www.regionalexpress.com.au), which does daily flights between Adelaide and Coober Pedy ($169, two hours), and Olympic Dam ($149, 1½ hours).

### BUS

The long-distance buses are licensed to operate only parts of the route between Adelaide and Alice Springs. Premier Stateliner go no further than Woomera, while Greyhound Australia continue up to Alice Springs via Coober Pedy.

**Greyhound Australia** (☎ 13 14 99; www.greyhound .com.au) operates a passenger coach each day from Adelaide to Alice Springs ($129, nine hours), stopping at Pimba ($93, 6½ hours), Glendambo ($103, 7½ hours) and Coober Pedy ($129, 10½ hours). **Premier Stateliner** (☎ 08-8415 5555; www.premierstateliner.com.au) runs from Port Augusta to Roxby Downs ($45.70, three hours), which passes through Woomera ($33.40, 1¾ hours) Sunday to Friday.

### CAR & MOTORCYCLE

The well-maintained bitumen Stuart Hwy passes through Coober Pedy, but there are several interesting detours off this road. You can detour from Pimba through Woomera to Andamooka, and from Marla to Mintabie. There are minor roads from the highway across to the Oodnadatta Track.

Fuel and accommodation facilities for travellers are scattered along the highway at Pimba (171km from Port Augusta), Glendambo (285km), Coober Pedy (535km), Cadney Homestead (689km), Marla (771km) and Kulgera in the NT (949km). Pimba, Coober Pedy and Marla have 24-hour fuel sales.

---

### DRIVING IN THE OUTBACK

Driving in the outback has become a lot safer with new technology and better roads, but it's still a dangerous environment and its unique challenges can come as a shock after the predictability of SA's other roads. Even driving up the Stuart Hwy can get dangerous if you don't have enough petrol or water.

- Check weather and road conditions before heading out with **Transport SA Hotline Road Conditions** (☎ 1300 361 033), who have comprehensive reports on roads across the state, or the **Pink Roadhouse** (☎ 1800 802 074), who can give you updates on the Oodnadatta Track and other roads in the region. There's also useful information on the national parks with the **DEH** (www.environment.sa.gov.au/parks/outback.html), which has daily downloadable updates on conditions in the national parks.

- Always carry plenty of drinking water (the bore water on the Oodnadatta and Birdsville tracks is mainly undrinkable), and *never* camp near or pollute stock watering points.

- If you're going to drive SA's remoter tracks you should have a 50-watt (minimum) high frequency radio with Royal Flying Doctor Service (RFDS) frequencies – and know how to use it.

- Driving on dirt roads creates a whole new set of conditions for your car, so it pays to deflate your tyres a little (by no more than 10psi) to absorb the bumps. Also, if you're driving a big 4WD rig, be sure to pack your load low to avoid excessive weight on tyres and overturning.

- On really remote roads, such as the Birdsville and Strzelecki Tracks, there will be few stops and even fewer passing cars, so you'll need to be well-equipped for breakdowns by carrying spare parts including tyres, radiator hoses and fan belts. A winch is a vital addition to a 4WD in wet weather.

- You'd be mad to head out without a good map. The RAA has the best regional road map. Westprint's *Desert Parks* is good for the parks. The Desert Parks Pass package (p236) includes an indispensable map if you're thinking of taking on the parks.

- Driving at night is particularly dangerous with wildlife often attracted to bright lights, so plan your drives for daylight hours and avoid dusk and dawn when the light isn't good for drivers or wildlife.

For more info, see p273.

# STUART HIGHWAY

The Stuart Hwy was named after the explorer John MacDouall Stuart, whose expeditions in SA and the NT took him through much of the country traversed by the road today. You reach the NT border 930km from Port Augusta, after which it's 294km to Alice Springs.

## WOOMERA

☎ 08 / pop 1000

Established in 1948, Woomera was once the base for tests of experimental British rockets and secret nuclear weapons at nearby sites such as Maralinga and Emu. More recently it was a used as a detention centre for refugees awaiting judgement by the federal government, though this facility was closed in 2003 with detainees moved to Baxter Detention Centre outside Port Augusta (p220). It remains an oddly artificial oasis in the middle of this harsh environment (for contrast look at unattractive **Pimba** just 7km away), nourished as it has been by federal government projects.

The small **Woomera Heritage Centre** (☎ 8673 7042; Dewrang Ave; ◷ 9am-5pm) in the centre of town has several interesting displays on Woomera's past and present roles. Outside is a collection of old military aircraft, rockets and missiles. It also sells coffees and sandwiches in the Outback Diner.

**Olympic Dam Tours** (☎ 8671 0788; www.flinders outback.com/odtours; 4hr tour $45) is the best way to see the controversial missile range with a tour that takes in the town, Koolymilka camp, and the rocket launch site at Lake Hart. Tours may not be available if the range is being used to test weapons.

### Sleeping & Eating

**Woomera Travellers' Village** (☎ 8673 7800; www .woomera.com; Wirruna Ave; unpowered/powered 2 people $16/22, dm $25-30, units $68, cabins $58-68; ☒ ) This friendly place, near the town entrance, has a good range of accommodation with a small extra charge for air-con even in backpacker rooms.

**Eldo Hotel** (☎ 8673 7867; Kotara Ave; s/d $83/100, mains $12-24 ◷ breakfast Mon-Fri, lunch & dinner daily) This hotel has comfortable rooms with shared facilities, and counter meals or restaurant meals off the á la carte menu. This

place once hosted hundreds of workers here for missile research ('Eldo' is the acronym for the European Launcher Development Organisation).

**Spud's Hotel/Motel** (☎ 8673 7473; Stuart Hwy, Pimba; s/d $44/55, meals $10-25; ◷ dinner) In Pimba, this place has basic units.

## WOOMERA TO COOBER PEDY

Just 114km northwest of Pimba with another 253km to go before Coober Pedy, **Glendambo** was created in 1982 as a service centre on the new Stuart Hwy. Fuel is available from 6am to midnight. You can bunk down in the **Glendambo Outback Resort** (☎ 08-8672 1030; s $83-94, d $85-96) which also has bars, a restaurant and 60 motel units each sleeping up to five people. Right next door, the **Woody's BP Roadhouse & Caravan** (☎ 08-8672 1035; unpowered/powered sites per 2 people $14.50/18.50, dm $20) has a basic backpackers bunkhouse which has two beds in each room.

From Glendambo you can take the unsealed road west to fast-fading Kingoonya (43km), then south to the Gawler Ranges and on to the Eyre Peninsula coast. Alternatively, travel west from Kingoonya for another 80km to the old gold-mining centre of **Tarcoola**, where the *Ghan* and *Indian-Pacific* trains part company.

OUTBACK

If you're heading north, there are no petrol stations in between Glendambo and Coober Pedy.

# COOBER PEDY

☎ 08 / pop 2624

Coming into Coober Pedy you'll definitely notice the dry desolate desert suddenly becomes pocked with holes – reputedly more than a million around the township. The reason for all this digging is opals – the 'fire in the stone' that has made this small town a mining mecca.

The lure of the precious stone draws diggers up into this harsh dry landscape where temperatures sizzle right up to 50°C during summer and can drop below zero at night during winter. The town's name reputedly means 'white fellow's hole in the ground', aptly describing a town where more than half the population live in underground dugouts.

The surrounding country is stunningly desolate and dry, making it the perfect locale to shoot 'end of the world' films such as *Mad Max III* and *Stark*. Other location scouts have seen it as another planet, making it the setting for otherworldly movies including *Red Planet* and the sci-fi cult film, *Pitch Black*, which has left its mark on the town (see p243). A more recent Australian film, *Pobby & Dingan*, gives the town an autobiographical role, focusing on the unique characters and people drawn to Coober Pedy. Film crews also shoot beer advertisements or car commercials up here to represent the thirst-quenching or rugged-toughness of products in this harsh desert environment.

Coober Pedy is actually very cosmopolitan, with more than 40 nationalities represented. Greeks, Serbs, Croats and Italians form the largest groups among the miners, while gem buyers are drawn from as far away as Scotland and Hong Kong.

## Orientation

Turning off the Stuart Hwy will put you on Hutchison St, Coober Pedy's main drag which has most of the town's other streets branching off it. Buses stop at the Ampol Roadhouse on Hutchison St. The airport is 2km further along the Stuart Hwy; a shuttle bus ($7) from the airport drops off at the Desert Cave Hotel.

## Information

### BOOKSHOPS

**Underground Books** ( ☎ 8672 5558; Post Office Hill Rd; ☽ 8.30am-5pm Mon-Fri, 10am-4pm Sat) The town's only bookshop has an expansive range and loads of information on the area.

### INTERNET ACCESS

There is no broadband access in Coober Pedy and no dedicated Internet cafés. Radeka's Downunder Dugout Motel & Backpackers (p244) offers Internet access.

### LAUNDRY

**Laundrette** (Hutchison St; ☽ daily) Attached to the real estate agent.

### MEDICAL SERVICES

**Coober Pedy Hospital** ( ☎ 8672 5009; Hospital Rd) Has a 24-hour emergency room.

### MONEY

Banking facilities are limited, though there are several Eftpos cash-withdrawal facilities (including an ATM at the Opal Inn), a Westpac branch with ATM, and a Commonwealth Bank agency in the post office. All are on Hutchison St.

### POST

**Post office** ( ☎ 8672 5062; Hutchison St; ☽ 9am-5pm Mon-Fri)

### TOURIST INFORMATION

**Coober Pedy visitors centre** ( ☎ 1800 637 076; www .opalcapitaloftheworld.com.au; Council offices, Hutchison St; ☽ 9am-5pm Mon-Fri) In the council offices diagonally opposite the Ampol Roadhouse at the entrance to town on Hutchison St. Outside these times, Underground Books is always very helpful.

## Dangers & Annoyances

With several large holes around (usually well-signposted), you'd have to be an absolute idiot to go wandering around outside of the town centre at night. The main street and surrounding streets are fine, but further out there are large mine shafts.

Visitors may also be confronted by beggars, though they are mostly harmless.

Bottled water is an expensive commodity here and you'll need plenty of it to avoid dehydration. For those headed into the outback, it's cheap to refill water bottles at the coin-operated **24-hour water dispenser** (30L for

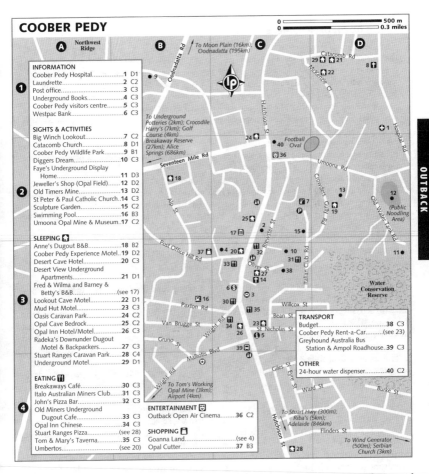

# COOBER PEDY

**INFORMATION**

| | |
|---|---|
| Coober Pedy Hospital.....................**1** | D1 |
| Laundrette........................................**2** | C2 |
| Post office.......................................**3** | C3 |
| Underground Books.........................**4** | C3 |
| Coober Pedy visitors centre.............**5** | C3 |
| Westpac Bank...................................**6** | C3 |

**SIGHTS & ACTIVITIES**

| | |
|---|---|
| Big Winch Lookout...........................**7** | C2 |
| Catacomb Church.............................**8** | D1 |
| Coober Pedy Wildlife Park..............**9** | B1 |
| Diggers Dream.................................**10** | C3 |
| Faye's Underground Display | |
| Home...........................................**11** | D3 |
| Jeweller's Shop (Opal Field)...........**12** | D2 |
| Old Timers Mine.............................**13** | D2 |
| St Peter & Paul Catholic Church......**14** | C3 |
| Sculpture Garden............................**15** | C2 |
| Swimming Pool...............................**16** | B3 |
| Umoona Opal Mine & Museum.......**17** | C2 |

**SLEEPING**

| | |
|---|---|
| Anne's Dugout B&B..........................**18** | B2 |
| Coober Pedy Experience Motel........**19** | D2 |
| Desert Cave Hotel...........................**20** | C3 |
| Desert View Underground | |
| Apartments.................................**21** | D1 |
| Fred & Wilma and Barney & | |
| Betty's B&B.............................(see 17) | |
| Lookout Cave Motel........................**22** | D1 |
| Mud Hut Motel...............................**23** | C3 |
| Oasis Caravan Park.........................**24** | C2 |
| Opal Cave Bedrock.........................**25** | C2 |
| Opal Inn Hotel/Motel.....................**26** | C3 |
| Radeka's Downunder Dugout | |
| Motel & Backpackers..................**27** | C3 |
| Stuart Ranges Caravan Park............**28** | C4 |
| Underground Motel.........................**29** | D1 |

**EATING**

| | |
|---|---|
| Breakaways Café..............................**30** | C3 |
| Italo Australian Miners Club...........**31** | C3 |
| John's Pizza Bar..............................**32** | C3 |
| Old Miners Underground | |
| Dugout Cafe................................**33** | C3 |
| Opal Inn Chinese............................**34** | C3 |
| Stuart Ranges Pizza....................(see 28) | |
| Tom & Mary's Taverna.....................**35** | C3 |
| Umbertos.................................(see 20) | |

**ENTERTAINMENT**

| | |
|---|---|
| Outback Open Air Cinema..........**36** | C2 |

**SHOPPING**

| | |
|---|---|
| Goanna Land.............................(see 4) | |
| Opal Cutter....................................**37** | B3 |

**TRANSPORT**

| | |
|---|---|
| Budget............................................**38** | C3 |
| Coober Pedy Rent-a-Car...........(see 23) | |
| Greyhound Australia Bus | |
| Station & Ampol Roadhouse..**39** | C3 |

**OTHER**

| | |
|---|---|
| 24-hour water dispenser...............**40** | C2 |

---

$0.20) by the **Oasis Caravan Park** ( ☎ 8672 5169; Seventeen Mile Rd).

## Sights
### OPAL MINING

In a town where even the barber cuts hair and opals, everyone is distracted by the appeal of the magnificent stones. Diggings surround Coober Pedy for more than 30km in every direction with most locals having a small fossicking claim.

Unlike all other forms of mining there are no big operators, so every other ute around town will have an automatic hoist mounted on the back. You might also spot the massive tunnelling machines or giant truck-mounted vacuum cleaners known as

'blowers'. Wherever there are columns of white dust rising like smoke above the waste dumps, you'll know that a blower is sucking up earth.

The best place to check out an excavation that is up and running is 1km north of town at **Tom's Working Opal Mine** ( ☎ 1800 196 500; Stuart Hwy; tours adult/child $15/5; ☼ tours 10am, 2.30pm & 4pm), which gives excellent tours detailing what mining equipment does as it continues to search for the big vein. Visitors are encouraged to noodle – or fossick – through the mullock (waste pile) for their fortunes.

Mining in Coober Pedy itself is no longer legal, which means there are several great mines in town to tour. The fascinating **Old Timers Mine** ( ☎ 8672 5555; www.oldtimersmine.com;

**OUTBACK**

---

### LIVING DOWN DEEP UP HERE

Fierce temperatures mean that living and working underground is the way to go. No matter what the mercury is doing outside, the temperature inside remains a steady 23°C. Most locals reckon they don't need air-conditioning because of this year-round cool. It's tough to live up here, though, with water at least four times the price it is in Adelaide and electricity similarly pricey. Some extremely power-conscious retailers even switch lights off when customers leave.

The mining lifestyle has affected almost every aspect of life with most townsfolk having a claim that they'd work at least as a hobby if not as a serious business. Even the most amateurish of claims will be fiercely protected by owners, so trespassing is not a good idea. As few people make their money solely from mining, there's a lot of diversification. This means the bloke who fuels the plane at the airport might also run the bookshop and be working his own little claim on weekends so he can retire from both jobs.

The ready access to explosives has sometimes meant that local spats have become, well, explosive. Locals have become so known for making 'sausages' (homemade bombs, usually used for mining) that an advertisement in the cinema used to reminded them not to bring explosives with them to see films – perhaps they just wanted action movies to be more interactive. Even the odd misguided letter to the editor or editorial has resulted in blowing up the newspaper's office. Though these incidents are rare, some waggish locals may tell you the real reason for living underground is to make their homes better bomb shelters.

---

near Crowders Gully Rd; adult/child $10/5; 9am-5pm), was an early (1916) mine hidden by miners who left several opals still embedded in the stone. The mine was rediscovered when an underground home extended into a labyrinth of tunnels, which make a great tour.

The **Umoona Opal Mine & Museum** is a large complex right in the centre of Coober Pedy, with informative tours of the mine and displays of Aboriginal mythology and traditions, as well as exhibitions about the early mining days.

Outside of town, most of the area is defined as claims which are legally owned by miners and often fiercely defended. Tour operators and friendly locals may invite you out to their claim to noodle, sifting through the mullock for stones. Watch out for shafts that dot the landscape and never wander the fields around at night.

### DUGOUT HOMES

Many of the early dugout homes were simply worked-out mines, but these days they are often cut specifically as residences. No-one's sure whether the homes were originally built for temperature (subterranean temperatures hover between 20-25°C no matter what the mercury is doing outside) or due to lack of building materials in this treeless environment.

Today many residents open their homes to visitors. Chintzy, but endearing **Faye's**

**Underground Display Home** ( ☎ 8672 5029; Jeweller Shop Rd; admission $4; 9am-5pm Mon-Sat) was originally the postman's residence until three women renovated and expanded it by hand. It features a fantastic bottle collection (especially the plasma port) and – a must-have for every home – a living-room swimming pool. **Digger's Dream** ( ☎ 8672 5442; Nayler Pl; admission $4; sunrise-sunset) is more modern if a little characterless. An old-school character resides at **Crocodile Harry's** ( ☎ 8672 5872; Seventeen Mile Rd; admission $2; 9am-6pm), known for its large collection of women's underwear on the roof and Harry's strange sculpture. Some readers have found it sleazy, others sad, but this quirky dugout has featured in the movies *Mad Max III* and *Ground Zero*, and the miniseries *Stark*.

### UNDERGROUND CHURCHES

If you're going to live underground then you may as well worship underground. You can visit most of Coober Pedy's five **underground churches**, but as these are functioning churches you should be sensitive to services and worshippers. While the churches are ostensibly free, a donation seems only fair with many having an honesty box near the entrance. The **Serbian Church** (off Stuart Hwy; 11am-6pm) is the largest and most spectacular, but you can only visit this building on a guided tour. The **Catacomb Church** (Catacomb Rd) has a bush austerity, summed up by its stick cross and natural furnishings. The **St Peter & Paul Catholic Church** (Oliver St) was the first church in Coober Pedy and still has a sweet appeal.

**OTHER ATTRACTIONS**

The action isn't all underground in Coober Pedy. To get close to the fauna, head for the **Coober Pedy Wildlife Park** ( ☎ 8672 5405; Tom Cat Hill Rd; admission by gold coin donation; ☺ sunrise-sunset) which has euros, kangaroos and lizards, many so used to humans they can be held. Most of these animals are abandoned pets or rescued animals so it would be cruel to tease the one-eared rabbits.

You can't miss the **Big Winch**, which is also a prominent lookout over the town. Here you find the sculpture of a tree made from the remains of a burnt-out truck; it's reputedly the first 'tree' in town. Further south there's a **sculpture garden** (admission by donation) that incorporates technology into some bizarre art and some leftover props from *Pitch Black*.

Finally, there is the strangeness of the **golf course**, which features bitumen 'greens' and dustbowl fairways.

## Tours

There are heaps of tour options that can take you around town or further afield to the majestic Breakaways (p246) or distant stations.

Most accommodation places offer a tour of the town that can be booked with them. Definitely the most convenient is **Desert Cave Tours** ( ☎ 8672 5688; 4hr tour adult/child $52/26) which takes in town attractions and a few further out such as the Dog Fence and Moon Plain, and leaves from the reception of the Desert Cave Hotel. **Stuart Range Tours** ( ☎ 8672 5179, 0418-890 736; 2hr tour adult/child $30/15, 4hr tour adult/child $40/20) has a more budget-conscious option that takes in a similar range of sights. **Radeka's Downunder Dugout Motel & Backpackers** ( ☎ 8672 5223; 4-5hr tour adult/child $40/20) has a wandering tour that includes Crocodile Harry's, Catacomb Church, the desert golf course and a little fossicking in Radeka's claim. **Oasis Tours** ( ☎ 8672 5169; 3hr tour adult/child $30/15) does a good budget tour taking in the major in-town sights plus a spot of fossicking and (in the afternoon only) a Devonshire tea. **Riba's Evening Mine Tour** ( ☎ 8672 5614; 1½hr tour adult/child $16/8) is an informative wander through this mine/camping area

that lets you play with divining rods and see embedded opals.

Clear outback skies lend **Martin's Night Sky Tour** ( ☎ 8672 5223; 1¼hr tour adult/child $22/11) a good backdrop for stargazing, and the tour gets rave reviews from readers who've enjoyed the nightly trips out to Moon Plain. If you're after an in-car guide **Opal Cave Tag-Along Tours** ( ☎ 8672 5028; 1hr tour adult $15-20) can provide a knowledgeable companion or for an extra $10 you can borrow their vehicle.

Venturing further out, the **Outback Mail Run** ( ☎ 1800 069 911, 8672 5226; www.desertdiversity.com; 12hr/9hr tours $125/$145-155) delivers the mail to outlying areas like Oodnadatta and William Creek (with several stops in between) on an exhaustive bash through the bush that leaves 9am Monday to Thursday. Under the name Desert Diversity, this group also offers nine-hour tours out to Lake Eyre and the Painted Desert (Saturday only). This colourful sandscape is as harsh as it is beautiful, so a tour is ideal for exploring it. For a more indepth exploration of the desert, try the **Painted Desert Mail Run** ( ☎ 8670 7991; 24hr tour $200-375) with spectacular looks at the Painted Desert and insights into life at isolated cattle stations, especially Evelyn Downs Station where you can stay overnight.

To see it all from camelback (or by 4WD if you prefer), **Explore the Outback** ( ☎ 1800 064 244, 8672 3968; www.austcamel.com.au/explore.htm; 4-day trek $1025) does specialised conservation-based tours of the desert.

To get the big picture, **Wrightsair** ( ☎ 8670 7962, 8670 6080; www.wrightsair.com.au; 1hr/2hr flight $135/260) takes you on a stunning tour over Lake Eyre, the vast waterland that is the breeding ground for pelicans. **Opal Air** ( ☎ 8672 3067, 0427-304 599; Breakaways $65, Lake Eyre $390) does a variety of tours from a short town hop to the extensive spanning of Lake Eyre.

## Sleeping

Bunking down in Coober Pedy gives you the unique opportunity to sleep underground in dugout accommodation, from hand-carved homes to machine-bored hotels. Underground places generally don't need air-con, because the temperatures are around 20-25°C year round. The downside is that there is a dearth of cheap options, with most motel rooms costing more than you'd pay in other towns.

### BUDGET

**Radeka's Downunder Dugout Motel & Backpackers** ( ☎ 1800 633 891, 8672 5223; Hutchison St; dm $22, d & tw $55, motel units $99; 🅿 🖳 ) At this underground complex, you'll find some of the best budget beds in town – bunks in open alcoves, as well as good individual rooms and motel units. The shared kitchen is handy for self-caterers as are other facilities such as bar, barbecue, restaurant, games room and laundry. Staff are very helpful and will do drop-off/pick-ups from the airport.

**Riba's** ( ☎ 8672 5614; William Creek Rd; underground/ above-ground camping per 2 people $7.50/11, powered sites per 2 people $18, tour free with accommodation or $16) Just 5km from town on the William Creek Rd, Riba's has the unique option of underground camping or above ground (for traditionalists). There are cool underground extras such as a TV lounge, free showers and an interesting one-hour evening tour (which is included in the cost of camping).

**Opal Cave Bedrock** ( ☎ 8672 5028; Hutchison St; dm $17.50) This offshoot of the Umoona Opal Mine (see them to check-in) has four-bed alcoves opening from a wide central passageway with curtains for privacy. Toilets and showers are located in another area, but there is a kitchen and TV room in the main cave. A bonus for sci-fi fans is a huge abandoned spaceship out the front, not from previous alien guests, but another prop from the movie *Pitch Black*.

**Oasis Caravan Park** ( ☎ 8672 5169; Seventeen Mile Rd; unpowered/powered sites per 2 people $19/23, on-site vans $32, r $34, cabins $70-89) Reasonably central to the action, this place has the best shade and shelter, as well as an undercover swimming pool in a big old storage tank.

**Stuart Ranges Caravan Park** ( ☎ 8672 5179; Hutchison St; unpowered/powered per 2 people $16/20, d $50-60) The first park as you're coming off the Stuart Hwy, this place is the largest in town with good facilities, including big shaded areas, a good park for frolicking kids and a well-regarded pizza kitchen (opposite).

### MID-RANGE

**Mud Hut Motel** ( ☎ 1800 646 962, 8672 3003; St Nicholas St; s/d/units $90/105/145; 🅿 ) The rustic looking walls are actually packed earth and despite the grubby name this is one of the cleanest places in town. Units are well tricked-out with cooktops, large fridges and silent air-conditioning.

**Coober Pedy Experience Motel** ( ☎ 8672 5777; www.cooberpedyexperience.com.au; Crowders Gully Rd; dm/d $24/126) Another buried treasure, this subterranean place is the largest motel in Coober Pedy yet maintains it homey feel. Attached to next-door's Revival Church, its wholesomeness pervades this place – even their bottleshop is a display the of discarded bottles of boozy miners.

**Opal Inn Hotel/Motel** ( ☎ 8672 5054; Hutchison St; unpowered/powered sites per 2 people $20/25, hotel s/d $60/70, motel s $73-103, d $80-110; 🅿 🖳 ) A diverse venue like the Opal Inn is a jack of all trades with basic, smoky pub rooms with TVs and fridges; more sophisticated motel rooms with kitchens; and a caravan park that can be cramped. Regardless of where you're staying in the Opal Inn, they have an excellent information pack presented on check-in.

**Fred & Wilma's and Barney & Betty's B&B** ( ☎ 8672 5028; Hutchison St; d $110) You can book these cute Flintstones-inspired places through the Umoona Opal Mine & Museum. Fred & Wilma's is underground, while Barney & Betty's is above ground, but both places come with full kitchens, fold-out beds and continental breakfasts.

Also recommended:

**Underground Motel** ( ☎ 1800 622 979, 8672 5324; Catacomb Rd; s $80-90, d $100-110) Choose between standard and suites (includes separate lounge and kitchen) at this pleasant spot with a great panorama towards the Breakaways.

**Desert View Underground Apartments** ( ☎ 8672 3330; Shaw Pl; s/d $70/80) This homey venue has natural

---

### THE AUTHOR'S CHOICE

**Anne's Dugout B&B** ( ☎ 08-8672 5541; www .annesdugoutbandb.com; Koska St; d/f $80/110) If you want to really feel like you're living in a dugout, then Anne's is definitely the go. Rooms include a hefty cooked breakfast (with Anne's homemade quandong jam) and a shared bathroom. The main bedroom has a shaft extending up where an original mine was sunk and are relics (newspapers and picks) retrieved from the mine that was dug in the 1960s. Anne herself is a delightfully well-informed resident and member of the local historical society so she can give you lots of interesting historical titbits. It even features a good garden, by Coober Pedy's barren standards.

light in the front, full kitchens and videos, but is a little far from town.

**Lookout Cave Motel** ( ☎ 8672 5118; McKenzie Cl; s/d/tw $82/102/95) There's an impressive lookout up top and rooms are smallish with overhead fans.

**TOP END**

**Desert Cave Hotel** ( ☎ 8672 5688; www.desertcave.com .au; Hutchison St; d $187; 🍴 🖥 ) Fancy oasis-style luxury? With a pool, gym, in-house movies, formidable minibar and great restaurant, Umberto's (below), this underground palace won't disappoint. Staff are well-informed and there are plenty of tours that leave right from reception.

## Eating

With over 40 nationalities in town, food is relatively cosmopolitan for an outback town, but shipping pushes prices up.

**Umberto's** ( ☎ 08-8672 5688; Hutchison St; mains $22-28; 🍴 dinner) The Desert Cave Hotel's in-house restaurant maintains the quality with first-class dishes such as grilled barramundi with *beurre blanc* sauce or kangaroo served in a juniper *jus*. Service is swift and friendly in the town's best eating spot.

**Tom & Mary's Taverna** ( ☎ 8672 5622; Hutchison St; meals $6-15; 🍴 lunch & dinner) This popular Greek tavern does everything from yiros to hearty Greek salads to pastas with traditional Hellenic flair. The décor is distinctly lo-fi: faux wood panelling and vinyl chairs.

**Italo Australian Miners Club** (Italian Club; ☎ 8672 5101; Italian Club Rd; mains with salad bar $9; 🍴 dinner Wed-Sat) This local institution attracts drinkers most nights, but meals (steak, schnitzels and damn fine pastas) make an appetising appearance from Wednesday to Saturday nights with regular specials (expect the ubiquitous steaks and schnitzels to figure strongly).

**Old Miners Underground Dugout Cafe** ( ☎ 8672 3552; 335 Trow St; lunch $6-17, dinner $10-24; 🍴 lunch & dinner Mon-Sat) You pay a little extra for the underground ambience, but the menu here is internationally imaginative with sausages and sauerkraut or drunken snapper all making for some good eating.

**Opal Inn Chinese** ( ☎ 8672 5430; Wright Rd; mains $10-15.50; 🍴 lunch & dinner) For a small Chinese place attached to the Opal Inn, this joint really packs locals in with all-you-can-eat on Thursday and Friday nights.

Also recommended:

**Stuart Ranges Pizza** ( ☎ 8672 5179; Hutchison St; pizzas $7-20; 🍴 dinner) To feed a family, this caravan-park kitchen makes a mean pizza that locals love.

**John's Pizza Bar** ( ☎ 8672 5561; Hutchison St; mains $8-16; 🍴 10am-10pm) Serving up huge pizzas, good pastas and heat-beating gelato, it's hard to go past John's for a quick, easy meal.

**Breakaways Café** ( ☎ 8672 3177; cnr Wright Rd & Hutchison St; meals $5-9; 🍴 7am-7pm) A friendly and popular café serving value-packed cooked breakfasts, burgers, and specials such as schnitzel with salad ($7.50).

## Drinking

There's no excuse for dehydration with plenty of watering holes around town. The **Opal Inn Hotel/Motel** ( ☎ 8672 5054; Hutchison St) is the most reliable pub, while the **Italo Australian Miners Club** (Italian Club; ☎ 8672 5101; Italian Club Rd) is also a good place for a couple of beers. The most salubrious spot for a drink is the **Desert Cave Hotel** ( ☎ 8672 5688; Hutchison St), which has a good wine list.

## Entertainment

The best place for updates on what's happening in town is the *Coober Pedy Regional Times*, which can tell you when bands are playing. You can catch all the newest releases at the **Outback Open Air Cinema** (Hutchison St; per car or walk-in $12; 🍴 from 7pm Sat), which is a volunteer-run drive-in, although walk-ins are welcome. Thursday night sees a disco/dress-up night at the Italian Club (check the club noticeboard to avoid dressing up when you'll be needing your disco-pants). On Friday nights the Desert Cave Hotel has a video jukebox that pumps out a variety of hits.

## Shopping

There are numerous reputable – and some not so reputable – opal outlets in town. It's best to shop around and be wary of anyone offering too-good-to-be-true discounts (as they usually are). Some of the best buys are found at the **Opal Cutter** ( ☎ 8672 3086; Post Office Hill Rd), but you should definitely compare a few prices around town before purchasing.

For less opal-like souvenirs, **Goanna Land** ( ☎ 8672 5965; Post Office Hill Rd) produces unique silk-screen designs which feature Australian fauna and craft from around the region. Worth heading out of town for, **Underground Potteries** ( ☎ 8672 5226; Rowe St; 🍴 8.30am-6pm) has impressive ceramic and clay creations;

OUTBACK

plus the friendly potters will let you watch them at work.

## Getting Around
You can rent cars – including 4WDs and camping vehicles – from **Budget** ( ☎ 8672 5333; cpdbudget@ozemail.com.au; Oliver St) and **Coober Pedy Rent-a-Car** ( ☎ 8672 3003; Mud Hut Motel, St Nicholson St). Budget offers convenient one-way rentals, although you'll pay an additional rate over 100km.

**Opal Cave Bedrock** ( ☎ 8672 5028; www.opalcave coober pedy.com; Hutchison St) rents out mountain bikes for $12 a day.

## AROUND COOBER PEDY
The **Breakaways Reserve** is a stark but colourful area of arid hills and scarps about 33km away on a rough road north of Coober Pedy – you turn off the highway 22km from town. You can drive to a lookout in a conventional vehicle and see the white-and-yellow mesa known as the **Castle**, which featured in the films *Mad Max III* and *Priscilla, Queen of the Desert*. Entry permits ($2 per person) are available at the visitors centre or Underground Books in Coober Pedy or at the self-registration station. Late afternoon is the best time for photographs.

An interesting loop of 70km on mainly unsealed road from Coober Pedy takes in the Breakaways, the **Dog Fence** and the tablelike **Moon Plain** on the Coober Pedy–Oodnadatta Rd. You can get a free leaflet about this from the visitors centre.

## NORTH TO THE NORTHERN TERRITORY
On the Stuart Hwy 82km south of Marla and 151km north of Coober Pedy, **Cadney Homestead Roadhouse** ( ☎ 08-8670 7994; www.cad neyhomestead.com.au/default.htm; powered sites per 2 people $20, d $96.50, cabins $33) has caravan sites, serviceable motel rooms and basic (no linen) cabins. They can also organise tours of the Painted Desert.

In mulga scrub about 82km on from Cadney Homestead, **Marla** replaced Oodnadatta as the official regional centre when the Ghan railway line was rerouted in 1980. Fuel and provisions are available here 24-hours a day; there's also an Eftpos cash-withdrawal facility. **Marla Travellers Rest** ( ☎ 08-8670 7001; unpowered/powered sites per 2 people $10/17, cabins s/d $30/40, motel d $75-85) has a good range of rooms with motel rooms that are cheaper with no

---

**DETOUR: PAINTED DESERT**

If you're heading for Oodnadatta and you can handle rough roads, turn off the Stuart Hwy at Cadney for a shorter run (172km) on dirt roads, rather than going via Marla (209km) or Coober Pedy (193km). As a bonus, you travel through the spectacular Painted Desert en route.

There are basic huts and bush camping at **Copper Hills Tourist Park** ( ☎ 08-8670 7995; unpowered & powered sites per 2 people $6, dm $12, d huts $25-35), about 32km east of the roadhouse. Alternatively you can stay on a working cattle property at **Evelyn Downs Station** ( ☎ 08-8670 7991; www.senet.com.au /~apttours; s/f $50/99, 1-day tour $99) with a tour that includes the desert. To get to Evelyn Downs Station, turn right about 10kms after Copper Hills. About 50km after the Cadney turn-off is **Ackaringa Station** ( ☎ 08-8670 7992; unpowered sites per 2 people $5, cabins $30-45) with basic cabins within 10-minutes' drive of the Painted Desert itself.

---

TV and phone. The **café** (mains $6-10; ☺ breakfast, lunch & dinner) does basic meals, or there's a supermarket for self-caterers.

The frontier-style **Mintabie** opal field is on Aboriginal land 35km to the west of Marla. It has a general store, restaurant and caravan park.

From Marla, the NT border is still another 180km, with a fuel stop not far over the border.

# OUTBACK TRACKS

The Birdsville, Oodnadatta and Strzelecki tracks are minor, unsealed routes which are tracks in name only these days – unless, of course, it rains. Their loneliness and the fact that they cross some of Australia's most inhospitable country draws adventurous travellers keen to get some red dust on their 4WDs. When conditions are good, you can get by with a sturdy conventional vehicle with good ground clearance. Conditions can be difficult for even the most experienced drivers, so prepare well (see p238).

Marree is the gateway to both the Birdsville and Oodnadatta tracks, though you could take Oodnadatta track south from

Marla and head back to Port Augusta via Marree, Lyndhurst and the Flinders Ranges. The Birdsville Track extends all the way up through the Sturt Stony Desert, ending just over the Qld border in (unsurprisingly) Birdsville.

Lyndhurst is the beginning of the Strzelecki Track, which weaves its way north to Moomba and Innamincka.

All these tracks are comprehensively covered in Lonely Planet's *Outback Australia*. They are summarised only briefly in this travel guide.

## MARREE
☎ 08 / pop 80
It's hard to believe sleepy Marree was once a vital hub for camel teams and the Great Northern Railway (which closed in 1980). Signs of the town's former prosperity remain, like the grand two-storey **Marree Hotel**, built in the 1880s, or the expansive railway complex. Date palms, a mud-brick mosque and a large squatting camel sundial (made entirely from railway sleepers) recall the Afghan camel teams of yesteryear.

Reminders of indigenous history are at the **Arabunna People's Community Centre and Museum** ( ☎ 8675 8351; admission by donation; 8am-5pm Mon-Fri), which includes an informative video and several cultural displays.

Today, the town has modern travellers' facilities including a small hospital, fuel station, small supermarket and post office. The whole town goes wild for the **Marree Australian Camel Cup**, held on the first Saturday in July.

For a worthwhile day trip, the Muloorina **scenic drive** takes you to Lake Eyre and a beautiful deep waterhole in Frome River, where there's bush camping, $2 per vehicle, paid into an honesty box. **Muloorina Station** ( ☎ 8675 8341; dm $35) also offer accommodation in their shearing quarters from April to October for groups of six or more. You can grab a mud map (a rough map that is usually hand drawn) of the drive at Oasis Cafe in Marree.

Also at the Oasis Cafe, you can book **scenic flights** ( ☎ 8675 8352; 1hr flights $170) over Lake Eyre and **Marree Man**, the 4km-long outline of an Aboriginal warrior etched into the desert sands near Lake Eyre, which is beginning to wash away. One of the best land-based tours of the area is **Reg Dodd's**

**Arabunna Tours** ( ☎ 8675 8351; 1-day $90), which are tailored to individual visitors, but usually take in Lake Eyre and the Aboriginal history of the area, with a barbecue lunch thrown in.

In town, the **Oasis Caravan Park** (Oasis Cafe ☎ 8675 8352; unpowered/powered sites per 2 people $12/15, s/d $37/55; ) has several good campsites as well as motel-style rooms with TVs and fridges. The somewhat dustier **Marree Drovers Rest Caravan & Campers Park** ( ☎ 8675 8371; unpowered/powered sites per 2 people $16/20; on-site vans no linen $30, budget rooms $20, cabins d/f $80/100) is at the start of the Birdsville Track about 1km south of town. There's a campers' kitchen, and the park sells fuel and tyres (as well as repairing them).

Alternatively, **Marree Hotel** ( ☎ 8675 8344; Railway Tce South; s/d $50/70; ) has good rooms and can also organise flights out to Marree Man.

## OODNADATTA TRACK
Stretched 615km from Marree to Marla, the Oodnadatta Track is the historic and more rugged alternative to the Stuart Hwy. From Marree and Oodnadatta, the road traces the route of the old Overland Telegraph Line and the Great Northern Railway, taking in ruins of fettlers' huts (fettlers were stationed at sections of railway line to maintain tracks and sleepers), railway sidings and telegraph stations evoking its pioneering heritage. Lake Eyre (the world's sixth largest lake) is just off the route and scattered along the way are small oases watered by mound springs that are natural outlets for the Great Artesian Basin.

If you're finding the unsealed road hard going, there are several routes across to the bitumen Stuart Hwy, including from William Creek to Coober Pedy, or Oodnadatta to Coober Pedy.

Fuel, accommodation and meals are all available at Marree, William Creek (204km from Marree), Oodnadatta (406km) and Marla.

Just 60km from Marree, the old township of Alberrie Creek has become a monumental sculpture park known as **Mutonia** (admission by donation), featuring a gate made from a Kombi van cut in half and several planes welded together with their tails buried in the ground to form 'planehenge'. It's a truly strange site in the middle of nowhere.

Some 130km from Marree, **Coward Springs Camp Ground** ( ☎ 08-8675 8336; www.cowardsprings .com.au; unpowered sites per 2 people $14) is the first stop at the old Coward Springs railway siding. A natural hot spring is a good spot to soak weary muscles in a tub made from old rail sleepers. You can do **camel rides** or a full five-day camel trek to Lake Eyre from here. A few kilometres back down the road towards Marree, the **Wamba Kadurba Conservation Park** includes artesian mound springs such as the Bubbler and Blanche Cup.

In another 70km you'll hit William Creek, best enjoyed in the heritage-listed **William Creek Hotel** ( ☎ 8670 7880; www.williamcreek hotel.net.au; unpowered sites per 2 people $7, units d $60, dm $14, main $8-14; ☒ ), which has a dry camping ground, modest motel rooms (euphemistically called a 'box') with air-con and a bunkhouse. It also sells fuel, cold beer, basic provisions and meals, and stocks spare tyres.

If you just need to pitch a tent or stock up on supplies, head for the **William Creek Store & Campground** ( ☎ 08-8670 7746; www.williamcreek campground.com; unpowered/powered sites per 2 people $15/20, s $40, tw & d $49; ☼ Mar-Nov), which also has basic huts.

Operating about 100km north of William Creek, **Explore the Outback camel safaris** ( ☎ 08-8672 3968; www.austcamel.com.au/explore.htm; 4-day trek $1025) give you the chance to hitch a camel ride with a research team exploring the Denison Ranges and further afield.

## OODNADATTA
☎ 08 / pop 200
This small outpost is situated at the point where the main road and the old railway line diverged. The heart of the town today is the **Pink Roadhouse** ( ☎ 1800 802 074, 8670 7822; www.pinkroadhouse.com.au; Main St; ☼ 8am-5.30pm), an excellent source of travel information on track conditions, plus they serve meals. Owners Adam and Lynnie Plate installed road signs and kilometre pegs all over the district – even in the inhospitable Simpson Desert. Their mud maps are authoritative and can be found on their colourful website. They also run the attached **Adam & Lynnie's Oodnadatta Caravan Park** ( ☎ 8670 7822; www.pinkroadhouse.com.au; Main St; unpowered sites per 2 people $15, on-site vans $28, s/d/cabins $38/48/80; ☒ ) which has basic camping through to self-contained cabins.

Alternatively, there's the **Transcontinental Hotel** ( ☎ 8670 7804; webeze.au/oodnadatta/; Main St; s/d/tw $40/65/70; ☒ ), which has reasonably good pub rooms. The old train station (by far the most impressive building in town) has been converted into an interesting little **museum**. The pub and roadhouse both have keys to the museum.

From Oodnadatta you can head northwest to Marla (209km) or north to the 771,000 hectare **Witjira National Park** (below), on the western fringes of the Simpson Desert.

## BIRDSVILLE TRACK
From the early 1880s, huge mobs of cattle from southwest Qld were herded along the

---

### DETOUR: WITJIRA NATIONAL PARK & MT DARE

About 17km out of Oodnadatta on the Oodnadatta Track, turn north towards Hamilton, which is about another 100km along. From Hamilton, turn right onto an even rougher road that goes the 60km into **Witjira National Park** ( ☎ 08-8670 7901; admission per car $20) and **Dalhousie Springs**. In a barren area of dunes and often dry floodplain, this large group of artesian springs is the only permanent surface water, attracting waterbirds and raptors (birds of prey). You can **camp** ( ☎ 08-8670 7901; per vehicle $20) here by prior arrangement with the ranger. The park is jointly managed by the Irrwanyere Aboriginal Corporation, so rangers are well-informed Aboriginals who conduct guided cultural walks of the springs area.

Further into the park, **Mt Dare Hotel** ( ☎ 08-8670 7835; www.mtdare.com.au; unpowered site per 2 people $12, s/d $35/70) provides the last place for fuel if you're going further out. It has basic rooms in the old homestead and a camping ground – book ahead if you want a room or casual meals.

If you want to be even more daring there's the **Rig Rd** (4WD only) across the Simpson Desert connecting Mt Dare Homestead to Birdsville. Alternatively, take the **Old Andao Track** (also 4WD only) from Mt Dare to Alice Springs via Old Andado Homestead.

A 4WD is recommended on the roads into Witjira, but you should definitely call Mt Dare Hotel or the rangers to get advice on road conditions.

---

**DETOUR: THE INNER TRACK**

Just after **Clifton Hills**, about 200km south of Birdsville, there is an option to north on the **Inner Track**. The roughly 130km route is suitable only for 4WD vehicles as it crosses Goyder Lagoon, a vast seasonal swamp that makes for intrepid driving. When it's wet, the track is impassable, so be sure to check conditions before heading out.

---

520km Birdsville Track to Marree, where they were loaded onto trains to Adelaide. While motor transport put the drovers out of a job in the 1960s, Australians still romanticise this epic overland journey.

The Birdsville Track takes in some of the nation's harshest and driest land as the route weaves between the western sand dunes of the Simpson Desert to the west and desolate gibber wastes of the Sturt Stony Desert to the east. Despite the apparent desolation, you'll pass scattered homesteads and austere ruins, while artesian bores gush boiling-hot, sulphurous water at several points.

Despite these bores, water is extremely scarce on the track and you should carry sufficient to survive in the event of a breakdown. Traffic is light on the track particularly in summer when days can go by without a vehicle passing, so ensure your vehicle is in good repair and plan on taking a UHF/HF radio or satellite phone (there is definitely no mobile phone coverage).

The only refuelling stop is 205km north of Marree (315km to Birdsville) at **Mungeranie Hotel** ( ☎ 08-8675 8317; s/d $45/70; ☺ 8am-8pm), which offers camping, decent rooms, mechanical repairs, meals and a hot-spring pool to soak away road weariness.

**Birdsville**, just across the Qld border, has an excellent range of facilities, including a police station, small hospital, hotel, vehicle repairs, caravan park and general store.

## STRZELECKI TRACK

The Strzelecki Track spans 460km from Lyndhurst to the tiny outpost of Innamincka, meandering through the sand hills of the Strzelecki Desert. Discovery of oil and gas at **Moomba** saw the upgrading of the road from a camel track to a decent dirt road, though heavy transport travelling the road makes for bone-rattling corrugation.

Accommodation, provisions and fuel are available at Lyndhurst and Innamincka, but there's nothing between.

Hunkering in the low, barren hills at the southern end of the Strzelecki Track, **Lyndhurst** marks the end of the bitumen, 300km north of Port Augusta. You can get fuel and meals at the **Lyndhurst Roadhouse** ( ☎ 08-8675 7782; main $6-10; ☺ 7am-9pm). **Elsewhere Hotel, Motel & Caravan Park** ( ☎ 08-8675 7781; unpowered/powered sites per 2 people $10/15, s/d $40/60, meals $9-16; ☺ lunch & dinner) has basic rooms and does the standard counter meals (mixed grills, steaks etc). Approximately 1km along the track is the eccentric home and workshop of Cornelius Alferink, otherwise known as Talc Alf, producer of abstract carvings from local talc.

The track skirts the northern Flinders Ranges, crossing the **Dog Fence**, and eventually coming to the ruins of **Blanchewater Homestead** on MacDonnell Creek (157km from Lyndhurst). Established in 1857, it was once the largest Australian horse-breeding enterprise, but was abandoned after flooding devastated the homestead in 1940. The station is associated with the notorious cattle duffer (thief) Harry Redford, who trailblazed the track to smuggle a stolen mob of cattle from Qld in 1870.

The Moomba–Strzelecki Track is better kept, but longer and duller than the old track, which follows Strzelecki Creek. The mining town of Moomba, run by the Santos Corporation, is a closed town, where travellers cannot buy fuel or supplies.

## INNAMINCKA
☎ 08 / pop 10

At the northern extreme of the Strzelecki Track, Innamincka is on Cooper Creek close to where the ill-fated Burke and Wills expedition of 1860 came to its tragic end. The famous **Dig Tree** marks the expedition's base camp and although the word 'dig' is no longer visible, the expedition's camp number is still visible. The Dig Tree is over the Qld border, though memorials and markers – commemorating where Burke and Wills died, and where sole-survivor King was found – are downstream in SA. There is also a memorial where Howitt's rescue party made their base on the creek.

Cooper Creek flows only rarely – it takes big rains in centralwest Qld to bring

**OUTBACK**

---

**THE DOG FENCE** *George Dunford & Denis O'Byrne*

Erected as a barrier against sheep-killing dingoes, the Dog Fence stretches for thousands of kilometres across southeastern Australia, from the Nullarbor cliffs on the Great Australian Bight to Jimbour, in southeast Qld. Originally a whopping 8614km long, it was shortened to around 5500km in 1980.

Made of wire-netting and reaching 1.8m high, the fence meanders for 2250km across SA – you pass through it on the Eyre Hwy near Yalata, on the Stuart Hwy north of Coober Pedy and on the Oodnadatta and Birdsville Tracks.

Maintenance is an ongoing headache. The job is shared by individual landholders and the state government, which spends $500,000 on upkeep each year. Parts of the fence are more than 100 years old and in need of replacement, while even the newest sections are under constant assault from emus, kangaroos, livestock, floods and shifting sand.

A stretch of this fence recently had a star turn in the Phillip Noyce film, *Rabbit Proof Fence*. Set in Western Australia (WA), the film tells of two Aboriginal girls who were stolen from their families for domestic service. In the film the girls try to find their way home by following WA's stretch of fence, but in real life the crew set up at the Dog Fence in SA as this stretch of wire was thought to be more photogenic.

The film's release in 2002 has meant that many Australians have come to look at the Dog Fence as a symbol of racial division rather than an agricultural necessity.

---

it down in flood – but has deep, permanent waterholes and the semipermanent **Coongie Lakes**. These lakes are significant habitats for aquatic fauna and water birds, a major reason for founding the surrounding **Innamincka Regional Reserve**. Prior to European settlement, the area had a large Aboriginal population, so relics such as middens and grinding stones can be seen around the area.

The former **Australian Inland Mission Hospital** now houses the **DEH ranger's office** ( ☎ 8675 9909; ⏰ 8am-6pm), and also has displays on Innamincka Regional Reserve.

You can take 2WD vehicles over the unsealed road to Birdsville via **Cordillo Downs Homestead**. Originally constructed in 1883, the station's huge stone shearing shed, which had stands for 120 shearers, is an outstanding pastoral relic.

### Sleeping & Eating

**Innamincka Hotel** ( ☎ 8675 9901; fax 8675 9961; dm/s/d/tr $30/50/70/90, mains $15-24; ⏰ dinner; 🖳 ) There are good motel-style rooms in this old-style hotel as well as the basic bunkhouse for the

budget conscious. They serve takeaway and hefty counter meals – its Wednesday night bush barbecues and Sunday night roasts ($18) are a real treat for bigger bellies. They also have canoes and dinghies for hire and can give you some fishing tips.

**Innamincka Trading Post** ( ☎ 8675 9900; fax 8675 9920; s/d/tr $45/70/100; 🖳 ) There are three two-bedroom cabins sleeping up to four with bathrooms, and a barbecue. Fuel and provisions are also available here.

**Cooper Creek Homestay** ( ☎ 8675 9591; fourmat thews@bigpond.com.au; s/d $60/80; 🖳 ) About 400m from Cooper Creek, this friendly family offers rooms in a private home. All meals are available including the outdoor evening meal ($30), a three-course feast cooked over an open fire and eaten under the stars.

There are plenty of shady places to camp among the coolabahs along the **Cooper Creek** system – see the ranger or Innamincka Trading Post about a permit ($20 per vehicle per night), though facilities are extremely basic here. You can also camp on the **town common** for $5 per car per night, with fees paid into an honesty box.

# Directory

## CONTENTS

| | |
|---|---|
| Accommodation | 251 |
| Business Hours | 253 |
| Children | 253 |
| Climate | 254 |
| Customs & Quarantine | 255 |
| Dangers & Annoyances | 255 |
| Disabled Travellers | 256 |
| Discount Cards | 257 |
| Embassies & Consulates | 257 |
| Festivals & Events | 258 |
| Gay & Lesbian Travellers | 259 |
| Holidays | 259 |
| Insurance | 259 |
| Internet Access | 259 |
| Legal Matters | 260 |
| Maps | 260 |
| Money | 260 |
| Post | 262 |
| Telephone | 262 |
| Time | 263 |
| Tourist Information | 263 |
| Visas | 263 |
| Women Travellers | 264 |

### PRACTICALITIES

- Plugs have angled pins; the electricity supply is 220–240V AC, 50Hz.

- The *Advertiser*, Adelaide's daily, offers light reading with local-interest stories. The *Age*, *Sydney Morning Herald* and *Australian* newspapers are widely available.

- On TV, you'll find the government-sponsored ABC, the multicultural SBS, Imparja (an Aboriginal-owned station), and the three major commercial stations: Seven, Nine and Ten.

- Televisions (including videos and DVDs) use the PAL system; Australian DVDs are encoded as Region 4.

- The metric system is used for weights and measures. See the Quick Reference (inside front cover) for conversion information.

## ACCOMMODATION

South Australia (SA) has the full gamut of lodgings, from tent-pegged of camping grounds and the communal space of hostels to standard hotels and motels, gourmet B&Bs and everything-at-your-fingertip resorts.

Listings in the Sleeping sections of this guidebook are ordered from budget to mid-range to top-end options. Places that charge up to $40/80 per single/double are categorised as budget accommodation. Mid-range prices are from $80 to $140 per double, and top end is anything above this.

In most areas you'll find seasonal price variations. During summer and at other peak times, particularly school and public holidays, prices generally peak, whereas outside these times useful discounts and lower walk-in rates can be found. In peak holiday periods and during special events, it's advisable to book accommodation in advance.

### B&Bs

Many people opt for the atmosphere and privacy of B&Bs, which include everything from restored stone cottages and converted boat sheds to upmarket country houses, romantic escapes and simple bedrooms in family homes. The majority of B&Bs are 'self-catering' –that is, the breakfast provisions are provided for you to cook. Rates are typically in the $100 to $150 range, though they can climb much higher. Some are listed in this book, otherwise check with local visitors centres.

The South Australian Tourist Commission (SATC) publishes a booklet detailing various B&Bs around the state. For online information, try www.bnbbookings.com, www.ozbedandbreakfast.com or www.sabnb.org.au.

### Camping & Caravan Parks

Whether you're carrying a tent, driving a campervan or towing a caravan ('house trailer' in North American–speak), camping in the bush is a highlight of travelling in SA. In the outback you won't even need a tent most of the time as it hardly ever rains. Swags are the way to go. A night spent around a campfire under the Southern Cross is unforgettable; the silence is immense, the stars magnificent. There are plenty of places where you can camp for free, such as roadside rest areas where overnight camping is permitted. Stays at designated campsites in national parks generally cost around $4 to $8 per person.

Generally speaking, SA's plentiful caravan parks are well kept, conveniently located (often right on the foreshore) and excellent value, charging from $14 to $25 for two people camping, slightly more for a powered site. Most have on-site caravans (usually around $35 to $45), basic cabins with shared facilities (from $40) and cabins with en suite and cooking facilities ($70 to $110). Additional adults/children incur a fee of around $6/3 per night.

## Farm & Station Stays

For a true country experience, consider a rural getaway on a farm or station anywhere from the Fleurieu Peninsula and Kangaroo Island to outback regions. At some you can kick back and watch other people raise a sweat, while others like to rope you in to the day-to-day activities. Most accommodation is very comfortable – in the main homestead (B&B-style, many providing dinner on request) or in self-contained cottages on the property. Some farms also provide budget options in outbuildings or former shearers' quarters. The SATC has a brochure with listings or you can check the options online at www.farmstaysa.com.au and www.australiafarmhost.com.

## Hostels

Hostels are a highly social and low-cost fixture of the SA accommodation scene.

### HOSTEL ORGANISATIONS

The **Youth Hostel Association** (YHA; Map pp64–5; ☎ 08-8414 3010; www.yha.com.au; 135 Waymouth St, Adelaide) is part of the **International Youth Hostel Federation** (IYHF; www.hihostels.com), also known as Hostelling International (HI). Nightly charges are between $10 and $30 for members; most hostels also take non-YHA members for an extra $3.50. Purchase a HI card in your country of residence, or buy one at major local YHA hostels at a cost of $35 for 12 months.

**VIP Backpacker Resorts** (☎ 07-3395 6111; www.backpackers.com) has a few members in SA and many more around Australia and overseas. Membership (12 months, $39) entitles you discounts on accommodation, air and bus transport, tours and activities. You can join online, at VIP hostels or backpacker travel agencies.

**Nomads Backpackers** (☎ 1800 819 883, 08-8363 7633; www.nomadsworld.com; 43 The Parade, Kent Town) has a handful hostels; membership ($29 for 12 months) entitles you to numerous discounts. Join at participating hostels, backpacker travel agencies or online.

### INDEPENDENT HOSTELS

South Australia has numerous independent hostels, with the fierce competition for the backpacker dollar prompting fairly high standards and plenty of enticements, such as free breakfasts, supper and courtesy buses. However, some places are run-down hotels trying to fill empty rooms, while others are converted motels where each four- to six-bed unit has a fridge, TV and bathroom, but communal areas and cooking facilities may be lacking. The best places tend to be the smaller, more intimate hostels where the owner is also the manager.

Independent backpacker establishments typically charge $19 to $26 for a dorm bed and $40 to $60 for a twin or double room (usually without bathroom).

Some Adelaide hostels admit only travellers from overseas as a way of keeping unwanted customers out. This can be annoying, patronising and discriminatory for genuine travellers trying to explore their own country. Also keep an eye out for hostels catering expressly to working backpackers, where facilities are minimal but rents are high.

## Houseboats

You can cruise the Murray River on a fully self-contained houseboat, with standards ranging from budget to luxury. On average, the weekly hire of a two-berth/four-berth houseboat start from around $550/600 in winter and $720/800 in peak holiday periods.

There are many listings in the **Houseboat Hirers Association** (☎ 08-8395 0999; www.houseboat-centre.com.au) booklet *SA Houseboat Holidays*, available from SATC.

## Hotels & Motels

Except for pubs, the hotels that exist in Adelaide or places visited by lots of tourists are generally of the business or luxury variety where you get a comfortable, anonymous room filled with mod cons in a multistorey block. These places tend to have a pool, restaurant/café, room service and various other facilities. We quote 'rack rates' (official advertised rates) throughout this book, but often hotels/motels will offer regular discounts and special deals.

For comfortable mid-range accommodation that's available all over the state, motels (or motor inns) are the places to stay. Prices vary and there's rarely a cheaper rate for singles, so motels are better for couples or groups of three. Motels are usually low-rise and have similar facilities (kettle, fridge, TV, air-con, bathroom) but the price will indicate the standard. You'll mostly pay between $60 and $120 for a room.

## Pubs

For the budget traveller, hotels in Australia are the ones that serve beer – commonly known as pubs (from the term 'public house'). In country towns, pubs are invariably found in the town centre. Many pubs were built during boom times, so they're often among the largest and most extravagant buildings in town. In tourist areas some of these pubs have been restored as heritage buildings, but generally the rooms remain small and old fashioned, with a long amble down the hall to the bathroom. You can sometimes rent a single room at a country pub for not much more than a hostel dorm, and you'll be in the social heart of the town to boot. But if you're a light sleeper, never book a room above the bar. Standard pubs have singles/doubles with shared facilities starting from around $30/50, more if you want a private bathroom. Few have a separate reception area – just ask in the bar if there are rooms available. For women travellers, see p264.

## Rental Accommodation

Serviced apartments and holiday flats bear some resemblance to motels but usually contain cooking facilities. Basically, holiday flats are found in holiday areas, serviced apartments in Adelaide. In some holiday flats you have to provide your own sheets and bedding, while others are fully equipped.

If you're interested in sharing a flat or house for a longer-term stay in Adelaide, check the classified section of the *Advertiser*. Notice boards in universities, hostels, bookshops and cafés are also good to check out. See individual Sleeping sections in destination chapters for holiday rentals and price indicators.

## BUSINESS HOURS

Most shops and businesses open around 9am and close at 5pm or 6pm Monday to Friday, and at either noon or 5pm on Saturday. Sunday trading is becoming increasingly common, but it's currently limited to the major towns and Adelaide. In most towns there are usually one or two late-shopping nights each week, normally Thursday and/or Friday, when doors stay open until 9pm or 9.30pm. Supermarkets are generally open from 7am until at least 8pm and sometimes 24 hours. You'll also find delis (general stores) open until late.

Banks open from 9.30am to 4pm Monday to Thursday, and until 5pm on Friday. Most Adelaide Bank branches also open on Saturday morning. Post offices are open from 9am to 5pm Monday to Friday, but you can also buy stamps from newsagents and delis.

Restaurants typically open around noon for lunch and from 6pm for dinner; most dinner bookings are made for 7.30pm or 8pm. Restaurants typically serve until at least 9pm, later on Friday and Saturday. That said, restaurants in Adelaide and some other popular areas keep longer hours throughout the week. Cafés tend to be all-day affairs that either close around 5pm or continue their business into the night. Pubs usually serve food from noon to 2pm and from 6pm to 8pm. Pubs and bars often open for drinking at lunch-time and continue well into the evening, particularly from Thursday to Saturday. For more dining information, see p43.

Keep in mind that nearly all businesses are closed on Christmas Day.

## CHILDREN
### Practicalities

You'll find public rooms where mothers (and sometimes fathers) can go to nurse their baby or change its nappy in Adelaide (try Myer and David Jones in Rundle Mall) and major towns; check with the local visitors centre or city council for details. While many Australians have a relaxed attitude about breast-feeding or nappy changing in public, others frown on it. As anywhere, children should be accompanied in all public toilets, including shopping centres.

Motels and some caravan parks have playgrounds and swimming pools, and can supply cots and baby baths – motels may also have in-house children's videos and childminding services. Top-end hotels and many (but not all) mid-range hotels are well versed in the needs of guests who have children, often accommodating children up to 14 free in their parents' room. However, B&Bs often market themselves as child-free zones. See 'Whining & Dining' (p46) for dining information.

Some childcare agencies have places set aside for casual care, and babysitting agencies provide private services. To find them, check under Baby Sitters and Child Care Centres in the *Yellow Pages* telephone book, or phone the local council for a list. **Dial-An-Angel** ( ☎ 08-8267 3700) has a network of nannies and babysitters.

Child concessions (and family rates) often apply for tours, admission fees, and air, bus and train transport, with some discounts as high as 50% of the adult rate. However, the definition of 'child' can vary from under 12 to under 18 years. On the major airlines, infants travel free provided they don't occupy a seat – child fares usually apply between the ages of two and 11 years.

Medical services in SA are of a high standard, and items such as baby-food formula and disposable nappies are widely available (plan ahead if heading to remote regions). Major hire-car companies will supply and fit booster seats, for which you'll be charged around $16 for up to three days' use, with an additional daily fee for longer periods.

Enlisting kids' help in the planning the day's activities can have plenty of positive benefits. Lonely Planet's *Travel with Children* contains plenty of useful information.

### Sights & Activities

There's plenty of active or amusing things for children to focus on in SA. Adelaide has parkland with play equipment and nearby beaches, and most towns have a playground. One of the most appealing aspects of travelling in SA is the opportunity to get up close (and sometimes cuddly) with natural wildlife; see the Adelaide Hills (p86), Kangaroo Island (p113) and Fleurieu Peninsula (p98) chapters. Books-on-tape (available at ABC Shops) are the perfect accompaniment for long drives. For information see Adelaide for Children, p70.

## CLIMATE

The southern portion of SA experiences cold (though not freezing) winters (June through August). Summers (December to

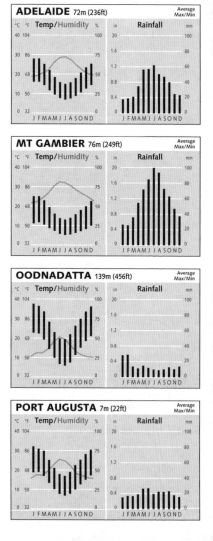

February) are pleasant and warm, although sometimes quite hot. Spring (September to November) and autumn (March through May) are transition months, much the same as in Europe or North America. The arid north of SA is hot and dry during the day, but often bitterly cold at night. See When to Go on p9 for more on the seasons. For current forecasts, see the **Bureau of Meteorology** (www.bom.gov.au) website.

## CUSTOMS & QUARANTINE

For comprehensive information on customs regulations, contact the **Australian Customs Service** ( ☎ 1300 363 263; www.customs.gov.au).

When entering Australia you can bring most articles in free of duty, provided that customs is satisfied that they are for personal use and that you'll be taking them with you when you leave. There's a duty-free quota per person of 2.25L of alcohol, 250 cigarettes and dutiable goods up to the value of A$900.

With regard to prohibited goods, there are two areas you should be particularly conscientious about. The first is drugs, which customs authorities are very good at sniffing out – unless you want to make first-hand investigations of conditions in Australian jails, don't bring any with you. And note that all medicines must be declared.

The second is food, plant material and animal products. You will be asked to declare all goods of animal or vegetable origin (wooden spoons, straw hats, the lot) and show them to a quarantine officer. The authorities are naturally keen to protect Australia's unique environment and important agricultural industries by preventing weeds, pests or diseases getting into the country – Australia has so far managed to escape most pests and diseases prevalent elsewhere in the world. See also the boxed text 'Interstate Quarantine' on p269.

Weapons and firearms are either prohibited or require a permit and safety testing. Other restricted goods include products made from protected wildlife species, and unapproved telecommunication devices.

Australia takes quarantine very seriously. All luggage is screened or x-rayed – if you fail to declare quarantine items on arrival and are caught, you risk an on-the-spot fine of $220, or prosecution which may result in fines over $60,000, as well as up to 10 years imprisonment. For more information on quarantine regulations contact the **Australian Quarantine & Inspection Service** (AQIS; www .aqis.gov.au).

## DANGERS & ANNOYANCES
### Animal Hazards
#### INSECTS

For four to six months of the year you'll have to cope with those two banes of the Australian outdoors: the fly and the mosquito (mozzie). Flies aren't too bad in Adelaide but they're more prevalent in the outback, and the further 'out' you go, the more numerous and persistent they seem to be. In the north, where they can be particularly troublesome, flies emerge with the warmer spring weather (early September) and last until winter. Embrace the 'Aussie Wave' or don the humble fly net (very effective, but not terribly glamorous). Widely available insect repellents such as Aerogard and Rid may also help to deter them, but don't count on it. Mozzies are a problem in summer, especially near wetlands, and some species are carriers of viral infections (see p278). Try to keep your arms and legs covered as soon as the sun sets, and make liberal use of insect repellent.

#### SHARKS

Shark attacks are extremely rare – you're more likely to be involved in a car accident (if that's any comfort). Great whites are known to inhabit some surf spots in SA. Seek local knowledge and swim where surf patrols are operative.

#### SNAKES

There are many venomous snakes in the Australian bush, the most common being the brown and tiger snakes. Few are aggressive – unless you're interfering with one or have the misfortune to stand on one, it's extremely unlikely that you'll be bitten. The golden rule if you see a snake is to leave it alone. For information on treating snake bites, see p279.

#### SPIDERS

The redback is the most common poisonous spider in SA. It's small and black with a distinctive red stripe on its body; for bites, apply ice and seek medical attention. The whitetail is a long, thin black spider with a white tail, and has a fierce bite that can lead to local inflammation and ulceration. The disturbingly large huntsman spider, which often enters homes, is harmless, though seeing one for the first time can affect your blood pressure. Look under the seat for spiders before sitting down in bush dunnies, particularly the long-drop variety.

## Bushfires & Hypothermia

Bushfires are an annual event in SA. Don't be the mug who starts one. In hot, dry and windy weather, be extremely careful with any naked flame – cigarette butts thrown out of car windows have started many a fire – and make sure your fire's out before you leave. On a total fire ban day it's forbidden even to use a camping stove in the open. Locals won't be amused if they catch you breaking this particular law; they'll happily dob you in, and the penalties are severe.

Campfires are banned in conservation areas during the Fire Danger Period (FDP), which varies from region to region but is usually from 1 November to 31 March (30 April in some places).

Bushwalkers should seek local advice before setting out. When a total fire ban is in place, delay your trip until the weather improves. If you're out in the bush and you see smoke, even a long distance away, take it seriously – bushfires move very quickly and change direction with the wind. Go to the nearest open space, downhill if possible. A forested ridge, on the other hand, is the most dangerous place to be.

More bushwalkers die of cold than in fires. Exposure in even moderately cool temperatures can sometimes result in hypothermia – for more information on how to effectively minimise the risk of developing hypothermia, see p279.

## Crime

South Australia is a relatively safe place to visit but you should still take reasonable precautions. Lock hotel rooms and cars, and don't leave your valuables unattended or visible through a car window.

In response to several reports of drugged drinks in pubs and clubs, authorities are advising women to refuse drinks offered by strangers in bars and to drink bottled alcohol rather than from a glass.

## On the Road

As a rule, South Australian drivers are a courteous bunch, but risks can be posed by rural petrolheads, inner-city speedsters and fatigue- or alcohol-affected drivers. Take regular breaks to avoid fatigue and be aware of animals, which can be a real hazard on country roads – kangaroos can leap out in front of your vehicle, mainly at dusk. Driving on dirt roads can also be tricky if you're not used to them. For more information on these and other potential dangers see Road Conditions (p274) and Road Hazards (p275).

### OUTBACK TRAVEL

If you're keen to explore outback SA, it's important not to embark on your trip without careful planning and preparation. Travellers regularly encounter difficulties in the harsh outback conditions, and trips occasionally prove fatal. For tips and advice on travelling in the outback, see p273.

## Swimming

Popular beaches are patrolled by surf lifesavers and patrolled areas are marked off by the red-and-yellow flags. Even so, surf beaches can be dangerous places to swim if you aren't used to the conditions. Undertows (or 'rips') are the main problem. If you find yourself being carried out by a rip, the important thing to do is just keep afloat; don't panic or try to swim against the rip, which will exhaust you. In most cases the current stops within a couple of hundred metres of the shore and you can then swim parallel to the shore for a short way to get out of the rip and make your way back to land. If you swim between the flags, help should arrive quickly if you get into trouble; raise your arm (and yell!) if you need help.

A number of people are paralysed every year by diving into waves in shallow water and hitting a sand bar; check the depth of the water before you leap.

## DISABLED TRAVELLERS

Disability awareness in SA is pretty high and getting higher. Legislation requires that new accommodation meets accessibility standards, and discrimination by tourism operators is illegal. Many of the state's key attractions provide access for those with

**DIRECTORY**

limited mobility and a number of sites have also begun addressing the needs of visitors with visual or aural impairments; contact attractions in advance to confirm the facilities. Reliable information is the key ingredient for travellers with a disability and the best source is the **National Information Communication & Awareness Network** (Nican; ☎/TTY 02-6285 3713, TTY 1800 806 769; www.nican.com.au; 4/2 Phipps Cl, Deakin, ACT). It's an Australiawide directory providing information on access issues, accessible accommodation, sporting and recreational activities, transport and specialist tour operators.

The **Disability Information & Resource Centre** (DIRC; Map pp64-5; ☎ 08-8223 7522; www.dircsa.org.au; 195 Gilles St, Adelaide) provides information on accommodation, venues, tourist destinations and travel agencies for people with disabilities.

The *Easy Access Australia* (www.easyaccessaustralia.com.au) publication is available online or from various bookshops around the state and provides details on easily accessible transport, accommodation and attraction options.

## DISCOUNT CARDS

Senior travellers and travellers with disabilities with some form of identification are often eligible for concession prices. Travellers over 60 years of age (both Australian residents and visitors) will simply need to present current age-proving identification to be eligible for discounts of up to 70% off regular airfares.

The **International Student Travel Confederation** (ISTC; www.istc.org) is an international collective of student travel organisations. It is also the body behind the internationally recognised International Student Identity Card (ISIC), which is issued only to full-time students aged 12 years and over, and gives the bearer discounts on accommodation, transport and admission to various attractions. The ISTC also produces the International Youth Travel Card (IYTC or Go25), which is issued to people who are between 12 and 26 years of age and not full-time students, and has benefits equivalent to the ISIC. Another similar ISTC brainchild is the International Teacher Identity Card (ITIC), which is available to teaching professionals. All three cards are available from student travel companies.

## EMBASSIES & CONSULATES
### Australian Embassies & Consulates
The website of the **Department of Foreign Affairs & Trade** (www.dfat.gov.au) has a full listing of Australian diplomatic missions overseas.

**Canada** ( ☎ 613-236 0841; www.ahc-ottawa.org; Suite 710, 50 O'Connor St, Ottawa, Ontario K1P 6L2) Also in Vancouver and Toronto.

**France** ( ☎ 01 40 59 33 00; www.austgov.fr; 4 Rue Jean Rey, 75724 Paris Cedex 15)

**Germany** ( ☎ 030-880 0880; www.australian-embassy.de; Friedrichstrasse 200, 10117 Berlin) Also in Frankfurt.

**Ireland** ( ☎ 01-664 5300; www.australianembassy.ie; 2nd fl, Fitzwilton House, Wilton Tce, Dublin 2)

**Japan** ( ☎ 03-5232 4111; www.australia.or.jp; 2-1-14 Mita, Minato-Ku, Tokyo 108-8361) Also in Osaka, Nagoya and Fukuoka City.

**Netherlands** ( ☎ 070-310 82 00; www.australian-embassy.nl; Carnegielaan 4, The Hague 2517 KH)

**New Zealand** Wellington ( ☎ 04-473 6411; www.australia.org.nz; 72-78 Hobson St, Thorndon); Auckland ( ☎ 09-921 8800; Level 7, Price Waterhouse Coopers Bldg, 186-194 Quay St)

**Singapore** ( ☎ 6836 4100; www.singapore.embassy.gov.au; 25 Napier Rd, Singapore 258507)

**South Africa** ( ☎ 27 12 342 3781; www.australia.co.za; 292 Orient St, Arcadia, Pretoria 0083)

**UK** ( ☎ 020-7379 4334; www.australia.org.uk; Australia House, The Strand, London WC2B 4LA) Also in Edinburgh and Manchester.

**USA** ( ☎ 202-797 3000; www.austemb.org; 1601 Massachusetts Ave NW, Washington DC 20036) Also in Los Angeles, New York City and other major cities.

### Embassies & Consulates in Australia
It's important to realise what your own embassy – the embassy of the country of which you are a citizen – can and can't do to help you if you get into trouble. Generally speaking, it won't be much help in emergencies if the trouble you're in is even remotely your own fault. Remember that while in Australia you are bound by Australian laws. Your embassy will not be sympathetic if you end up in jail after committing an offence locally, even if such actions are legal in your own country.

The principal diplomatic representations to Australia are in Canberra; some countries have consular representation in Adelaide also:

**Canada** ( ☎ 02-6270 4000; www.dfait-maeci.gc.ca/australia; Commonwealth Ave, Canberra, ACT 2600)

**France** ( ☎ 02-6216 0100; www.ambafrance-au.org; 6 Perth Ave, Yarralumla, Canberra, ACT 2600)

**Germany** ( ☎ 08-8231 6320; www.germanembassy.org
.au; 23 Peel St, Adelaide, SA 5000)
**Ireland** ( ☎ 02-6273 3022; irishemb@cyberone.com.au;
20 Arkana St, Yarralumla, Canberra, ACT 2600)
**Italy** ( ☎ 08-8337 0777; 398 Payneham Rd, Glynde, SA 5070)
**Japan** ( ☎ 02-6273 3244; www.japan.org.au; 112 Empire
Crt, Yarralumla, ACT 2600)
**Netherlands** ( ☎ 08-8232 3855; www.netherlands.org
.au; Level 1, 147 Frome St, Adelaide, SA 5000)
**New Zealand** ( ☎ 02-6270 4211; nzhccba@austarmetro
.com.au; Commonwealth Ave, Canberra ACT 2600)
**UK** ( ☎ 08-8212 7280; www.uk.emb.gov.au; Level 22, 25
Grenfell St, Adelaide, SA 5000)
**USA** ( ☎ 02-6214 5600; http://usembassy-australia.state
.gov; 21 Moonah Pl, Yarralumla, Canberra, ACT 2600)

# FESTIVALS & EVENTS

Adelaide prides itself on being Australia's festival epicentre, in a state that excels in putting
on a show – arts, music, culture, food and
wine, or high adrenaline sport. Typically
Australian events also mark the calendar,
including surf–life-saving competitions
and outback race meetings, which draw
together isolated town and station folk and
plenty of eccentric bush characters. Annual
events are listed in the events section on
www.southaustralia.com. Following is a selection of events.

## January
**Jacob's Creek Tour Down Under** (www.tourdown
under.com.au) South Australia's six-stage version of the
Tour de France.
**Tunarama** ( ☎ 08-8682 1300; www.tunarama.net) Port
Lincoln's celebration of the tuna industry.

## February
**Barossa Under the Stars** ( ☎ 1300 852 982, 08-8563
0600; www.barossaunderthestars.com.au) A weekend of
live entertainment and night picnics held in the Barossa.
**German Oompah Fest** ( ☎ 1300 852 982, 08-8563
0600; www.barossa-region.org) Celebrates German culture
in Tanunda, in the Barossa Valley.

## March
**Adelaide Festival of Arts** (www.adelaidefestival.com.au;
even-numbered years) Culture vultures absorb international
and Australian dance, drama, opera and theatre
performances.
**Adelaide Fringe** (www.adelaidefringe.com.au; even-
numbered years) A biennial independent arts festival,
second only to Edinburgh Fringe.
**Adelaide Hills Harvest Festival** Celebrates the hills'
food and wines.

**Clipsal 500** (www.clipsal500.com.au) Rev heads rejoice
as Adelaide's streets become a four-day Holden versus Ford
racing track.
**Womadelaide** (www.womadelaide.com.au; odd-numbered
years) One of the world's best live-music events with more
than 400 musicians and performers from around the globe.

## April
**Anzac Day** (25 April) This national holiday commemorates
the landing of Anzac troops at Gallipoli in 1915. Memorial
marches by veterans of the various conflicts in which
Australia has been involved are held all over the state.
**Barossa Vintage Festival** ( ☎ 1300 852 982, 08-8563
0600; www.barossa-region.org/vintagefestival; odd-
numbered years) Includes processions, maypole dancing,
traditional dinners and much wine tasting.
**Kapunda Celtic Festival** ( ☎ 08-8892 2154; first
weekend before Easter) Celebrating Celtic culture.

## May
**Clare Valley Gourmet Weekend** ( ☎ 08-8843 0222)
A festival of fine wine and food put on by local wineries
and some of SA's top restaurants.
**Kernewek Lowender Festival** ( ☎ 1800 654 991,
08-8821 2333; www.kernewek.org) Held at Kadina, Moonta
and Wallaroo, the festival celebrates the Cornish heritage of
Yorke Peninsula's 'Copper Triangle' with plenty of Celtic fun.
**Sorry Day** (www.journeyofhealing.com) On 26 May each
year, the anniversary of the 1997 tabling of the *Bringing
Them Home* report, concerned Australians acknowledge the
continuing pain and suffering of indigenous people affected
by Australia's one-time child-removal practices and policies.

## June
**Sea & the Vines Festival** (June long weekend)
A celebration of wine and seafood in McLaren Vale.
**South Australian Country Music Festival & Awards**
( ☎ 08-8341 0979; www.riverlandcountrymusic.com) Held
at Barmera, on the Murray.

## July
**Marree Australian Camel Cup** (first Saturday) The
Camel Cup is held at Marree, in the outback.
**National Aboriginal & Islander Day Observance
Committee (Naidoc) Week** (www.atsic.gov.au)
Communities across Australia celebrate Naidoc (inaugurated
in 1957); performances, exhibitions, talks etc are held by
communities around SA.

## September
**Royal Adelaide Show** (www.adelaideshowground.com
.au) A seven-day major agricultural show.
**Shakespeare in the Caves** ( ☎ 08-8762 1518) Shakespeare performed in Naracoorte's World Heritage–listed
wonder caves.

## October

**Barossa Music Festival** (www.barossa.org) A celebration of food and wine featuring jazz and classical music.
**Bartercard Glenelg Jazz Festival** Adelaide's beachside suburb celebrates jazz and food.
**Coober Pedy Races** Transforms Coober Pedy's townsfolk into mad punters on the Labour Day weekend.
**Riverland Food & Wine Festival** ( ☎ 08-8582 3321) Sip and savour some regional goodies in Berri.
**Wine Bushing Festival** McLaren Vale's main festival is held in late October to early November, and celebrates the new vintage with wine, food, art and music.

## November & December

**Credit Union Christmas Pageant** (www.cupageant.com .au) An Adelaide institution for more than 70 years – floats, bands and marching troupes take over the city streets for a day in November.
**Lobethal Lights** Lobethal, in the Adelaide Hills, hosts a spectacular display of decorative Christmas lights in December.

## GAY & LESBIAN TRAVELLERS

Attitudes in Adelaide towards homosexuality are fairly relaxed. However, as you'd probably expect, you have a much greater chance of meeting homophobes the further you travel into the country. Homosexual acts between consenting adults are legal in SA, and state legislation prohibits discrimination on the basis of sexual preference. Adelaide has plenty of gay-friendly venues (see p77) and a dedicated annual gay and lesbian cultural festival, **Feast** (www.feast.org .au), held over three-weeks in November.

The long-standing, Adelaide-based **Gay & Lesbian Counselling Service of SA Inc** ( ☎ 1800 182 233, 08-8334 1623; www.glcssa.org.au; ☻ phone line 7-10pm daily & 2-5pm Sat & Sun) offers a free and confidential counselling and referral service, provides information on the gay scene, and has an extensive library.

For details on the local scene, pick up a copy of **Blaze** (www.blazemedia.com.au), available around Adelaide; reviews, community news and popular gay and lesbian venues are listed on its website, and it publishes an accommodation and business directory.

## HOLIDAYS
### Public Holidays

Main national and state public holidays include the following:
**New Year's Day** 1 January
**Australia Day** 26 January
**Easter** (Good Friday to Easter Monday inclusive) March/April
**Anzac Day** 25 April
**Adelaide Cup Day** 3rd Monday in May
**Queen's Birthday** 2nd Monday in June
**Labour Day** 1st Monday in October
**Proclamation Day** Last Tuesday in December
**Christmas Day** 25 December
**Boxing Day** 26 December

### School Holidays

The Christmas holiday season, from mid-December to late January, is part of the summer school holidays – it's the time you're most likely to find transport and accommodation booked out, and long, restless queues at tourist attractions. There are three shorter school holiday periods during the year. They fall roughly from early to mid-April, late June to mid-July, and late September to early October. South Australian families take to the road (and air) en masse at these times.

## INSURANCE

Don't underestimate the importance of a good travel-insurance policy that covers theft, loss and medical problems – nothing is guaranteed to ruin your holiday plans more quickly than an accident or having that brand-new digital camera stolen. There is a wide variety of policies available, so compare the small print.

Some policies specifically exclude designated 'dangerous activities' such as scuba diving and even bushwalking. If you plan on doing these things, make sure the policy you choose fully covers you for your activity of choice.

You may prefer a policy that pays doctors or hospitals direct, rather than one that requires you to pay on the spot and claim later. If you have to claim later make sure you keep all documentation. Some policies ask you to call back (reverse charges or collect) to a centre in your home country where an immediate assessment of your problem is made. Check that the policy covers ambulances and emergency medical evacuations by air.

See also Insurance on p276. For information on vehicle insurance, see p273.

## INTERNET ACCESS
### Access Points

Most public libraries have Internet access, but generally there are a limited number of terminals and these are provided for research needs, not for travellers to check their emails – so book ahead or head for a cybercafé. You'll find plenty of Internet cafés in Adelaide and pretty much anywhere that travellers congregate. The cost ranges from less than $6 an hour to $10 an hour. Most youth hostels can hook you up, as can many hotels and caravan parks.

### Hooking Up

If you're bringing your palmtop or notebook computer check with your Internet Service Provider (ISP) to find out if there are access numbers you can dial into in SA. Most large international ISPs have numbers for Adelaide. Australia primarily uses the RJ-45 telephone plugs although you may see Telstra EXI-160 four-pin plugs – electronics shops such as Tandy and Dick Smith should be able to help.

### LEGAL MATTERS

Most travellers will have no contact with the police or legal system. Those who do are likely to experience it while driving. There is a significant police presence on the region's roads; they have the power to stop your car and see your licence (you're required to carry it), check your vehicle for roadworthiness, and insist that you take a breath test for alcohol – needless to say, drink-driving offences are taken very seriously here.

First offenders caught with small amounts of illegal drugs are likely to receive a fine rather than go to jail, but the recording of a conviction against you may affect your visa status. Speaking of which, if you remain in Australia beyond the life of your visa, you will officially be an 'overstayer' and could face detention and expulsion, and then be prevented from returning to Australia for up to three years.

Legal aid is available only in serious cases and only to the truly needy (for links to

---

#### COMING OF AGE

For the record:

- You can drive when you're 16½.
- The legal age for voting is 18.
- The age of consent for sex is 17.
- The legal drinking age is 18.

---

Legal Aid offices see www.nla.aust.net.au). However, many solicitors do not charge for an initial consultation.

### MAPS

The SATC publishes a range of brochures on individual regions, each containing a handy fold-out map. These are available at local visitors centres. For more detailed maps, try the **Royal Automobile Association of South Australia** (RAA; Map pp64-5; ☎ 08-8202 4600; 55 Hindmarsh Sq, Adelaide).

Gregorys and UBD both produce Adelaide street directories (around $28) that are useful if you intend to stay a while and do lots of city driving. Also, UBD has a street directory covering numerous country centres.

Hema and Westprint produce maps of the Simpson Desert region, the Flinders Ranges, Yorke Peninsula, Adelaide Hills, Kangaroo Island, the Barossa and the outback.

South Australia has been topographically mapped at 1:250,000, with most settled areas at 1:50,000 or 100,000; sheets are available from **Carto Graphics** ( ☎ 08-8357 1777; 147 Unley Rd, Unley) and the **Map Shop** (Map pp64-5; ☎ 08-8231 2033; 6 Peel St, Adelaide). The latter also provides special-interest maps and guides for cyclists and bushwalkers (including individual segment maps on the Heysen and Mawson trails), which are also available at shops specialising in bushwalking gear and outdoor equipment (see p80).

### MONEY
#### ATMs, Eftpos & Bank Accounts

Adelaide Bank, Bank SA, ANZ, Commonwealth, National and Westpac bank branches (and branches of affiliated banks) are found throughout the state and many have 24-hour ATMs attached. But don't expect to find ATMs *everywhere* – certainly not off the beaten track or in very small towns. Most ATMs accept cards from other banks and are linked to international networks.

Electronic Funds Transfer at Point of Sale (Eftpos) is a convenient service that many Australian businesses have embraced. It means you can use your bank card (credit or debit) to pay direct for services or purchases, and often withdraw cash as well. This system is available practically everywhere these days, even in roadhouses on the Nullarbor where it's a long way between banks. Just like an ATM, you need to know your Personal Identification Number (PIN) to use it.

## Credit Cards

Except in some remote areas, credit cards are widely accepted in SA and are a convenient alternative to carrying a wad of travellers cheques. Credit cards such as Visa and MasterCard are widely accepted for accommodation, tours, restaurant meals and any kind of merchandise, and are pretty much essential for car hire. They can also be used to get cash advances at banks and from many ATMs, depending on the card, but be aware that these incur immediate interest. Charge cards such as Diners Club and Amex are not as widely accepted.

## Currency

Australia's currency is the Australian dollar, which comprises 100 cents. There are coins for 5c, 10c, 20c, 50c, $1 and $2, and notes for $5, $10, $20, $50 and $100.

There are no notable restrictions on the importing or exporting travellers cheques. However, cash amounts in excess of the equivalent of A$10,000 (any currency) must be declared on arrival and departure. All prices given in dollars refer to Australian dollars in this book.

## Exchange Rates

The Aussie dollar tends to act a little insecure around the US dollar and can fluctuate wildly. In early 2001 it nosedived below US$0.50, then soared to US$0.78 in 2004, but has stabilised around the US$0.73 mark. See the Quick Reference (inside front cover) for a list of exchange rates.

## Moneychangers

Exchanging foreign currency or travellers cheques is usually no problem at banks throughout the state or at licensed moneychangers such as Thomas Cook or Amex in Adelaide.

## Taxes & Refunds

The Goods and Services Tax (GST), introduced by the federal government in 2000 amid much controversy, is a flat 10% on all goods and services – accommodation, eating out, transport, electrical goods, books, furniture, clothing and so on. There are, however, some exceptions, such as basic foods (milk, bread, fruits and vegetables etc). By law the tax is included in the quoted or shelf prices, so all prices in this book are GST-inclusive. International air and sea travel to/from Australia is GST-free, as is domestic air travel when purchased outside Australia by nonresidents.

If you purchase new or second-hand goods with a total minimum value of $300 from any one supplier no more than 30 days before you leave Australia, you are entitled under the Tourist Refund Scheme (TRS) to a refund of any GST paid. The scheme only applies to goods you take with you as hand luggage or wear onto the plane or ship. Also note that the refund is valid for goods bought from more than one supplier, but only if at least $300 is spent in each. For more information, contact the **Australian Customs Service** ( ☎ 1300 363 263, 02-6275 6666; www.customs.gov.au).

## Travellers Cheques

If your stay is short, then travellers cheques are safe and generally enjoy a better exchange rate than foreign cash in Australia. Also, if they are stolen (or you lose them), they can readily be replaced. However, there's a fee for buying travellers cheques (usually 1% of the total amount) and there may be fees or commissions when you exchange them.

Thomas Cook, Amex and other well-known international brands of travellers cheques are easily exchanged. You need to present your passport for identification when cashing them.

Fees per transaction for changing foreign-currency travellers cheques varies depending on the bank. Of the 'big four' banks, ANZ charges $7; Commonwealth Bank charges a minimum of $8 or 1% of the total dollar amount; Westpac charges $8; and the National Australia Bank charges its account holders $15 and noncustomers an extortionate $30. Clearly you're better off using an Amex or Thomas Cook exchange bureau, which are commission-free if you use their cheques.

Buying travellers cheques in Australian dollars is another option. These can be exchanged immediately at banks without being converted from a foreign currency or incurring commissions, fees and exchange-rate fluctuations.

DIRECTORY

# POST

Australia's postal services are efficient and reasonably cheap. It costs $0.50 to send a standard letter or postcard within the country. **Australia Post** (www.auspost.com.au) has divided international destinations into two regions: Asia-Pacific and Rest of the World; airmail letters up to 50g cost $1.10 and $1.65, respectively. The cost of a postcard (up to 20g) is $1 and an aerogram to any country is $0.85. There are five international parcel zones and rates vary by distance and class of service.

All post offices will hold mail for visitors, and Adelaide's GPO (main or general post office) has a busy poste restante section. You need to provide some form of identification (such as a passport) to collect mail. You can also have mail sent to you at city Amex offices if you have an Amex card or travellers cheques. Post offices are open from 9am to 5pm Monday to Friday.

# TELEPHONE

The two main providers in Australia are the mostly government-owned **Telstra** (www.telstra.com.au) and the fully private **Optus** (www.optus.com.au). Both are also major players in the mobile (cell) phone market, along with **Vodafone** (www.vodafone.com.au).

## Information & Toll-Free Calls

Numbers starting with ☎ 190 are usually recorded information services, costing anything from $0.35 to $5 or more per minute (more from mobiles and payphones). To make a reverse-charge (collect) call from any public or private phone, just dial ☎ 1800-REVERSE (738 3773), or ☎ 12 550.

Toll-free numbers (prefix ☎ 1800) can be called free of charge from anywhere in the country, though they may not be accessible from certain areas or from mobile phones. Calls to numbers beginning with ☎ 13 or ☎ 1300 are charged at the rate of a local call; the numbers can usually be dialled Australia-wide, but may be applicable only to a specific state or STD district. Numbers beginning with ☎ 1800, ☎ 13 or ☎ 1300 cannot be dialled from outside Australia.

## International Calls

Most pay phones allow International Subscriber Dialling (ISD) calls; the cost and international dialling code will vary depending on which provider you're using. International calls from Australia are cheap and subject to specials that reduce the rates even more, so it's worth shopping around – look in the *Yellow Pages* for a list of providers.

The **Country Direct service** ( ☎ 1800 801 800) connects callers in Australia with operators in nearly 60 countries to make reverse-charge (collect) or credit-card calls. When calling overseas you need to dial the international access code from Australia ( ☎ 0011 or ☎ 0018), the country code and the area code (without the initial 0). For a London you'd dial ☎ 0011-44-20, then the number. Also, certain operators will have you dial a special code to access their service.

If dialling Australia from overseas, the country code is ☎ 61 and you need to drop the 0 (zero), such as from the 08 in SA, in the state/territory area codes.

## Local Calls

Calls from private phones cost from $0.15 to $0.25; local calls from public phones cost $0.40. Both provide unlimited talk time. Calls to mobile phones cost more and are timed. Blue or gold phones usually cost a minimum of $0.50 for a local call.

## Long-Distance Calls & Area Codes

Australia uses four Subscriber Trunk Dialling (STD) area codes for long-distance calls; STD calls can be made from virtually any public phone and are cheaper during off-peak hours. Broadly, the main Australian area codes are as follows:

| State/territory | Area code |
| --- | --- |
| ACT & NSW | ☎ 02 |
| NT, SA & WA | ☎ 08 |
| QLD | ☎ 07 |
| TAS & VIC | ☎ 03 |

## Mobile (Cell) Phones

Mobile phones have the prefixes ☎ 04xx or ☎ 04xxx. Australia's two mobile networks – digital GSM and digital CDMA – service more than 90% of the population but leave vast tracts of the country uncovered. Adelaide and most of SA's settled areas get good reception, but as the towns thin out so does the service.

Australia's digital network is compatible with GSM 900 and 1800 (used in Europe), but generally not with the systems used in the USA or Japan. It's easy and cheap enough to get connected short term though, as the main service providers (Telstra, Optus and Vodafone) all have prepaid mobile systems.

## Phonecards
A range of phonecards ($10, $20, $30 etc) is available from newsagents and post offices, and can be used with any public or private phone by dialling a toll-free access number and then the PIN on the card. It's worth shopping around, as call rates vary from company to company. Some public phones also accept credit cards.

## TIME
Australia is divided into three time zones: Central Standard Time (Northern Territory, SA) is GMT/UTC plus 9½ hours, Eastern Standard Time (Tasmania, Victoria, New South Wales, Australian Capital Territory, Queensland) is GMT/UTC plus 10 hours, and Western Standard Time (Western Australia only) is GMT/UTC plus eight hours. When it's noon in SA it's 10.30am in the west and 12.30pm in the east.

During summer daylight saving (from the last Saturday of October to the last Saturday of March in SA), clocks are put forward one hour. This does not operate in WA, Queensland or the NT. In Tasmania it lasts for two months longer than in the other states.

For information on international timing, see www.timeanddate.com/worldclock.

## TOURIST INFORMATION
Australia's and SA's highly self-conscious tourism infrastructure means that when looking for information you can easily end up being buried neck-deep in brochures, booklets, maps and leaflets, or get utterly swamped with detail during an online surf.

**Australian Tourist Commission** (ATC; ☎ 1300 361 650, 02-9360 1111; www.australia.com; Level 4, 80 William St, Woolloomooloo, NSW 2011) is the national government tourist body. A good place for pre-trip research is the commission's website, which has information in nine languages (including French, German, Japanese and Spanish).

**South Australian Tourism Commission** (SATC; Map pp64-5; ☎ 1300 366 7701, 08-8303 2033; www.south australia.com; 18 King William St, Adelaide), as well as

having enough tourist and general information to bury you, can book transport, tours and accommodation. Its website has some excellent planning information (including map PDFs) and links to other useful sights.

## Local Visitors Centres
Within SA, tourist information is disseminated by various local offices. Almost every decent-sized town in SA maintains a visitors centre of some type with a proliferation of brochures on everything the region offers. They're usually staffed by (over-) friendly volunteers (some with little knowledge of tourism). If you're going to book accommodation or tours from local offices, bear in mind that they often only promote businesses that are paying members of the local tourist association. Local tourism offices are listed in destination chapters.

## VISAS
Visitors to Australia must have a visa; only New Zealand nationals are exempt, and even they receive a 'special category' visa on arrival. Visa application forms are available from Australian diplomatic missions overseas, travel agents or the website of the **Department of Immigration & Multicultural & Indigenous Affairs** ( ☎ 13 18 81; www.immi.gov.au). There are several types of visa.

### Electronic Travel Authority (ETA)
Many visitors can get an ETA through any International Air Transport Association (IATA) – registered travel agent or overseas airline. They make the application direct when you buy a ticket and issue the ETA, which replaces the usual visa stamped in your passport – it's common practice for travel agents to charge a fee for issuing an ETA (usually US$15). This system is available to passport holders of some 33 countries, including the UK, the USA and Canada, most European and Scandinavian countries, Malaysia, Singapore, Japan and Korea. You can also make an online ETA application at www.eta.immi.gov.au, where no fees apply.

### Tourist Visas
Short-term tourist visas have largely been replaced by the Electronic Travel Authority (ETA). However, if you are from a country

not covered by the ETA, or you want to stay longer than three months, you'll need to apply for a visa. Standard visas (which cost $65) allow one (in some cases multiple) entry, stays of up to three months, and are valid for use within 12 months of issue. A long-stay tourist visa (also $65) can allow a visit of up to a year.

### Visa Extensions

Visitors are allowed a maximum stay of 12 months, including extensions. Visa extensions are made through the Department of Immigration & Multicultural & Indigenous Affairs and it's best to apply at least two or three weeks before your visa expires. The application fee is $160 – it's nonrefundable, even if your application is rejected.

### Working Holiday Maker (WHM) Visas

Young, single visitors from Canada, Cyprus, Denmark, Finland, Germany, Hong Kong, Ireland, Japan, Korea, Malta, the Netherlands, Norway, Sweden and the UK are eligible for a WHM visa, which allows you to visit for up to 12 months and gain casual employment. 'Young' is defined as between 18 and 30 years of age and visa-holders are only supposed to work for any one employer for a maximum of three months.

There is an application fee of A$160, and visas must be applied for only at Australian diplomatic missions abroad. For more information on the WHM, see www.immi.gov.au/e_visa/visit.htm.

## WOMEN TRAVELLERS

South Australia is generally a safe place for women travellers, although the usual sensible precautions apply. It's best to avoid walking alone late at night in Adelaide and major towns. And if you're out on the town, always keep enough money aside for a taxi back to your accommodation. The same applies to outback and rural towns where there are often a lot of unlit, semideserted streets between you and your temporary home. When the pubs and bars close and there are inebriated people roaming around, it's not a great time to be out and about. Lone women should also be wary of staying in basic pub accommodation unless it looks safe and well managed. Lone female hitchers are tempting fate – hitching with a male companion is safer.

The **Women's Information Service** ( ☎ 08-8303 0590; www.wis.sa.gov.au; Station Arcade, 136 North Tce, Adelaide) provides information, advice and referrals on just about anything of specific interest to women.

# Transport

CONTENTS

| | |
|---|---|
| **Getting There & Away** | **265** |
| Entering Australia | 265 |
| Air – International | 265 |
| Air – Domestic | 268 |
| Land | 268 |
| **Getting Around** | **270** |
| Air | 270 |
| Bicycle | 270 |
| Boat | 271 |
| Bus | 271 |
| Car & Motorcycle | 271 |
| Local Transport | 275 |
| Tours | 275 |
| Train | 275 |

# GETTING THERE & AWAY

Australia's a long way from most places and a long-haul flight is usually required to get here. The majority of international flights service Australia's eastern states, from where you can take a regular domestic flight or travel overland to South Australia (SA).

## ENTERING AUSTRALIA
Disembarkation in Australia is generally a straightforward affair, with only the usual customs declarations (p255) and the fight to be first to the luggage carousel to endure. If you're flying in with Qantas, Air New Zealand, British Airways, Cathay Pacific, Japan Airlines or Singapore Airlines, ask the carrier about the 'Express' passenger card, which will speed your way through customs.

Recent global instability has resulted in conspicuously increased security in Australian airports, both in domestic and international terminals, and you may find that customs procedures are now more time consuming.

## AIR – INTERNATIONAL
### Airlines
The east coast of Australia is the most common gateway for international travellers, however there are some airlines that fly directly into **Adelaide airport** (www.aal.com.au; noise tax $4). If you do choose to fly to the east coast first, it's usually possible to book a same-day domestic flight to Adelaide. Airlines that visit Australia include the following (please note all phone numbers mentioned here are for dialling from within Australia).

**Air Canada** ( ☎ 1300 655 757; www.aircanada.ca; airline code AC) Flies to Sydney.

**Air New Zealand** ( ☎ 13 24 76; www.airnz.com.au; airline code NZ) Flies to Melbourne, Perth, Sydney.

---

**THINGS CHANGE**

The information in this chapter is particularly vulnerable to change: prices for international travel are volatile, routes are introduced and cancelled, schedules change, special deals come and go, and rules and visa requirements are amended.

Airlines and governments seem to take a perverse pleasure in making price structures and regulations as complicated as possible. You should check directly with the airline or a travel agent to make sure you understand how a fare (and ticket you may buy) works. In addition, the travel industry is highly competitive and there are many lurks and perks.

At the time of writing, many airlines were facing an uncertain future due to a worldwide decline in air travel. Many have reduced schedules and some have gone under, and it seems likely that more will follow. This will only add to pricing uncertainty.

The upshot of this is that you should get opinions, quotes and advice from as many airlines and travel agents as possible before you part with your hard-earned cash – consult the airline and travel agent websites listed throughout this book for current fares and schedules. The details given in this chapter should be regarded as pointers and are not a substitute for your own careful, up-to-date research.

**Air Paradise International** ( ☎ 1300 799 066; www
.airparadise.com.au; airline code AD) Flies to Adelaide,
Brisbane, Melbourne, Perth, Sydney.

**Australian Airlines** ( ☎ 1300 799 798; http://austra
lianairlines.com.au; airline code AO) Flies to Cairns,
Melbourne, Sydney.

**British Airways** ( ☎ 1300 767 177; www.britishairways
.com.au; airline code BA) Flies to Sydney.

**Cathay Pacific** ( ☎ 13 17 47; www.cathaypacific.com;
airline code CX) Flies to Adelaide, Melbourne, Perth,
Sydney, Brisbane, Cairns.

**Emirates** ( ☎ 1300 303 777; www.emirates.com; airline
code EK) Flies to Brisbane Melbourne, Perth, Sydney.

**Freedom Air** ( ☎ 1800 122 000; www.freedomair.com;
airline code SJ) Flies to Brisbane, Melbourne, Sydney.

**Gulf Air** ( ☎ 13 12 23; www.gulfairco.com; airline code
GF) Flies to Melbourne, Sydney.

**Japan Airlines** ( ☎ 02-9272 1100; www.jal.com; airline
code JL) Flies to Brisbane, Cairns, Melbourne, Sydney.

**Qantas** (Map pp64-5; ☎ 13 13 13; www.qantas.com.au;
144 North Tce; airline code QF) Flies to Adelaide, Brisbane,
Melbourne, Perth, Sydney.

**Royal Brunei Airlines** ( ☎ 08-8941 0966; www.bruneiair
.com; airline code BI) Flies to Brisbane, Darwin, Perth.

**Singapore Airlines** ( ☎ 13 10 11; www.singaporeair
.com.au; airline code SQ) Flies to Adelaide, Brisbane,
Melbourne, Perth, Sydney.

**South African Airways** ( ☎ 1800 099 281, 08-9216 2200;
www.flysaa.com; airline code SA) Flies to Perth, Sydney.

**United Airlines** ( ☎ 13 17 77; www.unitedairlines.com
.au; airline code UA) Flies to Melbourne, Sydney.

## Tickets

Be sure you research the options carefully
to make sure you get the best deal. The
Internet is an increasingly useful resource
for checking airline prices.

Automated online ticket sales work well
if you're doing a simple one-way or return
trip on specified dates, but are no substitute
for a travel agent with the low-down on
special deals, strategies for avoiding stop-
overs and other useful advice.

Paying by credit card offers some protection if you unwittingly end up dealing with
a rogue fly-by-night agency in your search
for the cheapest fare, as most card issuers
provide refunds if you can prove you didn't

---

**DEPARTURE TAX**

There is a $41 departure tax when leaving
Australia. This is included in the price of
airline tickets.

---

get what you paid for. Alternatively, buy a
ticket from a bonded agent, such as one
covered by the **Air Travel Organiser's Licence**
(ATOL; www.atol.org.uk) scheme in the UK. If you
have doubts about the service provider, at
the very least call the airline and confirm
that your booking has been made.

Round-the-world tickets can be a good
option for getting to Australia, and Adelaide
is an easy inclusion on your ticket. For online
bookings, start with the following websites.

**Airbrokers** (www.airbrokers.com) This US company
specialises in cheap tickets. To fly LA–Hong Kong–Bangkok–
Bali–Adelaide–Auckland– Fiji–Los Angeles costs around
US$1800.

**Cheap Flights** (www.cheapflights.com) Very informative
site with specials, airline information and flight searches
from the USA and other regions.

**Cheapest Flights** (www.cheapestflights.co.uk) Cheap
worldwide flights from the UK; get in early for the
bargains.

**Expedia** (www.expedia.msn.com) Microsoft's travel site;
mainly US-related.

**Flight Centre International** (www.flightcentre.com)
Respected operator handling direct flights, with sites for
Australia, New Zealand (NZ), the UK, the USA and Canada.

**Flights.com** (www.tiss.com) Truly international site
for flight-only tickets; cheap fares and an easy-to-search
database.

**Roundtheworld.com** (www.roundtheworldflights.com)
This excellent site allows you to build your own trips from
the UK with up to six stops. A four-stop trip including Asia,
Australia and the USA, costs from UK£800.

**STA** (www.statravel.com) Prominent in international
student travel but you don't have to be a student; site
linked to worldwide STA sites.

**Travel Online** (www.travelonline.co.nz) Good place to
check worldwide flights from NZ.

**Travel.com** (www.travel.com.au) Good Australian site;
look up fares and flights into and out of the country.

**Travelocity** (www.travelocity.com) This US site allows
you to search fares (in US$) to/from practically anywhere.

## Asia

Most Asian countries offer fairly competitive airfare deals, with Bangkok, Singapore
and Hong Kong being the best places to
shop around for discount tickets.

Flights between Hong Kong and Australia
are notoriously heavily booked. Flights to/
from Bangkok and Singapore are often part
of the longer Europe-to-Australia route so
they are also sometimes full. The motto of
the story is to plan your preferred itinerary
well in advance.

Typical one-way fares to Adelaide are $820 from Singapore, $1100 from Penang or Kuala Lumpur, $630 to $950 from Denpasar in Bali and $1100 from Bangkok. From Tokyo, fares start at $1250. There are several good local agents in Asia:

**Hong Kong Student Travel Bureau** ( ☎ 852-2730 3269)

**STA Travel Bangkok** ( ☎ 02-236 0262; www.statravel .co.th)

**STA Travel Singapore** ( ☎ 65-6737 7188; www.statravel .com.sg)

**STA Travel Tokyo** ( ☎ 03-5391-3205; www.statravel.co .jp in Japanese)

## Canada

The air routes from Canada are similar to those from mainland USA, with most Toronto and Vancouver flights stopping in one US city such as Los Angeles or Honolulu before heading on to Australia. Air Canada flies from Vancouver to Sydney via Honolulu and from Toronto to Melbourne via Honolulu.

Canadian discount air ticket sellers are known as consolidators and their airfares tend to be about 10% higher than those sold in the USA. **Travel Cuts** ( ☎ 800-667-2887; www .travelcuts.com) is Canada's national student travel agency and has offices in all major cities.

For flights from Vancouver to Sydney or Melbourne fares start from C$1650/2100 in the low/high season via the US west coast. From Toronto to Sydney or Melbourne, fares cost approximately C$1800/ 2200.

## Continental Europe

From the major destinations in Europe, most flights travel via one of the Asian capitals. Some flights are also routed through London before arriving in Australia via Singapore, Bangkok, Hong Kong or Kuala Lumpur. Return fares from Paris in the low/high season cost from €1000/1200. Some agents in Paris:

**Nouvelles Frontières** ( ☎ 08 25 00 08 25; www .nouvelles-frontieres.fr) Also has branches outside of Paris.

**OTU Voyages** ( ☎ 01 40 29 12 12; www.otu.fr) Student/ youth oriented, with offices in many cities.

**Usit Connect Voyages** ( ☎ 01 43 29 69 50; www .usitconnections.fr) Student/youth specialists, with offices in many cities.

A decent option in the Dutch travel industry is **Holland International** ( ☎ 070-307 6307; www.hollandinternational.nl). From Amsterdam, return fares start at around €1500. In Germany, good travel agencies include the Berlin branch of **STA Travel** ( ☎ 030-311 0950; www.statravel.de). Return fares start at around €900/1000 in the low/high season.

## New Zealand

Air New Zealand and Qantas operate a network of flights linking Auckland, Wellington and Christchurch in NZ with Adelaide and other Australian gateway cities. Fares from NZ to east coast Australia start at approximately NZ$350/700 one way/return. Other trans-Tasman options:

**Flight Centre** ( ☎ 0800 243 544; www.flightcentre.co.nz) Has a large central office in Auckland and many branches throughout the country.

**Freedom Air** ( ☎ 0800 600 500; www.freedomair.com) An Air New Zealand subsidiary that operates direct flights and offers excellent rates year-round.

**House of Travel** (www.houseoftravel.co.nz) Cheapest airfares on any airline from NZ to Australia. Note you can only book for travel out of NZ.

## UK & Ireland

There are two routes from the UK: the western route via the USA and the Pacific, and the eastern route via the Middle East and Asia. Flights are usually cheaper and more frequent on the latter. Some of the best deals around are with Emirates, Malaysia Airlines and Japan Airlines. Unless there are special deals on offer, British Airways, Singapore Airlines and Qantas generally have higher fares but may offer a more direct route.

A popular agent in the UK is the ubiquitous **STA Travel** ( ☎ 0870-160 0599; www.statravel .co.uk). Typical direct fares from London to Adelaide are UK£400/700 one way/return during the low season (March to June). In September and mid-December fares go up by as much as 30%, while the rest of the year they're somewhere in-between. High-season fares start at around UK£450/800 one way/return.

From Australia you can expect to pay around $900/1650 one way/return in the low season to London and other European capitals (with stops in Asia on the way), and $1100/2050 in the high season.

## USA

Airlines directly connecting Australia with San Francisco or Los Angeles include Air

New Zealand, Qantas and United Airlines. There are also numerous airlines offering flights via Asia, with stopover possibilities including Tokyo, Kuala Lumpur, Bangkok, Hong Kong and Singapore; and via the Pacific with stopover possibilities such as Nadi (Fiji), Rarotonga (Cook Islands), Tahiti (French Polynesia) and Auckland (NZ). In most cases, you will need to purchase an additional fare to Adelaide, as the usual gateway is the east coast of Australia. However, it is also possible to change flights at your Asian or Pacific stopover for Adelaide.

As in Canada, discount travel agents in the USA are known as consolidators. San Francisco is the ticket consolidator capital of America, although some good deals can be found in Los Angeles, New York and other big cities.

**STA Travel** (☎ 800-777 0112; www.statravel.com) has offices around the country, and can assist with tickets. Typically you can get a return ticket to Melbourne or Sydney from the west coast for US$1300/1700 in the low/high season, or from the east coast for US$1600/1900. Numerous domestic services fly between each capital city in Australia and Adelaide daily.

## AIR – DOMESTIC

The major Australian domestic carrier, **Qantas** (Map pp64-5; ☎ 13 1313; www.qantas.com.au; 144 North Tce, Adelaide), and highly competitive **Virgin Blue** (☎ 13 67 89; www.virginblue.com.au) fly all over Australia, operating flights between Adelaide and other capital cities and major centres, but do not offer a service within the state (see p270 for regional airlines). Qantas' cut-price **Jetstar** (☎ 13 15 38; www.jetstar.com.au), set up to counter the challenge from Virgin Blue, services capital cities and holiday destinations. All airports and domestic flights are nonsmoking.

**Regional Express** (Rex; ☎ 13 17 13; www.regional express.com.au) flies to Broken Hill in New South Wales (NSW) direct from Adelaide ($260).

### Fares

Few people pay full fare on domestic travel, as the airlines offer a wide range of discounts, particularly for Internet bookings (sometimes around 60% off the full fare). These come and go and there are also regular special fares, so keep your eyes peeled.

Approximate one-way fares include: Melbourne ($120), Sydney ($150), Perth ($170), Alice Springs ($200) and Darwin ($250).

Advance-purchase deals provide the cheapest airfares. Some advance-purchase fares offer up to 33% discount off one-way fares and up to 50% or more off return fares. You have to book one to four weeks ahead, and you often have to stay away for at least one Saturday night. There are restrictions on changing flights and you can lose up to 100% of the ticket price if you cancel.

There are also special deals available only to foreign visitors (in possession of an outbound ticket). If booked in Australia these fares offer a 40% discount off a full-fare economy ticket. They can also be booked from overseas (which usually works out a bit cheaper).

**Regional Express** (Rex; ☎ 13 17 13; www.regional express.com.au) has a 'Rex Backpacker' scheme, where international visitors (Australian visitors are ineligible) pay $500/950 for one/two month's worth of unlimited travel on the airline – standby fares only.

## LAND

Bitumen roads in generally good condition link the vast distances between Adelaide and other Australian cities.

### Border Crossings

Main routes into SA include Hwy 1 across the Nullarbor Plain from Western Australia (WA). The Stuart Hwy comes south from Alice Springs in the Northern Territory (NT) and runs through Coober Pedy (p240). From Victoria, there are two main crossings: the Princes Hwy (and Great Ocean Rd) runs via Mt Gambier (p150) while the more direct route, the Dukes Hwy crosses via Bordertown (p158) from Victoria's Western Hwy.

### Bus

Many travellers prefer to see SA by bus because it's one of the best ways to come to grips with the state's size – also the bus companies have far more comprehensive route networks than the railway system.

Adelaide's **central bus station** (Map pp64-5; 101-111 Franklin St) contains terminals and ticket offices for all major interstate and statewide services. It also has left-luggage lockers. For bus timetables see **State Guide** (www.bussa.com .au). Discounts for backpacker associations/

**INTERSTATE QUARANTINE**

When travelling in Australia, whether by land or air, you'll come across signs (mainly in airports, interstate train stations and at state borders) warning of the possible dangers of carrying fruit, plants and vegetables (which may be infected with a disease or pest) from one area to another. Certain pests and diseases – such as fruit fly, cucurbit thrips, grape phylloxera and potato cyst nematodes, to name a few – are prevalent in some areas but not in others, and so for obvious reasons authorities would like to limit them spreading.

There are quarantine inspection posts on some state borders and occasionally elsewhere. While quarantine control often relies on honesty, many posts are staffed and the officers are entitled to search your car for undeclared items. Generally they'll confiscate all fresh fruit and vegetables, so it's best to leave shopping for these items until the first town past the inspection point.

international student ID card holders are available.

**V/Line** ( ☎ 13 61 96, 08-8231 7620; www.vlinepassenger.com.au; ✆ 7.30am-5pm Mon-Fri) runs daily bus/train services to Melbourne ($62, 11½ hours), and Sydney ($155, 21 hours). Melbourne passengers take the train to/from Bendigo in Victoria.

**Firefly Express** ( ☎ 1300 730 740; www.fireflyexpress.com.au; ✆ 7am-8.30pm) departs at 7.30am and 8.30pm for Melbourne ($50, 11 hours) and Sydney ($100, 24 hours).

**Greyhound Australia** ( ☎ 13 14 99; www.greyhound.com.au; ✆ 6am-8.30pm) runs services between Adelaide and Melbourne ($65, 11 hours), Sydney ($145, 25 hours) via Broken Hill or Renmark, Alice Springs ($215, 21 hours) and Perth ($290, 35¼ hours). All buses have air-conditioning, toilets and videos, and smoking is forbidden. Australian and international students, holders of VIP and Nomads cards and children under 14 receive 10% discounts on passes. See also Bus Tours (right) for information on companies that provide hop-on/hop-off bus services.

**PASSES**

If you're planning to travel around Australia, check out Greyhound Australia's excellent Aussie Pass deals.

The **Aussie Kilometre Pass** is purchased in kilometre blocks, starting at 2000km ($330), in 1000-kilometre blocks up to 10,000km ($1260); 5000km costs $685. You can get off at any point on the scheduled route and have unlimited stopovers within the life of the pass. Backtracking is also allowed.

Choose from 25 preset routes covering the east coast, central Australia and WA, or a combination traversing the continent with

an **Explorer Pass** (valid six or 12 months). For passes that follow a circular route, you can start anywhere along the loop, and finish at the same spot. The main limitation is that, while you can travel in whichever direction you like, you can't backtrack, except on 'dead-end' short sectors. Passes include the following:

**All Australian Pass** ($2485) Takes you right around the country, including up or down through the Centre.

**Aussie Highlights** ($1470) Allows you to loop around the eastern half of Australia from Sydney taking in Melbourne, Adelaide, Coober Pedy, Uluru (Ayers Rock), Alice Springs, Darwin (and Kakadu), Cairns, Townsville, the Whitsundays, Brisbane and Surfers Paradise.

**Best of the East** ($1200) Allows you to loop around east coast Australia, through SA & the Centre, with detours to Uluru and King's Canyon.

**Best of the Outback** ($700) Allows you to travel from Adelaide to Darwin via Alice Springs.

**Best of the West** ($1480) Allows you to travel from Adelaide to Perth, along the coastal highway to Broome and Darwin and return to Adelaide via the Red Centre.

**Central Explorer** ($595) Loops around Sydney, Victoria and SA, then up to Uluru and the Centre.

**Country Road** ($835) Sydney, Victoria, SA, central Australia, Townsville and Cairns in Queensland.

## Bus Tours

Backpacker-style bus tours offer a great way to get from A to B and see the sights on the way. The buses are often smaller and not necessarily as comfortable as those of the big bus companies. Outback tours generally include Flinders Ranges, Coober Pedy and Uluru. Operators include:

**Groovy Grape** ( ☎ 1800 661 177, 08-8371 4000; www.groovygrape.com.au) Three-days Melbourne–Adelaide ($285) along the Great Ocean Rd, seven-days Adelaide–Alice Springs ($750), stopping in the Flinders Ranges,

Coober Pedy and Uluru. Includes all meals, camping ground charges and national park entry fees. Small groups.

**Heading Bush** ( ☎ 1800 639 933; www.headingbush .com) These rugged, small group 10-day Adelaide–Alice Springs expeditions (with/without VIP or YHA $1195/1400) are all-inclusive. Tours pass through the Flinders Ranges, William Creek, Coober Pedy, the Simpson Desert and aboriginal communities, into the NT, Uluru and West MacDonnell Ranges.

**Nullarbor Traveller** ( ☎ 08-8390 3297; www.the -traveller.com.au) Relaxed camping and hostelling trips between Adelaide and Perth (7/9 days $770/990) which include bushwalking, surfing and whale-watching. Prices include accommodation, national park entry fees and almost all meals.

**Oz Experience** ( ☎ 1300 300 028, 02-9368 1766; www.oz experience.com) A hop-on/hop-off backpackers transport network with frequent services in a big loop around the eastern half of Australia including Darwin, Adelaide and the east coast. There's a range of passes (valid for six or 12 months). Sydney to Darwin via Melbourne, Adelaide and Alice Springs costs around $1100.

**Wayward Bus** ( ☎ 1800 882 823; www.waywardbus .com.au) Melbourne–Adelaide via the Coorong and Great Ocean Rd ($295, 3½ days); weekly Adelaide–Alice Springs ($790, eight days; $180, 3 days) via Clare Valley, Flinders Ranges, Oodnadatta Track, Coober Pedy and Uluru. Prices include sightseeing, food kitties are generally extra.

### Car & Motorcycle

See opposite for details on car travel in SA.

### Hitching

Hitching is never entirely safe – we do not recommend it. Hitching to or from SA across the Nullarbor is definitely not advisable as waits of two or three days are common.

People looking for travelling companions for the long car journeys interstate often leave notices on boards in hostels and backpacker accommodation. Ask around. Just as hitchers should be wary when accepting lifts, drivers who pick up fellow travellers to share the costs should also be aware of the possible risks involved.

### Train

The interstate train terminal is at Railway Tce, Keswick, southwest of the city centre (Map pp64–5). **Skylink** ( ☎ 08-8332 0528; www.sky linkadelaide.com; ⊙ bookings 7am-10pm) will pick up prebooked passengers on its airport–city runs ($4).

**Great Southern Railway** ( ☎ 13 21 47, 08-8213 4444; www.trainways.com.au; ⊙ 7.30am-8pm Mon-Fri, 8am-

6pm Sat, 9am-5pm Sun) operate all train services in and out of SA. Backpackers are eligible for huge discounts (around 50%) and cheap six-month passes ($450) with specific ID.

The following trains depart from Adelaide regularly:

**Ghan** To Alice Springs (economy seat/twin-berth sleeper $215/680, 19 hours)

**Ghan** To Darwin (economy seat/twin-berth sleeper $440/1390, 47 hours)

**Indian Pacific** To Perth (economy seat/twin-berth sleeper $310/960, 39 hours)

**Indian Pacific** To Sydney (economy seat/twin-berth sleeper $223/450, 25 hours)

**Overland** To Melbourne (economy seat/twin-berth sleeper $60/150, 11 hours)

The fastest service between Sydney and Adelaide is Speedlink (approximately 20 hours) – you travel from Sydney to Albury on the XPT train, and from Albury to Adelaide on a V/ Line bus.

# GETTING AROUND

## AIR

See Transport sections in destination chapters for details on small airlines that fly to country destinations.

**Airlines of SA** ( ☎ 13 13 13, www.airlinesofsa.com.au) Flies twice each weekday from Adelaide to Port Augusta ($140).

**O'Connor Airlines** ( ☎ 13 13 13, 08-8723 0666; www .oconnor-airlines.com.au) Flies between Adelaide, Melbourne, Mildura, Mt Gambier and Whyalla.

**Rex** ( ☎ 13 17 13; www.regionalexpress.com.au) Flies between Adelaide and Kingscote on Kangaroo Island ($120), Coober Pedy ($167), Ceduna (from $305), Mt Gambier ($205), Port Lincoln ($185) and Whyalla ($165). Special fares can be 30% the price of fully-flexible fares.

## BICYCLE

Whether you're hiring a bike to ride around the city or wearing out your chain-wheels on a Mt Gambier to Marla marathon, you'll find that SA is a great place for cycling. There are some excellent bike tracks in Adelaide, thousands of kilometres of quiet road (many without hills of any real consequence) in the country, converted railway tracks in wine regions and the Mawson Trail (see p40), an 800km track from Adelaide to Blinman.

Note that bicycle helmets are compulsory in Australia. Make yourself as visible

as possible to other road-users by wearing light-coloured and (at night) reflective gear, and mounting white front lights and red rear lights.

If you're coming specifically to cycle, it makes sense to bring your own bike – check with your airline for costs and the degree of dismantling/packing that's required. While you can load your bike onto a bus to skip the boring bits, the bus companies require you to dismantle your bike, and some don't guarantee that it will travel on the same bus as you. Adelaide metropolitan buses do not carry bikes at all.

Bicycles can be hired in Adelaide and scenic areas including McLaren Vale, Victor Harbor, Hahndorf, the Barossa and Clare Valleys and the Flinders Ranges.

Dehydration is no joke and can be life-threatening. No matter how fit you are, water is still vital. It can get very hot in summer, and you should take things slowly until you're used to the heat. Cycling in 35°C-plus temperatures isn't too bad if you wear a hat and plenty of sunscreen, and drink *lots* of water.

Outback travel needs to be properly planned, with the availability of drinking water the main concern – those isolated water sources (bores, tanks, creeks and the like) shown on your map may be dry or un-drinkable, so you can't depend entirely on them. Also make sure you've got the necessary spare parts and bike-repair knowledge. Be aware of the blistering northerlies that make north-bound cycling a nightmare in summer. In April, when the clear autumn weather begins, the southeast trades prevail, and you can have (theoretically at least) tailwinds all the way to Darwin.

Check with locals if you're heading into remote areas, and let someone know where you're headed before setting off.

For information on bike touring around the state contact **Bicycle SA** ( ☎ 08-8410 1406; www .bikesa.asn.au).

## BOAT

The only passenger services in SA are the ferries that operate from Cape Jervis and Wirrina to Kangaroo Island. See p118.

## BUS

Adelaide's **central bus station** (Map pp64-5; 101-111 Franklin St) has ticket offices and termi-nals for all major interstate and statewide services, and left-luggage lockers. For bus timetables see **State Guide** (www.bussa.com.au), which is also available in brochure format at the bus station. Discounts are available for backpacker associations/international student ID card holders. For details of bus passes, see p269.

The main bus services provider within SA is **Premier Stateliner** ( ☎ 08-8415 5555; www.premier stateliner.com.au; 7am-9pm). Its services from Adelaide include: McLaren Vale and Victor Harbor on the Fleurieu Peninsula; Mt Gambier; Nuriootpa in the Barossa Valley; the Clare Valley; Whyalla; Port Lincoln on the Eyre Peninsula; Ceduna on the west coast; Port Augusta to Roxby Downs via Woomera; Port Augusta via Port Broughton; Kadina, Wallaroo and Moonta; Port Wakefield and Port Pirie; the Riverland; Waikerie, Kingston OM, Berri Loxton, Barmera and Renmark; Mt Gambier via the Coorong and Robe, or via Bordertown, Naracoorte and Penola. Other bus companies include:

**Barossa Valley Coaches** ( ☎ 08-8564 3022; bvcoach@bvcoach.com) Services from Adelaide to Lyndoch, Tanunda, Nuriootpa and Angaston; also to Kapunda via Gawler.

**Bute Buses' Mid-North Passenger Service** ( ☎ 08-8826 2346) Services Orroroo and Peterborough from Adelaide.

**Greyhound Australia** ( ☎ 13 14 99; www.greyhound .com.au) Travels daily to Perth via Ceduna; Alice Springs via Pimba, Glendambo and Coober Pedy; and Sydney via Barmera, Berri and Renmark.

**Gulf Getaways** ( ☎ 1800 170 170; Augusta Fisheries, Marryatt St, Port Augusta) Services between Port Augusta and Broken Hill.

**Mid-North Passenger Service** ( ☎ 08-8823 2375) Services from Adelaide to Auburn, Clare and Peterborough. Other services to Burra, Jamestown and Orroroo.

**Murray Bridge Passenger Service** ( ☎ 08-8415 5579; www.premierstateliner.com.au) Adelaide to Murray Bridge and Mannum.

**Southlink** ( ☎ 08-8186 2888; www.southlink.com.au) Services the Fleurieu Peninsula.

**Transit Plus** ( ☎ 08-8339 7544; www.transitplus .au) Adelaide Hills region.

**Yorke Peninsula Coaches** ( ☎ 1800 625 099, 08-8666 2255) Services Peterborough from Adelaide; Quorn, Wilmington and a few smaller towns in the southern Flinders Ranges from Port Augusta.

## CAR & MOTORCYCLE

Travelling by car is the best option in SA because it gives you the freedom to explore off the beaten track. Many towns have bus services only two or three days a week, and much of the state has no public transport at all, such as the Flinders Ranges where, if you haven't got your own transport, the only realistic options are to take a tour or to hire a vehicle. With several people travelling together, costs are reasonable and, provided that you don't experience any major mechanical problems, there are many benefits.

Motorcycles are another popular way of getting from place to place. The climate is good for bikes for much of the year, and the many small tracks from the road into the bush lead to perfect spots to spend the night. A fuel range of 350km will cover fuel stops up the Centre and on Hwy 1 around the continent. The long, open roads are really made for large-capacity machines above 750cc, which Australians prefer once they outgrow their 250cc learner restrictions. But that doesn't stop enterprising individuals from tackling the length and breadth of the continent on 250cc trail bikes. Doing it on a small bike is not impossible, just tedious at times.

Beware of dehydration in the dry, hot air – force yourself to drink plenty of water, even if you don't feel thirsty. In the outback, where it can be a long way between drinks, you'll need to carry at least 4L per day in warm weather.

## Automobile Associations

The **Royal Automobile Association of South Australia** (RAA; Map pp64-5; ☎ 08-8202 4600; www.raa .net; 55 Hindmarsh Sq, Adelaide) has lots of useful advice on statewide motoring, including road safety, local regulations and buying or selling a car. It also offers emergency breakdown services. The RAA has reciprocal arrangements with similar organisations overseas and other state automobile associations:

**Automobile Association of the Northern Territory** (AANT; ☎ 08-8981 3837; www.aant.com.au; 79-81 Smith St, Darwin 0800)

**National Roads & Motorists Association** (NRMA; ☎ 13 11 22; www.nrma.com.au) In NSW.

**Royal Automobile Club of Victoria** (RACV; ☎ 13 19 55; www.racv.com.au)

**Royal Automobile Club of Western Australia** (RACWA; ☎ 13 17 03; www.rac.com.au; 228 Adelaide Tce, Perth)

## Driving Licence

You can usually use your own country's driving licence in SA for up to three months, as long as it carries your photo for identification and is in English (if it's not, you'll need a certified translation). Alternatively, it's a simple matter to arrange an **International Driving Permit** (IDP), which should be supported by your home licence. Just go to your home country's automobile association and it can issue one on the spot. The permits are valid for 12 months, and cost approximately $20.

## Fuel

Fuel (super, diesel and unleaded) is available from service stations that sport the well-known international brand names. Gas (LPG) is not always stocked at more remote roadhouses – if your car runs on gas it's safer to have dual fuel capacity. Prices vary from place to place and from price war to price war, but basically fuel is heavily taxed and continues to hike up. Unleaded petrol (used in most new cars) is now hovering above $1 a litre, even in the cities. Once you get out into the country, prices soar – in outback SA it was as high as $1.50 a litre at the time of writing. Distances between fill-ups can be long in the outback but there are only a handful of tracks where you'll require a long-range fuel tank. On main roads there'll be a small town or roadhouse roughly every 200km or so.

## Hire

Competition between car-rental companies in SA is pretty fierce, so rates tend to be variable and lots of special deals come and go. The main thing to remember when assessing your options is distance – if you want to travel far, you need unlimited kilometres. As well as the big firms, there are a vast number of local firms, or firms with outlets in a limited number of locations. These are almost always cheaper than the big operators – sometimes half the price – but cheap car hire can often come with serious restrictions.

One-way hire into or out of the NT, WA, Victoria or NSW may be subject to a hefty repositioning fee; however, some big rental firms offer good deals from Alice Springs to Adelaide or Adelaide to Melbourne. Ask plenty of questions about this before deciding on one company over another.

The major companies offer a choice: either unlimited kilometres, or 100km or so a day free plus however many cents per kilometre over this. You must be at least 21 years old to hire from most firms – if you're under 25 you may only be able to hire a small car or have to pay a surcharge. It's cheaper if you rent for a week or more and there are often low-season and weekend discounts. Credit cards are the usual payment method.

Note that most car rental companies do include insurance in the price (see Insurance, right), but in the event of an accident the hirer is still liable for a sometimes-hefty excess. Most offer excess-reduction insurance on top of the rental rate. Major companies all have offices or agents in Adelaide and larger centres.

**Avis** ( ☎ 13 63 33; www.avis.com.au)
**Budget** ( ☎ 1300 362 848; www.budget.com.au)
**Hertz** ( ☎ 13 30 39; www.hertz.com.au)
**Thrifty** ( ☎ 13 61 39; www.thrifty.com.au)

If you want short-term car hire, smaller local companies are generally the cheapest and are pretty reliable. See p80 for details of hire companies in Adelaide.

#### 4WD & CAMPERVAN RENTAL
Renting a 4WD enables you to get right off the beaten track and out to some of the natural wonders that most travellers miss. Check the insurance conditions carefully, especially the excess, as they can be onerous. Even for a 4WD, the insurance offered by most companies does not cover damage caused when travelling 'off-road', which basically means anything that is not a maintained bitumen or dirt road. Hertz, Budget, Thrifty and Avis have 4WD rentals. Hertz and Avis offer one-way rentals between Adelaide and the NT. Most companies provide larger vehicles, such as Toyota Landcruisers and Nissans, including basic insurance and 200km free.

The following companies have fitted-out 4WDs and vans, offer one-way rental and have offices in other cities, including Alice Springs:

**Britz Rentals** ( ☎ 1800 331 454; www.britz.com)
Fully equipped 4WD vehicles fitted out as campervans are available for hire – just the thing if you're going to 'do' the outback and the Flinders Ranges. They start at around $90/130 per day for a 2-/4-wheel drive. Minimum five-day rental.

**Caudell's** ( ☎ 08-8410 5552; 121 Currie St, Adelaide) Associated with Thrifty.
**Wicked Campers** ( ☎ 1800 246 869; 07-3257 2170; www.wickedcampers.com.au) Fitted-out vans from $60/48 per day for one/eight weeks' rental.

### Insurance
In Australia, third-party personal injury insurance is always included in the vehicle registration cost. This ensures that every registered vehicle carries at least minimum insurance. You'd be wise to extend that minimum to at least third-party property insurance as well – minor collisions with other vehicles can be amazingly expensive. When it comes to hire cars, know exactly what your liability is in the event of an accident.

Rather than risk paying out thousands of dollars if you do have an accident, you can take out your own comprehensive insurance on the car, or (the usual option) pay an additional daily amount to the rental company for an 'insurance excess reduction' policy. This brings down the amount of excess you must pay in the event of an accident from between $2000 and $5000 to a few hundred dollars.

Be aware that if you're travelling on dirt roads you will not be covered by insurance unless you have a 4WD – in other words, if you have an accident you'll be liable for all the costs involved. Also, most companies' insurance won't cover the cost of damage to glass (including the windscreen) or tyres. Always read the small print.

### Outback Travel
The outback offers some great touring experiences on remote dirt roads and tracks. In fact, the Stuart Hwy and the main roads to Lyndhurst, Roxby Downs and Wilpena Pound are the only bitumen roads in the entire outback and northern Flinders Ranges. All other routes are dirt or gravel surfaced; their condition varies depending on factors such as when it last rained and when the last grader went through.

It's common sense to make sure your vehicle is in first-class mechanical shape before attempting to drive on any remote roads or tracks. Garages (and fuel supplies) are few and far between in these places; if you break down and become stranded in some small town waiting for parts, the experience could wreck your holiday budget. The SA Royal

TRANSPORT

Automobile Association (RAA) can advise on the essential spares and tools to carry. Always pack extra water for the radiator – you may need it if you blow a hose, and it's best not to use up your drinking ration.

When travelling to very remote areas, it's advisable to carry a high-frequency (HF) radio transceiver equipped to pick up the relevant Royal Flying Doctor Service bases. A satellite phone, Global Positioning System (GPS) finder and an EPIRB (Emergency Position Indicating Radio Beacon; ensure it's a Digital 406 MHz) can also be useful. Of course, all of this equipment comes at a cost, but it's wise to keep in the back of your mind the fact that travellers have perished in the Australian desert after breaking down.

Always carry plenty of water. In warm weather allow 5L per person per day and an extra amount for the radiator, carried in several containers. It's wise not to attempt the tougher routes during the hottest part of the year (October to April inclusive) – apart from the risk of heat exhaustion, simple mishaps can easily lead to tragedy at this time. Conversely, there's no point going anywhere on dirt roads in the outback if there has been recent flooding (this is particularly common in the north during the wet season). Get local advice before heading off into the middle of nowhere.

If you do run into trouble in the back of beyond, always stay with your car. It's easier to spot a car than a human being from the air, and you wouldn't be able to carry a heavy load of water very far anyway. Police suggest that you carry two spare tyres (for added safety) and, if stranded, try to set fire to one of them (let the air out first) – the pall of smoke will be seen for miles.

Of course, before you set out on your trip, let family, friends or your car-hire company know where you're going and when you intend to be back.

For information on some favourite outback tracks through SA see p246.

## Purchase

If you're planning a stay of several months that involves lots of driving, purchasing a second-hand car will be much cheaper than renting.

You'll probably get any car cheaper by buying privately rather than through a car

dealer. Buying through a dealer does have the advantage of some sort of guarantee, but this is not much use if you're buying a car in Adelaide one week and setting off for Perth the next. In SA there are no compulsory safety checks prior to the registration of a vehicle in a new name.

**Boomerang Cars** ( ☎ 0414-882559; www.boomerang cars.com.au; 261 Currie St, Adelaide) cater for the travelling market.

Make use of the RAA. They can advise members on local regulations, give general guidelines about buying a car, and perform on-site mechanical inspections of a car before you agree to purchase it. They also offer car insurance.

If you'd like to purchase your own motorcycle and are fortunate enough to have time on your hands, getting mobile on two wheels in SA is quite feasible. The beginning of winter (June) is a good time to start looking. Local newspapers and the bike-related press have classified advertisement sections.

See p273 for information about vehicle insurance.

## Road Conditions

This vast state is not criss-crossed by multilane highways; there's not enough traffic and the distances are simply too great to justify them. On all of the main routes, roads are well surfaced and maintained and have two lanes.

Driving on unsealed roads requires special care – a car will perform differently when braking and turning on dirt. Under no circumstances should you exceed 80km/h on dirt roads; if you go faster you will not have enough time to respond to a sharp turn, stock on the road or an unmarked gate or cattle grid. So take it easy: take time to see the sights and don't try to break the land speed record.

Travelling by car within SA means sometimes having to pass road trains. These articulated trucks and their loads can be up to 53.5m long, 2.5m wide, and they travel at around 100km/h. Overtaking them is a tricky process; at times you will have to drive off the bitumen to get past. Exercise caution – and remember that it is much harder for the driver of the larger road train to control their vehicle than it is for you to control your car.

## Road Hazards

Signposting on the main country roads is generally OK, but around Adelaide and other large towns it can be less so. In fact, you can spend a lot of time trying to find street name signs and, as for finding your way out of the city, the best thing to do is buy a street directory and try to remain calm.

Cows, horses, sheep and kangaroos are common hazards in many country areas, particularly in the outback where land tends to be unfenced – even if there are fences, kangaroos easily leap over or crawl underneath them. Often the only green grass in sight is along the side of the road, so grazing animals tend to congregate there. Wedge-tailed eagles may fly up directly in front of you from where they've been feasting on roadkill.

None of these animals has any road-sense whatsoever, so be careful; a collision is likely to kill or injure the animal (you may have to put it out of its misery) and could seriously damage your vehicle.

Being nocturnal, kangaroos are most active from dusk to dawn, but you also see them out and about on overcast days. They usually travel in family groups, so if you see one hopping across the road in front of you, slow right down – mum and the kids are probably just behind. Many Australians avoid travelling in country areas at night because of the hazard posed by animals. If you travel at night, keep the speed down.

If a kangaroo or cow does appear out of the darkness in front of you, hit the brakes, dip your lights (so you won't continue to dazzle it, making it even more confused) and sound the horn. Only take more extreme evasive action if it is safe to do so. Many people have died in accidents caused by the driver swerving to miss an animal – it's better to damage the car than kill yourself and others with you.

A not-so-obvious hazard is driver fatigue. Driving long distances (particularly in hot weather) can be so tiring that you might fall asleep at the wheel – it's not uncommon and the consequences can be unthinkable. So on a long haul, stop and rest every two hours or so – stretch, do some exercise, change drivers or have a coffee.

## Road Rules

Driving in SA holds few surprises. Australians drive on the left-hand side of the road, and cars 'give way to the right', meaning that if an intersection is unmarked (unusual), you *must* give way to vehicles entering the intersection from your right.

The speed limit in built-up areas was 60km/h but has been reduced to 50km/h on residential streets in most states – keep an eye out for signs. Near schools, the limit is 40km/h in the morning and afternoon. On the open highway it's 110km/h. Traffic police have speed radar cameras and are fond of using them in hidden locations – in the outback they often use aircraft to detect speedsters.

Oncoming drivers who flash their lights may be giving you a friendly indication of a speed camera ahead; they may also be telling you that you've left your headlights on, or they may just be flashing a greeting. The accepted thing to do is flash back – and slow down if you're speeding.

All new cars in Australia have seat belts back and front; if your seat has a belt you're required to wear it. You'll be fined if you don't. Small children must be belted into an approved safety seat.

## LOCAL TRANSPORT

See Adelaide (p80) and individual chapters for local transport within those areas.

## TOURS

Taking an organised tour is a useful way to get around if you don't have your own transport, have only limited time or would like the commentary. South Australia has a large number of tour operators specialising in all sorts of activities. See Tours sections in regional chapters.

## TRAIN

Other than Adelaide suburban trains and a handful of tourist trains (see p90, p109 and p206), there are no intrastate train services in SA. You can, however, get on and off the interstate trains as they travel through the state.

See the Adelaide (p81) chapter for details on trains running in and around the city.

# Health Dr David Millar

## CONTENTS

| | |
|---|---|
| **Before You Go** | **276** |
| Insurance | 276 |
| Recommended Vaccinations | 276 |
| Medical Checklist | 276 |
| Internet Resources | 277 |
| Further Reading | 277 |
| **In Transit** | **277** |
| Deep Vein Thrombosis (DVT) | 277 |
| Jet Lag & Motion Sickness | 277 |
| **In South Australia** | **277** |
| Availability & Cost of Health Care | 277 |
| Infectious Diseases | 278 |
| Environmental Hazards | 278 |

Australia is a remarkably healthy country in which to travel, considering that such a large portion of it lies in the tropics. Tropical diseases such as malaria and yellow fever are unknown, diseases of insanitation such as cholera and typhoid are unheard of and, thanks to Australia's isolation and quarantine standards, even animal diseases such as rabies and foot-and-mouth disease have yet to be recorded.

Few travellers to South Australia (SA) should experience anything worse than an upset stomach or a bad hangover, and if you do fall ill, the standard of hospitals and health care is high.

# BEFORE YOU GO

Since most vaccines don't produce immunity until at least two weeks after they're given, it's advisable to visit a physician four to eight weeks before departure. Ask your doctor for an International Certificate of Vaccination (otherwise known as the yellow booklet), which will list all the vaccinations you've received. This is mandatory for countries that require proof of yellow-fever vaccination upon entry (sometimes required in Australia, see right), but it's a good idea to carry it wherever you travel.

Bring your medications in their original, clearly labelled containers. A signed and dated letter from your physician describing your medical conditions and medications, including generic names, is also a good idea. If carrying syringes or needles, be sure to have a physician's letter documenting their medical necessity.

## INSURANCE

Health insurance is essential for all travellers. While health care in SA is of a high standard and not overly expensive by international standards, considerable costs can build up and repatriation is extremely expensive. If your health insurance doesn't cover you for medical expenses abroad, consider getting extra insurance; checkout Subwwway on www.lonelyplanet.com for more information. Find out in advance if your insurance plan will make payments directly to providers or reimburse you later for overseas health expenditures. See opposite for details of health care in SA.

## RECOMMENDED VACCINATIONS

Proof of yellow-fever vaccination is required only from travellers who enter Australia within six days of having stayed overnight or longer in a yellow-fever-infected country. For a full list of these countries visit the website of the **World Health Organization** (WHO; www.who.int/wer) or that of the **Centers for Disease Control and Prevention** (www.cdc.gov /travel/blusheet.htm).

If you're really worried about your health when travelling there are a few vaccinations you could consider for SA. The WHO recommends that all travellers should be covered for diphtheria, tetanus, measles, mumps, rubella, chickenpox and polio, as well as hepatitis B, regardless of their destination. When planning travel, it is a great time to ensure that all routine vaccination cover is complete. The consequences of these diseases can be severe and while Australia has high levels of childhood vaccination coverage, outbreaks of these diseases do occur.

## MEDICAL CHECKLIST
- antibiotics
- antidiarrhoeal drugs (eg loperamide)
- acetaminophen/paracetamol or aspirin

- anti-inflammatory drugs (eg ibuprofen)
- antihistamines (for hay fever and allergic reactions)
- antibacterial ointment to treat cuts and abrasions
- steroid cream or cortisone (for poison ivy and other allergic rashes)
- bandages, gauze, gauze rolls
- adhesive or paper tape
- scissors, safety pins, tweezers
- thermometer
- pocket-knife
- DEET-containing insect repellent to protect the skin
- permethrin-containing insect spray for clothing, tents and bed nets
- sunscreen
- oral rehydration salts
- iodine tablets or a water filter (for water purification)

## INTERNET RESOURCES

There is a wealth of travel health advice on the Internet. For further information, the **Lonely Planet website** (www.lonelyplanet.com) is a good place to start. The **WHO** (www.who.int/ith) publishes a superb book called *International Travel & Health,* which is revised annually and is available online at no cost. Another website of general interest is **MD Travel Health** (www.mdtravelhealth.com), which provides complete travel health recommendations for every country and is updated daily.

## FURTHER READING

Lonely Planet's *Healthy Travel Australia, New Zealand & the Pacific* is a pocket-sized guide packed with useful information including pretrip planning, emergency first aid, immunisation and disease information and what to do if you get sick on the road. *Travel with Children* from Lonely Planet includes advice on travel health for younger children.

---

**TRAVEL-HEALTH WEBSITES**

It's usually a good idea to consult your government's travel-health website before departure, if one is available:

**Australia** www.dfat.gov.au/travel
**Canada** www.travelhealth.gc.ca
**UK** www.doh.gov.uk/traveladvice
**USA** www.cdc.gov/travel

---

# IN TRANSIT

## DEEP VEIN THROMBOSIS (DVT)

Blood clots may form in the legs (deep vein thrombosis) during flights, chiefly because of prolonged immobility. The longer the flight, the greater the risk. Though most blood clots are reabsorbed uneventfully, some may break off and travel through the blood vessels to the lungs, where they could cause life-threatening complications.

The chief symptom of DVT is swelling or pain of the foot, ankle or calf, usually – but not always – on just one side. When a blood clot travels to the lungs, it may cause chest pain and breathing difficulties. Travellers with any of these symptoms should immediately seek medical attention.

To prevent the development of DVT on long-haul flights, take walks around the cabin, perform isometric compressions of the leg muscles (ie flex the leg muscles while sitting), drink plenty of fluids and avoid alcohol and tobacco.

## JET LAG & MOTION SICKNESS

Jet lag is common when crossing more than five time zones, resulting in insomnia, fatigue, malaise or nausea. To avoid jet lag try drinking plenty of (nonalcoholic) fluids and eating light meals. Upon arrival, get exposure to sunlight and re-adjust your schedule (for meals, sleep etc) as soon as possible.

Antihistamines such as dimenhydrinate and meclizine are usually the first choice for treating motion sickness. Their main side effect is drowsiness. A herbal alternative is ginger, which works like a charm for some people.

# IN SOUTH AUSTRALIA

## AVAILABILITY & COST OF HEALTH CARE

Australia has an excellent health-care system with a mixture of privately run medical clinics and hospitals, and a system of public hospitals funded by the government. The Medicare system covers Australian residents for some health-care costs. Visitors who come from countries with which Australia has a reciprocal health-care agreement (New Zealand, the UK, the Netherlands, Sweden, Finland, Italy, Malta and Ireland) are eligible for benefits to the extent specified under the Medicare programme. If you are from one of these countries, check the details before departure. In general, the agreements provide for any episode of ill-health that requires prompt medical attention. For further details visit www.health.gov.au/pubs /mbs/mbs3/medicare.htm.

There are excellent, specialised public health facilities for women and children in Adelaide. If you have an immediate and serious health problem, phone or visit the casualty department of the nearest public hospital.

Over-the-counter medications are available at chemists (pharmacies) throughout SA. These include painkillers, antihistamines for allergies and skin-care products. You may find that medications readily available over the counter in some countries are only available in Australia by prescription. These include the oral contraceptive pill, some medications for asthma and all antibiotics. If you take medication on a regular basis bring an adequate supply and ensure you have details of the generic name as brand names may differ between countries.

In very remote locations in SA, there may be a significant delay in emergency services reaching you in the event of serious accident or illness – do not underestimate the vastness between most major outback towns. An increased level of self-reliance and preparation is essential: consider taking a wilderness first-aid course, such as those offered at the **Wilderness Medicine Institute** (www .wmi.net.au); take a comprehensive first-aid kit that is appropriate for the activities planned; and ensure that you have adequate means of communication. South Australia has extensive mobile phone coverage, but additional radio communications are important for remote areas. The Royal Flying Doctor Service provides an important backup for remote communities.

## INFECTIOUS DISEASES
### Giardiasis
Drinking untreated water from lakes and streams is not recommended due to the widespread presence of the parasite giardia in the waterways around Australia. Water filters, and boiling or treating water with iodine, are effective in preventing the disease giardiasis. Symptoms consist of intermittent bad smelling diarrhoea, abdominal bloating and wind. Effective treatment is available (tinidazole or metronidazole).

### Meningococcal disease
Meningitis occurs worldwide and is a risk with prolonged, dormitory-style accommodation. A vaccine exists for some types of this disease, namely meningococcal A, C, Y and W. No vaccine is presently available for the viral type of meningitis.

### Ross River Fever
The Ross River virus is spread by mosquitoes living in marshy areas and is widespread throughout Australia. In addition to fever the disease causes headache, joint and muscular pains and a rash, before resolving after five to seven days.

### Sexually Transmitted Diseases
Sexually Transmitted Diseases occur at rates similar to many other Western countries. The most common symptoms are pain while passing urine and a discharge. Infection can be present without symptoms so seek medical screening after any unprotected sex with a new partner. In SA, you'll find sexual health clinics in all of the major hospitals. Always use a condom with any new sexual partner. Condoms are readily available in chemists and through vending machines in many public places, including toilets.

### Viral Encephalitis
Also known as Murray River encephalitis, this virus is spread by mosquitoes. Although the risk to most travellers is low, it is a potentially serious disease normally accompanied by headache, muscle pains and light insensitivity. Residual neurological damage can occur and no treatment is available.

## ENVIRONMENTAL HAZARDS
### Bites & Stings
Calamine lotion or Stingose spray will give some relief to bites and stings and ice packs will reduce the pain and swelling. Wash well and treat any cut with an antiseptic. Where possible avoid bandages and Band-Aids, which can keep wounds moist.

#### MARINE ANIMALS
Marine spikes, such as those found on sea urchins, catfish and stingrays, can cause severe

local pain. If this occurs, immediately immerse the affected area in hot water (as hot as can be tolerated). Keep topping up with hot water until the pain subsides and medical care can be reached.

## SHARKS

Despite extensive media coverage, the risk of shark attack in Australian waters is no greater than in other countries with extensive coastlines. The risk of an attack from sharks on scuba divers in SA is low. Check with local surf life-saving groups about local risks.

## SNAKES

Australian snakes have a fearful reputation that is justified in terms of the potency of their venom, but unjustified in terms of the actual risk to travellers and locals. Snakes are usually quite timid in nature and in most instances will move away if disturbed. They are endowed with only small fangs, making it easy to prevent bites to the lower limbs (where 80% of bites occur) by wearing protective clothing (such as gaiters) around the ankles when bushwalking. The bite marks are small and preventing the spread of toxic venom can be achieved by applying pressure to the wound and immobilising the area with a splint or sling before seeking medical attention. Application of an elastic bandage (you can improvise with a T-shirt) wrapped firmly – but not tight enough to cut off the circulation – around the entire limb, along with immobilisation, is a lifesaving first-aid measure.

## SPIDERS

Australia has a number of poisonous spiders although the only one to have caused a single death in the last 50 years (the Sydney funnel-web) isn't found in SA. Redback spider bites cause increasing pain at the site followed by profuse sweating and generalised symptoms. First aid includes application of ice or cold packs to the bite and transfer to hospital. Some paranoia revolves around the bite of the whitetail (brown recluse) spider, which has been blamed for causing slow-healing ulcers; clean the wound thoroughly and seek medical assistance.

## Heat Sickness

Very hot weather is experienced year-round in some parts of SA. When arriving from a temperate or cold climate, remember that it takes two weeks for acclimatisation to occur. Before the body is acclimatised an excessive amount of salt is lost by perspiring, so increasing the salt in your diet is very important.

Heat exhaustion occurs when fluid intake does not keep up with fluid loss. Symptoms include dizziness, fainting, fatigue, nausea or vomiting. On observation the skin is usually pale, cool and clammy. Treatment consists of rest in a cool, shady place and fluid replacement with water or diluted sports drinks.

Heatstroke is a severe form of heat illness that occurs after fluid depletion or extreme heat challenge from heavy exercise. This is a true medical emergency with heating of the brain leading to disorientation, hallucinations and seizures. Prevention is by maintaining an adequate fluid intake to ensure the continued passage of clear and copious urine, especially during physical exertion.

A number of unprepared travellers die from dehydration each year in outback Australia. This can be prevented by following these simple rules:
- Carry sufficient water for any trip, including extra in case of breakdown.
- Always let someone, such as the local police, know where you are going and when you expect to arrive.
- Carry communications equipment of some form.
- In nearly all cases it's better to stay with your vehicle rather than walking for help.

## Hypothermia

Hypothermia is a risk during the winter in SA. Despite the absence of high mountain ranges, strong winds produce a high chill factor that can result in hypothermia in even moderately cool temperatures. Early signs include the inability to perform fine movements (such as doing up buttons), shivering and a bad case of the 'umbles' (fumbles, mumbles, grumbles and stumbles). The key elements of treatment include changing the environment to one where heat loss is minimised, changing out of any wet clothing, adding dry clothes with wind- and waterproof layers, adding insulation and providing fuel (water and carbohydrates) to allow shivering, which helps build the internal temperature. In severe cases of hypothermia, shivering actually stops – this indicates a medical emergency requiring rapid evacuation in addition to the above measures.

## Insect-Borne Illness

South Australia's most significant insect-borne diseases are Ross River fever and viral (Murray River) encephalitis. Outbreaks are likely to occur in January and February, but the chances of infection are slight. Protection from mosquitoes, sandflies and ticks can be achieved by a combination of the following strategies:

- Wearing loose, long-sleeved clothing.
- Application of 30% DEET on all exposed skin, repeating application every three to four hours.
- Impregnation of clothing with permethrin (an insecticide that kills insects but is safe for humans).

## Surf Beaches & Drowning

The surf can be unpredictable is SA. Check with local surf life-saving organisations before entering the surf, and be aware of your own limitations and expertise before entering the water.

## Ultraviolet Light Exposure

Australia has one of the highest rates of skin cancer in the world. Monitor exposure to direct sunlight closely. Ultraviolet light exposure is at its greatest between 10am and 4pm so avoid skin exposure during these times. Wear a wide-brimmed hat, long-sleeved shirt with a collar and always use 30+ sunscreen, applied 30 minutes before exposure, and repeat regularly to minimise sun damage. Protect your eyes with good-quality sunglasses at the beach or in the outback.

## Water-Borne Illness

Tap water is universally safe in SA. Increasing numbers of the state's streams, rivers and lakes, however, are being contaminated by bugs that cause diarrhoea, making water purification advisable. The simplest way of purifying water is to boil it thoroughly. Consider purchasing a water filter. It's very important when buying a filter to read the specifications indicating exactly what it removes from the water and what it doesn't. Simple filtering will not remove all dangerous organisms, so if you cannot boil water it should be treated chemically. Chlorine tablets will kill many pathogens, but not some parasites such as giardia and amoebic cysts. Iodine is more effective in purifying water and is available in tablet form. Follow the directions carefully and remember that too much iodine can be harmful.

# Glossary

**ACT** – Australian Capital Territory
**Adnyamathanha** – an Aboriginal people of the Flinders Ranges, also known as the *'Hill People'*; a collection of the Wailpi, Kuyani, Jadiaura, Philadappa and Pangkala tribes
**Aussie rules** – Australian rules football: a game vaguely resembling rugby, played by teams of 18

**B&B** – 'bed and breakfast' accommodation
**barbie** – barbecue
**barrack** – cheer on a team at sporting event, support ('Who do you barrack for?')
**big mobs** – large amount, heaps
**bikies** – motorcyclists
**billabong** – a stagnant pool or backwater
**billy** – tin container used to boil water in the *bush*
**bitumen** – surfaced road
**bloke** – man
**blowies, blow flies** – large flies
**bodyboard** – half-sized foam surfboard
**bogan** – young, unsophisticated person
**bonzer** – great
**boogie board** – see *bodyboard*
**boomerang** – a curved, flat, wooden instrument used by Aborigines for hunting game and by souvenir shops for hunting tourists
**booze bus** – police bus used for random breath testing for alcohol
**bottle shop, bottle 'o** – liquor shop, off-licence
**brekky** – breakfast
**Buckley's** – no chance at all
**bull dust** – fine and sometimes deep dust on *outback* roads; also *bullshit*
**bullshit** – untrue, nonsense, balderdash
**bush, the** – country, anywhere away from the city
**bush tucker** – native foods
**bushwalking** – hiking, trekking
**butcher** – 200mL glass of beer
**BYO** – bring your own; a type of restaurant licence that permits customers to drink *grog* they have purchased elsewhere

**Cabernet Sauvignon** – popular red wine grape; requires ageing
**cask wine** – wine packaged in a plastic bladder surrounded by a cardboard box (a great Australian invention); also known as 'chateau cardboard'
**catch ya later** – goodbye, see you later
**cellar doors** – Wineries that have a section open to the public for wine-tasting and sales
**Chardonnay** – most popular white wine grape used for sparkling and still wines
**chocka** – completely full, from 'chock-a-block'
**chook** – chicken

**chuck a U-ey** – make a U-turn; turn a car around within a road
**corroboree** – Aboriginal festival or gathering for ceremonial or spiritual reasons
**counter meal, countery** – pub meal
**crook** – ill or substandard
**Crow-eater** – resident of South Australia
**cuppa** – as in cup of tea, an *outback* institution

**dag** – dirty lump of wool at the back end of a sheep; also an affectionate or mildly abusive term for a socially inept person
**damper** – bush loaf made from flour and water
**DEH** – Department for Environment & Heritage
**deli** – milk bar, corner store
**didgeridoo** – wind instrument made from a hollow piece of wood, traditionally played by Aboriginal men
**dinkum** – honest, genuine
**donga** – small, transportable building widely used in the *outback*
**doorstop** – a sandwich made with large cuts of bread and toasted
**Dreamtime** – complex concept that forms the basis of Aboriginal spirituality, incorporating the creation of the world and the spiritual energies operating around us; 'Dreaming' is often the preferred term as it avoids the association with time
**dunny** – outdoor lavatory

**Esky** – insulated box for keeping food and drinks cool

**fair dinkum** – see *dinkum*
**flake** – shark meat, the fish in fish and chips
**fossick** – hunt for gems or semi-precious stones
**freshie** – freshwater crocodile (harmless unless provoked)

**galah** – noisy parrot, thus noisy idiot
**g'day** – good day; traditional Australian greeting
**grey nomads** – self-funded retirees travelling the country, usually in a caravan, campervan or motor home
**grog** – general term for alcoholic drinks

**Hill People** – see *Adnyamathanha*
**hoon** – idiot, hooligan

**icy pole** – frozen lollipop, ice lolly
**iffy** – dodgy, questionable

**jackaroo** – male trainee on an *outback station*
**jillaroo** – female trainee on an *outback station*

**KI** – Kangaroo Island
**Kiwi** – New Zealander
**knackered** – broken, tired
**Kombi** – a classic (hippies') type of van made by Volkswagen ('*Mate*, that Kombi is *knackered*!')

**GLOSSARY**

**lamington** – square of sponge cake covered in chocolate icing and desiccated coconut
**lollies** – sweets, candy
**loo** – toilet

**mallee** – Grassy woodland found in semiarid parts of Australia; also describes the multistemmed eucalypts that dominate this habitat
**marron** – large freshwater crayfish
**mate** – general term of familiarity, whether you know the person or not; may take a long vowel: 'maaaaate! '
**Merlot** – ('mer-low') grape often blended with *Cabernet Sauvignon* to make softer red wine
**mobile phone** – cell phone
**Mod Oz** – modern Australian cuisine influenced by a wide range of foreign cuisines, but with a definite local flavour
**mozzies** – mosquitoes
**mud map** – rough map that is usually hand drawn
**mug** – a big, 570mL beer
**mullock** – a pile of waste left over from mining

**no worries!** – no problems! That's OK!
**noodle** – to *fossick* for opals missed by the miner ('Can I have a noodle in your *mullock*?')
**NSW** – New South Wales
**NT** – Northern Territory
**Nunga** – collective term used to identify Aborigines from South Australia

**outback** – remote part of the bush

**PADI** – Professional Association of Diving Instructors
**parma** – short for chicken *parmigiana*, a chicken breast, coated in breadcrumbs and fried, then covered with Napoli sauce, cheese, and possibly ham; considered by many to be the ultimate accompaniment to a *schooner*
**pavlova** – (pav) traditional Aussie meringue dessert
**perve** – to gaze with lust; to check something out
**pie floater** – meat pie served in green pea soup; a South Australian favourite
**Pinot Noir** – light red wine grape; grown in colder regions
**pint** – not actually a pint but 425mL of beer
**piss** – beer
**pissed** – drunk
**pissed off** – annoyed
**plonk** – cheap wine
**pokies** – poker machines

**quandong** – a sourish, peachlike fruit; a form of *bush tucker*

**Riesling** – good dry-to-light, sweet white wine
**rip** – a strong ocean current or undertow
**road train** – semitrailer truck towing several trailers
**'roo** – short for kangaroo, especially when it's dinnertime…

**root** – to have sexual intercourse
**rubbish** – to deride or tease

**SA** – South Australia
**saltie** – saltwater crocodile (the dangerous one)
**sanger** – sandwich
**Sauvignon Blanc** – a strong, crisp cooler-climate white wine
**scallops** – shellfish
**schooner** – regular beer glass; 285mL
**scrub** – *bush*
**sealed road** – *bitumen* road
**shark biscuit** – inexperienced surfer
**sheila** – woman
**Shiraz** – the most commonly grown red grape, synony-mous with Australian wines
**shout** – to buy a round of drinks ('Your shout')
**slab** – two dozen *stubbies* or *tinnies*
**snag** – sausage
**station** – large farm
**stickybeak** – nosy person ('That stickybeak was having a *perve* in the back of my *Kombi*')
**story** – tale from the *Dreamtime* that taps into the con-cepts of legend, myth, tradition and the law; carries more weight than an ordinary historical account
**Stubbies** – popular brand of men's work shorts
**stubby** – 375mL bottle of beer
**sunbake** – sunbathe (well, the sun's hot in South Australia)
**swag** – canvas-covered bed roll used in the *outback*

**take the piss** – make fun of, often as social sport
**tea** – evening meal; also a *cuppa* tea
**thongs** – flip-flops or jandals
**Tim Tam** – a commercial chocolate biscuit that lies close to the heart of most Australians
**tinny** – 375mL can of beer; a small aluminium fishing dinghy
**tinny holder** – insulating material used to keep the *tinny* ice-cold

**trucky** – truck driver
**tucker** – food

**unsealed road** – dirt road
**ute** – utility, a pick-up truck

**WA** – Western Australia
**walkabout** – lengthy walk away from it all
**whinge** – to complain, moan
**whoop-whoop** – *outback,* miles from anywhere
**wowser** – an puritanical person; teetotaller; killjoy

**yabbie** – small freshwater crayfish
**yonks** – a long time
**youse** – (pronounced 'yooze') the plural form of 'you' ('That *ute's knackered*. Do youse want a lift in the *Kombi*?')

# Behind the Scenes

## THIS BOOK

The first two editions of *South Australia* were researched and written by local lad, Denis O'Byrne. This edition (renamed *Adelaide and…* to reflect an increased focus on the Festival City and its surrounding regions!) was researched on the ground by diehard SA fan Susannah Farfor, Adelaidian Jill Kirby and the intrepid George Dunford. Susannah was our coordinating author, also writing the Adelaide and surrounds chapters. Jill wrote about areas east and south of Adelaide (including wine regions Barossa, Clare Valley and the Coonawarra…tough gig Jill!) and wrote the new wineries special section. George ranged widely around the state's north and west, rigorously testing rural mechanics' skills regarding flat tyres and blown manifold gaskets.

## THANKS from the Authors

**Susannah** Thanks to navigator Ian Malcolm – surf buddy, hiker, feaster and Shiraz quaffer extraordinaire. Warm thanks for the great local knowledge from Elizabeth and Melanie Dankel, Mark Potter, Annie McColl and family, Jason and Louise James, winery cellar-door staff and the many friendly South Australians who helped answer questions. Thanks also to Matthew Evans for his food/drink expertise, Denis O'Byrne, co-authors George Dunford and Jill Kirby, and the great production team.

**Jill** Firstly, thanks to Denis O'Byrne for his thorough research on previous editions of this guide. My appreciation goes to commissioning editor Errol Hunt for his straightforward direction and support, and to managing cartographer Corie Waddell for her good cheer. David Burnett is a lifesaver!

Jodie van Deventer of the South Australian Tourism Commission (SATC) was a brilliant help, as were many of her colleagues; much gratitude to you all.

Thanks to Peter Tucker of the Houseboat Hirer's Association Inc; Karen Ronning of the Coonawarra Vignerons Association; Katie Cameron of the Adelaide Hills Wine Region Inc; Anne Weddell of the Clare Valley Winemakers Inc; and Marcia Burnett of the SA Wine Industry Association Inc.

Members of our Wine Club are consistently knowledgeable and hedonistic; an inspiring combination, while Nigel & Gwendolyn Schmidt offered many useful tips, with a healthy Barossa bias!

My greatest appreciation has to go to my greatest support and constant love, John Allen; you always make it possible for me, thank you.

**George** Thanks to the ultimate travelling companions Nikki and Jemima who kept me company most of the way; Bob Tulloch for his expertise on the quandong; Alex Kelly in Coober Pedy; Ann and Jeff for advice, accommodation and footy tips; Beryl and Fred for their hard research assisting; and Jocelyn P for a few more tips. Toasting a Coopers to Susannah F for some low-stress coordinating, raising a glass of something jaunty from the Barossa to commissioning editor Errol Hunt and washing it all down with a West End with map mistress, Corie Waddell. Cheers to the wonderful folks of SA, who patched up the car, handed out speeding tickets, gave fishing tips and generally extended their warm hospitality.

### THE LONELY PLANET STORY

The story begins with a classic travel adventure: Tony and Maureen Wheeler's 1972 journey across Europe and Asia to Australia. There was no useful information about the overland trail then, so Tony and Maureen published the first Lonely Planet guidebook to meet a growing need.

From a kitchen table, Lonely Planet has grown to become the largest independent travel publisher in the world, with offices in Melbourne (Australia), Oakland (USA) and London (UK). Today Lonely Planet guidebooks cover the globe. There is an ever-growing list of books and information in a variety of media. Some things haven't changed. The main aim is still to make it possible for adventurous travellers to get out there – to explore and better understand the world.

At Lonely Planet we believe travellers can make a positive contribution to the countries they visit – if they respect their host communities and spend their money wisely. Every year 5% of company profit is donated to charities around the world.

## CREDITS

*Adelaide & South Australia* 3 was commissioned and developed in Lonely Planet's Melbourne office by commissioning editor Errol Hunt, with help from Stefanie DiTrocchio and Darren 'Dazza' O'Connell. Series publishing manager Susan Rimmerman and regional publishing managers Virginia Maxwell and Kate Cody oversaw various periods of its development. Jennifer Mundy-Nordin handed on the invaluable feedback from readers, Anna Bolger did likewise with feedback from booksellers and Karen Emmerson (PASU) handled contracting. Cartography was developed by Corie Waddell.

Inhouse, this book was coordinated by Kate Evans and Imogen Bannister (editorial), Amanda Sierp (cartography), Katherine Marsh (prelayout) and Margie Jung (layout). Ray Thomson and Charles Rawlings-Way managed the project inhouse. Kate was assisted by Julia Taylor and Lucy Monie. Amanda was assisted by Damien Demaj, Kusnandar and Jacqueline Nguyen. Simon Bracken designed and prepared the cover, with help from Brendan Dempsey, Wendy Wright and Jane Hart. Overseeing production were managing editor Martin Heng, managing cartographer Shahara Ahmed and layout manager Adriana Mammarella.

## THANKS FROM LONELY PLANET

**Many thanks to the travellers who used the last edition and contacted us with helpful hints, useful advice and interesting anecdotes:**

**A** Laura Addison, Olof Aerts, Paul Anderson, Ian Arnold, Scott Arnold, Erin Joseph Arsenault **B** Judith Babka, Hamish Barrett, Elke Behrens, Anthea Bell, Julien Benney, Carie Biggs, Shai Biran, Tom Bond, Kathy Bowden, Adrian Boyle, Hayden Brace, Felicity Branton, Daniela Brechbuehler, Tim Britza, Leak Bronte **C** Kacie Chang, Cynthia Chua, Abbi Clark, Gary Clarke, Becca Collins, Nigel Cropp **D** Paul Dale, Andrew Dawes, Marielle de Bakker, Elisa de Santis, Rick de Vries, Claire Dedman, Walter Denzel, Jerry & Lisa Diccox, Lies Dieben, Brenda Drinkwater, Kate Durey **E** Roger Paul Edmonds, Glenda Edwards, Alistair English **F** Alan Farleigh, Lisa Feege, Marvin Feldman, Simon Fielder, Louise Forbes, Claire Frost **G** Kathleen Gallichan, Emily George, Dave Gerrish, Cary Giakmoz, Emmett GIll, Anne Glazier, Erik Graafland, Jesse Grainger, Simon Greenway, Dianne Groves, Paul Guzyk **H** Ulrike Haeussler, Robert Hantzsch, Jon Harper, Ian Harrison, Carole Herbert, Robert Hia, Catriona Hickson, Trevor Hills, Siobhan Homan, D R Howlett, Haydn Hughes, Julia Humphries **I** Stephen Ireland **J** Loretta Jakubiec, Heather K James, Nancy Jenkins **K** Shannon Kardi, Andrew Kaye, Erik & Maayke Kazemier, Sue Kemp, Filip & Kristel Kennis-Verbeek, John Kerigan, Paul Key, Paul Knight, Jean Kramer, Daniel Kusterer **L** James Lambert, John Lawlor, Debbie Lawrence, Debbie & John Lawrence, Audrey Leeson, Milton Lever, Dayna Lynch **M** Julian Malone, Hayley Manning, Michaela Matross, Richard Mayo, Angela McKay, Gill and Neil McKay, Diane Meige, Ido Bar Meir, Alexandra

& Beverly Meyer, Martin Mickan, Tom Miller, Maxwell Millowick, Verity Millward, Heather Monell, W A A Monna, Meike Mueller, Luis Muller, Raphael Müller **N** Amy Newton, Chris Newton, Hanne Nielsen **O** David Oake, Angela Odermann, Rachel Ott, Alexandra Overbeck **P** Lynda Paananen, Robert Payne, David Peck, Christina & Marc Peeters, T A Petersen Gillespie, Kirstie Petrou, Irena Predalic, Hilton Purvis **R** Markus Reischl, Abe Remmo, Amy Reynolds, Carolyn Rich, Sean Richardson, Carol & Sean Richardson, Diana Rigg, John Ruehorn **S** Amy & Todd Sattersten Buckley, Peter Saundry, Maarten Schellingerhout, Ann Schioldann, Stefan Schmidt, Jochen Schneider, John & Thelma Schrader, Elke Schunck, Michal Silber, John Silby, Martin Smith, Steph Smith, John Snell, Gary Spinks, Karin Stadtländer, Alexandra Stiertz, Cindy & Greg Strauss, Kathy Strauss, Martin Sullivan, Bev & Lucy Sydney **T** David Talalla, Joshua Telser, Elke Thoma, Adrian Tschaeppeler **V** Miranda van der Gronde, Guido van Garsse, Andries van Wallinga, Michelle Vella, Ludwig Vogler, Marco Vronik **W** Anna Ward, Ben Watson, Sarah Watson, Klaus-Oliver Welsow, Irene Westendorp, Ling Weston, Chris Whitten, Catrin Williams, Paula Williams, Andy Wilson, Alexander Winwood, Gaynor Wood, Michelle Worm **Y** Doris & Trebor Yensen, Goh Yixuan **Z** Natacha Zana

## ACKNOWLEDGMENTS

Many thanks to the following for the use of their content:

Globe on back cover © Mountain High Maps 1993 Digital Wisdom, Inc.

### SEND US YOUR FEEDBACK

We love to hear from travellers – your comments keep us on our toes and help make our books better. Our well-travelled team reads every word on what you loved or loathed about this book. Although we cannot reply individually to postal submissions, we always guarantee that your feedback goes straight to the appropriate authors, in time for the next edition. Each person who sends us information is thanked in the next edition – and the most useful submissions are rewarded with a free book.

To send us your updates – and find out about Lonely Planet events, travel news and newsletters – visit our award-winning website: **www.lonelyplanet.com/feedback**.

Note: We may edit, reproduce and incorporate your comments in Lonely Planet products such as guidebooks, websites and digital products, so let us know if you don't want your comments reproduced or your name acknowledged. For a copy of our privacy policy visit www.lonelyplanet.com/privacy.

BEHIND THE SCENES

# Index

## A

Aborigines
art 28
books 10
cultural centres 66, 214, 247
Dreamtime *stories* 211
history 18, 22
rock carvings 213
abseiling 37
accommodation 251-3, *see
also individual locations*
activities 37-42, *see also individual
activities*
Adelaide 59-85, **61**, **64-5**, **82**, 4, 7
accommodation 72-5, 83
activities 68-9, 83
attractions 63-70, 82-3, 85
children, travel with 70
clubbing 78-9
cycling 85
drinks 77-8, 84
emergencies 62
entertainment 78-80, 84
festivals & events 71
food 75-7, 83-4, 85
Glenelg 81-4, **82**
Internet access 62, 82
Internet resources 60
itineraries 62
maps 61-2
medical services 62-3
money 63
music 79-80
North Adelaide 66, 67, 76-7,
78, **67**
Port Adelaide 70, 85
postal services 63
shopping 62, 70, 80, 81
tourist information 63, 82
tours 69-72
travel to/from 265-70
travel within 80-1, 84
walking tour 69-70, **69**
Adelaide Hills 86-97, **88**
Internet resources 87
travel around 89-90
travel to/from 89-90
Adelaide Hills wineries 49-50, **49**
Adelaide Oval 25, 67, 7
Adelaide Zoo 67

Admirals Arch 126
air travel
to/from South Australia 265-8
travel within South Australia 270
Aldgate 90-1
American River 120-1
Angaston 168-9
animal hazards 255-6, 278-9
animals 31-4, *see also individual species*
antechinus 33
architecture 26
Ardrossan 185-6
Arkaroo Rock 210
Arkaroola Wildlife Sanctuary 215
Arno Bay 222
art galleries, *see* galleries
arts 26-9
ATMs 260-1
Auburn 175
Australian Museum of Childhood 70

## B

B&Bs 251
bank accounts 260-1
Barmera 135-7
Barossa Gold Fields 164
Barossa Valley 159-69, **161**, 6
accommodation 161
Internet resources 160
tours 161-2
travel to/from 162
travel within 162
Barossa Valley wineries 54-6, 162,
**55**, 6
Baudin, Nicholas 114
Baxter Detention Centre 220
beaches
Aldinga Beach 103-4
Arno Bay 222
Back Beach 228
Brighton 84
Cactus Beach 232
Carrickalinga 104
Christies Beach 84
Coles Beach 227
Convention Beach 227
Coobowie 187
Emu Bay 119, 123
Farm Beach 227
Gallipoli Beach 227

Goolwa Beach 110
Greenly Beach 227
Henley Beach 84
Horseshoe Bay 109
Largs Bay 85
Locks Well Beach 227
Long Beach 147
Maslin Beach 103
Moana 84
Ninety Mile Beach 146
Normanville 104
O'Sullivan Beach 84
Pennington Bay 121
Port Neill 222
Port Willunga 103-4
Rapid Bay 104
Rifle Butts Beach 190
Seacliff 84
Seaford 84
Second Beach 190
Sellicks Beach 103-4
Semaphore 85
Shelley Beach 224
Snelling Beach 123
Stansbury 186
Stokes Bay 123
Vivonne Bay 124
West Beach 84
Western River Cove 123
Wool Bay 186
Beachport 148-50
Beachport Conservation Park 149
Belair National Park 88-9
Berri 138-40
Bethany 164
bicycle travel, *see* cycling
Big Bend 134
Big Galah 229
Big Kangaroo 233
Big Lobster 147
Big Rocking Horse 96
Big Winch 243
Billiatt Conservation Park 140
birds 32
Birdsville (Qld) 249
Birdsville Track 248-9
bird-watching 32-3
Flinders Chase National Park 126
Gluepot Reserve 136
Goolwa 110

**INDEX**

bird-watching *continued*
   Kangaroo Island 122
   Mannum 133
   Port Augusta 201
   Sir Joseph Banks Group of Islands 222
   Troubridge Island 187
   Tumby Island Conservation Park 222
Birdwood 96-7
bites 278-9
Blanchetown 135
Blinman 212-13
Blue Lake 152, **8**
boat trips, *see also* houseboats
   Adelaide 67, 68
   Murray River 131-2, 134, 140
Bookmark Biosphere Reserve 139
books
   Aboriginal 10
   bushwalking 37, 38
   culture 24
   environmental issues 35
   fauna 33
   flora 34
   food 43
   health 277
   history 19
   language 24
   literature 10, 27-8
   natural history 30
   surfing 42
   travel 10
   wines 44
Bool Lagoon Game Reserve 156
border crossings 268
Border Village 233
Botanic Gardens (Adelaide) 66
Bradman, Sir Donald 65
Breakaways, the 246, **7**
Brookfield Conservation Park 135
Burra 180-2, **181**
bus travel
   to/from South Australia 268-9
   within South Australia 271
bushfires 256
bushwalking 37-8
   Adelaide Hills 89
   Arkaroola Wildlife Sanctuary 215
   Barossa Valley 166
   Bookmark Biosphere Reserve 139
   Coffin Bay National Park 226

Edithburgh 187
Flinders Ranges National Park 211-12
Heysen Trail 38-9
Internet resources 39
Lincoln National Park 226
Mt Brown Conservation Park 208
Mt Remarkable National Park 205
Whyalla 219
business hours 253, *see also inside front cover*
Bute 186

**C**
Cactus Beach 232
Callington 93
camel riding 41
   Oodnadatta Track 248
campervan rental 273
camping 251-2
canoeing 39
   Loxton 138
   Mannum 133
   Murray River 129
Cape Gantheaume Conservation Park 124
Cape Jervis 104-5
car hire 272-3
car purchase 274
car travel 271-5
   outback driving 238, 256, 273-4
caravan parks 251-2
caves
   Engelbrecht Cave 152
   Kelly Hill caves 124-5
   Murrawijinie Caves 232
   Naracoorte Caves National Park 157
   Talia Caves 227
   Tantanoola Caves 149
caving 39-40
   Engelbrecht Cave 152
   Piccaninnie Ponds Conservation Park 149
Ceduna 229-32, **230**
Central Market 67-8
children, travel with 253-4
   food 46
Chowilla Game Reserve and Regional Reserve 140
Christianity 26
cinema 11, 27
Clare 176-7
Clare Valley 174-8
   Internet resources 171
   tours 173

travel to/from 174-5
travel within 174-5
Clare Valley wineries 56-8, 174, **57**
Clarendon 95
Clayton 111-12
Cleland Conservation Park 89
Cleland Wildlife Park 89
Clifford's Honey Farm 124
climate 9, 31, 254-5
Clinton Conservation Park 185
Coffin Bay 226-7
Coffin Bay National Park 226-7
conservation 36
conservation parks, *see also* national parks
   Beachport Conservation Park 149
   Billiatt Conservation Park 140
   Black Hill Conservation Park 89
   Brookfield Conservation Park 135
   Calpatanna Waterhole Conservation Park 228
   Cape Gantheaume Conservation Park 124
   Charleston Conservation Park 89
   Chowilla Game Reserve and Regional Reserve 140
   Cleland Conservation Park 89
   Clinton Conservation Park 185
   Danggali Conservation Park 140
   Deep Creek Conservation Park 105
   Dutchmans Stern Conservation Park 207
   Ewens Ponds Conservation Park 149
   Hacks Lagoon Conservation Park 156
   Hale Conservation Park 166
   Kaiser Stuhl Conservation Park 166
   Kelly Hill Conservation Park 124
   Kenneth Stirling Conservation Park 89
   Lake Newland Conservation Park 227
   Leven Beach Conservation Park 190
   Little Dip Conservation Park 147
   Mark Oliphant Conservation Park 89
   Martin Washpool Conservation Park 146
   Martindale Hall Conservation Park 173
   Messent Conservation Park 145
   Morialta Conservation Park 89
   Mt Boothby Conservation Park 146
   Mt Brown Conservation Park 208
   Mt Magnificent Conservation Park 102-3

Newland Head Conservation Park 107
Ngarkat Group of Conservation Parks 158
Pandappa Conservation Park 182
Piccaninnie Ponds Conservation Park 149
Pinkawillinie Conservation Park 229
Red Banks Conservation Park 173
Scott Creek Conservation Park 89
Seal Bay Conservation Park 124
Spring Gully Conservation Park 173
Swan Reach Conservation Park 134
Talisker Conservation Park 105
Telowie Gorge Conservation Park 203
Tumby Island Conservation Park 222
Wamba Kadurba Conservation Park 248
Warren Conservation Park 166
Western River Conservation Park 123
consulates 257-8
Coober Pedy 240-6, **241**
Coobowie 187
cooking
  courses 47
Coonawarra 153-8
Coonawarra wineries 52-4, 154, **53**
Coorong National Park 46-7, 5
Copley 214
costs 10
Cowell 221-2
Crafers 90-1
credit cards 261
crime 256
culture 17, 24-9
currency 261
Currency Creek 111
customs regulations 255
cycling 40, 270-1
  Adelaide 68
  Barossa Valley 162
  Clare Valley 175
  Encounter Coast 107
  Internet resources 40
  McLaren Vale 102
  Mt Lofty Summit 89

**D**

Deep Creek Conservation Park 105
deep vein thrombosis 277
deforestation 35
disabled travellers 63, 256-7
diving, see scuba diving

Dog Fence 250
dolphin-watching 42
drinks 43-4, 46. 48-58
driving licence 272
Dudley Peninsula 121-2
Dukes Highway 158
Dunstan, Don 17, 23
Dutchmans Stern Conservation Park 207

**E**

Echunga 94
economy 17
Eden Valley 169
Edithburgh 187-8
Eftpos 260-1
electricity 251
Elliston 227
email services 260
embassies 257-8
Emu Ridge Eucalyptus Distillery 124
environmental issues 17, 35-6
  Internet resources 10
events, see festivals & events
Ewens Ponds Conservation Park 149
exchange rates 261, see also inside front cover
Eyre Peninsula 218-28, **218**
  Internet resources 217

**F**

farmstays 252
festivals & events 11, 258-9
  Adelaide 71
  Adelaide Hills 90, 92, 94, 96
  Barossa Valley 163
  Eyre Peninsula 219
  Fleurieu Peninsula 101, 102, 110, 111
  McLaren Vale 101
  Mid-North, the 173
  Murray River 131
  outback region 237
  Southeast, the 145
  Yorke Peninsula 191
fishing 40-1
  Cape Jervis 105
  Coffin Bay 226
  Edithburgh 187
  Innes National Park 189
  Kangaroo Island 116
  Locks Well Beach 227
  Mannum 133
  Marion Bay 188
  Moonta 192
  Mt Schank Fish Farm 149

Ninety Mile Beach 146
Parsons Beach 107
Pennington Bay 121
Point Tinline 124
Port Broughton 194
Waitpinga Beach 107
Wallaroo 194
West Bay 126
Fleurieu Peninsula 98-112, **100**
  Internet resources 99
  travel to/from 100-1
  travel within 100-1
Flinders Chase National Park 125-6, 8
Flinders Ranges 195-215, **197**
  Internet resources 196
  tours 198, 212
  travel around 198-9
  travel to/from 198-9
Flinders Ranges National Park 210-12, **210**, 5
Flinders, Matthew 18
food 43, 46
  courses 47
  customs 46, 47
  Internet resources 46
  pubs 45
  restaurants 45
  vegetarian travellers 45-6
Fowlers Bay 232
fuel 272

**G**

galleries
  Art Gallery of South Australia 63
  Barossa Regional Gallery 164
  Burra Art Gallery 180
  Carine Turner Studio Gallery 206
  Cockatoo Dreaming Gallery 151
  Corella Hill Studio 178
  Dridan Fine Arts 101
  Experimental Art Foundation 63
  Fountain Gallery 199
  Glenelg Fine Art Gallery 83
  Goolwa Maritime Gallery 110
  Greenaway Art Gallery 63
  Gunner Bill's Museum & Gallery 186
  Jam Factory Craft & Design Centre 63
  Junction Art Gallery 206
  Kapunda Gallery 178, 179
  KI Gallery 120
  Medika Gallery 178
  Naracoorte Art Gallery 156
  Ocean Art Gallery 107
  Old Mill Gallery & Café 167
  Outback Colours 206

galleries *continued*
  Riddoch Art Gallery 151
  South Coast Regional Art Centre 110
  Stationmasters' Gallery 94
  Studio One 151
  Tandanya Indigenous Cultural
    Institute 66
  Yulgilbar Wood Gallery 157
Gammon Ranges National Park
  214-15, **215**
gardens
  Australian Arid Lands Botanic
    Garden 201
  Beechwood Heritage Garden 90
  Botanic Gardens (Adelaide) 66
  Himeji Gardens 67
  Mt Lofty Botanic Garden 89, 6
  Ruston's Rose Gardens 140
  Veale Gardens 67
Gawler Ranges National Park 229
gay travellers 77, 259
geography 36
geology 30-1
giardiasis 278
Glendambo 239
Glenelg 81-4, **82**
Gluepot Reserve 136
Goolwa 110-11
Granite Island 107, 8
Great Australian Bight Marine Park
  34, 232

**H**
Hacks Lagoon Conservation Park 156
Hahndorf 91-3
Haigh's Chocolates 68
Hale Conservation Park 166
Hallett 182
Hawker 208-9
Head of Bight 232
health 276-80
health retreats 116
heat sickness 279
Henley Beach 84
Heysen Trail 37, 38-9
Heysen, Hans 28-9, 92
hiking, *see* bushwalking
Hindmarsh Island 110
history 18-23
hitching 270
holidays 9, 259

horse riding 41
  Naracoorte 157
  Normanville 104
Horseshoe Bay 109
hostels 252
hotels 253
houseboats 130, 252, *see also* boat trips
hypothermia 256, 279-80

**I**
Iga Warta 214
Innamincka 249
Inner Track 249
Innes National Park 189-90
insects 280
insurance
  car 273
  health 276
  travel 259
Internet access 259-60
Internet resources 10-11
  activities 41
  Adelaide 60
  air tickets 266
  Barossa Valley 160
  bushwalking 39
  Clare Valley 171
  Coober Pedy 235
  culture 11, 28, 29
  cycling 40
  environment 10
  Eyre Peninsula 217
  Fleurieu Peninsula 99
  Flinders Ranges 196
  flora 34
  food 46
  health 277
  history 18
  Kangaroo Island 114
  outback region 235
  rock-climbing 37
  scuba diving 41
  Southeast, the 143
  surfing 42
  travel 10, 11
  weather 11
  Yorke Peninsula 184
Iron Knob 228
Island Pure Sheep Dairy 123
itineraries 12-14, 15
  Adelaide 62

**J**
Jamestown 178
jet lag 277

**K**
Kadina 193
Kangaroo Island 113-26, **115**
  accommodation 115-16
  activities 116-17
  Internet resources 114
  tourist information 115
  tours 117-18, 122
  travel to/from 118
  travel within 118
kangaroos 33
Kanyaka 208
Kapunda 178-80
Katarapko Game Reserve 138
kayaking 39
Kelly Hill Caves 124-5
Kelly Hill Conservation Park 124-5
Kimba 229
Kingscote 118-20, **119**
koalas 31
Koppio 222
Kuitpo Forest 94

**L**
Lake Eyre National Park 247, 7
Lake Newland Conservation Park 227
Langhorne Creek wineries 112
legal services 260
Leigh Creek 214
lesbian travellers 77, 259
Lincoln National Park 226
literature 10, 27-8
Little Dip Conservation Park 147
Little Sahara 124
lizards 34
Lobethal 96
Loxton 137-8
Lyndhurst 249
Lyndoch 163-4

**M**
Macclesfield 94
MacKillop, Mother Mary 66, 154, 155
Maitland 190-1
Mannum 133-5
maps 61-2, 260
  Adelaide 61-2
Marion Bay 188-9
markets
  Central Market 67-8
  Fisherman's Wharf Market 85
  Heart of the Hills Market 96
  MarketEast 68
  Stirling Organic Market 91
  Willunga Farmers Market 103

Marla 246
Marree 247
Marree Man 247
Martin Washpool Conservation Park 146
Martindale Hall Conservation Park 173
Mary MacKillop Centre 66
McLaren Vale 101-2
McLaren Vale wineries 50-2, **51**, 50
Meadows 94
medical services 277-8
Melrose 204-5
meningococcal disease 278
Messent Conservation Park 145
metric conversions 251, *see also inside front cover*
Middleton 109-10
Mid-North, the 170-82, **172**
  accommodation 173-4
  tours 173
  travel to/from 174
Migration Museum 65
Milang 111-12
Minlaton 190
Mintabie 246
Mintaro 175-6
Monarto Zoological Park 131
money 10, 260-1, *see also inside front cover*
  discount cards 257
moneychangers 261
Moonta 191-2
Moorook Game Reserve 136
Morialta Conservation Park 89
motels 253
motion sickness 277
motorcycle travel 271-5
Mt Barker 94
Mt Boothby Conservation Park 146
Mt Brown Conservation Park 208
Mt Gambier 150-3, **150-1**, 8
Mt Lofty Botanic Garden 89, 6
Mt Lofty Summit 89
Mt Magnificent Conservation Park 102
Mt Remarkable 205
Mt Remarkable National Park 205
Murrawijinie Caves 232
Murray Bridge 130-3, **132**
Murray River 127-41, **129**, **136**
  houseboats 130
  tours 129-30
  travel to/from 130
museums
  Adelaide Hills Settlement Museum 92
  Arabunna People's Community Centre and Museum 247

Ardrossan National Trust Museum 186
Australian Museum of Childhood 70
Axel Stenross Maritime Museum 223
Banking & Currency Museum 193
Barossa Valley Historical Museum 164
Burra Mine Museum 181
Camp Coorong Cultural Museum 146
Captain's Cottage Museum 131
Ceduna Museum 229
CL Alexander Memorial Museum 222
Cowell folk museum 222
Edithburgh Museum 187
German Immigration Museum 92
Goolwa Museum 110
Homestead Park Pioneer Museum 201
Investigator Science & Technology Museum 70
Kadina Heritage Museum 193
Kapunda Museum 179
Koppio Smithy Museum 222
Maitland National Trust Museum 190
Mannum Dock Museum of River History 133
Maritime Museum 85, 190
Market Sq Museum 180
Migration Museum 65
Minlaton Museum 190
Model Train & Toy Museum 206
Moonta Mines Museum 191
Motorcycle & Heritage Museum 96
Museum of Economic Botany 66
National Costume Museum 96
National Motor Museum 96
National Railway Museum 85
Old Wool & Grain Store Museum 148
Penneshaw Maritime & Folk Museum 121
Port MacDonnell & District Maritime Museum 153
Rose-Wal Memorial Shell Museum 223
Seashells Museum 190
Sheep's Back Museum 156
South Australian Aviation Museum 85
South Australian Museum 63-5, 4
Streaky Bay Museum 228
Umoona Opal Mine & Museum 242

Wallaroo Heritage & Nautical Museum 194
Warooka folk museum 188
Whyalla Maritime Museum 219
music 26
Mylor 91

**N**
Nairne 93
Naracoorte 156-7
Naracoorte Caves National Park 157-8
national parks 34, *see also* conservation parks
  Belair National Park 88-9
  Coffin Bay National Park 226-7
  Coorong National Park 146-7, 5
  Flinders Chase National Park 125-6, 8
  Flinders Ranges National Park 210-12, 5
  Gammon Ranges National Park 214-15
  Gawler Ranges National Park 229
  Innes National Park 189-90
  Lake Eyre National Park 247, 7
  Lincoln National Park 226
  Mt Remarkable National Park 205
  Naracoorte Caves National Park 157-8
  Nullarbor National Park 232
  outback region 236-7
  Witjira National Park 248
National Wine Centre of Australia 48, 68
Newland Head Conservation Park 107
newspapers 62, 251
Ngarkat Group of Conservation Parks 158
Normanville 104
North Adelaide 66, 67, 76-7, 78, **67**
Norton Summit 96
Nullarbor National Park 232
Nuriootpa 167-8

**O**
Oakbank 94
Old Clarendon Winery Complex 95
Oodnadatta 248
Oodnadatta Track 247-8
outback region 234-50, **236**
  Internet resources 235
  national parks 236-7
  tours 237
  travel to/from 238
outback travel 238, 256, 273-4

**P**

Painted Desert 246
painting 28-9
Pandappa Conservation Park 182
Para Wirra Recreation Park 164, 166
parks, *see* national parks, conservation
    parks
Parndana 123
Penneshaw 121-2
Penola 154-6, **154**
Peterborough 203
petrol 272
phonecards 263
Piccadilly 90
Piccaninnie Ponds Conservation
    Park 149
Pichi Richi Tourist Train 206
Pinkawillinie Conservation Park 229
planning 9-11, *see also* itineraries
    discount cards 257
    holidays 9, 259
plants 34-5
population 17, 25, 60
Port Adelaide 70, 85
Port Augusta 199-203, **200**
Port Broughton 194
Port Elliot 109
Port Germein 203-4
Port Lincoln 222-5, **221**, **223**
Port MacDonnell 153
Port Neill 222
Port Pirie 174
Port Victoria 190
Port Vincent 186
postal services 262
Price 185
pubs 45, 253

**Q**

quarantine 233, 255, 269
Quorn 206-7, 5

**R**

Rapid Bay 104
Ravine des Casoars 126
Red Banks Conservation Park 173
religion 26
Remarkable Rocks 126
Renmark 140-1
rental accommodation 253, *see
    also* accommodation

**000** Map pages
**000** Location of colour photographs

restaurants 45
Riverton 176
Robe 147-8
rock carvings 213
rock-climbing 37
Ross River fever 278
Roxby Downs 239
Rymill Park 67

**S**

safe travel
    animal hazards 255-6, 278-9
    crime 256
    hitching 270
    outback travel 238, 256, 273-4
    road conditions 274
    road hazards 275
    surf beaches 256, 280
    water 280
St Ignatius Church 66
St Joseph's Convent 66
St Mary's Convent 66
salinity 35
scuba diving 41-2
    Adelaide 83
    Ardrossan 186
    Edithburgh 187
    Engelbrecht Cave 152
    Fleurieu Peninsula 105
    Innes National Park 189
    Internet resources 41
    Kangaroo Island 116-17
    Normanville 105
    Piccaninnie Ponds Conservation
        Park 149
    Port Lincoln 224
    Port Victoria 190
    Rapid Bay 104
    Victor Harbor 107
Seal Bay Conservation Park 124
sexually transmitted diseases 278
sharks 279
snakes 34, 279
snorkelling 41-2
    Adelaide 83
    Fleurieu Peninsula 105
    Kangaroo Island 116-17
South Australian Museum 63-5, 4
Southeast, the 142-58, **144**
    Internet resources 143
    travel to/from 145
special events, *see* festivals & events
spiders 255-6, 279
sports 17, 25-6
Spring Gully Conservation Park 173

Springton 169
Stansbury 186
State Library of South Australia 65
station stays 252
stings 278-9
Stirling 90-1
Strathalbyn 94-5, **95**
Strzelecki Track 249-50
surfing 42
    Adelaide 83
    Cactus Beach 232
    Daly Head 190
    Fleurieu Peninsula 105
    Innes National Park 189
    Kangaroo Island 117
    Parsons Beach 105
    Point Tinline 124
    Port Elliot 105, 109
    Trespassers 190
    Waitpinga Beach 105
Swan Reach Conservation Park 134
swimming 42, *see also* beaches
    Adelaide 68
    Kangaroo Island 117
    safety 256, 280

**T**

Talia Caves 227
Talisker Conservation Park 105
Tandanya Indigenous Cultural
    Institute 66
Tantanoola Caves 149
Tanunda 164-7
Tarlee 180
taxes 261
telephone services 262-3
television 251
time 263
Torrens Track 239
tourist information 263
tours 269-70
    Adelaide 70-2
    Barmen 136-7
    Barossa Valley 161-2
    Blinman 212
    Ceduna 230
    Clare Valley 173
    Coober Pedy 243
    Coorong National Park 146
    Flinders Ranges 198, 212
    Goolwa 110
    Granite Island 107
    Kangaroo Island 117-18, 122
    McLaren Vale 101-2
    Mid-North, the 173

Mt Gambier 152
Murray River 129-30
outback region 237
Port Augusta 201
Port Lincoln 224
Quorn 207
Whyalla 219
train travel 270
train trips 90, 109, 194, 206
tram travel 107, 6, 8
travellers cheques 261-2
trekking, *see* bushwalking
Tumby Bay 222
Tumby Island Conservation Park 222

**V**
vegetarian travellers 45-6
Victor Harbor 105-9, **106**
viral encephalitis 278
visas 263-4
Vivonne Bay 124

**W**
walking, *see also* bushwalking
   Adelaide 68, 69-70
walking tour
   Adelaide 69-70, **69**
Wallaroo 193-4
Wamba Kadurba Conservation Park 248
Warooka 188
weather
   Internet resources 11
Weirs Cove 126

West Beach 84
West Coast 228-33, **232**
Western River Conservation Park 123
whales 33
whale-watching 42
   Head of Bight 232
Whispering Wall 164
Whyalla 218-21
wildlife 31-5, *see also* animals, birds,
   plants and *individual species*
   Arkaroola Wildlife Sanctuary 215
   Bredls Wonderland of Wildlife 140
   Cleland Wildlife Park 89
   Coober Pedy Wildlife Park 243
   Dundee's Wildlife Park 131
   Flinders Chase National Park 125-6
   Gorge Wildlife Park 96
   Granite Island Nature Park 107
   Head of Bight 232
   Innes National Park 189
   Kangaroo Island 122
   Moorook Game Reserve 136
   Ngarkat Group of Conservation
      Parks 158
   Parndana Wildlife Park 123
   Point Labatt 227
   Port Augusta 201
   Urimbirra Wildlife Park 107
   Wallaroo Fauna Park 194
Willunga 102-3
Wilmington 205-6
Wilpena Pound 211-12
wine tasting 58

wineries 48-58
   Adelaide Hills wineries 49-50,**49**
   Barossa Valley wineries 54-6,
      162, **55**, 6
   Clare Valley wineries 56-8,
      174, **57**
   Coonawarra wineries 52-4,154, 53
   McLaren Vale wineries 50-2,
      **51**, 50
Wirrabara 204
Witjira National Park 248
wombats 32
women travellers 264
Woods, Father Julian 155
Woodside 93
Wool Bay 186-7
Woomera 239
work 135
Wudinna 229

**Y**
Yalata 232
Yankalilla 104
Yorke Peninsula 183-94, **185**
   accommodation 185
   Internet resources 184
   travel to/from 185
Yorketown 188

**Z**
zoos
   Adelaide Zoo 67
   Monarto Zoological Park 131

INDEX

## MAP LEGEND

### ROUTES

| | |
|---|---|
| Tollway | One-Way Street |
| Freeway | Street Mall/Steps |
| Primary Road | Tunnel |
| Secondary Road | Walking Tour |
| Tertiary Road | Walking Tour Detour |
| Lane | Walking Trail |
| Under Construction | Walking Path |
| Track | Pedestrian Overpass |
| Unsealed Road | |

### TRANSPORT

| | |
|---|---|
| Ferry | Rail |
| Metro | Rail (Disused) |
| Bus Route | Tram |

### HYDROGRAPHY

| | |
|---|---|
| River, Creek | Water |
| Intermittent River | Lake (Dry) |
| Swamp | Lake (Salt) |

### BOUNDARIES

| | |
|---|---|
| State, Provincial | Fence |

### AREA FEATURES

| | |
|---|---|
| Airport | Land |
| Area of Interest | Mall |
| Beach, Desert | Market |
| Building | Park |
| Campus | Reservation |
| Cemetery, Christian | Rocks |
| Cemetery, Other | Sports |
| Forest | Urban |

### POPULATION

| | |
|---|---|
| CAPITAL (NATIONAL) | CAPITAL (STATE) |
| Large City | Medium City |
| Small City | Town, Village |

### SYMBOLS

**Sights/Activities**
- Beach
- Christian
- Monument
- Museum, Gallery
- Pool
- Ruin
- Surfing, Surf Beach
- Winery, Vineyard
- Zoo, Bird Sanctuary

**Eating**
- Eating

**Drinking**
- Drinking
- Café

**Entertainment**
- Entertainment

**Shopping**
- Shopping

**Sleeping**
- Sleeping
- Camping

**Transport**
- Airport, Airfield
- Bus Station
- Cycling, Bicycle Path

**Other**
- Other Site
- Parking Area

**Information**
- Bank, ATM
- Hospital, Medical
- Information
- Internet Facilities
- Petrol Station
- Police Station
- Post Office, GPO
- Toilets

**Geographic**
- Lighthouse
- Lookout
- Mountain, Volcano
- National Park
- Pass, Canyon
- Shelter, Hut

## LONELY PLANET OFFICES

### Australia
Head Office
Locked Bag 1, Footscray, Victoria 3011
☎ 03 8379 8000, fax 03 8379 8111
talk2us@lonelyplanet.com.au

### USA
150 Linden St, Oakland, CA 94607
☎ 510 893 8555, toll free 800 275 8555
fax 510 893 8572, info@lonelyplanet.com

### UK
72-82 Rosebery Ave,
Clerkenwell, London EC1R 4RW
☎ 020 7841 9000, fax 020 7841 9001
go@lonelyplanet.co.uk

### Published by Lonely Planet Publications Pty Ltd
ABN 36 005 607 983

3rd Edition – June 2005

First Published – September 1996

© Lonely Planet 2005

© photographers as indicated 2005

Cover photographs by Lonely Planet Images: Vinyards and almond trees in McLaren Vale, Diana Mayfield (front); Dining alfresco on the pavement outside Austral Hotel, Rundle St, Chris Mellor (back). Many of the images in this guide are available for licensing from Lonely Planet Images: www.lonelyplanetimages.com

Printed through The Bookmaker International Ltd
Printed in China